THE FIRE WITHIN

*The Olympic Flame*

SHEILA METZNER

# THE FIRE WITHIN

12 PHOTOGRAPHERS' QUEST TO CAPTURE THE OLYMPIC SPIRIT
PRESENTED IN THE OFFICIAL COMMEMORATIVE BOOK OF THE

## SALT LAKE 2002

## OLYMPIC WINTER GAMES

FEBRUARY 8-24, 2002

INTRODUCTION • YOU KNEW WHEN THE SALT LAKE 2002 OLYMPIC TORCH RELAY WAS COMING TO TOWN, FOR CHILDREN LINED THE STREETS, LONG BEFORE DAWN. THEY WAVED FLAGS, STAMPED THEIR FEET IN THE COLD MORNING AIR AND CRANED THEIR NECKS FOR A GLIMPSE—JUST A GLIMPSE—OF THAT MAGICAL FIRE. AND WHEN THE OLYMPIC FLAME FINALLY ARRIVED, HELD ALOFT BY THE PROUDEST PERSON IN THE WORLD AT THAT MOMENT, THE KIDS WRIGGLED FROM THEIR PARENTS AND BEGAN TO CHASE THE FLAME. IT WOULD ALL BE GONE IN AN

*Delicate Arch, Moab, Utah*

SHEILA METZNER

instant. The convoy of cars, the torchbearer, the silvery shaft of light, all gone down the road, one step, one mile, one state closer to the Salt Lake 2002 Games. No matter. For now, there was this delightful feeling of hope, a belief that all things were indeed possible in the world. So the children chased the flame until they ran out of breath.

Thus it began, a winter of wonder, when the Olympic Spirit streaked across the country like fairy dust, and settled in the mountains and valleys of Utah for nothing less than a fairy tale.

In November 2001, a spark of fire was brought to life in the olive groves of ancient Greece, where the Olympic Games were born. After a brief stay in Athens, the Olympic Flame was on its way toward Salt Lake City in one of the most remarkable journeys in history. The theme of the Salt Lake 2002 Games, *Light the Fire Within*, began with the very first step of this unique Torch Relay, for the torchbearers had been selected for inspiring another. In their strength, their dedication and their bravery, they resembled the athletes who would compete in the Games: the very best of their country.

More than 12,000 torchbearers carried the Olympic Flame, and like tiny dots of pointillism, they painted a portrait of a nation. There were parents and police officers, soldiers and schoolteachers, heart surgeons and Hiroshima survivors who spoke to children about the value of forgiveness. For Olympic champions, it was an old flame rekindled, while would-be Olympians who had missed their shot at a Games—because of war, because of an unfortunate twist of fate—finally felt that moment of glory. They ranged in age from 12 to 103, bound together by the leap of faith that had brought them here, and now, joined by the leap of the flame from torch to torch. Some torchbearers who had once inspired each other ran in pairs, and never before had the human connection seemed so strong.

World-famous actors and musicians were among the torchbearers, but the biggest celebrity of all was the Olympic Flame itself. Guarded 24 hours a day, the flame toured with a royal itinerary: the White House and the Pentagon, the Statue of Liberty and the Golden Gate Bridge; monuments and national parks, ski resorts and hot springs, rivers, lakes and oceans. It traveled by truck and by train, by bicycle, canoe and kayak and even soared off ski jumps. It took rides in a hot-air balloon, airplanes

# THUS IT BEGAN, A WINTER OF WONDER, WHEN THE OLYMPIC SPIRIT STREAKED ACROSS THE COUNTRY.

and a dogsled. There were cattle drives and auto shows, Native American celebrations, and chili cook-offs and pancake breakfasts. Flags, hundreds of thousands of American flags, fluttered from front porches and shop windows. Somehow, the flame and the Olympic Spirit illuminated, inspired and helped to heal a country still reeling from the events of September 11, 2001.

And when you held that flame, you were transformed; it was as if you were holding all of humanity in your hands. If you couldn't hold a torch in your hands, you carried it in your wheelchair, or fashioned a carpenter's belt with a special holder and strapped it to your waist. You ran as fast as you could, fleet-footed with adrenaline, or sashayed slowly, relishing every second. It blew your mind, this feeling. You rolled and skipped and danced and laughed and cried, across 13,500 miles of America.

On February 4, the Olympic Flame arrived in the land of the XIX Olympic Winter Games, a place of ancient redrock formations and alpine peaks that touched azure skies. When the flame passed him at Delicate Arch, Governor Michael Leavitt said "Utah will never be the same," and he was right. By the time that flame arrived in Salt Lake, three days later, a spell had been cast on the city, a spell that would last for nearly three weeks, and in some ways, much longer. Downtown, and in the venues beyond, buildings and bleachers were hung with towering and luminous banners of athletes, the sky-line transformed by the Salt Lake 2002 theme of *Light the Fire Within*. Looking out from a ridgetop, or strolling the wide streets, you could not help but feel privileged to be in such a marvelous place at such an uncommon time. The city was aglow with Torch Relay festivities, from the State Capitol to Washington Square to the Wasatch foothills, where the five Olympic Rings were suddenly alight. The first curious fans peeked at the final touches being made to Salt Lake Olympic Square. And up in Park City, Main Street was strung with lights, closed to traffic, ready for the tens of thousands of visitors who would amble along its way, a cup of hot chocolate or soup in hand. The Games were here.

Like the Olympic Flame, which blazed to life in the cauldron the following night in a glorious Opening Ceremony, it would all pass us by in the blink of an eye: the athletes, the sea of spectators with their brightly colored parkas, the sparkling days and electric nights. But like the children who lined the Torch Relay route, we chased the Olympic Spirit until we ran out of breath.

We traveled up to the mountains to watch Janica Kostelić and Ole Einar Bjørndalen haul in heaps of medals, to see Bode Miller resurrect himself from reckless runs, to follow the snowboarders' flips and twists. In the early morning light, sunrise just peeking over the Rockies, we climbed up to the ski jumps of Utah Olympic Park, where we saw Swiss wunderkind Simon Ammann soar, and Team Germany win by a whisker. We felt the roar of the sleds, the rattle and hum of the track as women's bobsleigh made its spectacular debut. A snowstorm swirled around us as Jimmy Shea went sliding with a picture of his grandfather tucked in his helmet and a dream tucked in his heart. The Olympic Spirit had surely swept over Shea during his skeleton run. "It's about competing and bringing the world together in a peaceful, friendly competition," he reminded us.

Still chasing it, we caromed through the valley, from ice hockey in Provo to curling in Ogden, finding exhilaration in each. As the mighty hockey behemoths battled for gold, our loudest cheers often erupted for those who played in their shadows: Kazakhstan, Belarus, Latvia. We basked in the radiance of spangled figure skaters, witnessing a 16-year-old student leapfrog past the favorites. While we could not hear all those records falling, we listened to the rush and clap of skates on the fastest ice in the world at the Utah Olympic Oval. We watched the short track tumbles, the astonishing wins of Steven Bradbury and Apolo Anton Ohno. Each night, we gathered at Olympic Medals Plaza, where we witnessed the Olympic Spirit held high in the lanterns of the symbolic Children of Light and twin-kling in the watery eyes of the champions. Finally, late in the evening, we slept, impassioned, visions of our own potential dancing through our heads.

An extraordinary group of photographers, meanwhile, also went looking for the Olympic Spirit in the hills and dales of Utah. They brought myriad backgrounds, styles and visions to docu-ment the Salt Lake 2002 Games. And they were granted an artist's utmost wish: unprecedented access. Not since the 1936 Olympic Games and the legendary work of Leni Riefenstahl have photographers been so close to Olympians. And so, with old-fashioned cameras on their backs, these explorers moved out of the press box and onto the field of play. Their discoveries are surprising portraits of per-severance and patience, of speed and serenity, of beauty, light and hope. Above all, they are timeless and inspiring images that manage to capture the elusive and powerful Olympic Spirit, the fire within.

Cycling champion and cancer survivor Lance Armstrong helped welcome the Olympic Flame to
Atlanta, Georgia, on December 4, 2001. He would later cycle with the flame in his hometown of Austin,
Texas, while accompanied by a group of young cancer survivors.

STEVEN CURRIE

*"People always talk about bridges and dividers. Wearing no colors and no name, today I united the*

*world," said one torchbearer of carrying the Olympic Flame.*

STEVEN CURRIE

*To remember the victims and heroes of September 11, 2001, special events were held in New York City, Washington,*

*D.C., and Philadelphia. John Gill, above, joined several family members of victims to carry the flame through*

*New York Harbor and past the Statue of Liberty by ferry. His only son, Paul, 34, was a firefighter with Engine*

*54 in Manhattan and one of the first to respond to the attacks on the World Trade Center.*

J O H N   H U E T

*Torchbearer Mike Casey of Wellesley, Massachusetts, holds his 10-month-old daughter, Riley. Mike's wife, Neilie, was on the first plane to crash into the World Trade Center. Carrying the Olympic Flame "was an incredible connection with Neilie, because running was our thing," he says. "And it was a nice metaphor, because she was such a bright light. I don't even remember running, I felt like I was floating."*

ELISABETH O'DONNELL

*The Olympic Flame traveled with 50 vehicles and a staff of 150. Passengers in passing cars often honked and waved at the torchbearers: just this small glimpse of the flame had made their day.*

STEVEN CURRIE

*A North Carolina businessman steps from his office to wave an American flag for the Torch Relay.*

STEVEN CURRIE

*"Excellence—the sheer beauty of human excellence—is here, possible, part of us,*
*part of life." — Salt Lake 2002 President and CEO Mitt Romney*

 13

CHAD    HOLDER

More than 10,000 banners lined the streets of Salt Lake City and adorned the Olympic venues.

IAN LOGAN

OPENING CEREMONY · MOTHER NATURE, IT SEEMED, HAD JOINED THE CAST OF 3200 FOR THE OPENING CEREMONY ON FEBRUARY 8. AFTER BLANKETING THE WASATCH MOUNTAINS WITH SEVERAL INCHES OF POWDER, THE SKIES SUDDENLY CLEARED AS MORE THAN 50,000 SPECTATORS FILED INTO RICE-ECCLES OLYMPIC STADIUM. WHEN THE SHOW BEGAN, IT WAS UNDER A SOFTLY FALLING SNOW, A FEW FLAKES DRIFTING LIGHTLY INTO THE STANDS AS THE FIRST SKATERS CARRIED BANNERS NAMING AND YEARS OF OLYMPIC WINTER GAMES PAST AND PRESENT.

*The Olympic Cauldron, Rice-Eccles Olympic Stadium, February 8, 2002*

JOHN HUET

17

And there was something in the way the breeze blew when an honor guard of American athletes, flanked by firefighters and police officers, carried in a flag rescued from New York City's World Trade Center after September 11, 2001. "A gust of wind would come through and blow through the rips in the flag, and it billowed in the wind. It was so beautiful," said American snowboarder Chris Klug, one of the flag bearers. "But I could feel this little bit of shaking and it wasn't the wind, it was just all of the Olympians holding it, we were shaking." The stadium was shrouded in absolute silence, a silence broken only by the strains of "The Star-Spangled Banner" as a new American flag was raised, honoring the host country.

Moments later, a drama unfolded on the ice, spinning the fabric that would weave together each event of the Games: the theme of *Light the Fire Within*. No Opening Ceremony had so connected each element. A child, holding a lantern, battled and overcame a storm—representing life's adversities—because he found the courage to summon an inner force, the Fire Within. He shared his power with other children, who spilled into the stands with their lanterns. This Child of Light became "a little thread that went through all this tonight," said American astronaut and former senator John Glenn, chosen as one of the eight Olympic flag bearers. "He kept coming back and that's really what this is all about, encouraging young people to strive for excellence and do their very, very best."

The Child of Light led in the parade of athletes—the Greek team appearing first in honor of the birthplace of the Olympic Games—followed by some 2300 athletes from 76 delegations (Costa Rica's delegation of one would join the Games after the Opening Ceremony). Dressed in every type of uniform from Bermuda shorts to elaborate silver and red capes, they waved exuberantly at the crowd, taking photos and videotaping this extraordinary moment. It was a moment they had been dreaming of, working toward, for years, even lifetimes. Whether they won a medal in the next 16 days seemed to matter little: they were *here*, they were Olympians, and they were going to remember this forever. In past Opening Ceremonies, athletes had arrived toward the end of the program; this new, early entrance meant they could see the show, rather than wait backstage. After finding their seats, members of the French delegation began a spur-of-the-moment wave that rippled through the crowd, with other athletes, the audience and even the Mormon Tabernacle Choir, joining in.

The impromptu wave preceded a planned, and poignant, moment of unity. For the first time in history, Utah's five native tribes—Goshute, Navajo, Paiute, Shoshone and Ute—joined together in public celebration, to welcome the world to their homeland. In traditional dress and honoring Native American traditions and symbols, they performed a vibrant and colorful stomp dance, set to the beat of more than 100 drummers, and then accompanied by the music of Robbie Robertson, Sadie Buck and Walela. They were followed by a wondrous display of the wilderness that inspired thousands of settlers from many different cultures to band together and travel west, to a land of enchantment. Gossamer creatures—wild horses, jackrabbits and coyotes, even a herd of buffalo—skittered across a star field toward a watering hole, dazzling the settlers' children. The reverie was broken by the sunrise-like sparks of pyrotechnics, and the arrival of the Dixie Chicks, who sang and played the fiddle while skaters, clad in Western costumes, joined in an old-fashioned rendezvous. The suite culminated in a tribute to the driving of the Golden Spike at Promontory Summit, 40 miles north of Salt Lake City, which joined East and West and completed the first transcontinental railroad in 1869.

"It was a wonderful celebration of the American West," President of the International Olympic Committee (IOC) Jacques Rogge said later. Rogge and Salt Lake 2002 President and CEO Mitt Romney spoke shortly after the Mormon Tabernacle Choir and the Utah Symphony performed the official Salt Lake 2002 musical theme, "Call of the Champions," which had been composed by John Williams. "You remind us all that excellence—the sheer beauty of human excellence," said Romney to the athletes, "is here, possible, part of us, part of life." President of the United States of America George W. Bush opened the Games officially, his declaration followed by the arrival of the Olympic Flag.

The eight flag bearers had been chosen for their power to inspire the world and represented the three pillars of Olympism—sport, culture and environment—and the five continents of the Olympic Rings. Such a gathering had never been seen in any Olympic ceremony. Skiing legend Jean-Claude Killy was chosen for sport, filmmaker Steven Spielberg for culture and activist Jean-Michel Cousteau for environment. "It was such a feeling of renewal of faith and diversity, and I was just honored to be anywhere near the individuals I was selected to accompany," said Spielberg. He was also joined by John Glenn, representing the Americas; Nobel Laureate Lech Walesa, Europe; Nobel

# "It was like all three of us were standing there together. It was the most exciting night of my life."

Laureate Archbishop Desmond Tutu, Africa; Nagano 1998 ski jumper Kazuyoshi Funaki, Asia; and Sydney 2000's track and field star Cathy Freeman, Oceania. "It's been a very, very great exhilarating moment," Tutu later said, "to participate in what has turned out to be a tremendous extravaganza." In an unusual duet, pop artist Sting and celebrated cellist Yo-Yo Ma then took center ice, performing the song "Fragile" as dove-like skaters circled the ice, and thousands of flashlights flickered in the stands.

But the most-awaited moment of the ceremony—the arrival of the Olympic Flame—had yet to come. After its 65-day journey from Greece and throughout America, the flame was carried toward the Olympic Cauldron by pairs of athletes who had inspired one another, and the world, with their courage and conviction. Figure skaters Dorothy Hamill and Dick Button handed the flame to figure skaters Peggy Fleming and Scott Hamilton. Then, alpine skiers Phil Mahre and Bill Johnson carried it to speed skaters Dan Jansen and Bonnie Blair, who handed it to skeleton racer and third-generation Olympian Jim Shea Jr. and his father, Jim Sr. Missing from the Shea reunion was 91-year-old Jack, who had been killed in a car accident just weeks before the Opening Ceremony. But as his son and grandson held a torch aloft, they felt something peculiar. "It was like all three of us were standing there together," said Jim Shea Jr. "It was amazing. It was the most exciting night of my life."

Finally, alpine skier Picabo Street and hockey player Cammi Granato ran the Olympic Flame up the stairs to the most closely guarded secret of the Salt Lake 2002 Games: the person who would light the Olympic Cauldron. Mike Eruzione, captain of the 1980 U.S. Olympic hockey team, which overcame prodigious odds to win the "Miracle on Ice" game against the Soviet Union, emerged from the shadows and beckoned his former teammates to experience the honor with him. The moment symbolized sharing the fire within, and the flame roared up the cauldron, where it would burn for 16 more days, as a beacon to the athletes going to and from events, as a reminder of the Olympic Spirit.

As LeAnn Rimes and a choir of 600 children sang "Light the Fire Within," the evening drew to a close. Under a sky of fireworks, set to Igor Stravinsky's "Firebird Suite" and Beethoven's "Ode to Joy," athletes who had arrived as nations began leaving as fellow competitors. A final, luminous moment: The Olympic Rings emerged in flame from the center of the ice sheet, a brilliant symbol of the power of humankind when united as one. It was a moment when, as environmental crusader Jean-Micheal Cousteau said of the Olympic Games, "All the boundaries fall apart."

*Salt Lake 2002 President and* CEO *Mitt Romney, President of the United States of America*

*George W. Bush and President of the* IOC *Jacques Rogge watch as the American flag rescued from New York*

*City's World Trade Center after September 11, 2001, is brought into the stadium by U.S. athletes.*

SHEILA METZNER

*"When they opened the curtain to let us walk out, I couldn't believe so many people*
*could be so silent. You could hear a pin drop." – Lea Ann Parsley,*
*U.S. skeleton athlete and flag bearer*

S H E I L A   M E T Z N E R

The Child of Light, played by 13-year-old Ryne Sanborn, finds himself surrounded by

stormlike elements, representing life's adversities, in The Fire Within segment.

His appearance ushered in a thematic unity never before seen in an Olympic Games.

SHEILA METZNER

*Some 30,000 costume pieces were created for the Opening Ceremony.*

JOHN HUET

23

*More than 800 adults and children appeared in The Fire Within performance.*

DAVID BURNETT

*Conjuring a winter storm, skaters race around the ice in The Fire Within segment.*

JOHN HUET (TOP)

SHEILA METZNER (BOTTOM)

"Children around the world are dreaming, dreaming of daring performances, cheering friends and proud families." — Salt Lake 2002 President and CEO Mitt Romney

TIBOR NEMETH

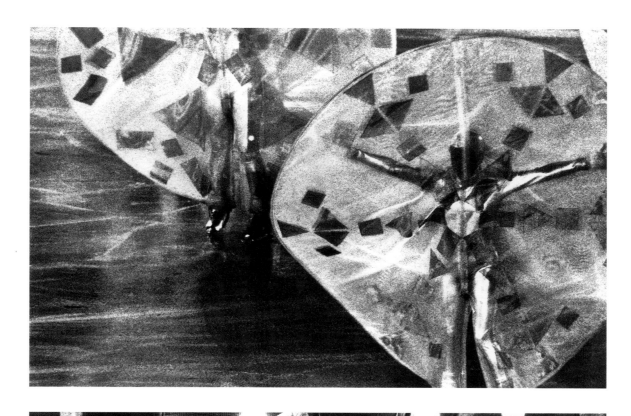

*Performers create the effect of snow and ice crystals, top, and ice shards, bottom.*

SHEILA METZNER

*The Olympic Cauldron still dark, Rice-Eccles Olympic Stadium is lit by fireworks in the shape*

*of XIX, marking the opening of the 19th Olympic Winter Games.*

TIBOR NEMETH

*As the Children of Light entered the stadium, beams of light illuminated flags*
*along the athletes' stand.*

JOHN HUET

*"There is no better feeling." – Freestyle mogulist Evan Dybvig, United States of America, on walking into*

*Rice-Eccles Olympic Stadium. Salt Lake 2002 organizers had persuaded the IOC to depart*

*from tradition and allow athletes to appear at the beginning of the ceremony and enjoy the show.*

IAN LOGAN

*Six hundred and eighty Children of Light symbolized the power to inspire.*

TIBOR NEMETH

"Deep in my heart it makes me feel very proud, my heart just swelled. It is so exciting and
impressive to see all the Indian tribes out there together for the first time, this has
never happened before." – Rupert Steele, Goshute Ceremonial Leader, on the gathering of the
Goshute, Navajo, Paiute, Shoshone and Ute tribes at the Opening Ceremony

TIBOR NEMETH

*After arriving in the stadium, the leaders of the five Utah native tribes were presented*

*with symbolic gifts from athletes representing five nations that have hosted*

*Olympic Games. In return, the tribal leaders offered blessings to the athletes.*

DAVID BURNETT

"The five [Indian] nations coming together shows the world that we can work side by side.
It is just amazing how the five [Olympic] Rings fit into the five nations that are part of Utah."
— Kenneth Maryboy, Navajo Ceremonial Leader

IAN LOGAN

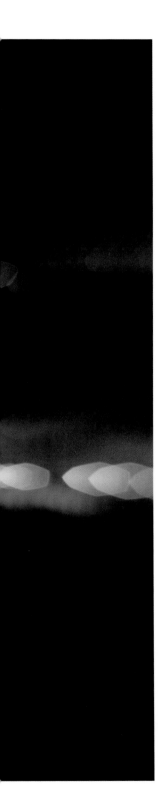

*The Native American Welcome began with the sounds of five distinct, ethereal tunes from five flute players. The final, unified chord signaled the landing of a live golden eagle in front of the athletes.*

JOHN HUET

*Appearing in the Native American Welcome were participants of every age, from infant to elder.*

SHEILA METZNER

*Sixty-six skaters swept around the ice, emulating the flight of the golden eagle.*

SHEILA METZNER

*"The mix of color, light and emotions surely lit the spirit of global unity across the world."* — *IOC President Jacques Rogge*

STEVEN CURRIE

*Square-dancing pioneers and a giant bison arrive on stage for the American West Suite.*

DAVID BURNETT

39

*A stampede of horses joins the wild beasts, birds and fish in the Land of Enchantment.*

MICHAEL   SEAMANS

Sting and Yo-Yo Ma perform "Fragile" on a star field of ice as 25 skaters form a flock of doves,
symbolizing the traditional release of doves as a sign of peace.

SHEILA METZNER

*The 1980 U.S. "Miracle on Ice" hockey team lights the Olympic Cauldron.*

DAVID BURNETT

*A sudden burst of flame creates the Olympic Rings on the ice as the Opening Ceremony*

*draws to a close. "I remember thinking, 'This is it. This is my dream. I'm finally an Olympian.'"*

*— Women's hockey player Julie Chu of the United States of America*

IAN LOGAN

*Fireworks explode over the athletes' stand, the moment accompanied by Beethoven's "Ode to Joy"*
*and Igor Stravinsky's "Firebird Suite."*

SHEILA METZNER

ALPINE SKIING · THEY CALLED THE COURSE
GRIZZLY. NEARLY TWO MILES OF SHEER TERROR FROM
START TO FINISH, LINED WITH 18 MILES OF FENCING TO
CATCH THE UNFORTUNATE SOUL WHO MIGHT SNAG AN
EDGE ON THE NASTY JOHN PAUL TRAVERSE OR LOSE CON-
TROL OFF THE BUFFALO JUMP. A DROP OF 74 DEGREES
MEANT ZERO TO 70 MILES PER HOUR IN 10 SECONDS. THIS
WAS THE MEN'S DOWNHILL AT SNOWBASIN SKI AREA, AN
UNPREDICTABLE RIDE OF SPEED AND SKILL IN WHICH RISK
WAS REWARDED WITH VICTORY—OR PUNISHED WITH PAIN

*"Skiing is all a matter of balance, of your position on the skis...You can feel the speed on the good*

*turns, you can be balanced," says women's downhill gold medalist Carole Montillet of France. "You're*

*on a peak, and then it seems easy. You love the speed, and you want to go faster."*

JOHN HUET

and loss. And on February 10, it was a fitting kickoff to the Salt Lake 2002 alpine events.

From the downhill, super-G and combined at Snowbasin Ski Area to the giant slalom at Park City Mountain Resort and the slalom at Deer Valley Resort, hundreds of skiers tore down Utah's mountains in a spine-tingling show of aggression and athleticism. Legends such as Picabo Street, Lasse Kjus and Stephan Eberharter returned, while new heroes were made of Janica Kostelić, Bode Miller and Anja Pärson. Tens of thousands of spectators shared the experience, cheering madly for each and every competitor, finding some element of truth or hope in their triumphs and struggles. "That is what the Olympics are all about," said Street. "We're making childhood dreams come true."

MEN'S DOWNHILL •

The grueling Grizzly course was Austrian Stephan Eberharter's chance at redemption. A spectacular breakthrough at age 21, when he became a double world champion in 1991, had been followed by a string of injuries that forced him to miss part of the 1992 and all of the 1994 Games and to fight his way back onto the Austrian team. Then he found himself skiing in the shadows of teammate Hermann Maier, often in second and so close to victory, but constantly edged out by the "Herminator." Perhaps this time it would be different. Maier had been severely injured in a motorcycle crash, unable to compete, and Eberharter, 32, was ready to crown his own comeback with gold at Snowbasin.

Incredibly, every competitor managed to complete his run and cross the finish line, the mighty Austrians taking the riskiest lines and sharpest turns. But when the top competitors had raced, Eberharter had again been bested by an Austrian teammate, Fritz Strobl, who had skied the course in 1:39.13. Norway's Kjus had earned the silver, with 1:39.35, and Eberharter was in third with 1:39.41. Kjus, who had been struggling with chronic sinus and bronchial problems that often interrupted his competition schedule, had earned his fourth Olympic medal. "I had a good day today," he said. "Everything went my way." Eberharter, meanwhile, shrugged off his disappointment at missing the gold and looked ahead. "There are plenty of races to collect," he said. "It's not over yet."

For gold medalist Strobl, a quiet policeman whose goal is to take over his parents' farm when he retires, shook his head at his victory. "Skiing, the fun of skiing—that's all I was thinking," he said, "and now my joy is even greater to have won."

LADIES' DOWNHILL •

The dangers of downhill may have been on Carole Montillet's mind as she careened down Wildflower (a misleading name, for the course was nearly as tough as the men's) on February 12. After all, her French teammate Régine Cavagnoud had been killed after crashing into a German coach during a training run in October 2001. But Montillet, known for her fearlessness and love of speed, showed no signs of even the slightest trepidation as she blazed through the course in 1:39.56, the fastest time of the day. "I chose the most direct line coming down," she said.

Her victory was a gift to a grieving team, and to a country that had not won ladies' alpine gold since 1968. "We had a difficult time this winter, but I really raced this race for myself," said Montillet. "However, I know that she [Régine] helped me because I know she was with me."

Close behind Montillet were silver medalist Isolde Kostner of Italy with a time of 1:40.01, who dedicated her victory to Amnesty International, and first-time medalist Renate Götschl of Austria, whose time of 1:40.39 earned her the bronze. American Picabo Street, who had been hoping for one more Olympic medal, finished 16th and announced her retirement from competitive ski racing. "I'm really relieved to be done with my career," she said. "I'm relieved to be safe."

MEN'S COMBINED •

American Bode Miller feared for his life. It was the downhill portion of the combined event, and his skis suddenly skipped out of control. "It was a crash," he said, remembering how, flooded with adrenaline, he somehow righted his body and avoided killing himself and officials in his path. "If it hadn't been a life-threatening situation, I probably wouldn't have been able to pull it off." The near disaster had landed Miller way behind the leaders in 15th place, with two slalom runs left to complete. In the first, he nearly slid off course again, ruining his chances at a medal by finishing a distant 2.44 seconds behind the leader, Norwegian Kjetil Andre Aamodt.

# "HE'S REVOLUTIONIZED THE WAY OF SKIING," SAID AAMODT. "NOBODY'S EVER SKIED THAT FAST...HE HAS NO LIMITS."

Or so we thought. In his final run of the day, Miller decided to forget about the fear and think about the fun. "I was looking at the slalom course, which for me is a lot like looking at a great golf course, or a playground if you're a kid," he said. "And I went out and charged the second run." Once again, Miller seemed out of control, but this time, his reckless style catapulted him into an incredible comeback—and a silver medal. He made up 2.16 seconds, grabbing the lead until Aamodt raced, winning the gold. Austria's Benjamin Raich won the bronze, his first Olympic medal.

Aamodt had broken his own record of 15 Olympic and world championship medals, becoming the most decorated alpine skier in history. But even the 30-year-old veteran was astounded by Miller's raw speed and ability to turn a potentially deadly day into a silver medal. "He's revolutionized the way of skiing. Nobody's ever skied that fast," said Aamodt. "When he's putting it all together, he's in a class of his own…He has no limits."

**LADIES' COMBINED** •

With all three runs on a single day for the first time in Olympic history, the combined event demanded versatile skiing skills and incredible mental toughness. Janica Kostelić, who would soon be known as the "Croatian Sensation," was the perfect match. She began ski racing at age 9 and soon fled her war-torn country to train in the mountains elsewhere in Europe. Beset by a lack of funds, Kostelić often slept in her father's car, while her brother Ivica, who also raced, slept beneath it.

Kostelić's stamina had guided her through a number of painful crashes and surgeries and on February 14, it would reward her with her first Olympic medal. After the two slalom runs (the event was held in the reverse order of the men's), Kostelić was a full 1.1 seconds ahead of Germany's Martina Ertl. Even a third-place finish in the downhill portion—her weakest discipline—couldn't knock Kostelić from atop the podium. She won the gold, Croatia's first-ever medal at an Olympic Winter Games. Two-time Olympian Götschl of Austria and two-time Olympic silver medalist Ertl of Germany took the silver and bronze, respectively.

"This is kind of a family medal, because it was always in the family—everything, always training," said Kostelić, who had her brother's name painted on the nails of her left hand before the race. "Everything was always me, my brother and my father. My mother was always on the side, but she's the boss. It's a great thing, and my family's dream came true."

**MEN'S SUPER-G** •

There are no practice runs in super-G, just an hour and a half to study the course and choose a line. That meant that Norwegian Aamodt's 10 years of experience could amount to little once he flew out of the start hut on February 16 at Snowbasin. Aamodt had won the gold in super-G at the Albertville 1992 Games and had since won a World Cup title in every discipline, one of only four men to accomplish such a feat. Nevertheless, he was not favored to medal in the 2002 super-G, thanks to the strength of teammate Kjus, Switzerland's Didier Cuche and Austrian Eberharter.

But Aamodt finished the race in 1:21.58, a time he would be astonished to see hold strong throughout the event. A tricky gate at the top of Rendezvous Face, with a 74 percent grade, cut the race short for both Kjus and Cuche. Eberharter slipped trying to make a hard right turn, but managed to stay on the course and finished second behind Aamodt by one-tenth of a second. "To win the super-G again after 10 years," said Aamodt, "is a dream come true."

Once again, Eberharter had just missed the gold, winning the silver. Teammate Andreas Schifferer, who finished just 0.25 seconds behind Aamodt, was elated by his bronze-medal performance after a difficult year recuperating from a knee injury. "You know, you have to be really patient," he said. "Now I think I'm harvesting the fruits of my work. If you know that there is something that you should fight for, then you must really do it."

Daniela Ceccarelli of Italy grew up in the sun-baked, gently rolling hills of Rocca Priora, just 20 minutes from Rome and five hours from the nearest major ski area. But she also grew up with a father addicted to thrills—an air-force pilot who spent his free time skiing and decided his children should be racers. So when Ceccarelli, a military police officer ranked 40th overall in the 2000–01 World Cup standings, rocketed to the top of the winner's podium in the super-G, with a time of 1:13.59, she turned to thank her mentor.

"I owe my victory to my father," she said. "This love for speed, this love for adrenaline comes from him." It was her first international victory and one of the biggest upsets of the alpine races. Favored to win were Germany's Hilde Gerg, No.1 in the World Cup super-G standings, Austria's downhill bronze medalist Götschl and France's downhill gold medalist, Montillet. They finished fifth, eighth and seventh, respectively.

# THE STEEP COURSE BECAME EVEN MORE BRUTAL, SENDING FRUSTRATED SKIERS FLYING OFF TOWARD THE FENCE.

Just behind Ceccarelli was Kostelić, winning the silver with a time of 1:13.64. For her second event, Kostelić had MAMA painted on the fingernails of her left hand. After finishing, she embraced her mother and asked, "Am I good? Am I good?"

Italy's Karen Putzer had skipped the combined event to train for super-G and was rewarded with the bronze. "It's like a dream," she said. "I can't believe it."

After nearly ideal, bluebird conditions for the first three alpine events, with only the ladies' downhill postponed due to high winds, the weather turned a corner. A snowstorm hit Deer Valley Resort on February 20, just in time for the ladies' slalom on the Know You Don't run. In the blinding snow and flat light, the steep course became even more brutal, sending frustrated skiers flying off toward the fence. American Kristina Koznick, a top contender who compared the race to a rodeo, was one of 19 skiers who failed to finish the first run. Eleven skiers fell during the second run. Simply put by Kostelić, "I think everyone skied really bad."

Kostelić, however, managed to remain on course for both runs, earning a combined time of

1:46.10 and her third Salt Lake 2002 medal—a gold. "I skied the best way through a bad course," she said. Just 0.07 seconds behind was France's Laure Péquegnot, who relished the conditions. "I like it like this," she said after her first run. "It will be a fight."

And Sweden's Anja Pärson, who was raised in the same town as the legendary skier Ingemar Stenmark, won bronze and her country's first alpine medal of the Games. "The course was very steep," she said, elated with her run. "When we're in the World Cup, it's flat hills. It's like skiing a parking lot. I just haven't raced on this kind of hill. But I'm happy with what I've done."

MEN'S GIANT SLALOM •

Eberharter stood in the start hut atop Park City Mountain Resort, awaiting his second run in the giant slalom. Three-quarters of a mile below, the 18,000 fans were still screaming for Miller, whose combined time of 2:24.16 had placed him in the lead. After a wild run in his signature, on-the-edge style, Miller had leapfrogged the field from seventh to first place. Now Miller waited for Eberharter. Near the finish line, he caught his breath and looked up at the ridgeline, toward Eberharter, the last of the top 15 competitors to race.

Despite the noise below, the Austrian heard nothing. "Actually, it was very quiet at the start," he said. "It was a bit unusual. I said to myself, 'I've got two medals, and on the other hand it's your last chance to win a gold medal.'" And so he charged the course in 1:11.30 for a combined time of 2:23.28. He had finally won his gold, and when he saw his time, he fell to the ground in joy and relief. "I knew I had to ski a near perfect run, and I made it," he said.

One of the first to congratulate Eberharter was Miller, who was in turn congratulated by Kjus, who had won the bronze. It seemed the American, despite missing the gold, had impressed his competitors. "He is a tough racer and has a great future," said Eberharter. "He has a crazy style of skiing, but he's fast and that's all that counts."

LADIES' GIANT SLALOM •

On February 22, Kostelić made history as she won the giant slalom and became the first alpine skier ever to win four medals at a single Olympic Winter Games. And with her winning combined time of 2:30.01, she also joined France's Jean-Claude Killy and Toni Sailer of Austria as the only skiers with three golds from one Games. Three days later, she was welcomed home to Croatia by 100,000 who skipped work and school to celebrate their hero, whom they had nicknamed the "Snow Queen."

Kostelić had barely prepared for the giant slalom event, logging only two training sessions in the weeks before the Games. She had never finished higher than fourth in a World Cup giant slalom. And that's precisely how she won. Like Eberharter the day before, Kostelić was the last of the top 15 skiers to race in the second run. She had heard that Pärson and Switzerland's Sonja Nef had skied well, and figured she wouldn't catch them. "I didn't have any pressure," she said. "I felt really relaxed."

She won by 1.32 seconds, while Pärson and Nef would earn silver and bronze, respectively. While shocked that she had beaten Nef, who was the giant slalom leader of the season, Kostelić remained sanguine about her historic feat. "I'm tired," she said. "For sure I am happy, but I'm tired. It's great but someone is going to break that record soon. The next Olympics maybe."

Pärson, it seemed, hoped to be that someone. "I'm very happy for Janica," she said. "We're good friends. But now she's the one to beat. I'm happy for her, yes. But I am still a competitor, and I'll try to do my best to beat her."

MEN'S SLALOM •

After blowing out both his knees in a 1999 training accident, France's Jean-Pierre Vidal didn't think he would walk, let alone ski. He was confined to a wheelchair, devastated and depressed. His career, it seemed, had come to an end. "I thought it was finished for me," Vidal said. "But after a few months, I had this passion to ski."

He spent day after day in rehabilitation, stubborn in his vision of competing again. "I've been dreaming about the Olympics since I was a child," he says. "After the accident, I came back. I prepared intensely."

The steep Know You Don't course struck again, with softening snow that tripped up some of the top skiers, including the first four competitors of the second run. Miller, hoping for a third Salt Lake 2002 medal and in second place behind Vidal after the first run, charged the course and missed a gate, finishing in 25th place. "That's what happens when you push hard," he said.

Among those who held on was Alain Baxter of Aviemore, Scotland, who won the bronze, Great Britain's first-ever Olympic alpine medal. Less than a month later, the medal was stripped and awarded to fourth-place finisher Benjamin Raich of Austria after it was discovered that Baxter had mistakenly, but illegally, used a banned substance found in a nasal inhaler.

And then there was Vidal, who clung ferociously to his lead and won the gold, 0.36 seconds ahead of teammate Sebastien Amiez, who earned the silver. Vidal was the first Frenchman in 34 years to win Olympic gold in the slalom; the last victory belonged to Jean-Claude Killy at the Grenoble 1968 Games. Looking back at his recovery and the road to gold, Vidal seemed inspired by the same passion that had fueled Killy.

"After two months in a chair, I feel that all is going to be OK," he said. "I knew that I had skiing in my heart, and I just had to light a fire in me."

*"It's downhill. It's just the best kick you can get. Where else can you go from top to bottom*
*with no people in your way?" – Ireland's Paul Patrick Schwarzacher-Joyce*

SHEILA METZNER

*Switzerland's Tobias Grünenfelder prepares to race the super-G.*

TIBOR NEMETH

55

*Canada's Anne Marie Lefrançois shoots out of the start house during the*

*second downhill training run on Snowbasin's Wildflower course.*

STEVEN CURRIE

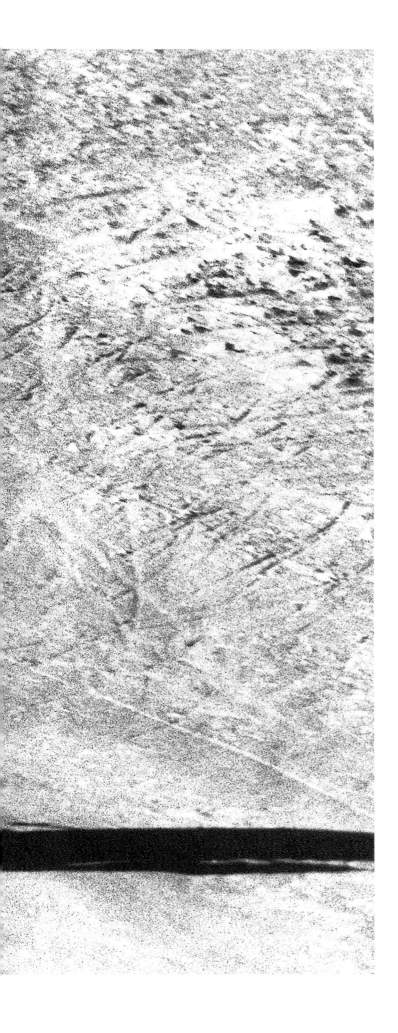

*"The Olympics are different for each person, but for me the medal is sort of a bonus. It's more for the crowd, the country and my family and coaches. For me, that feeling I had when I skied that second run was better than any medal." – Bode Miller of the United States of America (left). His second slalom run of the men's combined event was one of the greatest comebacks in the Games and earned Miller the silver medal.*

SHEILA METZNER

*The men's Grizzly downhill course, above, was named for a local legend about Old*

*Ephraim, a huge grizzly bear that roamed the area in the early 1900s, outsmarting shepherds and*

*hunters for years. Other parts of the course, such as Flintlock Jump and Trapper's Loop,*

*were named for the area's rich mining and hunting history.*

SHEILA    METZNER

Amazingly, every competitor in men's downhill managed to cross the finish line of a course

described by designer and Sapporo 1972 downhill gold medalist Bernhard Russi

as a roller coaster and a rodeo.

SHEILA METZNER

*"It's a long story. I was 9 when I started skiing, for serious. And I was skiing and skiing and skiing and I came here and I got a medal." – "Croatian Sensation" Janica Kostelić, who became the first alpine skier ever to win four medals at a single Olympic Winter Games.*

MICHAEL SEAMANS

*Anne Marie Lefrançois of Canada overcame a string of injuries to compete*

*in the downhill and super-G at Snowbasin.*

TIBOR NEMETH

"I love skiing and I always try to push myself, and those two things are the most important. If you love

skiing and you love competition and you still want to push yourself to win more, then you

can go a long way for a long time," – Kjetil Andre Aamodt of Norway. His gold in the Salt Lake 2002

super-G gave him a total of seven Olympic medals, the most ever for an alpine skier.

S H E I L A    M E T Z N E R    ( A B O V E )

T I B O R    N E M E T H    ( R I G H T )

*"I must admit that I was truly confused. I was so excited that I looked up at the screen, and I thought I
saw the number 9 next to my name. So I said, 'well, I'm last.' Then I saw the audience cheering, and I saw
my teammates cheering." – Super-G gold medalist Daniela Ceccarelli of Italy*

ALBERT  COLANTONIO

*Alexandra Munteanu represented Romania in four alpine events.*

MICHAEL SEAMANS

*Maui Gayme of Chile delivered the best South American performance of the*

*men's downhill with a time of 1:47.63.*

STEVEN CURRIE

FREESTYLE SKIING · IN THE WORLD OF SKI RACING, FREESTYLERS WERE ALWAYS DIFFERENT. THEY EMERGED ON THE SKI SLOPES IN THE 1970S WITH LONG HAIR AND BRIGHT, BAGGY CLOTHES, SHATTERING SKIING'S SERIOUS SIDE. THEY WERE SO-CALLED HOTDOGGERS, WHO BOUNCED OVER BUMPS AND FLIPPED OFF KICKERS, EVER PUSHING THE LIMITS OF HOW A HUMAN COULD SLIDE DOWN A SLOPE. AND AT THE SALT LAKE 2002 GAMES, THE FREESTYLE ATHLETES WERE ONCE AGAIN, WELL, DIFFERENT. THEY TALKED BIG AND SKIED BIG, ATTEMPTING NEW TRICKS

*"I wanted to get gold or last."* — Eric Bergoust, United States of America

ANDY ANDERSON

and flying faster than ever down the hill. Freestyle tickets were some of the hottest of the Games, thanks to the rock 'n' roll show displayed at Deer Valley Resort. With the course visible from top to finish, spectators could watch every minute of knee-bumping, death-defying action. They also saw moments of human drama from legends to newcomers, who proved that the sport will always be free.

WOMEN'S AERIALS •

Alisa Camplin trained with leeches. Literally.

"It made us tough," said the aerialist of her sessions in a leech-filled, scum-covered landing pool back home in Australia. Again and again, Camplin and teammate Jacqui Cooper worked on their flips and twists. After landing, they would have to hike through the mud, covered in leeches. They tried to feed the fish with bread so they would grow and eat the leeches. "I guess we did it the hard way," she said. Cooper, meanwhile, was drinking cockroach extract mixed with diet Coke to cure her bad back.

Having recovered from her back pain, Cooper broke her kneecap during training and pulled out of the Salt Lake 2002 competition. "It isn't just about my leg," she said. "I've got a broken heart."

But the leeches worked wonders for Camplin, who stunned the world—and herself—by winning the gold at Deer Valley Resort's White Owl course on February 18. After Cooper's injury, Australian coach Peter Judge had asked his team to step up and take her place. And so the 27-year-old Camplin, who had left her job at a major computer company to train and had sold her car to make ends meet, answered the call. She had placed second in the qualifying round on February 16, behind Switzerland's Evelyn Leu, who had set the world record by earning a total score of 203.16, and ahead of Belarusian Alla Tsuper. Two days later, during the first of two final jumps, she moved to third place, while Leu, one of only two competitors to try a triple flip, wiped out and Russia's Olga Koroleva advanced to first, with a back layout tuck full jump. Then, on Camplin's final run, she pulled off a second triple-twisting, double backflip jump, nailing the landing and then skidding to a stop. She stood in disbelief as she realized she had taken the lead. And then more disbelief, as Tsuper missed her landing and Koroleva fell just short of medal contention, finishing fourth. It was official. Gold. Camplin looked around in disbelief. "I won?" she said. "I won!"

She had become the first Australian woman to win gold in the Olympic Winter Games and part of a string of unexpected victories for her country. "This is the craziest thing that has ever happened to me," Camplin said later. "This is the first time I've ever won anything. It still doesn't seem real. I feel like a normal girl from Melbourne, Australia, who went out on a normal day and just landed two jumps. All of a sudden I've got people clapping for me every time I walk into a room."

Joining Camplin on the podium were Canadians Veronica Brenner and Deidra Dionne, who won silver and the bronze, respectively. Two-time Olympian Brenner was known for quoting Shakespeare while Dionne studied university courses during training. Looking back and forth between Brenner and Dionne, Camplin started to laugh. "We three girls up here are the dorkiest girls on the tour," she said, clutching Errol, a stuffed sheep who served as her good luck mascot. "Everyone always laughs at us. We never go out once. We sit inside and we read books. But it pays to be smart."

MEN'S AERIALS •

American Eric Bergoust defied the laws of gravity, but he arrived at the Salt Lake 2002 Games with the weight of the world on his shoulders. In the four years since he won gold at Nagano, Bergoust had been expanding the frontier of aerials, experimenting with new maneuvers, exhaustively training and drawing diagrams of the physics of flying. He mastered not only double and triple flips, but a quadruple flip, a move officials banned from competition until at least 2003. Bit by bit, the pressure was building on "Air Bergy" to win again. Olympic experts consistently picked him as the 2002 gold medalist. His father Don had written a poem that begins, "In aerial skiing one's known as the best."

Serious expectations, but Bergoust was just as serious about meeting them. In the qualification round, held just after the women's qualifiers on February 16, he was in second place after Belarusian Alexei Grichin (Bergoust's chief rival) and followed by American Joe Pack and nine other athletes.

As the finals began to unfold three days later, it was clear that the competition was fierce. One by one, the aerialists were landing difficult jumps. By the end of the first run, however, the leading lineup had barely shifted: Bergoust was in first with a score of 130.38—which almost guaranteed the gold—while Grichin had slipped to second and Pack remained in third. A Park City local, Pack was surrounded by friends and family. "This just allows me to go that much bigger," he said. "This is my backyard. This is my home. I know what's going on."

Aleš Valenta of the Czech Republic also knew exactly what was happening as he took off for a quint-twisting triple backflip, the first ever attempted at the Olympic Winter Games. If he landed the extremely tricky jump, he could vault from fifth to first place. There seemed nothing to lose: Valenta

# "I KNEW SOMETHING GREAT WAS GOING TO COME," SAID BAHRKE. "AND I JUST STOOD AT THE TOP, SMILING."

had missed the Lillehammer 1994 Games because he had been drafted to serve a year in the Czech army, and finished an agonizing fourth at Nagano in 1998. "I've landed that jump just three times," he admitted later. "I used it as my lucky shot at a medal."

Luck was on his side, and Valenta gained the lead. Deciding he could not afford to be conservative on his final jump, Bergoust took a step back from his starting position, starting higher to gain more air. But then, something went wrong. He accelerated too quickly and while his jump was strong, Bergoust slapped his back on the landing. The fans gasped. As the scores appeared, they gasped again: Air Bergy had earned just 218.5 points, tumbling from first to 12th place.

"I wanted to get gold or last," said Bergoust. "And I got last."

In a heartbeat, the pendulum of attention had swung to Valenta, who won not only gold but the same awe and admiration bestowed on Bergoust in 1998. "He's psycho, and he makes it look really easy," said Pack, who had earned the silver while Grichin won the bronze. "It's technique and confidence. Now, we're going to have to build bigger jumps and make it safer. Aleš is ahead of his time. I'm proud of him."

WOMEN'S MOGULS •

Champion, Deer Valley Resort's moguls course, stretched more than two football fields from top to bottom. Rippled with hundreds of moguls and two sets of kickers, it was easily one of the longest and most difficult courses in international competition. From where more than 13,600 fans sat for the women's competition on February 9, it looked daunting. From the start house, where the athletes tried to stay warm on the cold morning, prepped and pumped their fists, it looked like the future.

And it also looked like a whole lot of fun to the 29 women who bounced through the course during the qualifying round, heated by the climbing sun, the growing cheers of the crowd and the fluttering, colorful flags from around the world. In the ever-evolving sport—scored for turns, speed and maneuvers—the women pulled off more difficult moves from those displayed at the 1998 Games: triple position jumps and rotational spins with positions, which were rare at Nagano. By the end of the

7*1*

run, Norway's Kari Traa, the 1998 bronze medalist and reigning world moguls champion, was in first place, with Americans Ann Battelle and Hannah Hardaway in second and third, respectively. There were big expectations for newcomer Hardaway and for Battelle, who had competed in the first Olympic moguls competition in 1992 and nearly quit after a 10th place finish at Nagano. But she had come back to earn respectable finishes, and was giving a medal another shot. "I'm putting a lot of pressure on myself," she had admitted before the competition.

The pressure would prove too much for Battelle and Hardaway, who slipped to seventh and fifth place, respectively, in the finals. Then there was fellow American Shannon Bahrke, who was in fifth place after the qualifying round. Overcome by a severe back infection in 1999, Bahrke was told by doctors that she'd never ski at a world-class level again. Recovered and having climbed the international rankings, she would prove them wrong. Looking down the course and listening to the crowd, she did something unusual for an athlete about to begin the most important run of her life: She smiled. "I knew something great was going to come," she said later. "And I just stood at the top smiling, and the smile hasn't left yet."

Her performance—including a spectacular heli-iron cross—landed Bahrke in the lead, temporarily. And even when she was pushed to silver by Traa's superior run, with her own heli-iron cross and triple twister, Bahrke was overjoyed to have won America's first medal of the Games. In third was Tae Satoya, the surprise Nagano 1998 gold medalist who surprised the world again with her bronze. She had traded places with Traa, who had given up chocolate in 1999, lost 20 pounds and soon dominated the sport. Though she was expected to win gold, Traa spoke with the amazement of a rising star. "I was so nervous while I was waiting for my score," she said. "I'm just so happy that I made it."

MEN'S MOGULS •

 For three days, the Champion course underwent a slight metamorphosis, softening under the sunshine and freezing at night. The bumps were now even tougher for the men, who competed on February 12. "This is a really long course," said spectator Glen Plake, a pioneer of freestyle skiing in the 1980s. "This is going to be crazy. It's hard to tell what's going to happen. There are a lot of aces here and a few new tricks. Who knows?"

Among the new tricks expected was American Jonny Moseley's dinner roll, a controversial off-axis, horizontal 720-degree spin in which a skier rotates twice with his body parallel to the ground. Moseley, the Nagano 1998 gold medalist, had been practicing and performing the maneuver over and over, delighting spectators but earning few points from the judges. Inverted moves, where skis are above the athlete's head, are prohibited in moguls competition, and the dinner roll, to some, came dangerously close to breaking the rules.

But freestyle skiing began by breaking the rules, and in the qualifying round, the crowd of 14,300 chanting his name in unison, Moseley pulled off what he called a perfect dinner roll, and then jumped over a fence to embrace a group of fans. He had made the final round, earning an 11th place berth. Later, Sam Temple of Great Britain earned equally loud cheers when he fell halfway through the run and hiked back up the hill to gain more air off the second kicker. He had no chance at medaling, but there was still some room for fun. "I wanted to jump for the crowd, really," he said. Spectators were treated to sportsmanship and showmanship: Teppei Noda of Japan also clambered up the hill after a fall to retrieve his ski and complete the run, while 1994 gold medalist Jean-Luc Brassard wore bright yellow sleeves on his legs to draw attention to his bouncing knees.

American Travis Mayer was in first position after the first run, followed by four-time Olympian and Nagano 1998 silver medalist Janne Lahtela of Norway and then Finland's Mikko Ronkainen. In the finals, Lahtela, who had won nearly every major competition in the two years before the Games,

*Aerialist Deidra Dionne of Canada won bronze in the women's competition. "I just went for it.*
*I knew I could land it, I knew I could do it well," she said.*

JOHN HUET

Gold medalist Aleš Valenta of the Czech Republic slides to a stop. No other jumper attempted his trick, a quint-

twisting triple backflip. "I don't think I can really believe what I've really done, what I achieved," he said.

SHEILA    METZNER

*"In our sport, things change rapidly. A small mistake, a change of weather condition and in the wind*

*can mean a change in the result." — Bronze medalist Alexei Grichin, Belarus.*

SHEILA METZNER

*Aerialist Stanislav Kravchuk of the Ukraine placed fifth on February 19,*

*scoring a personal best of 246 points.*

ELISABETH O'DONNELL

*More than 13,000 fans filled the stands at Deer Valley Resort for aerials finals. "Unbelievable,"*
*said silver medalist Joe Pack of the United States of America. "To hear the crowd yell when I landed pushed*
*me back probably 10 feet."*

IAN LOGAN

*With sunny skies, music blasting and stands full of spectators who had been camped in their seats since the early morning, Deer Valley Resort's freestyle arena was part sporting venue, part rock concert.*

CHAD HOLDER

*"If you make the U.S. Olympic team, that's a life achievement. No one can ever take that away from you."*

*— Silver medalist Joe Pack, United States of America*

JOHN HUET

*"I am scared to do a triple here. This hill, it scares me."* – Aerialist Alla Tsuper of Belarus, above

D A V I D   B U R N E T T

*Aerialists must measure their takeoff from the kickers precisely or risk disaster. "You can take a half-meter step up and you can miss everything and land on your back," said bronze medalist Alexei Grichin of Belarus. "The wind changes every time, and it's so difficult to land the right way."*

IAN LOGAN

*Russian moguls skier Marina Cherkasova does a daffy at Deer Valley Resort.*
*"The course is very long and difficult," she said. "You have to be strong."*

A N D Y    A N D E R S O N

*"When you compete, you don't feel the pain." — Gold medalist Kari Traa of Norway, on the payoff*

*of exhaustive hours of training on knee-pounding mogul fields*

TIBOR NEMETH

*The men's moguls finalists are announced after qualifying for the medal round.*

JOHN HUET

"I heard the crowds cheering. It gave me such an energy boost. They spurred me on at the end, and it was an immense feeling." – Laura Donaldson of Great Britain (above), despite having placed last in the women's moguls event.

TIBOR NEMETH (ABOVE)

Deer Valley Resort's Champion course (right) measured 857 feet long, with a 28-degree pitch.

ALBERT COLANTONIO (RIGHT)

*American Jonny Moseley's dinner roll—an off-axis, horizontal 720-degree spin, above—won him adoration*

*from the crowd. After pulling off the tricky maneuever, he jumped into a group of cheering fans at the finish line.*

*"I just went and jumped into them and got so much love," he said. "It felt great."*

JOHN   HUET

"In 1992, I was 9 years old and I started dreaming about the Olympics then." — Men's moguls silver

medalist Travis Mayer, United States of America

IAN LOGAN

*The helicopter, an upright aerial spin of 360 degrees, was one*

*of several maneuvers displayed by 59 mogulists at Deer Valley Resort.*

TIBOR NEMETH

SNOWBOARDING · THE SPORT'S FIRST STEPS INTO THE OLYMPIC MOVEMENT WERE SHAKY. AT ITS DEBUT AT THE NAGANO 1998 GAMES, SNOWBOARDERS' ATTITUDES, FIERCE INDIVIDUALISM AND EVER-CHANGING MANEUVERS SEEMED TO CONFLICT WITH AGE-OLD OLYMPIC TRADITIONS. "THIS SPORT HAS ALWAYS BEEN ABOUT YOUTH AND PROGRESSION," SAID JAKE BURTON, A SNOWBOARDING PIONEER WHO POPULARIZED THE SPORT, BEFORE THE GAMES. "SNOWBOARDERS DON'T NEED THE OLYMPICS." · BUT AT THE SALT LAKE 2002 GAMES, SNOWBOARDING GREW UP.

Park City Mountain Resort's halfpipe venue elicited praise from nearly every competitor.

"This is completely different from anything I've ever seen before," said bronze medalist J.J. Thomas

of the United States of America. "It sets the standard for snowboarding."

TIBOR NEMETH

Athletes were impressed by Park City Mountain Resort's high-tech halfpipe and challenged by the new parallel format of the giant slalom. Inspired by the sold-out crowds, they threw down new tricks and flew down the course at record speeds. And the snowboarders, in turn, inspired spectators with their struggles, successes and genuine smiles. It was about youth and progression, but it was also about having fun, with the whole world watching.

The halfpipe event at Park City Mountain Resort often seemed more like a party than a competition. Just below the finish area and judges' tower, rock bands played in between rounds, the music blasting into the bleachers from giant speakers. Impromptu mosh pits formed: Some spectators surfed the crowd; others stripped down to T-shirts, smearing on sunblock while they danced under the bright blue skies.

But at the top of the course, there was no mistaking the intensity of this competition. As athletes strapped onto their boards, they peered down into their proving ground: the enormous halfpipe. At one time, riders made the best of snow-covered drainage ditches. But the halfpipe at the Salt Lake 2002 Games was a beast. Nearly 15 feet high and 55 feet wide, it was sculpted from 175,000 cubic feet of snow and stretched 200 feet longer than most halfpipes. The height allowed for tricks three-stories high, and the length allowed for seven tricks per run, with more air time than in any previous competition.

On February 10, the women took to the pipe. After the qualifying round, 12 riders advanced to the final two runs. As the athletes dropped into the course, having selected their own music, the sounds of Aretha Franklin, Madonna and Britney Spears spilled over the mountain. During the first final run, France's Doriane Vidal earned a score of 43.0 for her smooth riding and massive air, becoming the first woman of the day to break 40. She was soon followed by American Kelly Clark, who scored 40.8 points and landed in second. Switzerland's Fabienne Reuteler was in third with 39.7.

At the beginning of the last run, it appeared that Vidal, who had hitchhiked to the event after waiting fruitlessly for a cab that morning, would win the gold. It would be difficult to top her impressive score. One by one, the top riders reached scores in the mid-to-high 30s, but nothing near Vidal's 43. Even Vidal failed to surpass her mark, earning a 36.5 on the second run of the finals.

# "It's great to have all the people here, especially the young girls. Hopefully, I can be a hero for them."

The last to compete was Clark, a quiet teenager who had just graduated from high school. Riding with a mini-disc player blasting Blink 182's "This Is Growing Up," Clark tried to concentrate, drowning out the noise of 16,500 screaming fans. "The crowd was going wild," she said later. "I could hear it even over my headphones."

Clark's run was nearly flawless, a mix of seven difficult tricks that she pulled off with style and big air. After several tense seconds, her score popped up on the board. A 47.9; she had won the gold. The largely American crowd went even wilder.

"It's great to have all the people here today, and especially the young girls," said Clark. "Hopefully, I can be somewhat of a hero or a role model for them."

While the women's competition had thrilled snowboarding fans, nothing could prepare them for what would happen the following day. The men's halfpipe competition had a rough start, with several athletes crashing halfway down the pipe. But with the party atmosphere and energy of the huge crowd, even the athletes who fell began having fun. While waiting for his score—which he knew would be low—Japan's Kentaro Miyawaki fanned himself with a traditional Japanese fan and waved a Japanese flag.

The most fun, however, belonged to the Americans, who were riding higher and harder than ever before. In his first final run, Ross Powers' expertly delivered tricks and what he called "the biggest airs in my life" earned him a score of 46.1. With a 1080—three complete spins in the air—Danny Kass was in second place with 42.5 points, and Tommy Czeschin, with 40.6 points, held third.

During the second final run, J.J. Thomas pulled into third place, earning a 42.1, just 0.4 points behind Kass. It seemed as if an American medal sweep—a feat not accomplished in any Olympic Winter Games sport since 1956—might be possible. The other riders came close; Japan's Takaharu Nakai missed the podium by 1.4 points and Italy's Giacomo Kratter was off by 0.1 point. The last competitor and biggest threat to the Americans, Finland's Heikki Sorsa, who had used an entire bottle of hair spray to style his mohawk, dropped into the halfpipe. When his run was over, the scoreboard flashed 40.4, and the crowd erupted.

The Americans had swept the event.

"I couldn't ask for anything more," said gold medalist Powers, who had turned 23 the day before. "It's the best birthday present ever. These guys beside me are huge. Today was the perfect day."

For most Olympians, winning an Olympic medal is the achievement of a lifetime. But for American Chris Klug, simply being alive to compete at the Salt Lake 2002 Games was miraculous. In April 2000, he was diagnosed with a rare liver disease, and a transplant was his only hope. For three months, the snowboarder suffered from immense pain and waited to see if a donor might be found, knowing he would die if one wasn't.

Klug's hopes were answered by members of the Flood family of Denver, Colorado. Their 13-year-old son, Billy, had been killed in an accidental shooting, and Billy's mother Leisa wanted to donate his organs. Klug underwent the surgery, and seven weeks later was snowboarding again. "I thank you every day of my life," Klug wrote in a letter to the Floods. "I am forever grateful and humbled by your decision. It is impossible to express with words my gratitude to you."

His appreciation would be expressed in actions. First, Klug made the Olympic team. When Leisa heard the news, she visited Billy's grave. "Son," she said, "We're going to the Olympics."

On February 15, Klug had advanced from the qualifying round and competed against 15 other riders in the men's parallel giant slalom finals at Park City Mountain Resort. Among the favorites were Slovenia's Dejan Kosir, France's Mathieu Bozzetto and Austrian Alexander Maier, brother of legendary alpine skier Hermann Maier.

While snowboarding giant slalom was an event at Nagano in 1998, the parallel format was entirely new for 2002. Competitors glided from the start house in synchronized elegance, often just feet from one another as they leaned in and out of gates. Some riders lost control—by gaining too much speed or losing their fall line—cut each other off, shot out of the course and were disqualified. After the elimination and quarterfinal rounds, the field had narrowed to four: France's Nicolas Huet, Richard Richardsson of Sweden, Switzerland's Philipp Schoch and American Chris Klug. The results were a surprise: Schoch had been in 15th place from the qualifying round, and Klug had been trailing in several of the day's races, holding on tenaciously.

Then, as Klug raced against Schoch, the buckle on his five-year-old boots broke. Thinking quickly, he fixed the problem temporarily with a piece of scrap metal and some duct tape. "What I rigged up wasn't perfect or ideal," Klug said later. "But I just said to hell with it. If this buckle was going to decide whether I get third or fourth, to hell with it. If it works out it works out."

It worked out just enough for Klug to win the bronze, beating Huet in a photo finish. The gold would go to underdog Schoch, while Richard Richardsson won the silver.

"It's a miracle," said Klug. "I'm so lucky to be here today, and for it to have turned out like this is pretty special." The moment was also special for Leisa Flood, unable to attend the Games but supporting Klug from home. "They both won," said Flood of the snowboarder with the bronze medal and her son, who gave Klug the gift of life.

Maybe it was her singing that helped. Or perhaps the guitar she took with her on the road. Either way, French snowboarder Isabelle Blanc said her music helped grab the gold in the women's parallel giant slalom. Blanc had begun taking singing lessons while training for the Games, and found that they helped her to become stronger, and to express her emotions. "I can put all of those feelings into singing," she said. "I can get out all of those things and be Zen at competitions."

During the Games, Blanc was often seen playing her guitar at the CoffeeHouse in the Olympic Village. She dedicated one song, "Elle Glisse (She Slides)," to French alpine skier Régine Cavagnoud, who was killed earlier that season when she collided with a ski coach.

"My dream is to sing, and my sport is to go fast," she said. "So, I have to do both. I've been taking singing lessons, and I really think that's helped me as an athlete. It helps me believe in what I'm doing and the people around me."

On February 15, the people around her were the 15 other snowboarders who had advanced to the finals. Alternating heats with the men, the women raced head-to-head in eight races each. Isabelle Blanc's teammate Karine Ruby, who edged Blanc out for the gold medal at Nagano in 1998, was heavily favored to win again.

While other riders fell in the competition, Blanc managed to stay on her feet, blowing past Switzerland's Steffi Von Siebenthal in the first round and France's Julie Pomagalski in the quarterfinals. Poland's Jagna Marczulajtis nearly ended Blanc's streak in a neck-and-neck race in the semifinals, but was disqualified in her second run, allowing Blanc to move to the finals.

Meanwhile, Ruby, ill with a fever, had also advanced to the finals. But she faltered in the first of the two runs, giving Blanc the lead by nearly 2 seconds. It was a lead that Ruby could not recover. Blanc took the gold medal, Ruby the silver and Italy's Lidia Trettel captured the bronze.

The moment, Blanc would say, was pure Zen.

Park City Mountain Resort's halfpipe was 525 feet long with walls of 14.8 feet.

"I just dropped in and tried to get as much speed as I could," said American gold medalist Ross Powers.

"Those are probably some of the biggest airs I've ever done in a halfpipe, if not the biggest."

JOHN HUET

*Halfpipe silver medalist Danny Kass delivered just about every rotational trick in the book: an inverted 720, a corked 900 and a cab 1080, in which he did three complete spins in the air.*

IAN LOGAN

*"There's a certain fear factor. You really have to let go and be confident in yourself. You have to be really confident in the air because you're up there a long time." — Women's halfpipe gold medalist Kelly Clark, United States of America*

IAN LOGAN

*Riders compete in the women's qualification round at Park City Mountain Resort.*

T I B O R   N E M E T H   ( A B O V E )

*"I'm aiming for some big air." – Tommy Czeschin, United States of America*

I A N   L O G A N   ( R I G H T )

*Ross Powers displays his gold-medal moves over the historic town of Park City.*

TIBOR NEMETH

*"The whole thing has been great: the Opening Ceremony, the crowd here—the Olympics are huge. When*

*you're at the top, and can hear the crowd cheer and know that they're behind us. It's just awesome."*

*– Men's halfpipe gold medalist Ross Powers, United States of America*

ELISABETH O'DONNELL

*"I've competed there before, and I've seen maybe 50 people, and here there were 20,000. It was sold out. I thought it would be distracting, but it was like taking snowboarding and putting it in an arena."*
*— Parallel giant slalom racer Lisa Kosglow, United States of America*

107

S H E I L A   M E T Z N E R

*"Once you're in the Olympics, everything is really different. But once*
*you're in the race, it's the same as you do every other day." – Parallel giant slalom*
*silver medalist Richard Richardsson of Sweden (above)*

IAN LOGAN

*While snowboarding giant slalom was featured at Nagano in 1998, the parallel format*
*was entirely new for 2002. The result was a nonstop, action-packed*
*morning of head-to-head racing, with athletes often flying off the course.*

MICHAEL   SEAMANS

*"Usually I'm pretty good at handling the pressure. I think I just want to do well so badly that it can almost*
*be counterproductive sometimes. I just need to focus on relaxing and doing what I know*
*how to do best." – Liver transplant survivor Chris Klug, United States of America, one day before*
*he won the bronze medal in snowboarding parallel giant slalom*

SHEILA  METZNER

*"I'm not one who can do a really safe run. When my coach says to do 80
percent I say 'OK, I'll try,' but then I can't do it." – Gilles Jaquet of Switzerland*

SHEILA METZNER

*Swiss snowboarder Simon Schoch (above) was defeated in the elimination round of*
*parallel giant slalom. His brother Philipp, however, won the gold.*

MICHAEL SEAMANS

*Lidia Trettel of Italy, the fourth-place finisher at Nagano in 1998, and Jagna Marczulajtis of*
*Poland competed against each other for third place in the women's parallel giant*
*slalom. "When I was running for third or fourth, I thought that I cannot have another fourth*
*place. So I pushed harder," said Trettel, who won the bronze.*

MICHAEL SEAMANS

*"Snowboarders are athletes like any other athletes. I really feel the Olympic Spirit. I feel like I train hard all year.*
*We've proven that people should respect our sport." — Karine Ruby, France*

SHEILA METZNER

SKI JUMPING • FLIGHT HAS LONG FASCINATED
HUMANS. FROM THE MYTH OF ICARUS TO THE WRIGHT
BROTHERS' 1903 AIRPLANE, THERE HAS BEEN A QUEST
TO SOAR WITH THE BIRDS, TO SEE THE WORLD FROM ABOVE,
TO FLOAT FREELY IN THE SKY. IN 1860, A NORWEGIAN
BY THE NAME OF SONDRE NORHEIM DECIDED THAT SKIS,
NOT WINGS, COULD GRANT HIM THE POWER TO FLY.
HE LAUNCHED OFF A SNOW-COVERED ROCK AND FLEW
30 METERS, BECOMING THE WORLD'S FIRST-KNOWN SKI
JUMPER. SOON, MORE DAREDEVILS BEGAN COMPETING FOR

*Just two days after jumping to gold on the K90 hill, Switzerland's Simon Ammann (number 58) looks*

*down at 20,000 who gathered to see the K120 competition—and to see him soar once again.*

D A V I D   B U R N E T T

distance while the masses gathered to watch from below: Some 150,000 spectators gathered for ski jumping at the Oslo 1952 Games. Fifty years later, we assembled again, at Utah Olympic Park, to gaze upward as a few brave took flight through the thin air. We stargazers were treated not only to an athletic event, but to an amazing spectacle of men in silver and orange suits, of German electricians and Finnish students and Austrian soldiers laying down their tools, weapons and books to compete as equals. And we were bedazzled by a young Swiss jumper who resembled a flying wizard. His humility, good humor and gentility made our own hearts soar.

On the eve of Salt Lake 2002 Games, several names swirled in the air as K90 medal contenders. There was Adam Malysz of Poland, who had been competing since he was 6, and won back-to-back overall season titles in 2000–01 and 2001–02. Germany's Sven Hannawald was a two-time Olympic medalist who had just swept the prestigious Four Hills Tournament in Germany and Austria, the first jumper to do so in the 50-year history of the event. Strong showings were also expected from Finland and Austria, whose team featured four-time Olympic medalist Martin Hoellwarth. Missing from the buzz was Switzerland's Simon Ammann, a 20-year-old who had never won a World Cup event in his career. He had taken a terrible fall just one month before the Games, which left him with a concussion, a back injury and several cuts and contusions to his face.

But Ammann's bruises healed, and on February 10, it appeared that his confidence had never suffered. The field of ski jumpers had been whittled down from 60 to 50 in the qualification round on February 9. With clear blue skies, only a whisper of wind and the stands packed with 20,000 spectators, the athletes were ready to soar. In the first of two jumps, Ammann flew 98 meters and landed atop the leader board, ahead of Malysz, Hannawald and the others. For the second jump, athletes competed in order of scores from lowest to highest, so Ammann was slated to jump last. With three jumpers left, Finns held the top three spots. Malysz's jump of 98 meters was good enough to propel him past the Finnish athletes and into the top spot. Malysz had guaranteed himself a medal; the first Pole to do so in the Olympic Winter Games since Wojciech Fortuna won ski jumping gold in 1972.

Hannawald was next, and his 99-meter leap knocked Malysz down to second place with one jumper left. Ammann began his descent down the in-run—knees bent, leaning forward, hands clasped behind his back. Launching from the take-off point, his skis splayed in a perfect V position, Ammann soared through the crisp, thin air for 98.5 meters. Sliding to a stop, he knew that in order to best Hannawald, he needed near-perfect style points. Scarcely able to wait for the results, Ammann peered anxiously through his skis at the scoreboard, as if somehow hiding would lessen the impact of what he was about to see. But what he saw overjoyed him. A second-jump score of 135.5 points (based on distance and style) won him Olympic gold. It was the first ski jumping medal for Switzerland since Walter Steiner took silver in 1972. Ammann's teammates and coaches mobbed him in the snow.

Later, atop the podium at the Olympic Medals Plaza, he was ecstatic. In the shimmering silver cape of the Swiss uniform, with his tousled hair and eyeglasses, he bore more than a passing resemblance to Harry Potter, the immensely popular children's literature character who also shared Ammann's ability to fly. "I always thought, 'Go ahead and do your dreams,'" he said. "But the gold medal…I never expected. Never."

If Ammann was bewildered by his K90 win, nothing could have prepared him for the events of February 13, and the weeks following. Along with Hannawald and Malysz (who took silver and bronze, respectively, in the K90) and 11 more athletes, Ammann had already qualified for the K120 finals and thus took a few practice jumps during the qualifier on February 12. Thirty-six others jumped well enough to advance, including Japan's Noriaki Kasai, who proclaimed, "Tomorrow, I will perform a miracle."

But as the competition unfolded, it was clear the miracle had been bestowed elsewhere. Once again, the quest for gold came down to the last three jumpers. Malysz leaped 128 meters, good enough for the top of the list and another medal, guaranteed. Tied with Hannawald for the lead coming into the final round, Ammann skied next, his 133-meter jump topping his previous effort by half a meter. As he skidded to a stop in the outrun area, all eyes moved to the top of the in-run, where Hannawald sat on the starting bar. He needed to equal or surpass Ammann's score to claim gold. He shoved off and gained speed. As he jumped, things looked up for Hannawald—plenty of distance, good form. But then he touched ground and couldn't hold the telemark landing, falling back onto his skis and out of medal contention. It would be fourth for the German soldier and electrician. Finland's Matti Hautamäki took the bronze, aware that his medal was the result of a simple twist of fate. "I was lucky because Sven was unlucky," he said.

Malysz took second place, inflating his already considerable popularity in his homeland of Poland with a second podium appearance. "I can't find words to express how happy I am," Malysz gushed after the race. "My dream was to win a medal, and now I have two!"

# "TO CARRY ON QUIETLY," SAID SIMON AMMANN. "THAT'S ABOUT THE ONLY WAY TO GO ABOUT SKI JUMPING."

Simon Ammann, meanwhile, had soared into Olympic history. Against the odds, he became the first ski jumper since Finland's Matti Nykaenen at the Calgary 1988 Games to win both the K90 and K120 events. "I am trembling," he said, his voice cracking. "It's been a crazy day and a crazy week. I never would have believed that this could be possible."

Soon, Ammann took flight again—on a plane to his native Switzerland, where he was greeted as a national hero. Thousands of fans had been waiting for him at the Zurich Airport, and traveled with him on a specially decorated train toward the village of Unterwasser, where he was raised. There were breads, cakes, pizzas and two songs created in his honor, while admirers showered him with love letters, wedding proposals and such gifts as a car, a golden cell phone, even a live pig. (Having grown up on a farm, Ammann proclaimed he liked the pig best.) It was a magical ending to a magical tale, but the boy wonder remained grounded by his remarkable accomplishments and instant celebrity. "To carry on quietly," the Olympian said. "That's about the only way to go about ski jumping."

K120 TEAM •

The extraordinary happenings would only continue as the final ski jumping event unfolded. With four athletes per nation jumping just two times each in the K120 team, one poor jump threatened to damage a team's overall standing. So with Germany, Austria and Finland claiming nine of the top 11 jumpers in the world, the three medal positions seemed a near certainty. Japan, composed of the athletes who won four medals at the Nagano 1998 Games, including team gold, also hoped to be jumping into medal contention.

Throughout the competition, the leaderboard was in a constant state of change. After all the athletes had completed one jump, Germany and Finland sat in the first and second positions, respectively, less than 10 points apart. But it was not Austria in third, nor was it Japan. Thanks to Robert

Kranjec's jump of 133 meters—the longest jump of the day—it was Slovenia. In only its fourth Olympic Winter Games appearance, with only two jumpers in the top 20 World Cup standings, the tiny Baltic nation held a surprising 11.5-point lead over Austria heading into the final round of jumping.

As the second round progressed, strong jumps from Kranjec and teammates Damjan Fras, Peter Zonta and two-time World Cup champion Primoz Peterka widened the scoring gap with Austria, solidifying Slovenia's third-place standing. The gold medal, though, still hung in the balance. After three jumpers each, the margin between Germany and Finland had narrowed to just under six points. There were just two jumps left. Finland's Janne Ahonen went first, flying 125.5 meters to a score of 126.9 points. Germany's gold-medal hopes rested on Martin Schmitt, a student and four-time World Cup champion. Schmitt needed 121.3 points or more to capture gold for Germany. After gliding down the in-run and launching skyward, he stopped and waited for his score. Suddenly, the numbers on the board shifted.

In first: Schmitt and his teammates, with 974.1 points. They had edged out Finland by just one-tenth of a point for the gold, the closest Olympic team competition ever. Celebrating with the Germans at the base of the hill, Schmitt performed one more jump, a backflip. "They [the Finns] also deserve the gold medal," he said. "This is the kind of competition where one day you win, and one day you lose." Added teammate Michael Uhrmann, "Today, we were not better, we were the luckier ones."

The bronze was Slovenia's only medal of the Games, and Kranjec accepted third place with unbridled joy. "I knew we would do well, maybe as high as top six, but we were surprised to get the bronze," he said. "I'm going to sleep with my medal. Not just tonight, every night, always."

*Pine boughs spread across the landing hill provide athletes a sense of depth perception. Set five meters apart, the boughs also aid officials with the manual measurement of a jump should the electronic system fail.*

ELISABETH O'DONNELL

*"You tell us, without words but through your actions, that life is a beautiful thing, exciting and dramatic and full of the potential for joy." — Salt Lake 2002 President and CEO Mitt Romney*

RAYMOND MEEKS

*Finland's Veli-Matti Lindström soars off the K120 on February 13.*

STEVEN CURRIE

*Roar Ljøkelsøy of Norway trains on the K120 hill in the early morning.*

DAVID BURNETT

*"From the outside it probably looks like I am very relaxed and cool. But inside it is*
*completely different." – Gold medalist Sven Hannawald, Germany*

JOHN HUET

*After reaching speeds of 55 miles per hour on the in-run, ski jumpers launched off the highest-altitude jumps in the world and covered distances of 2.5 football fields.*

JOHN HUET

"The idea of flying is extraordinary. You don't need any extra assistance, any parachute. It's just taking off, and it's an extraordinary feeling." – Simon Ammann of Switzerland, gold medalist in the K90 and K120 events

ANDY ANDERSON

*A Korean ski jumper gathers the immense focus required for the task ahead.*

ANDY ANDERSON

*Unlike other ski jumping hills, Utah Olympic Park's K90 and K120 sites were carved into the natural*

*contours of the land, providing a stunning backdrop for competitors and spectators.*

JOHN HUET

*Finland's Matti Hautamäki, bronze medalist in the K120 individual event, takes his*

*turn in the team jump. It would be the closest such competition in Olympic history, with Germany*

*winning by just one-tenth of a point.*

JOHN HUET

"A champion is someone who surpasses personal limits. This means that all of you can be

champions, regardless of your final ranking." – IOC President Jacques Rogge

DAVID BURNETT

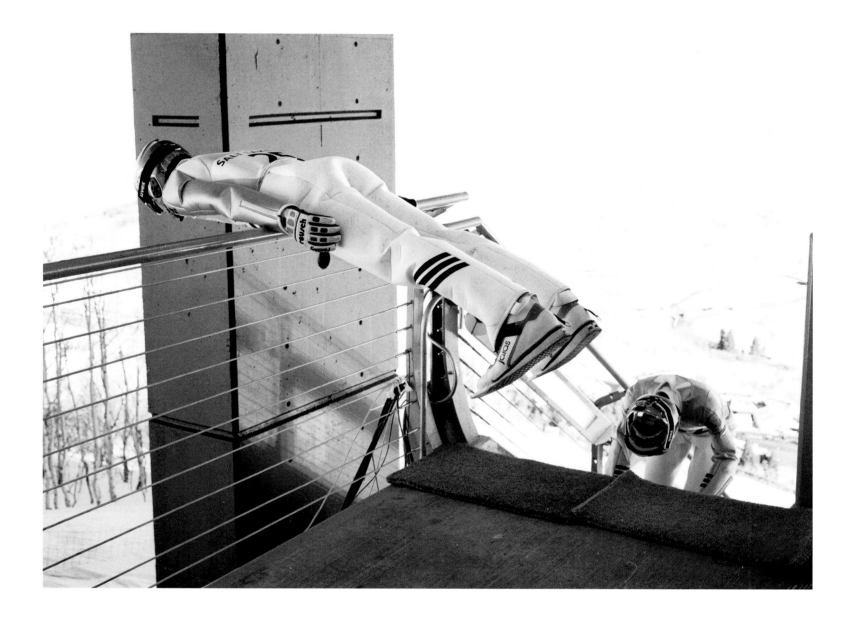

133

Michael Uhrmann of Germany prepares for the K120 individual event, in which he would place

16th, a disappointing finish after struggling through the season prior to the Salt Lake 2002

Games. But Uhrmann was soon elated by Germany's narrow defeat of Finland in the team competition.

"I would like to thank my coaches for trusting me," he said after the victory.

DAVID BURNETT

In the early 1990s, the aerodynamically superior V style of jumping replaced
the traditional method of keeping one's skis parallel in flight.

STEVEN CURRIE (ABOVE)

"You don't hear anything, in terms of little noises or people talking. All you do hear is the sound
of your skis sliding on the snow, the air moving around your helmet. When you actually
jump, all you hear is the air noise, and once you stop at the bottom of the hill, then everything comes
back, the sound of people." – Alan Alborn, United States of America

DAVID BURNETT (RIGHT)

*A Finnish jumper steadies himself after landing during the K120*

*team event. "Germany was a little better today, that's all." — Janne Ahonen, Finland*

ANDY ANDERSON

**NORDIC COMBINED** · HIS PERCH: A STEEL BAR ATOP A STEEP, SNOW-COVERED RAMP AT UTAH OLYMPIC PARK. HE IS MORE THAN 7000 FEET ABOVE SEA LEVEL AND HUNDREDS OF FEET ABOVE A WALL OF FANS. HE PAUSES A MOMENT AND CATCHES HIS BREATH. HE CHECKS HIS GEAR ONE LAST TIME, THEN LETS GO. WHERE THE RAMP ENDS, HE PUSHES OFF WITH MASSIVE FORCE. IN THE THIN AIR, HE SHIFTS HIS SKIS INTO A V SHAPE AND PRESSES HIS TORSO FORWARD, FLOATING ELEGANTLY UNTIL HIS SKIS SLAP THE PACKED SNOW. HE DROPS A KNEE IN THE TRADITIONAL,

*In the ski jumping portion of nordic combined, jumpers are scored on not just the distance but the style*

*—during flight, landing and runout—with which the jump is executed.*

MICHAEL   SEAMANS

telemark landing, a courtier bowing to the crowd. He spreads his arms and legs to slow down, spraying a fine mist of snow through the air.

But his job is only half done. His battlefield, the following day: Soldier Hollow, a beguiling land of meadows and aspens, and an infamous high-altitude cross-country course dreaded for its steep, unrelenting climbs and slick, sharp curves. Here, he assumes a new identity and turns his legs into powerful weapons. The gentleman has become a warrior, fighting for the finish.

Nordic combined athletes must have the precision and grace of a ski jumper, the power and endurance of a cross-country skier and nerves of steel. It is a delicate balance, and the competitors at the Salt Lake 2002 Games brought their own balancing acts. Finland's Samppa Lajunen played guitar in a rock band. Felix Gottwald of Austria and German Ronny Ackermann were soldiers. Ackermann was so focused on maintaining his balance, he had sworn off dating for a year before the Games. With Finn Jaakko Tallus, American Todd Lodwick and Japan's Daito Takahashi, these were the top contenders in three challenges: a K90 jump with a 15 km cross-country race, the team K90 and 4 x 5 km event, and the brand-new sprint event, a K120 jump with a 7.5 km race.

INDIVIDUAL K90/15 KM •

On February 9, nordic combined competition began. Forty-five athletes jumped three times each from Utah Olympic Park's K90 hill. Lajunen's performances landed him in third place, while his teammate Tallus was first and Austrian Mario Stecher was second. Ackermann earned a fifth place spot; Lodwick was just behind in seventh; Gottwald trailed in eleventh. Less than 24 hours later, at Soldier Hollow, the racers lined up for the 15 km race, consisting of three, 5-kilometer laps. According to the rules of nordic combined, each racer started a certain amount of time after the leader (Tallus) based on their scores from the jumping hill. Tallus started first, Stecher had a 48-second delay, Lajunen had a 53-second delay, and Gottwald was 2 minutes and 43 seconds behind.

Well before the 5-kilometer mark, Lajunen overtook Stecher to move into second place, 13.8 seconds behind Tallus. By the end of the second lap, he had taken a decisive lead, legs and arms pumping rhythmically with no signs of fatigue as he passed the stadium, head down, steady and unrelenting.

While Tallus clung stubbornly to second place, excitement built behind him. Gottwald, the World Cup leader from Austria, was making an incredible push from his 11th place start. By the second lap, he was closing in on the leaders—Finland's Lajunen and Tallus, German rival Ackermann and Austria's Stecher. By the last lap, he had a solid hold on third place behind Finns Lajunen and Tallus.

Lajunen, however, would not be overtaken. As he approached the finish line, he led Tallus by some 24 seconds—enough time to accept a Finnish flag from a fan and wave it as he skied the final meters, its vibrant blue cross matching not only the cloudless sky at Soldier Hollow, but also his hair, dyed blue for the Games. Lajunen took the gold, Tallus the silver and Gottwald the bronze. "That was one of the best competitions I have ever skied," Lajunen said. "This day was perfect."

TEAM K90/4 X 5 KM RELAY •

Nordic combined is often considered the toughest of winter sports, and the team event was tough even before it began. Jumps were postponed two days because of bad weather. When the event finally began on February 16, Finland—Lajunen and Tallus with Jari Mantila and Hannu Manninen—earned the top combined jump score. The Austrian team was second, thanks to Stecher's outstanding jumps. The Austrians would start 44 seconds behind Finland in the next day's race. The American team, led by Lodwick, would begin the race third (1:34 behind Finland) with high hopes for a first-ever nordic combined medal. Japan and Germany followed, respectively, in a close fourth and fifth.

The race started fast—so fast that Lodwick and several others collapsed, exhausted, just inches past the exchange line. Lodwick even needed an oxygen mask to recover. Finland held the lead, with

Austria in second, and Germany's Björn Kircheisen skied impressively, passing Lodwick and Japan's Gen Tomii to move into third. In the third leg, German skier Marcel Hoehlig passed Austria's Stecher and claimed second place. The last lap was a matchup between Finland's Lajunen, Germany's Ackermann and Austria's Gottwald. Lajunen kept Finland's lead and won the gold, but Ackermann was breathing down his neck: Thanks to skiing at an all-out sprint pace, the German finished just 7.5 seconds behind Lajunen, claiming the silver medal for his team. Gottwald clinched the bronze for Austria, finishing 11 seconds behind dominant Finland.

And so for Lajunen, another perfect day.

**INDIVIDUAL K120/7.5 KM SPRINT •**

With a cross-country distance of only 7.5 km, the K120 sprint demands more aggressive jumps and more furious racing than the K90 individual event. After the jumping on February 21, the 7.5 km course at Soldier Hollow became a showdown among Finland's Lajunen, Austria's Gottwald and Germany's Ackermann. Gottwald's jumping on the K120, or large hill, had again placed him in 11th at the race's start, 51 seconds—a considerable gap in a race this short—behind first-place Lajunen. Ackermann, who had dominated sprint events throughout the season, started 15 seconds after Lajunen, with Finland's Tallus, Japan's Takahashi and Austrians Mario Stecher and Christoph Bieler on his heels. "There was only one way for me to go," Ackermann would later recall, "and that was attack."

The strategy was apparently the same for Gottwald. Within the first lap, he had skied from 11th into fourth place, fighting to overcome Tallus, who had begun third, and Lodwick, who was skiing tenaciously from his 12th place start toward the front of the pack, even holding third place briefly. By the third lap, Gottwald's challengers for the bronze had fallen away. Lodwick finished fifth, the highest place ever for an American in the nordic combined.

# "THAT WAS ONE OF THE BEST COMPETITIONS I HAVE EVER SKIED," SAID SAMPPA LAJUNEN. "TODAY WAS PERFECT."

The event, however, and the six days of nordic combined competition, belonged to Lajunen. His head shaved of its Finnish-blue locks for the final day of racing, Lajunen displayed the confidence of a rock star and the physical power of a truly accomplished athlete. He maintained his lead to win yet another gold, nine seconds ahead of silver medalist Ackermann and a full 40 seconds ahead of bronze medalist Gottwald.

Asked if he was shocked by sweeping all three events, Lajunen shook his head. "When I was 17, I won a World Cup title," he said. "That was the year I was surprised."

"This sport is at its pinnacle. The best jumpers are skiing the best times right now, and they
do it every time." — Todd Lodwick, whose 5th place finish in the individual K120/7.5 km earned him
the highest spot ever for an American nordic combined athlete.

IAN LOGAN

*"There was only one way for me to go, and that was attack."* — *Silver medalist Ronny Ackermann of Germany*

D A V I D   B U R N E T T

*"You cannot win without being great at both sports."* – Gold medalist Samppa Lajunen of Finland

ELISABETH O'DONNELL

*Milan Kucera of the Czech Republic tests his limits against*

*the cross-country course at Soldier Hollow in the fast-paced 7.5 km sprint.*

SHEILA METZNER

At 7350 feet, Utah Olympic Park offered nordic combined athletes the highest
world-class ski jumping venue in the world.

CHAD HOLDER

*Nordic combined athletes hope for head winds, which help lift them higher and carry them farther.*

D A V I D   B U R N E T T

*Norihito Kobayashi of Japan, Sverre Rotevatn of Norway and Pavel Churavy of the*
*Czech Republic vie for position on one of the 7.5 km sprint's climbs, above.*

SHEILA METZNER

*"I won't forget the surroundings here anytime soon. It's just beautiful."* – *Björn Kircheisen, Germany*

ELISABETH O'DONNELL

CROSS-COUNTRY SKIING IS THE OLDEST OF WINTER SPORTS AND DECEPTIVELY BEAUTIFUL. FROM A DISTANCE, THERE IS THE ELEGANCE OF THE RACERS, AGAINST THE BACKDROP OF SNOW-LADEN FIELDS, PINES AND ASPENS. LEGS AND ARMS STRIDE IN PURPOSEFUL, SYMMETRICAL ANGLES, THIN SKIS SKIMMING ACROSS THE SNOW. THE ONLY SOUND IS THE SWOOSH OF THE POLES. · OR IS IT? MOVE CLOSER, AND THERE ARE THE GASPS FOR BREATH AND THE GRUNTS OF EXHAUSTION AS THE ATHLETES SUMMON THE VERY LAST OF THEIR ENDURANCE FOR THE PUSH TO THE

153

*"Everything is wonderful. It's like being in a fantasy.*

*I'm happy to represent my country."* — Isaac Menyoli, Cameroon

RAYMOND MEEKS

finish. Sweat is frozen to their cheeks, fear in their eyes as they glance over their shoulders to see a competitor approaching fast.

These were the cross-country skiers of the Salt Lake 2002 Games, who competed in 12 events ranging from the brand-new 1.5 km sprint to the arduous 50 km classical. At Soldier Hollow, they tested their lungs at high altitude and their legs on twisting, climbing trails. Each had a vision: to bring home another gold, to earn a first medal, to just finish at all. Their surprising performances embodied the Salt Lake 2002 theme of *Light the Fire Within*, as crowds packed into the stadium and lined the course, witnessing the power to inspire. From a distance or up close, it was simply beautiful.

## WOMEN'S 15 KM FREESTYLE •

Thirty-nine minutes and 54 seconds after the gun sounded in the women's 15 km freestyle, the first gold medal of the Salt Lake 2002 Games was earned on February 9. Italy's Stefania Belmondo, 33, and called the "Tiny Tornado" because of her 5-foot 3-inch stature and 101-pound weight, led the pack for the first 10.5 kilometers. For a woman whose coach says she skis 10,000 kilometers each year, 4.5 kilometers must have seemed a short distance to victory. But suddenly, she collided with another racer and looked down to see half her ski pole dangling from her wrist. She fell back to seventh place.

"At the moment when I broke my pole, I cried from the bottom of my heart," she later recalled. "I thought my Olympic race was over. Then a French coach handed me a pole, but since I am very short, the pole was too long. I again cried out." One of her coaches appeared and handed her the correct pole, and, skiing through her tears, she regained her stride and caught up to the front pack. In the final sprint, Belmondo surged past Russia's Larissa Lazutina to win the race. At the finish, she cried once more. "I am very, very happy," she said. "It's incredible."

## MEN'S 30 KM FREESTYLE •

Mass-start races leave little room for guessing: the leaders, and the trailers, are easy to pick out from the beginning. And in the first men's cross-country race of the Games, it was clear that Johann Muehlegg was the dominant force among the 78 athletes. The German-born Spaniard, who switched nationalities after a fallout with the German Ski Federation, led a breakaway group of five racers, and then pushed even farther ahead at the 6.2 kilometer mark. He finished more than two minutes ahead of his two Austrian pursuers, silver medalist Christian Hoffmann and teammate Mikhail Botvinov, who would win the bronze. Soldier Hollow's high altitude and terrain punished many favorites, including Sweden's Per Elofsson. He dropped out of the race at the 15-kilometer mark and would leave the Games placing no higher than fifth.

Far behind Muehlegg, a 43-year-old professor from Thailand who learned to ski while on breaks from school, had already won his own race. Prawat Nagvajara was the first athlete to represent Thailand at the Olympic Winter Games, and simply arriving at the Olympic Village was a victory. "I still can't believe it," he said. "I never imagined I'd be an Olympian." When the other racers bolted from the start, Nagvajara was already trailing by hundreds of yards, and midrace, he suffered a fall that would force him to drop out. No matter. "Marching in the Opening Ceremony was one of the best moments of my life," he said afterward. "But racing today is even better."

## WOMEN'S 10 KM CLASSICAL •

Three days later, on February 12, Norway won its first cross-country gold of the Games when Bente Skari crossed the finish line in the women's 10 km classical race. Known as the "Classical Queen" for her kick-and-glide skills, Skari finished just 2.5 seconds ahead of two Russians: Olga Danilova and bronze medalist Julija Tchepalova. For the 29-year-old Skari, Olympic glory ran in the family. Growing up in Oslo, she was inspired by her father, Odd Martinsen, who won a gold medal as a member of the Norwegian relay team at the Grenoble 1968 Games. "Tonight, I will tell my father I am a lot better than him," she joked, "because he won a relay gold but no individual competitions! And now we have two gold medals in our family."

Andrus Veerpalu won Estonia's first-ever Olympic Winter Games medal on February 12 as he took first place in the men's 15 km classical. Forty-three seconds later, his teammate Jaak Mae won the bronze. Norway's Frode Estil was the silver medalist. At the finish area, Veerpalu was busy receiving congratulations when his cell phone rang. It was the Prime Minister of Estonia. "He said people were cheering all around the country as the results flashed across the television," said Veerpalu. "Today is a great success for my country and the people of Estonia. I feel very proud."

For the first time at the Olympic Winter Games, both legs of the 10 km + 10 km pursuit were raced on the same day, which meant little rest for the athletes between the classical and freestyle portion. But Muehlegg apparently didn't need rest as he cruised to his second straight Olympic gold. Not even an early slipup in the first kilometer could derail the Spaniard, who continued to ski aggressively, only slowing down when a spectator handed him the Spanish flag to carry across the finish line.

Even as the crowd cheered for Muehlegg, a new drama was rapidly unfolding. After battling each other over the entire course, Norwegian teammates Frode Estil and Thomas Alsgaard entered the stadium in a head-on duel. The two skiers blasted around the final corner and dove across the line in a spectacular photo finish. The scoreboard went blank. Would it be Alsgaard or Estil for the silver? The race jury finally ruled the finish was too close to call and awarded both athletes the silver medal. Not since the 1982 Oslo World Championships had a major cross-country race ended in an outright tie. Joked Estil, "I need to work on my flexibility so I can reach for the finish line."

The day following the men's pursuit, Russia's top female skiers, 11-time world championship medalist Olga Danilova and her teammate Larissa Lazutina swept the two top spots on the podium of the women's 5 km + 5 km pursuit.

Beckie Scott from Vegreville, Alberta, skied the race of her life and won Canada's first-ever cross-country medal, a bronze. It was also the first North American medal in the sport since Bill Koch won the 30 km classical silver at the Innsbruck 1976 Games. Koch, who popularized the freestyle technique, had inspired Scott to pursue the sport. "It is a dream come true," she said. "This has been the best race of my life, and to have a race like this at the Olympics, it's incredible."

Every sport has its main event, the one defining competition that everyone dreams of winning. Soccer has the World Cup, baseball the World Series and for cross-country, it's the Olympic team relay, in which winners have been decided by mere inches. In 1994, Italy's Silvio Fauner stunned 100,000 spectators along the Lillehammer course when he beat Norway's Bjørn Dæhlie by a ski length; in 1998, Norway narrowly edged out Italy by *half* a ski length.

On February 17 the rivals faced off at Soldier Hollow. As the race progressed, an early Norwegian lead was broken on the third leg as Italy surged back to the front. When Thomas Alsgaard took the handoff on the final round, he was in a dead tie with his Italian foe, sprinting phenom Cristian Zorzi. Only 10 kilometers stood between the two skiers and a gold medal. Each, hoping to save strength by drafting, beckoned to the other to take the lead. Alsgaard reluctantly took it and was soon passed by Zorzi. But on the final corner, Alsgaard slingshotted around Zorzi to take gold by the second-smallest margin in men's Olympic relay history. "A sprint between Italy and Norway is a tradition," said Alsgaard at the finish. "But today shows we are the fastest team in the world."

MEN'S & WOMEN'S
1.5 KM SPRINT •

Wildly popular throughout Europe, sprint racing made its Olympic debut at Soldier Hollow in a short but thrilling show of athleticism. "It's three minutes of absolute adrenaline," said American Kikkan Randall. "You need to go all out and push your limits."

And push they did. As the four skiers in each heat jockeyed for the fastest angles, they bumped shoulders and dodged each other right down to the wire. After the qualifying round, 16 skiers advanced to the elimination heats and then the four fastest competed in the final. In the women's competition, Russia's Julija Tchepalova, using an old pair of skis she hadn't worn in two years, surged ahead from the field at the 500-meter mark and won her first gold of the Games. Anita Moen of Norway was edged out by Evi Sachenbacher of Germany, as she took the silver at the line.

In the men's race, Italy's Cristian Zorzi faced off against the world champion, Norwegian Tor Arne Hetland. The two other finalists, Björn Lind of Sweden and first-time Olympian Peter Schlickenrieder from Germany hoped to unseat the two favorites. (Schlickenrieder obviously liked to

# "WHEN I BROKE MY POLE, I CRIED FROM THE BOTTOM OF MY HEART. I THOUGHT MY OLYMPIC RACE WAS OVER."

drive even faster than he skied, later complaining about America, "I don't enjoy driving 65 miles per hour on the highways.") As the pack blasted into the stadium for the final 100 meters, Zorzi and Hetland squared off for the dash to the finish. Hetland appeared to be fading, but hung in there. Schlickenrieder and Zorzi made their move. With arms flailing and legs pumping the three blazed to the line, and the Norwegian fans erupted in applause when the announcer gave the results. Hetland had rallied and struck gold. He finished just one tenth of a second ahead of Schlickenrieder, who took silver, and less than a third of a second ahead of Zorzi, who won the bronze medal.

WOMEN'S 4 X 5
KM RELAY •

At the start of the women's 4 x 5 km relay, two lanes were empty. Both the Russian and Ukrainian women were unmistakably absent: Some of their skiers had failed a prerace blood doping test and were disqualified from the event. With the Russian favorites out of the picture, Norway and Germany were left to race for the gold. The two country's skiers traded the lead throughout the legs, with Norway leading after the third. Then, Germany's Evi Sachenbacher pulled ahead of Norway's Anita Moen, who then retook the lead. In the final 100 meters, Sachenbacher surged forward, passing Moen for the gold.

The Swiss team pulled off the surprise performance of the day and finished third. It was the country's first-ever women's Olympic medal in cross-country.

MEN'S 50 KM CLASSICAL
& WOMEN'S 30 KM
CLASSICAL •

Weary and battered from two weeks of fierce racing, the cross-country athletes faced their toughest challenge yet on the closing weekend of the Games: the ski marathon. The men would ski 50 km, and on the following and final day of competition, the women would ski 30 km. Starting at 30-second intervals, each skier had little company in the two or more hours of sheer pain and exertion.

For more than 40 kilometers of the men's race, Russia's Mikhail Ivanov cruised through the fields and hills, his splits indicating he was the clear leader. Muehlegg was chasing him the entire way. "I knew I was in the lead," Ivanov recalled, "but then the snow became damp, and I felt my speed decrease." His lead had been cut to just 3.3 seconds. In the final four kilometers, Muehlegg maintained a torrid pace, the pain clearly visible in his eyes, until he crossed the finish line first. Usually boister-ous, Muehlegg appeared too exhausted to celebrate. "This was the most difficult race of my life," he said, trembling, almost unable to stand upright. It would prove to be even more difficult: The follow-ing day, he was stripped of this gold medal after testing positive for a performance-enhancing drug.

On February 24, the women's field faced the tough 30 km classical. Russia's Larissa Lazutina, who had been disqualified from the relay after a blood test deemed her unhealthy to compete, was permitted to race. She skied with a fervor that no one could equal, and crossed the line almost two minutes ahead of her nearest competitors, Italians Gabriella Paruzzi and Stefania Belmondo, both ski-ing their last Olympic race. Skari, finishing fourth, saw her hopes for one more medal slip away. "Right now, I am just really tired," she said. "I am hoping for a better position next year."

Shortly after the finish, Lazutina and fellow Russian Olga Danilova were disqualified after it was revealed that they, like Muehlegg, had tested positive for performance-enhancing drugs. Lazutina was stripped of her 30 km gold—the 10th medal of her career and the most ever for a woman. The decision meant that Paruzzi won the gold, Belmondo the silver and Skari, the bronze. "I hope it will be remembered as my medal," said Paruzzi. "I have won it with my craft and with my hard work."

"The Olympics are a wonderful coming together. Even though I am not a
gold medalist, it's good to be here." — Paul O'Connor of Ireland, after placing 70th in the
men's 1.5 km sprint at Soldier Hollow

RAYMOND MEEKS

*Heber Valley, and Salt Lake 2002 decorations, created a spectacular backdrop for nordic events.*

DAVID BURNETT

*Spain's Haritz Zunzunegui battles through the men's 30 km on February 9.*

DAVID BURNETT

*"I think the mass-start format opens the race up. They will start together and go together, almost like a cycling race. It will be interesting to see who wins."*
*– Norwegian cross-country legend Bjørn Dæhlie*

STEVEN CURRIE

A skier trains at Soldier Hollow on February 10. The venue offered a

brand-new experience to Olympic spectators: the ability to wander along

the course as cross-country athletes competed.

IAN LOGAN

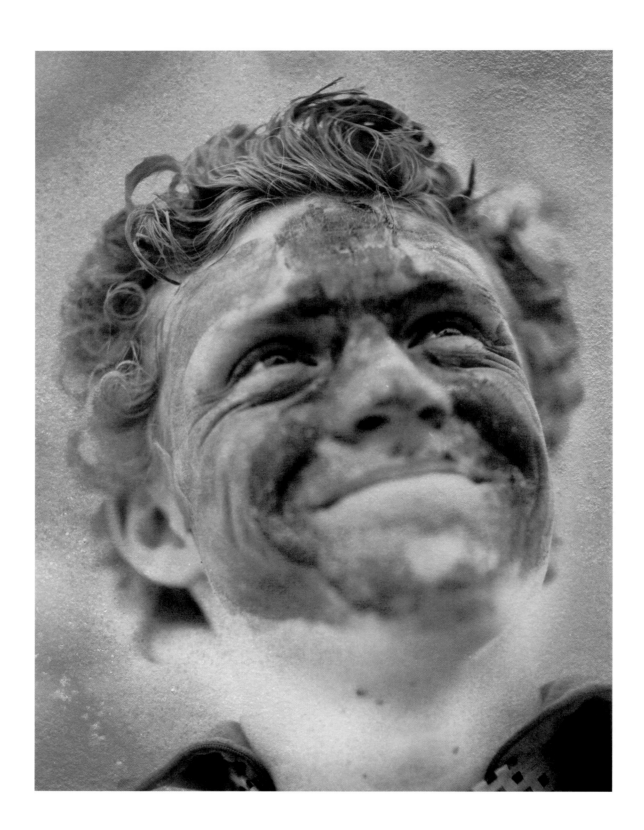

*A Norwegian fan watches the men's 50 km race on February 23.*

ANDY ANDERSON

*Andreas Schlütter helps his team toward a bronze medal in the men's 4 x 10 km relay on*

*February 17. It was Germany's first relay medal since the Innsbruck 1976 Games.*

DAVID BURNETT

*"In Europe, the courses are more up and down. Here you've got long uphills,*

*followed by long flat sections. You really have to fight after the uphills.*

*I think the strong guys will really be able to open up the gap on the flat sections. That's*

*where the races will be won." – Kristen Skjeldal, Norway*

SHEILA METZNER

Cross-country skiers glide down one of Soldier Hollow's rolling hills.
"This is a very hard course because you go one to two kilometers
uphill with steep and fast downhills. You never have time to relax. And if you
get tired, you are finished." — Markus Hasler, Liechtenstein

SHEILA METZNER

*Athletes endure the exhausting men's 50 km event on February 23.*

J O H N   H U E T

"In cross-country, it's not the fastest skier that wins, it's the person with the freshest legs. And that was me today." — Thomas Alsgaard of Norway who anchored his team to an historic win over Italy in the men's 4 x 10 km relay

JOHN HUET

*A team service member tests the Soldier Hollow course for Spanish athletes.*

TIBOR NEMETH

*More of Spain's team service members examine the particulars of Soldier Hollow*

*snow. Each cross-country team traveled with a substantial support crew, which skied courses*

*and chose from hundreds of waxes the perfect application for that day's conditions.*

TIBOR NEMETH

*On the last day of competition at Soldier Hollow, Italy's Stefania Belmondo ended a brilliant Olympic career.*

*"These will be my last Olympics," said the 30 km silver medalist. "But I've learned that in life, you can also*

*win outside of sport. So I will continue to find gold—with my family."*

ALBERT COLANTONIO

**BIATHLON** IS A GRUELING COMBINATION OF CROSS-COUNTRY SKIING AND PRECISION SHARP SHOOTING. TO SUCCEED, ITS CHAMPIONS MUST PUSH THEIR BODIES TO THE LIMIT OF HUMAN ENDURANCE, AND IN AN INSTANT, BRING THEM BACK FROM THE BRINK. THEY NEED MASSIVE LUNGS TO POWER UP MOUNTAINS, AND ICE-COLD NERVES TO TRAIN THEIR RIFLES ON FIVE COIN-SIZED TARGETS HALF A FOOTBALL FIELD AWAY. AND ALL OF THIS IN THE HEAT OF COMPETITION. WELCOME TO THE WORLD OF BIATHLON. ' IF THERE WAS ONE MAN STANDING ON TOP OF THIS WORLD

*Norway's Ann-Elen Skjelbreid takes aim in the women's 7.5 km sprint on*

*February 13. Five days later, she would help her teammates,*

*including her sister Liv Grete Poirée, win silver in the women's relay.*

SHEILA METZNER

in 2002, it was Norway's Ole Einar Bjørndalen. The 28-year-old biathlete came to Soldier Hollow looking to win all four of his events, a feat achieved only twice before, in 1964 by Russian speed skater Lydia Skoblikova and in 1980 by American speed skater Eric Heiden. A place in history awaited him.

Meanwhile, Sweden's Magdalena Forsberg had won practically every major biathlon title except one, an Olympic medal. On the verge of retirement, she had one final chance to face down her Olympic demons. The German women, captained by the veteran Uschi Disl, planned to defend their title as the strongest team in the world, a title that would be fiercely contested. Soldier Hollow, once an encampment for the American military, would once again host rifle-toting pioneers: some real soldiers, some civilians, all with their eyes set on glory.

On February 11, the 10-year anniversary of women's biathlon debut in Olympic competition, Germany's Andrea Henkel shot a near flawless race to eclipse Norway's Liv Grete Poirée by only 7.9 seconds. At the finish, the gold medalist received an emotional bear hug from her sister Manuela, who was competing in the cross-country events. "I didn't know whether I had won bronze, silver or gold," Henkel said with tears in her eyes. "I was just so unbelievably happy to have my sister there with me."

Magdalena Forsberg recorded the fastest ski time of the day, blazing the course in slightly more than 46 minutes. But skiing alone wouldn't win her a medal; she had to survive the shooting range. The pressure mounted. And it almost got the best of her.

Forsberg stepped to the range with the bronze medal on the line. (Poirée won the silver.) The stadium fell silent. One miss. Then another. With each mistake, she incurred a 1-minute penalty added to her race time. Would she hold on? Forsberg hit her last shot and attacked the final three kilometers of the course, poling harder and pushing faster with each stride. At the finish, she held on to third place, just 6 seconds ahead of fourth-place finisher Olga Pyleva of Russia. Her quest for an Olympic medal was complete. "Today means so much," she said. "I feel the pressure is finally over."

That afternoon in the men's 20 km race, Bjørndalen also had a double miss at the range. He hoped his time of 51:03 would be enough to overcome the 2-minute penalty. With the final challengers still out on the course, all he could do was wait. As each skier crossed the line, the Norwegian remained in the lead. It would all depend on his teammate Frode Andresen, the only one left who could take away the gold. Andresen had led the race and shot perfectly through the first three shooting rounds. Just four shots remained.

Bjørndalen waited in suspense. "When I was watching Frode, my pulse was higher than in the race," he later said. But disaster soon struck for Andresen. Three straight misses added a 3-minute penalty to his time, ending any hopes for a medal. He finished the day in seventh. Bjørndalen won the gold and Germany's Frank Luck barely edged out Russia's Victor Maigourov by 1.2 seconds for silver.

Two days later, the men's field faced the intensity of the 10 km sprint competition, an event that penalizes skiers with a 150-meter lap for each missed shot. In the physically taxing, yet relatively short event, penalty laps on the course would be a deciding factor. There was bound to be a shuffle on the scoreboard.

Bjørndalen shot flawlessly in both rounds, continuing his gold medal streak with a winning time of 24:51.3. With one missed shot, German veteran Sven Fischer finished 28.9 seconds behind for silver. The astonishing Austrian team placed three skiers in the top 10, including bronze medalist Wolfgang Perner. "It was the biggest surprise of my career," Perner said. "Today I concentrated."

The women's 7.5 km sprint was promoted as a battle between Sweden's Forsberg and Norway's Poirée, a strong sprinter whose husband Raphaël was the French World Cup biathlon champion. But

Germany's Kati Wilhelm, a former cross-country skier who began biathlon in 1999, soon took control of the race. She skied well and hit every target to win her first Olympic gold medal. Her teammate Uschi Disl joined her on the podium in second position after an amazing recovery from a missed shot.

Forsberg had fallen behind and when she missed a first-round shot, Poirée was poised to take the bronze. Both skiers approached the range for the final round. Poirée faltered. Forsberg shot cleanly, skied aggressively to the finish and earned her second medal of the 2002 Games, a bronze. "No matter what else happens, I'll go home satisfied," she said. "I have finally achieved Olympic success."

MEN'S 12.5 KM PURSUIT & WOMEN'S 10 KM PURSUIT •

Can you make it any harder? That's what the rest of the field was asking as it started a full 29 seconds behind Bjørndalen in the Olympic debut event of men's pursuit. In the new format, racers started at intervals based on the results from the sprint competition. With the sprint winner starting first and the rest of the field chasing for gold, it was a thrilling addition to the lineup of events at Soldier Hollow.

Bjørndalen was relentless. Although he missed a pair of shots and skied two 150-meter penalty loops, his superior endurance pulled him to a 32:34 victory, 43 seconds ahead of Raphaël Poirée. With this third consecutive victory, Bjørndalen became the first biathlete in Olympic history to win three golds in one Games. "I didn't set out thinking about the record," he said. "Today, I had fun, and that is what is most important to me."

Silver medalist Raphaël Poirée had secured his first-ever place on the Olympic podium by hitting every target on the final round while his German challenger Ricco Gross lost his focus and missed twice. "When you want an Olympic medal," said Poirée, "You have to give your maximum." Thirteen seconds behind, Gross finished for the bronze.

"I DIDN'T KNOW WHETHER I HAD WON BRONZE, SILVER OR GOLD. I WAS JUST SO HAPPY TO HAVE MY SISTER THERE."

In the women's race several hours later, all of the prerace favorites, including medalists Wilhelm, Liv Grete Poirée and Forsberg, made critical shooting mistakes that opened up the race. Starting more than one minute behind race leader Kati Wilhelm, Russia's Olga Pyleva seized the moment. She shot a nearly perfect race and caught up to Wilhelm, holding on during the final sprint to win by 5.3 seconds. "When I approached the last shooting, I realized I had a real chance to win this race," she said. Crying, she spoke with her mother in Siberia with the news. Wilhelm took the silver. Liv Grete Poirée made a strong push to come back from four penalty loops, but lost the bronze to Bulgaria's Irina Nikoultchina by 2.5 seconds.

WOMEN'S 4X7.5 KM RELAY •

Biathlon challenged these athletes in every way possible. Skiing taxed their bodies. Shooting was a battle of the mind. And the relay threw national pride into the mix. For the German women, it would be their chance to prove their continued dominance in biathlon as they defended their 1998 relay gold. But Norway, captained by double medalist Liv Grete Poirée, had its own agenda. So did the Russians. A fast and furious fight was inevitable.

At the sound of the gun, the pack of 15 skiers charged out of the stadium. The first round at the range was next. When Germany's lead-off skier Katrin Apel took aim from the standing position, the team's medal chances nearly vanished. The early race leader missed four shots on the opening round and plummeted back to 12th position. The German fans fell silent in disbelief. "When I missed those targets, I thought we lost the gold because of me," Apel said later. It was now up to her teammate and captain Disl, who took the handoff on the second leg. She shot brilliantly and skied into the lead. What looked like ruin was fast becoming a possible victory. In the final stretch, anchor skier Wilhelm overcame two missed shots and held on for the win. "When I missed twice," she said, "I realized Liv Grete was right there next to me, and she would do anything in her power to catch up with me on the shooting. It was a tough moment."

Norway stayed in contention most of the race, but a valiant effort in the final stretch by Liv Grete Poirée fell short. The team ended the day 30 seconds behind Germany for silver. The Russians, still riding high from Pyleva's gold in the pursuit event, took home the bronze.

If Bjørndalen was going to win a record fourth gold medal, he needed his teammates to pull through with their best performance yet. Besides Bjørndalen, no other Norwegian had medaled in biathlon at the Salt Lake 2002 Games. It would be a tough fight to unseat the formidable German team, the winner of the past three Olympic biathlon relays.

But when the gun went off and the pack surged, Germany's athletes realized they faced a serious challenge. The pack stayed bunched together through the first portion of the race. On the second lap, Norway's Andresen skied into the lead. Germany lagged behind with France in close pursuit. Fans rose to their feet. Norway's final dash for gold was on.

Bjørndalen took the handoff on the last lap and skied into history. Although a fall and broken pole caused him momentary panic, he recovered quickly when his coach handed him a replacement pole only seconds later. Twenty minutes and 30 seconds after he started, he crossed the finish line in victory. The historic fourth medal was his, along with Norway's first-ever relay gold in biathlon. Germany trailed in second. The French just missed the silver, when Raphaël Poirée finished the sprint seven seconds behind Germany's powerful anchor skier Luck.

Afterward, Bjørndalen's elated teammates piled on top of their captain. "The last gold was the most important," he said, "because it was the whole team—something we did together as a team."

*Irina Nikoultchina of Bulgaria won her first-ever Olympic medal when*

*she finished third in the 10 km pursuit. "After my first two*

*races, I was so disappointed," she said. "But then I thought to myself, I have*

*no more pressure, so I just tried to ski and shoot my best."*

SHEILA METZNER

*"In Salt Lake City, there is so much color and flags. The people are so welcoming, I*
*feel like I am finally racing in the Olympic Games." – Raphaël Poirée, France.*

JOHN    HUET

181

*Competitors line up at the range to shoot from the standing position. Since 1978,*

*biathletes have used standard 0.22 caliber rifles in international events.*

JOHN HUET

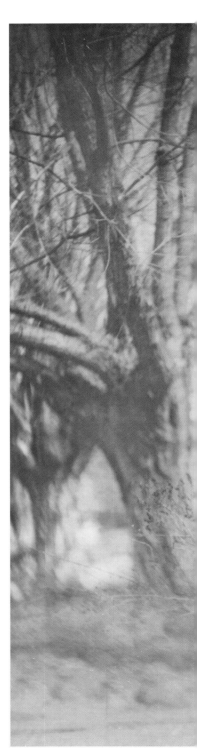

*"I was so exhausted, I had nothing left in the last part of the race. I have never been this tired before, but it is the Olympics, and you need to try your hardest." — Magdalena Forsberg of Sweden, a five-time world champion who finally won her first Olympic medal at Soldier Hollow.*

RAYMOND MEEKS

*In a Scandinavian duel, Sweden's Björn Ferry chases Norway's Egil Gjelland during*

*the men's 12.5 km pursuit. Ferry finished the race 24th; Gjelland, 15th.*

RAYMOND MEEKS

A racer slides under the spectator bridge. Soldier Hollow's unique design
allowed fans to traverse the course with outstanding views of the action.

JOHN HUET

Soldier Hollow's stunning beauty was deceptive. "This venue is very difficult.
We did several high-altitude training sessions before coming to Salt Lake,
but today proved challenging. The trails here are very demanding." — Julien Robert
of France after the men's 10 km sprint on February 13.

ELISABETH O'DONNELL

*Biathlon has been compared to sprinting up 25 flights of stairs*

*—and then trying to thread a needle at the top.*

SHEILA METZNER

*A racer crests one of Soldier Hollow's relentless hills in the women's 4 x 7.5 km relay.*

SHEILA METZNER

Oleksander Bilanenko of Ukraine races the men's 4 x 7.5 km relay, above.

Right: "This is the finest biathlon venue I've ever seen. It's a unique
setting. There are no others like it. Environmentally, it's absolutely fabulous."
— IOC President Jacques Rogge

TIBOR NEMETH

A German athlete trains on Valentine's Day, 2002. That day, France's
Raphaël Poirée and Norway's Liv Grete Poirée celebrated becoming the first married
couple from different nations to win Olympic biathlon medals.

ELISABETH O'DONNELL

*Vyacheslav Derkach of Ukraine skates across a meadow in the men's 20 km.*

ELISABETH O'DONNELL

*Nearly 6000 spectators journeyed to Soldier Hollow on the "Heber Creeper,"*

*a historic steam train that once carried pioneers through the valley.*

DAVID BURNETT

On February 20, Michael Dixon of Great Britain closed a biathlon career that
spanned a record six Olympic Winter Games. While he never medaled,
Dixon hoped his dedication would inspire others. "After so many Games, I've realized
that when you believe in your dreams," he said, "anything can work out."

ELISABETH O'DONNELL

Some 10,000 rounds were shot at Soldier Hollow. All were recycled, and the brass

shell casings were collected to make commemorative cheering bells.

SHEILA METZNER

BOBSLEIGH · HOW DOES IT FEEL TO ROCKET DOWN THE ICE IN A 1200 POUND SLED? FOR TWO 39-YEAR-OLDS ENDING THEIR CAREERS AT THE SALT LAKE 2002 GAMES, IT FELT LIKE A LAST CHANCE AT GLORY. FOR 30 WOMEN, COMPETING IN THE DEBUT WOMEN'S OLYMPIC BOBSLEIGH EVENT, IT FELT LIKE A FIRST CHANCE AT GREATNESS IN THE SPORT. FOR YUGOSLAVIA'S BORIS RADJENOVIĆ, A FORMER POLITICAL PRISONER WHO HAD RETURNED TO COMPETE WITH HIS SON, IT FELT LIKE FREEDOM. AND FOR TWO-TIME BREAST-CANCER SURVIVOR ILDIKO STREHLI,

*The Norwegian two-man team of Arnfinn Kristiansen and Bjarne Røyland trains at*

*Utah Olympic Park on February 15.*

TIBOR NEMETH

piloting a bright-pink sled that symbolized the struggle against the disease, it felt like hope.

Most of all, there was the feeling of adrenaline, a concoction of joy and fear. Riding in machines built with race-car technology, enduring gravitational forces of four Gs, timed to the 100th of a second, is like a roller-coaster ride with no safety bars. Prince Albert of Monaco, who crashed in the second heat of the four-man, knew the risks. But he had returned for his fifth Olympic Winter Games, he said, because "I've never wanted that feeling to go away. I still long to go faster."

TWO-MAN •

After winning three Olympic medals and nine world championships, Germany's Christoph Langen was still a perfectionist. His exacting nature explains why, at age 39, training for his last Games, he still built his own sleds. The combination of his precise knowledge of his sled and his unsurpassed driving skills made Langen and teammate Markus Zimmermann a favorite to win in the Salt Lake 2002 Games. It did not, however, guarantee anything. Two U.S. teams had trained long and hard to end the country's 46-year bobsleigh medal drought. Nobody knew the course better than drivers Todd Hays and Brian Shimer, who had navigated the twisting Utah Olympic Park track hundreds of times. Hays would compete with Garrett Hines, while Shimer would race with Darrin Steele. Each team hoped to turn its experience into gold in front of the home crowd. Then there was Christian Reich, a welder from Switzerland and a three-time Olympian. Distraught with his fourth-place finish in Nagano, Reich was out for revenge with brakeman Steve Anderhub. And Reich's countryman, cheesemaker Martin Annen, in the sled with Beat Hefti, was also a medal contender, having burst into bobsleigh in 2000 by earning seven medals and landing in first place overall in the two-man standings.

After the first run, Reich was in the lead over Langen, but only by 0.02 seconds. Another 0.02 seconds separated the third-place Annen from Langen, while the USA-1 sled piloted by Hays sat in the fourth position. As the race progressed, Langen and Reich slowly pulled away from the field, but not from each other. During the third heat, Langen drove his sled to a track-record time of 47.44 seconds, besting the record of 47.52 set the day before by Reich. Going into the final heat, there was not just one but two ties (a remarkable occurrence in bobsleigh): between Langen and Reich in first and between Hays and the Canadian team of Pierre Lueders and Giulio Zardo in fourth. Annen was in third.

Despite a strong final run in which he beat Lueders, Hays could not best Annen's combined time. "I thought we had a chance," he said, having missed the medal by 0.03 seconds. "But Annen rose to the occasion, and that's why he's the bronze medalist."

In the gold-medal runoff, Reich's sled went first and he crossed the finish line in 47.70 seconds. As Langen raced down the course, a lucky pig charm attached to his uniform, his split times indicated he was trailing Reich by fractions of a second. But navigating a sled built with his own hands and using 16 years of bobsleigh experience to his advantage, Langen made up time on the final portion of the course and clocked in at 47.61, winning the gold by less than one tenth of a second.

Reflecting on making up fractions of a second on his way to victory, Langen said, "In curves six to eleven the ride was superb. In curve eleven I thought, 'Oh my gosh, we might be able to make it,' and we did. Basically, I wanted Christian [Reich] and I to finish with the same time. We have fought like tigers, and this is a highlight of the whole program here."

WOMEN'S •

The first-ever women's Olympic bobsleigh competition began with letters. Long, passionate letters from five teams who dreamed of competing in 2002. In 1997, they were told that due to a lack of international interest in the sport, not to mention the dearth of teams, even inclusion at the 2006 Games was far-fetched. The year 2010 seemed a more reasonable goal. So athletes from Switzerland, Germany, Great Britain, Canada and the United States began a letter-writing campaign to the sport's international federation, the IOC and the Salt Lake Organizing Committee. These athletes recruited women from other nations to form their own teams. The movement grew, far exceeding anyone's expectations. Olympic status was granted to women's bobsleigh on October 2, 1999, for inclusion in the Salt Lake 2002 Games. A victory was won even before the 15 sleds from 11 nations took to the Olympic track on February 19, 2002.

Germany's team hoped for more victories on the Utah Olympic Park track. A soldier in her homeland of Germany and former luge athlete who won bronze in 1992 and silver in 1994, Susi-Lisa Erdmann was the overall World Cup champion for the 2001–02 season. With brakewoman Nicole Herschmann, she was a favorite for first place. Also favored to medal was Sandra Prokoff, another German soldier, who finished second to Erdmann in the World Cup standings and rode in with Ulrike Holzner in a sled painted as a hammerhead shark. Between these two sleds, Germany had won every World Cup race of the season.

# "I've never wanted that feeling to go away," said Prince Albert. "I still long to go faster."

American Jean Racine was ready for a comeback. She and brakewoman Jen Davidson had won overall World Cup titles in 1999–2000 and 2000–01 but began slipping in the standings in 2001–02. In a controversial move, Racine dumped Davidson and began competing with Gea Johnson, a top-ranked heptathlete from 1989–95. During their second race together, the duo set the track record in Park City. Said Racine before the race: "I'm going for the gold."

But winning gold in the two-heat event would require strong starts and early domination, and both would elude Racine. Johnson had pulled her hamstring three days before competition and struggled in pain during the first run push. She and Racine were in fifth place, 0.50 seconds off the lead. Erdmann and Herschmann sat in the third spot while Prokoff and Holzner were in second place. In the lead were Americans Jill Bakken and Vonetta Flowers, in a candy-apple red sled flecked with white snowflakes. With much of the attention paid to Racine, Davidson and Johnson, Bakken and Flowers had trained obscurely and exhaustively.

So it was a surprise when Bakken, the youngest member of the American team, and Flowers, a seven-time All-American track and field star from Alabama, set a new track record time of 48.81 seconds. Suddenly, the attention turned to what had come to be known as the "other" U.S. team for the second run. Could they hold on to first place?

Indeed, the Germans could not make up the lost time—0.29 seconds—in only one run. After their runs, Erdmann and Prokoff could only hope that Bakken would make a mistake. But the quiet driver negotiated the track quickly and cleanly, finishing in 48.95 seconds for the gold. Prokoff and Holzner took silver, 0.30 seconds behind the Americans, and Erdmann and Herschmann finished 0.53 seconds behind for the bronze.

At Olympic Medals Plaza the next night, Flowers cried silently. Two years earlier, she made it to the 2000 Olympic trials for track and field, but did not qualify. Her Olympic dreams temporarily shattered, she had responded on a whim to a flier seeking potential bobsled athletes. Now she was a gold medalist, the first African-American athlete ever to win gold at an Olympic Winter Games. And with their victory, Bakken and Flowers claimed the first U.S. Olympic medal in bobsleigh in 46 years.

"We feel honored to be the first ones to break the streak," she said. "Hopefully, this will encourage other African-American boys and girls to give winter sports a try."

The American men—specifically Todd Hays and Brian Shimer—were determined to break the medal drought in their own right. The 39-year-old Shimer, the veteran and five-time Olympian of the U.S. squad, had one last shot at an Olympic medal, a medal that had eluded him through four straight Olympic Winter Games. He had come close in the past, extremely close, missing a bronze in Nagano by just 0.02 seconds. But close wasn't good enough for Shimer, so he set his sights on Salt Lake. Hobbled by injuries throughout his career—he missed most of the 2000 season after two knee operations—Shimer was not even a sure bet to make the team for the 2002 Games.

But make it he did. After the first two runs he sat in fifth place, a relative long shot for a medal at 0.39 seconds behind the leader, teammate Hays. The fellow American had outraced stiff competition from the German sled driven by first-time Olympian André Lange and the two Swiss sleds, piloted by two-man bronze medalist Annen and two-man silver medalist Reich, respectively.

Warm temperatures slowed the track on the second day of competition and Hays, the first driver down, clocked a third heat time of 47.22, more than half a second slower than either of his runs the day before. But if the other sleds suffered the same fate, the top spot would remain his. And then Lange took to the course. A blistering run of 46.84 propelled his sled into the lead, by a hefty margin of 0.29 seconds. Minutes later, Annen moved into second, dropping Hays to third. Shimer, in the meantime, had gained ground and moved into fourth place. Would he suffer the same heartbreak as he did four years earlier?

It came down to the final heat, the excitement building as the top four teams raced from slowest to fastest. The day before, after the second run, Shimer was asked what it would take to make up time on the leader board on the final day. "This is my track," he declared. "Nobody is going to beat me down driving."

Shimer was right; he was the fastest in that final heat. In the last run of his career, he crossed the line in 47.23 and temporarily grabbed the lead. Hays came down next, fast enough to move into the top spot. Annen, who had struggled with his sled on the third run, faltered again on the final run. When the Swiss sled failed to crack the top two spots, the eight American athletes knocked one another down in exuberance. Even if Lange and the Germans won gold (which they did), there would still be two medals for the United States: silver for Todd Hays and his team of Garrett Hines, Randy Jones and Bill Schuffenhauer and bronze for Shimer, Mike Kohn, Doug Sharp and Dan Steele.

"I'm numb," said Shimer, smiling through his tears. "For 16 years this is all I ever dreamed for. To go out here, in the United States, in my last Olympic Winter Games, in my last race, in the last run of my career, it's a fairy-tale ending. As far as I'm concerned, that bronze is as shiny as gold."

*"I know that this is the most important race of any athlete's career. There's so much riding on it. Sometimes it gets a little overwhelming, but I wouldn't change it for the world." – Bronze medalist Brian Shimer, United States of America*

ANDY ANDERSON

201

*Driver Dan Janjigian and Jyorgos Alexandrou of Armenia take a training run
on the track. Prior to the Games, the pair had faced financial setbacks and practiced
with a wheeled sled on the streets of San Jose, California.*

ELISABETH O'DONNELL

*"What can I say? This is a dream come true for me." — Vonetta Flowers*
*of the United States of America, above, on winning the first-ever women's Olympic*
*bobsleigh gold with driver Jill Bakken on February 19.*

SHEILA METZNER

*The Czech Republic team prepares for the push on February 23.*

ALBERT COLANTONIO

*Austria's Wolfgang Stampfer and Martin Schützenauer navigate a turn during the*

*two-man competition. Salt Lake 2002 marked the fourth Olympic*

*Winter Games for the 39-year-old Schützenauer, who also competed in track and*

*field's 4 x 100 m relay at the Atlanta 1996 Olympic Games.*

DAVID BURNETT

*"I got goose bumps at the start. The atmosphere is just excellent. It's a lot of fun to compete here."* – Susi-Lisa Erdmann, Germany

STEVEN CURRIE

An Austrian team rockets through the track. In 2002, a remarkable number

of warm-weather delegations joined the traditional European powerhouses

in bobsleigh. "This sport is not only for people who live in the cold," said Winston

Watt, a driver and member of Jamaica's team since 1993.

TIBOR NEMETH

*A newcomer and a veteran pose at Utah Olympic Park just one day before winning*

*the gold. "I've been blessed to come into this sport and pick it up so quickly,"*

*said American Vonetta Flowers (left). Said Jill Bakken, "It's such an amazing feeling...It's*

*been eight years of hard work, and it's come down to this—the gold medal."*

JOHN   HUET

SKELETON · It was a unique and unlikely camaraderie, the skeleton community. It was a firefighter from Ohio and an air-traffic controller from Austria. A landscape architect from Calgary and an intelligence officer with the British Royal Air Force. They came together out of a pure love for the sport, for the rush of hurtling headfirst down a frozen track at nearly 80 miles per hour, chins scant inches from the ice. They trained together. They became a family. In February 2002,

*Kazuhiro Koshi of Japan gets ready to ride at Utah Olympic Park.*

S H E I L A  M E T Z N E R

skeleton returned to Olympic Winter Games competition after a 54-year absence. And so, on a snowy day at Utah Olympic Park, the skeleton family stepped onto the sporting world's grandest stage.

Jim Shea Jr. wasn't supposed to win the gold medal. He wasn't even the top-ranked slider competing for the United States. He was good, no doubt, but he wasn't Gregor Stähli, the slider from Switzerland who won four of the five races during the 2001–02 season. Shea didn't even have a major recent win, like teammate Chris Soule, who won the last World Cup race of the 2001–02 season in St. Moritz, Switzerland—the one race that Stähli didn't—and finished the season ranked second overall. And he wasn't the hometown favorite: That honor belonged to fellow American Lincoln DeWitt.

Shea, a third-generation Olympian, carried something with him on his sled, though, that the other athletes were missing: the spirit of his grandfather. Jim's father, Jim Sr., competed in nordic combined and cross-country skiing events at the Innsbruck 1964 Games. His grandfather, Jack, won two gold medals in speed skating at the Lake Placid 1932 Games. Ninety-one years old and America's oldest living winter Olympian, Jack was proud to see his grandson earn a spot on the Olympic team, and excited to travel to Utah to watch him compete at the Salt Lake 2002 Games. But on January 22, a tragic car accident—just blocks from Jack's Lake Placid, New York, home—claimed his life. Shea returned to Utah after the funeral, inspired to honor the memory of his grandfather with a victory.

On February 20, competition day, snow began to fall. This was a rare sight at the Games. For two weeks the sun had shined steadily, and some racers were nervous. Snow made the sliding tricky and slow, but the race—an event of two heats—was on. The effects of the weather were felt by the first competitor, the top-ranked Stähli. He navigated the course in 51.16 seconds, two seconds slower than normal for the sport's best athletes. Martin Rettl of Austria then slid in 51.02 seconds, a bit quicker than Stähli, but still much slower than his track-record run of 48.60 seconds from a year earlier.

At the start line, Shea jumped up and down. He ran in place. And then, with a photograph of his grandfather tucked inside his helmet, Jim Shea Jr. took off on the ride of his life. He blazed through the course, the spectators' cheers growing louder as each of his split times were posted. He was on a pace to take over the lead from Rettl. Shea slid flawlessly, given the conditions of the track, and when his final time of 50.89 seconds flashed on the video board, he pumped his fist triumphantly. He was 0.13 seconds ahead of the pack, a lead that would hold up throughout the remainder of the first run.

# SHEA REMOVED HIS HELMET, PULLED OUT A PHOTOGRAPH AND HELD IT HIGH. AND THEN HE LOOKED SKYWARD.

The snow continued through the second round. Soon, only the final three sliders remained. Clifton Wrottesley, in position to secure a first-ever Olympic Winter Games medal for Ireland, could not duplicate his strong first run and wound up finishing the race in fourth place. Rettl was next, putting up a 50.99. All Shea needed was a 51.12 or better for the gold. As he slid, it appeared that he wouldn't be able to pull it off. His split times showed that his lead had dwindled away to nothing. And then something incredible happened. He actually made up time at the end of the course—a feat rare at the track—as if a hand appeared out of nowhere and pushed him toward the finish. Shea crossed the line in 51.07, winning by just five hundredths of a second. The other sliders mobbed him. During the race they were his adversaries. Now, once again, they were a tight-knit skeleton family.

Pandemonium. Bittersweet euphoria. Dueling chants of "USA!" and "JIMMY SHEA!" merged into one. "U.S. SHEA! U.S. SHEA!" Shea removed his helmet, pulled out the photograph of a smiling Jack and held it high for all to see. And then he looked skyward. Near the finish line, Shea's mother, Judy, turned, her eyes overflowing with tears, and said to nobody in particular, "Grandpa would have loved it."

Thirteen athletes represented 10 nations in the first women's skeleton race in Olympic Winter Games history. Even in such a small group, a few sliders stood out from the rest. Great Britain's Alex Coomber, a lieutenant in the Royal Air Force, had dominated the sport, winning three straight overall World Cup titles. Maya Pedersen, a teacher in Switzerland, was the defending world champion, who ranked second in the 2001–02 World Cup standings. The best hope for a U.S. Olympic medal rested with Lea Ann Parsley, a 33-year-old firefighter from Ohio.

The first heat yielded some surprising results. Pedersen struggled on the snowy track and landed in seventh place. Michelle Kelly, a Canadian who set the Utah Olympic Park course record in February 2001, was in the 11th position. A solid run put Coomber, who had never practiced skeleton in the snow at Utah Olympic Park, in third place, 0.22 seconds out of the lead. Parsley, competing with a pulled hamstring, raced through the pain to a time of 52.27 seconds, fast enough for second place.

Sitting in the top spot after the first round was a small 21-year-old from Salt Lake City named Tristan Gale, just 5 feet 2 inches tall, 115 pounds, nicknamed "Twister" because she had accidentally spun in her sled while first trying the sport. Her performance was a surprise—Gale had never even heard of the sport until 1998, and had never finished higher than eighth place at a major event during her debut season in 2001–02. The snowy conditions on the track should have favored the heavier sliders. But there was Gale, waving to the fans and holding a precarious lead of 0.01 seconds.

With the excitement of Shea's gold medal-winning run minutes earlier still reverberating through Utah Olympic Park, one by one, the competitors for the final round slid down the course. It soon became clear that none of them would make up her time deficit. Showing more familiar form, Pedersen recorded the fastest time in the second run. It was not, however, enough to salvage her lack-luster first-round performance, and she settled for fifth place. Coomber completed a second solid run and secured herself at least the bronze. The chants for USA grew louder.

The race came down to the final two athletes—teammates and friends, racing each other for Olympic gold. Parsley slid first, and her time of 52.94 seconds moved her into first place. Not for long. With her hair streaked red, white and blue and the letters USA painted on her left cheek, Gale stormed the course in 52.85 seconds, winning the gold by one tenth of a second over Parsley. Coomber claimed the bronze, the first medal of the Salt Lake 2002 Games for Great Britain. Eleven days after her medal-winning race, Coomber admitted she had competed with a broken left arm. She had hid the injury from her coaches for fear they would prohibit her from competing.

At the finish area, the mood was giddy. Parsley jumped on Gale, and the two fell onto the track. Somehow, the exuberance and the camaraderie of the skeleton community had spilled over from the track, and strangers hugged each other and exchanged jubilant high fives. On one snowy February day, the crowd was inspired by not just the courage, but by the enthusiasm and the raw Olympic Spirit of a few athletes. And perhaps no one was inspired—or surprised—more than Gale, who was one of the first residents to check into the Olympic Village and the last to leave. "I didn't know I could slide well with international competition," she said, after her gold-medal run. "I just went out and did my best."

*"It's a dream come true. I have always said that the gold medal is possible for me. But even if I missed it by five-tenths of a second, I'm more than satisfied." – Silver medalist Martin Rettl, Austria*

JOHN HUET

*"If bobsleigh is the champagne of thrills, then skeleton is the moonshine of thrills."*
*— Gold medalist Jim Shea Jr., United States of America*

JOHN HUET

*Christian Steger of Italy takes a training run.*

ELISABETH O'DONNELL

*Jim Shea Sr. watched his son win gold with tears in his eyes, convinced that*
*"Gramp" was behind the remarkable run.*

JOHN HUET

*"I think he had some unfinished business before he went to heaven. Now I think he can go."*

*— Gold medalist Jim Shea Jr., United States of America*

JOHN HUET

*A snowstorm on February 20 added a dreamlike quality to the skeleton events.*

CHAD HOLDER

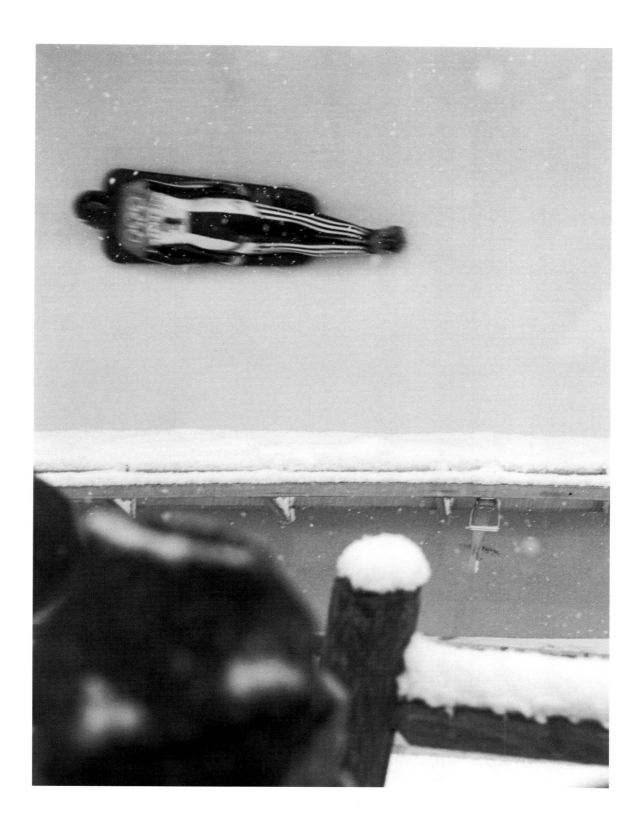

*Canada's Lindsay Alcock rides in the snow. "It's amazing to be a part*

*of this—to be in the first-ever women's skeleton. I never expected to be here," she said.*

IAN LOGAN

Several of the skeleton competitors were firefighters, including Canadian Duff Gibson,

shown at left during a training session. The Calgary, Alberta, resident is also a two-time winner

of the "Toughest Calgarian Alive" competition. Gibson placed 10th in the skeleton event.

TIBOR NEMETH (LEFT)

"This is going to be a blast. People don't know what they're going to see when they come to a skeleton race."

— Tristan Gale of the United States of America, just days before she won the gold.

ALBERT COLANTONIO (ABOVE)

"No one's heard of this sport, but everyone's done it. We've all had a Flexible Flyer that we hopped on at one time or another. When most people see the sport, it just takes them back to sled rides as a kid." – Silver medalist Lea Ann Parsley, United States of America

ANDY ANDERSON

*"You're the vehicle so you get to experience the whole thing."* – Luis Carrasco, Mexico

ANDY ANDERSON

*Troy Billington of the U.S. Virgin Islands, a schoolteacher, scraped together funds to buy a skeleton sled and often slept in his car to save money. Just 48 hours before the race, he was informed he could not compete because of a technicality in the qualification process. "I accept my fate, it wasn't my time. You snap back and you get to racing again," he said. Billington, who also runs an exchange program for kids, plans to compete in 2006.*

TIBOR NEMETH

**LUGE** · EVERY OLYMPIAN HAS A STORY. AND IN LUGE, THE MOST PRECISELY TIMED OLYMPIC SPORT OF ALL, MANY OF THOSE STORIES JUST SLIP BY IN FRACTIONS OF A SEC-OND. WE SEE THE TRIUMPH OF THE GIANTS AND MISS THE OTHER JOURNEYS, THE HUNDREDS OF SLOWER RIDES THAT ARE ALSO LINED WITH GUTS, PASSION AND NATIONAL PRIDE. BUT AT THE SALT LAKE 2002 GAMES, THE WORLD BEGAN TO PAY ATTENTION TO THE BACK OF THE PACK. YES, THERE WAS GLORY IN THE GIANT FEATS OF GEORG HACKL, ARMIN ZÖGGELER, THE GERMAN WOMEN AND THE AMERICAN

229

*Melanie Ougier of France slides down the Utah Olympic Park track on February 12.*

ANDY ANDERSON

men. For the nearly 70,000 spectators who stood by a mountainside to see a blur go by, however, there was also inspiration and humility in those who could not be defeated, no matter how far they fell behind. Athletes like 21-year-old Shiva Keshavan, who alone represented India in 1998 and 2002. Or Reto Gilly, who finished in 24th place, but beamed victoriously at the finish line because his wife had just given birth to a daughter back in Switzerland. Or the volunteer who courageously reached out to stop a runaway sled from injuring a fallen athlete and lost the tip of his finger. Or Anne Abernathy, who had survived cancer and was competing for the U.S. Virgin Islands. Why? "We all do it because we love the sport," said Abernathy. "That's the only reason you should be doing anything."

MEN'S SINGLES •

Georg Hackl of Germany is arguably the greatest slider in the history of luge. In 2002, he was attempting to become the first Olympic Winter Games athlete to win four consecutive gold medals in the same individual event. One man, though, had been gradually gaining ground on Hackl, trying to snap the streak. At Lillehammer in 1994, Hackl won his second consecutive gold medal while a 20-year-old rising star from Italy named Armin Zöggeler took the bronze. Four years later in Nagano, Hackl won again and Zöggeler claimed the silver. All Hackl had to do in Park City was to outrace Zöggeler to make history. But on February 10 and 11 at Utah Olympic Park, Zöggeler's time had come. The Italian slider and three-time world champion raced four solid runs to stake his claim of Olympic gold and to complete his multicolored collection of medals. Hackl finished 0.329 seconds behind Zöggeler to capture the silver, holding off Austria's Markus Prock—who took the bronze—by slightly more than a tenth of a second.

As Zöggeler crossed the finish line on his final run, Hackl stood next to the track, watching the scoreboard overhead. His reign as Olympic champion over, he smiled and clapped his hands together several times, cheering not for his silver but for another man's gold. At the flower ceremony a short time later, Hackl and Prock, the two elder statesmen of luge, hoisted the new champion onto their shoulders. "This second place is where I belong," said Hackl. "Armin is right behind me. And it's a pity that Markus Prock is once more behind me at the Olympics."

Prock, a 37-year-old corporal in the Austrian army, announced after the race that it had been his last, closing the door on an illustrious career—one that spanned six Olympic Winter Games and netted him three Olympic medals and 11 world championship medals. Hackl, who has designed and built all of his sleds since the age of 16, said he would race for one more year and then see how he felt about continuing. And then he tearfully dedicated the silver medal to his father, who died of a heart attack in December, 2001, just after watching his son win a race in Königssee, Germany, where Hackl fell in love with the sport at the age of 12.

There were others, of course, who had fallen in love with the sport, and missing a medal could hardly dampen their ardor or their courage. Patrick Singelton, the lone representative from Bermuda, crashed on his second run, ripping his suit, and had the tenacity to complete the race wearing a suit borrowed from the Latvian team. Werner Hoeger, 48, and Christopher Hoeger, 17, competed for Venezuela. A university professor and a high school honor student, they were the first father and son to compete in the same event in Olympic luge history. And American Adam Heidt thrilled the home crowd—and himself—with a surprising fourth-place finish, the best singles showing ever for an American. His response echoed the attitude of nearly every slider. Said Heidt: "I just had a great time."

WOMEN'S SINGLES •

When asked halfway through the competition if the German team could be toppled—a team that had won the previous 33 World Cup races—American slider Becky Wilczak proclaimed that "anything can happen. I've never slid on the track with a crowd like this." In that crowd, there was one person Wilczak was trying especially hard for: her father, Tom. Awaiting a liver transplant—with no donor in sight—and weak with fatigue, he had ignored his doctor's order not to travel. He made the 1400-mile trip from Illinois to see his daughter compete and, hopefully, win a medal.

"A crowd like this," meanwhile, referred to the 15,000 spectators who supported any team that happened to be on the track. If they knew the Germans might sweep the event, they didn't show it, or at least they didn't care. Pockets of Americans, Swiss and Canadians attempted to outchant each other with national pride. And nearly as loud as the "USA!" yells for the American sliders were the thunderous calls of "Latvia!" each time one of Latvia's women sliders came racing across the finish line.

Angelika Neuner of Austria was not as optimistic as Wilczak. "Germany's girls are so strong," she said before the event. "All of the others are happy to get the fourth place."

Her words proved to be prescient. Sylke Otto, Barbara Niedernhuber and Silke Kraushaar made it clear from the first run that the gold would belong to Germany. It became a question of who would wear it. Kraushaar, who cried the entire way down her first luge run at age 9, eventually overcame her fear to become a three-time World Cup champion and gold medalist at the Nagano 1998 Games. She took the bronze at Utah Olympic Park. Niedernhuber, a police officer in Rosenheim, Germany, who won the silver medal in Nagano behind Kraushaar, won another silver in 2002. And Otto, who had failed to even make the 1994 and 1998 Olympic teams, proved in a big way that she finally earned her spot. She flew past "Sylke Otto Fan Club" banners, German flags and T-shirts bearing her likeness straight to the gold, her first Olympic medal. And to put an exclamation point on her achievement, she set the new track record on her third run at 42.940 seconds. The Germans had, as expected, swept the event, recalling the German sweep of ladies' alpine combined at Nagano in 1998.

# HIS REIGN AS CHAMPION OVER, HACKL SMILED AND CLAPPED, NOT FOR HIS SILVER BUT FOR ANOTHER MAN'S GOLD.

But the unexpected moments proved equally as exciting and, at times, tense, as the race for the gold. Venezuelan Iginia Boccalandro, 41, lost control coming out of a turn during the first run and hit the wall hard. Knocked unconscious and thrown from her sled, she continued to slide, motionless, down the track. After 30 yards, she regained consciousness, and paramedics led her off the track. She was bruised, but otherwise was fine. She announced her retirement from the sport immediately after the race.

Another luge veteran, Anne Abernathy, drew some of the loudest cheers of the competition, even with a 26th—third to last—place finish. The 48-year-old crowd favorite from the U.S. Virgin Islands smiled and waved to shouts of "Grandma Luge!" Her teammate Dinah Browne, the first black woman to compete in Olympic luge, finished in last place, but you would never know from the look on her face afterward. "My first Olympics, and I can't stop smiling!" she said.

Angelika Neuner finished 1.297 seconds—an eternity in luge—behind the bronze medalist. Fourth place is a position of anguish for most athletes. But for Neuner, given the competition on this day, it was enough.

Wilczak finished fifth. But while her father didn't see her win a medal, a compatible donor was found shortly after the Games. He underwent a successful liver transplant, proving that as his daughter had said in February 2002, really, anything can happen.

In a sport that demands the ultimate precision, hurtling down an icy mountainside at 75 miles per hour with another person on board is a nerve-racking task. The athletes train together constantly and share together the thrill of the sport. Some even share the same name: At the Salt Lake 2002 Games, first cousins Tobias and Markus Schiegl of Austria raced on one sled, as did fellow Austrians Andreas and Wolfgang Linger, brothers.

But with nearly 500 pounds of mass trying to negotiate turns and looking for a few precious fractions of a second, doubles teams also share the inevitable crashes. Take Germany's Alexander Resch and Patric Leitner, both soldiers who were training happily—and fairly safely—as singles lugers when a nearby coach noticed them standing together. Their physical matchup seemed aerodynamically perfect: the smaller, lighter Resch could be in the back of the sled while Leitner, at 6 feet, 2 inches and 196 pounds, could provide the necessary momentum. But when they began practicing together, Resch and Leitner were so out of control, and crashed so often, they were nicknamed the Flying Bavarians.

On February 15, it proved to be an apt moniker, as the Germans flew to the doubles gold with a time of 1:26.082 after four runs. And even with the potential of crashing in front of 15,000 fans, the lugers hardly felt any jitters just before the race. Said Resch: "We thought like we always do in training and said, 'Let's hop on the luge and do our thing.'"

The Americans weren't quite so cavalier. "I have to admit to being a little nervous this morning," said Brian Martin after the race. He began racing after seeing a newspaper article on street luge and thinking it might be a fun thing to do for an afternoon. Fourteen years and many, many afternoons later, he found himself as the new Salt Lake 2002 doubles silver medalist, having earned a total time of 1:26.216 with teammate Mark Grimmette.

"I've never been more nervous in my life, and I don't think I could ever be that nervous again," said fellow American Chris Thorpe, who slid to the bronze with Clay Ives. The anxieties hit him during the second run. "In 17 years of sliding, I've never felt that much emotion or stimulus on the sled," he said. "Just bombing down the bottom part of the course, I felt like we could barely hold it together, I thought we might break apart."

In the brotherhood of doubles luge, that seemed nearly impossible.

*Lubomir Mick and Walter Marx of Slovakia compete in the doubles event.*

ELISABETH O'DONNELL

234

*A solitary athlete prepares to propel himself down the track. One of the most solitary lugers may*
*have been Shiva Keshavan, India's one representative at the Salt Lake 2002 Games. Keshavan*
*began the sport after attending a "luge on wheels" camp when he was 15. "I remember laughing all the*
*way down the track. Even more fun than that was the first time I crashed," he said.*

JOHN HUET

*Cousins Tobias and Markus Schiegl of Austria train for the doubles competition. They would place sixth.*

TIBOR NEMETH

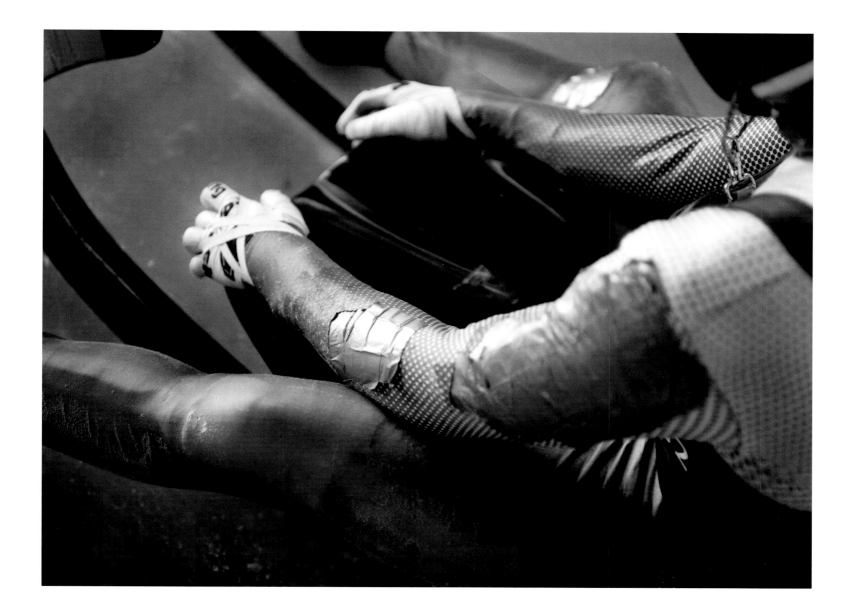

*"I never believed that fools like us could win the gold medal at the Olympics."— Germany's Patric Leitner after he
and Alexander Resch won the luge doubles gold.*

T I B O R   N E M E T H   ( L E F T )

*Accidents happen in luge. At Utah Olympic Park, Bermuda's Patrick Singelton crashed, ripped his suit and
returned with a borrowed outfit from a Latvian friend. Two days later, Iginia Boccalandro of Venezuela was
thrown from her sled and knocked unconscious after losing control during her first run.*

J O H N   H U E T   ( A B O V E )

*"I've seen athletes from Sarajevo dodge bullets to get on an airplane in order to go and train. The Olympics is a microcosm of the world. It brings the world together in the spirit of sportsmanship, competition and in games. Which is what this is. It's a game. It should be fun." – Five-time Olympian Anne Abernathy of the U.S. Virgin Islands, known as "Grandma Luge," above.*

ANDY ANDERSON

*Anders Söderberg and Bengt Walden of Sweden race in the doubles event.*

ELISABETH O'DONNELL

*"This is a very huge atmosphere with all the spectators shouting as we drive down the track."* – Karsten Albert, Germany.

RAYMOND MEEKS

*"I'm not looking to win medals. What I'm trying to do is encourage young kids from the islands to join the sport and to learn something from me." – U.S. Virgin Islands luger Dinah Browne, who placed last in the women's singles*

TIBOR NEMETH

243

*A Canadian team readies for the 17 curves and 4318 icy feet between this moment and the finish line.*

TIBOR NEMETH

*Resembling giant beetles, luge sleds are strictly monitored. Because doing so would*

*increase speed, heating the runners is prohibited. Officials check the weight of the sled*

*and the temperature of the runners at the start of each race.*

TIBOR NEMETH

**CURLING** · IT WAS A SCHOOL NIGHT IN THE TINY VILLAGE OF DUNLOP, SCOTLAND, BUT ON FEBRUARY 21, 8-YEAR-OLD JENNIFER MARTIN AND HER 5-YEAR-OLD BROTHER ANDREW WERE ALLOWED TO STAY UP PAST MID-NIGHT. THEY WERE AMONG THE 5.6 MILLION VIEWERS IN THE UNITED KINGDOM WHO SAT TRANSFIXED BEFORE THEIR TELEVISIONS TO SEE IF JENNIFER AND ANDREW'S MOTHER, RHONA, AND HER CURLING TEAMMATES WOULD MAKE SPORTS HISTORY FOR GREAT BRITAIN. · FIVE THOUSAND MILES AWAY, AT THE ICE SHEET AT OGDEN, THE

*"When you are playing in the Olympics, you are not allowed to think it's over. I just can't give up."*

*— Norway's skip, Pål Trulsen. Norway plays Canada for the gold medal, above.*

IAN LOGAN

score was 3–3 in the women's gold-medal match between Great Britain and Switzerland. It was the last round, and Switzerland's Luzia Ebnoether had thrown her team's last stone. Rhona Martin's hammer shot would end the match and decide the gold. She stepped into the hack to push off for the delivery and swiped at the bottom of the 42-pound granite stone, like a ballplayer knocking mud from her cleats. Then, gliding along the pebbled ice in a prolonged genuflection, she deftly released the stone with a subtle twist of the wrist. The stands went quiet. Rhona's husband, sitting with their children in Dunlop, couldn't look.

Moments like these are what earn curling its spot alongside downhill and luge and speed skating at the Olympic Winter Games. Moments like these when victory is lost in a heartbeat, when skill and strategy count more than brawn or bravery. There were hundreds of such moments during the Salt Lake 2002 curling tournaments. Each was a thrilling progression of surprises and upsets; each was a showcase of grace and dignity.

Although a strong contender along with Switzerland, Great Britain almost didn't make it to the gold-medal match when it lost to Germany in an earlier game. And then there was heavily favored Canada, where curling champions approach royalty status. On February 11, the Ice Sheet at Ogden hosted a traditional opening ceremony, during which Canada's "Queen of Curling," Sandra Schmirler, was remembered. She had led her team to the first-ever Olympic gold in curling at Nagano 1998 and died of breast cancer two years later. Her countrywomen hoped to carry on her legacy with another victory. As Marcia Gudereit, one of Schmirler's former teammates, explained, "With curling, everyone expects Canada to win a gold medal."

The pressure on Canada helps explain why the team hired a psychologist, in addition to a nutritionist and personal trainers. But while the Canadian women were able to slide into the semifinals, thanks to winning eight of nine round-robin matches, they lost in a dramatic 6–5 upset by Great Britain. Kelley Law and teammates Julie Skinner, Georgina Wheatcroft and Diane Nelson, with Cheryl Noble as alternate, were stunned and subdued. The only hope was for third place—unthinkable.

But Law soon had a change of heart. "I talked to my 10-year-old son and he said, 'You know, it's just nice that you're at the Olympics, Mom. I lost all my soccer games this year, like every single one. So it's great just to be there. You don't need to bring a medal home.' And I just started to cry. I thought, I need to bring a bronze home for that little guy." Suddenly, a bronze Olympic medal looked pretty good to the team. And they went after it with a vengeance, defeating the U.S. women's team 9–5.

# THOSE WHO HADN'T KNOWN THE DIFFERENCE BETWEEN A HOG LINE AND A HACK HELD THEIR HEADS HIGHER.

Great Britain, meanwhile, was equally stunned by its victory over Canada and its place in the gold-medal round. The team had struggled to stay strong in the standings, but here the women were, facing down Switzerland, with the shot of a lifetime, as their children watched from across the sea.

Rhona Martin's stone slowly slid into place, nudging a hair closer to the button (the bull's eye) than the stones played by Switzerland. It was enough. Great Britain had won the gold! Debbie Knox, Fiona MacDonald, Janice Rankin and alternate Margaret Morton jumped up and down while the fans shot from their seats. These Scottish women had earned the country's first winter gold in nearly 20 years. They were instant celebrities, congratulated by Prince Charles and Scotland's first minister, Jack McConnell, and invited to Edinburgh Castle. They inspired a country. Those who hadn't known the difference between a hog line and a hack held their heads a little higher because five women gave Great Britain international bragging rights. For Scotland, where the sport originated in the early 1500s, the victory by the all-Scottish team was especially sweet.

If the lingering image of the women's tournament is of a team that knew how to win, the highlight of the men's is of a team that knew how to lose. By February 22, Sweden's Peja Lindholm, Tomas Nordin, Magnus Swartling, Peter Narup and alternate Anders Kraupp had advanced to the bronze-medal match. They envisioned a place on the podium and were thrilled. As the match progressed, however, this vision began to fade. Switzerland, the defending champions who lost 7–6 to Norway in the semifinals, was equally determined to medal. In the eighth end, Swiss captain Andreas Schwaller knocked the Swedish stones out of the house. Lindholm had only one chance to score points: by landing his stone in the center of the house.

It didn't land there. The stone just kept going, past the button. And with it vanished Sweden's vision of victory.

Early in the next and final end, Lindholm was to deliver again. Focused on the other side of the ice sheet 146 feet away, Lindholm pushed off for the delivery. But instead of releasing the stone, he just kept going. In an unheard of and illegal move, he glided past the line, still clutching the stone. Spectators laughed and watched in amazement as, down the centerline, he slid all the way to the end of the ice sheet, never letting go of his grip.

The match was over. In this graceful and lighthearted moment, a classic moment of Olympic sportsmanship, Lindholm had conceded. He placed his stone in the center of the house and congratulated Switzerland. "I saw my sweepers," Lindholm said after the match. "They were very sad; they were almost crying. We will remember this Olympics. And it's not a great memory to cry at the end. It's better to have a good laugh. So I did it for the team."

Canada, too, was beginning to form its own great memory of the Games: a gold medal. The women had missed, but Kevin Martin, Carter Rycroft, Don Walchuk and Don Bartlett, with Ken Tralenberg as alternate, still had a shot. On February 22, the defending silver-medal winners faced Norway, the defending bronze medalists from the Nagano 1998 Olympic Winter Games, for the gold.

The mood inside the Ice Sheet at Ogden was intense. A hush had fallen over the crowd, and the only sounds were of the stones clicking and of the captain's orders to "sweep! sweep! sweep!" as Norway took the lead, 3–0, in the fourth end. Canada fought back, and by the ninth end, the score was tied, 5–5. Norway's last rock, thrown by Pål Trulsen, landed in the outer lip of the blue scoring area. So, it would be silver, it seemed, for Trulsen, Lars Vågberg, Flemming Davanger, Bent Ånund Ramsfjell and alternate Torger Nergård. No stones blocked the lane for Canada's Martin, who would throw the final stone of the game. He just had to deliver a clean shot to take the gold. And Martin had played this type of shot thousands of times.

The stone slid down the ice. It looked heavy, too fast. And as the stone slowed to a stop, it was too wide. Norway had won, 6–5.

It was a classic curling match. Sweden's Lindholm summed it up best. "The difference between disaster and success is very, very small," he said. "You have to be humble."

249

*A curler warms up for a round-robin match on February 15.*

DAVID BURNETT

*"It's pool, it's a boxing match, it's chess. In pool, there are so many angles out there. We'll pick a spot, and we'll try to hit it just like a pool ball. [Like] chess, we're strategically playing rocks to hit later on. It's a battle, it's a fighting match." — Myles Brundidge (left, with Mike Schneeberger), United States of America*

DAVID BURNETT

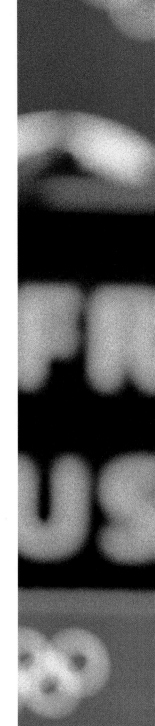

*Enthusiastic fans cheered curlers through 12 days of competition. "We've had the best time and we'll never, ever forget it," said Canadian bronze medalist Kelley Law. "The people of Salt Lake City have been wonderful."*

ELISABETH O'DONNELL

*France's Dominique DuPont Roc, skip, shouts encouragement to his teammates during a round-robin match*

*against the United States of America on February 15.*

DAVID BURNETT

*Norway defeated Germany 10–5 on February 16. Germany's skip, an ailing*

*Sebastian Stock, shown at right, left the match at the conclusion of the seventh end. Germany*

*opted to play with three men instead of using an alternate.*

ELISABETH O'DONNELL

"A shot takes about 25 seconds. In that 25 seconds, you may have an average of 10 pieces
of communication that you have to get across to each other. If you don't get it in those
25 seconds, then you can make the wrong decisions. It's those margins that make the difference
between a winning and a losing team." – Lisa Richardson, Denmark

TIBOR NEMETH

*Curlers compete in the semifinals of the men's tournament on February 20.*

ALBERT COLANTONIO

257

Canada advanced to the gold medal match, but then was defeated by Norway. "We lost to a great
team," said Canada's Don Walchuk. "I'm not going to hang my head."

ALBERT COLANTONIO

*With a nod to curling's Scottish roots, the Salt Lake Scots bagpipers escorted in*

*teams each day of competition at the Ice Sheet at Ogden.*

ALBERT COLANTONIO

ICE HOCKEY • IT WAS A FAST, FURIOUS AND PHYSICAL GAME, AT TIMES OVERWHELMING EVEN THE MOST SEASONED PLAYERS IN TWO EMOTIONAL TOURNAMENTS. EVERY SECOND COUNTED; ONE MISTAKE COULD COST THE GAME. WINNING REQUIRED TRUST OF TEAMMATES, RESPECT FOR THE OPPONENT AND UNWAVERING PASSION. "THE TEAM WITH THE BIGGEST HEART WILL WIN," PREDICTED SWEDISH FORWARD ERIKA HOLST. • THE MEN'S TOURNAMENT WAS DOMINATED BY THE "BIG SIX" HOCKEY COUNTRIES, PACKED WITH NATIONAL HOCKEY LEAGUE (NHL) PLAYERS; THE

*Switzerland practices before the men's preliminary round.*

*"No one knows what the next two weeks hold and that's the beauty of it. When everything's*

*at stake, you see what you are made of and that's really what the Olympic Spirit is*

*—athletes showing up when they have to." – Cammi Granato, United States of America*

IAN LOGAN

women's by the undefeated forces of the United States and Canada. The rest of the pack, however, wasn't planning to hold back. "We've got nothing to lose," said German forward Jan Benda. "We can only make a good impression, and that's what we're here for." There were lopsided losses and unbelievable upsets, every moment packed with a pure love of hockey.

WOMEN'S ICE HOCKEY •   On February 8, Cammi Granato, captain of the U.S. women's team, climbed the steps at Rice-Eccles Olympic Stadium, carrying the Olympic Flame toward the Cauldron at the Opening Ceremony. For her colleagues watching from the stands, it was an extraordinary moment that represented the progress of women's ice hockey. The sight transcended nationalism and even the bitter rivalry between the American and Canadian women's teams. "I was really happy for her," said Canadian Lori Dupuis. "It was really good for women's hockey."

It had not been an easy journey. Most of these women had grown up playing on boy's teams, changing in makeshift locker rooms, having to work twice as hard to prove themselves. Now here they were, competing in the second women's ice hockey tournament in the history of the Olympic Winter Games. Accustomed to playing before a small group of family and friends, they were now competing in arenas packed with up to 10,000 people, their games broadcast on national television back home. What every female player hoped was that a good performance would inspire young girls in their country to play hockey. Only then would the sport reach its potential.

During the preliminary round, the eight teams were divided into two groups of four and played a round-robin (teams in each group played each other once). The United States served up double-digit losses to Germany and China, as Canada did to Sweden. No team was able to score on Canada, and the U.S. team gave up only one goal, to China. The gap between the elite North American teams and the rest of the chasing pack reflected the wide disparity in funding, training time and most important, number of players. Canada had 50,000 girls and women playing hockey; China had 100.

But to assume this tournament was only about Canada, the United States and the gold medal was to miss the essence and some of the most exciting moments of women's ice hockey.

SEVENTH PLACE •   This was a final chance at redemption after a relentless tournament, a chance to avoid returning home with last place. The Kazakhstan team, making its Olympic debut, had lost every single game and scored only one goal. China had taken home fourth place from Nagano, had been on the road since January and hadn't won a game. The players were exhausted.

China protected a one-goal lead for almost the entire game, until Kazakhstan slipped one past goalkeeper Hong Guo, to tie the game 1–1. The final two minutes were intense as China received two successive penalties, giving Kazakhstan a two-player advantage and several scoring opportunities. But Guo, called the Great Wall of China, made great saves and sent the game into overtime. A minute and a half into overtime, Hongmei Liu, the team captain, scored the game-winning goal and secured the seventh-place win for China. "There was no way we could lose this game," said Guo. "The regret would have remained in our hearts forever."

FIFTH PLACE •   Russia's and Germany's teams were both playing in the Olympic Winter Games for the first time. The German players were excited to be playing for fifth, but the Russian team, having won the bronze in the 2001 world championship, had hoped for more. Russia's first game of the tournament was a disappointing 2–3 loss to Sweden, which dashed its medal hopes. "We are going to fight for fifth place as if it were first," said Russian goalie Irina Gachennikova. And they did. Forward Tatiana

Burina scored two goals less than eight minutes into the game, and forward Tatiana Tsareva scored one more in the second period.

Germany had earned this opportunity by edging out China in the preliminary round with an exciting three-goal comeback in the third period to tie the game 5–5. During the fifth-place game, the Germans again came alive in the third period, but against the more physical and determined Russians, it was too little, too late. The Russians scored two more goals to win 5–0. "We put all the effort we could. We were fighting our best," said Russia's Tsareva.

BRONZE MEDAL •  Finland had seven bronze medals—one from the Nagano Games and six more from world championships. At the Salt Lake 2002 Games, the players were determined to play in the gold-medal game. They came close. In the semifinal game against Canada, Finland led 3–2 early in the third period. But Canada came back and dominated, scoring five goals in the third period. Finland lost 3–7. The Finns would play Sweden, a team they had beaten seven times that season, for the bronze medal.

Sweden's preseason record, meanwhile, was so dismal (0–18 by mid-December 2001) that the Swedish Olympic Committee had publicly threatened to not send the team to Salt Lake City, and waited a month before officially giving the green light. Sweden also had one of the youngest and least experienced teams in the tournament (only five players were older than 25). But two of the team's youngest players became the stars of the bronze-medal game. Evelina Samuelsson, 17, knocked in two goals in the first period and 15-year-old rookie goaltender Kim Martin blocked 32 of Finland's

"THERE WAS NO WAY WE COULD LOSE THIS GAME. THE REGRET WOULD HAVE REMAINED IN OUR HEARTS FOREVER."

33 shots. In the final minutes, Finland, down 1–2, tried desperately to tie the game, peppering Martin with shots, but to no avail. When the clock ran out, the team piled on Martin, the youngest Swede ever to win an Olympic medal. Against tough odds, Sweden had won its first medal in women's hockey. "It's huge. I can't find the words . . . I'm just so happy," said Anna Andersson. "And for women's hockey in Sweden, I think it means a lot. I just hope that some more girls will start playing."

GOLD MEDAL •  For Canada and the United States, it was gold or nothing and the rivalry was intense. "We're out to win the gold medal," said Canadian defender Cheryl Pounder. "There are no friends in that." Canada had won all seven world championships, but the 1–3 loss to the United States in Nagano had haunted the team for four years. Team USA, meanwhile, boasted an untouchable record of 35–0 from the season, including an unprecedented 8–0 record in exhibition games against Canada. The Americans were the overwhelming favorites, the defending gold-medal champions with the home-team advantage, and the Canadians hoped they would crack under all that pressure.

The first fissure appeared just two minutes into the game, when Canadian Caroline Ouellette scored. "We wanted to get the first goal and put them back on their heels, and we did that," Ouellette said later. The Canadians' relentless defense prevented the Americans from scoring until the second period, when American Katie King tied the game 1–1, only to be answered minutes later by Hayley Wickenheiser (known in Canada as the female Wayne Gretzky), who scored another for Canada. With one second left in the second period, Canadian Jayna Hefford grabbed a bouncing puck with her glove, dropped it on the ice and scored. It turned out to be the back-breaking and game-winning goal, giving the Canadians a 3–1 lead and a psychological advantage, from which the Americans could never recover. "It was a huge goal," said Canada's Tammy Lee Shewchuk.

American Karyn Bye scored with less than four minutes left in the game, narrowing Canada's lead to one. The crowd cheered wildly as the Americans tried desperately to tie the game, but Canada's exceptional goaltending—Kim St. Pierre finished with 25 saves—and penalty killing had dominated the game. Thirteen penalties were called against the Canadians, eight of them in a row, yet they prevented the Americans from scoring on all but two of them.

"With five seconds to go, I actually had to look up at the clock, because I couldn't believe it was really happening. It was like a dream," said Canada's Lori Dupuis. Canada had won. The ice was soon littered with gloves, sticks and helmets as the Canadian players piled on St. Pierre and celebrated the win they had been working toward every day for the past four years.

The Americans quietly endured the celebration from their bench. "It's definitely heartbreaking," said Natalie Darwitz, an 18-year-old rookie, and one of the tournament's leading scorers. "But we're not hanging our heads. All 20 players gave it their all. We left everything out on the ice." They accepted the silver medals graciously, but many, especially the veterans, couldn't hold back tears of disappointment. "It's tough. I know what they're going through," said Canadian Vicky Sunohara, a Nagano veteran. "The medals are beautiful, but not the right color."

This time the medal was the right color for the Canadians. As the players lined up to receive Canada's first gold medal in Olympic hockey in 50 years, they embraced each other, laughed and cried. "I looked down the line and saw my teammates getting their gold medals," said Jennifer Botterill, "It felt like a moment I've dreamt about my whole life."

While many of the female ice hockey players saw the Salt Lake 2002 Games as a way to promote their sport, the tournament was yet another part of a busy hockey career for many of the men, who are paid—substantially—to play professional hockey. As the Games began, the top players were still competing in the NHL. Whether paid to play or not, however, all share a passion for the sport. "I love everything about hockey," said Martin Havlat of the Czech Republic. "It's my life, it's what I've been doing since I was 5. I love to compete, just go out there and compete against anybody."

The tournament began with a preliminary round. As the spotlight shined on the world's six best teams—the Czech Republic, Russia, Finland, Canada, Sweden and the United States, which had already qualified to play in the final round—eight other countries battled it out for one of two coveted spots in the finals. With many of these teams missing their top players, who were playing in the NHL until the season suspension on February 14, the odds of advancing were even tougher. Slovakia, for instance, was an early favorite to win pool A, but with fewer players per game struggled to pull together as a team. Germany, meanwhile, played almost-perfect defense, fending off competitors while taking advantage of opponents' mistakes to score. "Very low chances for us," said German defenseman Christian Ehrhoff before the tournament began. "But we will try our best. We are a well-balanced team and we are hard workers, and that's what our game is all about."

Their efforts paid off: Germany relied heavily on its defense and swept all three of its games, making the final round. In pool B, Belarus lost one game, to Switzerland, but managed to defeat the Ukraine (1–0) and France (3–1) for the spot in the finals. "I've got a feeling, maybe," foreshadowed Belarusian Alexander Zhurik. "We can do something more than just play."

After enjoying success in the preliminary round, Belarus lost three times in the final round: 4–6 to Russia, 1–8 to Finland and 1–8 to the United States. But Belarus had one more chance at the semifinals, by defeating Sweden. "Sometimes even a gun without the bullet shoots," said Belarusian Andrei Mezin.

Sweden was undefeated after three games, beating Canada 5–2, the Czech Republic 2–1 and Germany 7–1. Many attributed these victories to the team's "big ice" strategy, which Swedish coach Hardy Nilsson described. "What we want to do is keep the puck in the team and create a lot of ice to play on," said Nilsson, "and that's why our forwards are going to the offensive blue line. We keep the puck in the team and have fun."

And it was precisely this strategy that almost guaranteed Sweden another win against Belarus. But Belarus was focused and broke up the Swedish offense. Taking shots whenever it had the chance, the team also had a bit of luck. Outshot 47–19, Belarus goalie Andrei Mezin made 44 saves. "This was the biggest game of my career for sure," he said. "How can it be bigger than the Olympics against all NHL players?" The game was tied 3–3, and it was late in the third period. Suddenly, Belarus' Vladimir Kopat flew down the right side and launched a blast from the neutral zone. The puck hit Swedish goalie Tommy Salo's glove and bobbled up and off of his head. Seemingly in slow motion, the puck dribbled over his shoulder. Salo leaned forward, desperately hoping it would come to rest on his back, but it was too late. The puck had already crossed the goal line, and Belarus won the game, 4–3.

The upset put every team, including Canada, on edge. Handpicked by executive director and hockey legend Wayne Gretzky, the team had not only lost to Sweden, but had barely squeaked past Germany, 3–2, and tied the Czech Republic, 3–3. In its quarterfinal game, the team came together to defeat Finland, 2–1.

In the other two quarterfinal games, Russia narrowly defeated the Czech Republic, defending gold medalists, 0–1, and the United States beat Germany, 5–0. Belarus, Canada, Russia and the United States would advance to the semifinals.

In the first semifinal game, Belarus faced Canada. The underdog with nothing to lose, the Belarus team members played with everything they had. They had hope when Canada was ahead only 2–1 after the first period. But the Canadians soon came back to dominate—with skillful puck control, fast skating and sharp shooting. Canada won, 7–1, and advanced to the gold-medal game, while the Belarusians turned their thoughts to bronze.

In the second semifinal, it was Russia and the United States. The game was played exactly 22 years to the day after the famed "Miracle on Ice" game at the Lake Placid 1980 Games, when the United States beat the Soviet Union, 4–3, and inspired many children to begin playing hockey. U.S. coach Herb Brooks, who had also coached the 1980 team, was now back behind the bench. But both sides were less concerned with history than they were with the future: the gold-medal game on February 24. "There's nothing ever going to be like that again," said U.S. forward Bill Guerin. "But to say that it's less important to us is crazy. We're all Olympic athletes, we all want to grab the gold."

To observers, the United States seemed to control the game in the first two periods, leading 3–0 while outshooting Russia 38–11. Russian coach Vyacheslav Fetisov, however, blamed the Canadian referee for favoring his fellow North Americans, a complaint dismissed by the International Ice Hockey Federation. During the third period, Russia came back to score two goals, but it was too late. When the clock ran out, the United States had won 3–2, and prepared to face Canada for the gold.

With 11 Olympic medals (some as the Soviet Union), including four straight golds from 1964 to 1976 and silver in 1998, Russia was still dragging from its loss to the United States. Once again, there was a flicker of hope for Belarus, when the team tied the February 23 game at 2–2 early in the second period. Then, Russia's Oleg Tverdovsky and Pavel Datsyuk scored 23 seconds apart, followed by three more goals. Russia was determined to go home with something, and charged Belarus for a 7–2 victory to take the bronze. "We knew that we had to concentrate a lot to win this game," said Russian goalkeeper Nikolai Khabibulin. "Nobody gave us these bronze medals for free."

GOLD MEDAL •

On February 24, the last day of the Games and just hours before the Closing Ceremony, Canada and USA played in one of the most anticipated hockey games of all time. Each team felt the weight of a nation on its back: Canada had not won Olympic gold in men's hockey since 1952, while the United States had not won a medal of any color for 22 years. USA had also not lost an Olympic hockey game on home ice in 70 years—at the Lake Placid 1932 Games. "As soon as we strapped on the skates when we were young kids, it's been a goal of ours to beat the Canadians," said American defenseman Tom Poti before the game. Both teams were aching to win. But for Canada, the stigma of losing would have been unbearable. And Canadian coach Pat Quinn knew that north of the border, millions of his countrymen were watching his players' every move on television. "Somehow in Canada they expect more," he said. "If you get anything but gold, you're a failure."

When the puck dropped on the ice, almost nobody knew what lay buried beneath: a golden Canadian dollar coin, hidden by ice specialists from the Edmonton Oilers for good luck as they prepared the rink. The United States scored the first goal, but soon after, fate seemed to work in favor of the Canadians. Eight minutes into the game, American Tony Amonte scored a goal, but Canada's Paul Kariya—assisted by Chris Pronger and Mario Lemieux—and Jarome Iginla each scored to end the first period at 2–1 for Canada. U.S. goalie Mike Richter later recalled Pronger's centering pass to Lemieux, who faked a shot and let the puck go to Kariya, who then blasted the puck into the net. "It was a beautiful play, a play you have to honor as a goalie. Obviously, I honored it a bit too much."

By the start of the second period, the game was still anyone's to win. Brian Rafalski scored for the United States to tie the game. But less than three minutes later, Canadian Joe Sakic scored what turned out to be the game-winning goal. USA might have tied it up again in the third, but Canadian goaltender Martin Brodeur, whose father Denis, a former goalie, had helped Canada win the bronze in 1956, made several improbable saves. Canada then scored two more to seal the victory.

Just three days before, the E Center had been filled with the sounds of the Canadian national anthem when the women's team won the gold. Now, "O, Canada" reverberated through the stands once again in the final minute of the game. "We took a lot of inspiration from how the women's team played," said defenseman Chris Pronger.

And that Canadian coin? Said Gretzky, still beaming, "I dug it up, and we're going to give it to the Hockey Hall of Fame."

*The United States of America defeats Finland 6-0 in the men's final round.*

IAN LOGAN

*Russia lost 0–7 to the United States of America in a women's exhibition game.*
*"Obviously, the U.S. and Canada are way ahead of everyone else, but*
*we are learning from them and the day will come when we will be able to compete*
*with them." – Larisa Mishina, Russia*

IAN LOGAN

*"Nobody believed in us, and we came out as a whole team, we believed in
each other, we proved it to the whole world. We're thrilled, especially
now that we're going to play against the big boys." — Jan Benda, Germany.
Above, Germany faces the United States of America on February 20.*

MICHAEL  SEAMANS

*"Everybody just goes nuts over there about hockey. No other sports interest people there, just*

*hockey. The president of Belarus plays hockey twice a week, and for Belarus, hockey is everything."*

*— Alexander Zhurik, Belarus (Team captain Alexander Andrievski is shown above.)*

IAN LOGAN

271

*The crowd watches the United States of America play Germany on February 20.*

STEVEN CURRIE

*Finland's Teemu Selänne slips a goal past Sergei Shabanov of Belarus on February 16. Belarus lost 1–8.*

MICHAEL SEAMANS

*Canada scores on Finland in the women's tournament, February 19.*

IAN LOGAN

"The whole aura around the Olympics is something special. To get here and experience that with other athletes
who have dedicated themselves and their whole lives to reaching this level is something very special."
— Mark MacKay, Germany

IAN   LOGAN

*"I'd rather be a silver medalist from America than a gold medalist from*
*any other country." – U.S. goaltender Sarah Tueting, above*

IAN LOGAN

*"It's an empty feeling, and there's not much you can do about it." – Nicklas Lidström
of Sweden, above, whose team was eliminated after a 3–4 loss to Belarus.*

DAVID BURNETT

*"You start each game like a painter. You've got a blank sheet of paper, and you don't know*

*how it's going to end until 60 minutes are over." — Theo Fleury, Canada.*

*The Peaks Ice Arena, above, hosted more than 1400 minutes of ice hockey in February 2002.*

CHAD HOLDER

The Kazakhstani players had come to Salt Lake City with $30 in their pockets and a dream to compete in the Olympics. They were going home with last place but with the hearts of the fans and the community. Spectators fell in love with the players' fighting spirit. They cheered for every save and exploded when Kazakhstan scored its two goals. When a volunteer heard the players couldn't find any affordable souvenirs, she and the local community responded. After a tough 0–7 loss to Sweden, the players boarded the team bus to find gifts, money and letters. Momentum built and their schedule became packed with brunches, receptions and parties—all thrown in their honor. Said forward Dinara Dikambayeva: "We felt the warmth of strangers here. And it inspired us."

JOHN HUET

*Hockey fans often encouraged teams to play harder. "I don't think this building has*

*ever been as loud as it is when we're on the ice, and it definitely gives us more momentum."*

*— Forward Jeremy Roenick, United States of America*

IAN LOGAN

SPEED SKATING IS THE FASTEST HUMAN-POW-
ERED SPORT IN THE WORLD. WITH JUST THE STRENGTH OF
THEIR LEGS AND THE SWINGING OF THEIR ARMS, SKATERS
GO NEARLY 40 MILES PER HOUR. AND FOR 12 DAYS IN
2002 AT THE UTAH OLYMPIC OVAL, THE SPORT WAS THE
FASTEST EVER. ˒ THE OVAL SITS AT A HIGHER ALTITUDE
THAN ANY OTHER SUCH VENUE IN THE WORLD. SKATERS
CUT THROUGH THE AIR WITH LESS RESISTANCE. BECAUSE OF
UTAH'S DESERT CLIMATE, THE ICE IS HARDER. IT IS ALSO
DENSER AND SLICKER AS THE DRY ATMOSPHERE PRODUCES

*The Utah Olympic Oval's ice is kept at a constant surface temperature of 17 degrees Fahrenheit with*

*a system of more than 30 miles of cooling pipes and 74 miles of reinforced steel, embedded in*

*a concrete slab under the 3/4-inch-thick ice. The meticulous maintenance produces superior ice.*

A L B E R T   C O L A N T O N I O

less frost. The result? The smoothest, fastest ice on earth. During the Salt Lake 2002 Games, every Olympic record and eight out of 10 world records fell. And nearly 300 personal and national records were broken. "It's a special place to compete," said Dutch skater Jochem Uytdehaage, the "Flying Dutchman" who would emerge as the king of the Utah Olympic Oval.

MEN'S 5000 M •

Records began falling in the first speed skating event of the Games, with Jens Boden of Germany setting a new Olympic mark of 6:21.73, only to be eclipsed two hours later by American Derek Parra. A former in-line skating champion, Parra doubted he would perform well in the 5000 m. He had even asked his wife to stay home with their newborn daughter because he probably wouldn't win a medal. And then, in what he described as the best 5K of his life, Parra set a new Olympic and world record with a time of 6:17.98. "When you see someone else finish well, it encourages you," he said. "You say to yourself, 'I can skate as fast as he can.'"

Which is exactly what Uytdehaage must have been thinking when he blasted from the starting line 30 minutes later. He shattered Parra's time—and won the gold—by skating the course in 6:14.66. Boden, meanwhile, took home the bronze and Parra, earning the silver, became the first Mexican-American ever to medal in the Olympic Winter Games. It was a day of emotions. When Uytdehaage was asked why he shed tears after finishing, he responded, "Why shouldn't I cry? Why not?"

LADIES' 3000 M •

Like many other athletes at the Oval, German Claudia Pechstein and Canadian Cindy Klassen turned to speed skating after trying another sport. Pechstein began figure skating at age 3, but became bored by the ballet training. Klassen had played ice hockey, but failed to make the 1998 Olympic team. She tried speed skating reluctantly, only at the urging of her parents. Their second choice would prove to be the wisest. On February 10, Pechstein skated the tough 3000 m race in 3:57.70, breaking the world record (a 3:59.26, which she also set in 2001 in Calgary) and taking the gold. While Dutch skater Renate Groenewold won silver, Klassen found herself on the podium for bronze. "I never expected to medal," she said. "I just wanted to have fun."

MEN'S 500 M •

The 500 m is the only speed skating event in which athletes race twice, in two consecutive days. This gives competitors twice the chance to win—but also twice the chance to lose. For Canada's Jeremy Wotherspoon, it was a double disappointment. On February 11, the gold-medal favorite was just five steps into his first race when he tripped and fell. "It's one of the hardest things I've had to watch in competition," said American Casey FitzRandolph, whose interest in speed skating was sparked after he saw Eric Heiden win five gold medals in Lake Placid. "He's one of my best friends."

On February 12, Wotherspoon's time of 34.63 was the day's fastest, but by failing to finish the previous day's race, he had already missed his shot at glory. The gold would instead go to friend and training partner, FitzRandolph. He was joined on his victory lap by teammate Kip Carpenter, who won the bronze. Hiroyasu Shimizu of Japan, the Nagano 1998 gold medalist, won silver.

"It's a combination of art and grace," said FitzRandolph of speed skating. "And it's also power and strength."

LADIES' 500 M •

During the two days of competition in the ladies' 500 m, Catriona Le May Doan of Canada showed little emotion. As the defending gold medalist, she was the favorite for the event. Even she admitted that she would be surprised not to win. The pressure was enormous, but Le May Doan kept it inside. "I am in a sport where I am just going against the clock," she said. "I wouldn't want it any other way."

Although she set an Olympic record of 37.30 in the first race, she remained stoic until the next day when she crossed the finish line in 37.45 and knew she had won the gold once again. She smiled as she skated a victory lap with a Canadian flag. Her intense spirit was echoed by silver medalist Monique Garbrecht-Enfeldt of Germany, who had won bronze at the Albertville 1992 Games but had been struggling to reach the podium again for 10 years. Sabine Völker of Germany won the bronze, her first Olympic medal.

MEN'S 1000 M •

Gerard van Velde of the Netherlands was about ready to give up—again. In 10 years of Olympic competition, he had just missed a medal several times, and didn't race in 1998, because he couldn't adapt to the new klap skate. After taking a job as a car salesman, he was lured back to the ice and decided to give speed skating another shot at the Salt Lake 2002 Games. In the 500 m on February 11 and 12, van Velde, 30, finished fourth by 0.02 seconds. His expectations were low for the 1000 m. "I'm here for fun," he decided. "I'll do my best and give it everything I have."

After a mediocre start that left him 0.14 seconds behind Russia's Sergey Klevchenya at the first split, van Velde skated the fastest lap in any distance ever in speed skating. And he destroyed the world record with a time of 1:07.18. His first full lap was 36 miles per hour, nearly as fast as a grey-hound runs. The car salesman had made history, and teammate Jan Bos, who won silver, could only watch in admiration. "After Gerard put in such a great time, I could only skate for second place," said Bos. "He skated the race of his life."

LADIES' 1000 M •

Speed skating is tough. Speed skating while suffering from an exhaustive case of mononucleosis? Impossible. Or so one would think until witnessing American Chris Witty's performance in the 1000 m. Feeling drained in the months leading up to the Games, Witty found out just three weeks before the Opening Ceremony that she had the virus. Her training and competition days were cut down dramatically, and she was unsure of how she would perform in the Games. "I was happy just to be able to skate the 1000 m," she said later.

Paired with Canadian Catriona Le May Doan—the 500 m gold medalist—Witty felt shaky at the start. Fellow American Jennifer Rodriguez, a former in-line skater from Miami, had nearly stumbled coming out of the first corner, but made up the lost time to win the bronze. Could Witty manage the same kind of comeback? Her weakness seemed to vanish as she began skating around the track, trailing just behind Le May Doan at the 600-meter mark. "I was just happy to be so close to her," Witty later said. And then came the last lap, when Witty pushed forward to take the lead and break the world record in a time of 1:13.83.

MEN'S 1500 M •

While Witty fought fatigue, Norway's Ådne Søndrål battled pain. While training just before the Games, he dislocated not one but both of his shoulders—an excruciating experience for one who must swing his arms for speed, balance and momentum. "So far, I've mostly seen hospitals at the Olympics," he joked after the 1500 m, an event in which sprinters and long-distance skaters participate. The competition is so fierce, explained American J.P. Shilling, "The last lap, you just try to hang on, when your tongue is hanging out of your mouth and your eyes are crossed."

On February 19, Søndrål hit the ice and hoped for the best. Just minutes before, American Parra had set a new world record of 1:43.95, landing him a gold medal and knocking Uytdehaage into second for a silver. Søndrål was paired with American Joey Cheek to battle it out for bronze. Cheek quickly gained the lead. The already noisy crowd began cheering even louder for Cheek. But in the final 200 m of the last lap Søndrål hung on. He passed Cheek and finished in 1:45.26, good enough for the bronze medal, by simply ignoring the pain. "When you're racing, you don't feel anything," he said. "You could cut off both arms and not notice."

LADIES' 1500 M •

Anni Friesinger was famous, and she was flashy. Long before she arrived in Salt Lake City, her fellow Germans had been following her times, her training—and her tattoo—in the pages of celebrity magazines. But the child of two speed skating parents (her mother competed for Poland in the Innsbruck 1976 Games) also had a softer side. Her tattoo of a flame was created in memory of her father, who died in 1996 after a stroke and had always wanted a tattoo. "He was my coach, my best friend, my father," she said. And on February 20, when she beat her own world record to win the gold medal in the 1500 m, the so-called glamour girl began to cry.

Friesinger's race impressed more than her fans. "After Anni," said American Jennifer Rodriguez, "we were all going for second place." Rodriguez won the bronze medal, while that second-place spot would go to Germany's Sabine Völker, who finished the Salt Lake 2002 Games having won a medal in every race in which she competed.

MEN'S 10,000 M •

The 10,000 m is the marathon of Olympic speed skating: a long, 25-lap race where many athletes collapse or vomit or both at the finish line, a race where altitude hits hard. This marathon was dominated by the Dutch skaters. Gianni Romme, the gold medalist at Nagano in the 5000 and 10,000 had failed this year to qualify for the 5000, which meant the 10,000 was his only Olympic race. He aimed to break his own world record of 13:03.40.

But before Romme was even halfway through the race, his legs began to throb. He started losing his technique—and time. When he crossed the line, the clock read 13:10.03, which would eventually earn him the silver. Teammate Jochem Uytdehaage, whom Romme couldn't bear to watch win the 5000, set a new world record of 12:58.92, earning him his second gold and third medal of the Games. "Halfway, I saw the scoreboard and I thought 'Oh, it is going good,' and I started to increase my pace," he said. As Derek Parra, who was paired with the flying Dutchman in the 10,000 m said, "He's the king of these Olympics in speedskating...he's on fire."

The bronze went to Norwegian Lasse Sætre.

LADIES' 5000 M •

While German teammate Anni Friesinger stole the speed skating spotlight, Claudia Pechstein preferred to remain in her shadow, training steadily and seriously. So while the world turned to Friesinger to win her second gold of the Games in the 5000 m, Pechstein, the defending gold medalist, kept a low profile.

In the first pairing of the day, Gretha Smit of the Netherlands skated a 6:49.22, breaking the world record by more than three seconds, and secured a silver. Canadian Clara Hughes, a two-time Olympic bronze medalist in cycling, finished in the next fastest time, 6:53.53, for another bronze.

In the next heat, Pechstein, who was paired with Japan's Maki Tabata, exploded from the start and skated the 12.5 laps in 6:46.91. The time was more than 10 seconds faster than her personal best, and shattered the world record by more than two seconds. As Tabata, her only threat, finished far behind her, Pechstein realized she had won. It was her third consecutive Olympic gold medal in the 5000 m, a feat not accomplished since Bonnie Blair won her third consecutive in the 500 m. Pechstein stepped from the shadows to skate a victory lap, wearing a wig in Germany's colors and tossing flowers to the crowd. "I'm not really thinking about the future right now," she said. "I just want to celebrate."

*Kevin Marshall of Canada glides through the men's 1000 m on February 16.*

SHEILA METZNER

*Joey Cheek of the United States of America races in the 1500 m. He would place*

*fourth, missing the bronze by 0.08 seconds.*

TIBOR NEMETH

*"I have never dug so deep. With three or four laps, I thought, 'Please just let me stand up.*

*I just want to stand up and finish.'" — American Jason Hedstrand*

T I B O R   N E M E T H

Canadian Patrick Bouchard, who set a personal record in the 1000 m, has a
black belt in kung fu and a master's degree in electrical engineering.

291

SHEILA METZNER

*Canada's Catriona Le May Doan began speed skating when she was 9. On February 14,*

*the Saskatchewan native won the ladies' 500 m, giving Canada its first gold medal of the Games.*

SHEILA METZNER

*Christian Breuer of Germany catches his breath.*

SHEILA METZNER

*"Dreams come true. If you think it, you believe it." – Derek Parra, right, who on February 9 became the first Mexican-American to win a medal in the Olympic Winter Games. Ten days later, he set a new world record of 1:43.95 in the 1500 m.*

TIBOR NEMETH

*China's Fengtong Yu, 17, was the youngest speed skater to compete at the*

*Salt Lake 2002 Games. He set a personal record in the 1000 m.*

ANDY ANDERSON

297

*In 1998, Gerard van Velde of the Netherlands (center) gave up speed skating to*
*sell cars. In 2002, he came back to destroy the 1000 m record. "That I could do it here*
*is so incredibly beautiful," he said. "It's a crown on my career."*

S H E I L A   M E T Z N E R

*Korea's Seung-Yong Choi, above, set a new national record on the first day of*

*competition in the ladies' 500 m.*

TIBOR NEMETH

299

*American Derek Parra paces himself in the grueling 10,000 m.*

J O H N   H U E T

300

*Belarusian Aleksey Khatylyov takes off in the explosive 500 m.*

DAVID BURNETT

*The Dutch team warms up. Before the Salt Lake 2002 Games, the Netherlands had*
*won 61 Olympic Winter Games medals, 58 of which were in speed skating.*
*"It's definitely a Dutch sport," said fan Bart Schenk, who traveled to Utah from Holland*
*carrying a suitcase stuffed with orange cheering gear.*

DAVID BURNETT (TOP)

JOHN HUET (BOTTOM)

*Each day of competition, athletes treated 4600 spectators to history in the making, as world, Olympic,*

*national and personal records fell, one by one.*

ALBERT COLANTONIO

**SHORT TRACK ·** ONE BY ONE, THE SKATERS GLIDE INTO THEIR STARTING POSITIONS, SHAKING THE LAST JITTERS FROM THEIR POWERFUL LEGS AS THE ANNOUNCER CALLS THEIR NAMES. ON THE LINE, THEY CROUCH, MOTIONLESS, BALANCED ONLY ON THE PINPOINT TIP OF ONE SKATE AND THE RAZOR-THIN BLADE OF THE OTHER, WHICH THEY'VE WEDGED INTO THE ICE PARALLEL TO THE START LINE FOR MAXIMUM LEVERAGE. THE CROWD HUSHES. SKATES GLINT. MUSCLES TENSE. THIS IS HOW ALL SHORT TRACK RACES BEGIN. BUT THE WAY IN WHICH THIS ONE—THE

*Canada's Marc Gagnon, the United States of America's Apolo Anton Ohno*
*and Korea's Kim Dong-Sung jockey for the lead in the dramatic 1500 m final.*

SHEILA   METZNER

men's 1000 m final—ends is stunning, even in the fast, furious and notoriously unpredictable world of short track speed skating.

Starting on the inside is Canadian and two-time Olympian Mathieu Turcotte. Next to him is Ahn Hyun-Soo, 16-year-old junior world champion from South Korea; then American Apolo Anton Ohno, a rebellious teenager turned skating dynamo. To Ohno's right is Li Jiajun, China's defending Olympic silver medalist in this distance. And in the outside lane is Steven Bradbury, Australia's four-time Olympian, but a long shot for a medal.

The start gun sounds, and the skaters vie for position in a sudden jumble of skates, arms and legs, then fall into an orderly line that moves with unexpected serpentine grace. Korea's Ahn takes an early lead. Ohno moves into second place with a sleek inside pass, then explodes into the lead with Ahn on his heels, Li and Turcotte close behind. Ohno sprints toward the finish line, a gold medal just meters away. But suddenly everything changes: Li makes contact with him, then catches a skate and tumbles to the ice helplessly. Tripped up by Li's fall, Ahn goes down, too, arms flailing in a desperate attempt at recovery, which takes down both Ohno and Turcotte. Only straggler Steven Bradbury is still on his feet, and in a matter of seconds he has moved from last to first. "Hang on a minute, I've just won!" he thinks, crossing the finish line, both stunned and elated. Behind him, Ohno, whose thigh has been sliced by a skate and will require stitches, struggles to his feet and flings his body over the line to claim the silver. Turcotte follows him, winning the bronze.

It was a shocking race, but for Bradbury, just part of the topsy-turvy sport. Short track nearly killed him in 1994, when a blade cut through his leg, causing a serious loss of blood and requiring 111 stitches. At the Salt Lake 2002 Games, the Australian, who makes Ohno's skates, hoped the American might mention his handiwork upon winning. Instead, Bradbury found *himself* in the spotlight, earning his country's first-ever gold medal in an Olympic Winter Games and trying to defend his good-luck win. "Anything can happen," says Bradbury. "Sometimes it's a very cruel sport, and other times it's a sport that you smile a lot about, which is my case at the moment."

Delighted spectators experienced short track's fickle nature again and again at the Salt Lake Ice Center. First, there was the ladies' 1500 m event, held three nights before Bradbury's surprising win. The final round was a matchup of the world's best: Chinese favorites Yang Yang (A), the world's top female skater, and Yang Yang (S), ranked third in the world; Korea's Ko Gi-Hyun, just 15, and Choi Eun-Kyung, who had set a world record in the semifinals; Canada's Alanna Kraus, 23, from Calgary, Alberta; and Evgenia Radanova of Bulgaria, who had just swept the European championships.

Ko led for most of the race. Behind her, with about eight laps to go, Yang (S) and Kraus clipped skates and fell. Then Yang (A) tumbled, too, and Choi moved into second. With two laps to go, Radanova, in third, tried to pass both Ko and Choi, but they clung to their positions, Choi tucked in tightly behind her teammate. Ko took the gold medal, becoming the youngest individual gold medalist in short track history; Choi followed her for the silver, and Radanova took the bronze.

By February 16, the next night of competition, the word was out: Short track was a wild card, a rough-and-tumble, high-speed thrill ride. Fans donned stick-on "soul patch" beards in honor of Ohno or scooped up Korean and Chinese flags to wave from the bleachers. The show-stopping men's 1000—with its mass tumble and its come-from-behind-victory—provided drama. So did the ladies' 500—an all-out sprint. In the final round of the event, China's Yang Yang (A) achieved what she called her greatest victory: earning her country's first-ever gold medal of the Olympic Winter Games. She won by staving off Bulgaria's Evgenia Radanova, who won silver. Behind Radanova was China's Wang Chunlu, who, with a bronze medal, shared in her country's glory, a moment that coincided with the Chinese New Year. "We want to take this back to China as the best gift ever," said Wang. "This has been a dream for two generations," said Yang Yang (A). "Happy New Year!"

MEN'S 1500 M

LADIES' 3000 M RELAY •

On February 20, the thrills and spills continued as competitors in the final round of the men's 1500 m took to the ice. As the race began, Korean Kim Dong-Sung led the pack. He had come to Salt Lake City as a major threat, with two 1998 medals from Nagano and the highest top speed of any skater on his formidable team among his credentials. But Ohno was on the move after a slow start, passing skaters one by one until he was on Kim's shoulder, jockeying for the lead with an inside pass. Kim aggressively defended his position and finished first, with Ohno close behind.

Kim threw his fists into the air triumphantly and grabbed a Korean flag from the sidelines. But as he began a victory lap, the news came over the loudspeaker: He was disqualified for illegally blocking Ohno's pass attempt, and the gold would go to Ohno. Kim threw down the flag and kicked at the ice in anguish. China's Li Jiajun, who had finished third, won the silver; and the fourth finisher, Canada's Marc Gagnon, won the bronze. While Kim and his fans were angered, Ohno was elated by his fortune. "They can just go throw me in the desert and bury me," said Ohno. "I got a gold medal."

Korea was luckier in the ladies' 3000 m relay final, in which the team, made up of Choi Eun-Kyung, Choi Min-Kyung, Joo Min-Jin and Park Hye-Won—four first-time Olympic competitors in the event—pulled well ahead of China in the final two laps to set the world record and win the gold— Korea's third straight Olympic victory in the event. "I feel it was a great match," said Choi Min-Kyung later. "We finally did as we wished we could," added Joo Min-Jin.

MEN'S 500 M

MEN'S 5000 M RELAY

LADIES' 1000 M •

Short track's last night, February 23, began with the fast-paced men's 500 m. A much anticipated rematch between Ohno and Kim never happened; Kim was eliminated and Ohno was disqualified during the semifinals. In the elegantly skated final round, Canada's Gagnon stole American Rusty Smith's lead with a powerful inside pass—which Smith would later call "beautiful"—and won the gold medal, making him Canada's most decorated Olympian of all time. Fellow Canadian Jonathan Guilmette also passed Smith in the race's last seconds to win the silver, and Smith took the bronze. This proud moment for Canada would only be outshined later that evening, when the Canadian team (Gagnon, Guilmette, Eric Bédard, François-Louis Tremblay and Turcotte) won the men's 5000 m relay, making Gagnon the most medal-winning male short track skater in Olympic history.

But Canada wasn't the only nation celebrating. In the ladies' 1000 m, Yang Yang (A), already a national hero for winning her country's first Olympic gold in the 500 m, won again. Yang Yang (S) led early, but she was soon passed by Yang (A). Korea's Ko Gi-Hyun pushed for the lead, but Yang (A) held her at bay and took first place; Ko finished second, and Yang (S) third. "Each day, I have more passion for my sport," said the jubilant Yang (A). "This gold medal is very important to me, but the value of the experience of being here exceeds even the value of the gold medal."

For four memorable nights at the Salt Lake Ice Center, first became last and last became first. A nation's greatest hope was realized. Another's expectations were shattered. History was made. And the differences between first and last, elation and devastation, glory and infamy, were the tiniest of margins: one width of a paper-thin steel blade, a few hundredths of a second, a skate thrust over the finish line just barely ahead of another, a shoulder shifted inches off course. Unlikely gold-medal winner Steven Bradbury was right about short track: Just about anything can happen. And at the Salt Lake 2002 Olympic Winter Games, just about everything did.

*New Zealand's Mark Jackson, Bulgaria's Miroslav Boiadiev, Japan's Satoru Terao*

*and Belgium's Wim de Deyne compete in the men's 1000 m.*

MICHAEL SEAMANS

309

*The United States of America's Apolo Anton Ohno leads Italy's Fabio Carta and*

*Korea's Kim Dong-Sung on the 111.12-meter oval at the Salt Lake Ice Center.*

JOHN HUET

*Men's 1500 m: Korea's Kim Dong Sung and New Zealand's Mark Jackson (top) and the*
*Netherlands' Cees Juffermans and Canada's Marc Gagnon (bottom) compete in the preliminary heats.*

SHEILA METZNER

*"I just gave my best and I shined, like a star or something. I saw my chance and took it."*

*— American Apolo Anton Ohno, above, on his victory in the bizarre 1500 m.*

SHEILA METZNER

*"I don't know if everything sits perfectly well in my stomach about how I won the race. But, I'm justifying it within myself through the last 10 or 12 years of what I've put into this sport. I've been on a massive roller-coaster ride...I've paid my dues, I reckon." – Gold medalist Steven Bradbury of Australia*

TIBOR NEMETH

*"I need to think about having won two gold medals first," said Canada's Marc Gagnon*

*when asked how it felt to be the most decorated man in Olympic short track history.*

TIBOR NEMETH

On turns in short track, skaters lean inward at an angle of almost 50 degrees.

TIBOR NEMETH

*Canada's Alanna Kraus and Japan's Chikage Tanaka battle for position in the ladies' 1000 m.*

IAN LOGAN

*Members of China's and Canada's teams compete in the men's 5000 m relay.*

CHAD HOLDER

*Short track skaters start each race by sprinting on the ice to try to claim a position near the front of the pack.*

IAN LOGAN

*China's Yang Yang (A), in front, claimed her country's first-ever gold*
*in the Olympic Winter Games by winning the ladies' 500 m.*

MICHAEL SEAMANS

*Korea's Choi Eun-Kyung leads a serpentine pack of skaters in the ladies' 1500 m.*

MICHAEL SEAMANS

*Canada would leave Salt Lake City with six short track speed skating medals.*

SHEILA METZNER

FIGURE SKATING BEGINS IN COMPLEXITY —
THE LAWS OF PHYSICS TESTED, THE HUMAN BODY A PRECISE
MACHINE THAT JUMPS, SPINS AND GLIDES ACROSS THE
SLICKEST OF SURFACES. BY THE END OF A PERFORMANCE,
THOUGH, THE MECHANICS MELT AWAY INTO THE SIMPLEST
OF FORMULAS, WHERE GRACE AND POISE TAKE AWAY ONE'S
BREATH. DURING THE SALT LAKE 2002 GAMES, FIGURE
SKATING BEGAN IN A COMPLICATED TANGLE, WHEN A CON-
TROVERSIAL JUDGING DECISION SHOOK THE SALT LAKE ICE
CENTER. TEN DAYS LATER, IT ENDED IN THE SIMPLEST OF

*"When someone gives you a kick in the butt, you go forward, right?" – David Pelletier.*
*He and Jamie Salé, who won a dual pairs gold after a controversial judging decision, relax*
*backstage after their exhibition performance on February 22.*

J O H N   H U E T

ways, when a 16-year-old girl took our breath away with grace, polish and raw exuberance.

PAIRS •

On February 9, Russians Elena Berezhnaya and Anton Sikharulidze, two-time pairs world champions, skated a nearly flawless short program. They performed a triple loop side-by-side spin in perfect unison and completed the program with solid athletic technique. They earned the first-place spot going into the long program. "Many things happened in the last four years, good and bad ones," said Sikharulidze. "To be here and skate well is just great."

When the Russian pair first teamed up in 1996, Berezhnaya could barely walk. During a training session, she and a skating partner had become unsynchronized during a side-by-side camel spin. His skate blade pierced her skull. The gash required emergency brain surgery, leaving her speech impaired and the right side of her body partially paralyzed for some time. Her boyfriend Sikharulidze kept vigil at the hospital and when Berezhnaya recovered, the two decided to skate together.

Canadians Jamie Salé and David Pelletier were in second place after the short program. Before they met, he was selling hot dogs in a Montreal stadium and she was waitressing at an Edmonton restaurant. Salé couldn't find the right partner and thought about hanging up her skates. But when she first skated with Pelletier, they clicked instantly. "I feel like I'm one with him," said Salé. "I feel his energy, and he feels mine." In the short program, they nailed a side-by-side triple toe loop, a difficult lift and a triple twist. But in their pose at the finale, the 2001 champions slipped and fell. They lay on the ice laughing. "I just thought, 'I came all the way to the Olympics to do that?!'" Pelletier said later.

The lighthearted moment would soon end. The following evening, 20 pairs skated before the final three pairs—in first, second and third place, respectively—took to the ice: Berezhnaya and Sikharulidze would be followed by Salé and Pelletier, and then China's Xue Shen and Hongbo Zhao.

The Russians' performance, set to the opera piece "Meditation," was strong. But the pair made four mistakes, including Sikharulidze stepping out of the landing in the double Axel. Skating to the theme from the film *Love Story*, a program they had created two years prior to the Games, Salé and Pelletier seemed to have outperformed the Russians. Their throw triple Salchow, double Axel double toe loop and a triple throw loop were impeccable, and at the finish, an exuberant Pelletier kissed the ice in triumph. Fans, expecting a perfect score from the judges, chanted "Six! Six!"

But when the marks appeared, silence fell on the crowd. Salé and Pelletier were awarded a string of 5.8s and 5.9s and a second-place spot, not the first they were expecting.

What had happened? Had the Canadians been penalized for skating an old program? Or had something gone wrong with the judging process? Rumors of French judge Marie-Reine Le Gougne being pressured to vote a certain way began to swirl. The bronze medal, won by China's Xue Shen and Hongbo Zhao, was clear, but the gold remained murky for days. (Later, the International Skating Union suspended Le Gougne and banned her from the 2006 Games.) Finally, on February 15, a compromise was reached. Berezhnaya and Sikharulidze would keep their gold medal, while Salé and Pelletier would exchange their silver for a tie gold medal.

It was a significant moment in Olympic history, but for both pairs, simply one of relief. Said Berezhnaya, "I'm very happy it's all over, and it's closed."

The controversy had also turned competitors into colleagues. "The four of us were part of history," said Pelletier. "Obviously, it was a tough few days, but now we're happy to put some closure to it and we can go on and be athletes. Our gold medal is everybody's."

MEN'S •

While the world debated the outcome of the pairs competition, it nearly missed the men's event, in which Russia's Alexei Yagudin skated one of the most outstanding performances of the

Games. Before the short program, held just one night after the pairs free skate, it seemed that the gold-medal matchup would be between Yagudin and Evgeni Plushenko, three-time Russian champion. Though countrymen, they were known for a fierce rivalry in which each tried to outjump, out-choreograph and outperform the other.

But Plushenko fell on the opening quadruple toe loop in the short program, landing in fourth place. For Yagudin, whose complicated spins and original moves had earned him first place, the coast was suddenly much clearer. And when he reappeared two evenings later for the free program, skating to music from *The Man in the Iron Mask,* Yagudin seemed ready to end the duel with Plushenko. With incredible timing and execution, he performed no less than five triple jumps, with fast and furious footwork between each one. Having been prescribed skating lessons at age 4 because he was so small and sickly, Yagudin's moment had arrived. He was already crying with joy when his scores, including four 6.0s, flashed on the board. It was the first time in history any singles skater had earned more than one 6.0. "I was in a fog," he said. "I heard that I was the only guy who got 6.0s in the Olympics...I became not just a jumper, but also an artist on the ice."

Plushenko, meanwhile, had recovered sufficiently to earn the silver, with a flamboyant performance and complex moves. American Timothy Goebel, known as the "Quad King" for his ability in jumps of four revolutions, skated just after Plushenko and earned the bronze with a strong technical program and a carefree attitude as he skated to *An American in Paris.* He also became the first male figure skater to land a quadruple Salchow (in the short program) and three quads (in the free) in an Olympic competition. Goebel was the first U.S. athlete in 10 years to win a medal in men's Olympic figure skating. "It's great we've got an American man back on the podium," he said. "Any of the three of us [U.S. skaters for the men's event] could have medaled, and I'm just really happy it was me."

**ICE DANCING •**

If figure skating is a balance between artistry and athleticism, ice dancing tips to the side of artistry. Before the Salt Lake 2002 Games, some questioned whether the sport, part of the Olympic program since 1976, belonged there. With fewer compulsory moves than pairs skating, and rules requiring at least one foot on the ice at all times, except during circumscribed lifts or jumps (and therefore limiting highly technical moves), ice dancing was prone to highly subjective judging. And when the pairs controversy heated up, the sport gained even more intense scrutiny.

The three-part competition began with the compulsory program, in which all 24 couples were required to perform one dance each of the quickstep and the blues. France's Marina Anissina and Gwendal Peizerat emerged as the leaders. Their story fit well in a sport known for its drama: Anissina was born in the Soviet Union and had been winning junior titles with Ilia Averbukh until he fell in love with another skater named Irina Lobacheva and abandoned Anissina. Six months later, Anissina began practicing with Peizerat, a skater who liked to scuba dive and rock climb in his free time. She moved to France to try skating and eventually compete with him.

Finishing second in the Salt Lake 2002 compulsories were none other than Irina Lobacheva and Ilia Averbukh, now married, who were hot on Anissina's and Peizerat's heels. Italy's Barbara Fusar Poli and Maurizio Margaglio, the defending world champions, were in a close third place. Two nights later, the three pairs returned to the ice to battle it out in the original dance, set to a Spanish medley for all competitors. Anissina and Peizerat danced the flamenco and the tango, earning another first-place finish. Lobacheva and Averbukh, also in a tango and flamenco-inspired performance, again landed in second while the Italians held on to third.

There was just one more element to conquer: the free skate program. Anissina and Peizerat chose to honor the United States with a dance that began with Anissina posing as the Statue of

Liberty, set to music mixed with parts of Martin Luther King Jr.'s "I Have a Dream" speech. Their performance was packed with spins, spirals and synchronized movements, including the "gender bender" pose with Anissina lifting Peizerat. Barely edging out Averbukh and Lobacheva, who were second and the silver medalists by a 5–4 judging split, the duo captured France's first Olympic ice dancing gold medal. Winning bronze was Fusar Poli and Margaglio of Italy.

Often considered the marquee event of any Olympic Winter Games, the ladies' figure skating competition was in 2002 dominated by four names—Michelle Kwan, Irina Slutskaya, Sasha Cohen and Sarah Hughes—even before it began. Kwan, the United States of America's silver medalist at Nagano in 1998, was more determined than ever to win a gold medal. So determined, in fact, that she fired her longtime choreographer, and then her coach of nine years, shortly before the Games. Her career included six national and four world championships and 27 scores of 6.0. All it was missing was Olympic gold, and she would go for this final piece without a coach.

Russia's Slutskaya began figure skating to cure chronic bronchitis and ended up becoming the four-time European champion. She was poised to become Russia's first woman to win the Olympic figure skating gold. Known for landing difficult jumps, Slutskaya was the first woman to perform a double Biellmann spin with a foot change, a move in which she grasps the blade of a skate behind her back, pulls it over her head and spins, switching feet halfway through the move.

Cohen of the United States was a 17-year-old whose grace and flexibility had already commanded serious attention from judges in the figure skating circuit. And then there was Hughes, an American figure skating prodigy who learned to tie her own skates at age 3 and performed her first double Salchow (a distinctive move that requires taking off and landing on different edges of the skate) at age 5. Her natural prowess was tempered by a down-to-earth attitude: Unlike most skaters, Hughes trained from home. She was an excellent student, and hoped to become a doctor someday.

There were few surprises in the short program, with Kwan finishing first, Slustkaya second, Cohen third and Hughes in fourth. In the long program, everything changed. Of the four, Hughes skated first, in a stunning, flawless performance, landing seven successful triple jumps and nailing a difficult triple toe loop–triple loop combination. As the crowd roared and flowers rained down, Hughes threw her arms upward, radiant, with the overwhelming joy of an athlete who has just performed at her very best.

But there was more to come. Cohen fell on her triple-jump combination, only to be followed by Kwan, who fell out of a triple flip and landed poorly on another. Encouraged by cheers from the spectators, she landed three more triple jumps: Salchow, Lutz and toe loop. "I made a few mistakes," she said, "but I kept on going strong." Then, Slutskaya skated, with a shaky triple flip in a program that lacked her usual strength and speed.

Hughes, who was backstage with her coach Robin Wagner at this point, still didn't think it was possible to win gold. Suddenly, a nearby cameraman, who had heard the judges marks, told her she had won the gold. Hughes and Wagner fell to their knees, shrieking, completely in shock. She was the first figure skater ever to vault from fourth to first place in a tricky scoring system introduced in 1992. "In the past, I've held back, not always given it my all," said Hughes, still trying to grasp this truly Olympic moment. "Tonight, I just said, 'I have nothing to lose.'"

Nothing to lose, indeed. After causing one of the biggest upsets in Olympic history (Slutskaya won silver, Kwan, the bronze) and celebrating her gold medal with her brothers and sisters late into the night, Hughes was already turning her attention toward conquering another challenge: her college entrance exams. "My next goal," she said, "is to get in the high 1500s on my SATs."

*Russia's Elena Berezhnaya and Anton Sikharulidze, who were awarded the first pairs gold, performed their free*

*skate to music from the opera "Thais," the story of a seductress who courts a Cenobite monk.*

MICHAEL SEAMANS

*U.S. skater Michelle Kwan captured first place in the ladies' short program on February 19.*

*"I felt America behind me—and that was incredible!" she said.*

ELISABETH O'DONNELL

*While preparing for the Salt Lake 2002 Games, American Sarah Hughes was most looking*

*forward to sharing meals with other athletes at the Olympic Village cafeteria. Shown here during the*

*short program, Hughes was soon sharing gold with the world.*

ELISABETH O'DONNELL

*A powerful jumper, Russia's Irina Slutskaya was the first woman to land a*

*triple Lutz-triple loop, the first woman to land a Salchow-triple loop combination and the*

*first woman to perform a double Biellman spin with a foot change.*

IAN LOGAN

*Known for her classical elegance, Russia's Maria Butyrskaya*

*assists in designing her costumes.*

IAN LOGAN

*"When I got on the ice, I couldn't believe it was finally here. The moment I waited for my whole life."*

*— Sasha Cohen, United States of America*

JOHN HUET

*"I can't be perfect all the time," said Russia's Alexei Yagudin. "I'm not a machine." Yagudin was near*

*perfect in Salt Lake City, however, earning a record four 6.0s and winning the men's gold.*

JOHN HUET

*Yosuke Takeuchi of Japan performs a camel spin during the men's free program.*

MICHAEL SEAMANS

*Alexander Abt of Russia landed in fifth place after the men's free program.*

MICHAEL SEAMANS

*Slovakians Olga Bestandigova and Jozef Bestandig, siblings, compete in the pairs competition.*

MICHAEL SEAMANS

*Bestandig tosses his sister in a throw triple loop move during the pairs*

*competition. The two are five-time national champions.*

MICHAEL SEAMANS

*Gold-medaling ice dancers Marina Anissina and Gwendal Peizerat of France teamed up after
Anissina, deserted by her partner, wrote a letter to Peizerat from her native Russia. She remembered
seeing him at a competition. He answered six months later, when his own partner retired.*

MICHAEL SEAMANS

*Anissina, above, followed in the footsteps of her mother, Irina Cherniyeva, who*

*competed in pairs skating at the Sapporo 1972 Olympic Winter Games.*

IAN LOGAN

*Ice dancers Marika Humphreys and Vitali Baranov of Great Britain present their routine for original dance.*

IAN LOGAN

*Naomi Lang of the United States, shown here with ice dancing partner Peter Tchernyshev, is a member of*

*the Karuk tribe and the first female Native American to compete in the Olympic Winter Games.*

IAN LOGAN

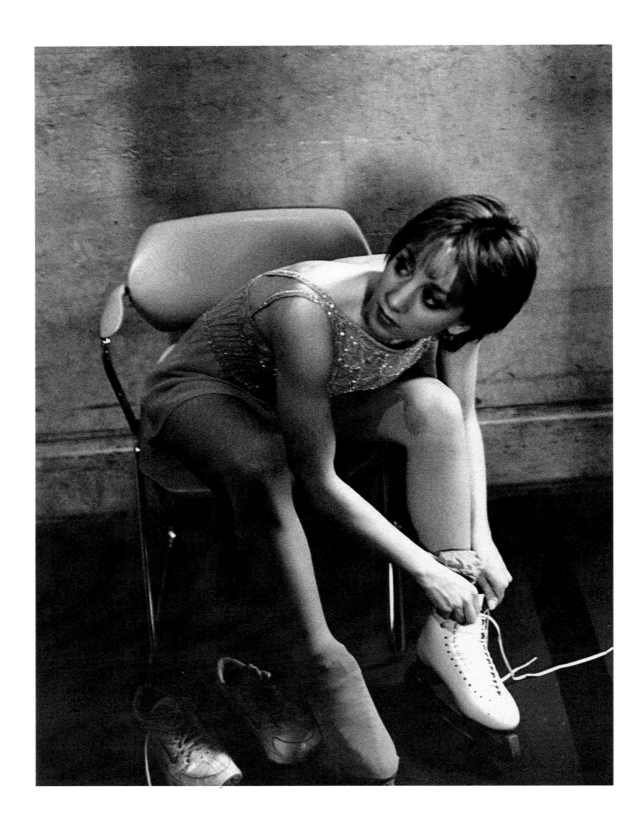

*Gold medalist Sarah Hughes dedicated her exhibition performance, one night after she won gold,*

*to those who suffered from the attacks of September 11, 2001.*

JOHN HUET

OLYMPIC VILLAGE • As fortresses go, the Salt Lake 2002 Olympic Village, located in the city's historic Fort Douglas area, was among the finest. Set high in the foothills of the Wasatch Mountains, in the glow of the Olympic Cauldron, it was a mythical land filled with the world's greatest athletes—but kept strictly off-limits to outsiders. Miles of fencing, security guards and surveillance cameras did not just protect thousands of men and women, they preserved peace of

*Andreas Morczinietz and Marc Seliger, Germany, Ice Hockey*

RAYMOND MEEKS

mind. Inside its walls, individuals from 77 delegations were united as one community as they unfurled flags from dormitory windows, unpacked good luck charms and began to unwind. Tomorrow, or the next day, or even next week, they would compete, with overwhelming expectations pinned on a blip in time. But for now, there were glorious, unfettered hours in which they could contemplate, focus and simply imagine, in a place that soon became less of a fort and more of a blessed sanctuary. These were the hours in which Olympians could simply be Olympians.

It was a place of peace and a place of discovery. Night and day, athletes found camaraderie, comfort—and the musical talents of their fellow residents—in the CoffeeHouse. From Prince Albert of Monaco, a five-time Olympian, to Jayaram Khadka, representing Nepal in its first Olympic Winter Games, they found equality in the simple dormitory lodging and along snow-covered walkways. Families, such as Argentinian siblings and alpine skiers Macarena, Maria Belen and Cristian Javier Simari Birkner, found a second home in the Olympic Village. Individuals such as Kenya's Philip Boit and Cameroon's Isaac Menyoli—their country's sole athletes at the Games—found family. Shiva Keshavan of India found an old friend: Kang Kwange-Bae of Korea, from whom he had borrowed crutches after becoming injured in a 1997 luge event. They had not seen each other since the Nagano 1998 Games. And most everyone found a little bit more about hope, about dreams and about courage.

Photographers could enter the Olympic Village only through tight restrictions, with one exception: Montana-based artist Raymond Meeks. He invited athletes to his small studio in the International Zone, where they could have their picture taken, if they pleased. The result is a remarkable collection of relaxed and intimate portraits, which reveal athletes beyond the boundaries of their sports and capture some of the most precious moments of the Salt Lake 2002 Games.

*Stéphanie Bouvier, France, Short Track Speed Skating*

RAYMOND MEEKS

*Aika Klein, Germany, Short Track Speed Skating*

RAYMOND MEEKS

*Georg Hackl, Germany, Luge*

RAYMOND MEEKS

*Gwendal Peizerat, France, Figure Skating*

RAYMOND MEEKS

*Jana Schreckenbach, Germany, Ice Hockey*

RAYMOND MEEKS

*Dinah Browne, U.S. Virgin Islands, Luge (Center)*

RAYMOND MEEKS

*Sisters Amanda and Jaime Fortier, Canada, Cross-Country Skiing*

RAYMOND MEEKS

*Liutauras Barila, Lithuania, Biathlon (Left)*

RAYMOND MEEKS

*Nicolas Fontaine, Canada, Freestyle Aerials*

RAYMOND MEEKS

*Trennon Paynter, Australia, Freestyle Moguls*

RAYMOND MEEKS

*Michel André, France, Bobsleigh*

RAYMOND MEEKS

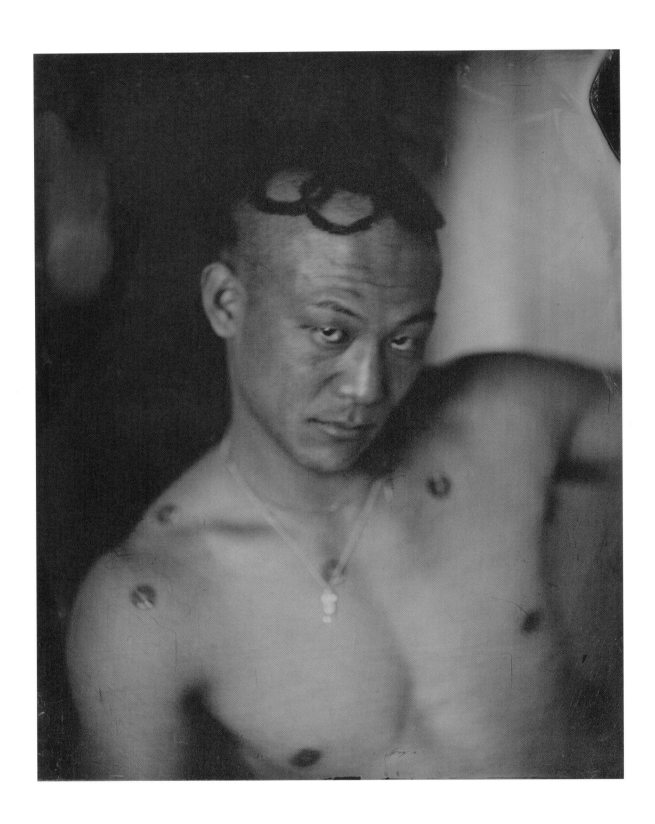

*Masanori Inoue, Japan, Bobsleigh*

RAYMOND MEEKS

*Irina Terentjeva, Lithuania, Cross-Country Skiing*

RAYMOND MEEKS

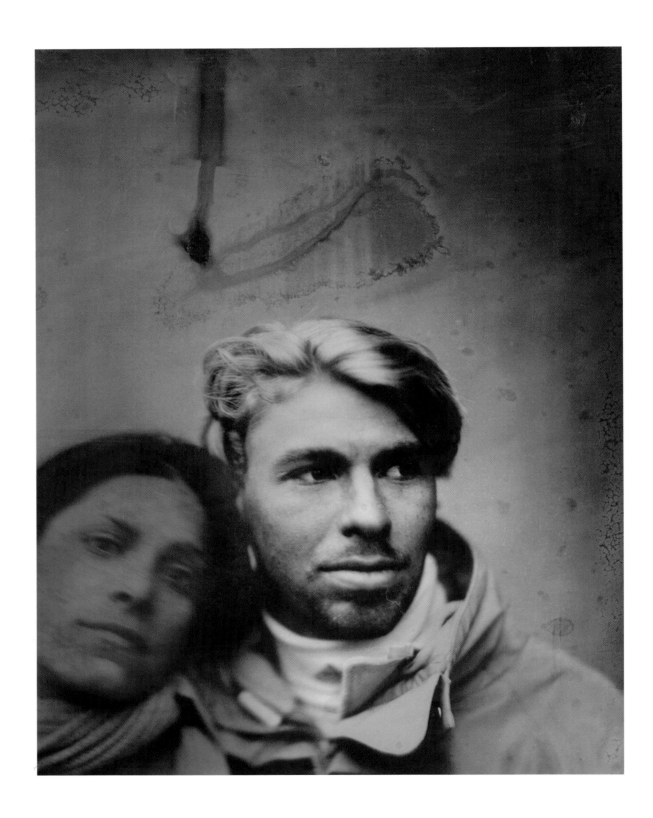

*Isabelle Delobel and Olivier Schoenfelder, France, Figure Skating*

RAYMOND MEEKS

OLYMPIC MEDALS PLAZA • IT WAS THE
HEARTBEAT OF THE OLYMPIC SPIRIT: AN AMPHITHEATER
IN DOWNTOWN SALT LAKE CITY CREATED FOR THE SOLE
PURPOSE OF HONORING OUR NEWEST OLYMPIC HEROES
AND SHARING THEIR GLORY WITH THE WORLD. OLYMPIC
MEDALS PLAZA WAS FREE TO THE PUBLIC, OPEN TO THE
STARRY SKIES—AND THE HOTTEST PLACE TO BE FOR TWO
WEEKS IN FEBRUARY 2002. NEVER BEFORE HAD OLYMPIC
LAURELS BEEN PRESENTED ON SUCH A SCALE: 20,000 FANS
FLOCKED TO THE VENUE EACH EVENING FOR MEDALS

*Women's downhill gold medalist Carole Montillet of France waves to the Olympic Medals Plaza crowd.*

ALBERT COLANTONIO

Ceremonies, concerts and fireworks. An extraordinary line up of headline artists, including Dave Matthews Band, Macy Gray, *NSYNC, Alanis Morrissette and Marc Anthony, paid tribute to the inspiring achievements of the athletes with rock-the-house shows.

As dramatic and memorable as the shows it hosted was the stage itself, encapsulated by the giant Hoberman Arch. Made of 96 translucent panels and symbolizing the Salt Lake 2002 theme of *Light the Fire Within*, the Arch suspended acrobatic dancers, dangling by silk sheets, from its silver beams. It retracted to reveal the Heroes' Cauldron, lit from the Olympic Flame on February 9 and illuminating the podium. Medalists were led to the stage by a Child of Light. For the first time in Olympic history, gold medals were presented last, allowing a prolonged celebration of bronze and silver medalists before culminating in the gold medalist and the playing of his or her national anthem.

Standing on the podium, surrounded by such grandiosity—and by so many people—was an experience for which the athletes were often wholly unprepared, despite their extraordinary accomplishments. Members of the Finnish nordic-combined team battled pre-Medals Plaza jitters by donning business suits to accept their medals because, as team member Jari Mantila said, "You want to look good up there." American Tristan Gale, having just won gold for a fearless, bone-rattling skeleton ride, could barely find the courage to walk toward the podium. "Lea Ann [Parsley] had to drag me out there," she said. "This was way harder than what I did today. We practice our sport over and over. We never practice standing up in front of our home crowd and hearing our national anthem."

These were times of overwhelming emotion, when speed skater Derek Parra, the first Mexican-American to win a medal in the Olympic Winter Games and bobsledder Vonetta Flowers, the first African-American to win winter gold, cried silently, the tears running down their faces and dripping from their chins. These were times of wonder, when the newly crowned Olympian champions looked down to inspect their medals, to see if they were real. Surprise Swiss ski jumping phenomenon Simon Ammann laughed and laughed at this peculiar but pleasant predicament, winning not one but two gold medals. Australian Alisa Camplin simply bounced on the podium. "I was so excited, I didn't know what to do," said the gold-medaling aerialist. "I just started jumping up and down."

But above all, Olympic Medals Plaza provided times of transcendence for all who gathered there, nights of glitter and splendor, when all things seemed possible. "I feel like I sprouted wings, and I'm showered with joy," said Germany's Silke Kraushaar, after receiving the bronze medal for women's luge. "I'm in heaven right now."

*"I should enjoy what I'm seeing right now, because this is just amazing. The people in America are great.*
*They cheered for us just as much as they did for their own." — Doubles luge gold medalist Alexander Resch of*
*Germany, on what ran through his mind as he stood on the Olympic Medals Plaza podium*

IAN LOGAN

*Creating a cathedral of champions, towering banners of athletes*

*surrounded Olympic Medals Plaza, reminding audiences of the power to inspire.*

CHAD HOLDER

*Olympic Medals Plaza was the most ambitious project of its kind in Olympic history. Its centerpiece was the*

*Hoberman Arch, a 30,000-pound structure that spiraled outward and upward.*

IAN LOGAN

*Designed to open like the iris of an eye, the Hoberman Arch revealed the Olympic Medals Plaza stage and*

*Heroes' Cauldron, which was lit from the Olympic Flame.*

IAN LOGAN

*Dave Matthews Band performed at Olympic Medals Plaza on opening night, February 9.*

DAVID BURNETT

*In a city of less than 1 million, more than 1 million visitors, total, strolled through Salt Lake Olympic Square,*

*the pedestrian-only festival surrounding Olympic Medals Plaza.*

D A V I D   B U R N E T T

*"It was mind boggling," said silver medalist Danny Kass (left) of the Medals Ceremony he, gold medalist*

*Ross Powers (center) and J.J. Thomas (right) experienced after the American sweep of*

*men's halfpipe. It was the first U.S. sweep of any Olympic Winter Games sport since 1956.*

IAN LOGAN

*Only two nations swept events at the Salt Lake 2002 Games: the United States*

*of America in men's snowboarding halfpipe and Germany in women's luge.*

IAN LOGAN

*"To win as a team is different than to win as an individual. Today, it was the team that won, and not just the four racers." — Cross-country men's 4 x 10 km relay gold medalist Frode Estil, Norway, shown here with teammates and silver and bronze medalists from Italy and Germany, respectively.*

STEVEN CURRIE

OLYMPIC ARTS FESTIVAL • IN ANCIENT GREECE, THE OLYMPIC GAMES WERE FESTIVALS OF NOT ONLY SPORT, BUT ART. TOP MUSICIANS WERE PRAISED ALONGSIDE CHARIOT-RACE WINNERS FOR THEIR TALENTS. THE SALT LAKE 2002 OLYMPIC ARTS FESTIVAL CONTINUED THIS TRADITION BY SHOWCASING SOME OF AMERICA'S BEST ART AND ARTISTS, WHILE EMBRACING THE CULTURE OF THE AMERICAN MOUNTAIN WEST. FROM ICE-CARVING COMPE-TITIONS AND POETRY READINGS TO BUD GREENSPAN'S DOCUMENTARY FILMS AND CONCERTS BY THE MORMON

*"We can't say we are the best artists in the world in 2002, but we can say we are a*
*part of a long tradition of mankind thinking about himself and his inner experience."*
*— Michael Tracy, Co-Artistic Director, Pilobolus Dance Theatre*

J O H N   H U E T

Tabernacle Choir and the Utah Symphony, the arts events were as diverse as the nations participating at the Games. Athleticism, sportsmanship and teamwork—words that usually describe skiers and skaters—became synonymous with the artists of the Olympic Arts Festival. Dancers, sculptors, musicians, poets, filmmakers, cowboys and chefs gathered in Salt Lake City to embrace the human spirit and, in their own way, to *Light the Fire Within*.

Energizing a synthesis of sport and art, Alvin Ailey American Dance Theater, one of the United States' premiere modern dance companies, created "Here…Now." specially for the Olympic Arts Festival. Choreographed by Ailey Artistic Director Judith Jamison, the dance was a tribute to the late Olympian Florence Griffith-Joyner. Joyner, or Flo-Jo, as she was called, won three gold medals at the Seoul 1988 Olympic Games. In her brief life—she died in 1998 at the age of 38 from complications during an epileptic seizure—Flo-Jo gained a reputation as a strong athlete and a powerful woman, but little else was known about her. "I had to deal with the surface because of the things that we don't know about her," said Jamison, "but I did know about how gorgeous she was and the kind of speed she had." Set to an original score by jazz trumpeter and composer Wynton Marsalis, the piece featured dancers clad in stylized running gear who leaped, ran and slid over and across a mirrored ramp center stage. "Dancers and athletes do the same kind of things," said Jamison. "Overstretching, going to the wall and through the wall when your strength is completely sapped. But yet you are still relying on this inner faith that you'll be able to get to the finish line…the curtain coming down or winning a gold medal."

Equally athletic was the performance of Tony Award-winning dancer and choreographer Savion Glover, who bounded onto the Abravanel Hall stage to a funky, extended version of "The Star-Spangled Banner." Glover, with a group of young dancers called TiDii, tap-danced to music by Stevie Wonder, John Coltrane, Sade and other musicians. Glover, known for his hard-hitting tap solos and ability to make music with his tap shoes, shared the spotlight with younger dancers he had inspired and who proved they could keep up with Glover and his distinctive style.

Set to the music of Scott Joplin and traditional ragtime jazz, meanwhile, Pilobolus Dance Theater's Olympic Arts Festival commission, "The Brass Ring," featured six dancers in an ode to Olympic athletes. The group has been collaborating for more than 30 years on work that explores

# "DANCERS AND ATHLETES DO THE SAME KIND OF THINGS… RELYING ON THIS INNER FAITH TO GET TO THE FINISH."

basic human emotions through theater, movement and athleticism. "Hopefully, artists bring something new to those who appreciate the physical world of athletes," said Pilobolus' cofounder and artistic director Michael Tracy, as he thought about his role in the Olympic Arts Festival. Creating Pilobolus "was really a perfect blend between theater and sports. Dancers certainly aspire to physical grace—they approach that level of physical achievement that athletes aspire to. But, we also have this other interest of creating imagery and theatrical content."

But with some 75 events taking place around town, there was far more than dance to choose from for the 350,000 people who enjoyed the Olympic Arts Festival. Musical collaborations brought together some of the finest musicians from Utah and around the world. The famed Mormon Tabernacle Choir, known for its 325-voice strong arrangements, invited clarinetist Richard Stoltzman, opera diva Frederica von Stade, *a cappella* men's group the king'singers and percussionist Evelyn Glennie for free concerts in Temple Square. The Utah Symphony accompanied Elaine Paige, the first lady of British musical theater, singing her favorite tunes by Andrew Lloyd Webber; three-time Tony Award winner Audra McDonald sang pieces from American composers. Jazz pianist Marcus Roberts and his trio also played with the 99-member symphony, performing his version of the George Gershwin classic, "Rhapsody in Blue." And one evening, Keith Lockhart, the symphony's music director, lent his baton to violin virtuoso Itzhak Perlman to guest conduct.

Some of Utah's own performing companies shared their world-class talents. Legendary folk singer Pete Seeger joined Salt Lake City's Children's Dance Theatre. Ririe-Woodbury Dance Company performed "Prelude de l'Olympiad," created by gifted choreographer Daniel Ezralow and Repertory Dance Theatre presented three masterpieces by the founders of modern dance: Martha Graham, Doris Humphrey and Helen Tamiris. One of America's leading ballet companies, Ballet West, located in Salt Lake City, celebrated 20th century choreographers Jerome Robbins, Hans van Manen and George Balanchine.

And as the contemporary arts were being appreciated across the Wasatch Front, the unique culture of the American West was also celebrated. From an exhibit exploring the art of Utah's indigenous American Indian tribes and appearances by the original Navajo Code Talkers to a rodeo featuring the best cowboys and cowgirls in North America and an evening of cowboy poetry and music, the Olympic Arts Festival honored these distinctive traditions.

Even those simply on their way to Olympic Medals Plaza could catch a glimpse of the Arts Festival, with glass artist Dale Chihuly's "Sun" and "Moon" sculptures gracing the Abravanel Hall plaza while thousands more delicate pieces were on display at the Salt Lake Arts Center. The 27-foot-high "Olympic Tower," a fiery column of twisted glass, had been created specially for the Games and lured passersby to stop and stare in wonder. "So many people will get to come by and see it," said Chihuly of the artwork's proximity to Salt Lake Olympic Square and Olympic Medals Plaza. "Glass is a very magical medium to be working in. It is both fragile and strong."

For these artists there were no podiums, no Medals Ceremonies, no press conferences. But there was much applause. As athletes returned home to recuperate and think about the next step after the 2002 Games, artists returned to their studios to create new dreams. As different as they appeared on the surface, these two groups were remarkably similar. Hard work and determination drove each. Judith Jamison believes artists and athletes share "the same thought process. Put your nose to the grindstone. Keep your eye on the prize. And work." Medals are not the point; the reward "is that you are burning your flame as hot as you can burn it, while you can," said Jamison. "That's the joy of it. That's the passion of it."

*"He likes to get the kids involved, whether it's singing or clapping. He has fun with it."*

*— Children's Dance Theatre's Laura Moyer, 16, of folk singer Pete Seeger (above)*

TIBOR NEMETH

*Children's Dance Theatre costume designers Cynthia Turner and Nancy Cook*
*created more than 600 costumes by hand for the group's performance on February 11.*

TIBOR NEMETH

*Linda-Denise Fisher-Harrell performs Alvin Ailey American Dance Theater's "Revelations."*

*"We have no ice, but we are still trying to glide." – Artistic Director Judith Jamison*

J O H N   H U E T

*Renee Robinson has been dancing with Alvin Ailey American Dance Theater for 20 years.*

JOHN HUET

*Benny Greene on piano and Bob Cranshaw on bass perform as part of the Russell Malone Quartet.*

DAVID BURNETT

*Jazz guitarist Russell Malone, center, with Bob Cranshaw on bass and*

*E.J. Strickland on drums, performs at the Rose Wagner Performing Arts Center.*

DAVID BURNETT

*Chihuly's "Olympic Tower" consisted of 1119 pieces of red glass.*

DAVID BURNETT

*More than 1300 pieces of blown glass meticulously arranged on*

*Plexiglas and suspended overhead created Dale Chihuly's "Persian Pergola Ceiling."*

DAVID    BURNETT

*Tony Award-winning dancer Savion Glover danced to a version of*
*"The Star-Spangled Banner" on February 22 at Abravanel Hall.*

TIBOR NEMETH

*Along with his size 12.5 feet, Glover uses jazz, funk and*
*hip-hop rhythms to create his own style of dance called "hitting."*

TIBOR NEMETH

*Participants in the Olympic Command Performance Rodeo enter the*
*ring at the Davis County Legacy Center in Farmington, Utah.*

ALBERT COLANTONIO

*Kyle Bowers of Brooks, Alberta, prepares for the bareback riding competition.*

ALBERT COLANTONIO

*"Athletes who wish to participate in the Olympic Games devote their years to training mentally*

*and physically. Allan, too, sought to make his art the best, to meet Olympic standards."*

*— Anna Marie Houser, widow of the late sculptor Allan Houser (1914-1994), whose "Meeting on*

*the Trail," above, was displayed at Washington Square in downtown Salt Lake City.*

STEVEN CURRIE

**CLOSING CEREMONY** • WE WERE BEWILDERED BY THE SUDDEN ARRIVAL OF THE CLOSING CEREMONY ON FEBRUARY 24. HAD 16 DAYS REALLY PASSED SINCE WE LAST GATHERED IN RICE-ECCLES OLYMPIC STADIUM TO LIGHT THE CAULDRON AND WELCOME THE WORLD? WAS IT REALLY TIME TO SAY GOODBYE? AS WE TOOK OUR SEATS, WE TRIED TO MAKE EACH MOMENT LAST JUST A LITTLE LONGER, SNAPPING OUR FINAL PHOTOS OF THE OLYMPIC FLAME AGAINST THE BLUE AND BURNISHED SKY OF SUNSET, ALREADY REPLAYING IN OUR MINDS HIGHLIGHTS OF THE GAMES. FROM JIM

*"Far and away, the most successful Olympics, summer or winter, in history."*

*— Dick Ebersol, Chairman of NBC Sports*

ALBERT COLANTONIO

Shea Jr.'s skeleton run to Janica Kostelić's medal haul to Canada's hockey victory that day, more than 2500 Olympians had shown us their power to inspire and had taught us about our own potential to *Light the Fire Within*, with their courage and their capacity for greatness.

And tonight, these heroes would lift our heavy hearts with their abundant joy. As they entered the stadium, the athletes did not march, but spilled forth, arm in arm, no longer separated by nation but bound by friendship. Some wore costumes; others danced and skipped their way to the stands. Sixteen nights ago, they had walked this stadium as athletes; they now marched as Olympians.

A sense of celebration, mixed with a bit of sadness, continued throughout the evening. Two giant dinosaur puppets, voiced by legendary Utahns Donny and Marie Osmond, cracked jokes and swung an enormous tail in the northeast corner of the stadium. *NSYNC kicked off an unprecedented, nightlong concert from a variety of artists by singing the national anthem, which was followed by the sweeping American Musical set. Kurt Browning skated to Dianne Reeves' jazz; a moving platform carried KISS around the ice, with Kristi Yamaguchi and Katarina Witt skating and pyrotechnics exploding to the sounds of "Rock and Roll All Nite." Earth, Wind & Fire, Gloria Estefan, Harry Connick, Jr. and tap dancer Savion Glover with skaters Ilia Kulik and Dorothy Hamill all added to the medley. Later, in a surprise appearance, Willie Nelson sang "Bridge Over Troubled Water," adding a note of melancholy to an otherwise lighthearted lineup.

We were also sobered, momentarily, by the passing of the Olympic Flag to Torino, Italy, host of the 2006 Olympic Winter Games. Salt Lake City Mayor Rocky Anderson's hand lingered on the flagpole during the handover, but as Torino presented singers and slides of Italian culture, we understood that the Olympic Spirit would carry on. We sighed in protest when Jacques Rogge announced that the Olympic Flame would be extinguished, but were reassured by his words. "Keep this flame alight," said Rogge, who called the Salt Lake 2002 Games superb and inspiring. "Promote the Olympic dream in your countries. You are the true ambassadors of the Olympic values."

And the final chapter of the story of the Salt Lake 2002 Olympic Winter Games was concluded with the Children of Light, who had symbolically carried the fire within during the past two and a half weeks, returning with skater Scott Hamilton to say goodbye and sing "Happy Trails to You" with the audience. The Child of Light passed his lantern to a child from Torino, representing the transfer of hope, peace and honor to the next host.

The Olympic Flame disappeared into the night sky, with Renee Roca and Gorsha Sur skating to the sounds of Charlotte Church and Josh Groban. We knew the Games were gone. The party, however, had only just begun, with Moby, Christina Aguilera and Bon Jovi rocking the stadium while skaters covered the ice in ultraviolet paint and giant, white "snow" balls bounced through the audience. The athletes poured onto center stage, dancing long into the night, long after a fireworks extravaganza of 10,000 explosives launched throughout the city and along the Wasatch Front at a rate of 37 shells per second. They, too, weren't quite ready to say goodbye. Said Canadian luge athlete Mike Moffat, "It's for sure been the greatest two weeks of my life."

*Six hundred and eighty Children of Light held up lanterns one last time.*

I A N   L O G A N

*In a state known for its archaeological discoveries, "Utah's First Family,"*

*75-foot-tall dinosaurs, entertained the audience.*

J O H N   H U E T

*The audience marveled as aerialists suddenly tumbled out of giant white balloons that*

*floated across the stage.*

JOHN HUET

*Representing figure skating, snowboarding, skeleton, freestyle skiing and ice hockey,*
*the balloon performers reminded fans of the hundreds of incredible moments they had*
*seen in these and other sports of the Salt Lake 2002 Olympic Winter Games.*

STEVEN CURRIE

*Eric Singer, Gene Simmons, Paul Stanley and Ace Frehley of* KISS *perform "Rock and Roll All Nite," as fireworks explode from their revolving platform and from the ice.*

J O H N  H U E T

"Olympians, we cheered all of you, not just our own. We saw in you the universal greatness of the human family." – Salt Lake 2002 President and CEO Mitt Romney

MICHAEL SEAMANS

*Giant white "snow" balls bounce through the audience and onto the athletes, who*

*spilled from the stands onto the field.*

TIBOR NEMETH

*"The Stick Man Ballet" kicked off an all-star party for the athletes, which included*

*performances by Moby, Christina Aguilera and Bon Jovi.*

JOHN HUET

*Nearly 2000 cast members joined together for the Closing Ceremony.*

IAN LOGAN

"Volunteers, you are, with the athletes, also champions of these Games. Your generosity
and profound kindness has won our hearts. You were marvelous." – IOC President
Jacques Rogge at the Closing Ceremony. A volunteer, above, celebrates with short track
gold medalist Apolo Anton Ohno of the United States of America.

IAN LOGAN

*"These were passionate Games, heartfelt Games, perfect Games. Salt Lake City, we*
*will never forget you." — Legendary Olympic alpine skier Jean-Claude Killy*

ALBERT COLANTONIO

**SALT LAKE 2002**

# A C K N O W L E D G M E N T S

JOHN HUET *worked for two years assembling a team of photographers to create The Fire Within. His ability to move sports imagery into the realm of art and to recognize photographers who could do the same, make this book unique in Olympic publishing. Huet also created the iconic images of athletes that were the key element of Salt Lake 2002's Look of the Games, appearing throughout the Salt Lake area. Huet's signature style is perhaps best represented in the award-winning book Soul of the Game, which chronicles the history of street basketball. With more than 15 years experience as a successful commercial photographer, he has worked for the world's leading advertising agencies and design firms.*

ANDY ANDERSON *lives with his family in Idaho but travels the world to photograph his subjects. His commercial clients include Nike and Harley Davidson, and his work has been featured regularly in such magazines as Audubon and Men's Journal. Among his awards are Life's coveted Alfred Eisenstadt Award for Magazine Photography and several nominations from Communication Arts. During the Salt Lake 2002 Games, Anderson shot with a vintage Graflex 4 x 5 camera: "I wanted to challenge myself to use the same equipment photographers used 50 years ago," he says.*

DAVID BURNETT *has been shooting for more than 35 years. After covering the Vietnam War for Time and Life, the Utah native traveled extensively for the Gamma agency and then founded Contact Press Images in 1975. His images of summer Olympic Games since Los Angeles 1984 are world-renowned, and he has won such awards as the World Press Photo of the Year and the Robert Capa Award from the Overseas Press Club. Among the cameras he used at the Salt Lake 2002 Games was a $30 Holga, chosen for its unpredictable, sometimes charming results.*

ALBERT COLANTONIO *grew up in Boston's North End and studied at the New England School of Photography. He shoots primarily location assignments, landscapes and sporting events as well as photographs for his advertising clients. For the Salt Lake 2002 Games, Colantonio aimed "to be a quiet spectator" and used a Graflex camera from the 1920s. "I wanted to get into the head of the athletes," he says, "and show the silent beauty of their sport."*

STEVEN CURRIE *was born in Salt Lake City and studied photography at Langara College in Vancouver, British Columbia. An avid fan of the Montreal 1976 Games, Currie was thrilled to work tirelessly on the Salt Lake 2002 Games. "The culmination of four years of training for the athletes and the pressure of all that time riding on one day of competition," says Currie, who now works out of his Park City, Utah, home, "is inspiration to shoot for 17 days in a row."*

CHAD HOLDER *is a native of San Diego, California, and studied at Utah's Brigham Young University. He currently lives in Minneapolis, Minnesota, where he works mainly as a commercial photographer. His work has been featured in Communication Arts, SOMA, Dwell and Lurzer's International Archive. Photo District News selected Holder as one of 2000's "Thirty under 30: Young Photographers to Watch." During the Salt Lake 2002 Games, Holder focused on the beauty of the venues and the cityscape decorations, capturing the Olympic Spirit beyond the athletes.*

IAN LOGAN *was born in London and moved to Seattle with his family when he was 8. His work covers a wide range of subjects, from celebrities to still-life images, and has appeared in the Los Angeles Times Magazine, Men's Journal, Bikini and Muscle and Fitness, among others. Shooting the Games was a dream come true for Logan, who is an avid snowboarder and surfer and currently resides in Hermosa Beach, California, with his wife and dog.*

RAYMOND MEEKS *prefers making his pictures in black and white and has recently begun experimenting with the wet plate ambrotype process. His sensual, timeless images of Salt Lake 2002 athletes were taken in the Olympic Village and at various venues, most notably, Soldier Hollow. Meeks lives in Montana with his wife and their two children.*

SHEILA METZNER *was born in Brooklyn, New York. Her fine-art photographs are featured in many private and museum collections, including the Metropolitan Museum of Art, the Museum of Modern Art, the International Center of Photography and the Getty Museum. She has published four monographs: Objects of Desire, which won the American Society of Magazine Photographers Ansel Adams Award for Book Photography, Sheila Metzner's Color, Inherit the Earth, and Form and Fashion. Says Metzner of her Salt Lake 2002 experience: "One after another, the superheroes appeared. I never stopped shooting."*

TIBOR NEMETH *studied photography at the Columbus College of Art and Design in Ohio. After traveling around the world as a camera assistant for five years, Nemeth opened his own studio in Boston in 1998. Nemeth's clients include The Boston Globe, Esquire, Fortune Small Business, Volkswagen, Coca-Cola and Converse. He shot events at every Salt Lake 2002 venue. "Being one foot from the athletes is an amazing rush," he says. "It was the closest thing to being starstruck."*

ELISABETH O'DONNELL *is a native of Oklahoma City, Oklahoma, and now lives in Salem, Massachusetts. She began her career assisting commercial photographers and traveling throughout Europe and the United States shooting portraits and landscapes. For the Salt Lake 2002 Games, she shot primarily with fully manual, single-shot cameras using wide-angle lenses. Her favorite was a 4 x 5 Speed Graphic from the 1940s. "I was surrounded by sports photojournalists with digital cameras and long lenses," she says. "And I got many strange looks."*

MICHAEL SEAMANS *received a B.F.A. degree in Photographic Illustration from the Rochester Institute of Technology. Since 1997, he has been a staff photographer for the Boston Herald, and his photographs have appeared in USA Today, Newsweek, Sports Illustrated and other publications. Seamans has covered major news, political and sporting events, including the 2000 Democratic National Convention, events in New York City following September 11, 2001, the National Football League playoffs and the 2002 Superbowl in New Orleans.*

SALT LAKE 2002

CREATIVE SERVICES •

LIBBY HYLAND, *Director*
RON STUCKI, *Design Manager*
SARAH J.M. TUFF, *Executive Editor*
PAULINE PLOQUIN, *Exec. Photo Producer*
ALEXANDRA HESSE, *Assoc. Photo Producer*
WHITNIE M. RASMUSSEN, *Account Exec.*
JARED SWEET, *Senior Designer*
RYAN ATWOOD, *Designer*
REBECCA MOORE, *Sr. Photo Coordinator*
LAURA SCHAFFER, *Sr. Photo Coordinator*
DAVID CLUFF, *Print Coordinator*

*Reporters and Writers*
AMY ALBO
JOHN CLARKE JR.
KATHY GURCHIEK
EUGENIE HERO
CLAIRE KNOPF
MATTHEW LAKENBACH
SCOTT LAURY
JAMIE MILLER
BRENDAN MORGAN
GABE SHERMAN
CLINT WADDELL

*Venue Photo Coordinators*
LAUREN ANDERSON
VINCENT GONZALES
MICHELLE GUYMON
ROGER JONES
MINE KASAPOGLU
ROBIN KROLL
LISA OLSON
IOLI PAPAGEORGIOU
LAURA RICKS
JENNIFER STAVROS

**M E D A L I S T S : A L P I N E S K I I N G** • **Ladies' Combined:** Gold / KOSTELIC, Janica / CRO • Silver / GOETSCHL, Renate / AUT • Bronze / ERTL, Martina / GER • **Ladies' Downhill:** Gold/ MONTILLET, Carole / FRA • Silver / KOSTNER, Isolde / ITA • Bronze / GOETSCHL, Renate / AUT • **Ladies' Giant Slalom:** Gold / KOSTELIC, Janica / CRO • Silver / PAERSON, Anja / SWE • Bronze / NEF, Sonja / SUI • **Ladies' Slalom:** Gold / KOSTELIC, Janica / CRO • Silver / PEQUEGNOT, Laure / FRA • Bronze / PAERSON, Anja / SWE • **Ladies' Super-G:** Gold / CECCARELLI, Daniela / ITA • Silver / KOSTELIC, Janica / CRO • Bronze / PUTZER, Karen / ITA • **Men's Combined:** Gold / AAMODT, Kjetil Andre / NOR • Silver / MILLER, Bode / USA • Bronze / RAICH, Benjamin / AUT • **Men's Downhill:** Gold / STROBL, Fritz / AUT • Silver / KJUS, Lasse / NOR • Bronze / EBERHARTER, Stephan / AUT • **Men's Giant Slalom:** Gold / EBERHARTER, Stephan / AUT • Silver / MILLER, Bode / USA • Bronze / KJUS, Lasse / NOR • **Men's Slalom:** Gold / VIDAL, Jean-Pierre / FRA • Silver / AMIEZ, Sebastien / FRA • Bronze / RAICH, Benjamin / AUT • **Men's Super-G:** Gold / AAMODT, Kjetil Andre / NOR • Silver / EBERHARTER, Stephan / AUT • Bronze / SCHIFFERER, Andreas / AUT • **B I A T H L O N** • **Men's 10 km Sprint:** Gold / BJOERNDALEN, Ole Einar / NOR • Silver / FISCHER, Sven / GER • Bronze / PERNER, Wolfgang / AUT • **Men's 12.5 km Pursuit:** Gold/ BJOERNDALEN Ole Einar / NOR • Silver / POIREE, Raphaël / FRA • Bronze / GROSS, Ricco / GER • **Men's 20 km Individual:** Gold / BJOERNDALEN, Ole Einar / NOR • Silver / LUCK, Frank / GER • Bronze / MAIGOUROV, Victor / RUS • **Men's 4 x 7.5 km Relay:** Gold / ANDRESEN, Frode; BJOERNDALEN, Ole Einar; GJELLAND, Egil; HANEVOLD, Halvard / NOR • Silver / FISCHER, Sven; GROSS, Ricco; LUCK, Frank; SENDEL, Peter / GER • Bronze / DEFRASNE, Vincent; MARGUET Gilles; POIREE Raphaël; ROBERT Julien / FRA • **Women's 10 km Pursuit:** Gold / PYLEVA, Olga / RUS • Silver/ WILHELM, Kati / GER • Bronze / NIKOULTCHINA, Irina / BUL • **Women's 15 km Individual:** Gold / HENKEL, Andrea / GER • Silver / POIREE, Liv Grete / NOR • Bronze / FORSBERG, Magdalena / SWE • **Women's 4 x 7.5 km Relay:** Gold / APEL, Katrin; DISL Uschi; HENKEL, Andrea; WILHELM, Kati / GER • Silver / ANDREASSEN, Gunn Margit; POIREE Liv Grete; SKJELBREID, Ann-Elen; TJOERHOM, Linda / NOR • Bronze / AKHATOVA, Albina; ISHMOURATOVA, Svetlana; KOUKLEVA, Galina; PYLEVA, Olga / RUS • **Women's 7.5 km Sprint:** Gold / WILHELM, Kati / GER • Silver / DISL, Uschi/ GER • Bronze / FORSBERG, Magdalena / SWE • **B O B S L E I G H** • **Four-Man:** Gold / EMBACH, Carsten; KUEHN, Enrico; KUSKE, Kevin; LANGE, André / GER • Silver / HAYS, Todd; HINES, Garrett; JONES, Randy; SCHUFFENHAUER, Bill / USA • Bronze / KOHN, Mike; SHARP, Doug; SHIMER, Brian; STEELE, Dan / USA • **Two-Man:** Gold / LANGEN, Christoph; ZIMMERMANN, Markus / GER • Silver / ANDERHUB, Steve; REICH, Christian / SUI • Bronze / ANNEN, Martin; HEFTI, Beat / SUI • **Women's:** Gold / BAKKEN, Jill; FLOWERS, Vonetta / USA • Silver / HOLZNER, Ulrike; PROKOFF, Sandra / GER • Bronze / ERDMANN, Susi-Lisa; HERSCHMANN, Nicole / GER • **C R O S S - C O U N T R Y S K I I N G** • **Men's 10 km Free Pursuit:** Gold / MUEHLEGG, Johann / ESP • Silver / ALSGAARD, Thomas / NOR; ESTIL, Frode / NOR • **Men's 15 km Classical:** Gold / VEERPALU, Andrus / EST • Silver / ESTIL, Frode / NOR • Bronze / MAE, Jaak / EST • **Men's 30 km Free Mass Start:** Gold / MUEHLEGG, Johann / ESP • Silver / HOFFMANN, Christian / AUT • Bronze / BOTVINOV, Mikhail / AUT • **Men's 4 x 10 km Relay:** Gold / ALSGAARD, Thomas; AUKLAND, Anders; ESTIL, Frode; SKJELDAL Kristen / NOR • Silver / MAJ, Fabio / PILLER COTTRER; Pietro; ZORZI, Cristian; di CENTA, Giorgio / ITA • Bronze / ANGERER, Tobias; FILBRICH, Jens; SCHLUETTER, Andreas; SOMMERFELDT, Rene / GER • **Men's 50 km Classical:** Gold / IVANOV, Mikhail; / RUS • Silver / VEERPALU Andrus / EST • Bronze / HJELMESET Odd-Bjoern / NOR • **Men's Sprint:** Gold / HETLAND Tor Arne / NOR • Silver / SCHLICKENRIEDER Peter / GER • Bronze / ZORZI, Cristian / ITA • **Women's 10 km Classical:** Gold / SKARI, Bente / NOR • Silver / DANILOVA, Olga / RUS • Bronze / TCHEPALOVA, Julija / RUS • **Women's 15 km Free Mass Start:** Gold / BELMONDO, Stefania / ITA • Silver / LAZUTINA, Larissa / RUS • Bronze / NEUMANNOVA, Katerina / CZE • **Women's 30 km Classical:** Gold / PARUZZI, Gabriella / ITA • Silver / BELMONDO, Stefania / ITA • Bronze / SKARI, Bente NOR • **Women's 4 x 5 km Relay:** Gold / BAUER, Viola; HENKEL, Manuela; KUENZEL, Claudia; SACHENBACHER, Evi / GER • Silver / BJOERGEN, Marit; MOEN, Anita; PEDERSEN Hilde G; SKARI, Bente / NOR • Bronze / ALBRECHT LORETAN, Brigitte; HUBER, Andrea; LEONARDI CORTESI, Natascia; ROCHAT, Laurence / SUI • **Women's 5 km Free Pursuit:** Gold / DANILOVA, Olga / RUS • Silver / LAZUTINA, Larissa / RUS • Bronze / SCOTT, Beckie / CAN • **Women's Sprint:** Gold / TCHEPALOVA, Julija / RUS • Silver / SACHENBACHER, Evi / GER • Bronze / MOEN, Anita / NOR • **C U R L I N G** • **Men's Curling:** Gold / DAVANGER, Flemming; NERGAARD, Torger; RAMSFJELL, Bent Ånund; TRULSEN Pål; VAAGBERG, Lars / NOR • Silver / BARTLETT, Don; MARTIN Kevin; RYCROFT, Carter; TRALNBERG, Ken; WALCHUK, Don / CAN • Bronze / EGGLER, Markus; GRICHTING, Damian; RAMSTEIN, Marco; SCHWALLER, Andreas; SCHWALLER, Christof / SUI • **Women's Curling:** Gold / KNOX, Debbie; MARTIN, Rhona; MORTON, Margaret; MACDONALD, Fiona; RANKIN, Janice / GBR • Silver / BIDAUD, Laurence ; EBNOETHER, Luzia; FREI, Tanya; OTT, Mirjam; ROETHLISBERGER, Nadia / SUI • Bronze / LAW, Kelley; NELSON, Diane; NOBLE, Cheryl; SKINNER, Julie; WHEATCROFT, Georgina / CAN • **F I G U R E S K A T I N G** • **Ice Dancing:** Gold / ANISSINA, Marina; PEIZERAT, Gwendal / FRA • Silver / LOBACHEVA, Irina; AVERBUKH, Ilia / RUS • Bronze / FUSAR POLI, Barbara; MARGAGLIO, Maurizio / ITA • **Ladies':** Gold / HUGHES, Sarah / USA • Silver / SLUTSKAYA, Irina / RUS • Bronze / KWAN, Michelle / USA • **Men:** Gold / YAGUDIN, Alexei / RUS • Silver / PLUSHENKO, Evgeni / RUS • Bronze / GOEBEL, Timothy / USA • **Pairs:** Gold / BEREZHNAYA, Elena; SIKHARULIDZE, Anton / RUS; SALE, Jamie; PELLETIER, David / CAN • Bronze / SHEN, Xue ZHAO, Hongbo / CHN • **F R E E S T Y L E S K I I N G** • **Men's Aerials:** Gold / VALENTA, Ales / CZE • Silver / PACK, Joe / USA • Bronze / GRICHIN, Alexei / BLR • **Men's Moguls:** Gold / LAHTELA, Janne / FIN • Silver / MAYER, Travis / USA • Bronze / GAY, Richard / FRA • **Women's Aerials:** Gold / CAMPLIN, Alisa / AUS • Silver / BRENNER, Veronica / CAN • Bronze / DIONNE, Deidra / CAN • **Women's Moguls:** Gold / TRAA, Kari / NOR • Silver / BAHRKE, Shannon / USA • Bronze / SATOYA, Tae / JPN • **I C E H O C K E Y** • **Men's Ice Hockey:** Gold / BELFOUR, Ed; BLAKE, Rob; BREWER, Eric; BRODEUR, Martin; FLEURY, Theo; FOOTE, Adam; GAGNE, Simon; IGINLA, Jarome; JOSEPH, Curtis / JOVANOVSKI Ed / KARIYA, Paul; LEMIEUX, Mario; LINDROS, Eric; MACINNIS, Al; NIEDERMAYER Scott; NIEUWENDYK, Joe; NOLAN, Owen; PECA, Mike; PRONGER, Chris; SAKIC, Joe; SHANAHAN, Brendan; SMYTH, Ryan;YZERMAN, Steve / CAN • Silver / AMONTE, Tony; BARRASSO, Tom; CHELIOS, Chris; DEADMARSH, Adam; DRURY, Chris; DUNHAM, Mike; GUERIN, Bill; HOUSLEY, Phil; HULL, Brett; LECLAIR, John; LEETCH, Brian; MILLER, Aaron; MODANO, Mike; POTI, Tom; RAFALSKI, Brian; RICHTER, Mike; ROENICK, Jeremy; ROLSTON, Brian; SUTER, Gary; TKACHUK, Keith; WEIGHT, Doug; YORK, Mike; YOUNG, Scott / USA • Bronze / AFINOGENOV, Maxim; BRYZGALOV, Ilja; BURE, Pavel; BURE, Valeri; DATSYUK, Pavel; FEDOROV, Sergei; GONCHAR, Sergei; KASPARAITIS, Darius; KHABIBULIN, Nikolai; KOVALCHUK, Ilya; KOVALEV, Alexei; KOZLOV, Viktor; KRAVTCHOUK, Igor; KVASHA, Oleg; LARIONOV, Igor; MALAKHOV, Vladimir; MARKOV, Daniil; MIRONOV, Boris; NIKOLISHIN, Andrei; PODOMATSKY, Yegor; SAMSONOV, Sergei; TVERDOVSKY, Oleg; YASHIN, Alexei; YUSHKEVICH, Dmitri; ZHAMNOV, Alexei / RUS • **Women's Ice Hockey:** Gold / ANTAL, Dana; BECHARD, Kelly; BOTTERILL, Jennifer; BRISSON, Therese; CAMPBELL, Cassie; CHARTRAND, Isabelle; DUPUIS, Lori; GOYETTE, Danielle; HEANEY, Geraldine; HEFFORD, Jayna; KELLAR, Becky; OUELLETTE, Caroline; PIPER, Cherie; POUNDER, Cheryl; SHEWCHUK, Tammy Lee; SMALL, Sami Jo; SOSTORICS, Colleen; ST-PIERRE, Kim; SUNOHARA, Vicky; WICKENHEISER, Hayley / CAN • Silver / BAILEY, Chris; BAKER, Laurie; BYE, Karyn; CHU, Julie; DARWITZ, Natalie; DECOSTA, Sara; DUNN, Tricia; GRANATO, Cammi; KENNEDY, Courtney; KILBOURNE, Andrea; KING, Katie; LOONEY, Shelley; MERZ, Sue; MLECZKO, Allison; MOUNSEY, Tara; POTTER, Jenny; RUGGIERO, Angela; TUETING, Sarah; WALL, Lyndsay; WENDELL, Krissy / USA • Bronze / AHLEN, Annica; ALMBLAD, Lotta; ANDERSSON, Anna; ANDERSSON, Gunilla; BERGGREN, Emelie; BERGSTRAND, Kristina; EDSTRAND, Ann-Louise; ELFSBERG, Joa; HOLST, Erika; JANSSON, Nanna; LARSSON, Maria; LINDBERG, Ylva; LINDSTROM, Ulrica; MARTIN, Kim; PETTERSSON, Josefin; ROOTH, Maria; RUNDQVIST, Danijela; SAMUELSSON, Evelina; SJOLANDER, Theresé VIKMAN, Anna / SWE • **L U G E** • **Doubles:** Gold / LEITNER, Patrick; RESCH, Alexander / GER • Silver / GRIMMETTE, Mark; MARTIN, Brian / USA • Bronze / IVES, Clay; THORPE, Chris / USA • **Men's Singles:** Gold / ZOEGGELER, Armin / ITA • Silver / HACKL, Georg / GER • Bronze / PROCK, Markus / AUT • **Women's Singles:** Gold / OTTO, Sylke / GER • Silver / NIEDERNHUBER, Barbara / GER • Bronze / KRAUSHAAR, Silke / GER • **N O R D I C C O M B I N E D** • **Individual K90 / 15 km:** Gold / LAJUNEN, Samppa / FIN • Silver / TALLUS, Jaakko / FIN • Bronze / GOTTWALD, Felix / AUT / • **Individual K120 / 7.5 km Sprint:** Gold / LAJUNEN, Samppa / FIN • Silver / ACKERMANN, Ronny / GER • Bronze / GOTTWALD, Felix / AUT • **Team K90 / 4 x 5 km Relay:** Gold / LAJUNEN, Samppa; MANNINEN, Hannu; MANTILA, Jari; TALLUS, Jaakko / FIN • Silver / ACKERMANN, Ronny / HETTICH Georg / HOEHLIG Marcel / KIRCHEISEN, Björn / GER • Bronze / BIELER, Christoph; GOTTWALD, Felix; GRUBER, Michael; STECHER, Mario / AUT • **S H O R T T R A C K** • **Ladies' 1000 m:** Gold / YANG (A), Yang / CHN • Silver / KO, Gi-Hyun / KOR • Bronze / YANG, (S) Yang / CHN • **Ladies' 1500 m:** Gold / KO, Gi-Hyun / KOR • Silver / CHOI, Eun-Kyung / KOR • Bronze / RADANOVA, Evgenia / BUL • **Ladies' 3000 m Relay:** Gold / CHOI, Eun-Kyung; CHOI, Min-Kyung; JOO, Min-Jin; PARK, Hye-Won / KOR • Silver / SUN, Dandan; WANG, Chunlu; YANG (A), Yang; YANG (S), Yang / CHN • Bronze / CHAREST, Isabelle; DROLET, Marie-Eve; GOULET-NADON, Amelie; KRAUS, Alanna; VICENT, Tania / CAN • **Ladies' 500 m:** Gold / YANG, (A) Yang / CHN • Silver / RADANOVA, Evgenia / BUL • Bronze / WANG, Chunlu / CHN • **Men's 1000 m:** Gold / BRADBURY, Steven / AUS • Silver / OHNO, Apolo Anton / USA • Bronze / TURCOTTE, Mathieu / CAN • **Men's 1500 m:** Gold / OHNO, Apolo Anton / USA • Silver / LI, Jiajun / CHN • Bronze / GAGNON, Marc / CAN • **Men's 500 m:** Gold / GAGNON, Marc / CAN • Silver / GUILMETTE, Jonathan / CAN • Bronze / SMITH, Rusty / USA • **Men's 5000 m Relay:** Gold / BEDARD, Eric; GAGNON Marc; GUILMETTE, Jonathan; TREMBLAY, François-Louis; TURCOTTE, Mathieu / CAN • Silver / ANTONIOLI, Michele; CARNINO, Maurizio; CARTA, Fabio; FRANCESCHINA, Nicola; RODIGARI, Nicola / ITA • Bronze / AN, Yulong; FENG, Kai; GUO, Wei; LI, Jiajun; LI, Ye / CHN • **S K E L E T O N** • **Men's:** Gold / SHEA, Jim / USA • Silver / RETTL, Martin / AUT • Bronze / STAEHLI Gregor / SUI • **Women's:** Gold / GALE, Tristan / USA • Silver / PARSLEY, Lea Ann / USA • Bronze / COOMBER, Alex / GBR • **S K I J U M P I N G** • **K120 Individual:** Gold / AMMANN, Simon / SUI • Silver / MALYSZ, Adam / POL • Bronze / HAUTAMAEKI, Matti / FIN • **K90 Individual:** Gold / AMMANN, Simon / SUI • Silver / HANNAWALD, Sven / GER • Bronze / MALYSZ, Adam / POL • **K120 Team:** Gold / HANNAWALD, Sven; HOCKE, Stephan; SCHMITT, Martin; UHRMANN, Michael / GER • Silver / AHONEN, Janne; HAUTAMAEKI, Matti; JUSSILAINEN, Risto; LINDSTROEM, Veli-Matti / FIN • Bronze / FRAS, Damjan; KRANJEC, Robert; PETERKA, Primoz; ZONTA, Peter / SLO • **S N O W B O A R D I N G** • **Men's Halfpipe:** Gold / POWERS, Ross / USA • Silver / KASS, Danny / USA • Bronze / THOMAS, Jarret / USA • **Men's Parallel Giant Slalom:** Gold / SCHOCH, Philipp / SUI • Silver / RICHARDSSON, Richard / SWE • Bronze / KLUG, Chris / USA • **Women's Halfpipe:** Gold / CLARK, Kelly / USA • Silver / VIDAL, Doriane / FRA • Bronze / REUTELER, Fabienne / SUI • **Women's Parallel Giant Slalom:** Gold / BLANC, Isabelle / FRA • Silver / RUBY, Karine / FRA • Bronze / TRETTEL, Lidia / ITA • **S P E E D S K A T I N G** • **Ladies' 1000 m:** Gold / WITTY, Chris / USA • Silver / VOELKER, Sabine / GER • Bronze / RODRIGUEZ, Jennifer / USA • **Ladies' 1500 m:** Gold / FRIESINGER, Anni / GER • Silver / VOELKER, Sabine / GER • Bronze / RODRIGUEZ, Jennifer / USA • **Ladies' 3000 m:** Gold / PECHSTEIN, Claudia / GER • Silver / GROENEWOLD, Renate / NED • Bronze / KLASSEN, Cindy / CAN • **Ladies 500 m:** Gold / LE MAY DOAN, Catriona / CAN • Silver / GARBRECHT-ENFELDT, Monique / GER • Bronze / VOELKER, Sabine / GER • **Ladies' 5000 m:** Gold/ PECHSTEIN, Claudia / GER • Silver / SMIT, Gretha / NED • Bronze / HUGHES, Clara / CAN • **Men's 1000 m:** Gold / VAN VELDE, Gerard / NED • Silver / BOS, Jan / NED • Bronze / CHEEK, Joey / USA • **Men's 10,000 m:** Gold / UYTDEHAAGE, Jochem / NED • Silver / ROMME, Gianni / NED • Bronze / SAETRE, Lasse / NOR • **Men's 1500 m:** Gold / PARRA, Derek / USA • Silver / UYTDEHAAGE, Jochem / NED • Bronze / SONDRAL, Ådne / NOR • **Men's 500 m:** Gold / FITZRANDOLPH, Casey / USA • Silver / SHIMIZU, Hiroyasu / JPN • Bronze / CARPENTER, Kip / USA • **Men's 5000 m:** Gold / UYTDEHAAGE, Jochem / NED • Silver / PARRA, Derek / USA • Bronze / BODEN, Jens (GER) •

**A T H L E T E S** • **A** • ANTTI AALTO, KJETIL ANDRE AAMODT, MEELIS AASMAE, NACHI ABE, ANNE ABERNATHY, ENVER ABLAEV, PAWEL ABRATKIEWICZ, TOBIAS ABSTREITER, ALEXANDER ABT, PAUL ACCOLA, RONNY ACKERMANN, GUIDO ACKLIN, MARCUS ADAM, MARGUS ADER, VIKTORIYA ADYYEVA, URS AEBERHARD, DAVID AEBISCHER, JEAN-JACQUES AESCHLIMANN, MAXIM AFINOGENOV, ERROL AGUILERA, ANNICA AHLEN, HYUN-SOO AHN, PIRJO AHONEN, JANNE AHONEN, ALEKSEI AIDAROV, RICHARD AIMONETTO, ALBINA AKHATOVA, SOFIA AKHMETELI, ANNA AKIMBETYEVA, CONSTANTIN ALADASHVILI, ATAKAN ALAFTARGIL, KARSTEN ALBERT, ALAN ALBORN, BRIGITTE ALBRECHT LORETAN, KILIAN ALBRECHT, GRANT ALBRECHT, LINDSAY ALCOCK, CHIMENE ALCOTT, JYORGOS ALEXANDROU, LYUBOV ALEXEYEVA, DANIEL ALFREDSSON, KATHLEEN ALLAIS, DAVE ALLARDICE, LOTTA ALMBLAD, THOMAS ALSGAARD, BAPTISTE AMAR, SEBASTIEN AMIEZ, SIMON AMMANN, TONY AMONTE, YULONG AN, JUNG-HYUN AN, LYUDMILA ANANKO, STEVE ANDERHUB, PETTER ANDERSEN, DAVID ANDERSON, JASEY JAY ANDERSON, ANNA ANDERSSON, GUNILLA ANDERSSON, LINA ANDERSSON, MICHEL ANDRE, GUNN MARGIT ANDREASSEN, FRODE ANDRESEN, TREVOR ANDREW, ALEKSANDR ANDRIEVSKY, ALEXEI ANDRYNIN, TOBIAS ANGERER, DANIL ANISIMOV, MARINA ANISSINA, MARTIN ANNEN, DANIELA ANSCHUETZ, DANA ANTAL, ZSOLT ANTAL, TIMO ANTILA, OLEG ANTONENKO, MICHELE ANTONIOLI, ELENA ANTONOVA, ANASTASIA ANTONOVA, ALEX ANTOR, KATRIN APEL, ALEXANDRE ARBEZ, PATRICE ARCHETTO, DMITRY ARKHIPOV, MIRELLA ARNHOLD, ERWIN ARNOLD, KEVIN ARNOULD, NICOLAS ARSEL, MAGNUS ARVEDSON, ESPEN ARVESEN, WILHELM ASCHWANDEN, JONAS ASPMAN, ANTONIDA ASSONOVA, KASPARS ASTASENKO, PAUL ATTWOOD, SUSAN AUCH, CHRISTIAN AUER, FRAENZI AUFDENBLATTEN, ANDERS AUKLAND, OLEG AVDEEV, ILIA AVERBUKH, PER-JOHAN AXELSSON, KELIME AYDIN, DAICHI AZEGAMI • **B** • ZUZANA BABIAKOVA, BENOIT BACHELET, VINCENT BACHET, SERGUEI BACHKIROV, ANDRZEJ BACHLEDA, SILKE BACHMANN, KRISTINA BADER, SHANNON BAHRKE, CHRIS BAILEY, SANDRINE BAILLY, MARTIN BAJCICAK, EUN-BI BAK, LAURIE BAKER, TRINE BAKKE-ROGNMO, JILL BAKKEN, NICOLAS BAL, HELENA BALATKOVA, KATERINA BALKABA, ZSOLT BALO, ONDREJ BANK, ALEXEI BANNIKOV, ALEXEJ BARANNIKOV, VITALI BARANOV, DON BARCOME, ANDERS BARDAL, IVAN BARIAKOV, LIUTAURAS BARILA, STEPHANE BARIN, TOM BARRASSO, CLAUDIA BARRENECHEA, LUBOS BARTECKO, DON BARTLETT, STEFAN BARUCHA, MARIA BARYKINA, VARVARA BARYSHEVA, PATRIZIA BASSIS, SLAVTSCHO BATINKOV, IVAN BATORY, ANN BATTELLE, FREDERIC BAUD, VERONIKA BAUER, VIOLA BAUER, LUKAS BAUER, JOHN BAUER, ALLISON BAVER, FLORENCE BAVEREL-ROBERT, ALAIN BAXTER, NOEL BAXTER, TINA BAY, JEFF BEAN, AJ BEAR, SYLVIE BECAERT, KELLY BECHARD, ENIS BECIRBEGOVIC, TIMOTHY BECK, MARITTA BECKER, FRANZISKA BECSKEHAZY, ERIC BEDARD, MATHIAS BEHOUNEK, VADIM BEKBULATOV, ZSUZSANNA BEKECS, ALEKSANDRS BELAVSKIS, ALEXEI BELETSKY, ED BELFOUR, SABINE BELKOFER, SCOTT BELLAVANCE, ANTONELLA BELLUTTI, STEFANIA BELMONDO, ALEXANDER BELOV, JAN BENDA, TESSA BENOIT, TONY BENSHOOF, KATERINA BERANKOVA, MANUELA BERCHTOLD, ELENA BEREZHNAYA, AKI-PETTERI BERG, GIANCARLO BERGAMELLI, EMELIE BERGGREN, JOHAN CARL BERGMAN, MONIKA BERGMANN, ERIC BERGOUST, KRISTINA BERGSTRAND, HEDDA BERNTSEN, INGRID BERNTSEN, SYLVIANE BERTHOD, CHRISTINA BERTRUP,

JANIS BERZINS, SANDRIS BERZINS, GUILLAUME BESSE, JOZEF BESTANDIG, OLGA BESTANDIGOVA, ELENA BIALKOVSKAIA, LAURENCE BIDAULD, LENE BIDSTRUP, CHRISTOPH BIELER, RADIK BIKCHANTAYEV, OLEKSANDER BILANENKO, ONDREJ BIMAN, EDSON BINDILATTI, RON BIONDO, TAHIR BISIC, DANIEL BIVESON, HAAVARD BJERKELI, MARIT BJOERGEN, BJOERGVIN BJOERGVINSSON, OLE EINAR BJOERNDALEN, STIAN BJORGE, KRISTINN BJORNSSON, MARIAN BLAJ, ROB BLAKE, ISABELLE BLANC, MASSIMILIANO BLARDONE, JEREMY BLOOM, KAROL BOBOWICZ, ELENA BOBROVA, VASYL BOBROVNIKOV, IGINIA BOCCALANDRO, JENS BODEN, CORINNE BODMER, ANNA BOGALJ, MIROSLAV BOIADJIEV, PHILIP BOIT, NATASA BOKAL, ANJA BOLBJERG, NIKOLAJ BOLCHAKOV, IGORS BONDAREVS, JEAN-FRANCOIS BONNARD, IGOR BORASKA, CATHERINE BORGHI, DIMITRI BOROVIK, VLADIMIR BORTSOV, JAN BOS, JENNIFER BOTTERILL, MIKHAIL BOTVINOV, PATRICK BOUCHARD, SARA-MAUDE BOUCHER, PIERRICK BOURGEAT, SHAE-LYNN BOURNE, KC BOUTIETTE, STEPHANIE BOUVIER, PHILIPPE BOZON, MATHIEU BOZZETTO, SPELA BRACUN, STEVEN BRADBURY, TAMI BRADLEY, CRAIG BRANCH, CHRISTOPH BRANDNER, TADEJA BRANKOVIC, JEAN-LUC BRASSARD, SIBYLLE BRAUNER, VERONICA BRENNER, CHRISTIAN BREUER, ERIC BREWER, ARNAUD BRIAND, ANZELA BRICE, ILMARS BRICS, ROWENA BRIGHT, JOERGEN BRINK, THERESE BRISSON, ERIC BRISSON, MARTIN BRODEUR, ILSE BROEDERS, JOANNE BROMFIELD, KRISTAN BROMLEY, NORMAN BROWN, CHRISTIAN BROWN, ONEIL BROWN GRASSA, DINAH BROWNE, ROBERT BRUCE, MYLES BRUNDIDGE, THERRY BRUNNER, COLIN BRYCE, EMILY BRYDON, PREBEN FIAERE BRYNEMO, ILJA BRYZGALOV, ILONA BUBLOVA, ION BUCSA, MARCO BUECHEL, JAROSLAVA BUKVAJOVA, GUNARS BUMBULIS, GION BUNDI, FRANCOISE BURDET, PAVEL BURE, VALERI BURE, RETO BURGERMEISTER, TATIANA BURINA, DELPHYNE BURLET, ELENA BURUKINA, MARIA BUTYRSKAYA, KARYN BYE, TRICIA BYRNES, LARS BYSTOEL, JONG MOON BYUN. • C • PETR CAJANEK, JEAN-FRANCOIS CALMES, JULIO CESAR CAMACHO, CASSIE CAMPBELL, DAN CAMPBELL, ALISA CAMPLIN, MARINELLA CANCLINI, FERREOL CANNARD, XIANMING CAO, ANDY CAPICIK, MARTA CAPURSO, MAURIZIO CARNINO, PASCAL CARON, KIP CARPENTER, BRETT CARPENTIER, LUIS CARRASCO, EMMA CARRICK-ANDERSON, ALLAN CARRIOU, DAVIDE CARTA, FABIO CARTA, RENE CATTARINUSSI, PHILIPPE CAUX, FRANCO CAVEGN, PHILIPPE CAVORET, DANIELA CECCARELLI, KRIS FREEMAN, TANYA FREI, SYLVAIN FREIHOLZ, YANN FRICHETEAU, ANNI FRIESINGER, JAN FRIESINGER, STEPHANIE FRUHWIRT, TIANYU FU, NIKI FUERSTAUER, EMMA CARRICK-ANDERSON

SHIMOYAMA, BYUNG-KOOK SHIN, MAMI SHINDO, YUGO SHINOHARA, KEIJI SHIRAHATA, SVETLANA SHISHKINA, YELENA SHTELMAISTER, VALERIY SHYRYAEV, KRZYSZTOF SIENKO, VLADISLAV SIEROV, ROBERTO SIGHEL, ANTON SIKHARULIDZE, HANNE SIKIO, TOMASZ SIKORA, ALEXEI SILAEV, JANIS SILARAJS, GENEVIEVE SIMARD, CRISTIAN JAVIER SIMARI BIRKNER, MARIA BELEN SIMARI BIRKNER, MACARENA SIMARI BIRKNER , KOSTYANTYN SIMCHUK, CHIARA SIMIONATO, GIAN SIMMEN, MATTHIAS SIMMEN, DOO SUN SIN, CHARLES SINEK, PATRICK SINGLETON, YULIA SIPARENKO, SAIJA SIRVIO, MARIUSZ SIUDEK, KENNETH SIVERTSEN, THERESE SJOLANDER, ANDREI SKABELKA, BENTE SKARI, STEFFEN SKEL, JULIE SKINNER, ANN ELEN SKJELBREID, KRISTEN SKJELDAL, JASON SKLENAR, VIBEKE W SKOFTERUD, ROMAN SKORNIAKOV, MARTIN SKOULA, ANASTASSIA SKOULTAN, KARLIS SKRASTINS, NAURIS SKRAUSTINS, NIKOLAY SKRIABIN, IRINA SKRIPNIK, ANASTASIA SKULKINA, WOJCIECH SKUPIEN, JAROSLAV SLAVIK, VADYM SLIVCHENKO, ASSOL SLIVETS, SUSANNE SLOTSAGER, IRINA SLUTSKAYA, SAMI JO SMALL, RICHARD SMEHLIK, PETR SMEJC, KATRIN SMIGUN, KRISTINA SMIGUN, GRETHA SMIT, CHRISTINA SMITH, WARWICK SMITH, RUSTY SMITH, EKATERINA SMOLENTSEVA, PETER SMREK, RYAN SMYTH, LEONARD SOCCIO, ANDERS SOEDERBERG, MATEJ SOKLIC, JOHN SOKOLOWSKI, IVAN SOLA, BJARNE SOLBAKKEN, JULIA SOLDATOVA, ALEXEY SOLOVEV, YULIYA SOLOVYEVA, TIM SOMERVILLE, RENE SOMMERFELDT, ADNE SONDRAL, LI SONG, MAJ HELEN SORKMO, OLEGS SOROKINS, HEIKKI SORSA, COLLEEN SOSTORICS, TATIANA SOTNIKOVA, CHRIS SOULE, JAROSLAV SPACEK, GEORG SPAETH, GREGOR SPAROVEC, DANE SPENCER, MILAN SPERL, RENE SPIES, JOHNNY SPILLANE, MARIA SPIRESCU, CHRISTINE SPONRING, ANDRIY SRYUBKO, KIM ST-PIERRE, GREGOR STAEHLI, WOLFGANG STAMPFER, RASTISLAV STANA, CRISTIAN STANCIU, DARIA STAROSTINA, SERGUEI STAS, PATRICK STAUDACHER, MAXIM STAVIYSKI, EKATERINA STCHASTLIVAIA, MARIO STECHER, DAN STEELE, DARRIN STEELE, RACHEL STEER, CHRISTIAN STEGER, ZALI STEGGALL, ZEKE STEGGALL, MARCO STEINAUER, MARTIN STEINEGGER, DMITRI STEPUSCHKIN, ANNA STERA-KUSTUSZ, MAGNUS STERNER, TOM STIANSEN, ANDREA STOCK, SEBASTIAN STOCK, CHRISTIAN STOHR, ELVIS STOJKO, VALERIJ STOLJAROV, KJELL STORELID, AURELIE STORTI, PICABO STREET, ILDIKO STREHLI, MARK STREIT, OLEXANDR STRELTSOV, FRITZ STROBL, OLE CHRISTIAN STROEMBERG, MILAN STUDNICKA, JOZEF STUMPEL, MARCO STURM, MELANIE SUCHET, NIKOLA SUDOVA, KEITH SUDZIARSKI, HAYATO SUEYOSHI, HIROMI SUGA, KYOJI SUGA, FUMIE SUGURI, MOJCA SUHADOLC, MARCO SULLIVAN, NICK SULLIVAN, KURT SULZENBACHER, CHRISTOPH SUMANN, DANDAN SUN, RIBO SUN, RUI SUN, GREGORY SUN, PATRIK SUNDBERG, MATS SUNDIN, KATI SUNDQVIST, BECKY SUNDSTROM, NIKLAS SUNDSTROM, VICKY SUNOHARA, GARY SUTER, KATHARINA SUTTER, PATRICK SUTTER, MICHAEL SUTTNIG, HIROSHI SUZUKI, CARSTEN SVENSGAARD, EVGENI SVIRIDOV, NATALIA SVIRIDOVA-K., MAGNUS SWARTLING, CARL SWENSON, ANN SWISSHELM, TOMASZ SWIST, MICHAL SYKORA, PETR SYKORA, JEROME SYLVESTRE, ALEKSANDR SYMAN, KRISZTIAN SZABO, KORNEL SZANTO, RYSZARD SZARY, IVETT SZOLLOSI, DAVID SZURMAN • **T** • MAKI TABATA, ELENA TAGLIABUE, IMRE TAGSCHERER, ZOLTAN TAGSCHERER, OKSANA TAIKEVICH, KUISMA TAIPALE, TOMISLAW TAJNER, RYOKO TAKAHASHI, DAITO TAKAHASHI, KEI TAKAHASHI, ATSUKO TAKATA, TOYOKI TAKEDA, TOMOKA TAKEUCHI, YOSUKE TAKEUCHI, YASUYUKI TAKISHITA, ROBERT TALEANU, JAAKKO TALLUS, LEONIDS TAMBIJEVS, ROBERTO TAMES, NAOYA TAMURA, CHIKAGE TANAKA, TAMAMI TANAKA, ANTONIO TARTAGLIA, RENE TAUBENRAUCH, DANIL TCHABAN, JULIJA TCHEPALOVA, SERGUEI TCHEPIKOV, PETER TCHERNYSHEV, JESSE TEAT, JEREMY TEELA, AXEL TEICHMANN, MIKAEL TELLQVIST, TOMAS TEMPIR, SAM TEMPLE, OLAF TER BRAACK, SATORU TERAO, IRINA TERELIA, SVETLANA TERENTIEVA, IRINA TERENTJEVA, IKUE TESHIGAWARA, MILAINE THERIAULT, ANNAMARIE THOMAS, BRUNO THOMAS, JARRET THOMAS, LAURENCE THOMS, PETER THORNDIKE, CHRIS THORPE, NICOLA THOST, ESTHER THYSSEN, MARIAN TICAN, DMITRI TICHKINE, ALEXEI TIKHONOV, MARIA TIKHVINSKAYA, VYACHESLAV TIMCHENKO, MARIANNE TIMMER, KIMMO TIMONEN, ANJELA TIOUVAEVA, MAIJA TIRUMA, VLADIMIR TIUMENTSEV, LINDA TJOERHOM, KEITH TKACHUK, INDREK TOBRELUTS, EVA TOFALVI, VICTORIA TOKOVAIA, DMITRI TOLKOUNOV, GEN TOMII, JIAN TONG, AKI TONOIKE, KRZYSZTOF TOPOR, JAROSLAV TOROK, FABRIZIO TOSINI, ZOLTAN TOTH, TATIANA TOTMIANINA, KARI TRAA, KEN TRALNBERG, TATYANA TRAPEZNIKOVA, MATTHIAS TRATTNIG, GARETH TRAYNER, SVETLANA TREFILOVA, ALEXIJ TREGOBOV, YORICK TREILLE, FRANCOIS-LOUIS TREMBLAY, LIDIA TRETTEL, OXANA TRETYAKOVA, JONDON TREVENA, ATVARS TRIBUNCOVS, ALEKSANDR TROPNIKOV, PAAL TRULSEN, NATALYA TRUNOVA, KAKHABER TSAKADZE, TATIANA TSAREVA, ORYSLAVA TSCUCLIB, PO YE CORDIA TSOI, IKUYO TSUKIDATE, YUGO TSUKITA, ALLA TSUPER, SERGEY TSYBENKO, VLADIMIR TSYPLAKOV, SARAH TUETING, MATHIEU TURCOTTE, MELANIE TURGEON, OLEG TVERDOVSKY, DANIEL TYRKAS • **U** • AIKO UEMURA, MICHAEL UHRMANN, MARTIN ULRICH, NIKOLAY ULYANIN, GERHARD UNTERLUGGAUER, SAMI UOTILA, GUNDARS UPENIEKS, GERHARD URAIN, KAMIL URUMBAEV, ELMIRA URUMBAEVA, SHIGEAKI USHIJIMA, STEFAN USTORF, MARKKU UUSIPAAVALNIEMI, JOCHEM UYTDEHAAGE, MATUS UZAK • **V** • LARS VAAGBERG, OSSI VAANANEN, PETRA VAARAKALLIO, LYUBOV VAFINA, SABINA VALBUSA, FULVIO VALBUSA, FLORINE VALDENAIRE, CESAR VALDIVIA, ALES VALENTA, MAREN VALENTI, RUSTAM VALIULLIN, ANNEMARIE VAN DONSELAAR, SONDRA VAN ERT , SIMON VAN VOSSEL, ARNOLD VAN CALKER, EDWIN VAN CALKER, GERARD VAN VELDE, CARL VAN LOAN, KEVIN VAN DER PERREN, POVILAS VANAGAS, MARIAN VANDERKA, CARLOS VARAS, KAISA VARIS, SERGEI VARLAMOV, STEFAN VASILEV, NADEJDA VASSILEVA, SVETLANA VASSINA, SEBASTIEN VASSONEY, MARTA VASTAGH REGOS, JULIEN VAUCLAIR, DESPINA VAVATSI, ANNICK VAXELAIRE-PIERREL, ANDRUS VEERPALU, ZDENKA VEJNAROVA, BART VELDKAMP, CARL VERHEIJEN, JURY VESELOV, TANIA VICENT, DORIANE VIDAL, VANESSA VIDAL, JEAN-PIERRE VIDAL, SONIA VIERIN, ANNA VIKMAN, VLADIMIR VILISSOV, ANNMARI VILJANMAA, PETER VINCZE, ROMAN VIROLAINEN, MARJA VIS, LUBOMIR VISNOVSKY, ZDENEK VITEK, HARIJS VITOLINS, VINCENT VITTOZ, DANIELA VLAEVA, TETYANA VODOPYANOVA, SABINE VOELKER, ACHIM VOGT, JILLIAN VOGTLI, OLEG VOIKO, VIKTORIA VOLCHKOVA, STEFFI VON SIEBENTHAL, MICHAEL VON GRUENIGEN, RETO VON ARX, THOMAS VONN, DENIS VOROBIEV, ELENA VORONA, IRINA VOTINTSEVA, MICHAEL PANAGIOTIS VOUDOURIS, MARJO VOUTILAINEN, RASO VUCINIC, RENE LAURENT VUILLERMOZ, KRISTINA VUTEVA • **W** • JUSTIN WADSWORTH, WENDY WAGNER, ACHIM WALCHER, MICHAEL WALCHHOFER, DON WALCHUK, BENGT WALDEN, LYNDSAY WALL, BRADLEY WALL, MARTIN WALTI, CHUNLU WANG, JIAO WANG, LINUO WANG, MANLI WANG, YING WANG, DEAN WARD, STEP. WARTOSCH-KURTEN, YUKARI WATANABE, WINSTON ALEXANDER WATT, PATRICK WEAVER, RYAN WEDDING, SABINE WEHR-HASLER, LARS WEIBEL, LINDSEY WEIER, DOUG WEIGHT, DANIEL WEINSTEIN, MICHAEL WEISS, GERDA WEISSENSTEINER, BRIAN WELCH, MARCEL WELTEN, KRISSY WENDELL, ERBEN WENNEMARS, GEORGINA WHEATCROFT, SIMON WHEELDON, QUINN WHEELER, PERNILLA WIBERG, HAYLEY WICKENHEISER, ANDREAS WIDHOELZL, HEIKE WIELAENDER, JULIA WIERSCHER, LISA THERESE WIIK, MARIEKE WIJSMAN, TORD WIKSTEN, BECKY WILCZAK, KATI WILHELM, JOANNA WILLIAMS, AASA WINDAHL, KATI WINKLER, CHRIS WITTY, STEFFEN WOELLER, MARION WOHLRAB, KATARZYNA WOJCICKA, JENNY WOLF, RAFFI WOLF, ALEXANDER WOLF, HANNE WOODS, JEREMY WOTHERSPOON, CLIFTON WROTTESLEY • **X** • AIHUA XING, LEI XU, NANNAN XU • **Y** • ALEXEI YAGUDIN, NATALYA YAKOVCHUK, OKSANA YAKOVLEVA, VALENTINA YAKSHINA, NOBUKO YAMADA, HIROKI YAMADA, (A) YANG YANG, (S) YANG YANG, CHUNYUAN YANG, XIUQING YANG, TAE-HWA YANG, ALEXEI YASHIN, SANG-YEOP YEO, JUHA YLONEN, SUMIKO YOKOYAMA, MIN HYE MIN YOO, MIKE YORK, YURI YOSHIKAWA, YANCHUN YOU, SCOTT YOUNG, SHUMEI YU, FENGTONG YU, STEVE YZERMAN • **Z** • COURTNEY ZABLOCKI, SERGEI ZACHARENKO, MATISS ZACMANIS, DOROTA ZAGORSKA, PETR ZAHROBSKY, OLGA ZAITSEVA, BOREK ZAKOURIL, PETRA ZAKOURILOVA, BOHDAN ZAMOSTYANYK, EDUARD ZANKAVETS, INESIS ZAPOROZECS, PAUL ZAR, EDOARDO ZARDINI, GIULIO ZARDO, VYACHESLAV ZAVALNYUK, KRYSTIAN ZDROJKOWSKI, WARWARA ZELENSKAJA, MARTINA ZELLNER, HENRIK ZETTERBERG, ALEXEI ZHAMNOV, STEPHANIE ZHANG, DAN ZHANG, JING ZHANG, WEINA ZHANG, XIAOLEI ZHANG, HAO ZHANG, MIN ZHANG, QING ZHANG, HONGBO ZHAO, GEORGI ZHARKOV, YURIY ZHURAVSKYY, ALEKSANDR ZHURIK, SVETLANA ZHUROVA, NINA ZIEGENHALS, WIESLAW ZIEMIANIN, EVGENIY ZIKOV, KSENIA ZIKUNKOVA, RAIVIS ZIMELIS, JOHN ZIMMERMAN, MARKUS ZIMMERMANN, KATIA ZINI, MARA ZINI, NATALJA ZJATIKOVA, VERA ZJATIKOVA, ARTEM ZNACHKOV, ARMIN ZOEGGELER, ZACHARY ZOLLER, PETER ZONTA, CRISTIAN ZORZI, ALEXANDR ZOUBKOV, ZSOLT ZSOMBOR, IGOR ZUBRILIN, OLENA ZUBRILOVA, ANNA ZUKAL, HARITZ ZUNZUNEGUI, NATASZA ZUREK, VERONIKA ZUZULOVA, ALEXEJ ZVETKOV, ROLAND ZWAHLEN, JONATHAN ZWIKEL, VLADISLAVAS ZYBAILO, PAWEL ZYGMUNT, TOMASZ ZYLA

**S T A F F** • **A** • SCOTT VANGENDEREN, SONDRA WEST, JOHN AALBERG, JAMES AARNODT, MICHAEL AARON, ANGELINA ABBATECOLA, DARIAN , FRANCES ABEL, JOSEPH ABEL, ROBERT ABEL, STEPHEN ABERCROMBIE, ROB ABERNETHY, DEIRDRE ABRAHAMSSON, ARNOLD ABRAMS, ABDOLREZA ABTAHI, JEFF ACERSON, LUIS ACEVEDO, ALLEN ACKERSON, DEAN ACKLES, JONATHAN ACKLES, DALE ACORD, ROBYN ADAIR, ELIZABETH ADAM, BENJAMIN ADAMS, BENJAMIN ADAMS, BRANDT ADAMS, DAVID ADAMS, JENNIFER ADAMS, JOE ADAMS, JOEL ADAMS, JONATHAN ADAMS, JULIE ADAMS, KANDY ADAMS, STACEE ADAMS, VALERIE ADAMS, VINCENT ADAMS, WILLIAM ADAMS, DAVID ADAMS JR, DUSTIN ADAMSON, MICHAEL ADDIS, TYSON ADDY, KIMBERLY ADOMANIS, RESHMA ADVANI, RESHMA ADVANI, KEVAN AEGERTER, NATALIA AFANASENKO, LUA AFATASI, FRANK AGAE, DAVID AGOSTO, CAMELA AGUERA, MICHAEL AGUILAR, ARTHUR AGUILERA, DANIEL AGUIRRE, DANIEL AHEARN, MELANIE AHLBORN, ALDO AHUMADA, SANDRA AIKEN, CYNTHIA AINGE, BENJAMIN AINSA, KIM AITKEN, BRYCE AKAGI, JAN AKRE, LOURDES ALARCON, RAMON ALARCON, JEFFREY ALBINO, NATHAN ALBISTON, AMY ALBO, ELMER ALBORNOZ, CHRISTIAN ALBRECHT, ERNESTO ALCALDE, AMY ALCORN, PAUL ALCUS, RICHARD ALDEN, ALFRED ALDER, JEFFREY ALDER, LINDSAY ALDER, ABDULLAH ALDOSSARI, KEVIN ALDRIDGE, JOSEPH ALEX, JEAN ALEXANDRE, JONATHAN ALFORD, PAMELA ALFORD, UVANNEY ALFORD, DEBORAH ALIFF, FRANCIS ALISAUG, PAUL ALLAN, ROBERT ALLEMAN, ANNMARIE ALLEN, COURTNEY ALLEN, CRAIG ALLEN, DENNIS ALLEN, JANET ALLEN, JOHN ALLEN, KAREN ALLEN, KEVIN ALLEN, KIMBERLY ALLEN, R MICHAEL ALLEN, RYAN ALLEN, SHARON ALLEN, SPENCER ALLEN, THOMAS ALLEN, SHIRLEY ALLIE, DOUGLAS ALLISON, MATTHEW ALLISON, ALISON ALLMAN, MICHAEL ALLRED, TARA ALLRED, KAYLENE ALLSOP, GAGAE ALOLU, RODRIGO ALOMIA, DIANE ALSERDA, NIDAL AL-SHARIF, BRIANNE ALTICE, DENNIS ALTON, MERY ALVAN-FRANCO, RAMON ALVAREZ, SOCORRO ALVAREZ-MITCHELL, MELISSA ALVES, DAVID ALVEY, NANCY AMADOR, EIGO AMAKATA, JAMES AMBERBOY, AMY AMINI, ROBERT AMONSON, ANTHONY ANASZEWICZ, ZACH ANDELIN, ARTHUR ANDERSEN, DEREK ANDERSEN, EGIL ANDERSEN, KIM ANDERSEN, KRISTY ANDERSEN, MARTIN ANDERSEN, MATTHEW ANDERSEN, WAYNE ANDERSEN, ART ANDERSON, BRIAN ANDERSON, BRUCE ANDERSON, DAVID ANDERSON, DOUGLAS ANDERSON, GERALD ANDERSON, GRANT ANDERSON, JACOB ANDERSON, JASON ANDERSON, JENNY ANDERSON, JESSE ANDERSON, LAUREN ANDERSON, LORI ANDERSON, MANDI ANDERSON, MATTHEW ANDERSON, NANCY ANDERSON, NATHANAEL ANDERSON, NICOLAS ANDERSON, PATRICIA ANDERSON, PRESTON ANDERSON, RICHARD ANDERSON, ROBERT ANDERSON, RUSSELL ANDERSON, SEAN ANDERSON, SHARNELLE ANDERSON, SHERRI ANDERSON, STEVEN ANDERSON, SUSAN ANDERSON, TALEESE ANDERSON, TARA ANDERSON, TERRY ANDERSON, TROY ANDERSON, WILLIAM ANDERSON, CHRISTOPHER ANDERTON, DALLAS ANDREEN, MICHAEL ANDREINI, DAVID ANDRENYAK, ANDREA ANDRES, ALVIN ANDREW, CHRIS ANDREWS, CURTIS ANDREWS, DERALD ANDREWS, KIRK ANDREWS, VONDA ANDREWS, WILLIAM ANDREWS, JENNIFER ANDRS, JOE ANDRUS, TIFFANY ANDRUS, TYLER ANDRUS, ROBERT ANGELO, LORI ANGLESEY, NICOLE ANHALT, MARK ANSDELL, ELLEN ANSON, ALYCIA ANTHONY, MICHAEL ANTONIUCCI, LYNNE APGOOD, LANCE APPERSON, EDUARDO ARAGON, VICTOR ARAGON, JORGE ARCE-LARRETA, APRIL ARCHIBALD, DOLORES ARCHULETA, MANUEL ARCOS RAMERE, ERYKAH ARDIS, MISTY ARELLANO, JOHN ARENBERG, JANET ARENDALL, CYNTHIA ARIAS, NEIL ARMER, JOHN ARMSTRONG, LARRY ARMSTRONG, LAURA ARMSTRONG, MELANIE ARMSTRONG, MELANIE ARMSTRONG, LEONCE ARNOLD, PAUL ARNOLD, DOUGLAS ARNOT, JUANITA ARRADONDO, GEORGE ARREDONDO, DAVID ARTIS, BART ARTZ, DAVID ASHBY, BRUCE ASHDOWN, STUART ASHE, VAL ASHLEY, WADE ASHTON, PETER ASHWIN, BRIANNE ASHWORTH, KEVIN ASHWORTH, THOMASINA ASKEW, CINDY ASLETT, DYLAN ASTILL, AARON ATKINS, TAYLOR ATWOOD, MARCEL AUBIN, JUAN AUGSPURGER, RICHARD AUGULIS, EMILY AUSTIN, JASON AUSTIN, KAREN AUSTIN, WALTER AUSTIN, KELLY AVEDOVECH, KYLE AVERY, SHAYLYN AVERY, WENDY AVERY, FRANCISCO AVILA, SOFIA AVILA, JAVIER AYALA, LUIS AYALA, MARC AYALA • **B** • GENE BAADSGAARD, SHANNA BAARZ, ELLEN BABERS, CYNTHIA BABINGTON, GREGORY BACCHETTI, ERICH BACHER, GARY BACK, MARK BACKMAN, ROBERT BACKMAN, KIMBERLI BACKUS, MARILYN BACON, TYREL BACON, ANNA BADGER, RYAN BADGER, BRIAN BAGGS, BRET BAGLEY, KENNETH BAGSHAW, CAMERON BAILEY, DARLENA BAILEY, JESSICA BAILEY, KIRSTEN BAILEY, NEIL BAILEY, RYAN BAILEY, ALYCIA BAILEY DEMAYO, PAMELA BAIN, BRAD BAIR, DENNIS BAIRD, GAIL BAIRD, GLORIA BAIRD, JAMES BAIRD, MATTHEW BAIRD, CATHERINE BAKER, CHRISTOPHER BAKER, CHRISTOPHER BAKER, JESSICA BAKER, JOSHUA BAKER, LISA BAKER, MIKE BAKER, TORI BAKER, NATHAN BAKES, FRANKLIN BAKKE, DAVID BAKKER, SUZETTE BALDAZO, GEORGE BALDINI, DANELL BALDWIN, PHYLLIS BALDWIN, RICHARD BALDWIN, SARA BALDWIN, BRUCE BALE, MATTHEW BALK, DAVID BALKCOM, JACOB BALL, TINA BALL, JULIE BALLARD, THOMAS BALLARD, JAMI BALLS, CLARISA BALOG, MICHAEL BALSIGER, KIMBERLY BANACH, HEATH BANBURY, EDWARD BANGS, BRYAN BANKER, KEVIN BANKER, SARA BANKER, DEREK BANKS, JENNIFER BANNICK, AIMEE BARBER, GAIL BARBER, ROBERT BARBER, MARVIN BARELA, RUEBEN BARELA, JOHN BARENBRUGGE, DENNIS BARKER, JACOB BARKER, BRETT BARLOW, JUDITH BARLOW, KATHLEEN BARLOW, PAUL BARLOW, CHRISTOPHER BARNES, HILARY BARNES, JAMES BARNES, RANDALL BARNES, TIFFANY BARNES, TODD BARNES, WARREN BARNES, AMY BARNETT, BRONWEN BARNETT, CRYSTAL BARNEY, HELEN BARNEY, RACHEL BARNEY, SPENCER BARNEY, LAURA BARNHART, ROBERT BARNHART, BRENDA BARNHURST, RICHARD BARON, CHAD BARRACLOUGH, REBECCA BARRACLOUGH, JOHN BARRACO, MARY BARRACO, COREY BARRETT, LISA BARRETT, MARK BARRETT, MATTHEW BARRETT, RICHARD BARRETT, WILLIAM BARRETT, LESLIE BARROWES, DAVID BARROWS, BRAD BARRY, DAVID BARRY, JEREMY BARRY, CASEY BARSON, POLLYANNA BARSS, DENNIS BARTHOLOMEW, DANIEL BARTLETT, JAMES BARTLETT, RENEE BARTLETT, BLAKE BARTON, BRENDON BARTON, GRANT BARTON, TED BARTON, TROY BARTON, RAY BARTON, IV, DAWN BARTYLLA, BRANDON BARZEE, MICHAEL BASHFORD, CRAIG BASS, STEVEN BASS, ROBERT BASSETT, SAGE BASSETT, STACI BATCHELOR, CHERYL BATEMAN, DALE BATES, LESLIE BATES, VICTORIA BATES, MEHMET BATMAZ, MEHMET ZAFER BATMAZ, DUSTIN BATT, CASEY BAUER, MANJA BAUER, BRAD BAUGH, ROGER BAUGH, TAMI BAUMGARTNER, KARL BAUTNER, WILLY BAUTNER, JEFFREY BAXTER, STEVEN BAXTER, EDWARD BAYLESS, CAROLINA BAYON, DANIEL BEACH, DAVID BEACH, NICOLE BEAL, WILLIAM BEAL, JAMES BEAN, ROBERT BEARDSHALL, HERMAN BEAUFORT, MISTI BEAUMONT, NANCY BEAUMONT, PETER BEAUPRE, MICHAEL BEAVAN, JAROM BECAR, AMNA BECIROVIC, ANGELA BECK, CHERYL BECK, JOAN BECK, LISA BECK, RYAN BECK, JOAN BECKER, JULIE BECKMAN, MIRANDA BECKMAN, TIMOTHY BECKMAN, TROY BECKMAN, VICKI BECKMAN, SIDNEY BECKSTEAD, AMMON BECKSTROM, ANDREW BEDINGFIELD, RUSSELL BEECHER, STEPHANIE BEER, ADAM BEESLEY, BRENT BEESLEY, PAUL BEGG, DANIEL BEHRINGER, LINDA BEITLER, PAUL BEKANICH, FLINT BELK, BREE BELL, PAUL BELL, STANLEY BELL, TIMOTHY BELL, TODD BELL, TYLER BELL, VERA BELL, MELANIE BELLETIERI, BEVERLEY BELLO, MELINA BELNAP, SARAH BEMIS, ROBERT BENCH, CHRISTINE BENDER, BYRON BENDFELDT, ROBERT BENGE, JANET BENJAMIN, BRYAN BENNETT, DAVID BENNETT, GARY BENNETT, GEORGE BENNETT, MARY BENNETT, STEVE BENNETT, WILLIAM BENNETT, JILL BENNION, JOHN BENNION, SCOTT BENNION, RANDY BENOIT, DIANNE BENSON, JAKE BENSON, JASON BENSON, MARGARET BENSON, RUTHANN BENSON, DONALD BENTLE, RONALD BENTON, RICHARD BERG, WILLIAM BERGERON, LAUREN BERGESON, JAYME BERGSENG, JAMES BERGSTEDT, MARK BERGSTROM, DENNIS BERKHOLTZ, RICHARD BERKLEY, FREDA BERMAN, TIVIA BERMAN, ANTONELLY BERMUDEZ, JODI BERRIS, DALLAS BERRY, DAVID BERRY, TERESE BERRY, GREGORY BERTOLA, JENNIFER BERTOLINA-TE, PEARL BERTRAND, JOANN BERZETT, CHARITY BEST, ROY BESTOW, ANDRE BETHEA, MICHAEL BETTIN, DAVID BETTINSON, PAUL BETZ, MELISSSA BEUCHERT, JILL BEVAN, TAMMIE BEVAN, CHANDLER BEY, TAMMY BEYMER, VIRGINIA BEYNON, RICHARD BEZEMER, MARIO BIANCHI, JAMES BIBLE, BENJAMIN BICKLE, KELLY BIELING, KARL BIESINGER, BETTINA BIGELOW, JARED BIGGS, ALLISON BIGSBY, ADAM BILLINGS, BONNIE BILLINGS, ANDREW BINGHAM, LEIGH-ANN BINGHAM, KYLE BIRD, MARK BIRDSILL, MIKE BIRDZELL, JULIE BIRKELAND, DUANE BIRKLAND, LEAH BISCHOFF, MELANIE BISCHOFF, MELANIE BISCHOFF, BONNIE BISHOP, BRENT BISHOP, DAVID BISHOP, ROBERT BISHOP, SCOTT BISHOP, KEVIN BISHOW, COURTNEY BIXLER, OTTO BJORNSTAD, ANTHONY BLACK, BONNIJANE BLACK, JAMES BLACK, JONATHAN BLACK, LUCE BLACK, MICAH BLACK, ROGER BLACK, SCOTT BLACK, STEVEN BLACK, TERANCE BLACK, CLEO BLACKBURN, DERRICK BLACKBURN, JAMES BLACKBURN, SCOTT BLACKWELL, DANIEL BLAIR, JAMES BLAIR, JAMES BLAIR, JASON BLAIR, MANDY BLAISDELL, DAVID BLAKE, KATHERINE BLAKE, RONALD BLAKE, APRIL BLAKELY, NORMA BLANCO, JASON BLANDI, DAVID BLANKESTYN, SAM BLATTER, DAVID BLESS, KATHRYN BLEVINS, MICHAEL BLOCKER, PATRICIA BLOMBERG, MARY BLONDE, CRYSTAL BLONQUIST, KELLY BLOOM, SCOTT BLUHM, JOURDAN BLUTH, MILENKO BOBAR, WILLIAM BOBO, APRIL BODELL, KARI BODELL, HEATHER BODRERO, KATHRYN BOELTER, SHEILA BOHARD, JOHN BOICE, LISA BOICE, EGON BOLDT, KELLEY BOLLINGER, STEVEN BOLTON, ERIC BONDURANT, JEFFREY BONDY, THOMAS BONERBO, JOSE BONILLA, CLAUDIA BONNER, CHRISTIAN BONNETTE, NINA BONNOYER, LISA BOOKER, ROBERT BOOKWALTER, MOLLY BOONE, WILLIAM BOONE, CHAKKRIT BOONVISETH, LISA BORCHERT, ROSS BORDERS, DICK BORG, PETER BORGERDING, JEFFREY BORN, VICKI BORN, GINNY BORNCAMP, ARON BOROS, EDWARD BORRELL, GREGORY BORROUSO, MARY BORROWMAN, ROBERT BORTISSER, JAMES BOS, MICHAEL BOSWELL, BLAINE BOTKIN, INGAR BOTTEN, SHAWN BOULEY, NICHOL BOURDEAUX, EDWARD BOUTTE, BRENN BOUWHUIS, ANNE BOVAIRD, SEAN BOVELSKY, GRANT BOWDEN, DENNIS BOWE, ELIZABETH BOWEN, JEREMY BOWEN, JEROME BOWEN, JONATHAN BOWEN, MICHELLE BOWER, BEN BOWERS, EDWARD BOWERS, JAMES BOWERS, KYLE BOWLER, DAVID BOWLES, ZANE BOWMAN, KASSIE BOWSER, ALISA BOYACK, AARON BOYCE, LEIA BOYCE, MATTHEW BOYCE, CHRISTOPER BOYD, DAVID R. BOYD, JAMES BOYD, WILLIAM BOYD, TIM BOYER, JASON BOYKIN, GEORGE BOYNTON, PAUL BRABANTS, HEATHER BRACE, ALAN BRADBURY, JONATHAN BRADFORD, TAMMARA BRADFORD, WENDY BRADFORD, WILLIAM BRADFORD, ADAM BRADLEY, DAPHNE BRADLEY, GEORGE BRADLEY, GERTRUDE BRADLEY, KATIE BRADLEY, MARY BRADLEY, PATRICIA BRADLEY, PETER BRADLEY, SIOBHAN BRADLEY, TAMMY BRADLEY, JEFF BRADSHAW, KEITH BRADSHAW, FREDERICK BRADY, JOHN BRADY, RICHARD BRADY, TONI BRADY, MICHAEL BRANDT, MIECHELLE BRANDT, BEN BRANNON, DAVID BRAUCHLER, DENISE BRAUN, JONATHAN BRAUN, EFREN BRAVO, ACE BRAWNER, KEITH BRAY, VAUGHN BRAZLE, CLIFTON BREAUX, LESLIE BRECKON, ALBERT BREEDEN, RICHARD BREEDEN, R SCOTT BREINHOLT, JAMES BREITINGER, RONALD BREIVIK, ANANDA BREMNESS, KERRY BRENNAN, DAVID BRESLAUER, BRADLEY BRETZING, KERRY BREWER, ROBERT BREWSTER, THAYNE BREWSTER, TODD BREY, JOHN BRIA, MONIKA BRICKSON, CONNIE BRIDGE, ANGELA BRIDGES, KATHLEEN BRIDWELL, LAUREN BRIEL, CHARLES BRIGGS, DELESE BRIGGS, KELLY BRIGGS, CHRISTIE BRIGHTWELL, JANIE BRIGODE, MERRY BRIM, BRITTANY BRINGARD, BRIAN BRINKERHOFF, JON BRINKERHOFF, DALIN BRINKMAN, MIKE BRINLEY, BENJAMIN BRINTON, DORIS BRISCOE, JOHN BRISTOL, JAMI BRKLACICH, BENJAMIN BROADBENT, DAVID BROADBENT, JASON BROCK, RICHARD BROCK, STEPHEN BROCK, LAWRENCE BROCK III, DAVID BROCKBANK, JAMES BROHM, WENDY BROKER, ALLEN BROOKS, BENJAMIN BROOKS, EFFIE BROOMHEAD, JENNIFER BROSCHINSKY, LAURA BROUGH, GREGORY BROWER, THOMAS BROWER, BRAD BROWN, CHERYL BROWN, DAVID BROWN, DON BROWN, DONALD BROWN, DONALD BROWN, EMMALEIGH BROWN, HAROLD BROWN, JACOB BROWN, JAMES BROWN, JANET BROWN, JARON BROWN, JESSE BROWN, KELLY BROWN, KIM BROWN, KIRK BROWN, KRISTEN BROWN, KYLE BROWN, KYLE BROWN, MICHELE BROWN, MIKE BROWN, NATHAN BROWN, NICHOLAS BROWN, NICHOLAS BROWN, REANNE BROWN, RICKY BROWN, ROY BROWN, RUSSELL BROWN, STACY BROWN, STUART BROWN, SUNNIE BROWN, ELISSA BROWNER, ALAN BROWNING, JOHN BRUCKNER, AMY BRUDERER, RICKEY BRUMMETTE, CORY BRUNER, MICAH BRUNER, ARTHUR BRUNISHOLZ, DARIN BRUNNER, KYLE BRUNNER, MYRIN BRUNO, TED BRUNSON, JAMES BRUNSWICK, SARA BRYAN, SARA BRYAN, ARMIN BUCAD, JAMES BUCCI, MICHAEL BUCHANAN, RICK BUCHANAN, TODD BUCHANAN, MARC BUCHANNAN, DERREK BUCHEI, JASON BUCHOVECKY, LARA BUCHTA, DAVID BUCK, JENNIFER BUCKLEY, THERESA BUCKLEY, THOMAS BUDGE, GAIL BUDINGER, ERIC BUERKLE, JAMES BUFFINGTON, ISAAC BUIE, KENNETH BULEY, MARGARITA BULL, ANGELA BULLOCK, DAVID BULLOCK, JARED BULLOCK, JENNIFER BULLOCK, KURTIS BULLOCK, SEAN BULLOCK, TIFFANY BULLOCK, BULENT BULUT, ROBERT BUNKALL, DAVID BUNKER, JARED BUNKER, KARL BUNNELL, JANE BUNTING, JUSTIN BURCH, BEN BURDETT, BRADY BURDETT, GRACE BURDETT, CONNIE BURGENMEYER, BENJAMIN BURGESS, LIZABETH BURGESS, NATHAN BURGESS, JEREMY BURGON, GLEN BURKE, JEREMIAH BURKE, KRISTIN BURKE, SUZANNE BURKHALTER, JOSEPH BURKHEAD, MIKE BURNETT, MELISSA BURNETTE, KELLY BURNHAM, BRUCE BURNS, MINDY BURNS, ROBERT BURNS, WILLIAM BURNS, ELIZABETH BURR, JEREMIAH BURRASTON, JOAN BURRELL, ELAINE BURROWS, WILFORD BURROWS, CAMERON BURRUP, DANYLLE BURRUP, ANGELA BURT, DOUGLAS BURT, JOHN BURT, STEVEN BURT, AMBER BURTON, JERRY BURTON, REBECCA BURTON, SPENCER BURTON, STACEY BURTON, JAMES BUSBY, NANCY BUSBY, JERRY BUSH, MARTHA BUSH, JESS BUSHMAN, DAVID BUSSER, ANDRIA BUTLER, BRANDEE BUTLER, JAMES BUTLER, PAUL BUTLER, ROBERT BUTLER, STANLEY BUTLER, TAREQ BUTLER, WING BUTLER, TERRY BUTT, JACOB BUTTERFIELD, JAMES BUTTERFIELD, LORI BUTTERFIELD-PHILLIPS, LARENE BUTTERS, JANELL BUTTON, DEBORAH BUTTS, ALEXANDER BUXTON, SICELY BUXTON, TROY BUYS, CHAD BYBEE, KAREN BYBEE, JONATHAN BYRD, MATTHEW BYRD, CURTIS BYRNE, KRISTIN BYRNE • **C** • LAUREN CABOT, LAWRENCE CABOT, MAGGIE CABRAL, ALEJANDRO CABUSORA, ROXANNA CACERES, CHERYL CAGLE, JONATHAN CAHOON, BRIAN CAIN, MICHAEL CAIN, BARBARA CAINE, DAVID CAINE, CHRISTINE CALDWELL, JEFFREY CALDWELL, JONATHAN CALDWELL, JULIE CALDWELL, KAREN CALDWELL, MICHAEL CALDWELL, ROBERT CALDWELL, LEVIL CALICO JR, SEBASTIAN CALIGIORE, EVAN CALL, KAREN CALL, MIKE CALL, MARK CALLAGHAN, JEFFRY CALLAHAN, SEAN CALLAHAN, TROY CALLANTINE, DONALD CAMERON, KIM CAMERON, RON CAMERON, RONALD CAMP, DAVID CAMPBELL, HEATHER CAMPBELL, JANEL CAMPBELL, JESSICA CAMPBELL, KENDRICK CAMPBELL, NICHOLAS CAMPBELL, RAY CAMPBELL, RICHARD CAMPBELL, SOPHIA CAMPBELL, STEVEN CAMPBELL, JOHN CAMPEAU, DEAN CAMPOLINI, SCOTT CAMPSIE, SCOTT CAMPSIE, BRIAN CANEPA, CONNIE CANFIELD, RICH CANNADAY, HYRUM CANNON, MARY CANNON, PAUL CAPOBIANCO, JUAN CARBALLO, TYSON CARBAUGH-MASON, SLOANE CARBONELL, NORMAN CARD, LARA CARDON, MATTHEW CARDON, MIKE CARDWELL, BEVERLY CAREY, CATHY CAREY, TOM CAREY, JACOB CARLEN, JEFF CARLON, DON CARLSON, JULIA CARLSON, AMY CARLSTON, KENNETH CARLSTON, WILLIAM CARLSTON, MICHAEL CARLUCCI, BRENT CARMAN, ANDY CARPENTER, CORY CARPENTER, DORISS CARPENTER, EDWARD CARPENTER, MIKE CARPENTER, ALEXIS CARR, JEANETTE CARR, KENNETH CARR, LANCE CARR, MORGAN CARR, NICHOLAS CARR, JULIAN CARRANZA, JAIME CARRASCO, CARL CARRIERO, KEVIN CARRILLO, LEE CARRY, SARA CARSTENSEN, ANNETTE CARTER, LORRAINE CARTER, WESLEY CARTER, NICHOLAS CARUSO, ANNA CARVER, JENEAN CARVER, KATIE CARVER, HARLAN CARY, JOSEPH CASALE, KEELY CASAUS, JOHN CASE, MARK CASE, SHILO CASE, JOSEPH CASHMAN, HENRY CASILLAS, JON-PHILLIP CASPER, KAY CASPER, MAUREEN CASSADY, JULIO CASSELS, BRANNYN CASSIDY, THOMAS CASSON, ALEJANDRO CASTANEDA, LOURDES CASTANEDA, MARIA CASTANEDA, TAMARA CASTELLANO, MADELEINE CASTELLANOS, LIVIA CASTILLEJA, GUSTAVO CASTILLO, RAYMOND CASTOLDI, CHRIS CATES, ANTHONY CATHEY, DAVID CATLIN, CURT CATMULL, CONSTANTIN CATU, EDWIN CAULFORD, MICHAEL CAVANAUGH, DUANE CAYWOOD, RAMIRO CEJA, KATHERINE CELAYA, ROBERT CHAFFEE JR, AMBER CHAIREZ, OLEG CHAKHOV, DAVID CHAMBERLAIN, BRADLEY CHAMBERS, KENNETH CHAMBERS, LISA CHAMPAGNE, WILLIAM CHAMPNEYS, ELENA CHAN, PETER CHANEY, GRACE CHANG, RICHARD CHANG, JACQUELYN CHANY, CRAIG CHAPPELL, ELDEN CHARD, ELDEN CHARD, MIA CHARD, RAHNDI CHARD, JASON CHARLES, ANDREW CHASE, RACHEL CHASE, GARY CHAULK, ANTHONY CHAVEZ, TREY CHAVEZ, SPENCER CHECKETTS, DANIEL CHELKO, JUSTIN CHELKO, BARBARA CHEN, KRISTINA CHEN, PATRICIA CHEN, JERICHO CHESLEY, BARNEY CHHOUN, MATTHEW CHIDESTER, GARRETT CHILD, JEFFREY CHILD, PAUL CHILD, STUART CHILD, LYNNE CHINEN, STEVEN CHIPMAN, BROOKE CHISHOLM, ROSEMARY CHITTY, LA CHIVERS, ANDREW CHO, LAWRENCE CHO, ANTHONY CHOICE, RENEE CHOICE, CAMI CHOPSKI, ALIISHA CHOUCAIR, SARIAH CHOUCAIR, CHRISTINE CHOW, LARS CHRESTA, BARBARA CHRISTENSEN, BROOKE CHRISTENSEN, BRYCE CHRISTENSEN, DEBBIE CHRISTENSEN, DIANE CHRISTENSEN, JACK CHRISTENSEN, KENNEY CHRISTENSEN, KEVIN CHRISTENSEN, KIM CHRISTENSEN, MELINDA CHRISTENSEN, RAY CHRISTENSEN, SCOTT CHRISTENSEN, SEAN CHRISTENSEN, TIFFINI CHRISTENSEN, VERLA CHRISTENSEN, ANN CHRISTENSON, DAWN CHRISTIAN, ASHLEY CHRISTIANSEN, JESSICA CHRISTIANSEN, JESSICA CHRISTIANSEN, PAUL CHRISTIANSEN, ROBERT CHRISTIANSEN, TYLER CHRISTIANSEN, REED CHRISTOFFERS, PHYLLIS CHRISTOPHER, FRED CHU, JEFFREY CHUMAS, SPERO CHUMAS, TINA CHUMAS, KENNETH CHUMLEY, ALLEN CHURCH, LISA CHURCH, BILLY CHURCHILL, CHRISTOPHER CIFERS, JAMES CIOFU, THOMAS CISEWSKI, DAMIEN CLAIBORNE, JENNIFER CLANTON, CHARLES CLAPHAM, ROBERT CLAPP, ANNA CLARK, ANNALEE CLARK, BRETT CLARK, CALUM CLARK, CAROL CLARK, CHRISTINA CLARK, DAVID CLARK, DOUGLAS CLARK, ERIN CLARK, JOHN CLARK, LACHLAN CLARK, MARK CLARK, MELANIE CLARK, PATRICE CLARK, RAYMOND CLARK, ROB CLARK, SHANNON CLARK, SHARON CLARK, STEPHANIE CLARK, STEPHEN CLARK, WILLIAM CLARK, ARDEN CLARKE, BOBBI CLARKE, DAVID CLARKE, KRISTEN CLARKE, ROBERT CLARKE, SCOTT CLARKE, TODD CLARKE, JOHN CLARKE JR, JAMES CLARKSON, PAULA CLARKSON, CAMILLE CLAUDON, EMILY CLAWSON, MICHAEL CLAWSON, RICHARD CLAWSON, KEVIN CLAYBAUGH, CATHERINE CLAYTON, G CLAYTON, ROBERT CLAYTON, SHAWN CLAYTON, NINA CLEERE, ALAN CLEGG, DOMINIQUE CLEMENT, THOMAS CLEMENT, PHILIPPE CLERC, JAMES CLIFFORD, KATHRYN CLIFFORD, BETTE JO CLINE, JOHNNIE CLINE, SHELLIE CLINE, BRIAN CLOCKSIN, JONATHON CLOUD, REBECCA CLOUGH, SUSAN CLOVE, AARON CLOWARD, DAVID CLUFF, ALEXANDER CLUNE, CHRIS CLUNE, DAMIEN COAKELEY, MELISSA COBAS, STEVEN COBB, SEAN COBERLY, KATHARINE COBERT-MORLA, VICTORIA COBLER, KRISTEN COCKRELL, STEVEN COCKRELL, AMY COFFEY, DAVID COHEN, ERIK COHEN, GREGG COHEN, ANTHONY COLACE, EDWARD COLBERT, MICHAEL COLBERT, STEVEN COLBURN, BILL COLEMAN, CHASE COLEMAN, CHRISTOPHER COLEMAN, TERRANCE COLEMAN, TREVER COLEMAN, MARCO COLINDRES II, HARRY COLLARD, PATRICIA COLLARD, JAMES COLLETON, CHELSEA COLLETT, ASHLEY COLLIER, WALTER COLLINGS, CLINT COLLINS, CRAIG COLLINS, KELLY COLLINS, MICHAEL COLLINS, MICHAEL COLLINS, RANDY COLLINS, ROBERT COLLINS, SARA COLLINS, VICTOR COLOROSO, DARREN COMER, ROBERT COMFORT, RICHARD COMITO, DAVID COMPANIONE, ANTHONY COMPORATO, JENNIFER COMPTON, KAREN COMSTOCK, THOMAS CONANT, JENNIE CONDER, SCOTT CONDIE, ANDREW CONE, SHAWN CONLIN, STEVEN CONLIN, JAMES CONN, BRIAN CONNAKER, DENNIS CONNELL, ALEXANDER CONNER, CAROLINE CONNER, EDMUND CONNOLLY, BRIAN CONRAD, CARA CONRAD, DIANE CONRAD, MICHELE CONSTANTINEAU, CLAUDIO CONTRERAS, RICHARD CONTRERAS, CAROL CONTRERAS-DENNY, AMY CONWAY, THOMAS CONZONE, BARRY COOK, BRIAN COOK, CAROLE COOK, CRAIG COOK, GREG COOK, KATIE COOK, NICOLE COOK, RON COOK, SCOTT COOK, SUE COOK, THOMAS COOK, SARAH COOKINGHAM, PAUL COOLEY, CHRISTOPHER COOMBS, PETER COOMBS, JENNY COON, MARITONA COOPER, MICHAEL COOPER, KIMBERLY COOPER WILLIAMS, ADAM COOTER, TIMOTHY COOVER, BENJAMIN COPE, SHERRIE COPE, TONINO COPENE, ROBERT COPSEY, ANITA CORBETT, STEVEN CORBIN, TED CORDINGLEY, BRANDON CORDNER, CHRIS CORDOVA, JEAN CORLEY, JAMES CORN, MARIA CORNEJO, JUDY CORNELL, TOM CORNWALL, DONNA CORRADO, CHARLES CORRELL, DONALD CORREN, JAMES CORRIGAN, ANDREW CORRY, CARLOS CORTEZ, MARCO CORVETTO, AMANDA COSBY, FRANCISCO COSTA, KATHLEEN COURT, WILLIE COUSIN, REYNALDO COUTS, LINDSEY COVINGTON, GARY COWAN, KRISTIN COWAN, KEARA COWLEY, KERIN COWLEY, KEVIN COWLEY, MARCIA COWLEY, ALISON COX, ANTONY COX, LARRY COX, PETER COX, TROY COX, JOHN COYLE, DAVID COYNE, SHARON COYNE, GORDON CRABTREE, SHANE CRABTREE, SPENCER CRABTREE, DAVID CRACROFT, KAMEE CRAIG, LISA CRAIG, REANNE CRAM, DENNIS CRANDALL, BRUCE CRANE, CRISTA CRANE, ERROL CRANE, MATT CRAPO, BRIAN CRAWFORD, DALLAS CRAWFORD, NATHANIEL CRAWFORD, DARRYLE CRAWLEY, THOMAS CRESCENZO, DAVID CREST, WILLIAM CRISSMAN, LANE CRITCHFIELD, MATTHEW CRITCHFIELD, RYAN CRITTENDEN, JUDITH CRITZ, DEVIN CRONISTER, JOHN CRONK, SAMUEL CROOK, TYSON CROOK, BENJAMIN CROSBY, GREGORY CROSBY, JACOB CROSBY, JOSH CROSBY, PATRICIA CROSLAND, PHIL CROSS, TARA CROULEY, ANDREW CROW, RHUPERDIA CROWE, CHRISTINE CROWELL, CHRISTOPHER CROWLEY, LUANN CROWTHER, MATT CROWTON, PRESTON CROXFORD, NORA CRUIKSHANK, WILLIAM CRUMLEY, CAROL CRUMP, CAROL CRUMP, FRANKLIN CRUZ, KENNETH CUDDEBACK, MARK CUGINI, BECKY CULLIMORE, MELISSA CUMMINGS, TIMOTHY CUMMINGS, DAVID CUMMINS, JENNIFER CUNNINGHAM, LOIS CUNNINGHAM, ANDREW CURRAN, MICHAEL CURRAN, STEVEN CURRIE, PEGGY CURRY, GARY CURTIS, LEX CURTIS, LEX CURTIS, SONNY CURTIS, STEVEN CURTIS, TONY CURTIS, RYMAN CURTIS-MCLAN, RICHARD CUSTER, MICHAEL CUTHBERT, BRYAN CUTLER, CAROLEE CUTLER, MARSHALL CUTLER, MARTIN CUTLER, DONALD CUTTER, RYAN CUTTER, JOSEPH CZERNY • **C** • REX DABLING, MICHAEL DAGES, JODY DAGGETT, NICK DAGNILLO, TERESA DAHL, TYLER DAHL, SETH DAHLE, LARRY DAHLIN, COLEMAN DAIGLER, ERIN DAILEY, THOMAS DAILEY, WILLIAM

DAILEY, DANIEL DAILY, TERRENCE DAILY, PENELOPE DAIN, JOHN DAKIN, THOMAS DALTON, CHARLES DAME, SHANNON DAMNAVITS, JARIN DANA, MICHAEL DANAHEY, JULIA DANCE, LINDA DANET, TAMANICA DANFORD-LEAF, TAMA D'ANGELO, BRYAN DANGERFIELD, CURTIS DANIEL, JEFFREY DANIELS, MELANIE DANIELS, VALERIE DANIELS, GARRETT DANKER, SUSAN DARCH, DAMON DARIENZO, BILL DARK, THOMAS DARK, J DARLEY, DIANE DARLING, WENDY DARLING, JACQUES DARMAGNAC, DEBORAH DARRAH, CARL DAUGHTRY, KEITH DAVENPORT, ELAINE DAVICA, JEFFREY DAVID, CRAIG DAVIDSON, JON DAVIES, RONALD DAVIES, GAIL DAVIES-SIGLER, PATRICIA DAVILA, AMBER DAVIS, BRUCE DAVIS, COLIN DAVIS, DEBORAH DAVIS, DONALD DAVIS, FRANCES DAVIS, HYRUM DAVIS, JAMES DAVIS, JASON DAVIS, JOSH DAVIS, KARA DAVIS, KARENE DAVIS, KATHLEEN DAVIS, LACEY DAVIS, LAEL DAVIS, MARK DAVIS, NEAL DAVIS, REGINA DAVIS, ROBERT DAVIS, ROBERT DAVIS, ROSHELLE DAVIS, RYAN DAVIS, SHELLIANNE DAVIS, TAYLOR DAVIS, TONY DAVIS, VENESTA DAVIS, ANDREA DAVIS-NICHOLS, ANGE DAVISON, ALLAN DAWKINS, BOSIE DAWSON, CAROLYN DAWSON, DUSTIN DAWSON, GARY DAWSON, MICHAEL DAWSON, BRYAN DAY, ROBERT DAY, MELISSA DAYTON, ANNE DE CHAMPLAIN, PATRICK DE FREITAS, SERGIO DE LA MORA, RICARDO DE LA TORRE, COLIN DEAKIN, JOSEPH DEAKIN, BRANDON DEAN, JAMES DEAN, LLOYD DEAN, MERRY DEAN, DOUGLAS DEANGELIS, KEVIN DEARDEN, LANCE DEARDEN, ELLEN DEATON, ROY DEATON, CHRISTOPHER DEAVER, REGAN DEBIE, LORI DEBOARD, HENRY DEBUSMANN, JOHN DECARVALHO, LAWRENCE DECHART, DENISE DECOITE, KASIDEE DECOL, DANIEL DECOOPMAN, BRAD DECOURSEY, SCOTT DEE, JASON DEELSTRA, MARY DEEM, CATHERINE DEFOER, SEAN DEFOER, JOHN DEGRAW, CHRISTIAN DEGREY, RYAN DEGREY, JANAE DEGUZMAN, BRENDA DEHERRERA, STEPHANIE DEHORNEY, KATHY DEJONG, INGRID DEKLAU, LUCIO DELCID, LIBBY DELIOTE, BELEN DELL, DANNY DELL, LUKE DELLENBACK, PHILLIP DELLINGER, RON DELMONT, CLAIRE DELNEGRO, SAMUEL DELONG, MICHAEL DELUCA, JESUS DELUNA, ROBERT DEMAYO JR, CARIN DEMILO, HERWIG DEMSCHAR, ANTON DENGLER, JOHN DENHAM, MAX DENNA, TODD DENNETT, DAVID DENNEY, JAMES DENTON, JOYCE DENTON, NICK DENUNZIO, MARCO DEPALMA, MATTHEW DEPAULA, SHANE DEROS, GAELYN DERR, STEVEN DERR, OLIVIA DERRIDINGER, DANNY DESMIDT, DONALD DESMOND, BRYCE DESPAIN, BRYSON DESPAIN, ERIC DESPAIN, MICHAEL DESPAIN, ROBINETTE DESROCHERS, RONALD DEUTCH, TASHA DEVAULT, TRENTON DEVENISH, CARRIE DEVINE, DAVID DEVRIES, HAROLD DEWEAVER, BRENT DEYOUNG, JAMES DIAMOND, KAY DIAMOND, ANTHONY DIANTONIO, CARLOS DIAZ, HECTOR DIAZ, KARL DIAZ, VICTOR DIAZ, BONNIE DIBBLE, PAUL DIBLE, DEANA DICENZO, KEITH DICK, ANTHONY DICKAMORE, TAMARA DICKAMORE, WILLIAM DICKERSON, KAREN DICKERT, DENNIS DICKINSON, TALMAGE DICKSON, SHANE DICOU, ALEX DIDANATO, JULIA DIEFFENBACH, JOSE DIEGUEZ, RONALD DIEHL, RICKIE DILLARD, ELLA DILLON, CHRIS DILSAVER, DAVID DINGER, MEIGHAN DINGLE, JAMIE DINSMORE, ANDREA DITTMORE, STEPHEN DITTMORE, MARGARET DIUBALDO, ANDREW DIXON, BEN DIXON, TIMMOTHY DIXON, DENNIS DOANE, KATHRYN DOBIS, BRYAN DODD, MORRIS DODD, DAVID DODDRIDGE, SUSAN DODGE, LEE DOEHNE, CHERYL DOERFLER-LAKE, BRIAN DOHERTY, EUGEUE DOHERTY, JUSTIN DOHERTY, SCOTT DOHN, CRYSTAL DOLAN, DAVE DOMAN, SAM DOMINGUES, MARK DONAHUE, GEORGANEE DONE, OLIVIER DONGIOVANNI, JOSEPH DONNELLY, BRIAN DONOVAN, JOHN DORBACOPOULO, CHRISTOPHER DORNY, DEBRA DORSEY, DONALD DORTON, CATHERINE DOTSON, PAUL DOTY, RICHARD DOTY, PAUL DOUD, DARIN DOUGLAS, JACK DOUGLAS, TONI DOUGLAS, KARYN DOWNING, KENT DOWNING, RYAN DOXEY, DIANE DOYLE, FRANCIS DOYLE, BRIAN DRABEK, SUSAN DRAKE, CRIS DRAPER, WILLIAM DRAPER, DAN DREIER, ALLISON DREITZLER, MARK DRENNEN, BESS DRESHER, JENNIFER DRIGGS, ANDREW DRILL, SAM DROSSOS, STEVE DROST, TRAVIS DROWN, HOWARD DRURY, MIKE DRURY, DANIEL DRYDEN, BENJAMIN DUBOIS, STEPHEN DUCKWORTH, NICHOLAS DUCLOS, JAMES DUFF, JOANNE DUFF, KATHY DUFF, MICHAEL DUFFY, DUANE DUFNER, MICHAEL DUFUR, KELLY DUKE, MARLON DUKE, NEIL DUKE, CHRISTIANE DUKES, KEITH DUMAS, GERALD DUMESTRE, DAVE DUNCAN, EMMA DUNCAN, SUZANNE DUNCAN, NALISA DUNFORD, ROBERT DUNHAM, WILLIAM DUNLEAVY, CARLTON DUNN, CRAIG DUNN, FIELDING DUNN, GARRY DUNN, GORDON DUNN, MATTHEW DUNN, SEAN DUNN, JOHN DUNNE, JAMIE DUNTON, CHARLES DUPAIX, FRED DUPAIX, MARK DUPCAK, LAWRENCE DUPRE, JOE DURAN, MARIA DURAN, TED DURDEN, JOHN DURKIN, THOMAS DURR, KATHERINE DURRANS, RONALD DURRANT, WYATT DURSTELER, LAWRENCE DURTSCHI, DARIUS DUSTIN, CHRISTOPHER DUTSON, MARSHALL DVORSCAK, BRUCE DWORSHAK, MARY DY, AIMEE DYER, JAMES DYER, KELLY DYER, ELLEN DZIENGELESKI • **E** • SCOTT EAGAN, STEVEN EAMES, RONALD EARL, KAREN EASLING, LEOLA EASON, JASON EASTER, CARLA EASTLAND, BRIAN EATON, CHRISTOPHER EATON, JANA EAVES, DAVID EBERT, JEFFREY EBERT, ROBERT ECCLES, SPENCER ECCLES, SHERRY ECKERT, TYSON EDDINGS, HEATHER EDGE, SHAWN EDGE, DOUGLAS EDGERTON, BENJAMIN EDGSON, HAYLEY EDGSON, HEIDI EDLEFSEN, ALLISON EDMUNDS, ANN EDMUNDS, BREE EDWARDS, ERIC EDWARDS, HEIDI EDWARDS, KENNETH EDWARDS, LEE EDWARDS, MELODY EDWARDS, MICHAEL EDWARDS, OSCAR EDWARDS, RONDA EDWARDS, TYSON EDWARDS, PATRICK EGAN, RALPH EGAN, TONYA EGAN, CLINTON EGELSTON, DAN EGELSTON, JAMES EGGERT, JAMES EGGERT, JESSICA EHAT, JOSEPH EHAT, RICK EHMCKE, TRACY EHRIG, TRACY EHRIG, JAMES EICHER, ANNA EICKMANN, SHERRI EINFELDT, BERND EISELE, AMY EKINS, DIANE EKINS, JAMES ELDER, JOSHUA ELDRIDGE, SARA ELGGREN, LARRY ELKINGTON, CAMILLE ELKINS, MARGARET ELKINS, TODD ELKINS, DEBORAH ELLERMEIER, BRUCE ELLINGER, CRAIG ELLIOTT, DWIGHT ELLIOTT, CLIFFORD ELLIS, RICHARD ELLIS, MICHAEL ELLISON, SHERRYL ELLISON, CHAD ELSKAMP, DOROTHY EMENS, DANA EMERICK, PETER EMERSON, ADRI EMERY, FRED EMERY, RACHEL EMERY, GRETCHEN EMMONS-KELLY, TRACY EMROE, ANDREA ENCE, HOLLY ENGAR, TIFFANY ENGAR, CODY ENGDAHL, DEBORAH ENGEN, EMILY ENGFER, DARREN ENGLEN, DEL ENGLEN, JOANNE ENGLISH, HEATHER ENNIS, WENDY ENNIS, MIGUEL ENRIQUEZ, CARLIE ERB, MELISSA EREKSON, JODY ERHARDT, BRANDON ERICKSON, BRUCE ERICKSON, CAROLYN ERICKSON, CHRISTOPHER ERICKSON, CHRISTOPHER ERICKSON, DAVID ERICKSON, MAURICE ERICKSON, MITCHEL ERICKSON, ROBERT ERICKSON, TIFFANI ERICKSON, JESSE ERNEST, STEPHEN ERNST, MARIE ERTEL, TROY ERTEL, MARY ESCALERA, GREG ESKEW, TINA ESPARZA, TANYA ESPINEL, VETO ESPINOLA, DAVID ESPINOSA, MANNY ESPINOZA, JEFFREY ESPLIN, TAI ESQUIBEL, BRENDA ESQUIVEL, ERIC ESSE, JONAH ESSERS, HOLLY ESSLER, SCOTT ESTAY, NATHAN ESTES, SHERILYN ESTES, JOHN ESTLE, RACHEL ESTLING, BEN ETHRIDGE, MARK EUBANK, SAMUEL EUBANKS, ANDREW EVANS, BECKY EVANS, DAVID EVANS, KAREN EVANS, KIRSTEN EVANS, LAWRENCE EVANS, PHILLIP EVANS, RAELYN EVANS, STEVEN EVANS, ZACKERY EVANS, TAUNI EVERETT, ERIN EVERS, LYLE EVERSTEN, PAUL EWALD, ELIZABETH EWASKIO, LYDIA EWING, EDWIN EYNON • **F** • ANDREW FABRIZIO, WILLIAM FAGERGREN, TRAVIS FAGO, VAL FAGRE, BENJAMIN FAIN JR, KERI FAIRBANKS, ANNE FAIRCHILD, JONN FAIRCREST, GAYLE FALARDEAU, DEBORAH FALCON, TYLER FALL, SHAUN FALLIS, CHIA JUNG FAN, KUO FAN, WENXIN FAN, KATHY FANGMANN, BRENT FARMER, JEFFERSON FARMER, SHANNON FARNER, JOEL FARNSWORTH, MICHAEL FARNSWORTH, TERESA FARNSWORTH, ANDREA FARR, CLAYTON FARR, JUSTIN FARR, MALISHIA FARR, NICHOLAS FARRELL, STEPHEN FARRELL, TONY FARRIS, BELINDA FATOVICH, MATTHEW FATOVICH, LORI FAUSETT, MICHELLE FAUSETT, GREGORY FAUVER, JACOB FEATHERSTONE, MELANIE FEATHERSTONE, MEREDITH FEATHERSTONE, OONA FEDDIS, TIM FEDEL, ALEX FEDORA, BRANDON FEELY, JASON FEIN, CHRISTIAN FEINAUER, DAVID FELD, VIRGINIA FELD, EDWARD FELDHAKE, RISA FELDMAN, SHELLEY FELDMAN, CRIS FELLOWS, ABRAM FELSCH, STEVE FENNER, JOHN FENTON, PATRICIA FENTON, GARRY FERA, HERBERT FERFUSON, JEFFREY FERGUS, ELDIN FERGUSON, JEREMY FERGUSON, JUSTIN FERGUSON, MELINDA FERGUSON, TRENT FERGUSON, MYRON FERNANDEZ, PAUL FERNANDEZ, ERIC FERNELIUS, ELLEN FEROLIE, LARRY FEROLIE, BILL FERRARA, AMILCAR FERRARI, REBECCA FERRIN, LEE FIELDING, KATHY FIELDS, PATRICK FIELDS, MICHAEL FIGUEROA, CURTIS FILLMORE, CHERE FINCH, MICHAEL FINDARLE, ROBERT FINLEY, MICHAEL FINNEGAN, SAPPHIRE FINNEGAN, EDWARD FINNERTY, MATTHEW FIRESTONE, EMILY FIRTH, TYLER FIRTH, BENJAMIN FISCHER, BETH FISCHER, ERIKA FISCHER, JAMES FISCHER, TIMOTHY FISCHER, CORBY FISHER, DAVID FISHER, JASON FISHER, JOANNA FISHER, KEVIN FISHER, PATRICIA FISHER, SCOTT FITZGERALD, STEPHANIE FITZGERALD, MATTHEW FITZPATRICK, GREGORY FIUME, DAVID FIVAS, GEORGE FIVAS, GORDON FLACH, PAUL FLACH, TATIANA FLADE, SARA FLADELAND, SEAN FLAGG, ROYCE FLANDRO, SUSANNE FLEMING, ALAN FLETCHER, JORDAN FLETCHER, SOPHIE FLICHY, LOU ANN FLICK, JOSEPH FLINN, KELLY FLINT, ARTHUR FLINTON, KEVIN FLINTON, PAMELA FLIPPIN, ROBERT FLISHER, DAVID FLISIK, JILL FLITTON, LARRY FLORENCE, MARIAN FLORENCE, PAUL FLORENCE, WILLIAM FLOTHMEIER, DENNIS FLUHRER, CHRISTIAN FLYGARE, MARY KATE FLYNN, PAUL FODOR, DIANE FOERSTER, MICHAEL FOESS, JOSEPH FOGG, JENNY FOLEY, PAUL FOLEY, JUDY FOLLETT, ALAN FONG, HOLLY FONTAINE, MICHAEL FONTANO, LEO FONTE, DEBRA FORBES, KELLIE FORBES, KELLIE FORBES, AIMEE FORCIER, ANDREW FORD, JOHN FORD, JONATHAN FORD, RICHARD FORGIE, SHAWN FORREST, RAE FORSETH, OLA FORSLUND, SHARON FORSTER, ANN FORTE, AUDRA FORTE, JOSEPH FORTENBERRY, CRAIG FOSTER, JOANN FOSTER, PAUL FOSTER, JARED FOTSCH, KATIE FOTSCH, ASHLEY FOWERS, BRANDON FOWERS, SHUPERT FOWLKES, WARREN FOWLKS, GAIL FOX, JOHANNA FOX, ROBERT FOX, ANDREA FRALEY, CHARLES FRANCIS, JARED FRANCIS, PAUL FRANCIS, RICHARD FRANCIS, RONALD FRANCIS, THOMAS FRANCIS, HILARY FRANCOM, STANLEY FRANCOM, JENNICA FRANDSEN, BENJAMIN FRANK, RICHARD FRANK, ROBIN FRANK, ROBERT FRANKE, TRACY FRANKEL, EARL FRANKLIN, GINGER FRANZMAN, ROGER FRASER, NICOLAS FRAZIER, VIRGINIA FRAZIER, SHARON FREDE, DAVID FREDERICKSON, JOSHUA FREDERICKSON, CHAD FREDRICKSON, RALPH FREDRICKSON, ANDREW FREEDMAN, LISA FREEDMAN, DEESHA FREEMAN, RONALD FREEMAN, JUSTIN FREER, LARRY FREEZE, SYDNEE FREI, FALKO FREIMANN, DOUG FREISS, TIMOTHY FREISS, ROSA FRESNEDO, KRISTEN FRESTEL, PAUL FREUDENSPRUNG, SHELLIE FREY, JAMES FRIDAL, ROBERT FRIEDEL, SONJA FRIEDMAN, STEVEN FRISCHLING, SABRINA FROHLICH, JACK FROST, KARIE FROST, MICHAEL FRY, JEFFERY FRYE, JEFFREY FRYE, SHAWN FRYE, OSCAR FUENTES, SANDRA FUGAL, RANDY FUGIT, LEONARD FUGLE, KATIE FULGHUM, MUA FULI, CASEY FULLER, JOHN FULLER, KENNETH FULLER, RUSSELL FULLER, TOBIN FULLMER, JANINE FULTON, DAVID FUNGAVARA, KYLIE FUNK, MARTIN FUREMAN, MITCHELL FURMAN, SETH FURTAW, • **G** • MICHAEL GABA, SHAROLYN GABBITAS, ANDY GABEL, JESSE GABOR, MEGIN GAENZLER, MICHELLE GAILLARD, PAUL GAINEY, KEN GAJEWSKY, NATASHA GALAVODAS, ELLEN GALBRAITH, MELISSA GALBRAITH, DONALD GALE, LIZA GALEA, BRIAN GALLACHER, JOHN GALLACHER, ALBERT GALLAGHER, JERRY GALLEGOS, PAUL GALLICK, PEGGI GAMBINO, WILLIAM GAMLEN, DENISE GANNON, HUMBERTO GANOZA, LARRY GANSON, ANA GARCIA, ANGELICA GARCIA, JAIR GARCIA, JOE GARCIA, JOHN GARCIA, JOSE GARCIA, JULIO GARCIA, MIGUEL GARCIA, RAFAEL GARCIA, ROGER GARCIA, VINCENT GARCIA, ALBERTO GARCIA-MENOO, KRISTINA GARDANIER, LINDA GARDENHIRE, JEFFREY GARDINER, MELISSA GARDINER, AARON GARDNER, DARCI GARDNER, EMILY GARDNER, HALEY GARDNER, IAIN GARDNER, JAMES GARDNER, PATRICIA GARDNER, RICKY GARDNER, RYAN GARDNER, STEPHEN GARDNER, NORTHROP GARFIELD, TONY GARINO, CINDY GARLICK, KATHERINE GARMEY, DAVID GARMIRE, PHILLIP GARNER, SALVADOR GARNICA, CORDELIA GAROFALO, ALEX GARRETT, BRYANT GARRETT, LILLIE GARRIDO BUTCHER, RALPH GARRITY, JASON GARVER, JOHN GARVER, MEGGHAN GARWOOD, MEGGHAN GARWOOD, AIREY GASPER, MICHAEL GAST, WILLIAM GAST, SHARON GATES, WILLIAM GATES, ANDREW GATHERUM, JOSHUA GATHERUM, LUIS GATICA, LUIS GATICA, BARTON GATRELL, WILLIAM GAUDET, GERI GAUFIN, REBEKAH GAUTHIER, RACHELLE GAY, JAMES GAYDEN, DARIUS GBEDO, SHAWN GEARHART, ERIC GEBS, CRAIG GEDDES, MATTHEW GEDDES, ROSSANA GEDDES, VICKI GEE, MATTHEW GEHRING, JONATHAN GEISLER, ANDREW GELINAS, ANDREW GEMPERLINE, WILLIAM GENTRY, CHRISTOPHER GEORGE, NICHOLAS GEORGE, THOMAS GEORGE, DAVID GERARD, ERIN GERBA, KATHARINE GERBA, MICHAEL GERBA, ROBERT GERBER, TERESA GERBER, ERIC GERHARDT, BEN GERLACH, BRADLEY GERRARD, GREGORY GERRITSEN, GARRY GERTMENIAN, CHARLES GERY, WAYNE GESSEL, DAVID GETTER, ROBERT GHALI, REZA GHAZIMORADI, CHRISTIE GIALLORETO, ROBERT GIALLORETO, MICHAEL GIAMP, ELDEN GIBB, GRANT GIBB, GREGORY GIBB, MARCIE GIBBONEY, ADAM GIBBONS, GUY GIBBONS, KURT GIBBONS, MARGARET GIBBONS, AMY GIBBS, JEFFREY GIBBS, ALDRED GIBSON, DANIEL GIBSON, GREGORY GIBSON, RICHARD GIBSON, MOLLY GICKLING, ROBERT GIERKE, RACIE GIFFEN, DAWN GILBERT, JASON GILBERT, JOHN GILBERT, SHAWN GILBERT, ALTON GILES, CHRISTIAN GILES, RUSSELL GILES, ALLISON GILL, AUDREY GILL, STEVE GILL, JACOB GILLEN, CYNTHIA GILLESPIE, RYAN GILLET, ALYCE GILLETT, AMBER GILLETTE, DORIS GILLETTE, ASHLEY GILLIAM, JOHN GILLIAM, SHELLEY GILLWALD, GLORIA GILMORE, MERLE GILMORE, SCOTT GINGERICH, EDDIE GIST, SCOTT GIVENS, NANCY GLAGOLA, ERIK GLANVILLE, RICHARD GLASS, ERIC GLASSER, DEVON GLAZIER, JONATHAN GLEISBERG, AMANDA GLENN, JIM GLENN, VERGIL GLISMANN, DANIEL GLON, DENNIS GLOVER, ERIN GLOVER, ERIN GLOVER, JERAMY GLOVER, STEVEN GLOVER, CARRIE GOBRECHT, CHRISTINE GODFREY, KRISTIE GODFREY, MARK GODFREY, ROSEMARY GODFREY, SHANNON GODFREY, STEPHEN GODFREY, MICHELLE GOEKE, CHERYL GOELLER, GUNNAR GOERLITZ, BRAD GOERTZEN, MARSHA GOFF, MARC GOLDBERG, MARK GOLDBERG, SALLY GOLDMAN, TIMOTHY GOLDSMID, SUSAN GOLDSMITH, DANIEL GOMEZ, FAUN GOMEZ, NELLIE GOMEZ, NANCY GONSALVES, DIANE GONZALES, JOSE GONZALES, VINCENT GONZALES, JULIA GONZALEZ, LUIS GONZALEZ, MARIO GONZALEZ, PABLO GONZALEZ, XAVIER GONZALEZ, KATHERINE GOOCH, SHERLYN GOODFELLOW, PEGGY GOODING, CHARLES GOODJOINES, ARI GOODLOE, EMMA GOODMAN, GREGORY GOODMAN, SUSAN GOODMAN, SUSAN GOODRIDGE, CORY GOODWIN, BEAU GORDON, EMERY GORDON, ROBERT GORDON, FREDERICK GORHAM, PETER GORTAT, TROY GOTTFREDSON, THERESA GOTZ, ALICE GOULD, DYAN GOULET, PATRICK GOVE, BRIAN GOWDY, DAVID GRABOWSKI, STEPHANY GRACE, CHRISTA GRAFF, MATTHEW GRAGE, CHARLES GRAHAM, HEATHER GRAHAM, TREECE GRAHAM, VANIA GRANDI, SHIRLEY GRANERE, LOUISE GRANGER, HELEN GRANT, JOANNE GRANT, JOSEPH GRANT, LINDA GRANT, PATRICK GRANT, RAYMOND GRANT, SHAUNA GRANT, TIMOTHY GRANT, TRAVIS GRANT, CAROL GRANTHAM, ANITA GRAVES, JEFFREY GRAVES, PETER GRAVES, ADAM GRAY, KENNETH GRAY, MICHAEL GRAY, RYAN GRAYSON, EDGAR GRAZZIANI, JANICE GRAZZINI, ANTHONY GRECO, CHRISTINA GREEN, DONALD GREEN, JORDAN GREEN, LAURA GREEN, MARGARET GREEN, RICHARD GREEN, DAVID GREENE, HARVEY GREENE, MELODIE GREENE, MELODIE GREENE, GREG GREENFIELD, PATRICK GREENHALGH, NICK GREENIG, COURTNEY GREENING, MICHAEL GREGA, ANNE GREGORY, BOBBI GREN, INA GRENNES, GOLDA GRIER, ANDREW GRIFFARD, EDWARD GRIFFIN, JARED GRIFFIN, KEVIN GRIFFIN, THOMAS GRIFFIN, WILLIAM GRIFFIN, MLISSA GRIFFIT, BENJAMIN GRIFFITHS, LANCE GRIFFITHS, NATALIE GRIFFITHS, JOHN GRILL, JOSHUA GRIMAUD, GEIR GRIME, DAVID GRIMES, SHEILA GRINDSTAFF, JODI GRIZZLE, MARSHA GROOME, BRIAN GROOS, ALEXIS GROS-PIRON, CORY GROSS, DAVID GROVER, KELLY GROVER, JULIE GROVES, MICHAEL GROW, CLIFFORD GRUBBS, PAUL GRUBER, TERESA GRUHN, ANDREW GRUMBEIN, DEREK GRUNANOER, ARTURO GUAJARDO, CHRIS GUELLER, PATRICIA GUENTHER, JUAN GUERRA, JANE GUINETTI, MARTHA GUKEISEN, FINN GUNDERSEN, JACOB GUNDERSEN, MONT GUNDERSEN, HUNTER GUNDERSON, BRANDON GUNN, GLENDA GUNN, NICOLE GUNN, TRAVIS GUNN, WENDY GUNNERSON, JEROME GUNSALUS, KATHLEEN GURCHIEK, DANIEL GURCHIK, JERALD GURR, DAVID GUSTAFSON, HENRY GUTIERREZ, INDOLFO GUTIERREZ, FLORINA GUTIERRIZ, BRYAN GUYMON, MICHELLE GUYMON, RACHEL GUYMON, WANDA GUYON, PIERRE GUZMAN, PIERRE GUZMAN, MATTHEW GWYTHER, TENZIN GYALTSEN, ROBERT GYGI, LYNDA GYORGY • **H** • EMILY HAAG, JAMES HAAPOJA, KATHRYN HABEGGER, GEORGE HABERSETZER, JANE HABIGER, SARAH HACKEBORN, ROGER HACKER, KENT HACKETT, TODD HADERLIE, JOSEPH HADFIELD, BRIAN HADLEY, GEORGE HADLEY, ELIZABETH HAGEN, JAY HAGGARD, KEVIN HAGGERTY, DANIELLE HAGLUND, MEGAN HAGLUND, CECILIA HAHN, CHRIS HAJDU, CHRIS HALBASCH, MICHAEL HALCHAK, DIANNE HALDER, ALFRED HALE, BRENT HALE, ANDREA HALES, ANGELA HALES, LINDSY HALES, SHARON HALES, JIM HALEY, CARRIE HALL, CORDELL HALL, DEREK HALL, GEORGE HALL, JACOB HALL, JEFFREY HALL, JOHN HALL, LAMORRIS HALL, LELAND HALL, MEGAN HALL, RANDALL HALL, SHAWN HALL, SEAN HALLERAN, THOMAS HALLERAN, LYNNE HALL-NEZ, RONALD HALLOCK, JEREMY HALLOWS, RAYMOND HAMADA, ROBERT HAMBERG, SANDRA HAMBERG, THOMAS HAMBERG, DAVID HAMBURGER, JAMES HAMILTON, JON HAMILTON, SANDI HAMILTON, MICHAEL HAMLIN, DANIEL HAMMARI, MELISSA HAMMATT, CHANTE HAMMOND, CRYSTAL HAMMOND, LEEROY HAMPSHIRE, MICHAEL HAMPSHIRE, DAVID HAMSON, BRUCE HANCOCK, ILENE HANCOCK, LINARD HANCOCK, GARRETT HANDY, CYNTHIA HANEY, CYNTHIA HANKS, MICHAEL HANNEBAUM, ROBERT HANNIBAL, ANGELA HANSEN, BENJAMIN HANSEN, BRIAN HANSEN, DAVID HANSEN, DEBI HANSEN, DENNIS HANSEN, DOUGLAS HANSEN, FORREST HANSEN, GERALD HANSEN, JARED HANSEN, MARLO HANSEN, PAUL HANSEN, ROBERT HANSEN, SHARON HANSEN, TINA HANSEN, TREVER HANSEN, DARELL HANSON, FAWN HANSON, JENNIFER HANSON, KARL HANSON, MICHAEL HANSON, RICHARD HANSON, JOHN HANUS, DANNIELLE HARDEN, WOLFGANG HARDER, SAMUEL HARDMAN, JEFF HARDWICK, KAREN HARDWICK, CHRIS HARDY, CHRISTINA HARDY, DONALD HARDY, GREGG HARDY, KATHY HARDY, MIKE HARDY, WIN HARDY, NICHOLAS HARGRAVE, DARREN HARLINE, DANNY HARMON, FRANCIS HARNDEN, SHARON HARNED, DAVID HARNSBERGER, BRYN HAROLDSEN, DAVID HARPER, KATHRYN HARPER, STEVEN HARPER, VICKI HARPER, WARREN HARPER, WILLIAM HARPER, THOMAS HARPER JR, MELISSA HARRELL, STEPHANIE HARRILL, ANDREW HARRIS, ANNE HARRIS, CAROL HARRIS, CHERIE HARRIS, CHERYL HARRIS, CYNTHIA HARRIS, DANIAL HARRIS, DENNIS HARRIS, JEFFREY HARRIS, LORENE HARRIS, LOUISE HARRIS, LYNETTE HARRIS, NICHOLAS HARRIS, RICCI HARRIS, RICHARD HARRIS, ROSE HARRIS, VAL HARRIS, DIANN HARRISON, JENNIFER HARRISON, NICOLE HARROP, MAXINE HARSCH, CATHLEEN HART, JACK HART, TERRI HARTLAUER, CINDY HARTLEY, GREGORY HARTLEY, KRISTEN HARTLEY, DOUGLAS HARTMAN, JEREMIE HARTRUP, JAMES HARTVIGSEN, ALAN HARVEY, RUSSELL HARWARD, STEVEN HARWARD, BRENT HARWOOD, BRANDON HASLAM, KENT HASLAM, SANDRA HASLAM, CHRISTOPHER HASLOCK, MICHAEL HASS, CHRIS HASTINGS, JASON HASWOOD, DEBORAH HATCH, ELIZABETH HATCH, JAMES HATCH, SONJA HATCH, JAMES HATHAWAY, JUSTIN HATTAWAY, FRED HAUK, LEWIS HAUPT, PETER HAUSER, PAUL HAUSMANN, TIM HAVENS, TIMOTHY HAVERLY, BRIAN HAVRON, CHARLES HAWKER, DANIEL HAWKINS, MARILEE HAWKINS, MICHAEL HAWKINS, JEREMY HAWKS, JEFF HAWS, JULIE HAWS, KENNETH HAWS, MILTON HAWS, RYAN HAWS, BRAD HAYCOCK, JOSH HAYCOCK, SHAWN HAYCOCK, NATALIE HAYES, RICHARD HAYNES, STEVEN HAYNIE, KATHERINE HEAD, RANDALL HEAD, PAULA HEADEN, RICHARD HEALEY, WILLIAM HEALEY, GENEVIEVE HEALY, JON HEALY, ARNELL HEAPS, DAVID HEARD, DONALD HEASLEY, HAYLEY HEATH, MICHAEL HEATH, SHAWNA HEATON, DON HEBBRING, HOLLIS HEBDON, TRACEY HEBERT, ADAM HECKERT, CHARLES HECKERT, JANNETT HECKERT, MATTHEW HECTOR, JOHN HEFFERNAN, JOEY HEGEMAN, KATHY HEGERHORST, TARA HEIDEN, NANCY HEIDT, ELLEN HEIGHT, WAYNE HEIMAN, BRUCE HEINE, KATHERINE HEINS, DARIN HELCO, STINE HELLERUD, WILBUR HELMER, BRANDON HELSOP, MATTHEW HEMMERT, VANDY HENCH, TIFFANY HENDEREN, DEREK HENDERSON, DOTTIE HENDERSON, HEATHER HENDERSON, KETHRYN HENDERSON, MICHAEL HENDERSON, DAVID HENDRICKS, RON HENDRICKS, DERIK HENDRICKSON, EVELYN HENKEL, MICHAEL HENNINGER, FRANCLENA HENNIS, ALISON HENRICKSEN, BILLY HENRY, HANNAH HENSEL, JASON HENSEL, ALBERT HEPTIG, JON HERBERGER, DONALD HERBISON, BRUNO HERDT, WIJNANDA HERMANS, KYLE HERMANSEN, AARON HERNANDEZ, ADOLPH HERNANDEZ, EMMANUEL HERNANDEZ, GINA HERNANDEZ, OLIVIA HERNANDEZ, EUGENIE HERO, NATHAN HERR, GENEVIEVE HERRERA, MICHELLE HERRERA, PAMELA HERRERA, PAUL HERRERA, ROMMEL HERRERA, SHERE HERRERA, ZACHARY HERRIES, KERI HERSMAN, BEN HERTZ, STEPHEN HERTZ, ALAN HERTZNER, NICK HERZOG, DIANNE HESLEPH, JACKIE HESLEPH, MARVIN HESLOP, BARBARA HESS, GARY HESS, PHILIP HESS, ALEXANDRA HESSE, JAN HETLETVED, JULIA HEUFT, JAMES HEYGSTER, MARGARET HEYGSTER, BRETT HIATT, JARROD HIATT, LOIS HIBBARD, LOIS HIBBARD, JASON HICKEN, JAMES HICKEY, JON HICKEY, PHILIP HICKEY, JOSEPH HICKEY II, JOSEPH HICKEY II, CAMILLE HICKMAN, BRIAN HICKS, MICHAEL HICKS, MARIO HIEB, RITA HIEBER, ERNEST HIGBEE, ROSEANN HIGGINS, JOSHUA HIGGINSON, DOUGLAS HIGGONS, ALAN HIGGS, SCOTT HILE, ALISON HILGER, ANGELA HILL, CHRISTEN HILL, DALLIN HILL, DENNIS HILL, HEATH HILL, JENNIFER HILL, KRISTEN HILL, LOREN HILL, NATHAN HILL, RICHARD HILL, TERENCE HILL, GREG HILLIS, GERRI HILLMAN, GERRI HILLMAN, SONJA HILLMAN, JOSE HILL-SOTO, FRED HILLYARD, COLIN HILTON, JUDY HINCKLEY, KRISTINE HINDALE, GLENN HINERMAN, DONALD HINES, JASON HINES, MATT HINKLEY, ALBERTO HINOJOS, SCOTT HINSCH, SCOTT HINSCH, MICHAEL HIPSHER, LAWRENCE HIRSCH, KENT HISLOP, SANDRA HISLOP, JASON HITT, NANCY HITT, AMY HIXSON, JOSEPH HJORTSHOJ, VICTORIA HOAGLAND, ALBERT HOBBS, KAREN HOBEL, NORMAN HOBSON, JAMES HODGES, DAVID HODGSON, SENAD HODZIC, TAUNYA HOEPPNER, NEIL HOESEL, THELMA HOESSLER, LAYNE HOFER, LAYNE HOFER, NATHAN HOFF, DANIEL HOFFMAN, ELLEN HOFFMAN, JOHN HOFFMAN, LESLIE HOFFMAN, TERRY HOFFMEYER, JAMES HOFHEINS, PAUL HOFHEINS, EMILY HOGANSON, THOMAS HOGGAN, CHRISTOPHER HOHMANN, MELISSA HOLAS, MATTHEW HOLBROOK, JENNIFER HOLDEN, CURTIS HOLDER, JANA HOLDER, BERT HOLFELTZ, ROBERT HOLFELTZ, RUTH HOLFELTZ, RICHARD HOLGATE, MANUEL HOLGUIN, BRICE HOLLADAY, DEBRA HOLLADAY, LOGAN HOLLADAY, CRAIG HOLLAND, ELIZABETH HOLLAND, REED HOLLAND, STEVE HOLLAND, TODD HOLLINGSWORTH, DAVID HOLLINS, CAROLYN HOLLOWAY, MARTIN HOLLOWAY, RICHARD HOLLOWAY, JONI HOLM, KIRK HOLMAN, ANN HOLMES, EPHRAIM HOLMES, JON HOLMES, SHELLI HOLMES, JOSHUA HOLSHOUSER, DWIGHT HOLT, HEATHER HOLT, LYNN HOLT, MIKE HOLT, PHYLLIS HOLT, KARI HOLT LARSON, JERRY HOMINDA, ANDREW HOOD, GREGORY HOOD, NICOLE HOOK, C BRETT HOPKINS, FREDDIE HOPKINS, HOWARD HOPKINS, JOHN HOPKINS, SPENCER HOPKINS, ANDERS HOPPERSTEAD, DAVID HORDER, CHARLES HORMAN, DOUGLAS HORMAN, DARIN HORNE, HOLLY HORNE, JESSE HORNE, KENT HORROCKS, MEG HORROCKS, TERESA HORROCKS, TOM HORROCKS, DAVID HORSPOOL, MICHAEL HORSPOOL, SHERYL HORSPOOL, GREG HORTON, GLENN HORVATH, CRYSTAL HOTH, MICHAEL HOTOPP, GREG HOUGH, JAMES HOUGHTBY, BEVERLY HOUSDEN, EDWARD HOUSE, EMMA HOUSTON, TROY HOUSTON, DERAINE HOWARD, JOHN HOWARD, LINDA HOWARD, NELLENE HOWARD, RHODA HOWARD, ROSS HOWDEN, DAVID HOWE, KEITH HOWE, KEITH HOWE, BRIAN HOWELL, DAVID HOWELL, KERRY HOWELL, STACY HOWELL, PAUL HOWELLS, JANET HOWES, EDWARD HOYLE, FONG HSU, NATASHA HUBBARD, CARL HUBER, DAVID HUBER, BETY HUBLER, LOREN HUBLER, JOSHUA HUCKABEE, MICHAEL HUERTA, TIM HUFALIN, CAROL HUFF, JUSTIN HUFF, RONNIE HUFF, WARREN HUFFAKER, JOHN HUFFMAN, DARREN HUGHES, GARY HUGHES, JAMES HUGHES, TIMOTHEN HUGHES, KIRK HUGHS, ROBERT HULST, DANIEL HULVERSON, COLLETTE HUMBLE, HEATHER HUME, DAVID HUMPHERYS, KIRK HUMPHERYS, MASON HUMPHERYS, JACOB HUMPHREYS, AARON HUNT, LANCE HUNT, RAYMOND HUNT, ROBERT HUNT, ROBERT HUNT, KATHLEEN HUNTER, KATRINA HUNTER, ROBERT HUNTER, SHEILA HUNTSMAN, TERREL HUPPI, ALAN HUSS, SUSIE HUSTED, GREGORY HUTCHESON, CARA HUTCHINGS, STEPHEN HUTCHINGS, COURTNEY HUTCHINS, BENJAMIN HUTCHINSON, AMY HYATT, DAVID HYDE, JAMES HYDE, MARK HYDE, LIBBY HYLAND • **I** • SHARON IACOFANO, DONALD IARUSSI, MOHAMMAD IBRAHIM, ADAM IHLER, DANIEL IHLER, GEORGE III, KIRSTEN ILLUM, FRANCINE ILUNGA, STEPHEN IMES, KEN INAGAKI, ALICIA INGERSOLL, JOE INGLES, JEFF INGMAN, DOUGLAS INGRAM, MICHAEL INGRAM, RONDA INGRAM, FAY INMAN, BRENT INNES, JORDAN INOUYE, ROBERT INTOCCIA, CLAY IORG, KENNETH IRBY, JOHN IRISH, LINCOLN IRUINE, TODD IRWIN, BOYD IVEY, CARALEE IVINS, CORALEE IVINS • **J** • BETH JACKENDOFF, STEVEN JACKMAN, BRANDON JACKSON, JAMES JACKSON, MATT JACKSON, MATTHEW JACKSON, MICHAELLE JACKSON, TAMRA JACKSON, TROY JACKSON, TAWNI JACO, DAVID JACOBS, DONALD JACOBS, ELANA JACOBS, JULIE JACOBS, LEO JACOBS, TERRI JACOBS, ANNE MARIA JACOBSON, CHAD JACOBSON, CRYSTAL JACOBSON, CYNTHIA JACOBSON, ERIC JACOBSON, SHANE JACOBSON, DANIEL JACOT, SUSAN JAGER, ERDMAN JAKE, JOSEPH JAMES, RICHARD JAMES, MINDY JAMESON, PAUL JAMISON, DEBORAH JANTHO, RETTA JAQUES, GABRIEL JARAMILLO, JULIE JARAMILLO, KEVIN JARDINE, JUNALEE JARQUE, ALISA JEFFERY, DIRK JELITTO, BRADLEY JENKINS, CHRISTOPHER JENKINS, KIMBERLY JENKINS, KRISTIN JENKINS, MICHAEL JENKINS, SPENCER JENKINS, CHAD JENKS, CATHERINE JENNINGS, JANICE JENNINGS, PAMELA JENNINGS, SCOTT JENNINGS, AL JENSEN, BRIAN JENSEN, CAMI JENSEN, CHRIS JENSEN, CLYDE JENSEN, DONA JENSEN, DONNA JENSEN, DUSTIN JENSEN, ELDEN JENSEN, ERIK JENSEN, GARY JENSEN, JAMES JENSEN, JEFFREY JENSEN, JENNIFER JENSEN, JEROLD JENSEN, K REX JENSEN, KARL JENSEN, KARL JENSEN, KENT JENSEN, MAREN JENSEN, MARK JENSEN, MARNE JENSEN, MICHAEL JENSEN, NATHAN JENSEN, PATRICIA JENSEN, ROBERT JENSEN, STEVEN JENSEN, STEVEN JENSEN, TYLER JENSEN, HEIDI JENSON, LLOYD JENSON, JASON JENTZSCH, RICHARD JEPPERSON, MARK JEPPESEN, KRISTEN JEPPESON, MANDY JEPPSEN, MICHAEL JEPSON, DIANE JERGENSEN, DEEDEE JESSEN, PAM JESSUP, JAMES JEWETT, DAVID JEWKES, ELENILSON JIMENEZ, KAREN JINE, BRION JOHANSEN, ERIN JOHANSON, ERIN JOHANSON, ADAM JOHNSON, ALAN JOHNSON, ANDREW JOHNSON, BARRY JOHNSON, BRETT JOHNSON, BRYANT JOHNSON, BURT JOHNSON, CHRISTENE JOHNSON, DEBRA JOHNSON, DEBRA JOHNSON, DENNIS JOHNSON, DIANE JOHNSON, GORDON JOHNSON, HELMER JOHNSON, JAMES JOHNSON, JANINE JOHNSON, JIMMY JOHNSON, JOHN JOHNSON, KENNETH JOHNSON, KRISTEN JOHNSON, LARS JOHNSON, LESLEY JOHNSON, LEXIA JOHNSON, LINDSEY JOHNSON, M DAVID JOHNSON, MARIE JOHNSON, MARTIN JOHNSON, MARY JOHNSON, MAX JOHNSON, MELANIE JOHNSON, MICHAEL JOHNSON, MONICA JOHNSON, NANCY JOHNSON, PHILIP JOHNSON, RICHARD JOHNSON, ROBERT JOHNSON, RUSSELL JOHNSON, RUTHANN JOHNSON, SCOTT JOHNSON, SCOTT JOHNSON, SETH JOHNSON, SHANE JOHNSON, SUSAN JOHNSON, THOMAS JOHNSON, TIFFANY JOHNSON, TIMOTHY JOHNSON, TRACY JOHNSON, WILLIAM JOHNSON, ANGELA JOHNSTON, JODY JOHNSTON, KIRBY JOHNSTON, SUSAN JOHNSTON, THOMAS JOHNSTON, DREW JOLLEY, MERLYN JOLLEY, AMBER JONES, ARNOLD JONES, BRADLEY JONES, CAPRICE JONES, CINDY JONES, DEBRA JONES, DENNIS JONES, ELLIOTT JONES, JOE JONES, JOHNATHON JONES, JUSTIN JONES, KENNETH JONES, LARRY JONES, LAURA JONES, LAURA JONES, LAYNEE JONES, MATT JONES, MELISSA JONES, MICHAEL JONES, MICHAEL JONES, MICHELLE JONES, REBECCA JONES, ROGER JONES, RUSTIN JONES, RUSTIN JONES, SEAN JONES, SHERIDAN JONES, SUSAN JONES, TAMIKO JONES, TANN JONES, WILLIAM JONES, NATALIE JONSSON, AMI JORDAN, DENNIS JORDAN, GLENN JORDAN, PATRICIA JORDAN, PHILIP JORDAN, RANDALL JORDAN, WENDY JORDAN, WESLEY JORDAN, BARBARA JORGENSEN, BRYCE JORGENSEN, WILLIAM JORGENSEN, DAVID JOSEPH, SHEREE JOSEPHSON, JOHN JUDD, JESSICA JUDGE, MARK JUDISH, COREY JUDKINS, CHRISTOPHER JULIAN, JENNIFER JURGENS, KURT JURGENS, JOHN JUST, ROSALIND JUSTER • **K** • ROBERT KAGGIE, WAYNE KAHALEKOMO, JIMMY KAHOLOAA, ERIK KALACIS, ERIC KALLESTAD, RONALD KAMINEN, CINDY KAMRADT, CHARLES KANE, SHAWN KANE, JOANNE KANEHARA, LEO KANELL, MERI KANO, TRUDY KAREUS, JACK KARFORD III, ELIZABETH KARGES, NATHAN KARGES, KENDRA KARLSON, JEREMY KARTCHNER, RIKARD KARTEVOLD, MINE KASAPOGLU, AMBRE KASSIS, MARVIN KASTELER, STANISLAW KATOWSKI, HIAM KATRIB, BRIAN KATZ, SANDRA KATZMAN, REID KATZUNG, MICHAEL KAUTZ, SHELLEANN KAUTZMAN, WILLIAM KAVANAGH, BETH KAVOUKAS, DALE KAWAI, CATHLEEN KAY, KELLI KAY, DANIKA KEARNEY, JEFFREY KEAS, DOUG KEATES, JULIANA KEENAN, MARK KEENEY, TERRY KEGLEY, BEATE KEHL, JAMES KEHL, THURMAN KEIFER, ALBERT KEIL, CHARLES KEITH, JASON KEITH, JASON KELLEHER, RYAN KELLEMS, CAROLINE KELLER, ROBERT KELLERMAN, JENNIFER KELLEY, KEVIN KELLEY, WILLIAM KELLGREEN, DOUG KELLY, JAMES KELLY, LUCINDA KELLY, MISHELL KELLY, PATRICIA KELLY, RUSSELL KELLY, MAAKE KEMOEATU, LARRY KEMP, AMANDA KEMPER, MIQUELLE KENDALL, THOMAS KENDALL, BRIAN KENDELL, KEVIN KENDIG, STEVEN KENER, DAVID KENNARD, CARRIE KENNEDY, CHRISTOPHER KENNEDY, KEITH KENNEDY, MARLA KENNEDY, SHANNON KENNEDY, ROBERT KENNISTON, KRISTA KENT, TERRY KENT, LONI KERNS, CHRISTOPHER KERR, KIM KERR, SEAN KERR, ANNE KERWIN, GARRY KESLER, LELAND KESLER, MARGIE KESTNER, LENKA KETTLE, NANCY KEY, MICHAEL KEYMER, SAFIA KHADERI, KAREN KHATCHADOURIAN, OYUNCHIMEG KHORLOO, JUSTIN KIGGINS, RYAN KIGGINS, CHARLOTTE KILLOUGH, ALISA KIM, MYUNG-GYU KIM, YU-RA KIM, JAMIESON KIMBALL, RANCH KIMBALL, REID KIMBALL, SARA KIMBALL, SUZANNE KIMBALL, DALE KIMSEY, SCOTT KINDERWATER, RICHARD KINDRED, BROC KING, JEFFREY KING, JOHN KING, JOHN KING, JONATHAN KING, LESLIE KING, LISA KING, STEPHANIE KING, STEPHANIE KING, SHARON KINGMAN, JENNY KINGSFORD, DAVID KINIKINI, KENT KIRBERG, PETER KIRKENDALL, ESTELLE KIRKHAM, RASHAUNA KIRKLAND, RICHARD KIRKWOOD, LISA KIRSCHNER, CONNIE KISH, BARBARA KISKIS, ZACH KISSELL, DAVID KITCHEN, LAURA KITCHEN, CONNIE KITCHENS, CHAD KITCHIN, RONAN KITCHING, SARAH KIZZIAR, DIETMAR KLIEM, RENEE KLINE, ALLYN KLINGONSMITH, ELIZABETH KLUMP, JACQUI KNIFE, CRAIG KNIGHT, ELMER KNIGHT, ANGELA KNIPS, ROBERT KNOBLAUCH, CLAIRE KNOPF, KAREN KNUDSEN, EMERY KNUDTSON, JEANINE KNUTESON, LANCE KOCHERHANS, L SUSY KOCHERHAUS, LAWRENCE KOEHLER, MICHAEL KOENIG, MICHAEL KOFOED, RUSSELL KOFOED, ISA KOHLER, JOHN KOHLER, RICHARD KOHLER, SHIRLEY KOHLER, MARK KOHLMAN, JOY KOHNKEN, MIKE KOK, CAROL KOLEMAN, GARY KOLL, ROBERT KOLLAR, KRISTEN KOOP MILES, KAREN KOPPEL, ALEXANDRA KORAB, KAREN KORFANTA, RICHARD KORGER, ANGELA KORMAN, JON KORTMAN, PAUL KORUNA, WILLIAM KOSCO, WAYNE KOSTEN, JEROME KOTRBA, YANN KOTTELAT, STEPHEN KOVACHEVICH, JOHN KOWALSKI, KURT KOZMOWSKI, ARNOLD KRABBENHOFT, ARNOLD KRABBENHOFT, DAVID KRACK, JAY KRACZEK, UTE KRAGL, GREGG KRAHULEC, ANDREAS KRALIOS, EMILY KRAMER, MATTHEW KRAMER, MARK KREITZ, ALICIA KREUTZKAMPF, KURT KRIEG, MARTHA KRIEG, NEAL KRISTOFFERSO, JENIFER KRIZMANIC, SUSAN KRUGER, DARLA KRUSEE, VIRGINIA KRUSIC, ALES KUBINA, LENKA KUBINOVA, JEANETTE KUCHARSKI, PETER KUENNEMANN, FAYE KUHN, SCOTT KUHN, NANCY KUIPER, ANJALI KULKARNI, STEVE KUN, WALTER KUNKLE, THOMAS KURILICH, LISA KUROSAWA, ANDREW KURTZ, BRADLEY KURTZ, MARTIN KUSS, KRIS KUTTERER, JEFF KYLE • **L** • CHRISTIAN LABARBERA, LORI LABRUM, TANYA LABUICK, MICHELLE LACEY, PAUL LACEY, EDWARD LACHMAN, JOHN LACOGNATA, FRED LACOSS JR, MICHEL LACROIX, DONALD LACY, BOBBI LADD, SANDRA LADD, KELLY LADYGA, NICHOLAS LAFASTO, PETER LAFAVE, ROTH LAFLEUR, GREGORY LAFRANCE, SHERI LAGORQUIST, MARK LAHR, CAROLYN LAI, PAMELA LAISHLEY, MARKO

LAITINEN, MATTHEW LAKENBACH, ROBERT LAM, TIM LAMARCHE, DARREN LAMB, JAMES LAMB, JOHN LAMB, ROBERT LAMB, TIM LAMB, THOMAS LAMBE, JEFFREY LAMBERT, MICHAEL LAMBERT, MANUEL LAMBOY, TANJA LAMMERS, VIVIAN LAMORIE, ROCHETTA LAMPTON, JOHN LAMUNYON, SUZANNE LANCE, ANGELA LANDEEN, BARBARA LANE, LINDA LANE, STEVE LANGE, MICHAEL LANGENBACH, MARY LANGLEY, GABRIELLE LANGMAN, THOMAS LANGSTAFF, TRACY LANIER, JULIE LANNING, CHARLIE LANSCHE, DAN LAPRAY, SAMUEL LARA, ROBERT LARABEE, MEGAN LARKIN, TIMOTHY LARKIN, HART LARRABEE, MARK LARROW, BRYAN LARSEN, CHRIS LARSEN, HOLLY LARSEN, JACOB LARSEN, JAMES LARSEN, JODY LARSEN, JULIE LARSEN, KRISTEN LARSEN, MICHELLE LARSEN, NATHAN LARSEN, ROGER LARSEN, SALLIE LARSEN, SIGRID LARSEN, BRIAN LARSON, CHRISTOPHER LARSON, GARY LARSON, LANCE LARSON, PEGGY LARSON, TRAVIS LARSON, STEVEN LARUE, MARY LASALLE, SCOTT LASKER, CHRISTINE LASSEN, IRA LATHAN, MARK LATIMER, RILEY LATIMER, CHRISTOPHER LAU, JOSHUA LAUDER, ELAINE LAUREN, ERIN LAURENCE, FRED LAURENTS, LOUIS LAURIA, SCOTT LAURY, SANDRA LAUS, JOHN LAVEDER, PAUL LAVIGNE, FRED LAW, MICHAEL LAW, REBECCA LAW, VARLIN LAW, AME LAWLOR, GRETCHEN LAWLOR, CRAIG LAWRENCE, LISA LAWRENCE, ROBERT LAWRENCE, COLIN LAWSON, DON LAWSON, KERRY LAWSON, SUZANNE LAWSON, TYSON LAWTON, LAURENCE LAYBOURNE, SHARI LAYNE, JARED LAYTON, J BRETT LAZAR, ANGELITA LAZARO, TALALELEI LEALA-TAIAO, RONALD LEARNED, DIANE LEARY, KENNETH LEATH, PERRY LEATHAM, KAHRE LEAVITT, JEFFREY LEAVY, RUSSELL LEBARRON, KATHLEEN LEBEAU, AMY BETH LEBER, PAULA LEBER, MARK LEBLANC, ALEXANDRE LECHENNE, JOYCE LEDELL, DALE LEDESMA, BART LEE, BRANDON LEE, BRETT LEE, CARRIE LEE, CHRISTINE LEE, CHRISTOPHER LEE, DARREN LEE, DARRIN LEE, DAVID LEE, JAMES LEE, LAURA LEE, PAUL LEE, PAUL LEE, RONALD LEE, RYAN LEE, SETH LEECH, MARTHA LEEKAM, AMY LEET, JILL LEGAULT, JILL LEGAULT, MATTHEW LEHMAN, CRAIG LEHTO, FRANK LEICHLITER, ISMAEL LEIRA, CHRISTIAN LELEPALI, VANESSA LENEHAN, WILLIAM LEOGAS, MATTHEW LEON, CRAIG LEONARD, EDWARD LEONARD, SVEND LERCHE, KATHERINE LESER, DON LESLIE, JAMES LESNESKI, KAREN LESTER, LANCE LEVINE, ANDREW LEWIS, CARL LEWIS, DAVID LEWIS, DAWN LEWIS, DOUGLAS LEWIS, ELISHA LEWIS, JEFFREY LEWIS, JORY LEWIS, MARK LEWIS, TINA LEWIS, SHIH-CHANG LI, VICTOR LIBERTY, LOUIS LIBIN, JUSTIN LICHFIELD, LANCE LIDDELL, SHEREZA LIEBLANG, LISA LIEBOW, CHRISTENA LIECHTY, TONI LIECHTY, WILLIAM LIERMANN, BOB LIGGET, MARIANNE LILJEBLAD, BRAD LILLEY, KELLI LIM, HAMILTON LIMA, DAVID LIMBERG, SHANNA LIMBERG, VICTOR LINARES, CHARLENE LIND, DENISE LIND, EDWARD LINDER, AMY LINDSEY, DAVE LINDSEY, DAVID LINDSEY, KIT LINDSEY, RICHARD LINDSEY, ROBIN LINDSEY, RONALD LINDSEY, STACEY LINDSEY, WILLIAM LINDSEY, LARRY LINEBAUGH, AMY LING, JUSTIN LINGARD, TRENT LINGARD, DENNIS LINGMANN, TASHA LINGOS, HEATHER LINHART ZANG, RICHARD LINIO, JANA LINNELL, RYAN LINNEMEYER, GILLIAN LINNEN, BRUCE LINSENMAYER, GREGOR LINSIG, JUSTIN LINTON, HARTFORD LINTZ, AARON LIPPARD, STEVEN LIPSIT, JOEDY LISTER, LINDA LISTER, BRANDON LITTLE, DANA LITTLE, LESLIE LITTLE, DAVID LITTLEFIELD, JACOB LIVSEY, TYLER LLEWLYN, BEVERLYE LLOPIS, MIKE LLOYD, ROBYN LLOYD, SHANE LLOYD, HARIANTO LNU, ADAM LOCKE, RICHARD LOCKHART, KRISTOPHER LODWICK, DONALD LOEBER, JEFFREY LOEFFLER, CHARLES LOGAN, CHRIS LOIBNER, DARREN LONG, ERICK LONG, FOREST LONG, JOYCE LONG, LINDA LONG, WILLIAM LONG, SANDRA LONGHURST, SCOTT LONGNECKER, SEAN LONNQUIST, LINDA LOOMIS, DIANE LOOSBROCK, AARON LOOSLI, CARLOS LOPEZ, HENRY LOPEZ, JOSE LOPEZ, BONNIE LORENGER, TIFFANIE LORENSEN, MARK LORENZO, MARC LORRAIN, IARA LORTON, A DAVID LOSEY, ANDREW LOVE, AARON LOVELAND, DAVID LOVELESS, EDGAR LOVELL, JEFFREY LOVELL, RONALD LOVETT, CORY LOVING, LAYNE LOWDER, BRADLEY LOWE, LISA LOWE, NATALIE LOWE, RUSSEL LOWE, DAVID LOWELL, DANIEL LOWMAN, ROBERT LOYND, DANIEL LOZANO, TYEHAO LU, STEPHEN LUBER, DAVID LUCAS, JOHN LUCAS, ALAN LUCCHETTI, LINDA LUCHETTI, PAULA LUCY, SHAUNA LUDWIG, RANDEE LUEKER, AMY LUKAS, JULIE LUKES, PHILLIP LUNA III, BRIAN LUNCEFORD, JAMES LUND, KENNETH LUND, LESLIE LUND, WENDI LUND, SONJA LUNDE, KRISTIN LUNDGREN, DANIEL LUNDWALL, SARAH LUNNEY, LAWRENCE LUTHER, SUSAN LUTHER, STEVEN LYBBERT, JASON LYMAN, CLARENCE LYNCH, KAREN LYNCH, MICHAEL LYNCH, ADAM LYNN, KIMBERLY LYNN, MATTHEW LYON, ROBERT LYON, JACQUELINE LYONS, THOMAS LYONS • **M** • JANET MABEY, JENNIFER MABLEY, PAUL MACDONALD, TINA MACE, RYAN MACFARLANE, CHANTAL MACHABEE, VINCENT MACHADO, ANGELA MACIAS, JOHN MACINNIS, LARRY MACINTOSH, SEAN MACKAY, SUMMER MACKEL, MATTHEW MACKEY, SARAH MACKEY, TURNER MADDEN, WARREN MADISON, DAVID MADRID, JOSH MADSEN, KERI MADSEN, LEAH MADSEN, RUSSELL MADSEN, SARAH MADSEN, VALERA MADSEN, RALPH MAESTAS, THOMAS MAESTAS, FRANK MAGLIOCCO, LISA MAGNANI, LINDA MAGNESS, ALAN MAGNIN, YUK-LIM MAH, STEVE MAHLSTEDE. ALICE MAHMOOD, LISA MAHON, BRAD MAHONEY, MARTHA MAHONEY, TINA MAIER-COX, TANIA MAKI, DAVID MAKINS, SCOTT MALAN, WILLIAM MALAN, PATRICK MALENDOSKI, RONALD MALIN, KATHERINE MALLORY, PAUL MALLORY, GLENN MALLROY, JEFFREY MALMON, WILL MALONE, DANIEL MALONEY, GERALDINE MALONEY, JEFFREY MALONEY, MICHAEL MALOVICH, KELLY MAMER, JAMES MANGAN, JEANETTE MANGRAM, DEWAIN MANGUM, VICTORIA MANN, CHRISTOPHER MANNING, KIMBERLY MANNING, SHAWNA MANNING, GEORGE MANTLE, JIM MANWILL, SANDRA MANWILL, KRISTEN MAR, NELSON MARCIAL, MATTHEW MARCINEK, LAURA MARCUS, DOUGLAS MAREADY, TODD MARGETTS, RANAE MARIETTI, DEBRA MARINCIC, JOSH MARKIEWICZ, ELLEN MARKOWITZ, ROBERT MARKS, LETICIA MARLEY, THOMAS MARLO, NANETTE MARLOWE, CHRISTINA MARQUEZ, GENE MARQUEZ, MICHAEL MARRAZZO, KEVIN MARSCHKE, ALMUT MARSCHNER, ANDREW MARSH, CHRIS MARSH, DON MARSH, DOUGLAS MARSH, LINDSAY MARSH, LYMAN MARSH, MARYANNE MARSHALL, MATTHEW MARSHALL, SCOTT MARSHALL, MARC MARSING, FERNANDO MARTICORENA, ALLISON MARTIN, BOB MARTIN, CARA MARTIN, CRAIG MARTIN, DANA MARTIN, DONALD MARTIN, EMMA MARTIN, JANET MARTIN, JON MARTIN, NIC MARTIN, RUSTY MARTIN, STEVE MARTIN, WANOS MARTIN, ALDO MARTINEZ, ANDY MARTINEZ, ANTHONY MARTINEZ, JUAN MARTINEZ, KELLY MARTINEZ, KIM MARTINEZ, MARIA MARTINEZ, MICHAEL MARTINEZ, TRAVIS MARTINEZ, TRINO MARTINEZ, VENEDICTA MARTINEZ, JOHN MARTINSEN, TIMOTHY MASIAS, ALFRED MASON, BRYAN MASON, DAVID MASON, RUTH MASON, CARL MASSY, SAM MAST, HEATHER MASTAKAS, MAEVA MATAALII-HOLLINGWORTH, MARK MATHER, SARAH MATHER, MARC MATHESON, ROBERT MATHEWS, SYLVIN MATHIAS, ALAN MATISOFF, JENNIFER MATISOFF, JESSICA MATSUMORI, DALLAS MATSUOKA, AUSTIN MATTHEWS, DEREK MATTHEWS, ALAN MATTHYS, MARY MATTHYS, DONALD MATTINGLY, LAURIE MATTOS, EMILY MAUGHAN, JAMES MAUGHAN, DAVID MAW, TRENTON MAW, KENNETH MAWHINNIE, RANDALL MAWHINNIE, JEANNINE MAXFIELD, MICHAEL MAXFIELD, CHARLES MAXWELL, PETER MAXWELL, KYLE MAYBERRY, HEIDI MAYER, MARCY MAYFIELD, DERYL MAYHEW, CHRIS MAYNES, ERIC MAYNES, NATALIE MAYNES, ARTHUR MAYO, WENDY MAYO, KELLY MAYOH, MOLLY MAZZOLINI, KEENA MCARTHUR, JULIE MCBETH, NOEL MCBRAYER, SARAH MCBRIDE, JAMES MCBRYDE, JOSEPH MCCAA, FELICIA MCCABE, KAREN MCCABE, JOSHUA MCCALL, PATRICK MCCALL, KEITH MCCALLIN, SEAN MCCALLISTER, DEBORAH MCCANDLESS, MAUREEN MCCANDLESS, CAROLINE MCCANN, JASON MCCARTHY, MICHAEL MCCARTHY, SHANNON MCCARTHY, PATRICK MCCARTY, SHERRY MCCARTY, SHANNA MCCARTY-FLETCHER, DARRICK MCCASLAND, CHARLENE MCCAULEY, ELIZABETH MCCAULEY, MICHAEL MCCAULEY, MICHAEL MCCLARLIE, DAVID MCCLINTOCK, RICHARD MCCLURE, BRIAN MCCOMBS, CHRISTOPHER MCCONNEHEY, STEVEN MCCONNELL, MICHAEL MCCONVILL, TAUNZIA MCCORMICK, JOHN MCCORQUINDALE, ORSON MCCOTTER, RICHARD MCCOY, DON MCCRACKEN, DAVID MCCRAE, SHARON MCCRIGHT, DAVID MCCROSKEY, REBECCA MCCULLOCH, JOEL MCCULLOUGH, SARA MCCURDY, DOREEN MCDADE, EDDY MCDANIEL, LAURIE MCDERMOTT, TIMOTHY MCDERMOTT, DEBRA MCDEVITT, CLAYTON MCDONALD, IAN MCDONALD, RONALD MCDONALD, JOHN MCFARLAND, ROSALIE MCFARLANE, STEVEN MCFARLANE, LARRY MCFERSON, RICHARD MCGEE, DEIDRE MCGILL, BRETT MCGLOTHLIN, ERIK MCGRATH, TIMOTHY MCGRAW, DANIEL MCGREGOR, CLYDE MCGUIRE, DEBORAH MCGUIRE, CINDY MCHALE, CATHERINE MCHENRY, SARAH MCHUGH, JULIE MCINTYRE, JENNIFER MCKAY, HENRY MCKEE, MICHAEL MCKELL, NICHOLAS MCKERNAN, BLAKE MCKIBBIN, TIFFANY MCKINNEY, MICHAL MCKINNON, DON MCKNIGHT, DALE MCLANE, RYAN MCLAUGHLIN, SHARON MCLEAN, DEBORAH MCLELLAND, KRISTIE MCLEOD, SUSAN MCMAHON, DIX MCMULLIN, DARIN MCNALLY, LORI MCNEELY, PATRICIA MCNICHOLAS, THERESE MCNICHOLAS, MARIA MCNULTY, MARK MCOMBER, JOHN MCPEEK, ANDREJA MCQUARRIE, PAUL MCWATERS, BRANDT MEAD, BETTY MEADOWS, MILITZA MEADOWS, TIMOTHY MEAGHER, JOSEPH MEAKIN, ROBERT MEALS, ANDREW MECHAM, JAIME MEDELLIN, TOMAS MEDINA, GLENN MEEK, PATRICK MEFFERT, WILLIS MELDRUM, COSTAS MELISSINOS, JEFFREY MELLINGER, HALLIE MELLON, AARON MELVILLE, EDSON MELVILLE, WENDELL MEMMOTT, CAROLINA MENDEZ, ROGELIO MENDIOLA, JACOB MENG, CRISTINA MENGS, MARK MENLOVE, FRANK MENONI, RUTH ANN MENTES, DANIEL MERCER, SCOTT MERCER, CHRISTINA MEREDITH, MILTON MERKEL, DANIEL MERKLEY, SHAWN MERLEN, JUAN MERLOS, JOHN MERRIHEW, ANDREA MERRILL, DEAN MERRILL, MARDEE MERRILL, MARDEE MERRILL, RUSSELL MERRILL, TONYA MERRILL, BLAIR MESSICK, SCOTT METCALFE, KRAIG MEWA, CARLA MEYER, ELDEN MEYER, GARY MEYER, JENNIFER MEYER, LARRY MEYER, STEVEN MEYER, STEVEN MEYER, KARL MEYERSICK, PIERRE MEYRAT, RACHEL MICHAEL, ALLEN MICHAELIS, LEONARD MICHAELSEN, PAUL MICKELSEN, PHILIP MICKEY, MICHELLE MIDDLETON, WAYNE MIDDLETON, LISA MIDGLEY, MATTHEW MIETCHER, VANJA MIKANOVIC, ANTHONY MILANO, KENNETH MILBURN, COURTENAY MILES, JOHN MILES, KRISTENE MILES, SARAH MILES, GUADALUPE MILES-EL, DANIEL MILEY, PAUL MILLBURN, ANDREA MILLER, ANDREW MILLER, BRIAN MILLER, CADE MILLER, CHANDRA MILLER, CRISTINA MILLER, DOROTHY MILLER, ERNEST MILLER, JAMIE MILLER, JOHN MILLER, KEITH MILLER, KENNA MILLER, LANE MILLER, LEAH MILLER, NATHAN MILLER, PERKINS MILLER, PHILLIP MILLER, ROBERT MILLER, STACY MILLER, STERLING MILLER, TATIANA MILLER, TEREVOR MILLER, THOMAS MILLER, THOMAS MILLER, TOBIAS MILLER, KEVIN MILLIGAW, BRAD MILLS, REBECCA MILLS, TERRI MILLS, PATRICK MILNER, STANLEY MILSTEIN, JASON MINCHEY, RACHEL MINER, TROY MINER, JED MINGO, CURTIS MINOLETTI, CHERYL MINOR, DARREN MINSON, NATALIE MINSON, STEPHEN MIRABILE, KEITH MISCHO, SARA MISSELHORN, LOSSIE MITCHEL, BRANDI MITCHELL, EDWARD MITCHELL, ERIN MITCHELL, IVAN MITCHELL, JAY MITCHELL, KELLEY MITCHELL, KORI MITCHELL, KORRINE MITCHELL, LISA MITCHELL, PATRICK MITCHELL, SCOTT MITCHELL, TIMOTHY MITCHELL, VICTORIA MITCHELL, DAVID MOBRATEN, JAMES MODESITT, JARRETT MOE, SHAWN MOELLER, STEINAR MOEN, RAY MOFFAT, SCOTT MOFFITT, DANIEL MOGENSEN, TRAVIS MOISE, NATALIE MOLDOVER, KIMBERLY MOLYNEUX, ROBERTO MONCADA, RUDOLFO MONCADA, JOSEPH MONDELLA, PAOLO MONELLI, ROBERT MONK, JOHN MONNETT, BEVAN MONROE, WAYNE MONROE, JARED MONSEN, ALAN MONSON, CAMILLE MONSON, KENDRA MONSON, LORI MONSON, MARVEN MONSON, REBECCA MONSON, WENDY MONSON, FRANKLIN MONTES, DANIELLE MONTFORT, GORDON MONTGOMERY, JAMES MONTGOMERY, MELISSA MONTGOMERY, KIM MONTI, EMMA MONTOYA, IGNACIO MONTOYA, NICHOLAS MOODY, ALAN MOONEY, MICHAEL RAY MOONEY, JENNIFER MOONEYHAN, ABIGAIL MOORE, CAROLYN MOORE, CAROLYN MOORE, CYNTHIA MOORE, DALE MOORE, REBECCA MOORE, REBEKAH MOORE, REGINALD MOORE, ROXI MOORE, THOMAS MOORE, JACINTO MORALES, JOHN MORELAND, LORI MORENCY, BILL MORETON, BRENDAN MORGAN, KEITH MORGAN, MELVIN MORGAN, THOMAS MORGAN, TIMOTHY MORIN, RANDY MORISHITA, LISA MORK, BETTY MORLAN, CHAD MORLEY, DAN MORO, MATTHEW MORRELL, RICHARD MORRELL, DANA MORRILL, DEBORAH MORRILL, JODY MORRILL, BRAD MORRIS, DAVID MORRIS, DELBERT MORRIS, LUANN MORRIS, MICHAEL MORRIS, SIOBHAN MORRIS, WALTER MORRIS. LAURLEE MORRISON, SCOTT MORRISON, JEAN-MARIE MORRISSEY, KEVIN MORSE, MICHAEL MORSE, PAULA MORSE, RICHARD MORSE, YVETTE MORSE, RONALD MORTENSEN, BRUCE MOSBERG, ANNE MOSER, SCOTT MOSES, DORIS MOSHER, ROBERT MOSHER, COREY MOSS, DAN MOSS, JESSICA MOSS, WILLIAM MOSS, BRIAN MOSTELLER, RAMIRO MOTA, RYAN MOTLEY, CORY MOULDEN, BRODIE MOWER, LISA MOWER, JOSHUA MUCCIARONE, MATTHEW MUDEK, CLYDE MUELLER, GAYLARI MUHLESTEIN, LEON MUHLESTEIN, TONY MUIR, JACOB MULDER, ENRIQUE MULGADO, LEANNA MULIPOLA, RICHARD MULLAN, MARY MULLEN, SEILEEN MULLEN MURPHY, LORETTA MULLINS, SHARLA MUMFORD, LEONARD MUMMERT, BRENNEN MUNFORD, GUY MUNFORD, PHILIP MUNHOLLON, GABRIEL MUNOZ, WAYNE MURAKAMI, KIMBERLY MURLEY, JACK MURPHY, MALLORY MURPHY, MATTHEW MURPHY, NORMAN MURPHY, VINCENT MURPHY, AMY MURRAY, GREGG MURRAY, JON MURRAY, SALLY MURRAY, TERRY MURRAY, ROBERT MURRILL, JESSICA MUSKEY, JONATHON MUSSEHL, FRITZ MUSSER, PHILIP MUSUMECI, KENNETH MUZTAFAGO, DALE MYERS, JESSE MYERS • **N** • MIKE NAANES, JOHN NABOS, FUKI NAGAKURA, JAMES NAGEL, URVASI NAIDOO, SUELI NAIMAT, ANNE NAPER ANDERSEN, CHRISTIAN NAPIER, MICHAEL NAPOLI, ADRIENNE NARDI, PHYLLIS NASSI, VICTOR NAVARRA, JOANNE NAVARRO, CHAD NAY, DAVID NDETO, THANE NEBEKER, ROBERT NEELEY, STACIE NEELEY, DAVID NEFF, NORMAN NEFF, WARREN NEFF, ADRIENNE NEIL, LEE NEIMAN, ALICE NELLESTEIN, ANTHONY NELSON, BARBARA NELSON, CAMILLE NELSON, CARL NELSON, CHERYL NELSON, CHRISTINE NELSON, CONNIE NELSON, DALE NELSON, DALE NELSON, ERIC NELSON, ERIC NELSON, ERIC NELSON, GREG NELSON, KELLYANNE NELSON, KIM NELSON, KIM NELSON, LORI NELSON, LYLE NELSON, NATHAN NELSON, NORMAN NELSON, STEVEN NELSON, WENDI NELSON, ROBERT NEMBHARD, MICHAEL NEMELKA II, ROSIL NESBERG, WENDY NESBITT, WES NESTOR, MICHAEL NETTESHEIM, JEFFREY NEU, PATRICK NEUMANN, ROBERT NEVE, DENNIS NEVELS, COURTNEY NEVILLE, PETER NEVIN, LANCE NEWARD, JILLIAN NEWBOLD, GERALD NEWCOME, PAUL NEWEY, JON NEWKIRK, CHRISTOPHER NEWMAN, KATHLEEN NEWMAN, WILLIAM NEWMAN, JEREMY NEWNS, ADELE NEWSOME, REBECCA NEWTON, DENELL NEY, CHARLIE NGUYEN, JAMES NICHOLAS JR, JOSEPH NICHOLLS, JOSH NICHOLLS, JENNIFER NICHOLS, JOHN NICHOLS, KARREN NICHOLS, MICHAEL NICHOLS, RICHARD NICHOLS, WESLEY NICKEL, BRIAN NICKERSON, TYLER NICKL, JANETTE NICKOLAISEN, JANETTE NICKOLAISEN, CHRISTY NICOLAY, JASON NIEDERHAUSER, BOYD NIELSEN, BRAD NIELSEN, BRITTANY NIELSEN, COLLEEN NIELSEN, DALE NIELSEN, JENNIKA NIELSEN, JOSHUA NIELSEN, KIMBERLY NIELSEN, ROBERT NIELSEN, CREIG NIELSON, EVAN NIELSON, KAREN NILSON, NANCY NILSSON, JOHN NIOVICH, WILLIAM NIXON, JAMES NJOROGE, CHARLES NOBLE, ERIC NOBUNAGA, TONI NOETZLI, LOUIS NOLAN, KEVIN NOLEEN, MARGARET NOLEN, DAVID NOLLEY, GERALDINE NOLLEY, STEVEN NOLTON, JAMES NORBERG, ROAR NORDBY, LARRY NORDENTOFT, BEN NORDERUM, MICHELE NORINE, PAUL NORINE, GARY NORMAN, MARC NORMAN, COLLEEN NORRIS, MARSHA NORRIS, RADFORD NORRIS, SCOTT NORRIS, COY NORTH, SHELLEY NORTH, ANNIE NORTON, JASON NORTON, LEE NORTON, MICHAEL NORTON, NICHOLAS NORTON, KEVIN NOSTROM, JENNIFER NOVACK, MARK NOVACK, CHRISTOPHER NOVAK, MICHAEL NOVAK, MIKE NOVAK, SANDRA NOVAK, MICHAEL NOVOTNY, CAROL NUGENT, DAVID NUGENT, TACKETT NUNNERY, CINDY NUQUI, KIMBERLY NYE • **O** • CHRIS OAKLEY, DOUGLAS OAKLEY, CANDACE O'BANNON, JENNI OBERAN, JAMIE OBERHOLTZER, JASON OBERHOLTZER, RONNY OBERMILLER, ALISA OBORN, RICHARD OBORN, JESSICA OCHS, JEAN OCKEY, MICHAEL OCONNELL, DAVID OCONNOR, STEVEN O'CONNOR, MICHAEL O'CONOR, SHANNON ODELL, HEATHER ODENDAHL, ANDREW O'DIERNO, PAULA ODOM, DENNIS O'DONNELL, LINDA OHLSON, DENNIS OKICICH, ROBERT OLDENBURG, STEVEN OLDHAM, BRIAN OLEARY, ERVIN OLER, ROBERTO OLIVARES, JOE OLIVER, MICHAEL OLIVER, WILLIAM OLIVER, CHARLES OLMSCHENK, DANIEL OLMSTEAD, DEANNA OLNEY, AMANDA OLSEN, BRENDA OLSEN, BRYAN OLSEN, CURTIS OLSEN, JAMES OLSEN, KYLE OLSEN, MEGGIN OLSEN, PAUL OLSEN, R BURKE OLSEN, RYAN OLSEN, SHERRIE OLSEN, SONNY OLSEN, BOYD OLSON, JOSEPH OLSON, LISA OLSON, MICHAEL OLSON, MICHAEL S OLSON, RAELYN OLSON, RAY OLSON, RUSSELL OLSON, STEWART OLSON, GERALD OLTMAN, PEDRO OLVERA JR, IVOR O'NEIL, RONALD O'NEIL, ROBERT ONEILL, ANTHONY ONOFRIETTI, ADAM OPALEK, DIANNE ORCUTT, SHANE ORDWAY, JUAN OROZCO, DANIEL ORR, JAMES ORSWELL, DAVID ORTEGA, JERRY ORTEGA, JESSE ORTEGA, TERI ORTEGA, RAMON ORTIZ, NICOLE ORTMAN, ERIC OSBORN, GARY OSBORN, ALEX OSBORNE, STEPHANIE OSBORNE, TARA OSBORNE, JAMES OSHUST, JOHN OSMOND, CYNTHIA OSMUN, BRYAN OSORO, BRUNO OSTARCEVIC, SCOTT OSTERLOH, AMANDA OSTLER, ULTAN OSULLIVAN, ALISON OSWALD, JOHN OTTAVIANO, DOMENICA OTTERO, DAVID OTTESON, KIM OTTO, MANUEL OVALLE, STEVEN OVARD, KELLI OVERY, COLBY O'VERY, FREDERICK OWENS, JAMES OWENS, EVAN OWNBY, LYNN OXLEY, RUTH OYLER • **P** • GARY PABEN, CHRISTOPHER PACE, DENISE PACE, JEFFREY PACE, ARNULFO PACHECO, DANIEL PACHECO, JIMMY PACHECO, MARCO PACHECO, ANTONELLA PACKARD, LESLEY PACKEL, ANDREA PACKER, MATTHEW PACKER, MASON PADILLA, RONALD PAGE, SHARON PAGE, HEIDI PAGET, CECELIA PAGLIA, ANTHONY PAIGE, KRISTY PAINTER, STACEY PALACIOS, ELSA PALANZA, KRISTINE PALAZZOLO, AMBER PALFREYMAN, MARIAN PALLER, KENNETH PALMER, MATILDA PALMER, R BRANDON PALMER, TIFFANY PALMER, TRAVIS PALMER, JAMES PALMERI, JOHN PANGLE, ZACHARIA PANHORST, JAMES PANKOW, SUI LANG PANOKE, JOEY PANTONE, ALLISON PARADISE, ISABELLE PARENT, CHRISTOPHER PARK, RANDY PARK, ARNOLD PARKER, CURTIS PARKER, ELIZABETH ROSE PARKER, ERIN PARKER, KRISTIE PARKER, LYNETTE PARKER, MAIKELLA PARKER, TRENT PARKER, TROY PARKER, RAVEN PARKER-HARTOG, ROBERT PARKES, AMITY PARKHILL, GRAHAM PARKS, JENNIFER PARKS, KRISTIN PARR, CHRISTINE PARRIS, KATIE PARRIS, RICHARD PARRIS, CHERYL PARRISH, CANNON PARRY, ROBERT PARRY, ERIC PARSHALL, ALANA PARSLOW, ROBERT PARSLOW, SILVIA PASQUINI, JOSEPH PASTEUR, KERRY PATE, RAJENDRA PATEL, RAVI PATEL, BOBBY PATHAMMAVONG, DAVID PATTERSON, LAWRENCE PATTERSON, MICHAEL PATTERSON, MICHAEL PATTERSON, TAYLOR PATTERSON, WILLIAM PATTERSON, PAULETTE PATTILLO, CHRISTY PATTON, JOHN PATTY, RONALD PATZER, DINESH PAUL, MELODEE PAUL, STEPHEN PAUL, CRISTINE PAULL, JASON PAULSEN, KATHRYN PAULSEN, CRAIG PAULSON, SIONE PAUNI, SPIVEY PAUP, DONALD PAVLACIC, DAN PAXTON, RENE PAYETTE, NATHAN PAYNE, PAUL PAYNE JR, DIANE PEACOCK, HELEN PEACOCK, JAYNE PEARCE, THOMAS PEARCE, JILL-ANN PEARL, COREY PEARS, NANETTE PEARSON, ROBERT PEARSON, ETHAN PEAVEY, BOB PEAY, ROBERT PEBLEY, BRADFORD PECK, ROBERT PECK, CRAIG PEDERSEN, DIXIE PEELER, CASSIE PEET, JIM PEHKONEN, ANGELA PEISLEY, NIKKI PEISLEY, ROBERT PEISLEY, MARYLINE PEIXOTO, SYLVIE PELESASA, KRISTEEN PELLUM, JAMES PENDLETON, PAUL PENDOLA, ROBERT PENNINGTON, FREDERICK PENT, KATHARINE PENTZ, TARA PEOPLES, MOLLY PEPPO, ANGEL PERALTA, GEORGE PERCHES, JORGE PEREA, RICHARD PERELMAN, DAVID PEREZ, HELEN PEREZ, JOSEPH PEREZ, LISA PEREZ, MANUEL PEREZ, DEREK PERKINS, KRISTIE PERKINS, SAMUEL PERKINS, SHERYL PERRIE, CARY PERRINE, JENNIFER PERRINE, FRANCOISE PERROUD, FRANCOISE PERROUD, ALMA PERRY, DANIEL PERRY, EMILY PERRY, JACOB PERRY, UTAHNA PERRY, CHRISTINA PETERSEN, GREGG PETERSEN, JAMES PETERSEN, ROBERT PETERSEN, TRAVIS PETERSEN, WILLIAM PETERSEN, ALISA PETERSON, ANN PETERSON, ANNETTE PETERSON, BEVERLY PETERSON, BRENT PETERSON, CARYN PETERSON, DAVID PETERSON, DOUGLAS PETERSON, EMILY PETERSON, EMILY PETERSON, HARVEY PETERSON, JERRY PETERSON, JOHN PETERSON, JULIE PETERSON, KATIE PETERSON, KEVIN PETERSON, LARS PETERSON, LORENCE PETERSON, LUCIE PETERSON, MATHEW PETERSON, MICHAEL PETERSON, MICHAEL PETERSON, NORALEE PETERSON, NORALEE PETERSON, PAULINE PETERSON, RANDE PETERSON, ROBERT PETERSON, RYAN PETERSON, SCOTT PETERSON, STEVE PETERSON, TAMSEN PETERSON, THOMAS PETERSON, WALLACE PETERSON, DARRICK PETON, SPENCER PETT, JULIE PETTIT, ADAM PETTY, SHANE PEW, CHERI PEWTRESS, LEIGH PEZZICARA, TIFFANY PEZZULO, RICHARD PFAFF, JASON PFEIFER, HANS PFEIL, BRANDON PHELPS, SEAN PHELPS, MONICA PHELPS-ZAMBRANO, AUBREY PHILLIPS, BRIAN PHILLIPS, ERNEST PHILLIPS, JAN PHILLIPS, NATHAN PHILLIPS, RANDALL PHILLIPS, STEPHEN PHILLIPS, STEPHEN PHILLIPS, WILFORD PHILLIPS, AUDRA PHILPOT, CONNIE PICKETT, SHERI PIECUCH, MICHAEL PIEKARSKI, BRANDON PIERCE, PATRICK PIERCE, CHERYL PIERSON, MILES PIERSON, JOHN PIESTER, SYLVIA PIGGOTT, KENN PILCH, CASEY PILLING, ADAM PINALES, SASHA PINEGAR, MARK PINELLI, LAMAR PINKNEY, JAMES PINKSTON, MANUEL PINO, PETER PIOTTO, KARLA PIPER, BRIAN PIPKIN, STUART PIPPIN, TAWNA PIPPIN, CAMMIE PIQUET, CHRISTOPHER PIRONI, COURTNEY PITCHER, HEATHER PITTS, JOHN PITTS, RICHARD PITZAK, KENNETH PIXTON, ELIZABETH PIZAC, JESSICA PLATT, PATRICIA PLATTS, MARGARET PLAVOCOS, RYAN PLEWE, PAULINE PLOQUIN, CLIFFORD PLOWMAN, PORTIA PLUMB, EUGENE POBOL, WILLIAM POFF, SUSAN POLAKOFF SHAW, ALAN POLGAR, EDGAR POLGAR, JASON POLLAN, ANTHONY POLLINGTON, ALICIA POLLOCK, JEFFERY POLLOCK, RICK POLLOCK, WENDY POLLOCK, TASHA POMERLEAU, DAVID POND, JAY POND, KRISTIN POND, SCOTT POND, BENJAMIN POOLE, JOAN POOLE, KATRINA POPE, ANGELA PORTER, JILL PORTER, KAREN PORTER, KEVIN PORTER, TODD PORTER, MICHAEL POTTER, MIKE POTTER, SHANTA POTTER, THOMAS POTTER, TIFFANY POTTS, CLAIRE POTVIN, SIONE POUHA, AARON POULSEN, DENNIS POULSEN, EMILY POULSEN, MELANIE POULSEN, STEVEN POULSEN, CARL POULSON, JENNIFER POULSON, MARIE POULSON, AHSLEIGH POUND, ALAN POWELL, AMY POWELL, BENJAMIN POWELL, BURDETTE POWELL, CRYSTAL POWELL, DAVID POWELL, ELAINE POWELL, KIM POWELL, KIRK POWELL, LEWIS POWELL, ROBERT POWELL, RYAN POWELL, SUSAN POWELL, PETER PRADER, GRETCHEN PRATLEY, SUE PRATLEY, CASEY PRATT, WILLIAM PRATT, JOHN PRAZAK, RAYMOND PREECE, KRISTINA PRENTISS, HELEN PRESCOTT, AIMEE PRESTON, DAVID PRESTWICH, MICHAEL PRESTWICH, BETTY PRICE, CARMEL PRICE, GARRISON PRICE, LARRY PRICE, LAUREN PRICE, THOMAS PRICE, DEBORAH PRIDE, LINTON PRIESKORN, CATHY PRIESTNER-ALLINGER, GUILLERMO PRIETO, TIFFANY PRIMM, TONIA PRINCE, WAYLON PRINCE, ROBERT PRINE, DONALD PRITCHARD, LAUREN PRITCHARD, STACY PROBASCO, MARGARET PROBST, JON PROCTOR, KRISTEN PROCTOR, LYNNE PROCTOR, STACEY PROCTOR, THOMAS PROCTOR, PAIGE PROTHERO, CAROL PROWS, JOHN PROWS, JAMES PRUITT, TODD PRYOR, CHARLES PUGH, VIRGIL PUGSLEY, JOHN PULKRABEK, AMBER PULLEY, RYAN PULLEY, OWEN PULLIAM, STEVEN PULSIPHER, MARK PULVER, ANDREW PUNZAL, CATHERINE PURCELL, MAJA PURCELL, OFISI PUTUTAU, MICHAEL PYSNAK • **Q** • BRITTNEY QUAI, ANDREA QUATTRY, ALEXANDER QUERNA, TAMARA QUICK, ROBERT QUIGLEY, ISABEL QUILANTAN, TIFFANY QUILTER, JAYNA QUINN, JESSIE QUINN, LANA QUINN, SHAUNA QUINN, WILLIAM QUINN, PAULA QUINONEZ, RUBEN QUIROZ, DAVID QUITTNER • **R** • VICTORITA RAAEN, SUSAN RABIGER, LOREN RACICH, SARA RADAMUS, DALE RADECKI, ALAN RADMALL, ALAN RADMALL, DAVID RAFFERTY, ANDREA RAIFORD, JEAN RAKISITS, BRIAN RALPH, LORRAINE RALSTON, FRANCISCO RAMIREZ, GILBERT RAMIREZ, REINA RAMIREZ, ROBERTO RAMIREZ, ARTURO RAMOS, BRIAN RAMOS, SIDNEY RAND, KRISTINE RANDALL, STEPHEN RANDALL, TODD RANDALL, JEFFREY RANKIN, DONNA RANSOM, HYRUM RAPPLEYE, WILLIAM RAPPLEYE, CAROLYN RASMUS, HOLLY RASMUSSEN, LINDA RASMUSSEN, VERENA RASMUSSEN, WHITNIE RASMUSSEN. IAN RASSMAN, DANETTA RATCLIFFE, WILLIAM RATCLIFFE, PETRA RAUCH, ED RAUSE, PETER RAVEN, TERRI RAWDIN, ANGELA RAWLINGS, MAX RAWLINGS, LARRY RAY, MARGARET RAY, MARY RAYMOND, MELISSA RAYMOND, LOGAN READING, DAVID REAM, JARON REAY, ROBERT RECKIS, RANDY RECORD, JENNIFER REDD, JANICE REDDAWAY. PHILLIPS REDDEN, DANIEL REDDING, DAVID REDFEARN, AMANDA REDINGTON, AMANDA REDINGTON, MICHAEL REDINGTON, JON REDLINE, EDDIE REDMAN, EDITH REDMOND, JANICE REDMOND, DIANA REED, EVA REES, MICHAEL REES, TIFFANY REES, RICHARD REEVE, KARINA REEVES, RANDALL REEVES, JAMES REGIS, MATTHEW REHWALD, GREG REID, MICHAEL REID, SAMANTHA REID, SHELLY REIF, SUSAN REIFER, CHRIS REILLY, KELLY REIMSCHIISSE, TERESA REINHARDT, WILLIAM REMBACZ, MICHAEL REMILLARD, JENNIFER RENCHER, SHERI RENDON, SCOTT RENNER, NICHOLAS RENO, KURT REPANSHEK, PAUL REPPUCCI, DAREN RESCHKE, ANTHONY REYES, LEO REYES, ROSENDO REYES, RUTH REYES, CRISTINA REYNAGA, DAVID REYNAGA, JENNIFER REYNOLDS, KERRY REYNOLDS, LEONARD REYNOLDS, SHANE REYNOLDS, STEPHANIE REYNOLDS, TIMOTHY REYNOLDS, VANESSA REYNOLDS, WAYNE REYNOLDS, STEPHANIE RHEAD, LESLIE RHINEHART, ANDREW RHODES, KIRK RHODES, LONNY RHODES, LORINN RHODES, MARSHA RHODES, LOUIS RICCI, JODI RICE, MICHAEL RICE, CATHRYNE RICHARDS, CHARLES RICHARDS, CLARK RICHARDS, HOLLEY RICHARDS, MARILYN RICHARDS, THOMAS RICHARDS, TIMOTHY RICHARDS, WILLIAM RICHARDS, HEIDI RICHARDSON, MARK RICHARDSON, PAUL RICHARDSON, ROBERT RICHARDSON, TERENCE RICHINS, FIONA RICHMOND, ENRICO RICHTER, CODY RICKS, LAURA RICKS, CHRISTIAN RIDDELL, DAVID RIDLEY, ELIZABETH RIDLEY, SARAH RIGBY, BRIAN RIGGS, AMELIA RILEY, DUSTON RILEY, LEXIE RILEY, MITCHELL RILEY, PATRICIA RILEY, RENEE RILEY-CHRISTENSEN, BERND RILK, ERIKA RINGER, LESLIE RINK, RAUL RIOS, JULIA RIPLEY, LESLIE RIPLEY, DAN RISCH, PAMELA RITCHIE, BRANDON RITTER, MARK RITTER, SHELLI RITTER, GUILLERMO RIVAS, LISA RIVAS, GEORGE RIVERA, MARTIN RIZER, CECIL ROACH, JAY ROBB, ADDELINE ROBBINS, HARVEY ROBBINS, SHARYN ROBBINS, TAYLOR ROBBINS, KECIA ROBERG, CORRINE ROBERGE, DALE ROBERGE, JEANETTE ROBERGE, BRANDON ROBERTS, CHERI ROBERTS, DAVID ROBERTS, HARRY ROBERTS, JIMMY ROBERTS, LISA ROBERTS, MINDY ROBERTS, PATRICIA ROBERTS, STEFANIE ROBERTS, DAVID ROBERTSON, JACQUALYON ROBERTSON, JOSHUA ROBERTSON, VERRETTA ROBERTSON, WESLEY ROBERTSON, JENNIFER ROBINS, RICHARD ROBINS, BEN ROBINSON, BRENDA ROBINSON, CASSANDRA ROBINSON, EDWARD ROBINSON, ELISHA ROBINSON, EMILY ROBINSON, GAYLE ROBINSON, JESSICA ROBINSON, MARK ROBINSON, NATHAN ROBINSON, PATRICIA ROBINSON, RICHARD ROBINSON, BARRY ROBISON, SCOTT ROBISON, DOUGLAS ROBSON, TRAVIS ROBSON, CHRISTINA ROCK, MICHAEL RODAK, CESAR RAUL RODARTE, DAN RODEN, JOHN RODERICK, NATALIE RODGERS, STEVEN RODGERS, JARED RODMAN, ROBERT RODMAN, AARON RODRIGUEZ, ALBERTO RODRIGUEZ, CHERIE RODRIGUEZ, CYNTHIA RODRIGUEZ, DENNIS RODRIGUEZ, HORACIO RODRIGUEZ, ROBERT RODRIGUEZ, SANTIAGO RODRIGUEZ, LOURDES RODRIGUEZ COOKE, BEATRIZ RODRIGUEZ-HE, TERRANCE ROEDELL, TONY ROEDER, CARL ROEPKE, MARCIA ROESBERRY, BOONE ROGERS, JOHN ROGERS, RANDAL ROGERS, TIMOTHY ROGERS, WILLIAM ROGERS, NATHAN ROHLING, BRIAN ROHLOFF, MIGUEL ROJAS, FRANK ROLDAN, WILLIAM ROLLER, DOUG ROLLINS, CRISTIAN ROMAN, TIM ROMAS, MANDY ROMERO, MITT ROMNEY, VINCENT ROMNEY, JUAN ROMO, GAYLE ROMOSER, ERIC ROMSEY, MARK ROONEY, CHRISTOPHER ROOT, STEVEN ROOT, KEVIN ROPER, GONZALO ROSAS, CELESTE ROSELL, RUTH ROSEWARNE, CHERYL ROSS, KELLY ROSS, NANCI ROSS, TERRY ROSS, AMY ROSZMANN, KONRAD ROTERMUND, DANIELLE ROTHE, PATRICIA ROTHERMICH, PAUL ROUNDY, LAUREN ROUTH, STANFORD ROVIG, LANCE ROWE, JULIA ROWELL, MURIEL ROWELL, LINDSAY ROWLES, BRENT ROWLEY, BRUCE ROWLEY, ELISE ROWLEY, JASON ROWLEY, KEVIN ROWLEY, KEVIN ROWLEY, STEPHEN ROWLEY, ERIC ROY, JACK ROYBAL, TERESA ROYCE, REBECCA ROYLANCE, YEZID RUBIO, DIETER RUEHLE, GILBERT RUIZ, LARRY RULON, RENEE RUMP, JAIME RUPERT, RONALD RUPERT, JULIA RUPKALVIS, KENNETH RUPPEL, RACHEL RUSBARSKY, CHARLES RUSHING, CHARLES RUSSELL, CHRISTIAN RUSSELL, JAMES RUSSELL, OSCAR RUSSELL, TODD RUTLEDGE, ANDREW RUTTER, DENISE RYAN, KATHLEEN RYAN, SHELLY RYAN, CORY RYDMAN, REBECCA RYSER • **S** • NADINE SAAGER, MATTHEW SABASTEANSKI, KIRBY SABET, DANIEL SACHSE, DEBBIE SACKIE, CHRISTINA SADLER, STEPHEN SADLER, SAMUEL SAEVA, LYNA SAFFELL, STEPHEN SAGERS, AMEL SAIED, REBECCA SAIZ, YUKI SAKUMA, PATRICK SALANDI, DAVID SALCIDO, WILLY SALINAS, MITCHELL SALING, DERRICK SALISBURY, SARA SALISBURY, CHAD SALMELA, JODIE SALMON, MAGALI SALOMON, ROBERT SALOSKI, HEATHER SALTER, ROBERT SALTZGIVER, WAYNE SALTZGIVER, KOURTNEY SALVATORI, BONNIE SAMPSON, BONNIE SAMPSON, MICHAEL SAMPSON, RALPH SAMPSON, CARMEN SAMUELSON, VINOD SANATHRA, KEITH SANBORN, LINDA SANBORN, ADOLPH SANCHEZ, ERIC SANCHEZ, MICHAEL SANCHEZ, SHASTA SANCHEZ, JOHN SANDBERG, HEATHER SANDERS, JEFF SANDERS, JIMMY SANDERS, KATHRYN SANDERS, NATHANIEL SANDERS, RHODA SANDERS, ROBERT SANDERS, TYLER SANDERS, MARK SANDERSON, LATONYA SANDLES, SABRINA SANDRY, RICHARD SANDS, LARS SANDSTROM, DALE SANDUSKY, BEVERLY SANTAMARIA, ROBERT SANTHOLZER, NATILY SANTOS, ELI SAPP, ROBERTO SARABIA, NICHOLAS SARGENT, NEIL SARIN, NARINE SARKISSIAN, NICHOLAS SARRIS, MARILYN SARZYNSKI, RICHARD SARZYNSKI, MEGAN SATHER, WENDY SATHER, EDUARDO SAUCEDO III, DANIEL SAUCIER, BRYAN SAUNDERS, JAMES SAUNDERS, NICOLE SAUNDERS, RICK SAUNDERS, SELENE SAUNDERS, LUCAS SAURES, CLAUDE SAUTER, JENNIFER SAVAGE, DANIEL SAVANT, JAVIER SAVEDRA, KONSTANTIN SAVICH, MICHAEL SAVITT, KIMBERLY SAWTELLE, CAMERON SAWYER, LAMAR SAYER, KEITH SAYERS, OMAR SAYIED, CLYDE SAYLER, MARY SCHAELLING, CAROL SCHAFF, GREGORY CHARLES SCHAFFER, LAURA SCHAFFER, BARBARA SCHAMEL, BENJAMIN SCHAPIRO JR, JOSEPH SCHEELE, NORMA SCHEELE, LINDY SCHELIN, MARK SCHELIN, JOEL SCHELINSKI, KRISTINE SCHELLENBERG, LIESL SCHERNTHANNER, JAMES SCHICKEL, URS SCHIENDORFER, ERIC SCHIFF, SHANNON SCHIFFGEN, GRAHAM SCHILDMEYER, MATT SCHILLER, WADE SCHILLO, MICHAEL SCHIML, TODD SCHIRMAN, MATTHEW SCHLAMBERGER, JAMES SCHLETER, ANDREA SCHMIDT, BETH SCHMIDT, DANIEL SCHMIDT, KEVIN SCHMIDT, LEONARD SCHMIDT, SHANNON SCHMIDT, WILLIAM SCHMITTEL, RYAN SCHMITZ, SIMONE SCHMUDDE, CHARLES SCHNETZLER, ROBERT SCHOCKER, LISA SCHOENEBERG, PAUL SCHOLZ, HARRY SCHOUTEN, KRISTI SCHRIEBER, ERIC SCHROEDER, BRADY SCHUCK, MARTIN SCHUEREN, JULIE SCHULDT, ALBERT SCHULTZ, JILL SCHUMACHER, MARK SCHUMACHER, BRYAN SCHUTZ, MORONI SCHWAB, RICHARD SCHWAB, CAROLYN SCHWAN, JACKIE SCHWARTZ, KERRY SCHWARTZ, WILLIAM SCHWARTZ, GEORGE SCHWEIGERT, SHELLY SCHWEIGERT, FRANCIS SCHWEITZER, HEATHER SCHWENDIMAN, JEFF SCHWENDIMAN, LORI SCHWILLING, KARL SCHWOLOW, ADAM SCOTT, BRYAN SCOTT, CARRIE SCOTT, GINGER SCOTT, GREG SCOTT, KYLI SCOTT, RICHARD SEALS, ANGELA SEAMONS, TEDI SEARLE, GALE SEARS, HENRY SEARS, JEFFREY SEARS, DEBRA SEAY, GAIL SEAY, MEAGAN SEAY, SANDRA SEBBANE, SANTIAGO SEDACA, ULF SEEHASE, ANDREW SEELEY, BENJAMIN SEELEY, SCOTT SEELY, ADNAN SEHOVIC, GREG SEIBOLD, NATHAN SEIDLE, MARC SEITZ, TRACY SEITZ, GREGORY SEKRETA, DRAKE SELF, ERIC SELLERS, ALBERT SEMADENI, MAFATINI SEMEII, SIMONE SEPOLVEDA-TO, SCOTT SEPPICH, RICHARD SEPTON, MARY SEPULVEDA, DAVID SERRANO, MARC SERRECCHIA, JONATHAN SERXNER, MARK SESSIONS, KRIS SEVERSON, TODD SEVERSON, JOE SEWARD, ROBERT SHABERT, PEGGY SHADEL, KARLA SHAFFER, SALLY SHAFFER, JENNIFER SHAH, NIKESH SHAH, CYNDI SHALHOUB, ALISA SHANK, JOHN SHANK, JOHN SHANK, LAWRENCE SHANK, RUSSELL SHANNON, LEON SHAPOSHNIKOV, KEVIN SHARKEY, ALAN SHARP, ERIC SHARP, LESLIE SHARP, STEPHEN SHARP, TYLER SHARP, PAUL SHARWELL, ZIANIBETH SHATTUCK-OWEN, FRED SHAVERS, ALAN SHAW, CAROLINE SHAW, GORDON SHAW, JAMIE SHAW, LENI SHAW, VICTOR

SHAW, WILLIAM SHAW, MARY SHEA, MICHAEL SHEA, JAMES SHEEHE, MARK SHEETS, KIMBERLY SHEFFIELD, GARY SHEIDE, TREVOR SHELDON, CHAD SHELLEY, TIMOTHY SHELSEA, DELMER SHELTON, JOSHUA SHELTON, JUSTIN SHELTON, MARIA SHELTON, FRANKIE SHEPHERD, LORI SHEPHERD, PETER SHEPHERD, SHILO SHEPHERD, DAVID SHER, BRETT SHERMAN, CYNTHIA SHERMAN, FRANCIS SHERMAN, GABRIEL SHERMAN, CRAIG SHERRER, ELIZABETH SHERRY, RYAN SHERWOOD, ADAM SHILAND, TYLER SHIMIZU, PETER SHINGLEDECKE, DONALD SHIPLEY, JOSHUA SHIRE, ANDREW SHIRLEY, MITCHELL SHIRLEY, MELVIN SHIVERS, JUDY SHOEMAKER, ALLEN SHORT, ALLEN SHORT, JEREMY SHOVAN, SUSAN SHREEVE, SHANE SHRUTLIFF, ERIKA SHUBIN, SCOTT SHUBIN, JASON SHUMAKER, BRANT SICHKO, JEREMY SIDES, MIKE SIEBER, STEPHEN SIEGEL, RICHARD SIEMERS, SANDRA SIFUENTES, BETHANY SIGEL, ANDREAS SIGURDSSON, BERGAN SILLITO, SHELI SILLITO, FELICIA SILVA, WANDA SILVER, KENNETH SILVERBERG, C CALEB SILVEY, ANN SIMMONS, COBIE SIMMONS, GEOFFREY SIMMONS, LINDA SIMMONS, VAN SIMMONS, ISABEL SIMOES, JOLENE SIMON, JONATHAN SIMON, STEPHEN SIMON, MICHAEL SIMONE, AMBER SIMONS, DAN SIMONS, PAUL SIMONS, HEATHER SIMONSEN, PAIGE SIMONSON, JENNIFER SIMPSON, MELISSA SIMPSON, PETER SIMPSON, SANDRA SIMPSON, SARAH SIMPSON, CORDELL SIMS, NOLAN SIMS, RUBY SINCLAIR, JOHN SINDELAR, DAVID SINGER, LOGAN SISAM, ROBYNN SISAM, LISA SISNEROZ, JARED SKELTON, LYNN SKENE, MICHAEL SKENZICH, DOUGLAS SKORDAS, MATTHEW SLACK, MICHAEL SLADE, DOUGLAS SLATER, GENE SLATER, STEPHANIE SLATER, SHAUN SLEEPER, MICHAEL SLINGER, JENNIFER SLOAN, MITCHEL SLOAN, DAVID SMART, HOWARD SMART, RICHARD SMART, CAROL SMEDLEY, LESLIE SMIDDY, AMANDA SMITH, AMY SMITH, ANGELA SMITH, BETTINA SMITH, BLAIR SMITH, BRIAN SMITH, BRODIE SMITH, CAMERON SMITH, COLLEEN SMITH, CONSTANCE SMITH, DANIEL SMITH, DANIEL SMITH, DAVID SMITH, DOROTHY SMITH, DOUGLAS SMITH, GREG SMITH, HOWARD SMITH, JAMI SMITH, JANIE SMITH, JOSEPH SMITH, JOSHUA SMITH, KARIN SMITH, KEVIN SMITH, KONI SMITH, KRISTIE SMITH, LOREN SMITH, MICHAEL SMITH, NANCY SMITH, NATHAN SMITH, PAMELA SMITH, PATRICIA SMITH, PATRICK SMITH, PATSY SMITH, PATSY SMITH, PAUL SMITH, PAUL SMITH, REED SMITH, RICK SMITH, ROD SMITH, ROLAND SMITH, SCOTT SMITH, SCOTT SMITH, STEVEN SMITH, SUSAN SMITH, TERRY SMITH, ZACH SMITH, LAURA SNARR, MARSHALL SNARR, LEE SNEDAKER, MARSHALL SNEDAKER, KRISTIN SNOW, MATTHEW SNOW, PAUL SNOW, RICHARD SNOW, SPENCER SNOW, ELIZABETH SNYDER, ERICH SNYDER, RICHARD SNYDER, ROBERT SNYDER, RODNEY SNYDER, JON SODERSTROM, SHERI SOHM, GAY SOHNREY, SHAWN SOLBERG, MARIA SOLOMON, MARK SOLUM, JASON SOMERS, CHRIS SOMERVILLE, LYNN SOMERVILLE, EDWARD SOMMERS, MARK SONGER, GORDON SOPER, DEBRA SOPHER, PETER SORCKOFF, CAMERON SORENSEN, CHARLES SORENSEN, ERIC SORENSEN, HILLARY SORENSEN, HOWARD SORENSEN, JENNIFER SORENSEN, JENNIFER SORENSEN, JESSICA SORENSEN, KARL SORENSEN, MAREN SORENSEN, SANDY SORENSEN, TENNILLE SORENSEN, DANIEL SORENSON, DIANE SORENSON, MARK SORENSON, KENNETH SORRENTINO, CARLOS SOSA, BRIGETTE SOSKIN, ABEL SOTELO, ELLENEY SOTER, HIAM SOUEIDI, JAKE SOUTHWORTH, SAMUEL SOUTHWORTH, KATHERYN SPAFFORD, SHAWN SPALDING, DEVIN SPANN, JOHANN SPARBER, RYAN SPARKS, GLORIA SPEARS, CHRISTINE SPENCER, DARREN SPENCER, MATTHEW SPENCER, MELISSA SPENCER, MICHAEL SPENCER, SYDNI SPENCER, ROBIN SPERA, NOLA SPICER, TIMOTHY SPIER, RONNIE SPIVEY, NANCY SPOONER, PATRICK SPORLEIN, KEVIN SPRAGUE, PETER SPRANSY, ROBERT SPRINGMEYER, SHERRY SPURLIN, LYNNE SPURWAY-YOST, GAYLEN SQUIRE, TIMOTHY SQUIRE, LEE ST. ONGE, RANDAL STABLER, JEFF STACK, PATRICK STACK, ELDON STAHL, KENNETH STAHL, EMILY STAHR, ROGER STAIR, STEVEN STAKER, JEFFREY STAMBAUGH, JAMES STANER, JOHN STANFIELD, JUDY STANFIELD, JUDY STANGER, LEESA STANSELL, ANNE-GRETHE STARHEIM, DAVID STARK, BRENDA STARR, TIMOTHY STARR, AUDREY STAUFFER, DORA STAUFFER, DORA STAUFFER, EMILY STAUFFER, JENNIFER STAVROS, DAVID STEADMAN, LINDON STEADMAN, PATRICK STEADMAN, BRIAN STEED, BRUCE STEED, DAVID STEED, WILLIAM STEEL, DWAYNE STEELE, EDNA STEELE, LEAH STEELE, TIMOTHY STEELE, MARY STEER, DOROTHY STEFANICH, MICHAEL STEHLE, JON STEIN, NANCY STEIN, STEPHANNE STEINHOFF, CHRISTINA STENFORS-STARK, PAUL STENOIEN, CRAIG STEPHENS, DERRICK STEPHENS, KENT STEPHENS, LARRY STEPHENSON, SANDRA STEPHENSON, ROBIN STEPS-KROLL, RONI STERN, BRETT STERRETT, KENNETH STERZER, ALEXA STEVENS, MICHELLE STEVENS, SANDRA STEVENS, ANNIE STEVENSON, FRANKLIN STEVENSON, GREGORY STEVENSON, MARK STEVENSON, MONT STEVENSON, STEVEN STEVENSON, TONY STEVENSON, GRAEME STEVERSON, BEVERLY STEWARD, BRIAN STEWART, DAVID STEWART, GARRY STEWART, JEFFREY STEWART, THOMAS STEWART, VICTORIA STEWART, WAYNE STEWART, JEROME STILLE, CAROLYN STINEMATES, CHARLES STINNETT, JACQUELINE STINNETT, DARREN STIRLAND, CHERIE STIRLING, DONALD STIRLING, JAY STIRLING, DAVID STITCHER, BRENT STODDARD, JON STODDARD, JUSTIN STODDARD, KATHRYN STODDARD, RALPH STOECKLI, JOSEPH STOGNER, CALEB STOKER, PHILLIP STOKES, RACHEL STOKES, STEVEN STOKES, JACOB STOLK, PETE STOLL, HALLIE STOLLER, DUSTIN STONE, MEREDITH STONE, MICHAEL STONE, MICHAEL STONE, KEVIN STONER, DAVID STONEY, DANIEL STORMONT, KELLIE STORMS, JENNIFER STORRER, RYAN STOSICH, DAVID STOTLAR, LAURA STOTT, DAWN STOUT, PAUL STOUT, VIRGINIA STOUT, NATHAN STOWELL, DONAVON STRAIN, JOHN STRANSKY, RACHEL STRATE, DANIEL STRATTON, WENDITH STRATTON, AMANDA STREAMS, ROBERT STREBEL, JAMES STRICK, RYAN STRINGFELLOW, ALESHA STRINGHAM, CHERISE STRINGHAM, KIRSTEN STRINGHAM, KIMBERLY STROMNESS, ALEXANDRA STROMVALL, BECKY STRONG, CODY STRONG, GARY STRONG, KAREN STRONG, TAMI STRONG, JUDD STROUD, MARIE STROYLS, MICHAEL STRUHS, CHRISTOPHER STUARD, JAMES STUART, JEFFREY STUART, PAMELA STUART, DANIEL STUBBS, RONALD STUCKI, TAMI STUMPF, DANIEL STUNKEL, DANIEL SUAREZ, DANIEL SUAREZ, BRIAN SUCHER, YOSHIKO SUDA, DAVID SUGDEN, CONNIE SUGIYAMA, TONY SUICH, LYNN SUKSDORF, BENSON SULIT, BILL SULLIVAN, CHRISTOPHER SULLIVAN, GLENN SULLIVAN, LAWRENCE SULLIVAN, MARK SULLIVAN, RUTH SULLIVAN, SANDY SUMMER, ANNETTE SUMMERS, DAVID SUMMERS, SUSAN SUMMERS, WILLIAM SUNDERMAN, NORMAN SUTTLES, MATTHEW SUTTON, ROBERT SUTTON, TY SUTTON, ERIC SWAIN, TARA SWAIN, STACY SWAINSTON, CHARLES SWALLOW, ROSEMARIE SWANEY, EARL SWANSON, GEORGE SWANSON, SID SWANSON, DANIELLE SWAPP, KELLY SWEAT, LEONA SWEDENHSELM, MAUREEN SWEENEY, PATRICK SWEENEY, CATHERINE SWEET, JARED SWEET, ALYSSA SWEETEN, CHRISTOPHER SWEETEN, JAMES SWEETEN, RACHEL SWEETOW, JAMES SWENSEN, JAMES SWENSEN, COLETA SWENSON, KRISTY SWENSON, MARK SWENSON, THOMAS SWENSON, KELLIE SWIATOCHA, EDWARD SYGUDA, SHERYL SYMONS, PAUL SYNOWIEC, KRISTEN SYPHUS, REBECCA SZMUKLER • **T** • PHILLIP TABIA, NORMA TABISH, LINDA TAFT, LOUIS TAGGART, TRACY TAGGART, TRACY TAGGART, STUART TAGUE, CETUS TAHL, SONJA TAKAC, GREGORY TALBERT, DAVID TALBOT, YVONNA TALERMO, NAITASIRA TALI, CHERI TALKINGTON, GLENN TANIS, PATRIA TANIS, JESSICA TANNER, PEGGY TANNER, TIM TANNER, KATHRYN TAPIA, THOMAS TARDY, LOUISE TARR, MASAHIKO TASAKI, BETHANY TATE, JAMIE TATE, MICHAEL TATE, KENNETH TAUA, PAULINE TAUTU, JENNIFER TAVARES, KIM TAYLER, AMY TAYLOR, ANDREW TAYLOR, BRETT TAYLOR, CALVIN TAYLOR, CHRISTA TAYLOR, ELISSA TAYLOR, GLENN TAYLOR, JASON TAYLOR, JENNIFER TAYLOR, JENNIFER TAYLOR, JERRY TAYLOR, JOHNNY TAYLOR, MARY TAYLOR, MICHAEL TAYLOR, MICHELLE TAYLOR, ROBERT TAYLOR, SHERILYN TAYLOR, STACY TAYLOR, TERRY TAYLOR, THOMAS TAYLOR, TRACY TAYLOR, TRAVIS TAYLOR, WILLIAM TAYLOR, KEVIN TEA, JOHN TEBALDI, DARYL TEEPLES, DARYL TEEPLES, ELIZABETH TEETER, GILBERT TENEN, MATTHIAS TENER, JUAN TERRIQUEZ, BEN TERRY, KEVIN TERRY, STEVE TERRY, STEVEN TERRY, BONNIE TEVIS, JENNIFER THACKER, TROY THACKER, AMY THALER, BRUCE THARALDSON, NATHAN THATCHER, JOHN THAYER, JOHN THAYER II, ERIKA THEW, AARON THOMAS, ALISHA THOMAS, ANGELIQUE THOMAS, BRUCE THOMAS, C THOMAS, DEBORAH THOMAS, DEBRA THOMAS, DENNIS THOMAS, DUSTIN THOMAS, DUSTIN THOMAS, GRANT THOMAS, JEN THOMAS, JENNIFER THOMAS, JULIAN THOMAS, KEITH THOMAS, MARJORY THOMAS, MARK THOMAS, MARK THOMAS, MORGAN THOMAS, NICHOLAS THOMAS, RICHARD THOMAS, SANDRA THOMAS, STEPHEN THOMAS, JAMES THOMASON, KENNETH THOMASON, NICK THOMETZ, ANDREW THOMPSON, BRENT THOMPSON, BRETT THOMPSON, BRIAN THOMPSON, CHANDRA THOMPSON, CLOYD THOMPSON, DENNIS THOMPSON, JOYCE THOMPSON, KEITH THOMPSON, KELLENE THOMPSON, MCSEAN THOMPSON, NATALIE THOMPSON, PAMELA THOMPSON, RUSSELL THOMPSON, SHERRY THOMPSON, TREVOR THOMPSON, V KEITH THOMPSON, VIRGIL THOMPSON, DANIEL THOMSON, DOUGLAS THOMSON, ZACHARY THOMSON, JOHAN THOREN, LARS THORN, RICHARD THORNBERRY, ANNE THORNBURY, DEVAN THORNE, MATT THORNE, NICK THORNE, RICHARD THORNTON, BRENDA THORPE, JOHN THRASHER, NATHAN THURGOOD, TAMARA TIALAVEA, KENT TIBBITTS, LISA TIBBITTS, KARIN TIDGEWELL, BEN TIDSWELL, COREY TIDWELL, DEIDRE TIDWELL, RUSSELL TIDWELL, ANN TIERNEY, RODNEY TIETSORT, MARCIE TIJERINA, INGUNN TILLERAAS, DONNA TILLERY, LOU TILLOTSON, SARIAH TILLOTSON, KENNETH TIMMS, NATHAN TIMMS, STEVEN TINGEY, MICHAEL TINSLEY, BOYD TIPPETTS, JASON TIPPETTS, JACKSON TISHER, PHILIP TISOVEC, JAMIE TITENSOR, BRUCE T'KACH, STEPHANIE TOBEY, ESTHER TODD, LINUS TOLAND, JIMMY TOLBERT, KAREN TOLBOE, MCKAY TOLBOE, ANGELA TOLER, JONATHAN TOLER, DONNA TOLES, MORTEN TOLLEFSEN, VIOLA TOLLIS, ERIN TOLMAN, NATHAN TOLMAN, WINIFRED TOMAN, SERGEI TOMIN, MARTIN TOMLIN, JOHN TOMLISON, ROGER TOMSCHIN, JASON TONIOLI, JEFFORY TOONE, KATHRYN TOONE, RYAN TOONE, SHAWN TORESDAHL, JUSTIN TOTH, BENJAMIN TOWERS, BRANDON TOWNER, CHARLES TOWNER, SCOTT TRACY, KAREN TRAMEL, NATE TRAUNTVEIN, GILBERT TRAVERS, ERIN TREACY, JAMES TREMEL, DARREN TRENCHER, DEANNA TRENCHER, VENNA TREPASSO, BILLY TRESNER, JOHN TRIANTAFYLLO, NORMAN TRIBBETT, RICH TRIPP, NORMAN TROSETH, ROBORT TROWBRIDGE, TERESA TROYER, TERRY TRUJILLO, ROBYN TRUMAN, HAI SAM PHI TRUONG, WILLIAM TRUPPE, CRAIG TRUSKEY, RANESSA TSINNIJINNIE, JESSICA TSOSIE, DEBORAH TSUCHIDA, TOSHIO TSURUNAGA, DANIEL TUBBS, ELIZABETH TUBBS, DONALD TUCKER, MARY TUCKER, MIKE TUCKER, ROBERT TUCKER, JESS TUCKETT, CANDICE TUELLER, SARAH TUFF, SEAN TUITE, K TULLIS, SHAUN TULLIS, TRICIA TULLOCH, FRANCIS TULLY, FRANK TUMAN, ANDREW TURCSANSKI, ROBERT TURGEON, DEMIL TURGESON, DEREK TURLEY, RYAN TURMAN, ANNETTE TURNER, CAROL TURNER, DORENE TURNER, GARY TURNER, KATHLEEN TURNER, KATHLEEN TURNER, STEPHANIE TURNER, TIMOTHEE TURNER, WADE TURNER, MAX TURNIER, BOB TUTTLE, DONNA TUVESON, EVA TWARDOKENS, LELAND TWITCHELL, TREVOR TWITCHELL, DLORAH TYLER, RICHARD TYLER, KEVIN TYO, JACQUELINE TYSON • **U** • RYAN UDELL, JOHN UDSETH, CHRISTOPHER UIGAESE, LINCOLN ULMER, GEORGE ULRICH, MARIE JINKY UMALI, COREY UNGER, TERESA UPTON, HOLLY URICK, MCCOY USELMAN, CRAIG UTIAN, DEAN UTIAN, TAKAYUKI UTSUNOMIYA • **V** • ELYSE VACCARO, GEORGE VAIELAND, LINDA VAILE, TEVITA VAKALAHI, ANTHONY VALCIC, ELIZABETH VALDEZ, PATRICK VALDEZ, GINA VALENCIA, RONNIE VALENCIA, BRANDON VALENTINE, ELMER VALLEJOS, RICHARD VALLEJOS, DIRK VAN ADRIGHEM, LAWRENCE VAN ATTA, EMILY VAN CAMP, JOEL VAN CAMPEN, SETH VAN COTT, JAN VAN DE ROEMER, JOHN VAN DER MEYDEN, GLENN VAN ORNUM, MICHAEL VANASSA, TARA VANATTA, DAVID VANBROCKLIN, ERIC VANBROCKLIN, LINDSAY VANBROCKLIN, MISTI VANBUSKIRK, MORGAN VANCE, MORGAN VANCE, BRIAN VANDENHOGEN, SARAH VANDERHOEF, AUBREY VANDERLINDEN, MICHAEL VANDERLINDEN, STEPHEN VANDERWALL, GREGORY VANDYKE, MARVIN VANN, JULIE VANO, ROBERT VANSOOLEN, ALONZO VANTASSELL, TRAVIS VANTASSELL, KAREN VARDENY, ERICKA VARGAS, JIMMY JR VARN, DARREN VAUGHAN, MICHAEL VAUGHAN, MARCHERIE VAZQUEZ, ADRIAN VELLINGA, JEFFREY VENEZIA, NICHOLAS VERHOEF, RICHARD VERNON, JILL VERON, RICHARD VERZANI, ROBIN VIAVANT, PAUL VIBERT, TERRY VICEK, DANIEL VIGANSKY, CAMILLE VIGIL, EUREKA VIGIL, JEFFREY VILARDI, DENISE VILLA, RAMON VILLARREAL, CONNIE VINCENT, RYAN VINCENT, SCOTT VINSON, MARITA VISELLI, TONY VITRANO, CHARLES VOGHELL, SHARKA VOKEL, MARTY VOLLA, PAUL VOLLSTEDT, NANCY VOLMER, JEFFREY VOLMRICH, GEORGE VON HOLTZ JR, KRISTI VON NIEDERHAUSER, DAROUNSAVAT VONGSAVATH, KARL VONNIEDERHAU, MARGARET VOS, CARL VOYLES, HENK VREDEVELD, JAN VREELING, GERALDINE VYBIRAL • **W** • JENNIE WACH, WENDY WACHTER, CLINT WADDELL, JACOB WADE, LUCIA WADE, STEPHEN WADE, BRIAN WADSWORTH, JENNIFER WAGENBACH, ROBERT WAGER, JOAN WAGGONER, JAN WAGNER, NICHOLAS WAGNER, PATRICK WAGNER, RICHARD WAGNER, PAUL WAIBEL, AMBER WALBECK, KEVIN WALD, ADIA WALDBURGER, PAUL WALDRON, GREGORY WALKENHORST, CHRISTIN WALKER, DANA WALKER, HARRY WALKER, JAMES WALKER, JASON WALKER, JOANNE WALKER, KAYLA WALKER, KYLE WALKER, LOUISE WALKER, MARK WALKER, MICHELLE WALKER, RAGAN WALKER, RYAN WALKER, THOMAS WALKER, DALE WALKOWSKI, ANNE WALL, ELLERY WALLACE, KENDRA WALLACE, LISA WALLACE, VINCENT WALLACE, DANIEL WALLENBERG, BRIAN WALSH, DONAL WALSH, LORAN WALSH, TREVOR WALSH, BOB WALTERS, DARLENE WALTERS, WARREN WALTERS, KENNETH WALTHER, RUTH WALTHER, JOHN WALTI, SHAWN WALTON, STANLEY WALTON, TERESE WALTON, MELISSA WAMSLEY, BILLY WANG, VIVIAN WANG, RAY WANLASS, RICHARD WANNINGER, DENNIS WANSOR, CHARLES WARD, DAVID WARD, DONNA WARD, EUGENE WARD, WESTON WARD, BEN WARDEN, BRIAN WARDEN, DONALD WARDLE, LISA WARDLE, KARIN WARE, WANDA WARE, WARREN WARE, RENAE WARNE, CLINTON WARNER, ERIC WARNER, GREGORY WARNER, KEITH WARNER, MATTHEW WARNER, MATTHEW WARNER, AMY WARNICK, CLARK WARNICK, MARC WARREN, DOUGLAS WASHINGTON, SHERRY WASSERMAN, JAMES WATANABE, CHELSEA WATEN, TIMOTHY WATERLYN, BRETT WATERMAN, JOE WATERS, JULIE WATERS, ALEISHA WATKINS, KERRY WATKINS, STEVEN WATKINS, TRES WATKINS, VANESSA WATKINS, JUSTIN WATSABAUGH, AARON WATSON, BENJAMIN WATSON, JULIE WATSON, LEILAH WATSON, NATHANAEL WATSON, TERRY WATSON, JEFF WATTERS, CARY WATTERSON, JASON WATTERSON, LELAND WATTS, WENDI WATTS, ALAN WAXMAN, JERRY WAY, STEPHEN WAYMAN, BRUCE WEARDA, KAREN WEAVER, VENIS WEAVER, CATHERINE WEBB, DAVINA WEBB, JAMES WEBB, JIM WEBB, KEVIN WEBB, MARGARET WEBB, REBECCA WEBB, SEAN WEBB, SHEILA WEBB, JACK WEBB JR, BRANDIE WEBBER, ADAM WEBER, ASHLEY WEBER, BENJAMIN WEBER, JUSTIN WEBER, STEPHEN WEBER, NANCY WEBSTER, ELIZABETH WEDGE, GREGORY WEEKS, KENDALL WEEKS, KRISTINA WEEKS, WILLIAM WEGESENT, KENNETH WEIDAUER, RYAN WEIERMAN, ROBERT WEIN, SUSAN WEINGARDT, KELLY WEINHARDT, JEFFREY WEINMEISTER, BRYCE WEIR, JULIE WEIR, MARY WEIR, RYAN WEIR, MICHAEL WEISER, ROBERT WEISFELD, RACHEL WEISHAAR, JUSTIN WEISS, TIM WEISS, ADAM WEITZELL, BRANDON WELCH, ERIN WELCH, ROSS WELCH, BRADFORD WELLER, KEVIN WELLS, TERRI WELLS, STEPHEN WELSH, AMY WELTER, BRIAN WENTE, MARIE WENTZ, FRANCIS WERNER, STEVEN WERTALIK, DAVID WESCOTT, GLENN WEST, JASON WEST, KRISTOFFER WEST, THOMAS WEST, ANTONIO WESTBROOKS, THOMAS WESTENBURG, ALAN WESTENSKOW, AMBER WESTENSKOW, SUSAN WESTERGARD, ALISON WEST-SCARPELLA, BRIAN WEST-SCARPELLA, MARTHA WETMORE, WARREN WETMORE, CLINTON WETZEL, CLIFFORD WHATCOTT, DEAN WHEADON, MIRANDA WHEADON, PETER WHEADON, DALE WHEALTON, JEFFREY WHEELER, LEWIS WHEELER, RONALD WHEELER, GEORGE WHELAN, CEDRIC WHETTEN, CHRISTOPHER WHETTEN, JESSE WHITAKER, SHAWN WHITAKER, AMY WHITE, AUDREY WHITE, ELIZABETH WHITE, JOHN WHITE, JOHN WHITE, KATHERINE WHITE, MEECHE WHITE, PAUL WHITE, PHILLIP WHITE, RICHARD WHITE, RUTH WHITE, RYAN WHITE, SPENCER WHITE, STACIE WHITE, STEPHEN WHITE, TYLER WHITE, WHITNEY WHITE, MARNIE WHITEAKER, JUSTIN WHITEAR, JOSEPH WHITEHEAD, WILLIAM WHITEHILL, WILLIAM WHITEHILL, LAURA WHITESIDES, MELANIE WHITESIDES, BRANDAN WHITING, KIP WHITING, JOHN WHITLOCK, ALLISON WHITMER, ELIZABETH WHITMIRE, TIFFANY WHITNEY, DELORES WHITTAKER, JOHN WHITTAKER, SHAUNI WHITTAKER, JASON WHITTLE, RANDY WHITTLE, KARA WHITTON, NICOLE WHYE, ALEXANDRIA WICHMAN, DAVID WICHOWSKI, ANGIE WICKHAM, LEON WIDDISON, CRAIG WIDMIER, NANCY WIEDEL, EHREN WIENER, AARON WIGGINS, ANNE WIGHT, GERALD WIGHT, PATRICIA WIGHTMAN, REBECCA WILBER, ADAM WILCOX, DIANE WILCOX, JOSHUA WILCOX, LAYNE WILCOX, NATE WILCOX, CHRIS WILDE, DARREN WILDE, JACQUELYN WILDE, ROBERT WILDE, ELIZABETH WILDER, WENDY WILEY, LEE WILKE, CURTIS WILKERSON, RITA WILKEY, JAIME WILKINS, JUSTIN WILKINS, ANDRIA WILKINSON, BRADLEY WILKINSON, BRIAN WILKINSON, CLYDE WILKINSON, LINDA WILKINSON, MICHAEL WILKINSON, DESICA WILLARD, PAGE WILLARD, R SCOTT WILLEY, ABBY WILLIAMS, ACIE WILLIAMS, ALBERT WILLIAMS, ANDY WILLIAMS, BRENT WILLIAMS, CARRIE WILLIAMS, CHRISTIAN WILLIAMS, CORAY WILLIAMS, CRAIG WILLIAMS, DIAN WILLIAMS, ELIZABETH WILLIAMS, ELIZABETH WILLIAMS, ERIN WILLIAMS, JAMES WILLIAMS, JEFF WILLIAMS, LEIGH WILLIAMS, LOUISE WILLIAMS, LYNN WILLIAMS, MARK WILLIAMS, MATTHEW WILLIAMS, MAX WILLIAMS, NATHAN WILLIAMS, PAUL WILLIAMS, PAUL WILLIAMS, PETER WILLIAMS, SHERRY WILLIAMS, SKIP WILLIAMS, STEPHEN WILLIAMS, JACOB WILLIAMSON, ADAM WILLIS, MARYLOU WILLIS, MARYLOU WILLIS, JOYCE WILLMORE, SCOTT WILLOUGHBY, AMANDA WILSON, BONNIE WILSON, CHRIS WILSON, ERIC WILSON, ERICK WILSON, GREGORY WILSON, ISAAC WILSON, JACK WILSON, JAMES WILSON, JAN WILSON, JENNIFER WILSON, JESSIE WILSON, KRISTINE WILSON, MARTIN WILSON, MATT WILSON, NATHAN WILSON, REGAN WILSON, RICHARD WILSON, SKIPPER WILSON, THOMAS WILSON, CHRISTOPHER WINCEK, LISA WIND, EDWIN WINDER, JANAE WINDER, JENNIFER WINDLEY, JEFF WINEGAR, MICHAEL WINGATE, STEPHANIE WINN, TIFFANY WINSLOW, PAUL WINSTON, CATHERINE WINTER, JEFFREY WINTERROTH, JONATHAN WINTERS, CHARLIE WINTZER, CINDY WINWARD, LEVI WINWARD, ANDREW WISE, MILLA WISECARVER, ALISA WISEMAN, EVELYN WISEMAN, MICHAEL WISOTZKE, THOMAS WITCZAK, THOMAS WITCZAK, BEN WITHERELL, LINDEE WITHERS, MICHAEL WITTE, ROBERT WITTEMORE, DAVID WOHLHUETER, FREDERIC WOJCIECHOWSKI, MICHAEL WOLF, GARY WOLFE, MARNIE WOLFGRAMM, JENNIFER WOLFSON, JENNIFER WOMACK, RACHEL WON, ANDREW WONDERS, MONIQUE WONG, ALAN WOOD, CHAD WOOD, CHARLES WOOD, DANIEL WOOD, GARY WOOD, HILARY WOOD, JORDAN WOOD, JUDY WOOD, KARL WOOD, LEO WOOD, ROGER WOOD, TREVIN WOOD, YANABAH WOOD, BRUCE WOODBURY, DEBORAH WOODBURY, LORI WOODBURY, MICHAEL WOODCOCK, HAROLD WOODHAM, KAREN WOODLAND, JAMES WOODMAN, LESLIE WOODMANSEE, SUSAN WOODRUFF, SUSAN WOODRUFF, TODD WOODRUFF, DEREK WOODS, LORETA WOODWARD, LUCY WOODWARD, SUSAN WOODWARD, FREDRICH WOOLLEY, JACQUELINE WOOLLEY, MICHAEL WOOLSTON, CAROLE WOOTEN, JANET WOOTEN, DAVID WORKMAN, JOSEPH WORTHEN, MICHAEL WREN, AMBER WRIDE, ALAN WRIGHT, AMY WRIGHT, ANDREA WRIGHT, AUSTIN WRIGHT, CHARLES WRIGHT, DELMER WRIGHT, GRANT WRIGHT, JAMES WRIGHT, JAMES WRIGHT, KAREN WRIGHT, KEVIN WRIGHT, KYLE WRIGHT, MELVIN WRIGHT, MICHAEL WRIGHT, MICHAEL WRIGHT, NATASHA WRIGHT, PAUL WRIGHT, RYAN WRIGHT, SIDNEY WRIGHT, WILLIAM WRIGHT, BRIAN WUCHER, WILLIAM WUNDERLICH, ANDREW WURTS, MARK WUTHRICH, MARIETTA WYNN • **X** • MING XIAO, DI XIE, ROBERT XIONG • **Y** • BONNIE YAN, ALICIA YANEZ, ANN YANG, JON YARRINGTON, ERIKA YASUDA, DAWN YATES, DONALD YATES, GREGORY YATES, DOROTHY YAZZIE, SHAWN YAZZIE, JEFFREY YEAGER, STELLA YEAW, CANDICE YEE, MARY YELANJIAN, DENNIS YEOMANS, ROGER YIN, SUYOUNG YOO, RUTH YORKE, MICHELLLE YOST, ROGER YOST, BROOKE YOUNG, CHRISTOPHER YOUNG, CHRISTOPHER YOUNG, COURTNEY YOUNG, DAVID YOUNG, JANICE YOUNG, JENNY YOUNG, JOHN YOUNG, KENNETH YOUNG, KEVIN YOUNG, LINDSAY YOUNG, MANDY YOUNG, MICHAEL YOUNG, PAUL YOUNG, SARAH YOUNG, SEAN YOUNG, SHANNON YOUNG, SHIRLEY YOUNG, WALTER YOUNG JR, LATOYA YOUNGER, CHARLES YOUNGKIN, JOHN YOUNGS JR, SARALEE YUEN, MATTHEW YURICK, KATHRYN YURK, RUSSELL YURK, AMINATU YUSUF • **Z** • BREEGE ZACHARY, BLAIR ZACKON, RIGOBERTO ZAMORA, CHARLES ZANDAZA, FRANK ZANG, CARL ZAPARANICK, DAVID ZAPATA, MATTHEW ZARIT, MICHAEL ZARRILLI, KENNETH ZEITS, ROBERT ZENDER, JERRY ZEPEDA, JIANYING ZHAO, DAVID ZIAREK, PHILIP ZIKE, CHARLOTTE ZIMMERMAN, SHANE ZIMMERMAN, PATRICE ZINDEL, JOANNA ZIPSER-GRAVES, ERIN ZITO, PACOME ZOKOU, JEFF ZORNOW, WENDY ZUERLEIN, SHAE ZUFELT, DAVID ZUMBRENNEN, DAVID ZUMBRENNEN, SEAN ZUZIK, SPENCER ZWICK,

**V O L U N T E E R S** • **A** • ADELE AADLAND, MIA AAGARD, VANESSA AAGARD, KIRSTEN AALBERG, ROBERT AAMODT, DANELLE AARDEMA, ALICE AARON, MICHAEL AARON, DAVID ABBOTT, DIANNE ABBOTT, JAMES ABBOTT, KEVIN ABBOTT, LEAH ABBOTT, ROGER ABBOTT, SARA ABBOTT, SCOTT ABBOTT, THOMAS ABBOTT, TIM ABBOTT, ALAN ABDULLA, TAYLOR ABEGG, JEFFREY ABEL, LEON ABEL, JOAN ABELE, GARRY ABER, RICHARD ABERLEY, WENDELL ABLES, KAI ABOULIAN, LESLIE ABPLANALP, RANDY ABPLANALP, HAZEL ABRAHAM, ELAINE ABRAMOWITZ, JAY ABRAMOWITZ, JAN ABRAMSON, RACHEL ABRASH, SUFIAN ABU-RMAILEH, DANIEL ACCROCCO, KAREN ACERSON, DAVID ACOCKS, BRIAN ACORD, VICENTA ACOSTA, RUSSELL ACTON, RANDY ADACHI, CARA ADAIR, AARON ADAMS, ALICIA ADAMS, ANN ADAMS, ANNABELLE ADAMS, BRADLEY ADAMS, BRIAN ADAMS, BRITT ADAMS, CAROLYN ADAMS, CONNIE ADAMS, CRAIG ADAMS, DANA ADAMS, DANIEL ADAMS, DAVID ADAMS, DENNIS ADAMS, ERIC ADAMS, GWEN ADAMS, HERBERT ADAMS, JAMES ADAMS, JAN ADAMS, JASMIN ADAMS, JOSH ADAMS, JUDITH ADAMS, KAREN ADAMS, KATHIE ADAMS, KENNETH ADAMS, KIM ADAMS, LAURILEE ADAMS, LYNN ADAMS, MARSHA ADAMS, MARY ADAMS, NATHANAEL ADAMS, REED ADAMS, RODNEY ADAMS, ROGER ADAMS, RUSSELL ADAMS, SHANNON ADAMS, TRACY ADAMS, ANDREW ADAMSON, CAROLYN ADAMSON, GREG ADAMSON, JASON ADAMSON, JEAN ADAMSON, JOHN ADAMSON, MARK ADAMSON, STEVE ADDICOTT, HIRAM ADELMAN, SCOTT ADELMAN, KYLE ADEMA, JOAN ADMIRAND, EVA-MARIA ADOLPHI, COLETTE ADORE, HENRY ADOVNIK, DONNETTE AFFLECK, JUDITH AGOS, DAWN AGREN, THELMA AGUAYO, ABERRA AGUEGNEHU, ENIO AGUERO, JOSEPH AHERN, JUDITH AHERN, RICK AHLANDER, CATHERINE AHLERS, JENNIFER AHLGREN, AMANDA AHLSTROM, CAMILLE AHLSTROM, DOUGLAS AHLSTROM, VERONICA AHMED, EUNGHO AHN, STEVE AHN, BARBARA (BUNNY) AIKEN, JULIE AIMAN, JULIE AINSCOUGH, RICHARD AINSCOUGH, RICHARD AIRD, REED AITKEN, MIYUKI AJIKI, FRANCES AKITA, KENNY ALA, HENRY ALAS, DIANA ALBA, JOSEPH ALBANO, WILLIAM ALBERS, PAUL ALBERT, CHARLES ALBERTI, ERIK ALBERTINE, MILLIE ALBERTSON, ROBERT ALBON, JEAN ALBRECHT, LEANN ALBRECHT, MARCY ALBRECHT, MITCHELL ALBRECHT, RICK ALBRECHT, ANITA ALBRIGHT, CODY ALBRIGHT, DIANNE ALBRIGHT, LESLIE ALBRIGHT, PHILLIP ALBRIGHT, UTAHNA ALBRIGHT, MARIO ALBURGES, AMY ALCORN, VERDENE ALCORN, CONNIE ALDER, CORALIE ALDER, ERIC ALDER, LINDSAY ALDER, RICHARD ALDERETE, SANDRA ALDOUS, JENNIFER ALDRICH, ROBERT ALDRICH, VIRGINIA ALEWINE, CYNTHIA ALEX, CONNIE ALEXAKOS, DENISE ALEXANDER, DENNIS ALEXANDER, DIANA ALEXANDER, KATHLEEN ALEXANDER, LAURA ALEXANDER, LAURIE ALEXANDER, MARIA ALEXANDER, MARILYN ALEXANDER, NATASHA ALEXANDER, ROD ALEXANDER, THOMAS ALEXANDER, TRAVIS ALEXANDER, MARIA ALFONSO, PAMELA ALFORD, UVANNEY ALFORD, AXEL ALFREDSSON, LOUIS ALGER, MAXINE ALGER, DAMIR ALIJAGIC, VICTORIA ALIMOV, PATRICIA ALJANICH, CAROL ALKIRE, LANCE ALKIRE, ANTHONY ALLAM, RICHARD ALLAM, DEAN ALLAN, KIM ALLARD, JERI ALLBEE, KATHRYN ALLDREDGE, KRISTIAN ALLEE, ALISA ALLEMAN, LISA ALLEMAN, ALEXIS ALLEN, AMY ALLEN, ANGELA ALLEN, ANNETTE ALLEN, BRENDA ALLEN, BRIAN ALLEN, CAROL ALLEN, CAROLYN ALLEN, CLYDE ALLEN, CONNIE ALLEN, CRAIG ALLEN, DANETTE ALLEN, DARREN ALLEN, DAVID ALLEN, DAVID ALLEN, DOUG ALLEN, DOUGLAS ALLEN, FRANK ALLEN, GARY ALLEN, IONE ALLEN, JEANETTE ALLEN, JOANNE ALLEN, JOHN ALLEN, JUDITH ALLEN, KANDEE ALLEN, KAREN ALLEN, KAREN ALLEN, KATHRYN ALLEN, KATHY ALLEN, KEVIN ALLEN, KORIE ALLEN, LEON ALLEN, LORRIE ALLEN, MARK ALLEN, MICHELLE ALLEN, NANCY ALLEN, NANCY ALLEN, NEDRA ALLEN, RICHARD ALLEN, SHERRY ALLEN, STEPHEN ALLEN, STEPHEN ALLEN, SUSAN ALLEN, THOMAS ALLEN, THOMAS ALLEN, TIMOTHY ALLEN, TODD ALLEN, TRAVIS ALLEN, CHARLENE ALLERT, MUTHU ALLETTO, PHIL ALLETTO, GARY ALLGAIER, JULIE ALLIE, KENNETH ALLIE, SHIRLEY ALLIE, ALLEN ALLIGOOD, ROELFIENA ALLIS-VAN ROSSUM, CHRIS ALLISON, JANE ALLISON, MARK ALLISON, WANDA ALLISON, BOHDANA ALLMAN, BRYAN ALLMAN, CLAUDIA ALLMAN, ALICE ALLMARK, WILLIAM ALLPHIN, ANDREA ALLRED, ANGELA ALLRED, BARRY ALLRED, BRUCE ALLRED, DEBRA ALLRED, DEREK ALLRED, DOUGLAS ALLRED, ELLEN ALLRED, ERIC ALLRED, GIGI ALLRED, KEITH ALLRED, KELLY ALLRED, KENT ALLRED, LAUREN ALLRED, LINDA ALLRED, MARILYN ALLRED, MARTIN ALLRED, MATHEW ALLRED, MICHAEL ALLRED, SHERRIE ALLRED, WILLIAM ALLRED, BRENT ALM, BRIAN ALM, WENDY ALMOND, SANDRA ALOIA, LARRY ALSERDA, SANDRA ALTHAUS, MARK ALTICE, PETER ALTMAN, DUSTIN ALTMANN, SCOTT ALTMAYER, MARK ALTOM, DAVID ALTOP, DONNA ALTOP, FRANKLIN ALVARADO, BRYON ALVAREZ, CARLOS ALVAREZ, LUIS ALVAREZ, MICHAEL ALVAREZ, SYLVIE ALVAREZ, HUGO ALVAREZ-DONGO, BEN ALVORD, DARRON ALVORD, JACOB ALVORD, JOHN ALVORD, MEKINZIE ALVORD, RYAN ALVORD, TIMOTHY ALVORD, NICHOLAS AMABILE, TRACY AMADIO, JENNIFER AMADOR, STEVEN AMANN, JEREMY AMAR, LAURA AMAR, PHILIP AMBARD, KATHRYN AMBROSE, M JENE AMBROSE, RICHARD AMBROSE, JIM AMBUEHL, TIMOTHY AMEEL, DAVID AMEETI, MARK AMENDOLA, COREY AMES, ROBERT AMES, BARBARA AMIDON, DAVID AMIDON, ALICE AMINI, ROBERT AMINI, STEVEN AMOIA, ANDREA AMOTT, DAVID AMOTT, JOAN AMOTT, ROBERT AMOTT, JUDITH AMSEL, JEFFREY AMUNDSEN, DINO AMUNDSON, FRANZ AMUSSEN, CAROLYN ANCTIL, DARYL ANDELIN, HEATHER ANDELIN, JENNIFER ANDELIN, DANIEL ANDEREGG, PETER ANDERS, CINDY ANDERSEN, CURTIS ANDERSEN, DAVE ANDERSEN, DELONNA ANDERSEN, DIANE ANDERSEN, ERIC ANDERSEN, ERIC ANDERSEN, JANITA ANDERSEN, MARK ANDERSEN, MATTHEW ANDERSEN, RUSTY ANDERSEN, RYAN ANDERSEN, VICKI ANDERSEN, WILLIAM ANDERSEN, AARON ANDERSON, AARON ANDERSON, ALBERT ANDERSON, AMY ANDERSON, ANDREW ANDERSON, ARNE ANDERSON, BARRY ANDERSON, BOBBIE ANN ANDERSON, BRANDON ANDERSON, BRENT ANDERSON, CARLI ANDERSON, CHAD ANDERSON, CHARMAINE ANDERSON, CHERYL ANDERSON, CLAUDIA ANDERSON, CLINT ANDERSON, CLINTON ANDERSON, COLBY ANDERSON, CRAIG ANDERSON, CURTIS ANDERSON, CYNDI ANDERSON, CYNTHIA ANDERSON, DALE ANDERSON, DARLENE ANDERSON, DAVID ANDERSON, DEANNA ANDERSON, DEBORAH ANDERSON, DEREK ANDERSON, DERYK ANDERSON, DESTINEE ANDERSON, DIANE ANDERSON, DIANE ANDERSON, DIXIE ANDERSON, DIXIE ANDERSON, EDWARD ANDERSON, ELIZABETH ANDERSON, ELLEN ANDERSON, ERIK ANDERSON, FLOYD ANDERSON, FRANCES ANDERSON, FRANKLIN ANDERSON, GARY ANDERSON, GEORGE ANDERSON, GREG ANDERSON, HAROLD ANDERSON, HEATHER ANDERSON, HEATHER ANDERSON, HEIDI ANDERSON, HEIDI ANDERSON, HELI ANDERSON, HOWARD ANDERSON, IDA ANDERSON, ILENE ANDERSON, IVAN ANDERSON, J.K. ANDY ANDERSON, JACQUELINE ANDERSON, JAMES ANDERSON, JAMES ANDERSON, JANAE ANDERSON, JANE ANDERSON, JAY ANDERSON, JENNIFER ANDERSON, JESSICA ANDERSON, JESSICA ANDERSON, JOSHUA ANDERSON, JOYCE ANDERSON, JUDY ANDERSON, JUDY ANDERSON, KARL ANDERSON, KARY ANDERSON, KASSIE ANDERSON, KATHLEEN ANDERSON, KATHRYN ANDERSON, KATHY ANDERSON, KELLI ANDERSON, KENNETH ANDERSON, KENNETH ANDERSON, KERRY ANDERSON, KEVIN ANDERSON, KIMBERLY ANDERSON, KRISTA ANDERSON, KRISTINE ANDERSON, KRISTY ANDERSON, KYLE ANDERSON, LARK ANDERSON, LORI ANDERSON, LOUIS ANDERSON, MARGARET ANDERSON, MARGERY ANDERSON, MARY ANDERSON, MARY ANDERSON, MARY LEE ANDERSON, MATTHEW ANDERSON, MELODIE ANDERSON, MERIDEE ANDERSON, MICHAEL ANDERSON, MICHELE ANDERSON, MICHELLE ANDERSON, MIKE ANDERSON, MIRIAM ANDERSON, NADINE ANDERSON, NIKKI ANDERSON, NOEL ANDERSON, NORMA ANDERSON, NORMAN ANDERSON, PAMELA ANDERSON, PATRICIA ANDERSON, PATRICIA ANDERSON, PAUL ANDERSON, PAUL ANDERSON, PAUL ANDERSON, PAULA ANDERSON, PENNY ANDERSON, PHIL ANDERSON, PHILIP ANDERSON, RAY ANDERSON, REBECCA ANDERSON, RICHARD ANDERSON, RICK ANDERSON, ROBERT ANDERSON, ROBERTA ANDERSON, ROGER ANDERSON, RUDY ANDERSON, SALLY ANDERSON, SARA ANDERSON, SARA ANDERSON, SCOTT ANDERSON, SCOTT ANDERSON, SEBASTIAN ANDERSON, SERENA ANDERSON, SETH ANDERSON, SHARISE ANDERSON, SHARREN ANDERSON, SHERMAN ANDERSON, SHERRY ANDERSON, STANFORD ANDERSON, STEVE ANDERSON, STEVENS ANDERSON, SUSAN ANDERSON, TALON ANDERSON, TAMARA ANDERSON, TAMI ANDERSON, TED ANDERSON, TERESA ANDERSON, THERON ANDERSON, THOMAS ANDERSON, TIM ANDERSON, VIC ANDERSON, VICTORIA ANDERSON, WILLIAM ANDERSON, MARK ANDERSON JR, ERIC ANDERSON MD, SYLVIA ANDERSSON, CHRISTINA ANDERTON, MICHELLE ANDERTON, RICHARD ANDERTON, RYAN ANDERTON, LA NEIL ANDES, ROBERT ANDES, YAMATO ANDO, ADRIANA ANDRADE, YVETTE ANDREASEN, CARRIE ANDREW, GREGORY ANDREW, BRENT ANDREWS, CAROLE ANDREWS, HOWARD ANDREWS, JEANINE ANDREWS, JENNIFER ANDREWS, JENNIFER ANDREWS, JILL ANDREWS, JILL ANDREWS, MARY BETH ANDREWS, MAUREEN ANDREWS, MICHAEL ANDREWS, RICHARD ANDREWS, ROBERT ANDREWS, KERRI ANDROES, ARLENE ANDRUS, CHRIS ANDRUS, CHRISTIAN ANDRUS, KRIS ANDRUS, MARY ANDRUS, ROBERT ANDRUS, VAUN ANDRUS, ZACHARY ANDRUS, ALICIA ANDRUS-OGLESBY, JORGE ANGEL, TROY ANGELI, JUDITH ANGELL, PATRICK ANGELL, RICHARD ANGELL, AMIE ANGER, LISA ANGERBAUER, TIFFANY ANGILAU, NATALIE ANGLE, JAMES ANGLESEY, JACK ANGUS, KEVIN ANGUS, PAM ANGUS, DAVID ANKENEY, TIHOMIRA ANKOVA, ALLAN ANOPOL. CAREY ANSON, NAOMI ANSON, LARISA ANSPAUGH, SHEILA ANTHIS, PETER ANTHONY, SANDY ANTHONY, GRIGORIOS ANTONAROS, GARY ANTONINO, ARLENE AOKI, DAWN AOKI, KAYE AOKI, RICHIE AOKI, TERESA AOKI, ALLISON APEDAILE, KENNETH APEDAILE, SHEILA APOSHIAN, DONALD APPELLE, JOSEPH APPIAH, SHERYL APPLEBY, JOHN APPLEGARTH, DIANA APPLEGATE, ELIZABETH APRILE, RICHARD APRILE, VINAYAK APTE, PEARLA AQUINO, RUDOLPH ARAKTINGI, VICTOR ARANA, JOHN ARANDA, CINDY ARANEDA, RICHARD ARBOGAST, CYNTHIA ARBON, ROBERT ARBON, LISA ARBON-TAGGE, GINA ARBUCKLE, MIGUEL ARCE CRUZ, CHRIS ARCHBOLD, GREGORY ARCHBOLD, MONIQUE ARCHBOLD. HAROLD ARCHER, WARREN ARCHER, AMY ARCHIBALD, CHRISTINE ARCHIBALD, DONALD ARCHIBALD, G MURRAY ARCHIBALD, JOYCE ARCHIBALD, MARK ARCHIBALD, MARY LOU ARCHIBALD, SCOTT ARCHIBALD, WAYNE ARCHIBALD, GERRI ARCHULETA, SAM ARCHULETA JR, MAXIMILIANO ARCIA, HEIDI ARCINIEGA, JULIO ARCINIEGA, TERESA ARD, JOHN ARENS, DONNA ARGYLE, JASON ARGYLE, LOUJEAN ARGYLE, KATIE ARISHITA, DELBERT ARKIN, NANCY ARMATA, CINDY

ARMER, WILLIAM ARMER, JIMMIE ARMITAGE, PENNY ARMITAGE, VICKI ARMITAGE, BONNIE ARMITSTEAD, CHAD ARMITSTEAD, LYNN ARMITSTEAD, BETTIE ARMSTRONG, CAMERON ARMSTRONG, CARA ARMSTRONG, DANIEL ARMSTRONG, DEBORAH ARMSTRONG, DOULGAS ARMSTRONG, EDWARD ARMSTRONG, ERNI ARMSTRONG, KIM ARMSTRONG, KRISTINE ARMSTRONG, MARGARET ARMSTRONG, MELANIE ARMSTRONG, ROSEMARY ARMSTRONG, MICHAEL ARNDT, INGVAR ARNESON, KOREY ARNESON, STEVEN ARNETT, ALLISON ARNOLD, GARN ARNOLD, KARMA ARNOLD, LEWIS ARNOLD, LYNN ARNOLD, MARY ARNOLD, NIKKI-ANN ARNOLD, PATRICIA ARNOLD, TRISHA ARNOLD, WILLIAM ARNOLD, SHANNON ARNOLDSEN, JEFFREY ARNSON, JOHN ARON, ARTHUR ARRINGTON, BRANDON ARRINGTON, DANIEL ARRINGTON, PHILIP ARRIOLA, WILLIAM ARTHUR, SKYE ARTHUR-BANNING, DONALD ARTICO, ELLEN ARTIST, GLENN ARTIST, MARY LOU ARVESETH, BRENT ASAY, DAVID ASAY, WILLIAM ASAY, KELLY ASBRIDGE, DENTON ASCHLIMAN, ALEEN ASH, KARA ASH, KEVIN ASH, RONALD ASH, ELIZABETH ASHBY, GARY ASHBY, LENORE ASHBY, MICHELLE ASHBY, GLEN ASHDOWN, MELISSA ASHDOWN, CATHY ASHMAN, JEANENE ASHMAN, ELIZABETH ASHTON, MICHELLE ASHTON, SPENCER ASHTON, DANNY ASKEW, REBECCA ASKEW, DALE ASKEY, JENNIFER ASKEY, PAUL ASKINS, BARBARA ASKVIG, SHIRLEY ASPINWALL, JOHN ASPINWALL II, PAUL ASTIN, STACEY ASTIN, TONYA ASTLE, JANET ASTON, BARBARA ATHENS-ZAPOTOCKY, JAMES ATHEY, XANTHI ATHOUSAKIS, ROBERT ATISME, KENNETH ATKIN, AMY ATKINSON, CINDY ATKINSON, CURTIS ATKINSON, KATHY ATKINSON, MICHAEL ATKINSON, MISTY ATKINSON, SCOTT ATKINSON, THOMAS (TOM) ATKINSON, TIFFANY ATKINSON, TISH ATKINSON, VENUS ATKINSON, SACHIN ATTAVAR, JULIE ATWATER, KAREN ATWATER, BETH ATWOOD, GENEVIEVE ATWOOD, STEVE ATWOOD, STEVE ATWOOD, STEFANIE AUGER, ELAINE AUGUSTINE, TANYA AUJLA, SCOTTY AULD, HAROLD AURE, REX AUSBURN, GREGORY AUSLAND, RANDALL AUSTILL, ALLAN AUSTIN, ASTA AUSTIN, BETTY AUSTIN, BEVERLY AUSTIN, DAWNEE AUSTIN, JARED AUSTIN, JULIANE AUSTIN, KRISTY AUSTIN, LARRY AUSTIN, LEROY AUSTIN, LLOYD AUSTIN, MARK AUSTIN, MICHAEL AUSTIN, MILTON AUSTIN, RICHARD AUSTIN, SHARI AUSTIN, SHARON AUSTIN, SUSAN AUSTIN, JANET AUTREY, MELISSA AUXIER, REBECCA AVANS, LEE AVERETT, ROBERT AVERILL, SUSAN AVERILL, CARL AVERY, STEPHEN AVERY, DAVID AXENTY, SHANE AXTELL, MARION AYERS, VICTOR AYERS, BRENT AYRE, SUSAN AYRES • **B** • CAROL BAAS, BOB BABALIS, MAXINE BABALIS, WILLIAM BABB, CHARLES BABBEL, TAMMY BABBITT, AMY BABCOCK, GARY BABCOCK, JUDD BABCOCK, NICHOLAS BABILIS, SAMUEL BABIN, KAE BABINCHAK, WILLIAM BABIONE, ANNETTE BABISZ, MAURINE BACHMAN, LINDA BACHMEIER, CASSANDRA BACHTELL, JANICE BACK, ROY BACK, JAMES BACKMAN, JANET BACKMAN, RICHARD BACKMAN, ROBERT BACKMAN, LEAH BACKSHALL, DON BACKSTROM, CINDY BACKUS, MARK BACKUS, BRYAN BACON, DARYL BACON, DONALD BACSO, JOAN BACSO, JASON BADELL, JAN BADERTSCHER, BYUNG BAE, AMANDA BAER, KRISTIN BAER KARTCH, TAMARA BAGGETT, GARY BAGGS, CAMILLE BAGLEY, DOUGLAS BAGLEY, KENT BAGLEY, LANE BAGLEY, LISA BAGLEY, STEVEN BAGLEY, CINDY BAGNELL, KENNETH BAGSHAW, TAMARA BAHR, NICKOLA BAIC, ALEXANDER BAILEY, BRANDEN BAILEY, BROOKE BAILEY, CARL BAILEY, CAROL BAILEY, CARY BAILEY, CONNIE BAILEY, DENNIS BAILEY, DOREENE BAILEY, DORINE BAILEY, ERIN BAILEY, EVELYN BAILEY, HIRAM BAILEY, JANET BAILEY, JEFF BAILEY, LON BAILEY, MELISSA BAILEY, MICHAEL BAILEY, MICHAEL BAILEY, MICHELLE BAILEY, ROBERT BAILEY, ROGER BAILEY, SCOTT BAILEY, STEVEN BAILEY, SUZANNE BAILEY, WENDY BAILEY, MARILYN BAILEY-STOWE, RONALD BAILOR, RYAN BAILOR, DAVE BAIN, BRAD BAIR, KATHRYN BAIR, LYLE BAIR, MARY BAIR, SHARON BAIR, TORY BAIR, VERLA BAIR, WENDY BAIR, ANDREW BAIRD, DAN BAIRD, GERRY BAIRD, MARLENE BAIRD, MICHAEL BAIRD, NICHOLAS BAIRD, SHANE BAIRD, SHANNA BAIRD, TERRY BAIRD, THERON BAIRD, DARLENE BAIRETT, AMBER BAKER, BARBARA BAKER, BENJAMIN BAKER, CHERYL BAKER, CINDY BAKER, CONNIE BAKER, DARRIN BAKER, DEAN BAKER, JEAN BAKER, JOHN BAKER, JOSEPH BAKER, KAREN BAKER, KRISTY BAKER, LAWRENCE BAKER, LINDA BAKER, MAUREEN BAKER, PAULA BAKER, RICHARD BAKER, RUSSELL BAKER, SUSAN BAKER, TIM BAKER, TRICIA BAKER, VIRGINIA BAKER, WILLIAM BAKER, JOHN BAKER III, ROBERT BAKER III, TERRY BAKES, MOHAMMAD BAKHTI, LAURA BAKKER, PAMELA BAKST, JUDY BALABAN, MIKE BALAVAGE, BERNARDINO D BALAY, JOANN BALAY, ELIZABETH BALCAZAR, REGINA BALD, DON BALDAZO, BRYCE BALDERAS, SHANTEL BALDONADO DE ARRAIZ, CONNIE BALDWIN, LYNN BALDWIN, MELVIN BALDWIN, PHYLLIS BALDWIN, REBECCA BALDWIN, RICHARD BALDWIN, STEVEN BALDWIN, MARK BALFOUR, DOUGLAS BALL, JOHN BALL, REBECCA BALLAM, DARYL BALLANTYNE, BRIAN BALLARD, DAVID BALLARD, DAVID BALLARD, ELIZABETH BALLARD, KATHRYN BALLARD, ROBERT BALLARD, JOHN BALLENTINE, BEN BALLESTEROS, KIRK BALLIF, REBECCA BALLIF, ANGIE BALLING, BRIAN BALLS, MARTIN BALLS, PAUL BALLSTAEDT, ALAIN BALMANNO, BARBARA BALTZELL, JEFFREY BALTZELL, JERRY BALTZELL, RONALD BAMBERG, MARY BAMBROUGH, JAMES BANAS, TOM BANAS, KATHRYN BANASKY, DANIEL BANCHIK, STEVE BANDIS, MARTIN BANFIELD, RICHARD BANFIELD, SHANNEN BANFIELD, DON BANFORD, SARAESSA BANGERT, CATHERINE BANGERTER, NATALIE BANGERTER, SHARON BANGERTER, SUSAN BANGERTER, CHRISTINE BANIEWICZ, CHRISTIE BANKS, CHRISTINE BANKS, EVELYN BANKS, GREGORY BANKS, KAY BANKS, MARCIA BANKS, RANDY BANKS, BHAKTI BANNING, MARILYN BANNING, MATT BANNING, CONNIE BANTA, TODDIE BANTA, CHRISTOPHER BANTRUP, CHRISTINA BANTUG, JACOB BANYAI, STELLA BARACH, JULIANNE BARAN, ROY BARAN, BILL BARANOWSKI, BRYAN BARANOWSKI, TODD BARBEE, DIANE BARBER, MELISSA BARBER, THOMAS BARBER, MARC BARBEZAT, JOHN BARCIK, LATRECE BARCIK, CRISTY BARCLAY, ANN BARDSLEY, ROBERT BARDSLEY, MARVIN BARELA, BOBBY BARENG, ANDREW BARFIELD, JEFF BARGAR, JOSEPH BARICH, AMIRALI BARKER, BOYD BARKER, JANET BARKER, JANET BARKER, KAREN BARKER, KIM BARKER, LAYNE BARKER, LYNDIE BARKER, MICHAEL BARKER, MIKE BARKER, NANCY BARKER, NATHAN BARKER, PAULA BARKER, RANDALL BARKER, RONALD BARKER, ROXANNE BARKER, TAMI BARKER, THOMI BARKER, VERNON BARKER, WENDI BARKER, LINA BARKEY, ALLESON BARKLEY, EILEEN BARLAGE, KRISTEN BARLAGE, BRUCE BARLOW, EMILY BARLOW, JEREMY BARLOW, JULIANNA BARLOW, KRISTIN BARLOW, LINDA BARLOW, LISA BARLOW, NATHAN BARLOW, RON BARLOW, RONALD BARLOW, RULON BARLOW, THOMAS BARLOW, WILLIAM BARLOW, JAMIE BARMORE, MARY ANN BARNARD, MICHAEL BARNARD, MICHELLE BARNARD, CAMERON BARNES, CARON BARNES, EMILY BARNES, JAMES BARNES, JAMES BARNES, JASON BARNES, JIMMIE BARNES, JOY BARNES, KELLIE BARNES, KENT BARNES, LANCE BARNES, LAYNE BARNES, LORILEE BARNES, MONTY BARNES, NEIL BARNES, PATRICIA BARNES, PATRICK BARNES, WAYNE BARNES, YOLANDA BARNES, BRIAN BARNETT, GARY BARNETT, GERRIE BARNETT, ANDREW BARNEY, BRANDON BARNEY, CAROLYN BARNEY, DEL BARNEY, ERIC BARNEY, KAREN BARNEY, KAROL BARNEY, KATHY BARNEY, KRISHELE BARNEY, LARRY BARNEY, LYNDA BARNEY, MORGAN BARNEY, PAULA BARNEY, RAY BARNEY, SUE DAWN BARNEY, DR GUY D. BARNICOAT, BRANDON BARNSON, DEANN BARNSON, FAYE BARNSON, ROGER BARNSON, THOMAS BARNSON, CALVIN BARNUN II, ANN BAROCO, BELINDA BARON, JOYCE BARON, LOUANN BARR, JOHN BARRACLOUGH, PAUL BARRACO, RENE BARRERA, APRIL BARRETT, BRAD BARRETT, JESSE BARRETT, JESSICA BARRETT, JULIE BARRETT, KELLY BARRETT, MELISSA BARRETT, SOSA BARRETT, TIMOTHY BARRETT, WHITNEY BARRETT, WILLIAM BARRETT, JOHN BARRICK, DUSTIN BARRINGTON, A BARROS, ANDY BARROS, SCOTT BARROW, GLENDA BARROWMAN, CYNTHIA BARRUS, DAVID BARRUS, GREG BARRUS, JOHN BARRUS, JULIA BARRUS, MICHAEL BARRUS, BOUBACAR BARRY, GORDON BARRY, JANET BARRY, KAREN BARRY, CHERYL BARSON, TIFFANY BARSON, JAMES BARTA, JULIE BARTA, PAUL BARTELL, ADAM BARTH, DANIEL BARTHOLOMEUSZ, HEIDI BARTHOLOMEUSZ, BETH BARTHOLOMEW, SAMUEL BARTHOLOMEW, THEODORE BARTKOSKI, CHERYL BARTLETT, JIM BARTLETT, JOE ANN BARTLETT, RICHARD BARTLETT, WM BARTLEY, MICHELE BARTMESS, ANNE-MARIE BARTON, DAVID BARTON, DEBRA BARTON, JANIECE BARTON, JOANN BARTON, KARL BARTON, KATIE BARTON, LAURIE BARTON, NANCY BARTON, NATALIE BARTON, SARAH BARTON, DEBBE BARTOW, RUSSELL BARTSCH, DAVID BARTSCHI, BENEDICT BARTUSH, MARY BARTUSH, AMANDA BARUSCH, BRANDON BARZEE, BRANDON BASCOM, CHRISIE BASCOM, MELVIN BASHORE, CAROLYN BASISTA, DEBBIE BASRAK, GREGORY BASRAK, GERALDINE BASS, JANET BASS, ROBERT BASS, JENNIFER BASSAREAR, DONALD BASSETT, EVAN BASSETT, HAL BASSETT, KEN BASSETT, NANCY BASSETT, KIM BASSHAM, WAYNE BASSHAM, DEBRA BASTIAN, KAREN BASTIAN, NEIL BASTIAN, KEVIN BATCHELOR, JOE BATEMAN, MATTHEW BATEMAN, ROBERT BATEMAN, ROBERT BATEMAN, RONDA BATEMAN, THERESA BATEMAN, ALLED BATES, ANDREA BATES, BETSY BATES, DAWN BATES, FRANK BATES, JANICE BATES, JEFFERY BATES, JEFFREY BATES, JOSHUA BATES, KIMBERLY BATES, MATT BATES, MATTHEW BATES, WENDY BATES, UDO BATHELT, JAMES BATLEY, JANEEN BATT, MELVIN BATT, SHERRI BATT, MARY ANN BATTLE, KRIS BATTLESON, GEORGE BATY, BOYD BAUER, CAROLYN BAUER, KAY BAUER, KEVIN BAUER, LESSLIE BAUER, SHANNON BAUER, ANDREW BAUGH, BRENT BAUM, ROSELLE BAUM, WILLOW BAUM, LESLIE BAUMAN, LAURIE BAUMBACH, WILLIAM BAUMGAERTNER, LYNDA BAUMGART, JANET BAUMGARTNER, PAUL BAUMGARTNER, KATHERINE BAUTER, KRISTIN BAUTER, RICHARD BAUTER, DENNIS BAXTER, JOHN BAXTER, LANCE BAXTER, LINDSY BAXTER, RONALD BAXTER, SHIRLEY BAXTER, STEVEN BAXTER, TEGSHEE BAYARSAIKHAN, KATHLEEN BAYER, GEORGE BAYLES, NEIL BAYLIE, JOHN BAYLIS, BARRY BEA, KATHERINE BEA, MARY BEACCO, ROY BEACH, STAN BEACH, JASON BEACHAM, ROGER BEACHLER, LIESEL BEAGLEY, LOLA BEAGLEY, KRISTINE BEAIRD, MICHELLE BEAIRD, KERRY BEAKE, BARBARA BEAL, JEFFREY BEAL, KAREN BEAL, NATALIE BEAL, STEVEN BEALER, BRUCE BEAM, CAROL BEAM, PATRICIA BEAMAN, CHARLES BEAMER, ALAYNA BEAN, BILL BEAN, CHARLES BEAN, DANIEL BEAN, DARREN BEAN, EVE BEAN, JACK BEAN, JAMES BEAN, JAMI BEAN, LINDA BEAN, STACEY BEAN, ALBERT BEANE, CYNTHIA BEARD, KAROL BEARD, MICHAEL BEARD, DANIEL BEARDALL, ROBERT BEARDSHALL, STEVEN BEARNSON, ANNA BEARS, NARDA BEAS-NORDELL, BEVERLY BEASLEY, MARISA BEASLEY, ROBIN BEASLEY, PATRICIA BEATY, TODD BEAUCHENE, STACEY BEAUDINE, TANYA BEAULIEU, ALICE BEAUMONT, GAIL BEAUREGARD, ROXANN BEAUREGARD, CONNIE BEAVER, GAYLEN BEAZER, DENNIS BECENTI, JAMES BECHER, ANDREW BECK, BRIAN BECK, DAVID BECK, ELIZABETH BECK, JAMES BECK, JULIE BECK, KAREN BECK, KRISTINE BECK, LAUREL BECK, LYNNE BECK, MARTHA BECK, MARY ANN BECK, MIKE BECK, MONTE BECK, OLLIE JEAN BECK, ROBBIE BECK, ROSALIE BECK, TERESA BECK, TERI BECK, TERRI BECK, TRUDY BECK, ADAM BECKER, BENJAMIN BECKER, DENNIS BECKER, E. BECKER, ROBERT BECKER, SALLY BECKER, THOMAS BECKER, DONALD BECKMAN, IRENE BECKMAN, LONI BECKMAN, LYNZI BECKMAN, KRISTIN BECKSTEAD, NEIL BECKSTEAD, KENNAN BECKSTRAND, CURTIS BECKSTROM, ERIKA BECKSTROM, GREGORY BECKSTROM, MARY BECKSTROM, SHANNON BECKSTROM, SHAWN BECKSTROM, ALEX BEDKE, SUSAN BEDKE, EWA BEDNAREK, PIOTR BEDNARSKI, ENOS BEEBE, EMILY BEECH, TARREN BEECH, ERIKA BEECHAM, SHELLEY BEECHER, CHRISTINA BEER, KRISTEN BEER, ROBERT BEER, STEPHANIE BEER, GAIL BEERE, RACHAEL BEERS, MARILYN BEESLEY, JASON BEESON, MARIDEE BEESTON, TANYA BEFUS, STEVEN BEHLING, SILVIA BEHREND, GLADLYN BEHRMANN, GRANT BEHRMANN, MICHELLE BEHRMANN, DARCIE BEHUNIN, SHAWN BEHUNIN, JOY BEIGHTOL, GARINE BEKEARIAN, KATHY BEKKEMELLOM, PAUL BEKKEN, DAVE BELANGER, SHELLY BELFLOWER, KAREN BELFORD-SPJELDVIK, GUILLAUME BELGIQUE, LAURA BELGIQUE, BETH BELL, BONITA BELL, BRENDA BELL, CHARLOTTE BELL, CYNTHIA BELL, DARRELL BELL, GREGORY BELL, HOLLY BELL, JENNIFER BELL, JEREMY BELL, JOSEPH BELL, KIMBERLY BELL, LARRY BELL, SHARON BELL, SITA BELL, THOMAS BELL, VAL BELL, VICKI BELL, BEVERLY BELL-PROFFETT, BILLY BELLAR, SHIRLEY BELLEVILLE, JENNIFER BELLISTON, VAL BELMONTE, LEANN BELNAP, MELINA BELNAP, JOHN BENCH, SHIRLEY BENCH, CHRISTINA BENDA, ROBERT BENDA, WILLIAM BENDA, KAREN BENDALL, CHERYL BENDER, EARL BENDER, GARY BENEDETTI, MOLLY BENEDICT, RICHARD BENEDICT, SHARON BENEDICT, GARY BENGTZEN, RAYNEE BENGTZEN, MARK BENIGNI, VICKIE BENINCOSA, NATALIA BENNER, NIC BENNER, BRENDA BENNETT, CHRISTOPHER BENNETT, CYNTHIA BENNETT, GARRY BENNETT, GARY BENNETT, GEORGE BENNETT, GEORGE BENNETT, HEATHER BENNETT, JOLENE BENNETT, KARL BENNETT, KATHY BENNETT, LINDA BENNETT, LINNEA BENNETT, MARGARET BENNETT, MARGARET BENNETT, MICHELLE BENNETT, MILES BENNETT, NANCY BENNETT, RACHAEL BENNETT, RICHARD BENNETT, STACY BENNETT, SUSAN BENNETT, TARYN BENNETT, TROY BENNETT, WILLIAM BENNETT, WENDI BENNINGTON, ALEXANDRA BENNION, DOUGLAS BENNION, KARYL BENNION, MARCIA BENNION, AARON BENSON, BARBARA BENSON, DEBORAH BENSON, ELDA BENSON, JAMES BENSON, JEFFREY BENSON, KATHLEEN BENSON, KERRY BENSON, MELINDA BENSON, RUTHANN BENSON, SARALYN BENSON, SARIAH BENSON, SCOTT BENSON, SHERYL BENSON, DAWN BENTLEY, JEAN BENTLEY, SHAWNA BENTLEY, WENDY BENTLEY, JUSTIN BERA, DON BERCUSON, SHERRIE BERCUSON, THOMAS BERETVAS, KELLY BEREZAY, BETTY BERG, DALE BERG, DELLA BERG, KRYSTAL BERG, SUZANNE BERG, TROY BERG, WILLIAM BERG JR, DANIEL BERGANTZ, DEREK BERGEN, STEPHANIE BERGER, PETER BERGESON, RENEE BERGESON, SHELTON BERGESON, DANIEL BERGIN, ARTHUR BERGLUND, DONALD BERGMAN, CAROLYN BERGQUIST, JAMES BERGSENG, PAT BERGSENG, DAN BERGSTROM, JACQUELYN BERGSTROM, MARK BERGSTROM, MELISSA BERGSTROM, RUSSELL BERGSTROM, VERNON BERGSTROM, VIC BERGSTROM, GEORGE BERKLEY, IRV BERLIN, JAN BERLIN, JILL BERMAN, FRANK BERNAL, SONIA BERNARD MCCALL, TERRY BERNER, MARGARET BERNHARDT, RAYMOND BERNIER, NICOLE BERNSHAW, JANICE BERNSON, TAMARA BERNSON, CHARLIE BERNSTEIN, KATHI BERNSTEIN, NANCY BERNSTEIN, CHRISTINA BEROUTI, RENE BEROUTI, CHAD BERRETT, GENE' BERRETT, MONICA BERRONDO, BARBARA BERRY, DAVID BERRY, HOWARD BERRY, JOSEPH BERRY, MARVIN BERRY, MYRIAM BERRY, RICHARD BERRY, HILARY BERTAGNOLE, CHRISTINE BERTIN, GREGORY BERTOLA, JASON BERTOLA, NANI BERTOLA, HEATHER BERTOTTI, BETTY BERTRAND, CYNTHIA BERTRAND, MARTIN BESANT, MARSHA BESLEY, JOHN BESSELIEVRE, PATTI BESSELIEVRE, DARRELL BEST, JENNIFER BEST, JULIE BEST, KIM BEST, LOUISE BEST, MARIE BEST, STEVEN BEST, THOMAS BEST, CAROL BESTE, WILLIAM BESTE, ROY BESTOW, DONALD BETENSON, JIM BETHEL, SCOTT BETHEL, JENNIE BETHERS, LEE BETHERS, JULIE BETTINSON, BRUCE BETTS, DAVID BETTS, RAYMOND BETTS, FREDRICK BETZ, RAMONA BEUK, LISA BEUS, BARRY BEUTLER, JEAN BEUTLER, LORI BEUTLER, CARLA BEVAN, CLAYTON BEVAN, CRAIG BEVAN, RENEE BEVAN, JEFFREY BEVANS, MICHAEL BEVERLY, HOPE BEVILHYMER, GREG BEYER, VIRGINIA BEYNON, LOUISE BEZDJIAN, DAVID BEZZANT, ELIZABETH BIAETT, JAKE BIAMONTE, ANDREW BIANCUR, DORIS BIAS, JAMES BICKLEY, JODI BICKLEY, RICHARD BIDDINGER, DIANA BIDDLE, KERRY BIDDLE, NATHANIAL BIDDLE, ROBERT BIDDLE, WILLIAM BIDDLE, JANIEL BIDEAUX, GARRETH BIEGUN, GARY BIEHL, VAL BIELECKI, QUINN BIESINGER, SHERRI BIGBY, CARRIE BIGGER, JAMES BIGGS, LILA BIGGS, ALLISON BIGSBY, ELIZABETH BIITTNER, GENEVIEVE BILANZICH, JESSICA BILANZICH, SHELLEY BILBAO, JULIE BILBREY, LORRI BILJANIC, CAROLYN BILLINGS, MARGARET BILLINGS, PETER BILLINGS, RICK BILLINGS, BRIAN BILLINGSLEY, KIRSTEN BILLINGSLEY, MICHAEL BILLINGSLEY, DREW BILLINGTON, ADA BILLS, ALEXANDRA BILLS, JON BILLS, LAURA BILLS, LORRAINE BILLS, NAMON BILLS, SANDRA BILLS, JAMES BINA, TOM BINDAS, ALICIA BINGGELI, ADAM BINGHAM, BONNIE BINGHAM, BRAD BINGHAM, CHRIS BINGHAM, CLARA BINGHAM, CRAIG BINGHAM, DAVID BINGHAM, ERIC BINGHAM, KAREN BINGHAM, KRISTEN BINGHAM, MICHAEL BINGHAM, WILLIAM BINGHAM, DERICK BINGMAN, JAYE BINKERD, RAYMOND BINKERD, BRIAN BINTZ, WENDY BINYON, MARLA BIRCH, HEATH BIRCHALL, KAREN BIRCHENOUGH, ROBERT BIRCHENOUGH, DEL BIRCHER, TAMARA BIRCUMSHAW, DANIEL BIRD, DONNI BIRD, IAN BIRD, LAURA BIRD, LAURIE BIRD, MARK BIRD, MARY ANN BIRD, RANDALL BIRD, REBECCA BIRD, ROBERT BIRD, SAMANTHA BIRD, SHEILA BIRD, STEPHANIE BIRD, TERESA BIRD, STEVEN BIRDSALL, KRISTEN BIRKELAND, RYAN BIRKES, SUE BIRRELL, GARY BIRTCHER, GERALD BISCHOFF, ORMA BISCHOFF, TAMMI BISCHOFF, LAURI BISH, BETSY BISHOP, BRANDON BISHOP, BRENT BISHOP, BRYAN BISHOP, CHRISTINA BISHOP, DAVID BISHOP, EDWARD BISHOP, JAMIE BISHOP, JENNIFER BISHOP, JEROLD BISHOP, JILL BISHOP, KEITH BISHOP, KRISTIN BISHOP, LINDSAY BISHOP, MILES BISHOP, NICOLE BISHOP, PAMELA BISHOP, SUNNEE BISHOP, WILLIAM BISHOP, RACHEL BISSELL, ROY BISSETT, SCOTT BISSEY, LELAND BITNER, JERRY BITTER, REED BITTER, FREDERICK BJERKE, PAMELA BJERNFALK, KEITH BJORK, DAVID BJORKMAN, GINGER BJORNSTAD, RONALD BLACHLEY, AMY BLACK, BONNIJANE BLACK, BROOKE BLACK, CARL BLACK, DOUGLASS BLACK, EDWARD BLACK, ELIZABETH BLACK, JED BLACK, KEITH BLACK, KENNARD BLACK, KENNETH BLACK, KRISTEN BLACK, MARY BLACK, ROSA BLACK, RYAN BLACK, STEVEN BLACK, STUART BLACK, TERRY BLACK, VALARIE BLACK, ROBB BLACKABY, ALLEN BLACKBIRD, JAMIE BLACKBURN, MAXINE BLACKBURN, MICHELLE BLACKBURN, ROAMELIA BLACKBURN, ANNA BLACKERBY, LESLIE BLACKHAM, NATHAN BLACKHAM, ELAINE BLACKHURST, THERESE BLACKMER, DOLORES BLACKMORE, LYNN BLACKMORE, SAUNDI BLACKNER, ANGELA BLACKWELL, BRENT BLACKWELL, MATTHEW BLAHNA, MICHAEL BLAIN, MICHELLE BLAIN, ADAIRE BLAIR, BONNIE BLAIR, GERRI BLAIR, JAMES BLAIR, MARILYN BLAIR, PRESTON BLAIR, CATHRINE BLAIS, DEBRA BLAISDELL, JASON BLAKE, LARRY BLAKE, LINDA BLAKE, LOLENE BLAKE, MARK BLAKE, STEPHEN BLAKE, TINA BLAKE, TRACIE BLAKE, WALTER BLAKE, GERALDINE BLAKELY, CONNIE BLAKEMORE, WILLIAM BLAKLEY, GARTH BLANCH, ASHLEY BLANCHARD, CHRISTINE BLANCHETTE, WALTER BLANCO, DIANNE BLANEY, BETHANY BLANK, SANDRA BLANK, THOMAS BLANK, LINDA BLANKENSHIP, LAURIE BLANSCETT, STEVEN BLANTHORN, LINDA BLASING, JOHN BLASKO, TERESA BLAUER, DENISE BLAYLOCK, PATRICIA BLAZEWICH, JOHN BLAZEY, BRIAN BLAZZARD, SHIRLEY BLEAK, PAMELA BLEAZARD, SHERRY BLEAZARD, IVY BLECHMAN, TERRY BLECKNER, CATHERINE BLEDSOE, NICKY BLEGGI, BILL BLEVINS, KATRINA BLEYL, WILLIAM BLEYL, LORI BLICKFELDT, KAREN BLISS, MICHAEL BLISS, SHIRLEY BLISS, ROBERT BLIX, BEVERLY BLOCK, WILLIE BLOCKER, QUENT BLODGETT, SPENCER BLODGETT, CLAUDE BLOMQUIST, DEBBIE BLOMQUIST, JESSICA BLOMQUIST, LACEY BLOMQUIST, MICHELLE BLOMQUIST, PHIL BLOMQUIST, JONATHAN BLONDER, CRYSTAL BLONQUIST, GILL BLONSLEY, LINDA BLONSLEY, RANDALL BLOOMDALE, WILFRED BLUM, JOHN BLUMENKAMP, CATHRYN BLUMENKRANTZ, BRAD BLUMENTHAL, DEBORAH BLUMENTHAL, RANDY BLUMENTHAL, JOAN BLY, ELLEN BLYTHE, RAYMOND BLYTHE, DIANE BOBACK, MARK BOBACK, MAURICE BOBST, BIRGIT BOCK, ROBERT BOCK, KERI BODELL, WILLIAM BODELL, MARIE BODENSTEDT, JASON BODIE, BETHALENE BODILY, BLAKE BODILY, CYNTHIA BODILY, DAVID BODILY, PATRICIA BODILY, FARRON BODILY-JOHNSON, TERRIE BODINE, MARIA BODKIN, BENJAMIN BODMER, JULIE BODTCHER, SKIJ BOERSMA, CAROLINE BOETTCHER, BILL BOGDAN, DEBORAH BOGENRIEF, BILLY BOGGS, CHRISTI BOGGS, ERNEST BOGGS, EVELYN BOGGS, HOLLY BOGGS, JACK BOGGS, ZACHARY BOHARD, BARBARA BOHM-BECKER, WILLIAM BOHMHOLDT, DEBBIE BOHN, MARC BOHN, MICHAEL BOHNE, JILL BOHNEY, CRESS BOHNN, FREDERICKA BOICE, STEPHEN BOICE, SUSAN BOITANO, AMIE BOIVIN, LAEF BOKISH, DEBORAH BOLAMPERTI, JIM BOLDON, KARL BOLDT, BOB BOLDUC, DENISE BOLDUC, JAMES BOLEY, EUGENE BOLINDER, SHARON BOLL, RONALD BOLLINGER, JOHN BOLLOW, JAY BOLLWINKEL, SOMMER BOLMAN, JOHN BOLOGNA, PARK BOLOS, DANIEL BOLZ, THOMAS BOLZ, AL BOMAN, BROOKE BOMAN, DEBRA BOMAN, RICHARD BOMBARD, JANE BOMMERSBACH, SANDAE BONARE, BECKY BOND, KIM BOND, MARSHA BOND, VICTORIA BOND, ERIC BONDER, JOHN BONDS, NADINE BONE, MICHAEL BONELLO, JEFFREY BONHAM, SUZANNE BONHAM, JOHANNA BONISTEEL, JEANETTE BONNELL, STEVE BONNEMORT, CARMA BONNER, KATHY BONNER, TODD BONNER, KENNETH BONNEY, DENISE BONVOULOIR, TERRY BONYNGE, BETH BOOKMAN, MOLLY BOONE, BRUCE BOOTH, CHAD BOOTH, ELAINE BOOTH, JEFFREY BOOTH, STANLEY BOOTH, SCOTT BORCHARD, TRACIE BORDER, CRAIG BOREN, DOLORES BOREN, GARY BOREN, LINDA BOREN, MELANI BOREN, SHERRY BOREN, WILFORD BOREN, DANETTE BORG, JANET BORG, LEEANN BORN, RICHARD BORNCAMP, MIKE BORREGO, CHARLES BORRENPOHL, SHARON BORROR, THOMAS BORROR, GINA BORROWMAN, LAREAN BORROWMAN, SAMUEL BORROWMAN, THOMAS BORROWMAN, HEATHER BORSKI, KERI BORST, GARY BORTOLUSSI, HAYLEY BOS, BETTE BOSCARENO, DOROTHY BOSHARD, ANGHELA BOSKOVICH, JEFFERY BOSSARD, JOY BOSSI, DONALD BOST, BARBARA BOSTIC, SONDRA BOSTON, JOHN BOSWELL, LISA BOSWELL, WILLIAM BOTH, W BOTHE, BARBARA BOTKIN, CASEY BOTKIN, ED BOTKIN, DAVID BOTSFORD, JOSEPH BOTT, MARIE BOTT, REBECCA BOTT, HARRIET BOUCHARD, RYAN BOUCHE, DAVID BOUCHER, WILLIAM BOUCHER, ANA BOUCK, MICHAEL BOUD, THOMAS BOUD, RODNEY BOUDRERO, RICK BOUILLON, ROBERT BOULTER, STEVE BOUNOUS, HEIDI BOURCIER, GLADYS BOURGEOIS, JOHN BOURGUIGNON, CARRIE BOURNE, BLAKE BOUVANG, LEE BOUWHUIS, MICHAEL BOUWHUIS, SHIRLEY BOUWHUIS, VICKY BOUY, CHARLES BOVA, LYNNE BOVAY, GERALD BOWCUT, STEFANIA BOWCUT, THOMAS BOWCUT, JOSEPH BOWCUTT, THOMAS BOWCUTT, JOANNE BOWDEN, BILLIE BOWEN, ELIZABETH BOWEN, GARY BOWEN, HOLLY BOWEN, MATHEW BOWEN, MICHELLE BOWEN, TANYA BOWERBANK, DOROTHY BOWERS, ROBERT BOWERS, ROXANNE BOWERS, STEVEN BOWLING, MARC BOWMAN, MICHAEL BOWMAN, SHERRI BOWMAN, ANNETTE BOWTHORPE, DENNIS BOWTHORPE, SHERENE BOWTHORPE, REGINA BOY, AMY BOYACK, ASHLEY BOYACK, GEORGE BOYACK, VERL BOYACK, LYNN BOYAKIN, ELAINE BOYCE, JOHN BOYCE, NEAL BOYCE, CHRISTOPER BOYD, DAVID R. BOYD, JAMES BOYD, LINDA BOYD, MARNIE BOYD, NANCY BOYD, REXENE BOYD, ROBERT BOYD, STUART BOYD, PAMELA BOYDSTON, CATHERINE BOYE, ASHLEY BOYER, CAROLYN BOYER, KATHLEEN BOYER, ROCK BOYER, SUSAN BOYER, THEODORE BOYER, KENT BOYINGTON, VIVIAN BOYINGTON, DOUGLAS BOYLAN, CHRIS BOYLE, JASON BOYLE, ROBERT BOYLE, SIDNEY BOYLE, SUSAN BOYLE, KATHLEEN BOYSEN, LANCE BOZEK, JOHN BOZUNG, TODD BRAATEN, DAVID BRABY, EULA BRABY, LARRY BRABY, JACOB BRACE, JOANN BRACE, MATTHEW BRACE, ROBERT BRACE, NORMA BRACETTI, ANNETTE BRACKEN, BRYAN BRACKEN, ELIZABETH BRACKEN, KATHY BRACKEN, MATTHEW BRACKEN, MICHAEL BRACKEN, JUDY BRACKETT, JAMI BRACKIN, CHANTELLE BRADE, DARWIN BRADFIELD, JEANETTE BRADFIELD, RANDALL BRADFIELD, SHERADEE BRADFIELD, SHIRLEY BRADFIELD, DAVID BRADFORD, JOHN BRADFORD, MISHA BRADFORD, WILLIAM BRADFORD, CRAIG BRADLEY, JANICE BRADLEY, JOHN BRADLEY, MARGARET BRADLEY, MICHAEL BRADLEY, PATRICIA BRADLEY, PAUL BRADLEY, SALLY BRADLEY, TERRY BRADLEY, THOMAS BRADLEY, WENDY BRADLEY, ELIZABETH BRADSHAW, JED BRADSHAW, JEFF BRADSHAW, JOSEPH BRADSHAW, MARYANNE BRADSHAW, MICHAEL BRADSHAW, TOM BRADSHAW, WILLIAM BRADSHAW, BRYAN BRADY, DEBI BRADY, HEIDI BRADY, JOSLYN BRADY, KEITH BRADY, LORALYNN BRADY, NATALIE BRADY, RACHELLE BRADY, RICHARD BRADY, ROBERT BRADY, SCOTT BRADY, WILLIAM BRADY, ERIN BRAGG, JIM BRAGG, KATHLEEN BRAGG, JACQUELINE BRAIDECH, LISA BRAIDECH, THOMAS BRAIDECH, MIRIAM BRAITHWAITE, JULIE BRAMHALL, ROBERT BRAMHALL, EUNICE BRAMWELL, JANE BRAMWELL, JENNIFER BRAMWELL, GABRIEL BRAN, LINDA BRANCH, CAROL BRAND, CHRISTINE BRAND, KARL BRAND, SAMUEL BRAND, STEVE BRAND, CARLOS BRANDARIS, GEORGE BRANDENBURG, JARED BRANDLEY, BRUCE BRANDOL, JOE BRANDON, MAUREEN BRANDON, DAVID BRANDT, JAMES BRANDT, JOHN BRANDT, LEANNE BRANDT, PATRICIA BRANN, MARLYS BRANNAN, DAYNA BRANSCUM, VERA BRANSON, SHANNON BRANSON FULLER, SHERRIE BRANZ, STEVE BRANZ, LADORA BRASEL, WILLIAM BRASEL, CHARLES BRASHER, SUSAN BRASHER, PAULA BRASHIER, MARTA BRASSEAUX, DAVID BRAUN, JOHN BRAUN, JUDITH BRAUN, MICHELLE BRAUNBERGER, CHARLOTTE BRAY, CHRIS BRAY, EMBER BRAY, NANCY BRAZELTON, JUNE BRAZEROL, JAMES BREARTON, KAREN BREAU, DARL BRECKENRIDGE, KATHRYN BRECKENRIDGE, MARK BREDEMANN, NICOLE BREDER, LINDA BREDIN, MARCIA BREEDING, BEVERLY BREEN, DAVID BREEN, PATRICIA BREEN, UDO BREHM, NATHANIEL BREIGHNER, NEIL BREINHOLT, DARLENE BREITENFELD, ROBERT BREITENFELD, DAVID BREITER, MELISSA BREITER, CHRISTINA BRENCHLEY, DAVID BRENCHLEY, TANIA BRENES, RICHARD BRENKMANN, SARAH BRENNA, EILEEN BRENNAN, KATIE BRENNAN, AMY BRENNER, JIM BRENTZ, MICHAEL BRESNAHAN, MICHELLE BRESTER, ALICE BREW, DAVID BREWER, DIANA BREWER, GAYLE BREWER, GLEN BREWER, JANE BREWER, JOHN BREWER, RICH BREWER, JOSEPH BREWERTON, TEDDY BREWERTON, NATALIE BREWSTER, JANET BRIAN, SUSAN BRIAN, APRIL BRICE, LARRY BRICE, DAVID BRICKEY, ALLYSON BRICKLEY, MATTHEW BRICKLEY, CONNIE BRIDGE, CORA BRIDGE, JEAN BRIDGE, JONATHAN BRIDGE, LARRY BRIDGE, STEWART BRIDGE, ANDREW BRIDGEMAN, JEAN BRIDGEMAN, WILLIAM BRIDGES, OREN BRIESE, BENJAMIN BRIGGS, BETTY BRIGGS, GARTH BRIGGS, JANAE BRIGGS, JOHN BRIGGS, LISA BRIGGS, ROBERT BRIGGS, THOMAS BRIGGS, DALE BRIGHT, DEBORAH BRIGHT, SHELBY BRIGHT, MERRY BRIM, JAN BRIMHALL, JASON BRIMHALL, MERRILL BRIMHALL, REBECCA BRIMHALL, TERRY BRIMHALL, KENNETH BRIMLEY, STEPHEN BRIMLEY, SARAH BRINEY, ELOISE BRINGHURST, INGER BRINGHURST, LANCE BRINGHURST, STEVEN BRINGHURST, JEFF BRINKER, CHARLES BRINKERHOFF, DARLENE BRINKERHOFF, GARTH BRINKERHOFF, JOHN BRINKERHOFF, KIRK BRINKERHOFF, MARK BRINKERHOFF, KRISTEN BRINKS, BRANSON BRINTON, CATHERINE BRINTON, DANIEL BRINTON, DANIEL BRINTON, DAVID BRINTON, JON BRINTON, SHARON BRINTON, STEPHEN BRINTON, TWYLA (DIANE) BRINTON, WHITNEY BRINTON, SUZANNE BRISCOE, EDWARD BRISSON, RICHARD BRISSON, JOHN BRISTOL, HEATHER BRISTOW, LYNDON BRITTNER, RONNY BROADAWAY JR, BERNE BROADBENT, CARMA BROADBENT, DAVID BROADBENT, DEBORAH BROADBENT, GEORGE BROADBENT, PHILIP BROADBENT, TROY BROADBENT, PHILIP BROADBENT JR., ANGIE BROADHEAD, KANDIS BROADHEAD, DAVE BROBERG, KENT BROBERG, JANET BROCK, KELVIN BROCK, SHANE BROCK, DIANE BROCKBANK, JOHN BROCKERT, CARRIE BRODERICK, SAMUEL BRODERICK, JEFFREY BRODIE, AMY BROEKEMEIER, PAULA BROG, JANET BROHM, MATT BROKAW, MARCIE BRONCHELLA, LINDY BRONSON, PAULA BRONTE, JUDITH BROOKE-GREEN, PRISCILLA BROOKENS, ROBERT BROOKER, JAMES BROOKES, SUSAN BROOKHART, CHRIS BROOKS, DEAN BROOKS, DORLENE BROOKS, EDWARD BROOKS, EUGENE BROOKS, FRANK BROOKS, HEATHER BROOKS, JOHN BROOKS, KARIN BROOKS, MICHAEL BROOKS, NATE BROOKS, RUDOLPH BROOKS, STEPHEN BROOKS, TRACIE BROOKS, ERLON BROOMHALL, HEIDI BROOMHALL, RAYMOND BROOMHALL, SCOTT BROOMHALL, WENDALL BROOMHALL, JENNIFER BROSCHINSKY, KURT BROSIG, TOM BROTHERS, DAVID BROTHERSEN, DIANE BROTHERSEN, KATHLEEN BROTHERTON, RACHELLE BROUGH, GEORGE BROUSARD, MICHAEL BROUSSEAU, ALAN BROWER, CINDIE BROWER, DANIEL BROWER, KRISTY BROWER, LEE BROWER, ALAN BROWN, ALLAN BROWN, BENJAMIN BROWN, BEVERLY BROWN, BLAIN BROWN, BRANDON BROWN, BRANT BROWN, CAROLE BROWN, CARYL BROWN, CHALEN BROWN, CHRISTINE BROWN, CHRISTOPHER BROWN, CORY BROWN, CURTIS BROWN, CYNTHIA BROWN, DARRYL BROWN, DAVE BROWN, DEANN BROWN, DEBORAH BROWN, DENNIS BROWN, DIANA BROWN, DIANE BROWN, DONALD BROWN, DONALD BROWN, DOUGLAS BROWN, EARL BROWN, ELISABETH BROWN, FRANK BROWN, FRANK BROWN, GAYLEN BROWN, GAYLENE BROWN, GEORGINA BROWN, GERALD BROWN, GLORIA BROWN, HELEN BROWN, HERBERT BROWN, JACKIE BROWN, JAMES BROWN, JANALIE BROWN, JANENE BROWN, JANET BROWN, JARED BROWN, JAY BROWN, JEAN BROWN, JESSICA BROWN, JOAN BROWN, JOYCE BROWN, JOYCE L. BROWN, JUDITH BROWN, KATHRINE BROWN, KAY BROWN, KELLY BROWN, KENNETH BROWN, KIM BROWN, KRISTIN BROWN, KRISTINA BROWN, LINDA BROWN, LISA BROWN, LISETTE BROWN, LORRAINE BROWN, MARI DEE BROWN, MARILYN BROWN, MARK BROWN, MARK BROWN, MARY BROWN, MICHAEL BROWN, MIKE BROWN, NICHOLAS BROWN, PATRICIA BROWN, PAUL BROWN, PAULINE BROWN, PEGGY BROWN, RAY BROWN, RAYLENE BROWN, REBECCA BROWN, RICHARD BROWN, ROBERT BROWN, ROBERT BROWN, ROBERT BROWN, ROBERT BROWN, ROBIN BROWN, RORY BROWN, SAMUEL BROWN, SCOTT BROWN, SHARMAN BROWN, SHERMA BROWN, SHIRLEY BROWN, STACEY BROWN, STEVE BROWN, STEVE BROWN, TAMRA BROWN, THERESA BROWN, THOMAS BROWN, TIM BROWN, TINA BROWN, TODD BROWN, TRACY BROWN, WALLACE BROWN, WAYNE BROWN, WILLIE BROWN, FRANK BROWN MD, DAMON BROWN WESTBROOK, JEREMY BROWNE, TED BROWNE, GARY BROWNING, PEGGY BROWNING, ROBERT BROWNING, COREY BROWNSON, JOHN BRUBAKER, JOSEPH BRUBAKER, REBECCA BRUBAKER, SCOTT BRUBAKER, MAX BRUCE, STEPHANIE BRUCE, SUZAN BRUCE, JEANNE BRUCKNER, JOHN BRUCKNER, ROSANNE BRUEGMANN, ROB BRUENDL, MARK BRUENING, TIMOTHY BRUETT, BRENDA BRUEY, ASHLEE BRUFORD, WILLIAM BRUGGER, MERIDETH BRUIN, LYNDA BRUINGTON, ROBERT BRUINGTON, JOHN BRUMMETT, NANCY BRUMMETT, DENNIS BRUNATTI, IDA BRUNATTI, EMILY BRUNER, JANA BRUNER, LUCAS BRUNER, ANDY BRUNET, ANDREW BRUNISHOLZ, DEBORAH BRUNISHOLZ, EDWARD BRUNISHOLZ, PETER BRUNJES, MARGARET BRUNN, DONOVAN BRUNNER, MARIAM BRUNNER, MARY BRUNNER, BARBARA BRUNO, JOHN BRUNS, TERESA BRUNT, JAN BRUNVAND, DAVID BRUSKE, CHRISTOPHER BRUST, LEONIE BRUTSCH, WERNER BRUTSCH, ELANA BRYAN, JOHN BRYAN, JOHNNY BRYAN, KATHERINE BRYAN, SARA BRYAN, GARRY BRYANT, JACQUIE BRYANT, PAUL BRYANT, SHANNA BRYANT, BLAINE BRYNER, WAYNE BRYNER, JARED BRYSON, LYNN BRYSON, MICHAEL BUCH, ALFRED BUCHANAN, BENNION BUCHANAN, KARLA BUCHANAN, MICHAEL BUCHANAN, MYRA BUCHANAN, NATHAN BUCHANAN, TERESA BUCHANAN, WILLIAM BUCHANAN, JESSICA BUCHI, RANDALL BUCHMILLER, ANGELA BUCIO, DANIEL BUCIO, MICHAEL BUCK, NATHAN BUCK, RUBY BUCK, SUSAN BUCKALEW, MARILYN BUCKHOLTS, LEONARD JR BUCKLAND, ALLISON BUCKLEY, MICHAEL BUCKLEY, TINA BUCKLEY, JACQUELINE BUCKMINSTER, CARLOS BUCKNER, CHRIS BUCKNER, KENNETH BUCKWALTER, BEVERLY BUCKWAY-ROSALES, ANA BUDD, JOANNE BUDD, KIMBERLY BUDD, SUANNE BUDDEN, FRANCES BUDDLE, MARGARET BUDGE, TREVOR BUDGE, DAN BUDZYNSKI, HANS BUEHLER, SUSAN BUEHLER, WOLFRAM BUEHLER, CHARLES BUEHNER, BRANDON BUHLER, DIANE BUHLER, DOUGLAS BUHLER, ERIC BUHR, RICHARD BUIST, MARGARITA BULL, CYNTHIA BULL-RICKARDS, GRANT BULLOCH, ALAN BULLOCK, ANGELA BULLOCK, COREY BULLOCK, DARRELL BULLOCK, DEAN BULLOCK, JAMES BULLOCK, JONYCE BULLOCK, JULIA BULLOCK, LAURY BULLOCK, MARY BULLOCK, SABRINA BULLOCK, SHAWNA BULLOCK, WILLIAM BULLOCK, BENJAMIN BULLOUGH, RICHARD BULLOUGH, MICHELLE BUMP, ERIC BUMSTEAD, TANAUNA BUNCH, BRUCE BUNDERSON, LUCY BUNDY, INA BUNE, ALAN BUNKER, JULIE BUNKER, CHAD BUNN, SANDRA BUNN, EMILY BUNNELL, JACKIE BUNTING, TATYANA BUNYATOVA-BAUER, DEBORAH BURBACK, SHANNON BURBANK, JANEAL BURBANK-SCHULTZ, BRINTON BURBIDGE, EMILEE BURBIDGE, WILLIAM BURBRIDGE, MICHAEL BURCH, SUSAN BURCH, WILLIAM BURCH, HEATHER BURCHETT, ASHLEY BURDEN, ANTHONY BURDETT, BEN BURDETT, JOAN BURDETT, KIMBERLI BURDETT, SUSAN BURDETT, JACOB BURDETTE, JOSEPH BURDS, DOUGLAS BURGAN, MATTHEW BURGEMEISTER, ROBIN BURGENER, RON BURGERS, KENNETH BURGESS, MOANA BURGESS, JOHN BURGGRAF, ANGELLA BURGON, MARK BURGON, CHRISTOPHER BURGOYNE, LEIGH BURK, SARAH BURKART, AMBER BURKE, GERALD BURKE, HUBERT (JACK) BURKE, JOHN BURKE, KAREN BURKE, KAREN BURKE, SUSANNE BURKETT, LYLE BURKHART, JOSEPH BURKHEAD, GREG BURKHOLDER, JIM BURKHOLDER, SALLY BURKHOLDER, HOWARD BURKHOLZ, CORBY BURKINSHAW, ROBERT BURKS, DANIEL BURLEIGH, BRIANNE BURLEY, JOAN BURLINGAME, ANN BURNETT, BECKY BURNETT, BERNICE BURNETT, DOUG BURNETT, JILL BURNETT, JULIE BURNETT, MARK BURNETT, RICHARD BURNETT, ROBERT BURNETT, TRACIE BURNETT, CHARLES BURNHAM,

EMMY LOU BURNHAM, JET BURNHAM, LEE BURNHAM, EDWARD BURNHETER, GLEN BURNINGHAM, LAUREN BURNINGHAM, MARILYN BURNINGHAM, BECKY BURNS, CAROL BURNS, DALE BURNS, GEORGE BURNS, JACALYN BURNS, JAMES BURNS, JOSEPH BURNS, LARRY BURNS, LOREN BURNS, MARY BURNS, MICHELLE BURNS, MARY BURRASTON, ALONZO BURRELL, BARTON BURRESS, LYNNMARIE BURRESS, STEPHEN BURRESS, DONALD BURRIGHT, BROCK BURROWS, ELAINE BURROWS, JASON BURROWS, WILFORD BURROWS, RONALD BURRUP, JAMES BURRUSS, ROCHELLE BURSON, AMBER BURT, CAROLYNN BURT, MARILYN BURT, MARYEE BURT, ROBERT BURT, DOROTHY BURT-COBURN, BRENT BURTON, DAVID BURTON, DONNA BURTON, GRANT BURTON, JAMES BURTON, JAMES BURTON, JED BURTON, JEFF BURTON, JEFFREY BURTON, JERRED BURTON, KENNETH BURTON, LEONARD BURTON, MARK BURTON, NOLAN BURTON, S. BURTON, SANDEE BURTON, SHERRY BURTON, SUSAN BURTON, TARYN BURTON, THOMAS BURTON, THOMAS BURTON, LISA BURY, DALE BUSATH, DAVID BUSBY, NICHOLAS BUSBY, LISA BUSCH, ALISA BUSCHE, KENT BUSH, ROBERT BUSH, GARY BUSHMAN, BILL BUSHNELL, VICTORIA BUSHNELL, JENNIFER BUSTILLO, PIPER BUTCHER, REY BUTCHER, JIM BUTERBAUGH, NANCY BUTERBAUGH, GINNY BUTIKOFER, ALDEANA BUTLER, ANNA BUTLER, ANTHONY BUTLER, JEFFREY BUTLER, JUDITH BUTLER, JULIA BUTLER, RACHEL BUTLER, RICHARD BUTLER, ROBERT BUTLER, TRENT BUTLER, BRIAN BUTTARS, JANE BUTTARS, TRACY BUTTARS, BRET BUTTERFIELD, MICHELLE BUTTERFIELD, SHARON BUTTERFIELD BUTTERFIELD, BOBBIE BUTTERS, KENT BUTTERS, JOHN BUTTLES, LINDA BUTTLES, JANELL BUTTON, FERD BUTTSCHARDT, ENRICO BUZON, ALAN BYBEE, COREY BYBEE, GLEN BYBEE, JAMES BYBEE, LAURA BYBEE, LYNETTE BYBEE, NANCY BYBEE, PAMELA BYBEE, RAYMON BYBEE, SUSAN BYBEE, BROOKE BYERS, CLAY BYINGTON, DEBORAH BYLSMA, MICHAEL BYLSMA, STEPHANI BYLUND, INGRID BYRAM, HARRY BYRD, MARTHA BYRD, JOSHUA BYRNE, MARY BYRNE, STEPHEN BYRNE, JUDY BYRON. TOM BYRON, ALVIN BYTHEWAY, ANEGELA BYTHEWAY, TIMOTHY BYWATER • C • LAURALYN CABANILLA, ARTHUR CADJAN, DANIEL CAFFEE, JAMES CAGE, CHERYL CAGLE, BARBARA CAHILL, CLIFFORD CAHOON, GARY CAHOON, JACOB CAHOON, ELIZABETH CAIN, TOBY CALAFETTI. MAHALA CALAME, MARY CALAME, RUSSELL CALAME, TARA CALANCEA, ROBERT CALAS, PATSY CALAWAY, JOAN CALDER, MONIQUE CALDER, COLLETTE CALDERWOOD, CHRISTINE CALDWELL, JILL CALDWELL, LYNNE CALDWELL, RICHARD CALDWELL, ALISA CALHOON, CORY CALL, DEBRA CALL, DREW CALL, ELAINE CALL, JAN CALL, JANEAL CALL, JOEL CALL, JUANITA CALL, JUDY CALL, KEITH CALL, KIRSTEN CALL, LAURIE CALL, LEVI CALL, MATTHEW CALL, PETER CALL, RICHARD CALL, SCOTT CALL, SHANNON CALL, STEPHANIE CALL, WILLARD CALL, GAYLE CALLAHAN, LESLIE CALLAHAN, THERESA CALLANAN, JERRI CALLANTINE, STEVEN CALLANTINE, LENNIT CALLEN, MICHAEL CALLES, SHERRIE CALLES, TAMMY CALLIHAN, NEIL CALLISTER, THOMAS CALTON, LUCINDA CALVERT, JOSEPH CAMALICHE, ROBERT CAMARGO, JOAN CAMARRO SIMARD, ANGELIA CAMERON, GRACE CAMERON, HENRY CAMERON, JAMES CAMERON, RENEE CAMEROTA, STEVE CAMEROTA, VICKIE CAMMACK, COLLEEN CAMP, CRAIG CAMP, JEFFERSON CAMP, PAMELA CAMP, ALISHA CAMPBELL, ANGELA CAMPBELL, BENJAMIN CAMPBELL, BRENT CAMPBELL, BRYAN CAMPBELL, BRYAN CAMPBELL, CONNIE CAMPBELL, DAVID CAMPBELL, DEMETRIOS CAMPBELL, DOUGLAS CAMPBELL, DUREECE CAMPBELL, EDWARD CAMPBELL, EILEEN CAMPBELL, GLENN CAMPBELL, JACQUALINE CAMPBELL, JEAN CAMPBELL, JEFFREY CAMPBELL, JESSICA CAMPBELL, JOHN CAMPBELL, JONI CAMPBELL, KAREN CAMPBELL, KATHLEEN CAMPBELL, KATHY CAMPBELL, LAURA CAMPBELL, LINDSAY CAMPBELL, LLOYD CAMPBELL, LURALEE CAMPBELL, MARTIN CAMPBELL, MICHELLE CAMPBELL, PETER CAMPBELL, RANDY CAMPBELL, REGINA CAMPBELL, ROBERT CAMPBELL, ROBERTA CAMPBELL, TAWNY CAMPBELL, WILLIAM CAMPBELL, WILLIAM CAMPBELL, CONRAD CAMPOS, EMILY CAMPOS, JEANNE CAMPSIE, MICHAEL CANAAN, TERRI CANCHOLA, TONI CANCRO, MATHEW CANDLAND, ANDREA CANDRIAN, JOY CANDRIAN, JEAN CANESTRINI, ROBERT CANESTRINI, CONNIE CANFIELD, ELAINE CANFIELD, PAIGE CANFIELD, DICK CANNADAY, THOMAS CANNING, ALYSA CANNISTRA, BARBARA CANNON, CHELSEA CANNON, COURTNEY CANNON, EMY CANNON, HEATHER CANNON, JOSEPH CANNON, KATRINA CANNON, LESA CANNON, LINDSAY CANNON, NANCY CANNON, ROGER CANNON, RUSSELL CANNON, RUTH CANNON, STEPHANIE CANNON, SUSAN CANNON, SUZETTE CANNON, THOMAS CANNON, TRICIA CANNON, JENNIFER CANTER, ROBERTO CANTU VILLARREAL, DONALD CAPERTON, LINDA CAPOBIANCO, BRIAN CAPPEL, ROGER CAPPS, DAVID CAPUANO, MARY CAPUTO, CHRIS CARAS, JEAN-PIERRE CARAVAN, MORY CARAWAY, BENJAMIN CARD, BENJAMIN CARD, CYNTHIA CARD, DOUGLAS CARD, TERRIE CARD, MARGARET CARDALL, DANIEL CARDELL, JENNIFER CARDELL, WILLIAM CARDEN JR, BARTELL CARDON, CHAD CARDON, CHANTAL CARDON, DAVID CARDON, DENICE CARDON, JEREMY CARDON, KATHLEEN CARDON, KATHY CARDON, PETER CARDON, RONALD CARDON, KAREN CARDOZA, SCOTT CARDWELL, CATHY CAREY, COLLEEN CAREY, DAVID CAREY, STEPHANIE CAREY, STEVE CAREY, THOMAS CAREY, BRIAN CARISCH, SHAUNA CARL, DAVE CARLILE, LUCY CARLILE, MARK CARLILE, WAYNE CARLILE, LEE CARLING, EDWARD CARLISLE, DAVID CARLQUIST, JENNIFER CARLQUIST, BRIAN CARLSEN, THOMAS CARLSEN, ANDREW CARLSON, CAROL CARLSON, CARRIE CARLSON, CONNIE CARLSON, GARY CARLSON, JAMES CARLSON, JANICE CARLSON, JOHN CARLSON, KAREN CARLSON, KATHLEEN CARLSON, KIMBERLEE CARLSON, MELANIE CARLSON, NORMAN CARLSON, SARAH CARLSON, STU CARLSON, TERRY CARLSON, ABIGAIL CARLSTON, CHARLES CARLSTON, CHRISTOPHER CARLSTON, PETER CARLSTON, STEPHEN CARLTON, JANET CARMER, OWEN CARNEY, MARY CAROFANELLO, DAVID CARPENTER, GERALD CARPENTER, LISA CARPENTER, LORRAINE CARPENTER, MELISSA CARPENTER, PAUL CARPENTER, CHRISTINE CARPER, DIANNE CARR, EMILY CARR, EUGENE CARR, IRENE CARR, MARY CARR, NATHAN CARR, NORMA CARR, VALERIE CARR, JAMES CARRABRE, ANGELLA CARRIER, ALYSON CARRIERE, LORI CARRIG, SHAWN CARRIGAN, LEE CARRILLO, CARRIE CARROLL, CHERI CARROLL, DANIEL CARROLL, HOLLY CARROLL, KATHY CARROLL, ROBERT CARROLL, DAVID CARRUTH, MICHELLE CARRUTH, ROBERT CARRUTH, AERIAL CARSEY, KATHRYN CARSON, MARJORIE CARSON, BECKY CARTER, BRIANT CARTER, BRYAN CARTER, CONNIE CARTER, CORY CARTER, DAN CARTER, DAVID CARTER, DON CARTER, JANE CARTER, JASON CARTER, JEFFERY CARTER, JEFFERY CARTER, JODY CARTER, KAREN CARTER, KATHRYN CARTER, KEVIN CARTER, KEVIN CARTER, LARRY CARTER, LINDSAY CARTER, LISA CARTER, MARY CARTER, MARY ANN CARTER, MATTHEW CARTER, MICHAEL CARTER, MICKEY CARTER, PAUL CARTER, RAQUEL CARTER, REED CARTER, SHIRLEEN CARTER, STEVEN CARTER, STEVEN CARTER, SUSAN CARTER, TANIELLE CARTER, TARA CARTER, TERESA CARTER, TIFFANY CARTER, JAMES CARTER JR, DEBORAH CARTMILL, TODD CARTON, KATHLEEN CARTWRIGHT, MARGIE CARTWRIGHT, VICTOR CARTWRIGHT II, CAROLYN CARTY, GABRIELLE CARUSO, JOSE CARVAJAL, GERARD CARVALHO, GRANT CARVER, ROY CARVER, EVAN CASE, LORI CASE, MICHAEL CASE, AARON CASEBOLT, CARLIE CASEY, KEVIN CASEY, MACKENZIE CASEY, TRACY CASH, MARGARET CASHELL, KIT CASHMORE, JOHN CASIAS, CARRIE CASKEY, ASPEN CASPER, BRIAN CASPER, MARY JANE CASPER, MATTHEW CASPER, SABRINA CASPER, DAVEN CASSADY, MATTHEW CASSEL, DAVID CASSETT, JAMES CASSIDY, JOHN CASSIDY, LEE CASSITY, PATRICK CASSITY, TODD CASSITY, ERNEST CASSLER III, BRUNO CASTAGNO, RICHARD CASTAGNO, RICK CASTEEL, MADELEINE CASTELLANOS, CHRISTINE CASTILLO, IRENE CASTILLO, CHARLES CASTLE, LARRY CASTLE-FERICKS, CHARLES CASTLETON, PAMELA CATES, SCOTT CATES, SEAN CATHERALL, ANTHONY CATINELLA, JOHN CATMULL, STEVE CATMULL, STACY CATTELAIN, JOSEPH CATTEN, LAURA CATURIA, JENNY CAULK, KATHI CAVALIERE, CHARLES CAVANAH, CORINNA CAVANAUGH, PATRICIA CAVANAUGH, PAMELA CAVERS, MARCUS CAZIER, STEPHEN CAZIER, IRAJA CECY, MARY JANE CECY, JOHN CEDENO, KATHERINE CEDERGREEN, GLEN CELLA, BONNIE CELONA, W IVAN CENDESE, RAND CENTER, CLAUDIA CENTONZE, TINA CEPELNIK, CHRISTOPHER CERVANTES, JULIE CERVANTES, PETRA CERVENKOVA, MELISSA CESSNA, JAMIE CETRARO, YULIYA CHADOVICH, ALICIA CHADWICK, DAWNETTE CHADWICK, HAROLD CHADWICK, LYNN CHADWICK, NATALIE CHADWICK, AMBER CHAIREZ, ALEXANDRIA CHAMBERLAIN, BRAD CHAMBERLAIN, BRADLEY CHAMBERLAIN, DILWORTH CHAMBERLAIN, KELLIE CHAMBERLAIN, KAYLEEN CHAMBERLIN, CHAD CHAMBERS, DALLIN CHAMBERS, EUGENE CHAMBERS, JENNIFER CHAMBERS, JOSEPH CHAMBERS, KENT CHAMBERS, LYNN CHAMBERS, ROBERT CHAMBERS, SHELLY CHAMBERS, SHERRIE CHAMBERS, STU CHAMBERS, CATHERINE CHAMBLESS, DOMINIQUE CHAMBLESS, ROSS CHAMBLESS, TIMOTHY CHAMBLESS, JONELLE CHAMPION, WILLIAM CHAMPNEYS, TANYA CHAN, MAGGIE CHAN-ROPER, DEVON CHANDLER, JAYLENE CHANDLER, STEVEN CHANDLER. DENNIS CHANG, FAUSTINA CHANG, RICHARD CHANG, SUZIE CHANG-HIGHLEY, DALE CHAPLIN, BRADLEY CHAPMAN, CAMILLE CHAPMAN, CYNTHIA CHAPMAN, DEBORAH CHAPMAN, JAMES CHAPMAN, JEFFREY CHAPMAN, JOSHUA CHAPMAN, MARY JANE CHAPMAN, PAMELA CHAPMAN, VICKIE CHAPMAN, ANNELISE CHAPPELL, CARL CHAPPELL, DANIEL CHAPPELL, JANALEE CHAPPELL, JENNIFER CHAPPELL, BRUCE CHAPPLE, JACQUES CHAPPUIS, MARCIA CHARD, JACOB CHARLES, ROBERT CHARLESON, ANGIE CHARLESWORTH, MINDY CHARLESWORTH, PATSY CHARLESWORTH, PAUL CHARTIER, BRENT CHASE, JOHN CHASE, MICHELLE CHASE, PAUL CHASE, ROBERT CHASE, ANDREW CHASTAIN, KATHY CHATELAINE, BRADLEY CHATLIN, SARAH CHATTERLEY, EDWARD CHAUNER, CARLOS CHAVES, ROBSON CHAVES, JULIE CHAVEZ, JOE CHAVIS, BRADLEY CHECKETTS, PAMELA CHECKETTS, SANDRA CHECKETTS, TERRI CHECKETTS, DAVID CHEEK, RONALD CHEESMAN, ROSS CHEESMAN, RUBY CHEESMAN, CHAING-LIU CHEN, CHIH-HUI CHEN, MARTY CHEN, XIN CHEN, CAROLYN CHENEY, MELANIE CHENEY, REBECCA CHENEY, RICHARD CHENEY, STEPHANI CHENEY, EMIL CHENG, KINGPUN CHENG, PAMELA CHERRINGTON, BERT CHERRY, CLAIR CHERRY, HARDY CHERRY, JANET CHERRY, KEPA PETER CHERTUDI, NATHAN CHESHIRE, LEZLIE CHESLER, NORMAN CHESLER, JULIE CHESNEY, NORA CHETTERBOCK, JEFFREY CHEVALIER, HIRO CHHATPAR, BRUCE CHIDESTER, DEBBIE CHIDESTER, DIANNE CHIDESTER, LORI CHIDESTER, MICHAEL CHIDESTER, RICHARD CHIDESTER, SANDRA CHIDESTER, ANTONIETTE CHILD, DARREN CHILD, DENNIS CHILD, EVAN CHILD, JASON CHILD, JOHN CHILD, LAURIE CHILD, MARY JAYNE CHILD, RYAN CHILD, THOMAS CHILD, JAMIE CHILDS, TODD CHILDS, AMELIA CHIPMAN, COLLEEN CHIPMAN, ELIZABETH CHIPMAN. LARRY CHIPMAN, BROOKE CHISHOLM, JUDYTH CHISM, RICHARD CHITWOOD, EDWARD CHIVERS, LEANN CHLARSON, JAMES CHLUMSKY, IRENE CHO, TONY CHOATE, CHUNG RYONG CHOI, RICHARD CHOLODOWSKI, JEFF CHOW, RONALD CHOWEN, ILEEN CHRIS, TAMERRA CHRIS, WILLIAM CHRIS, TIFFANY CHRISMAN, DANIEL CHRIST, AMY CHRISTEN, ALLISON CHRISTENSEN, ANGELA CHRISTENSEN, BARRY CHRISTENSEN, BRENDA CHRISTENSEN, BRENT CHRISTENSEN, BRENT CHRISTENSEN, BRUCE CHRISTENSEN, BRUCE CHRISTENSEN, BRYCE CHRISTENSEN, CAROLYN CHRISTENSEN, CHARLES CHRISTENSEN, CLINT CHRISTENSEN, CYNTHIA CHRISTENSEN, DANYALE CHRISTENSEN, DAVID CHRISTENSEN, DAVID CHRISTENSEN, DAVID CHRISTENSEN, DIANE CHRISTENSEN, DONALD CHRISTENSEN, EARL CHRISTENSEN, ELAINE CHRISTENSEN, ELAINE CHRISTENSEN, ELISE CHRISTENSEN, ELIZABETH CHRISTENSEN, ELWOOD CHRISTENSEN, ERIC CHRISTENSEN, EUGENE CHRISTENSEN, EVELYN CHRISTENSEN, GARRET CHRISTENSEN, GARY CHRISTENSEN, GAYLE CHRISTENSEN, GERALD CHRISTENSEN, GLEN CHRISTENSEN, HEATHER CHRISTENSEN, HERBERT CHRISTENSEN, ILENE CHRISTENSEN, JACQUELINE CHRISTENSEN, JAN CHRISTENSEN, JANIS CHRISTENSEN, JEFFREY CHRISTENSEN, JERRY CHRISTENSEN, JON CHRISTENSEN, JOYCE CHRISTENSEN, KAREN CHRISTENSEN, KAREN CHRISTENSEN, KATUSKA CHRISTENSEN, KAYE CHRISTENSEN, L. BRUCE CHRISTENSEN, LARISA CHRISTENSEN, LEEANN CHRISTENSEN, LILLY CHRISTENSEN, LISA CHRISTENSEN, LOIS CHRISTENSEN, LUCILLE CHRISTENSEN, MAILE CHRISTENSEN, MARY CHRISTENSEN, MATTHEW CHRISTENSEN, MERRILL CHRISTENSEN, MICHAEL CHRISTENSEN, MICHAEL CHRISTENSEN, NATHAN CHRISTENSEN, NECIA CHRISTENSEN, NICHOLAS CHRISTENSEN, PATSY CHRISTENSEN, PAUL CHRISTENSEN, PETER CHRISTENSEN, RAYLENE CHRISTENSEN, RICHARD CHRISTENSEN, ROGER CHRISTENSEN, RON CHRISTENSEN, RON CHRISTENSEN, SHANE CHRISTENSEN, SHARI CHRISTENSEN, TANNA CHRISTENSEN, TARALEE CHRISTENSEN, TERRI CHRISTENSEN, THAMINA CHRISTENSEN, THOMAS CHRISTENSEN, VALERIE CHRISTENSEN, VON CHRISTENSEN, DAVID CHRISTENSON, KATHERINE CHRISTENSON, JANET CHRISTIAANSEN, KEITH CHRISTIAN, MICHAEL CHRISTIAN, STEPHANIE CHRISTIAN, CAROLE CHRISTIANSEN, CRAIG CHRISTIANSEN, KAREN CHRISTIANSEN, KAREN CHRISTIANSEN, KELLY CHRISTIANSEN, LISA CHRISTIANSEN, MICHELLE CHRISTIANSEN, ROBERT CHRISTIANSEN, SHANNON CHRISTIANSEN, STEVEN CHRISTIANSEN, CHARLEY CHRISTIANSON, PETER CHRISTIE, WILLIAM CHRISTIE, GARY CHRISTLEY, HOLLY CHRISTLEY, ANGIE CHRISTMAN, THOMAS CHRISTMAN, JULIE CHRISTOFFERSON, JESSICA CHRISTOPHER, BONNIE CHRISTOPHERSEN, SUSAN CHRISTOPHERSON, TYLER CHRISTOPULOS, LYNNE CHRONISTER, ANDREAS CHRYSIKAKIS, MELINA CHRYSOVOULOU, DARIN CHUGG, GENE CHUN, HYE JIN CHUNG, NELSON CHUNG, ALISON CHUNTZ, ANDREW CHURCH, CASEY CHURCH, KALI CHURCH, LISA CHURCH, MATTHEW CHURCH, GORDON CHURCHILL, JON CHUTICH, DARLENE CHYTRAUS, JULIE CHYTRAUS, TODD CHYTRAUS, LENKA CIBULOVA-REMES, GARY CICHOWSKI, CYNTHIA CIMA, SCOTT CIMA, ANDY CINDRICH, SAM CIRCO, GREGORY CISCO, KARYN CLAFFEY, VICTOR CLAMPITT, HEATHER CLANCY, JUANITA CLAPHAM, PATRICIA CLAPHAM, JUDITH CLAPP, ALLEN CLARK, ANNALEE CLARK, BARB CLARK, BARBARA CLARK, CHRIS CLARK, CINDY CLARK, CYNTHIA CLARK, DAVID CLARK, DEXTER CLARK, DOROTHY CLARK, DUANE CLARK, ELI CLARK, FRANCIS CLARK, GARY CLARK, GLENYS CLARK, H. SCOTT CLARK, HERBERT CLARK, JASON CLARK, JENNIFER CLARK, JESSE CLARK, JOHN CLARK, JOSEPH CLARK, KARALIE CLARK, KELLER CLARK, LINDA CLARK, LOUANN CLARK, MARGARET CLARK, MARTI CLARK, MARYANN CLARK, MATT CLARK, PAMELA CLARK, PAUL CLARK, RAY CLARK, REED CLARK, SCOTT CLARK, SHIRLEY CLARK, SPENCER CLARK, THOMAS CLARK, WENDY CLARK, WESTON CLARK, WILLIAM CLARK, WILLIAM CLARK, WILLIAM CLARK, CARLYLE CLARKE, DARRELL CLARKE, DAVID CLARKE, JAMES CLARKE, KEITH CLARKE, MARILYN CLARKE, MIKE CLARKE, PATRICIA CLARKE, ROBERT CLARKE, STEPHEN CLARKE, THOMAS CLARKE, BARBARA CLASEN, RICHARD CLASEN, SCOTT CLASEN, PAT CLAUSSE, JACK CLAWSON, ODEN CLAWSON, TIMOTHY CLAWSON, EDMUND CLAXTON JR, BARBARA CLAY, RAYNA CLAY, CHRIS CLAYBURN, CORINNE CLAYPOOL, MARTHA CLAYSON, BEVERLY CLAYTON, MARILYN CLAYTON, WILLIAM CLEAIR, SUSANN CLEARWATER, AMANDA CLEAVINGER, HOWARD CLEAVINGER, ANNE CLEGG, CHRISTIAN CLEGG, DEANNE CLEGG, DUSTY CLEGG, JAMES CLEGG, JANICE CLEGG, MELISSA CLEGG, SHANNON CLEGG, STANLEY CLEGG, CINDA CLEMENT, KELLY CLEMENT, STEPHANIE CLEMENT, BRADLEY CLEMENTS, CINDY CLEMENTS, GERALDINE CLEMENTS, PATRICIA CLEMENTS, MITCHELL CLEMENTSON, SHARON CLEMENTSON, HAROLD CLEMMER, BRENT CLEVERLY, TAMMIE CLEVERLY, CHRISTOPHER CLIFFORD, EMILY CLIFFORD, JAYNE CLIFFORD, KENNETH CLIFFORD, NICOLE CLIFFORD, GARY CLIFT, CHRISTINE CLINE, DAVID CLINE, DAVID CLINE, DENISE CLINE, DERRICK CLINE, ENRIQUETA CLINE, KEITH CLINE, SCOTT CLINE, PHILLIP CLINGER, SUSAN CLINGER, JOAN CLISSOLD, WESLEY CLOCK, BRAD CLONTZ, TIFFANY CLOSE, JODI CLOUSE, CARL CLOWARD, SHERMAN CLOWARD, SPENCER CLOWARD, JONE CLUFF, KARIE CLUFF, TARA CLUFF, WILLIAM CLUFF, CHRIS CLUNE, BRENDA CLUSTER, JOHN CLYDE, CAROLYN CLYNE, RALPH COATES, ERIC COATS, MITT COATS, DOUGLAS COBABE, FREDRICK COBABE, GEORGE COBABE, JEFFREY COBABE, SYLVIA COBABE, HANK COBB, RONALD COBBLEY, JASON COBLE, DARRIN COBLER, BRIAN COBURN, ROYAL COBURN, LARRY COCHRAN, BELINDA COCHRAN-BARENBRUGGE, DIANE COCKER, RAYDEN CODY, WAYNE CODY, NANCY COE, SHIRLEY COE, ANDREW COEN, JULIE COEN, DONALD COFER, JOHN COFER, BRAD COFFEY, JEROME COFFEY, DEANNE COFFIN, JANE COFFIN, WILLIAM COFFIN, DAVID COFFMAN, KIMBERLEY COHEE, CHRISTINE COHEN, MARK COHEN, BARI NAN COHEN ROTHCHILD, PAT COHN, BRUCE COHNE, LYNN COHNE, ANDY COIL, MORRIS COILE, JOHN COKER, LINDA COLBURN, DEBRA COLBY, ERMA COLBY, MICHAEL COLBY, MONICA COLBY, RONALD COLBY, TAMMY COLBY, LORETTA COLE, MATTHEW COLE, MICHAEL COLE, PAEA COLE, RITA COLE, RONALD COLE, TYLER COLE, WAYNE COLE, WENDY COLE, ARTHUR COLEMAN, DANIEL COLEMAN, JOHN COLEMAN, KATIE COLEMAN, MARINA COLEMAN, THOMAS COLEMAN, JAMES COLEMAN JR, JEFFREY COLEMERE, CYNTHIA COLES, RICHARD COLES, DAWNETTA COLLAR, CATHY COLLARD, KENT COLLARD, PATRICIA COLLARD, SANDRA COLLARD, KIRK COLLEDGE, LORRAINE COLLEDGE, AARON COLLETT, BECKY COLLETT, CHARLES COLLETT, CLARK COLLETT, LINDA COLLETT, MARK COLLETT, MARVIS COLLETT, OWEN COLLETT, DAVID COLLIER, PATI COLLIER, CHERI COLLIGAN, THOMAS COLLIGAN, NICK COLLIN, CHELSEY COLLINS, CRAIG COLLINS, DEBORA COLLINS, ELIZABETH COLLINS, JARED COLLINS, JOHN COLLINS, JULIA COLLINS, LACY COLLINS, LISA COLLINS, MARINA COLLINS, MARY COLLINS, ROLAYNE COLLINS, TIFFANY COLLINS, JASON COLLOTZI, MERCEDES COLOMINES, MARY SUE COLONY, KELLY COLOPY, KATHIE COLOSIMO, CARMEN COLOTLA, SHERRON COLTHARP, BOYD COLTON, CHARLES COLTRAIN, SHIRLEE COLTRAIN, JANET COLVIN, STEPHEN COLVIN, GINGER COMARELL, ANDREA COMBE, COREY COMBE, GLENNA COMBE, JESSICA COMBE, NANETTE COMBE, KAMILLE COMBS, FRANK COMER, EDWIN COMPTON, TREVOR COMPTON, JONNA COMSTOCK, JULIE COMSTOCK, WES COMSTOCK, BRODIE CONDIE, JAMES CONDIE, JUDITH CONDIE, NANCY CONDIE, SHANNON K CONDIE, MARCI CONDIE-GUNNELL, JUDY CONDON, STEPHEN CONDON, CHARLES CONDRAT, BRANDON CONDREN, DIANE CONGDON, JUNE CONGDON, WILLIAM CONGDON, WENDY CONGLETON, ROBIN CONK, SHELLEY CONKEY, CARITA CONKLIN, DWAYNE CONLIN, JEREMY CONLIN, SPENCER CONNELLY, WENDY CONNELLY, MICHAEL CONNER, RICHARD CONNER, SCOTT CONNER, DAVID CONNER JR, EDMUND CONNOLLY, LARRY CONNOLLY, KATHRYN CONNOR, CHARLES CONNOY, BART CONRAD, CARA CONRAD, CONRAD CONRAD, GEORGANN CONRAD, CONNIE CONROY, RICHARD CONTE, JAMES CONTOS, UNIFORMED CONTRACTORS, JAMES CONWAY, JOHN CONWAY, MARY CONWELL, ADAM COOK, ALENE COOK, BENJAMIN COOK, CALENE COOK, CAMILLE COOK, CARLA COOK, CAROLE COOK, CLIFTON COOK, CRAIG COOK, CRAIG COOK, DAVID COOK, DELL JEAN COOK, DOUGLAS COOK, GREG COOK, KAREN COOK, KATHLEEN COOK, KIMBERLY COOK, KURDELL COOK, LISA COOK, MIRIAM COOK, PALMA COOK, ROBERT COOK, SACHA COOK, SPENCER COOK, STEPHANIE COOK, THOMAS COOK, VICKY COOK, ANDREW COOKLER, GAY COOKSON, MICHAEL COOL, JANET COOLEY, STEPHANIE COOLEY, VERNON COOLEY, JOANNA COOLIDGE, SALLY COOLLEY, MATTHEW COOMBES, BRIENNE COOMBS, VERN COOMBS, EARL COOMBS II, MIKE COON, RICHARD COON, CARLA COONRADT, CHARLES COONRADT, KELLY COONRADT, CAMILLE COONS, MIRIAM COONS, BARB COOPER, JOLAYNE COOPER, LARRY COOPER, LAURIE COOPER, LYNN COOPER, RUSS COOVER, CHERYL COPE, DAVID COPE, ROBERT COPE, STANLEY COPE, MARK COPELAND, NANCY COPLEN, PHILLIP COPLEN, TRACY CORAM, JACKE CORBETT, KEN CORBETT, MARILYN CORBETT, JACKIE CORBRIDGE, JONATHAN CORCHNOY, SARA CORDERY, BONNIE CORDON, MICHAEL CORDON, SHELLY CORDOVA, KAREEN COREA, DARREN COREY, HEATHER CORLESS, MAUREEN CORMIER, ROBERT CORN, LINDA CORNABY, KIMBERLY CORNELIUS, BARBARA CORNELSEN, BRIAN CORNETT, JOAN CORNISH, CLAUDE CORNU, BETSY CORNWALL, FELICIA CORNWELL, CARRIE ANN CORONA, RORY CORONA, DONALD CORRADO, MARGARET CORRADO, MICHAEL CORRELL, CARRIE CORRIGAN, JAMES CORRIGAN, BARBARA CORRY, CASEY CORRY, CINTHIE CORRY, JACQUELINE CORRY, JENNIFER CORRY, LAUREN CORTES, ROBERTA CORTEZ, NIKKI CORUM, CAROLINE CORWIN, GEORGE CORWIN, MITSI CORWIN, ROGER CORYER, MICHAAEL COSGRAVE, MARIANNE COSPER, RICHARD COSTANZA, JOHN COSTELLO, MARYSUE COSTELLO, CORY COSTLEY, DEBRA COSTLEY, JOHN COSTLEY, LAUNA COSTLEY, NOLAN COSTLEY, SHANNA COTE, STEPHEN COTE, LAUREL COTTAM, BARBARA COTTER, SHARON COTTERILL, RICHARD COTTINO, ADAM COTTLE, JENNIFER COTTLE, KEVIN COTTLE, DANIEL COTTON, VERNE COTTON, DALE COTTRELL, MICHAEL COTTRELL, RAEGAN COTTRELL, STEPHANIE COTTRELL, BILLY COTTS, SANDY COUCH, PATRICK COUGILL, MICHAEL COULTHARD, SCOTT COURSER, JEFFREY COURSEY, SUZANNE COURTRIGHT, LINDSEY COVINGTON, ROGER COVINGTON, JACOB COWAN, MARY COWAN-KLEIN, JASON COWER, JOAN COWLES, BETTY COWLEY, CRIS COWLEY, JAMES COWLEY, MARK COWLEY, PAUL COWLEY, ROCIO COWLISHAW, ALISA COX, ANTONY COX, BLAIR COX, BREANNA COX, BRYAN COX, CHANTELLE COX, CHRISTOPHER COX, CYNTHIA COX, DANA COX, DEAN COX, JASON COX, KIRSTIN COX, LADAWN COX, LINDA COX, MICHAEL COX, NEIL COX, PATRICIA COX, REBECCA COX, SHAWN COX, SUSAN COX, VALERIE COX, MELISSA COXEY, JOHN COY, DAVID COYLE, JOHN COYLE, TROY COYLE, GINA COZZA, SHERRIE COZZENS, BERNELL CRABTREE, CHERISSE CRABTREE, MARISHA CRABTREE, RICHARD CRABTREE, JOEL CRAFT, AMI CRAGUN, MARC CRAGUN, MICHAEL CRAGUN, MICHAEL CRAGUN, SHAWNA CRAGUN, WALLACE CRAGUN, BONNIE CRAIG, CAY CRAIG, DAN CRAIG, DAVID CRAIG, LAYNE CRAIG, LISA CRAIG, MARY CRAIG, MELISSA CRAIG, JOHN CRAIGLE, STEPHEN CRAIN, KELLY CRAM, CHRISTINE CRANDALL, GREGORY CRANDALL, NAN CRANDALL, ROBIN CRANDALL, CHRISTINE CRANDELL, CREIGHTON CRANE, JASON CRANE, ROBYN CRANE, BARBARA CRANER, BRANDON CRAPO, CRAIG CRASE, ALLEN CRAWFORD, CAROLYN CRAWFORD, D. BOYD CRAWFORD, ELIZABETH CRAWFORD, GARY CRAWFORD, GEORGE CRAWFORD, JANET CRAWFORD, KATHRYN CRAWFORD, MARK CRAWFORD, MARYLOU CRAWFORD, PAULA CRAWFORD, BARBARA CRAWLEY, SHEREEN CRAYTHORN, RAMONA CREBS, RANDY CREBS, RICHARD CREBS, JOHN CREER, KENNETH CREER, MARGARET CREER, NATHAN CREER, SHIRLEY CREER, TROY CREER, HENRY CRELLIN, KIM CRELLIN, VICKIE CRENO-WHITING, CINDY CRETEAU-MILLER, CASSANDRA CREWS, EMILY CRIBBS, RICHARD CRIBBS, KELI CRICHFIELD, DAVID CRIM, JULIA CRIM, BILLIE CRINO, MICHAEL CRINO, ANNETTE CRISMON, MAUREEN CRISMON, SUSAN CRISMON, JAN CRISPIN-LITTLE, BRIAN CRITCHFIELD, TROY CRITCHFIELD, JAMES CRITTENDEN, THOMAS CRITTENDEN, KEITH CROCHIERE, PAMELA CROCKER, ALAN CROCKETT, DIANNE CROCKETT, JEFF CROCKETT, GREGORY CROFOOT, CAROL CROFT, LINDA CROFT, LYNN CROFT, DAREL CROFTS, JOHN CROFTS, DOUGLAS CROMAR, KEVIN CROMAR, KATHY CROMPTON, KELLY CROMPTON, JOE CRONIN, STACY CRONINGER, BRIAN CROOK, RUSSELL CROOK, STANLEY CROOK, TRACY CROOK, LAUREN CROOKS, HEATHER CROPPER, NANCY CROPPER, AMANDA CROSBY, BRADLEY CROSBY, CARL CROSBY, CARL CROSBY, JACOB CROSBY, BETTE CROSHAW, CONNIE CROSHAW, IVA M. CROSHAW, ROSEANN CROSHAW, JAN CROSLAND, JEFFERY CROSLAND, KYLE CROSLAND, PATRICIA CROSLAND, TRAVIS CROSLAND, CARRIE CROSS, CHRISTOPHER CROSSETT, JED CROSSLEY, JERRY CROSSLEY, MICHAEL CROSSLEY, RICHARD CROSSLEY, TRUDI CROSSLEY, LAURIE CROSSWELL, DENNIS CROUCH, SUZANNE CROW, CHRIS CROWE, CHRIS CROWE, ELIZABETH CROWE, TERRENCE CROWE, BRENDA CROWLEY, BRIAN CROWLEY, KENNETH CROWTHER, LESLIE CROWTHER, MICHELE CROWTHER, SUZANNE CROWTHER, TED CROWTHER, TERRY CROWTHER, NATHAN CROWTON, CAROL CRUMP, COBY CRUMP, JENELLE CRUMP, PEGGY CRUMP, ROY CRUMP, STEVE CRUMP, VALENE CRUMPLEY, ALBA CRUZ, HILARIO CRUZ, MISTY CRUZ, PAM CRUZ, TERESA CRUZ, WENDY CRYAN, GENE CTIBOR, ERNEST CUATTO, KENNETH CUDDEBACK, RICHARD CULATTA, JOHN CULBERSON, KAREN CULBERSON, LARRY CULBERSON, MATT CULBERSON, NAN CULBERT, CHRISTOPHER CULLEY, SHEILA CULLEY, KATHLEEN CULLIMORE, CASSANDRA CULLISON, GARY CULLOP, PATRICIA CUMBERLAND, FRANK CUMBERLAND JR, CASEY CUMMINGS, CURTIS CUMMINGS, DAVID CUMMINGS, DOUGLAS CUMMINGS, JOYE CUMMINGS, MARK CUMMINGS, ROBERT CUMMINGS, RYAN CUMMINGS, ROBERT CUMMINGS JR, BRENDAN CUMMINS, BETSY CUNDICK, DENISA CUNDICK, RYAN CUNDICK, THOMAS CUNDICK, ALAN CUNNINGHAM, BRIGGS CUNNINGHAM, DARRELL CUNNINGHAM, DOUGLAS CUNNINGHAM, JAMIE CUNNINGHAM, KEVIN CUNNINGHAM, PENELOPE CUNNINGHAM, WILLIAM CUNNINGHAM, SHARON CUPIT, WILLIAM CUPIT, QUINTEN CUPPS, JAMES CURNEAL, FRANK CURRAN, NATHAN CURRIER, ALEXANDER CURRY, KAREN CURRY, MATT CURRY, MICHAEL CURTIN, ANDREW CURTIS, BOYD CURTIS, BRENDA CURTIS, BRENDA CURTIS, BRENT CURTIS, BRYAN CURTIS, CLARK CURTIS, DAVID CURTIS, DEBBIE CURTIS, ERIN CURTIS, FRANK CURTIS, GUY CURTIS, KENT CURTIS, KEVIN CURTIS, MACRAY CURTIS, MARK CURTIS, MATTHEW CURTIS, MICHAEL CURTIS, SEAN CURTIS, STEVEN CURTIS, TAIN CURTIS, VARDELL CURTIS, ERIN CUTCHEN, JENNIFER CUTLER, KAREN CUTLER, KIRT CUTLER, CHARLIE CUTTER, AMY CUTTING, HEINZ CUVELIER, LUDOMIR CZYNSKI • D • KELLY D'ALESSIO, JULIANN D'AMORE, STEPHEN D'EUSTACHIO, DAVID D'HULST, KEVIN DABB, JERI DABLING, DANNY DABNEY, KURT DAEMS, RICHARD DAEMS, LARRY DAGLEY, FREDRICK DAGNER, GINA DAGOSTINO, ALLISON DAHL, JEFFREY DAHL, JOLENE DAHL, KIM DAHL, MAX DAHL, LESLIE DAHLBERG, KATHERINE DAHLE, MARY DAHLE, HEATHER DAHLEEN, RODNEY DAHLEEN, PATRICIA DAHLIN, PAMELA DAHLKAMP, ESTELLE DAHLKEMPER, RICHARD DAHLKEMPER, JUDY DAHLQUIST, JAMES DAHLSTROM, MARYLIN DAHLSTROM, MICHAEL DAHLSTROM, DIANE DAHM, VICKY DAHN, JOHN DAILEY, RONALD DAILEY, SHERRILYN DAILEY, THOMAS DAILEY, ZACHARY DAILEY, KARI DAINES, ROBERT DAINES, CHRISTOPHER DAKE, LISA DAKE, RUSSELL DALBY, JENNEAN DALE, JEAN DALEBOUT, MATTHEW DALEBOUT, DIANE DALEY, PHILIP DALEY, RULEN DALEY, RUSSELL DALEY, RANAE DALGLEISH, DELIA DALLAS, CATHERINE DALLEY, MELISSA DALLEY, ROBERT DALLEY, RUTH H. DALLEY, SUSAN DALLEY, CLY'TA DALLING, DANNAH DALLING, JILLIAN DALLON, PATRICIA DALPIAZ, PAUL DALPIAZ, ROBERT DALPONTE, CRISPIN DALSING, AMIE DALTON, BRAD DALTON, DONNA DALTON, GEORGE DALTON, JESSICA DALTON, JON DALTON, MICHELLE DALTON, NAN DALTON, NAOMI DALTON, RON DALTON, SHAUNA DALTON, SYBILLA DALTON, LESLEY DALUZ, ANGIE DALY, CANDACE DALY, KAREN DALY, CARL DAMBMAN, RICHARD DAME, OTT DAMERON, RALPH DAMMANN, JOHN DAMON II, JULIE DANA, BETTY DANCE, EVA DANFORS, PER DANFORS, DEBI DANG-KUWADA, ANN DANGERFIELD, DAVID DANGERFIELD, ENOCH DANGERFIELD, MD, CAROLYN DANIELS, CHERIE DANIELS, DENNIS DANIELS, ESTEN DANIELS, JOANNE DANIELS, KAREN DANIELS, LINDA DANIELS, MICHAEL DANIELS, PATTI DANIELS, RICHARD DANIELS, RON DANIELS, WENDY DANIELS, CADY DANIELS III, MEG DANIELSON, WENDY DANIELSON, FRED DANNEMAN, HOLLY DANNEMAN, CHAD DANSIE, DANE DANSIE, DOUGLAS DANSIE, MICHELLE DANSIE, TRISHA DANSIE, PHONESAVANH DAOHEUANG, SHAWN DARBY, ROBIN DARK, BRANDI DARLINGTON, DOUGLAS DARRINGTON, GENEAL DART, DIANE DATTERI, JEFFREY DAUBE, LORRIE DAUBE, ROBERT DAUDT, DARELL DAVENPORT, NANCY DAVERIO, RUSSELL DAVEY, ALEX DAVIDSON, BENJAMIN DAVIDSON, CINDY DAVIDSON, DONALD DAVIDSON, ELIOTT DAVIDSON, JANET DAVIDSON, KRISTEN DAVIDSON, RETA DAVIDSON, ANGELA DAVIES, BECKY DAVIES, DAVID DAVIES, GEORGE DAVIES, JEANNIE DAVIES, LAURA DAVIES, ROBERT DAVIES, S DAVIES, SANDRA DAVIES, ELVIN DAVILA, JEAN DAVIN, ADAM DAVIS, ALAN DAVIS, ANITA DAVIS, BETTY LYNN DAVIS, BEVERLY DAVIS, BRENT DAVIS, BRETT DAVIS, BRIAN DAVIS, CHARLENE DAVIS, COREY DAVIS, DALE DAVIS, DALE DAVIS, DANIELLE DAVIS, DAVID DAVIS, DAVID DAVIS, DIANE DAVIS, DONALEE DAVIS, GEORGE DAVIS, GLENN DAVIS, HOWARD DAVIS, IAN DAVIS, JACKI DAVIS, JACQUELINE DAVIS, JANN DAVIS, JEFF DAVIS, JEFFREY DAVIS, JENI DAVIS, JENNY DAVIS, JIM DAVIS, JUDY DAVIS, JULIE DAVIS, KAAREN DAVIS, KARENE DAVIS, KATHLEEN DAVIS, KELLY DAVIS, KENT DAVIS, KENT DAVIS, KEVIN DAVIS, KIMBERLY DAVIS, KIRBY DAVIS, LARRY DAVIS, LINDA DAVIS, LYNNE DAVIS, MANDY DAVIS, MARK DAVIS, MATTHEW DAVIS, MICHAEL DAVIS, MICHAEL DAVIS, MICHAEL DAVIS, MICHELLE DAVIS, MONA DAVIS, MONICA DAVIS, PEGGY DAVIS, PHILLIP DAVIS, ROBERT DAVIS, ROBERT DAVIS, ROBERT DAVIS, ROBIN DAVIS, ROY DAVIS, SANDRA DAVIS, SCOTT DAVIS, SCOTT DAVIS, SHANA DAVIS, SHERWOOD DAVIS, STEVEN DAVIS, TAD DAVIS, TERESSA DAVIS, TERRI DAVIS, THOMAS DAVIS, WAYNE DAVIS, ANDREA DAVIS-NICHOLS, JAN DAVISON, MIKE DAVISON, DAVID DAWES, BARBARA DAWSON, COLLEEN DAWSON, DAVID DAWSON, JANET DAWSON, MEILING DAWSON, OLGA DAWSON, SHIRLEY DAWSON, STEVEN DAWSON, ANGELA DAY, BRITTANY DAY, CHRISTINE DAY, DEBI DAY, FORREST DAY, GINA DAY, JACQUELINE DAY, JOANN DAY, JOSEPH DAY, KAREN DAY, KEVIN DAY, MARIANNE DAY, MARK DAY, MILDRED DAY, MORGAN DAY, SALLIE DAY, STEPHANIE DAY, SUZANNE DAY, THELL DAY, THOMAS DAY, ANDREW DAY III, MERRILL DAY JR, CRAIG DAYHUFF, RICHARD DAYHUFF, LANAE DAYLEY, TAMRA DAYLEY, SUSAN DAYNES, CHERYL DE CASTRO, ROBERTO DE GIORGIO, ALMA DE GUZMAN, KRISTINA DE HAAN, STANLEY DE JONG, SUSANA DE LA CRUZ, AARON DE LA ROSA, EUGENE DE MARTA, NANCY DE MASI, EDUARDO DE RODA, RENATA DE ROSIS, MARIANELLA DE SOLA, PERRY DE VLUGT, DAVID DEAKIN, HOMER DEAL, BRENDA DEAN, FRANK DEAN, JENNIFER DEAN, JENNY DEAN, JILL DEAN, JOHN DEAN, KAY DEAN, KELSEY DEAN, KENNETH DEAN, MARK DEAN, NORMA DEAN, SAMUEL DEAN, DIANE DEARDEN, HUGH DEARDEN, VIVIAN DEARDEN, MICHAEL DEARDEUFF, BRIAN DEAVER, CHRISTINE DEAVER, DARYL DEBACKER, KATRIN DEBACKER, JESSICA DEBENHAM, JULIE DEBENHAM, REGAN DEBIE, ANITA DEBOER, VANESSA DEBROECK, GUY DECARLO, JOSEPH DECASTRO, CYNTHIA DECHART, CARL DECKER, CHRIS DECKER, DAVID DECKER, JEFFREY DECKER, MARIN DECKER, RANDALL DECKER, ANTHONY DECOITE, CORINE DECRION, BELINDA DEDOW, BRYAN DEEM, MARY DEEM, ANNETTE DEFRIES, DOUGLAS DEFRIES, CHIARA DEGLI ESPOSTI, PAUL DEGREY, NICHOLAS DEIEN, TRACINE DEIMER, CLAUDIA DEINES. GAIL DEJONG, RUSSELL DEJONG, PAUL DEJONG JR, INGRID DEKLAU, CAROL DEL GIUDICE, VERLENE DEL PORTO, BRYAN DELAGE, CATHIE DELEWSKI, RICHARD DELEWSKI, LULU DELGADO, RAYMOND DELGADO, SONIA DELGADO, JOHN DELGROSSO, LORI DELIO, PAULA DELIS, KAMILA DELL, JAMIE DELONG, KENNETH DELONG, ANTHONY DELPRETE, GLORIA DELPRETE, RAQUEL DELUCA, WILLIAM DELVIE, GEORGIA DEMARCO, WENDI DEMILLE, GARY DEMILT, JARED DEMING, MATT DEMING, DOT DEMMER, BERNIE DEMOSS, DAVID DEMOULPIED, JEFF DEMPSEY, PATRICIA DEMPSEY, CINDY DENAMUR, GREGORY DENARO, ALI DENHAM, TERESA DENISON, TIM DENISSON, SUSAN DENNETT, BLAIR DENNEY, MICHELLE DENNEY, ANNETTE DENNIS, LEROY DENNIS, SUZANNE DENNIS, SHIRLEY DENNISON, LISA DENNY, KORY DENOS, MARANATHA DENOS, WENDY DENSLEY, ARVELLA DENT, JEAN DENTON, TAMERA DENTON, JOHN DEPHILLIPS, MICHAEL DEPUTY, SHEILA DEPUTY, JAMES DERBY, LORI DERBY, TED DERBY, JAMES DEREAMER, SHARON DEREAMER, RANAE DERICO, ZACHARY DERR, KAREN DERRICK, ORVILLE DERRICK III, BRITTNEY DERRICOTT, KENT DERRICOTT, MATHIEU DES ROBERT, CHRISTOPHER DESANTIS, DOM DESANTIS, KIMBERLY DESAUTELS, MICHAEL DESCH, JANET DESCHAMP, RENE DESCHAMPS, ROBERT DESIMONE, STEPHEN DESIO, MATT DESJARDINS, ARLO DESPAIN, DON DESPAIN, KATHLEEN DESPAIN, RICHARD DESPAIN, W GLEN DESPAIN, DMITRY DESSIATNIKOV, GENESIS DESTINY, ALISHA DETEMPLE, DANIEL DETEMPLE, KATHERINE DETEMPLE, JACKLYN DETMERS, DONNA DETTMAN, GARY DETTMAN, DONNELL DETWEILER, ROBERT DETWEILER, BEVERLY DETWILER, MARITZA DEVALLY, ELIZABETH DEVANEY, LEE DEVER, JOHN DEVERALL, THOMAS DEVEREUX, CATHERINE DEVERS, MARIE-ODILE DEVILLERS, SANJIV DEVNANI, BOB DEVORE, CHRISTINE DEVOY, ANNE DEVRIES, DEBORAH DEVRIES, DEREK DEVRIES, GRACE DEVRIES, MICHELLE DEVRIES, PIA DEVRIES,

RHONDA DEVRIES, MARY DEWAAL, MICHAEL DEWAAL, REBECCA DEWAAL, STEPHANIE DEWAAL, LESLIE DEWALD, JAMES DEWEERD, GEORGE DEWEY, KATHY DEWEY, MELISSA DEWEY, ROBBI DEWEY, STEVE DEWEY, SYLVIA DEWEY, NORM DEWITT, JAMES DEWOLFE, LINDA DEWOLFE, ALESHA DEXTER, JEFFREY DEXTER, JOAN DEYLE, WILLIAM DEYLE, LINDA DEYOUNG, TOMMY DIAL, BARRY DIAMOND, DIANE DIAMOND, DICK DIAMOND, JUDIE DIAMOND, MARTA RAE DIAMOND, WAYNE DIAMOND, JODEE DIARTE, ARTHUR DIAS III, MICHAEL DIAZ, VICTOR DIAZ, VICTOR DIAZ, LAURA DIAZ DE LEON, CARMEN DIAZ-ALVERSON, BRUCE DIBB, COLLEEN DIBB, LELAND DIBBLE, LORI DICARLO, SANDRA DICHARO, ILENE DICKAMORE, DOUGLAS DICKENS, DEBORAH DICKERSON, DORIS DICKERSON, LINDA DICKEY, NICHOLAS DICKEY, TRAVIS DICKEY, CHRIS DICKINSON, EDITH DICKINSON, LINDSAY DICKINSON, RICK DICKINSON, SANDRA DICKINSON, MARJORIE DICKSON, STEVEN DICKSON, JULIE DIDERICKSEN, HUGO DIEDERICH, MARY DIEDRICH, CLAIRE DIETERLE, LORRAINE DIETERLE, MARGUERITE DIETRICH, EDUARDO DIEZ DE MEDINA, SALLIE DIFRANCESCO, VICKY DIGREGORIO, ELAYNA DIKEOU, MCKELL DILG, GREG DILL, TOM DILLER, CHARLES DILLIER, JOYCE DILLIER, RACHELLE DILLINGHAM, CARTER DILLMAN, ELLA DILLON, PATRICIA DILLON, SUSAN DILLON, JACQUELINE DILLON GAYER, PETER DIMAROGONAS, TATIANA DIMC - CERNIGOJ, LEWIS DIMLER, PENELOPE DIMLER, CINDY DIMOND, MARITA DIMOND, VICKIE DIMOND, SAM DIMSDALE, KHAJA DIN, TERRY DINGBAUM, MEIGHAN DINGLE, CHERYL DINSDALE, CECILE DINSMORE, JAMES DINSMORE, SUE DINTELMAN, SUSAN DINTER, WARREN DINTER, BOB DION, ANGELA DIRKMAAT, GERRIT DIRKMAAT, DEYA DISHMAN, NORMA DISZ, THOMAS DISZ, DARRON DITTMORE, JANE DITTMORE, KATHY DITTMORE, WILLIAM DITTMORE, HILLARY DIVEN, ALEX DIVERS, BARRY DIXON, BONNIE DIXON, CARL DIXON, JAMES DIXON, JOAN DIXON, KAREN DIXON, KELLY DIXON, REED DIXON, SCOTT DIXON, SUSAN DIXON, MICHAEL DJUNAEDI, MELITA DJURISIC, ARTHUR DOBBE, SHELLEY DOCKSTADER, KRISHNACHANDRA DODBALLAPUR, ANDY DODDS, JULIANN DODDS, MICHAEL DODDS, TERRY DODDS, TIFFANY DODDS, HEIDI DODENBIER, JEFFREY DODENBIER, ROBBIE DODENBIER, KATHY DODGE, JEFFREY DODSON, WILLIAM DODSON, DENISE DOEBBELING TURKANIS, CINDY DOEBLER, PATRICIA DOERMANN, MICHELLE DOHERTY, DELORAH DOHNER, STEVE DOHNER, AMBER DOI, JOHN DOLAN, RACHEL DOLAN, AMY DOLBIN, FRANCIS DOLCE, MICHELLE DOLINAR, CAROLYN DOLL, DREW DOLL, DARRIN DOMAN, KAREN DOMAN, WAYNE DOMAN, ANDRES DOMINGUEZ, WILLIAM DONACHIE, DAVID DONAHOE, TIM DONAHOE, BILLIE DONALDSON, CHRISTOPHER DONALDSON, LAUREN DONALDSON, LESLIE DONAVAN, TANIA DONE, DEVON DONEY, LILIN DONG, JAMES DONNELLS, SUSAN DONNELLS, MATTHEW DONNELLY, KATHLEEN DONNER, JANET DONOVAN, JOHN DONOVAN, PETER DONOVAN, BRENT DOOLEY, JOHN DOOLEY, LORI DOOLEY, SHARLENE DOOLIN, ALAN DOONAN, JOSEPH DOORNEK, BRENT DOPP, JANET DOPP, NATHAN DOPP, HENK DORENBOSCH, BARBARA DORNSEIF, ADELE DORSEY, BRIDGET DORSEY, BRAD DOSCH, STEVE DOSEN, GRADY DOTSON, HELEN DOTSON, VALERIE DOTY, SUSAN DOUCETTE, CYNTHIA DOUGHERTY, KATHY DOUGHERTY, STEVE DOUGHERTY, JASON DOUGLAS, PAMELA DOUGLAS, PATRICIA DOUGLAS, CATHERINE DOUGLASS, CRAIG DOUGLASS, JIM DOUSSARD, ARVA DOVER, SHARON DOVER, DEBORAH DOWD, MARCIA DOWDALL, DOUGLAS DOWDING, SHARON DOWDLE, WENDY DOWDY, ALICE DOWLING, BARBARA DOWNEY, JOYE DOWNEY, KIM DOWNEY, KARYN DOWNING, KENT DOWNING, CANDACE DOWNS, CHRISTINE DOWNS, ERRON DOWNS, HEATHER DOWNS, KATHY DOWNS, LISBETH DOWNS, TRACY DOWNS, HEIDI DOXEY, MATHEW DOXEY, SAMUEL DOXEY, SCOTT DOXEY, TERRY DOXEY, PATRICIA DOYLE, DOUGLAS DRAESEKE, DEBERA DRAGE, SHELLY DRAGE, DEBORAH DRAIN, ANDREW DRAKE, CATHERINE DRAKE, HENRY DRAKE, MAGGIE DRAKE, PAUL DRAKE, TENNILLE DRAKE, WENDY DRAKE, DAVID DRANSFIELD, ALLYN DRAPER, ANGELA DRAPER, BRENT DRAPER, DAVID DRAPER, HELEN DRAPER, LESA DRAPER, RICHARD DRAPER, ROBERT DRAPER, SCOTT DRAPER, JACK DRAXLER, DOUG DREDGE, RUTA DREIJMANIS EHLERS, DEBRA DREITZLER, CONNIE DRENKER, PENNY DRENNAN, ANNA DRESEL, RONDA DRESSEN, LAURA DREW, ROBERT DREW, DAVID DREWES, KENNETH DREYER, NANCY DREYER, ROBERT DREYER, DAN DRIGGS, DAVID DRIGGS, LEONARD DRIGGS, RICHARD DROESBEKE, APRIL DROGE, JILL DROWN, JOHN DRUCE, LINDA DRUCE, DANIEL DRUMILER, KAREN DRUMMOND, CASSIE DRYSDALE, DAVID DRYSDALE, ROBIN DRYSDALE, SCOTT DRYSDALE, TAWNY DRYSDALE, MARCELLO DUARTE, CINDY DUBOIS, NANCY DUBOIS, CHARLES DUBUC, JENNIFER DUBUC, SANDRA DUBUC, CARL DUCKWORTH, LARRY DUCKWORTH, DAVID DUDEK, JAMES DUDLESTON, DONALD DUDLEY, KATHY DUDLEY, KURT DUDLEY, PAMELA DUDLEY, DENISE DUECK-STUEBER, JANICE DUEHLMEIER, STEPHANIE DUEHLMEIER, CLORY DUERDEN, KELLIE DUERDEN, MATHEW DUERDEN, MARA DUERING, JANALYN DUERSCH, LORNA DUFF, KREIGHAN DUFFIELD, TROY DUFFIN, SHERYL-LEE DUFFY, MIKAELA DUFUR, GUY DUGAL, MARY JO DUING, BLAINE DUKE, LISA DUKE, MICHAEL DUKE, ROBERT DUKE, SHAUNA DUKE, JONATHAN DUKES, JAMES DUKETTE, JONATHAN DULEY, PAMELA DULIN, RACHEL DULL, MARIA DULZIADES, MARKUS DUMMERMUTH, GEORGE DUMOND, JOY LYNN DUNAJ, D LANETTE DUNBAR, CHRISTINE DUNCAN, EMMA DUNCAN, LARETTA DUNCAN, LINDA DUNCAN, MARK DUNCAN, MICHAEL DUNCAN, ROBERT DUNCAN, CAROLYN DUNFORD, JILL DUNFORD, TRACI DUNFORD, WILMA DUNFORD, DEANNA DUNKER, JODIE DUNKLEY, SCOTT DUNKLEY, SEAN DUNKLEY, STEPHANIE DUNKLEY, BARBARA DUNN, BARBARA DUNN, CARLTON DUNN, CAROLYN DUNN, DONALD DUNN, JERRY DUNN, LINDA DUNN, LORI DUNN, MARK DUNN, MICHAEL DUNN, MICHAEL DUNN, ROSE DUNN, VALENTINA DUNN, MARYANA DUNNING, THOMAS DUNNING, THOMAS DUNNING, WILLIAM DUNNING, MEGAN DUNPHY, DENNIS DUNSMORE, PAULA DUPIN-ZAHN, ROBERT DUPONT, BRANDON DUPUIS, ERIC DUPUIS, EUGENE DUQUETTE, MARIE DENISE DUQUETTE, JOE DURAN, MARIA DURAN, LOUIS DURANTE III, JOAN DURFEE, LYNN DURHAM, NORA DURHAM, PHILIP DURIAN, WILLIAM DURNEY, DANIEL DURRANT, DAVID DURRANT, DOUGLAS DURRANT, EARLENE DURRANT, JANE DURRANT, KELLEY DURRANT, SCOTT DURRANT, TODD DURRANT, NICK DURST, ERIC DURSTELER, AMY DURTSCHI, SHIRLEY DURTSCHI, MARY DURWARD, BARBARA DUSENBERRY, JEREMY DUSTIN, TRACY DUSTIN, JOHN DUTCHER, MELANIE DUTCHER, DENNIS DUTSON, LANA DUTSON, SUSAN DUTSON, RON DUYKER, ERIN DWAN, SCOTT DWIRE, SHRINATH DWIVEDI, MARY DWORSHAK, STEVEN DWYER, NEOMI DYAL, DAVID DYATT, ROYCE DYE, DIANA DYER, JANE DYER, KELLY DYER, RONALEE DYER, TIMOTHY DYER, ROGER DYKE, DIANE DYKMAN, SHERRY DYMOCK, TYSON DYMOCK, RUSSELL DYRENG, CHRISTOPHER DYSON, LUCIA DZUGAS • **E** • CYNTHIA EAGAR, RICHARD EAMES, SHARELL EAMES, FREDRICK EANES, KY EAP, ALAN EARL, BONNY EARL, BOYD EARL, CAROL EARL, CHARMALEE EARL, CORTNEY EARL, DEAN EARL, GARRY EARL, JULIANNE EARL, KAREN EARL, LISA EARL, LOIS EARL, MELISSA EARL, SUSAN EARL, ALLISON EARNSHAW, COLLEEN EARNSHAW, CRAIG EARNSHAW, CHARLES EARWOOD, REX EASLEY, BRANTLEY EASON, CHARLOTTE EAST, SUSAN EAST, CARLA EASTLAND, ERICA EASTMAN, JAMES EASTMAN, JANELL EASTMAN, LUCAS EASTMAN, STEPHANEE EASTMAN, CRISTI EASTON, TORI EATON, APRIL EBBERT, ARNOLD EBERHARD, DINEEN EBERHARD, ERNEST J. EBERHARD, NICOLLE EBERHARD, PAUL EBERLE, HOLLY EBERT, JEFFREY EBERT, MARILYN EBERT, ROBERT EBERT, SHELLY EBERT, TAY EBERT, GARY ECCLES, ALVIN ECHEVERRIA, PATRICE ECHOLA, NANCY ECHOLS, CAROL ECKARDT, WILLIAM ECKARDT, JOHN ECKELS, LIAHONA ECKHARDT, TRACE EDDINGTON, BRENT EDDY, DIANNE EDDY, JERRY EDDY, JUDY EDDY, NORMAN EDDY, QUENTON EDDY, RYAN EDDY, SUSAN EDDY, REX EDGEL, BECKY EDGELL, MARY LYNNE EDISON, BETTY EDLEFSEN, DAVID EDLUND, JAMI EDMAN, CARLOS EDMUNDS, CYNTHIA EDMUNDS, DAVID EDMUNDS, JANET EDMUNDS, LEIF EDMUNDS, RYAN EDMUNDS, BONNIE EDSON, LAWRENCE EDSON, CYNTHIA EDSTROM, NOAH EDVALSON, DEBBIE EDWARD, ARLOU EDWARDS, BECKY EDWARDS, BENJAMIN EDWARDS, BRUCE EDWARDS, BRUCE EDWARDS, DAMON EDWARDS, DAVE EDWARDS, DONALD EDWARDS, ELEANOR EDWARDS, FRED EDWARDS, JACK EDWARDS, JAMES EDWARDS, JAMES EDWARDS, JOHN EDWARDS, JOSHUA EDWARDS, JOYCE EDWARDS, KAREN EDWARDS, KERRY EDWARDS, LINDA EDWARDS, LINDA EDWARDS, MARGARET EDWARDS, MICHAEL EDWARDS, PATRICIA EDWARDS, ROBERT EDWARDS, TYLER EDWARDS, WENDY EDWARDS, CAROL EGAN, JERI EGAN, KAREN EGAN, RICHARD EGAN, DONALEA EGBERT, LON EGBERT, MELETA EGBERT, ANN EGELAND, PETRA EGGENBERGER, JASON EGGERS, CHRISTINE EGGERT, SUE EGGERT, BRYANT EGGETT, FRANK EGGINTON, BRUCE EGGLESTON, PAULINE EGGLESTON, LORI EHAT, CATHERINE EHLERT, CHRISTIE EICHENTOPF, GRETCHEN EICHENTOPF, ERNST EICHLER, SHERRI EINFELDT, YO-AT EINGAL, SHAWN EINZINGER, DON EISELE, JANICE EISELE, FRANCES EISENBERG, MICHAEL EISENBERG, RICHARD EISNER, GARY EKKER, CAROLEE ELDER, JO ANNE ELDER, JON ELDER, ROBERT ELDER, VALERIE ELDER, WHITNEY ELDER, LAWRENCE ELDREDGE, MARION ELDREDGE, MICHAEL ELDREDGE, SCOTT ELDREDGE, JOHN ELDRIDGE, CHARMAINE ELEGANTE, JOYCE ELFORS, CLAUDIA ELIASON, DAVID ELIASON, SCOTT ELIASON, BARBARA ELIESON, PATRICK ELIOT, HOLLY ELISON, BEVERLY ELKINGTON, PAMELA ELKINGTON, RUTHANN ELKINGTON, AMY ELKINS, BARBARA ELKINS, BRIAN ELKINS, CAMILLE ELKINS, CAROL ELKINS, MARK ELKINS, MELISSA ELKINS, CODY ELLEFSEN, DIANE ELLENSON, ROBERT ELLENSON, DEBORAH ELLERMEIER, LARRY ELLERTSON, LINDA ELLERTSON, KASSANDRA ELLINGSON, GREG ELLIOT, ANGELA ELLIOTT, ANNE ELLIOTT, CONNIE ELLIOTT, DONALD ELLIOTT, F RICHARD ELLIOTT, JASMIN ELLIOTT, JOAN ELLIOTT, LESLIE ELLIOTT, MARK ELLIOTT, MICHAEL ELLIOTT, PAMELA ELLIOTT, ANN ELLIS, CHRISTOPHER ELLIS, DAVID ELLIS, ERIKA ELLIS, JAMES ELLIS, JAMES ELLIS, JULIE ELLIS, LAURIE ELLIS, LISA ELLIS, LYN ELLIS, MARTELL ELLIS, RICHARD ELLIS, RONALD ELLIS, SHANNON ELLIS, STEPHEN ELLIS, TROY ELLIS, JANICE ELLISON, MARC ELLISON, STEPHANIE ELLISON, CAROL ELLSWORTH, JEFFREY ELLSWORTH, JONATHAN ELLSWORTH, JON ELMEN, RONALD ELMEN, CHARLES ELMER, ELIZABETH ELMER, GEORGE ELMER, KATHRYN ELMER, PENNY ELMER, RICHARD ELMER, STEVEN ELMER, NICOLE ELPHINSTON, DERENE ELS, JENNIFER ELSKEN, MARK ELSTAD, GLORIA ELSTON, TERRY ELSTON, CRAIG ELTON, RODNEY ELWOOD, BEATE ELY, DOROTHY EMENS, BRUCE EMERSON, KATHY EMERSON, ANASTASIA EMERY, GARRETT EMERY, PAMELA EMERY, RAY EMETT, LUPE EMLET, TRACY EMMANUEL, NATHAN EMMER, ALVA EMMERTSON, BLAIN EMPEY, RYAN EMPEY, ILONA ENCE, JOHN ENCE, MATTHEW ENCE, MARK ENDERS, THEODORE ENDRIZZI, ANN ENGAR, DEBORAH ENGEBRETSEN, CARLA ENGEL, KATHRYN ENGELBERT-FENTON, MICHAEL ENGELBERT-FENTON, SCOTT ENGELSTAD, ALAN ENGEN, KIP ENGER, SVEIN ENGER, JUDY ENGH, ANNE ENGLAND, COLLEEN ENGLAND, E. GARY ENGLAND, ELAINE ENGLAND, RONALD ENGLAND, LYNN ENGLE, SCOTT ENGLE, CHRIS ENGLERT, YVETTE ENGLERT, JOANNE ENGLISH, KATHLEEN ENGLISH, MARTHA ENGLISH, MONA ENGLISH, MICHAEL ENGSTROM, ERIN ENKE, LIESEL ENKE, MARNIE ENKE, ALVA ENNISS, ENID ENNISS, GERALDINE ENNISS, LORI ENRIGHT, DOUGLAS ENSIGN, EMILY ENSIGN, RICHARD ENSIGN, DONALD ENTERLIN, KITTY ENTWISLE-SHERER, DANIEL EPPERSON, JULIE EPPERSON, EVA ERCANBRACK, MONICA ERCANBRACK, CHERI EREKSON, CHERI ERICKSEN, KENNETH ERICKSEN, THOMAS ERICKSEN, ADAM ERICKSON, CHARLES ERICKSON, DEAN ERICKSON, HEIDI ERICKSON, JENNIFER ERICKSON, JILL ERICKSON, JOHN ERICKSON, JON ERICKSON, KRISTI ERICKSON, LESLIE ERICKSON, LINDA ERICKSON, LOREN ERICKSON, LYNETTE ERICKSON, MARGIE ERICKSON, MARY ANN ERICKSON, PATRICIA ERICKSON, PAUL ERICKSON, WILLIAM ERICKSON, JOHN ERICSON, PATRICIA ERICSON, STANLEY ERIKSEN, BRUCE ERKKILA, RONDA ERNEST, STEVEN EROR, MARK ERSKINE, EILEEN ERTEL, HEINZ ERTEL, ROBERTA ESCARCESGA, ARTHUR ESENBERG, ELIZABETH ESENBERG, MAX ESKELSON, SANDRA ESLINGER, CYNDY ESPARZA, EDWARD ESPARZA, DANIEL ESPERSON, ANNETTE ESPINOZA, JULIO ESPINOZA, MARCELLA ESQUIVEL, SUZANNE ESSER, GREGORY ESTEP, NORVEL ESTEP, PHILLIP ESTES, LEEANN ESTEVEZ, JOHN ESTLE, KATHRYN ETCHEVERRY, SHELLEY ETHERINGTON, KATHRYN ETHINGTON, KRISTINE ETTER, RICHARD ETTER, MICHAEL ETTINGER, SARA EUBANK, PAUL EUBANKS, JOHN EVANICH, ALAINA EVANS, ANDREW EVANS, ANNA EVANS, BECKY EVANS, BRENDA EVANS, DAVID EVANS, DAVID EVANS, DAVID EVANS, DOUGLAS EVANS, ED EVANS, G KENT EVANS, GREG EVANS, HEIDI EVANS, JAMES EVANS, JANELLE EVANS, JAYCILYN EVANS, JEFF EVANS, JEFFREY EVANS, JOHN EVANS, JOHN EVANS, LINDA EVANS, LORA EVANS, MAUREEN EVANS, MICHAEL EVANS, MICHAEL EVANS, MICHAEL EVANS, MICHELLE EVANS, NAN EVANS, PAT EVANS, PAUL EVANS, PAUL EVANS, ROBERT EVANS, SHEELAGH EVANS, TERI EVANS, THOMAS EVANS, TRENT EVANS, WARREN EVANS, WAYNE EVANS, WILLIAM EVANS, YVETTE EVANS, ZACHARY EVANS, LEE EVANS DMD, GERALD EVERETT, JOHN EVERETT, MICHAEL EVERETT, RANDY EVERETT, RICHARD EVERETT, SALLY EVERETT, SUSAN EVERETT, SUSAN EVERETT, HAL EVERETT D.D.S., MORGAN EVERSHED, STEVEN EVERSMEYER, ROBERT EVERSON, MARY ANN EVERTON, SANDRA EVERTSEN, ROSS EVESON, PAULA EWERS, MARCIE EWING, SHARON EWING, ALLYSON EYNON, AMANDA EYNON, PATRICIA EYNON, RONALD EYNON, STEPHEN EYNON, EMILY EYRE, JAMES EYRE • **F** • MICHELLE FABERT, CHANDY FABRIZIO, KERRI FABRY, JOHN FACER, PEGGY FACER, JIM FADDEN, KELLY FADDIS, REBECCA FADDIS, SUSAN FAGER, BRIAN FAGERGREN, PAUL FAGERGREN, SANDRA FAGERGREN, PAULA FAGNANT, MARTIN FAHJE, JOHN FAIDIGA, GRANT FAIRBANKS, TAMARA FAIRBANKS, DEBORAH FAIRBOURN, MICHELLE FAIRBOURN, AMY FAIRCHILD, BRAD FAIRCHILD, CARLA FAIRCHILD, DON FAIRCHILD, CHRISTINE FAIRCLOUGH, FRED FAIRCLOUGH JR, COREY FAIRHOLM, KERI FAKATA, CASANDRA FAKATOUMAFI, CAROLYN FALDALEN, MARYANN FALK, CAROL FALLON, ANITA FAN, SCOTT FANDRICH, LINDA FANKHAUSER, KRIS FANNIN, SHELLIE FARADAY, JOSHUA FARBER, CAROLINA FARFAL, BARBARA FARMER, FRED FARMER, JEREMY FARNER, JODY FARNES, ALLYCEN FARNSWORTH, FLORENCE FARNSWORTH, JEFFREY FARNSWORTH, KELLY FARNSWORTH, REED FARNSWORTH, SCOTT FARNSWORTH, WENDY FARNSWORTH, ANTHONY FARNUM, JOAN FARNUM, BRANDON FARNWORTH, SHAWN FARNWORTH, JULIE FARR, REBECCA FARR, SHARLENE FARR, JILL FARRELL, THERESA FARRELL, RHETT FARRER, LARRY FARRIS, JENNIFER FARRUGIA, JO ANN FASEN, CAROL FASLIJA, SILVIA FASSIO, ELAINE FAST, ELISABETH FATZINGER, BRUCE FAULKNER, NATHAN FAULKNER, SHARI FAULKNER, SHERRY FAULKNER, SUSAN FAULKNER, LORI FAUSETT, MONIQUE FAUSETT, SCOTT FAUSETT, JACQUELINE FAUST, ANN FAUX, EDWARD FAVERO, KERI FAWCETT, STANLEY FAWCETT, DANELL FAWSON, PETER FAWSON, TALANA FAWSON, LEROY FAY, MARDELL FAYER, DAN FAZZINI JR, SUSAN FEATHERSTONE, SARAH FEDDEMA, SUSAN FEDERMANN, LYNN FEDERSPIEL-YOUNG, MARYANNE FEHR, NATALEE FEHR, RALEIGH FEHR, JOHN FEIG, LAWRENCE FEIN, VIRGIL FEINAUER, JOYLENE FEIST, TRACY FEIST, DMITRY FELD, GEORGE FELIS, TED FELIS, CHET FELIX, LOUISE FELLER, CHAD FELLOWS, ROBERT FELLOWS, NEVA FELS, ALLISON FELSHAW, ANGELA FELSTED, JAMES FELT, KAREN FELT, NATHAN FELT, KAREN FELTZ, CLAIRE FENECH, GARY FENLEY, MARIE FENLEY, PAUL FENNESSEY, BARBARA FENSTERMAKER, BRANDON FENSTERMAKER, NICOLE FENSTERMAKER, DON FENTON, KIRK FENTON, MARCUS FENTON, CLINTON FERAGEN, DOLORES FERCH, DEANNA FERDIG, LARRY FERDIG, ALLEN FERGUSON, BRITTANY FERGUSON, CAROLE FERGUSON, HEATHER FERGUSON, JACKSON FERGUSON, JAMES FERGUSON, JANICE FERGUSON, JILL FERGUSON, KATHLEEN FERGUSON, LIBBY FERGUSON, MARC FERGUSON, PHILLIP FERGUSON, AARON FERGUSSON, MAUREEN FERKIN, FLYNN FERNANDES, ALAN FERNANDEZ, DAVID FERNANDEZ, KRISTI FERNEY, GARRET FERRARI, PASQUALE FERRARO, SHELLY FERRARO, CAMERON FERRE, JON FERRE, MATT FERRE, ANN FERREE, JULIE FERREIRA, CHARITON FERRIN, CHRISTINE FERRIN, GARY FERRIN, JOSEPH FERRIN, LOREL FERRIN, NANCY FERRIN, REED FERRIN, SCOTT FERRIN, ELLEN FERRIS, JOSEPH FERRITER, ROBERT FERROZZO, MILES FERRY, SUZANNE FERRY, PHILLIP FETCHIK, PAT FETTIG, CHRISTINA FICHTER, GARY FICHTER, NANCY FICHTER, KEITH FIDONE, PATRICIA FIDONE, JUDY FIEHLER, SANDRA FIELD, JANET FIELDS, FLOYD FIET, CHERYL FIFIELD, DEEELL FIFIELD, BRENT FIGGINS, JOHN FILANDER, MICHEL FILION, DRAGAN FILIPOVIC, RICHARD FILLMAN, ALISON FILLMORE, BOB FILLMORE, CHRISTOPHER FILLMORE, JIM FILLMORE, KAMERON FILLMORE, PAUL FILLMORE, SHARLA FILLMORE, ELINOR FINCH, HENRY FINCH, LAWRENCE FINCH, MELISSA FINCH, PAM FINCH, LEIGH FINCHER, DONALD FINDLAY, JOHN FINDLAY, NICOLE FINDLAY, GARY FINDLEY, MICHAEL FINE, PERRY FINE, TRICIA FINE, ALISON FINERFROCK, BARBARA FINK, ROBERT FINK, VAL FINLAYSON, ALYSON FINLEY, TIMOTHY FINLEY, SHARON FINLINSON, CATHY FINNEGAN, EDWARD FINNERTY, SUE ELLEN FINNEY, JONATHAN FINNOFF, MICHAEL FIORE, LINDA FIRNENO, CLIFFORD FIRTH, DONALD FIRTH, KATHRYN FIRTH, LISA FIRTH, RALPH FIRTH, VICTORIA FIRTH, RICK FISCH, BENJAMIN FISCHER, ERIKA FISCHER, JEFFREY FISCHER, KRISTA FISCHER, KRISTINA FISCHER, MELANIE FISCHER, CANDACE FISH, MERLIN FISH, PATRICIA FISH, RYAN FISH, DAVID FISHBACK, ANNE FISHER, CORBY FISHER, DOUGLAS FISHER, GWYNN FISHER, JACQUELINE FISHER, JANICE FISHER, JENNIFER FISHER, KELLY FISHER, KRISTA FISHER, KRYSTYL FISHER, MONICA FISHER, MORGAN FISHER, NANCY FISHER, RANDY FISHER, STEVEN FISHER, TODD FISHER, VIRGINIA FISHER, JIM FITLOW, PATRICIA FITT, RICHARD FITT, JANE FITTS, ALICE FITZGERALD, DONALD FITZGERALD, JOHN FITZGERALD, JUDY FITZGERALD, KENT FITZGERALD, KRISTIE FITZGERALD, BETH FITZGERALD-WEEKLEY, KEVIN FITZPATRICK, KRISTIN FITZPATRICK, TIMOTHY(CLINT) FITZPATRICK, ROSANNE FJELDSTED, ORMAN FLACK, SEAN FLAGG, PAUL FLAIG, DAVID FLAIM, SUSAN FLAIM, DEBORAH FLAMISH, DENISE FLAMM, MARTHA FLAMMING, KRISTIN FLANAGAN, LUANN FLANDERS, ROYCE FLANDRO, CARA FLANIGAN, JOHN FLANIGAN, LINDA FLANNERY, KATHLEEN FLATLEY, MICHAEL FLEGAL, DOROTHY FLEISCHMAN, CHARESE FLEMING, ELIZABETH FLEMING, JOHN FLEMING, JOLYNN FLEMING, STEPHANIE FLEMING, SUSANNE FLEMING, TIMOTHY FLEMING, VIDA FLEMING, CHERYL FLETCHER, GORDON FLETCHER, MICHAEL FLETCHER, PETER FLETCHER, STACEY FLETCHER, SUZANNE FLEURY, SOPHIE FLICHY, JAMES FLINDERS, MILTON FLINDERS, SHAUNA FLINDERS, LINDA FLINN, KEVIN FLINT, LOU JEAN FLINT, ROBERT FLINT, SHARIDEAN FLINT, BARRY FLITTON, DON FLITTON, JACKIE FLITTON, TODD FLITTON, MARY FLOOD, PAUL FLOOD, CHRISTINE FLOOR, ROBERT FLOOR, MARGARET FLORENCE, MARGARETHA FLORENCE, NONA FLORENCE, SCOTT FLORENCE, ENOC FLORES, SHARON FLORES, THOMAS FLORES, KERRY FLOREZ, CATHY FLOYD, KRISTINE FLUCK, MARILYN FLUCKIGER, VANESSA FLUCKIGER, TERESA FLUEGEMAN, CINDI HALL FLUEKIGER, LARRY FLUHARTY, SANDY FLURY, WILLIAM FLURY, CINDY FLYGARE, ROSE FLYGARE, TIFFANY FLYGARE, LEORA FLYNN, WILLIAM FOGARTY, EDITH FOGLIANO, JOSEPH FOGLIANO, RANDY FOILES, TODD FOISY, CAROLYN FOLEY, JENNY FOLEY, SHARI-LYNN FOLEY, JENNIFER FOLKERSON, RICHARD FOLKERSON, ANDREA FOLKMAN, WILLIAM D. FOLLAND, SHIRLY FOLTZ, JUDY FONDREN-TIPPETS, RUTH FONNESBECK, LETANE FONOTI, SHARIE FONOTI, JO FONTENOT, 'OFA FONUA, SHERYL FOOT, DONALD FOOT JR., DEBBIE FORAKIS, JOHN FORAKIS, SALLY FORAKIS, BRUCE FORBES, CHARLENE FORBES, KELLIE FORBES, MICHAEL FORBES, BRADLEY FORD, DAN FORD, DESMOND FORD, JOSHUA FORD, MARY FORD, MARY FORD, MAUREEN FORD, MICHAEL FORD, MOLLY FORD, PATRICK FORD, ROSS FORD, RUTH FORD, SUSAN FORD, VICTORIA FORD, WENDY FORD, BOB FORET, TASHA FORISKA, DIAN FORMAN, JANAE FORMAN, LAURI FORMAN, PETE FORMAN, PATRICIA FORMICHELLI, ALEXANDRA FOROGLOU, BARBARA FORREST, BETTE FORSBERG, DEREK FORSBERG, GEORGE FORSBERG, JUSTIN FORSBERG, CHARLENE FORSGREN, ADAM FORSLOFF, DIANE FORSTER-BURKE, SILJE FORSUND, MICHELLE FORSYTH, ERIN FORSYTHE, GRACE FORSYTHE, KIMBERLEE FORSYTHE, NELSON FORTIER, KIRSTEN FOSLI, SUSAN FOSS, CAROL FOSTER, DANIEL FOSTER, ELIZABETH FOSTER, GLEN FOSTER, JENNIFER FOSTER, JOANNE FOSTER, LELAND FOSTER, REBECCA FOSTER, ROBERT FOSTER, STAN FOSTER, TANA FOSTER, THOMAS FOSTER, TODD FOSTER, TYLER FOSTER, KEN FOSZCZ, DAVID FOULGER, PATRICIA FOULGER, DESSA FOUNTAINE, DEBRA FOUTS, MARIAN FOWDEN, MECHELL FOWDEN, MARSHA FOWERS, TYMM FOWERS, EDWARD FOWLER, HOLLY FOWLER, JEFFREY FOWLER, LAUREN FOWLER, PAUL FOWLER, SCOTT FOWLER, TAMSEN FOWLER, TINAMARIE FOWLER, TRACI FOWLER, CLYDE FOWLER III, SUZETTE FOWLKS, AMY FOX, ARTHUR FOX, CHERYL FOX, GAIL FOX, GEORGE FOX, HUBERT (HUB) FOX, RANDY FOX, WREN FOX, AARON FOY, JOANNE FOY, LESA FRAKES, SHELLY FRALIA, AMY FRAME, DONNA FRAME, JEFFERY FRAME, JESSICA FRAME, MICHAEL FRAME, ELIZABETH FRAMPTON, QUINN FRAMPTON, SADIE FRAMPTON, SCHYLAR FRAMPTON, JEAN FRANCES, DUANE FRANCIS, GARY FRANCIS, JARED FRANCIS, JEFFREY FRANCIS, JIM FRANCIS, JOSHUA FRANCIS, RICHARD FRANCIS, WENDELL FRANCIS, FARREL FRANCOM, KENT FRANCOM, ANTONE FRANDSEN, DAVID FRANDSEN, GALE FRANDSEN, JANET FRANDSEN, JENNICA FRANDSEN, JILL FRANDSEN, MICHAEL FRANDSEN, ELIZABETH FRANK, JANET FRANK, JEANNE FRANK, MATTHEW FRANK, THERESE FRANK, GENEVIEVE FRANK-MURPHY, KELLY FRANKLIN, MARGARET FRANKLIN, MONICA FRANKS, DAVID FRANSIOLI, MARION FRANSIOLI, LARA FRANSON, LON FRANSON, ANNE-LOUISE FRANTZ, MARION FRANTZ, SUSAN FRANTZ, HUGH FRASER, JOHN FRASER, JOHN FRASER, JOHN FRASER, MARGIE FRASER, MONICA FRASER, JOSEPH FRATTO, KATHY FRATTO, EDMOND FRATUS, EDWARD FRAZE, ALTON FRAZIER, BOYDEAN FRAZIER, CATHY FRAZIER, HILDEGUNDE FRAZIER, ROMAN FRAZIER, WENDY FRAZIER, JASON FREDERICK, ROGER FREDERICK, RAELYNN FREDERICKSON, FREDDY FREDERIKSEN, JAMES FREDRICKSON, VICTORIA FREDRICKSON, CARLA FREEBAIRN, JOHN FREEH, MARY FREEH, KIRT FREELAND, LEE FREELOVE, CRAIG FREEMAN, JOHN FREEMAN, JUSTIN FREEMAN, KENT FREEMAN, MATTHEW FREEMAN, PATTI FREEMAN, LINDA FREER, BRADLEY FREESTONE, DELORES FREESTONE, KIRSTEN FREESTONE, KIMBALL FREEZE, AURELIA FREI, CELESTIA FREI, DAN FREI, JACQUELINE FREI, LISA FREI, SHERRY FREI, NANCY FREIFELD, ALAN FREIGENBERG, MELINDA FREISS, JOSEPH FRENETTE, PAULETTE FRENYEA, TED FRENYEA, WILLIAM FREUTEL, PATRICIA FREY, ROBERT FREY, THOMAS FREY, WILMA FREY, WILLIAM FREYMAN, LARS FRIBERG, JUDY FRIED, GERHARD FRIEDEMANN, ADAM FRIEDMAN, BARRY FRIEDMAN, JEFFREY FRIEDMAN, JON FRIEDMAN, LAURA FRIEDMAN, ROBERT FRIEDMAN, SONJA FRIEDMAN, STEVEN FRIEDMAN, ANKE FRIEDRICH, ARTHUR FRIEDRICH, JAMES FRIEDRICH, HEIDI FRISCHKNECHT, KAYE FRISCHKNECHT, OTSO FRISTROM, CHRISTINA FRITZ, GARY FRITZSCHE, MARK FROELICH, NICHOLAS FROERER, TAMARA FROHNEN, HAL FROOT, BRIAN FROST, GAYLEEN FROST, JEFFERY FROST, SCOTT FROST, SEAN FROST, THOMAS FROST, TIMOTHY FROST, CAROL FROW, JON FRUEHAN, CLAUDIA FRUIN, MARIA FRUIN, JONI FRY, MARILYN FRY, RODGER FRY, JEFFREY FRYE, JACKIE FUAHALA, CAROL FUDYMA, JASON FUERST, SCOTT FUGATE, KARL FUGE, JR., DAVID FUHRIMAN, DOUGLAS FUHRIMAN, FRANK FUHRIMAN, SARAH FUHRMANN, KIPP FUIT, RICHARD FUIT, JASON FULGHUM, JAMES FULLEN, NANETTE FULLEN, BETTY FULLER, BLAIR FULLER, HARRY FULLER, JORDAN FULLER, LYLA FULLER, BETTY FULLMER, BRIAN FULLMER, DAWN FULLMER, JACQUELINE FULLMER, JOAN FULLMER, LISA FULLMER, NYLE FULLMER, RONALD FULLMER, SHARI FULLMER, SHEREE FULLMER, SHERRY FULLMER, DON FULTON, ARLA FUNK, DEBORAH FUNK, ELLEN FUNK, TESSA FURANO, AMBER FURBEE, JASON FURBEE, ROSEMARY FURDA, ANITTA FURLONG, DOUGLAS FURLONG, MARTIN FURMANSKI, SHELLY FURNER, DOROTHY FURNISS, SETH FURTAW, JENNIFER FYNBO • **G** • JAMES GAARDER, PATRICIA GABALDON, MICHAEL GABBITAS, WILLIAM GABBOTT, KRISTINE GABEL, GEORGE GABISCH, DON GABRIELE, JARED GABRISH, CHANTEL GADDIE, JERRY GADDY, PETER GADUE, CHRISTINA GAGE, LESLIE GAILEY, DONALD GAILLARD, JERAMIE GAILLARD, KIMM GAILLARD, LAURA GAILLARD, MARY GAJKOWSKI, BRUCE GALBRAITH, KIM GALBRAITH, MARY GALBRAITH, ALAN GALE, ALECIA GALE, GABRIELLE GALE, HEATHER GALE, JAMES GALE, JANET GALE, JODI GALE, MARSHA GALE, SALLY GALE, TORY GALI, ELINA GALKINS, ALETHEA GALLACHER, GAYLAN GALLACHER, ANNETTA GALLAGHER, JUDITH GALLAGHER, JULIA GALLAGHER, MAUREEN GALLAGHER, MICHAEL GALLANT, MAUREEN GALLEGOS, MICHAEL GALLEGOS, DWIGHT GALLOWAY, JULIE GALLOWAY, DAVE GALUSHA, WILLIAM GALWAY, ANNA GAMANGASSO, JOHN GAMBLE, AMELIA GAMETT, HAL GAMETT, LELAND GAMETTE, BLAKE GAMMELL, GAYLE GAMMELL, JOSHUA GANA, ROY GANDOLFI, WARREN GANE, BAT-ERDENE GANKHUYAG, CHRISTIE GANN, PAUL GAPINSKI, EDUARD GAPPMAIER, DAVID GARBRECHT, BONNIE GARCIA, CONNIE GARCIA, ELIGIO GARCIA, MARY GARCIA, PHIL GARCIA, RICHARD GARCIA, SANDRA GARCIA, STACI GARCIA, VANESSA GARCIA-DELZER, CAROL GARDEN, DEBRA GARDINER, HEIDI GARDINER, JESSIE GARDINER, KEVIN GARDINER, LORALEE GARDINER, MARILYN GARDINER, MERLIN GARDINER, FREDERICK GARDINIER, AARON GARDNER, BRAD GARDNER, BRANDON GARDNER, BRYAN GARDNER, DIANA GARDNER, DIANE GARDNER, DOUGLAS GARDNER, DUANE GARDNER, DUSTIN GARDNER, EMMA GARDNER, GREG GARDNER, GREGORY GARDNER, HENRY GARDNER, HOLLIANN GARDNER, ILLONA GARDNER, JAN GARDNER, JENNIFER GARDNER, JENNIFER GARDNER, KAREN GARDNER, KEN GARDNER, LAURA GARDNER, MART GARDNER, MATTHEW GARDNER, MICHAEL GARDNER, MINDY GARDNER, REBECCA GARDNER, RENEE GARDNER, RENEE GARDNER, ROBERT GARDNER, RONALD GARDNER, SHAWN GARDNER, STACIE GARDNER, WILLIAM GARDNER, KAREN M. GARFF, MATTHEW GARFF, MARK GARFIELD, CHRIS GARISON, ALISA GARLICK, JAY GARLICK, SHANE GARLICK, SPENCER GARLICK, MARY GARLITZ, SUELLEN GARN, ASHLEIGH GARNER, BRETT GARNER, MELISSA GARNER, ROCK GARNER, STEVE GARNER, ALFREDO GARNICA, BRAD GARR, CARALEE GARR, LENARD GARRARD JR, BRIAN GARRETT, CRAIG GARRETT, DEAN GARRETT, GARY GARRETT, GINGER GARRETT, JANA GARRETT, JANICE GARRETT, KIMBERLEY GARRETT, LILLIAN GARRETT, MAX GARRETT, MAXINE GARRETT, RALPH GARRETT, STASI GARRETT, LILLIE GARRIDO BUTCHER, DAN GARRISON, CRAIG GARRITSON, ANTON GARRITY, SCOTT GARROD, SHANNON GARSIDE, HELEN GARTRELL, AMANDA GARY, DOUGLAS GASKILL, LINDA GASSAWAY, TERRANCE GASSAWAY, CHRISTOPHER GASSMAN, EDWARD GASSMAN, KENT GASSMAN, ELIZABETH GASTELUM, JIM GASTELUM, REBECCA GASTER, LOU GASTON, DAVID GATELY, EDWARD GATELY, JEFFREY GATELY, DANIEL GATES, DAVID GATES, ERNEST GATES, GEORGIA GATES, JANET GATES, KENNETH GATES, LORI GATES, RICHARD GATES, ROBERT GATES, DEBBIE GATHERCOLE, KENNETH GATHERCOLE, CORDELL GATHERUM, CHRISTOPHER GATY, TRAVIS GAUCHAY, BARBARA GAUFIN, LORRAINE GAUFIN, CHRISTOPHER GAULT, LINDA GAUSE, ANN GAVIN, CAROLYN GAVIN, DOUG GAVIN, DANNIE GAVROS, PATRICIA GAY, RACHELLE GAY, THOMAS GAYHEART, ROBIN GAYLER, CLAIRE GAYLORD, PRESTON GAYLORD, WILLIAM GAYLORD, JOANNE GEALTA, CHARLES GEARY, RONALD GEBHART, GARY GEBS, NATHAN GEDGE, ANN GEDMARK, HELEN GEE, RICHARD GEE, RYAN GEE, VICKI GEE, JOEL GEHRETT, JULIE GEHRETT, MERCEDA GEHRKE, THOMAS GEHRKE, GAVIN GEHRT, PAUL GEIGER, COLETTE GEIS, RICHARD GEIS, WILLIAM GEISDORF, JAY GEISLER, SHEILA GELMAN, GLORIA GELSTEIN, CHARLES GELTZ, LOAJEAN GELTZ, JENNIFER GELWIX, DIANNE GEMMILL, CLAUDIA GENER, DENA GENNERMAN, FLOLRENCE GENNERMAN, RICHARD GENOVESE, ADRIAN GENTILCORE, THERESA GENTILE, CHERYL GENTLE, CHERYL GEORGE, JAMES GEORGE, JASON GEORGE, LAVINA GEORGE, MICHAEL GEORGE, RYAN GEORGE, FRANCES GEORGIADES, MARIYANA GEORGIEVA, DANIEL GERBEC, KATHRYN GERBER, KELLY GERBER, SIGNE GERBER, TRUDY GERBER, KRISTIN GERDY, DAVID GERHART, DEBORAH GERHART, ALEXANDRA GERICKE, ALECIA GERKE, CAROLYN GERLACH, KATIE GERLACH, KIMBERLY GERLACH, LINDA GERLACH, ROBERT GERLACH, WILLY GERLACH, SUZANNE GERMAIN, RUSSELL GERRARD, RUTH GERRITSEN-MCKANE, MICHAEL GERSHTENSON, RACHEL GERSON, ANITA GERSTLE, JOSEPH GERSTLE, LINDA GERSTUNG, LYNN GERTSCH, MINDY GERUN, RON GESE, JEFFREY GESLISON, MEGAN GESLISON, BONNIE GESSEL, STEVE GETZ, DALE GEURTS, GERALD GEURTS, JAMES GEURTS, KIM GEURTS, LYLE GEURTS, MAY GEURTS, SHARON GEURTS, KARI GHAFFARI, SIAVASH GHAFFARI, CURTIS GHENT, STEPHANIE GIACOLETTO, KAREN GIACOMINI, JOAN GIANNELLI, MIKE GIANNELLI, JENNIFER GIAUGUE, SHERILYN GIAUQUE, JAMES GIBAS, PATRICIA GIBAS, ROBERT GIBB, MARCIE GIBBONEY, ALICE GIBBONS, CORRIN GIBBONS, DEBBIE GIBBONS, JENNIFER GIBBONS, KIMBERLY GIBBONS, KYLE GIBBONS, LEAH GIBBONS, TRAVIS GIBBONS, BENJAMIN GIBBS, DIANE GIBBS, ENNIS GIBBS, GLORIA GIBBS, JANET GIBBS, LYN GIBBS, MELISSA GIBBS, NANCY GIBBS, SUSAN GIBBS, WADE GIBBS, SHAUNA GIBBY, GARY GIBERSON, NEAL GIBERSON, GREGORY GIBESON, CHAD GIBSON, DENISE GIBSON, DIANE GIBSON, GEORGE GIBSON, HUGH GIBSON, LINDSAY GIBSON, MATTHEW GIBSON, MICHAEL GIBSON, PAMELA GIBSON, PAUL GIBSON, RAYMOND GIBSON, SHAWN GIBSON, TAMMY GIBSON, ZACHARY GIBSON, DAVID GIECK, ESTHER GIEZENDANNER, LISA GIFFI, ROB GIFFING, BEN GIFFORD, DAVID GIFFORD, PETROS GIFOROS, MAUREEN GIGGEY, PHILIP GILANFARR, ALISON GILBERT, BARBARA GILBERT, DAWNA GILBERT, DENNIS GILBERT, HEIDI GILBERT, JAMES GILBERT, JERRY GILBERT, JOAN GILBERT, JON GILBERT, MAREN GILBERT, MAVIS GILBERT, MICHELE GILBERT, RICHARD GILBERT, ERIC GILBERT MD, AMY GILES, CURTIS GILES, DENNIS GILES, JACQUELINE GILES, JAMES GILES, KRISTEN GILES, LORRAINE GILES, MATTHEW GILES, MAURY GILES, PAMELA GILES, TAYLOR GILES, MELANY GILIVARY, ERIN GILL, RICHARD GILL, ALLAN GILLEN, DANIEL GILLESPIE, LEONARD GILLESPIE, MARILYNN GILLESPIE, MATTHEW GILLESPIE, MICHAEL GILLESPIE, PATRICK GILLESPIE, VALORIE GILLESPIE, KEITH GILLETT, ANNETTE GILLETTE, DAVID GILLETTE, DORIS GILLETTE, PAUL GILLETTE, WINSTON GILLIES, DAVID GILLILAND, TAMARA GILLILAND, VERONA GILLILAND, ANNETTE GILLIS, BENJAMIN GILLIS, DOTTI GILLIS, LADEAN GILLMAN, MARGIE GILLMAN, PETER GILLWALD, ANNE GILMARTIN, CHARLES GILMORE, MARYANN GILMORE, MELISSA GILMORE, SUSAN GILOMEN, AMY GILSON, GLEN GILSON, KELLIE GILSON, CAROLYN GILSTRAP, ROGER GINES, KAREN GINGERICH, SHARI GIRARD, KATHERINE GIROUARD, LEO GIROUARD, SUZANNE GIROUARD, JON GISLASON, MARY GISLASON, PAUL GITS, DAVID GITTINS, LARRY GITTINS, SHELLEY GITTINS, SUZANNE GITTINS, MORENO GIUDICETTI, JACOB GIVEN, JAY GLAD, HARVEY GLADE, LISA GLADE, CHARLES GLADWELL, KAYE GLADWELL, TIMOTHY GLADWELL, GLEB GLADWIN, NANCY GLAGOLA, CARLTON GLANTZ, DEAN GLANVILLE, JAMES GLASCOCK, YVETTE GLASCOCK, JOHN GLASDER, JONATHAN GLASGOW, JANA GLASS, MELISSA GLAUCH, ALFRED GLAUSER, BRADY GLAUTHIER, JEANETTE GLAZIER, STEVEN GLEASON, SUSAN GLEASON, JOHN GLEAVE, CURT GLEAVES, KATHERINE GLEAVES, ROBERT GLEDHILL, STEVEN GLEDHILL, THOMAS GLEDHILL, WAYNE GLEDHILL, KATHY GLEED, LISA GLEED-THORNTON, CARRIE GLESSNER, JOCELYN GLIDDEN, JUDY GLOMMEN, JUSTIN GLOMMEN, KARREN GLOVER, MERLENE GLOVER, STEVEN GLOVER, LAWRENCE GLUECK, MARGARET GLUECK, ROBERT GLUTZ, CORIANNE GOASLIND, DAVID GOATCHER, DAWN GOATCHER, MELANIE GOATES, MICHAEL GOATES, GREGORY GOCHNOUR, DAVE GODDARD, LINDA GODDARD, FRANCES GODDERIDGE, ANDREA GODFREY, BECKI GODFREY, CINDY GODFREY, COREY GODFREY, GARY GODFREY, GLEN GODFREY, KYLE GODFREY, PATRICE GODFREY, RENEE GODIN, KATHY GODWIN, WILLIAM GODWIN, ERIC GOEBEL, DAVID GOFF, DENNIS GOFF, ALEKSANDAR GOGIC, JEFFREY GOINS, ROBERT GOINS, BRET GOLD, MARIANNE GOLD, TAMARA GOLD, DON GOLDBERG, LAURA GOLDBERG, MICHELLE GOLDBERGER, ANDREW GOLDEN, JOHN GOLDEN, CAROL GOLDEN-THOMPSON, MIKE GOLDER, CAROL GOLDMAN, JAN GOLDMAN, ROBERT GOLDMAN, JANET GOLDSTEIN, JOAN GOLDTHWAIT, LISA GOLDY, JEROME GOLEMBIEWSKI, CYNTHIA GOLSAN, KALEV GOLUBJATNIKOV, MICHELE GOMEZ, CHRISTY GOMM, KENT GOMM, FABIAN GONYEA, CATHY GONZALES, CLARRISA GONZALES, EMMA GONZALES, JAMES GONZALES, DAVID GONZALEZ, GUILLERMO GONZALEZ, JOSEPH GONZALEZ, CHARLENE GOO, ANN GOOD, MARIA GOOD, ROGER GOODE, JOSEPH GOODIN, ARI GOODLOE, ROBERT

GOODLOE, CHARLES GOODMAN, DOROTHY GOODMAN, KATHLEEN GOODMAN, LISA GOODMAN, NAOMI GOODMAN, DANIEL GOODMANN, ROSA GOODNIGHT, DANIEL GOODRICH, MORRIS GOODRICH, STEVEN GOODRICH, TAMMRA GOODRICH, ZELVA GOODRICH, DEBRA GOODSON, CAROL GOODWIN, DAVE GOODWIN, SUSIE GOODWIN, MARY GOOLD, ROD GOOLD, ANN GORDON, BARBARA GORDON, CLAUDENE GORDON, DAVID GORDON, DOUGLAS GORDON, GREGORY GORDON, HEIDI GORDON, JAMES GORDON, KAREN GORDON, PAMELA GORDON, PATSY GORDON, RICHARD GORDON, STEPHEN GORDON, CHASE GORISHEK, TOM GORMAN, TAPPIN GORMAN III, JANE GORRELL, CLAY GORTON, JAMES GORTON, SUSAN GOSE, TERRY GOSE, GLENNA GOSEWICH, ANTON GOSKOWICZ, BRAD GOSKOWICZ, STEPHANIE T. GOSSELIN, DANIELA GOSSELOVA, MADGE GOSSMAN, ORVILLE GOSSMAN, BROOKE GOUDIE, KEN GOULD, RITA GOULD, TRAVIS GOULDING, CHRISTOPHER GOULET, KAREN GOWANS, MICHAEL GOWE, KRISTINA GOWEN, TINA GOYEN, DONALD GRABARZ, ROBERT GRABLE, DEAN GRACE, JODIE GRACE, STEPHANY GRACE, TAMI GRACE, KERRY GRACEY, ALEXANDRA GRAF, JASON GRAF, JUDY GRAF, BETTY GRAFF, ROBERT GRAFF, ALYSON GRAHAM, DANIEL GRAHAM, FRED GRAHAM, GARY GRAHAM, GLEN GRAHAM, JOHN GRAHAM, JOHN GRAHAM, NATALIE GRAHAM, PAMELA GRAHAM, SANDY GRAINGER, DAVID GRANADINO, COSTANTINO GRANDJACQUET, MICHAEL GRANDY, SHIRLEY GRANERE, PATSY GRANGE, WILLIAM GRANGE, CHRISTINE GRANT, CORINNE GRANT, HELEN GRANT, JAMES GRANT, JAMES GRANT, JEFF GRANT, JODI GRANT, JULIANNE GRANT, KAREN GRANT, PAMELA GRANT, PAUL GRANT, SCOTT GRANT, SHARON GRANT, DONALD GRANTHAM, JANELLE GRANTHAM, ELLEN GRAVES, JEFFREY GRAVES, PAMELA GRAVES, ROBERT GRAVES, ROGER GRAVES, STEVEN GRAVES, TATIANA GRAVES, TODD GRAVES, CHANTELE GRAY, E WARREN GRAY, GARY GRAY, HOWARD GRAY, JOSEPH GRAY, MICHAEL GRAY, RICHARD GRAY, ROBERT GRAY, LORALIE GRAY-RICHINS, DEBBIE GRAYBILL, CHARLES GRAYBILL III, MARILYN GRAYSON, ALLEN GRAZER, DEB GREATHOUSE, CHERI GREAVES, DAVID GREAVES, KAY GREAVES, ANTHONY GRECO, RICKY GRECO, ALAN GREEN, ALEXANDER GREEN, ARTHUR GREEN, CHARLES GREEN, DEL RAY GREEN, DOUGLAS GREEN, JACQUELYN GREEN, JULIE GREEN, KRISTI GREEN, KRISTINE GREEN, LAUREL GREEN, MARK GREEN, MARY GREEN, MATTHEW GREEN, PAMELA GREEN, RICHARD GREEN, ROBERT GREEN, ROGER GREEN, WILLIAM GREEN, LINDA GREENBERG, SUSAN GREENBERG, AMANDA GREENE, ANGELA GREENE, JOHN GREENE, DION GREENFIELD, G GREENFIELD, GEORGE GREENFIELD, KIM GREENFIELD, LYNADELL GREENFIELD, KAMI GREENHAGEN JONES, CHARLES GREENLAND, DOROTHY GREENLAND, ROB GREENLAND, JILL GREENLEAF, IAN GREENWALD, LESTELLE GREENWALT, DALE GREENWELL, JOSEPH GREENWELL, KAREN GREENWELL, LYNETTE GREENWELL, SCOTT GREENWELL, CHRISTOPHER GREENWOOD, GEORGE GREENWOOD, KEITH GREENWOOD, MELISSA GREENWOOD, NORIKO GREENWOOD, BILLY GREER, BROOKE GREER, DENNIS GREER, DOUGLAS GREER, KATHY GREER, KENNETH GREER, LUKE GREER, MICHELLE GREER, NATHAN GREER, NICHOLAS GREER, LOIS GREGERSON, AARON GREGORY, AMY GREGORY, JANALEE GREGORY, JASON GREGORY, MICHAEL GREGORY, NANCY GREGORY, NICHOLAS GREGORY, POLLY GREGORY, RUSSELL GREGORY, STUART GREGORY, SUMMER GREGORY, SUSAN GREGORY, T GREGORY, PATRICK GREIS, DAVID GREMILLION, RICHARD GREMILLION, BEATE GRESHAM, SHEILA GRESHAM, SUZANNE GREVSTAD, CARLY GREY, KENT GRIER, LORNE GRIERSON, MATTHEW GRIERSON, BERNARD GRIESEMER, FAITH GRIFFALL, JANET GRIFFEN, LINDA GRIFFEN STRICKLAND, CLAUDIA GRIFFETH, LISA GRIFFETH, AMANDA GRIFFIN, BARBARA GRIFFIN, GARY GRIFFIN, JARED GRIFFIN, JOHN GRIFFIN, LAURA GRIFFIN, BRANDI GRIFFITH, DARRYL GRIFFITH, JUDY GRIFFITH, KATHIE GRIFFITH, ROBERT GRIFFITH, RONALD GRIFFITH, BEAU GRIFFITHS, CALVIN GRIFFITHS, CHARLES GRIFFITHS, DAVID GRIFFITHS, LUCY GRIFFITHS, MAUREEN GRIFFITHS, ROY GRIFFITHS, TERESA GRIFFITHS, TIFFANY GRIFFITHS, ALLAN GRIGGS, BROOKE GRIGGS, ROSEMARY GRIM, PATRICIA GRIMME, RODNEY GRIMME, BENJAMIN GRINDSTAFF, ROSALIE GRIP, ALEXANDRA GRISPOU, COLIN GRISSOM, JANET GRISSOM, SHARON GRIX, STEVEN GRIZZELL, MARK GROENIG, KRISTA GROLL, DAVID GRONDEL, JON GRONEMAN, SHERYL GRONEMAN, KEN GRONSETH, MYRNA GRONWALD, MELISSA GROOM, WILLEM GROOT, TROY GROSE, BOB GROSS, DOROTHY GROSS, FLETCHER GROSS, MARK GROSS, STEPHANIE GROSS, RICHARD GROSSEN, GERALD GROSWOLD, DEIDRA GROTH, PAT GROUSTRA, BENJAMIN GROVER, HOLLY GROVER, KELLY GROVER, LOREN GROVER, EMILY GROVES, RICHARD GROVES, VICTOR GROVES, RONALD GROW, PAOLINA GRUBS, ERIC GRUENDELL, TERESA GRUHN, GARY GRULICH, LARRY GRULICH, JIRI GRYGAR, LUDMILA GRYGAR, NAN GUDGELL, PAULINA GUDGELL, HEIDI GUDMUNDSEN, HANS-RUDOLF GUENTER-SCHLESINGER, CINDY GUENTHER, JACQUELYN GUENTHER, PATRICIA GUENTHER, RICHARD GUENTHER, LORRAINE GUERINO, VIRGINIE GUERINOT, MARGARITA GUERRA, RAQUEL GUERRERO, DENNIS GUERTIN, JAMIE GUERTLER, JANET GUETSCHOW, ROBERT GUETSCHOW, SHAD GUFFEY, ANDRE GUILLEMOT, MARY GUILLORY, ALISON GUINN, CHRISTINE GUINN, WENDY GULCZYNSKI, DANA GULL, EMILY GUNDERSEN, DIRK GUNDERSON, LARS GUNDERSON, LISA GUNDERSON, ADI GUNDLAPALLI, SUSANNE GUNNARSON, MARILYN GUNNE, CAROL GUNNELL, ROBIN GUNNELL, ALLEN GUNNERSON, KAREN GUNNING, SHARYN GUNTER, WALTER GUNTER JR, MARK GUNTY, DEEPA GUPTA, MARJANN GUPTILL, BLAIR GURNEY, JERALD GURR, TIM GURR, ROBERT GURUNLIAN, DOUGLAS GUSE, NADINE GUSS, FRANK GUSTAFSON, JUDITH GUSTAFSON, LEO GUSTAFSON, PATRICIA GUSTAFSON, SANDRA GUSTAVESON, JULIE GUSTIN, ELLEN GUTHRIE, MELISSA GUTHRIE, TERRY GUTHRIE, JOSE GUTIERREZ, LIBBY GUTIERREZ, MICHELLE GUTIERREZ, RANDY GUTIERREZ, TERESA GUTIERREZ-MARTINEZ, GORDON GUTKE, SHIRLEY GUTKE, JIM GUTZWILLER, ANNA GUY, PIERRE GUZMAN, SANDRA GUZMAN, DAVID GUZY, DREXEL GUZY, SAMANTHA GWILLIAM, CHRISTINE GWYNN, MELISSA GYGI, PERRY GYGI, SUSAN GYGI • **H** • ELDON HAACKE, PAUL HAACKE, STEVEN HAACKE, BROOKE HAAG, TODD HAAG, ROBIN HAALAND, KRISTINE HAAS, CRAIG HAASER, JOHN HAASER, WILLIAM HAASER, GERALD HABECK, BARBARA HABERMAN, HORST HACKBARTH, CRAIG HACKETT, THOMAS HACKETT, RICHARD HACKING, SAMUEL HACKING, VICKIE HACKING, KEN HACKMEISTER, GEORGE HADDAD, MELISSA HADERLIE, JAMIE HADFIELD, STEVEN HADFIELD, BONNIE HADLEY, CAMILLE HADLEY, GAIL HADLEY, GEORGE HADLEY, JOHN HADLEY, MARK HADLEY, MARLENE HADLEY, SHARON HADLEY, STACIE HADLEY, DEBRA HADLOCK, KENNETH HADLOCK, PAUL HADLOCK, NANCY HADLOW, DAVID HAET, BRADLEY HAFEN, MARY JO HAFEN, WENDY HAFEN, ELAINE HAGAN, DONNA HAGBLOM, DOUGLAS HAGEMAN, JOHN HAGEN, HEATHER HAGEN-CLOWARD, KEIKO HAGERT, KELLEY HAGGARD, MARANDA HAGGERTY, MYKAL HAGLER, JOHN HAGLUND, SYDNEY HAGLUND, ANDREW HAHN, LAURA HAHN, MARK HAHN, MAURA HAHNENBERGER, EDWIN HAIDENTHALLER, BRENT HAIGHT, SHELLY HAIGHT, JAMES HAILEY, BLAKE HAINES, MICHAEL HAIR, NATHAN HAIR, JOHN HAIRE, JAMES HAISLEY, TIMOTHY HALASIMA, MATTHEW HALBLEIB, MARY HALBOSTAD, JENA HALDEMAN, DIANNE HALE, DIANNE HALE, ERIN HALE, GEORGE HALE, JASON HALE, JENNIFER HALE, JESSICA HALE, JONATHAN HALE, KENNAN HALE, MARY ANN HALE, NATALIE HALE, NICOLE HALE, PETER HALE, RICK HALE, SCOTT HALE, TIM HALE, ANGELA HALES, CHAZ HALES, DAWN HALES, DIANE HALES, ELIZABETH HALES, FRANK HALES, GARY HALES, HILARY HALES, MAVIS HALES, NICLAS HALES, SANDRA HALES, THOMAS HALES, TRACY HALES, KAREN HALEY, THOMAS HALEY, AMBER HALL, ANGELA HALL, CHAD HALL, CHRISTINA HALL, CHRISTINE HALL, CHRISTOPHER HALL, DAVID HALL, DEL HALL, DON HALL, DOUGLAS HALL, EMILY HALL, GEORGE HALL, H. HALL, JAMES HALL, JASON HALL, JOHN HALL, JOHN HALL, JOHN HALL, JOYCE HALL, JULIE HALL, KAREN HALL, MARLENE HALL, MARY HALL, MICHAEL HALL, PAMELA HALL, PERRY HALL, RENEE HALL, ROBYN HALL, SANDRA HALL, SANFORD HALL, SHARLYN HALL, STEPHEN HALL, TAMMY HALL, TERESA HALL, THOMAS HALL, VICTORIA HALL, CYNTHIA HALL-DUKE, BLAKE HALLADAY, AUBREY HALLAM, LAURA HALLAM, JOHN HALLENBERG, SUSAN HALLENBERG, GERALD HALLER, KENNETH HALLER, HEIDI HALLETT, ELIZABETH HALLEY, RANDALL HALLEY, ALLAN HALLIDAY, JAMES HALLIEN, LINDA HALLIEN, ANITA HALLOWS, LYNDA HALLS, GENE HALSALL, JULIE HALSALL, CHRIS HALTERMAN, JULIE HALTERMAN, CHRISTEN HALVERSEN, ANNA HALVERSON, CLARK HALVERSON, ERIC HALVORSEN, JARED HAM, GENE HAMBLE, BRENT HAMBLIN, CAROL HAMBLIN, JEFF HAMBLIN, MARCIA HAMBLIN, LEE HAMBLY, DAVID HAMBURGER, LORI HAMBURGER, RANDOLPH HAMBURGER, BOYD HAMILTON, BRAD HAMILTON, BRIANNE HAMILTON, CLARENCE HAMILTON, DIANE HAMILTON, JEANNE HAMILTON, KELLY HAMILTON, MELONY HAMILTON, NEIL HAMILTON, SHERI HAMILTON, TONUA HAMILTON, VINCENT HAMILTON, PATRICK HAMLER, DANIEL HAMMARI, DAMON HAMMER, LISA HAMMER, PAUL HAMMER, SANDRA HAMMER, DIANNE HAMMON, KARI HAMMON, BRUCE HAMMOND, CRISTINA HAMMOND, DORIAN HAMMOND, DOROTHY HAMMOND, GREGORY HAMMOND, HEATHER HAMMOND, JOHN HAMMOND, JOHN HAMMOND, JOHN HAMMOND, KARYN HAMMOND, REBECCA HAMMOND, SANDY HAMMOND, TED HAMMOND, ERIN HAMP, BRUCE HAMPSON, ANITA HAMPTON, CATHERINE HAMPTON, CINDY HAMPTON, SANDY HAMPTON, WES HAMPTON, CHARLES HAMSTRA SR, JASON HAMULA, DONG-HOON HAN, JEFFREY HANCEY, DEBBIE HANCOCK, LINDA HANCOCK, NATHANIEL HANCOCK, PAULINE HANCOCK, RACHEL HANCOCK, STEVEN HANCOCK, TERRY HANCOCK, LEIF HANDY, MATT HANDY, LARRY HANES, CYNTHIA HANEY, DARNEL HANEY, MARIE HANEY, GENE HANFLING, CARL HANKINS, DALENE HANKINS, KEITH HANKINS, KERRY HANKINS, CINDY HANKS, CYNTHIA HANKS, DORINE HANKS, JAMES HANKS, ROSEMARY HANKS, SAMUEL HANKS, ZINA HANKS, ELLEN HANLEY, STEVE HANLINE, ROBERT HANNA, MICHAEL HANNAN, MINDY HANNEMAN, JENNIFER HANNI, JOHN HANNI, DEAN HANNIBALL, PATRICK HANNIGAN, THOMAS HANRAHAN, BRETT HANSCOM, DAVID HANSCOM, GREG HANSCOM, ROSS HANSEEN, MARIA HANSELL, ALAN HANSEN, ALAN HANSEN, ALMA HANSEN, ALYSON HANSEN, ANNE HANSEN, ANNE HANSEN, ANNETTE HANSEN, ARTHUR HANSEN, BARBARA HANSEN, BOYD HANSEN, BRENDA HANSEN, BRENDA HANSEN, BRIAN HANSEN, CARLY HANSEN, CHRISTIE HANSEN, CORY HANSEN, CORY HANSEN, DANIEL HANSEN, DAVID HANSEN, DAVID HANSEN, DEANNA H HANSEN, DEBORAH HANSEN, DENNIS HANSEN, DOUG HANSEN, FINN HANSEN, FORREST HANSEN, GABRIEL HANSEN, GEORGE HANSEN, GEORGIA HANSEN, HEATHER HANSEN, HEATHER HANSEN, HENRY HANSEN, JAMES HANSEN, JAY HANSEN, JENNIFER HANSEN, JESS HANSEN, JOANNE HANSEN, JODIE HANSEN, JOHN HANSEN, JOHN-ERIK HANSEN, JON HANSEN, JON HANSEN, KAREN HANSEN, KATHLEEN HANSEN, KAYE HANSEN, KENA HANSEN, KIRK HANSEN, KIRSTI HANSEN, KRISTYN HANSEN, LAUNIE HANSEN, LEANN HANSEN, LESLIE HANSEN, LORI HANSEN, LOWELL HANSEN, LYNETTE HANSEN, MARK HANSEN, MATTHEW HANSEN, MATTHEW HANSEN, MCKEOWN HANSEN, MEGAN HANSEN, MELANIE HANSEN, MELISSA JOY HANSEN, MICHAEL HANSEN, MICHELLE HANSEN, NITA HANSEN, ORIS HANSEN, PAULETTE HANSEN, PENNY HANSEN, PRECINDIA HANSEN, RILLA HANSEN, SAUNDRA HANSEN, SCOTT HANSEN, SHANNON HANSEN, SHARON HANSEN, STEVEN HANSEN, THOMAS HANSEN, TODD HANSEN, TROY HANSEN, VICKIE HANSEN, KYLEE HANSEN-MITCHELL, ALAN HANSHAW, MARK HANSING, JOHN HANSMANN, BETH S. HANSON, BRITTANIE HANSON, CAROLYN HANSON, CINDY HANSON, DAVID HANSON, DENNIS HANSON, DENNIS HANSON, DOUGLAS HANSON, ERIC HANSON, IRJA HANSON, JAMES HANSON, JERRY HANSON, JOANN HANSON, KATHLEEN HANSON, KEITH HANSON, LEILA HANSON, MARILYN HANSON, MATTHEW HANSON, RICHARD HANSON, ROBERT HANSON, SUZANNE HANSON, TRACY HANSON, DALE HANSSEN, ARTHUR HANTLA, JAMES HANZELKA, DARREL HANZON, ANDREA HARBERTSON, ANN HARBERTSON, BRIAN HARBICAN, KAREN HARBOLD, TODD HARDCASTLE, BARBARA HARDEN, BILL HARDEN, JOHN HARDEN, JUDITH HARDESTER, WILLIAM HARDESTY, ALISON HARDING, ANNIE HARDING, DAWN HARDING, GARY HARDING, JAN HARDING, JEFFREY HARDING, JIM HARDING, KAYLENE HARDING, MELANIE HARDING, PAUL HARDING, SCOTT HARDING, SHARLON HARDING, SUSAN HARDINGER, LARRY HARDWICK, AARON HARDY, ANNETTE HARDY, DALE HARDY, DUANE HARDY, HIROKO HARDY, KATHLEEN HARDY, KEITH HARDY, KENNETH HARDY, LAURIE HARDY, LORRILEE HARDY, MONTY HARDY, ROBERT HARDY, SHARON HARDY, SHERRIE HARDY, STEVEN HARDY, HAROLD HARKEN, DANIEL HARKER, HEATHER HARKNESS, JOLENE HARLOW, BRUCE HARMON, CHARLENE HARMON, HAL HARMON, JUDY HARMON, LEISLY HARMON, MARK HARMON, MARY HARMON, NANCY HARMON, STEPHEN HARMON, TREV HARMON, ALLEN HARMS, DIANA HARMS, KATHLEEN HARMS, RANDALL HARMSEN, SHARON HARMSEN, STEVE HARMSEN, ERIC HARMSTON, EDWARD HARNESS, GENA HARNESS, ANGELINA HARNEY, ALISA HARPER, ANDREA HARPER, DENVER HARPER, GUDRUN HARPER, RICHARD HARPER, SANDRA HARPER, STUART HARPER, BRENDA HARR, DALE HARRELL, JANE HARRINGTON, REMI HARRINGTON, SARAH JANE HARRINGTON, STEPHEN HARRINGTON, ANN HARRIS, BRAD HARRIS, BRIAN HARRIS, CAROL HARRIS, CHAD HARRIS, CHARLES HARRIS, CHRISTOPHER HARRIS, CYNTHIA HARRIS, ELIZABETH HARRIS, JAMES HARRIS, JAMES HARRIS, JAMES HARRIS, JANALYN HARRIS, JAYME HARRIS, JEANETTE HARRIS, JENNIFER HARRIS, KEITH HARRIS, KEN HARRIS, KIMBERLY HARRIS, KIP HARRIS, LEROY HARRIS, LINDA HARRIS, LINDSAY HARRIS, LYNETTE HARRIS, MARILYN HARRIS, MARK HARRIS, MERRILL HARRIS, PATRICIA HARRIS, PHYLLIS HARRIS, POLLY HARRIS, R. HARRIS, RICHARD HARRIS, ROBERT HARRIS, SHELDON HARRIS, SUSAN HARRIS, TERRY HARRIS, ANN HARRISON, BELINDA HARRISON, CYNTHIA HARRISON, DANIEL HARRISON, DAVID HARRISON, DAVID HARRISON, DON HARRISON, DOUG HARRISON, JAMES HARRISON, JEFFREY HARRISON, KARLA HARRISON, KIM HARRISON, LINDA HARRISON, MARC HARRISON, MELISA HARRISON, RICK HARRISON, RUTHANNE HARRISON, SHAREN HARRISON, THERESA HARRISON, TODD HARRISON, WILLIAM HARRISON, WYNN HARRISON, KYLE HARRS, MICHAEL HARSTON, BARRY HART, BRUCE HART, CHARLES HART, CHRISTOPHER HART, CINDY HART, DAVID HART, JAY HART, JEFF HART, JOHN HART, JUDY HART, KAY HART, MICHAEL HART, JAMES HARTEN, DIANNE HARTER, GERALDINE HARTLEY, JEFFREY HARTLEY, RICHARD HARTLEY, SHERRY HARTLINE, BARBARA HARTMAN, KATHLEEN HARTMAN, WILLIAM HARTMAN, ANDREW HARTMANN, STEPHEN HARTSELL, JENNIFER HARTT, DAVID HARTVIGSEN, TELEEN HARTVIGSEN, TERESA HARTVIGSEN, CLIFFTON HARTY, GARY HARTZ, DAPHNE HARTZHEIM, RAGNAR HARTZHEIM, SANDRA HARTZHEIM, EILEEN HARVAT, ADRIAN HARVEY, ALAN HARVEY, ALVIN HARVEY, ANGELA HARVEY, CATHERINE HARVEY, CATHY HARVEY, DAWN HARVEY, JANICE HARVEY, KATHLEEN HARVEY, LEESA HARVEY, MICHELLE HARVEY, RICHARD HARVEY, ALVIN HARWARD, APRIL HARWARD, JILL HARWARD, PHYLLIS HARWARD-JONES, KELLY HARWOOD, BENJAMIN HASAN, ROBYN HASE, JAMIE HASHIMOTO, MIYOKO HASHIMOTO, HIROKO HASHITANI, SHINICHI HASHITANI, JASON HASKELL, LEE HASKELL, HARMONY HASKINS, VICCI HASKINS, BRYAN HASLAM, DIANE HASLAM, VALEEN HASLAM, MELISSA HASLAUER, CHRISTA HASLIP, THOMAS HASSARD, DEREK HASSELL, PATRICK HASSETT, ROBERT HASTINGS, ALICE HATCH, AMIE JO HATCH, AUDREY HATCH, BRIGHAM HATCH, CLAUDINE HATCH, DERYL HATCH, EKATERINA HATCH, JACKIE HATCH, JAMES HATCH, JEAN HATCH, JEFFREY HATCH, JOHN HATCH, JULIE HATCH, KATHIE HATCH, KENT HATCH, LAMAR HATCH, MARISSA HATCH, MARLENE HATCH, MARSHA HATCH, MARY ANN HATCH, MAXANNE HATCH, RICHARD HATCH, SANDRA HATCH, SHELLEY HATCH, SUSAN HATCH, JOHN HATCHER, KELLY HATFIELD, LAURIE HATHAWAY, ERIC HATTABAUGH, JULIE HATTABAUGH, EVONNE HATTON, STEPHANIE HATTON-WARD, BRIAN HATZEL, NORMA HAUBENSTOCK, MARY HAUG, ANDREW HAUGH, EVA LOY HAUN, LEWIS HAUPT, JACQUELINE HAUS, BONNIE HAUSKNECHT, RANAE HAVEMANN, TIM HAVENS, NANCY HAVERKAMP, CATHERINE HAVEY, MICHAEL HAVIG, ADELA HAVRANKOVA, JOANNE HAWES, ROGER HAWES, CHARLES HAWKER, DOUGLAS HAWKER, CANDIS HAWKES, JOHN HAWKES, MELANIE HAWKES, REED HAWKES, SARAH HAWKES, SHARLENE HAWKES, JOHN HAWKINS, JOSHUA HAWKINS, APRIL HAWKS, MELODY HAWKS, MONTY HAWKS, CONNIE HAWS, RALPH HAWS, SHIRLEY HAYCOCK, CHRISTY HAYES, CINDY HAYES, KATHRYN HAYES, LINDA HAYES, LU ANN HAYES, MARJIE HAYES, NANCY HAYES, NANCY HAYES, RUTH HAYES, RYAN HAYES, TIM HAYES, TOM HAYES, VICKI HAYES, ANGELA HAYMOND, BRETT HAYMOND, JOHN HAYMOND, MIRIAM HAYMOND, SHANNON HAYMORE, CLIFFORD HAYNES, MICHAEL HAYNES, SANDI HAYNES, GLEN HAYNIE, CHRISTOPHER HAYS, ELONA HAYWARD, LORI HAYWARD, MURRAY HAYWARD, REBECCA HAYWARD, ROSANNA HAYWARD, ROBERT HAYWOOD, SUSAN HAYWOOD, ERIC HAZARD, REVA HAZELRIGG, ELLA HAZELWOOD, GAYLE HAZEN, DARLENE HEAD, KATHERINE HEAD, MAUREEN HEAGANY, LAURIE HEALEY, RICHARD HEALEY, SHERRELL HEALEY, COLLETTE HEALY, FRANK HEALY, GARY HEALY, JACK HEALY, JEANETTE HEALY, LELA HEALY, MARY HEALY, NINA HEALY, RICHARD HEALY, ROBERT HEALY, TIMOTHY HEALY, WILLIAM HEALY, ROBERT HEANEY, KARL HEAP, COLBY HEAPS, DAVID HEAPS, STEVEN HEAPS, GEORGENE HEARE, LOIS HEART, SONDRA HEASTON, DUDLEY HEATH, EMALYNN HEATH, LINDSAY HEATH, MARY JO HEATH, TYLER HEATH, BRUCE HEATON, BRYSON HEATON, ERIC HEATON, KIMBERLY HEATON, MARILYN HEATON, MINDY HEATON, SHAUN HEATON, SHERRIE HEBERT, ROBERT HECK, JOSEPH HECKMAN, NIELS HEDBERG, ROBERT HEDDENS, RICHARD HEDENSTROM, HOLLY HEDGEPETH, RAMONA HEDGEPETH, GRANT HEDGES, KENNETH HEDIN, KERRY HEDIN, JENNIFER HEDMAN, PAUL HEDMAN, GREGORY HEDQUIST, SUSAN HEDQUIST, JULIE HEELIS, BEVERLEY HEFFERNAN, JAMES HEFFNER, STEPHANIE HEFFNER, TERI HEGEMANN, KATHY HEGERHORST, HEIDI HEGG, CAROL HEIDEN, SCOTT HEIDEN, DEBORAH HEIDERSCHEIT, JEFF HEIDERSCHEIT, JAMES HEIDT, MARINA HEIDT, ANDREW HEIL, JEFFREY HEILESON, MARY JO HEILMEIER, SUSANA HEIMULI, KLAUS HEIN, MONICA HEIN, SANDRA HEIN, DEBORAH HEIN-HELGREN, AMY HEINE, JACOB HEINER, JARED HEINER, THERESA HEINRICH, HEIDI HEINZE, STEVEN HEINZE, APRIL HEISELT, NATHAN HEISELT, ROBERT HEISER, JENNIFER HEISTERMAN, KENNETH HEITHOFF, PETER HELGREN, ROBERT HELLEKSON, ANDREAS HELLSTRAND, LAURA HELM, ADAM HELPS, KELLY HELTON, RACHEL HELWIG, SHERMA HEMINGWAY, HEATHER HEMINGWAY-HALES, KARL HEMMERICH, DANIEL HEMMERT, JONATHAN HEMMERT, LINDSEY HEMMERT, RUSSELL HEMMERT, TAMARA HEMMERT, BRENDA HEMPHILL, ANNETTE HEMSLEY, RAYMOND HEMSLEY, SHERI HEMSLEY, MEGAN HENDERSHOT, AMANDA HENDERSON, ANDREA HENDERSON, ANNA HENDERSON, BRENT HENDERSON, BRIAN HENDERSON, BRUCE HENDERSON, CAROL HENDERSON, EDGAR HENDERSON, ELIZABETH HENDERSON, GREGORY HENDERSON, JOANN HENDERSON, JOELLE HENDERSON, JOHN HENDERSON, KELLY HENDERSON, LIN HENDERSON, MERLE HENDERSON, MIKE HENDERSON, NEIL HENDERSON, PATRICK HENDERSON, RACHEL HENDERSON, ROBERT HENDERSON, SCOTT HENDERSON, BETTY HENDREN, FREDRICK HENDRICKS, JAN HENDRICKS, JOANN HENDRICKS, JULIEANNE HENDRICKS, KEVIN HENDRICKS, PHIL HENDRICKS, TAMRA HENDRICKS, MELANIE HENDRICKSEN, BRYAN HENDRICKSON, DAVID HENDRICKSON, DUANE HENDRICKSON, JULIA HENDRICKSON, KARLA HENDRICKSON, NOELE HENDRICKSON, RITA L HENDRICKSON, TIMOTHY HENDRICKSON, VIRGINIA HENDRICKSON, CLARK HENDRY, JEAN HENGESBAUGH, JOAN HENINGER, JERRY HENLEY, KATHRYN HENNEBRY, TIM HENNEY, CAROLINE HENRICHSEN, JAMES HENRICKSEN, RICHARD HENRICKSEN, ANN HENRIE, BRIAN HENRIE, CAROLYN HENRIE, HUTCH HENRIE, JANIS HENRIE, PAULA HENRIE, RYAN HENRIE, STEVEN HENRIE, TONYA HENRIE, VERNA HENRIE, XENIA HENRIE, CLARENCE HENRIKSEN, CLARENCE HENRIKSEN III, KRISTINA HENRIOD, JON HENRY, KATHLYN HENRY, SAM HENRY, SHAUNA HENRY, JEREMY HENSHAW, SUSAN HENSHAW, MICHAEL HENSLEY, SUSAN HENSLEY, WAUNALEE HENSLEY, DONGHO HEO, BRANDON HEPNER, JUSTIN HEPPLER, VIVIAN HERAS, MELISSA HERB, BRETT HERBERT, CRAIG HERGET, CORI HERMAN, ROBIN HERMAN, JONATHAN HERMANCE, MARJ HERMANSEN-ELDARD, GEORGIANN HERNANDEZ, JOE HERNANDEZ, MARTIN HERNANDEZ, ROBERTO HERNANDEZ, URSULITA HERNANDEZ, ANTONIO HERNANDEZ CONTE, WILLIAM HERODES, DEBBIE HERR, JEFFREY HERR, ROBERTO HERRERA, H. HERRICK, DAVID HERRING, GEORGE HERRMANN, HANS HERRMANN, KATHRYN HERSCHBERG, THOMAS HERSCHBERG, KERI HERSMAN, GERALD HERTWECK, SUSAN HERTZ, LANA HERTZKE, BRYANT HERTZOG, DALLEN HERZOG, EVELYN HERZOG, LARALEE HERZOG, TROY HERZOG, JON HESHKA, BETTY HESKETT, MERILYN HESLEPH, CAROLE HESLOP, AMY HESS, CAROL HESS, DARYL HESS, JEANNE HESS, MATT HESS, MICHAEL HESS, STACY HESS, BECKY HESTERMAN, JENNIFER HETTINGER, BRIAN HEUGLY, MARCI HEUGLY, GEORGE HEUMANN, JANET HEUMANN, TRACY HEUN, ENNO HEUSCHER, M.D., KELLY HEWARD, GENE HEWITT, GEORGE HEWITT, JESSICA HEWLETT, JUSTIN HEYDORN, SHANON HEYDORN, MICHAEL HEYDT, TERRY HEYER, ANTHONY HIATT, JACK HIATT, JAMES HIATT, JEANETTE HIATT, LORINA HIATT, SHON HIATT, TAMMY HIATT, LOIS HIBBARD, BEV HICKEN, CYNTHIA HICKEN, JULIE HICKEN, NILA HICKEN, DAVID HICKEY, JOSEPH HICKEY II, PAMELA HICKMAN, BILL HICKS, JOYCE HICKS, LISA HICKS, PETER HICKS, SONYA HIGBEE, CHERYL HIGGINS, JOHN HIGGINS, ALISHA HIGGINS-CARLSON, LAWRENCE HIGGINSON, ROBERT HIGGINSON, BRENDA HIGGS, DANIEL HIGGS, JANEEN HIGGS, JULIE ANN HIGGS, NORMAN HIGGS, OWEN HIGGS, REBECCA HIGGS, SYLVIA HIGH, DELILA HIGHAM, JOHN HIGHAM, VIRGINIA HIGHLEYMAN, LEONARD HIGHT, PATSY HIGHT, JILL HIGHTOWER, MARK HIGHTOWER, MIKE HIGHTOWER, WENDY HIGHTOWER, CONNIE HIGLEY, JONNIE HIGLEY, BARBARA HILBERT, BENTON HILDEBRAND, CATHERINE HILDEBRAND, MARILYN HILDEBRAND, RICHARD HILDERBRAND, ANDREW HILL, BONNIE HILL, BRIAN HILL, CASSIE HILL, CONNIE HILL, DAVID HILL, DEMAREE HILL, DONNETTE HILL, FERN HILL, JAMES HILL, JANET HILL, JO ANN HILL, JONI HILL, JOSEPH HILL, KAREN HILL, KAREN HILL, KATHRYN HILL, KERRY HILL, KRIS HILL, LIEZLE HILL, LISA HILL, LYNN HILL, MARTY HILL, MARVIN HILL, MELISSA HILL, MERRY HILL, MICHELLE HILL, PATRICIA HILL, ROMA HILL, STACEY HILL, STEPHEN HILL, TAMLYN HILL, TRACY HILL, WILLIAM HILL, DOUGLAS HILLAM, JULIE HILLEBRANT, JAMES HILLEGAS, CHARLIECE HILLERY, CAROL HILLIER, JOHN HILLIER, JUSTIN HILLIER, CHRISTOPHER HILLMAN, KERI HILLS, RONALD HILLS, GAIL HILTON, JEFF HILTON, LAURA HILTON, STEVE HILTON, GWENDOLYN HILYARD, JIM HILYER, ALAN HINCKLEY, BRENT HINCKLEY, GORDON HINCKLEY, LYNDA HINCKLEY, MARK HINCKLEY, TODD HINCKLEY, LIN HINDERMAN, KELLY HINDLEY, DAVE HINMAN, TIMOTHY HINRICHS, BETTY HINTZE, HENRY HINTZE, MARLA HINTZE, NICHOLAS HINTZE, RAYMOND HINTZE, RICHARD HINTZE, ZOE HINTZE, ISAAC HIPPLE, PAUL HIRAI, VIRGINIA HIRAI, STEVEN HIRCHAK, GINA HIRST, JAYNE HIRST, JERRY HIRST, MATTHEW HIRST, THOMAS HIRTZEL, JILL HISLOP, DEBBIE HITESMAN, EDWARD HITESMAN, BRIAN HIVELY, AARON HIXSON, VAUGHN HIXSON, JOHN HIZER, ERMA HJORTH, RICHARD HJORTH, TODD HLAVATY, BARBARA HOAG, VICTORIA HOAGLAND, NATALIE HOBBS, XYDELL HOBBS, DARYL HOBSON, DIANE HOBSON, RYAN HOBSON, BETTY HOCKIN, CHRISTOPHER HOCKING, DAVID HODGDON, RICHARD HODGES, RONALD HODGES, EARL HODGKINS, MICHELE HODGKINS, KAREN HODGSON, PATRICIA HODGSON, RYAN HODGSON, CONNIE HODSON, ELIZABETH HODSON, EUGENE HODSON, STEPHEN HOEKSTRA, STANLEY HOELLEIN, SCOTT HOELSCHER, LUANA HOFELING, LAYNE HOFER, MARK HOFERITZA, JACQUELINE HOFF, ANN HOFFMAN, CATHERINE HOFFMAN, CLYDE HOFFMAN, ERIC HOFFMAN, GARY HOFFMAN, KARIE HOFFMAN, MARGARET HOFFMAN, PEGGY HOFFMAN, SCOTT HOFFMAN, TONI HOFFMAN, JOSHUA HOFFMANN, RODNEY HOFFMANN, ANDREW HOGAN, DAVID HOGAN, ERIC HOGAN, ERIC HOGAN, MARY HOGAN, ROY HOGAN, THOMAS HOGARTY, LISA HOGG, ANDREW HOGGAN, LELAND HOGGAN, MALCOLM HOGGAN, SARAH HOGGAN, SUSAN HOGGAN, TUULA HOGGARD, DAN HOGGE, DARIN HOGGE, JENNIFER HOGGE, JAY HOGGINS, JO ANN HOGGINS, PATRICK HOGLE, TRISHA HOKANSON, BIRGITTA HOLBROOK, BLAIR HOLBROOK, CHANDLER HOLBROOK, DAVID HOLBROOK, JO LINN HOLBROOK, JOHN HOLBROOK, LEANN HOLBROOK, MELISSA HOLBROOK, SALLY HOLBROOK, KYLE HOLCOMBE, MARK HOLCOMBE, ADAM HOLDAWAY, JACLYN HOLDEN, TRICIA HOLDEN, RICHARD HOLDER, WINFRIED HOLDERIED, CHRISTINE HOLDING, RONALD HOLDSWORTH, KARA HOLLADAY, GARY HOLLAND, HEIDI HOLLAND, JILL HOLLAND, JOSEPH HOLLAND, JULANE HOLLAND, JUDITH HOLLBERG, BRIAN HOLLEN, DEBORAH HOLLENBEAK, LISA HOLLERBACH, DANETTE HOLLEY, JANICE HOLLEY, BROCHELLE HOLLIDAY, DANNELE HOLLINGER, LYRA HOLLINGER, APRIL HOLLINGSHEAD, HELEN HOLLINGSWORTH, JAMES HOLLINGSWORTH, STEVEN HOLLINGWORTH, HASSIE HOLLIS, JAY HOLLISTER, CAROLYN HOLLOWAY, ROBERT HOLLOWAY, WILLIAM HOLLROCK, CLAUDIA HOLM, JOHN HOLM, TERRY HOLM, NANCY HOLMAN, SCOTT HOLMAN, NANNETTE HOLMBERG, CHERYL HOLMES, DIXON HOLMES, LARRY HOLMES, LAURELL HOLMES, RANDOLPH HOLMES, SHARON HOLMES, THOMAS HOLMES III, EMILY HOLMGREN, HARMONY HOLMGREN, DAVID HOLMSTROM, LARRY HOLMSTROM, MARK HOLMSTROM, MICHAEL HOLMSTROM, SHERIE HOLST, CARL HOLT, DAVID HOLT, DAVID HOLT, HEATHER HOLT, HUGH HOLT, JENNIFER HOLT, JENNIFER HOLT, JEREMY HOLT, JOHN HOLT, MARK HOLT, NANCY HOLT, RANDY HOLT, ROBERT HOLT, SHELLY HOLT, WILLIAM HOLT, WILLIAM HOLT, JAMES HOLTKAMP, MARIANNE HOLTKAMP, JAMES HOLUB, AMY HOLYOAK, JOSH HOLYOAK, MELISSA HOLYOAK, JOHN HOLZ, VERNON HOLZER, BRIAN HOMER, KRISTIN HOMER, PAUL HOMER, RAYMOND HOMER, TIM HOMER, CONSTANCE HOMERSTAD, JOHN HOMERSTAD, STEVE HONE, YOUNG JOO HONG, ROBERT HONIG, JACQUI HOOD, MARTY HOOD, SUSAN HOOD, TIMOTHY HOOD, KATHLEEN HOOK, ANA HOOKER, DIANA HOOKER, ROBERT HOOKER, DAVID HOOPER, SARAH HOOPER, SHAUNA HOOPER, TAMMIE HOOPER, WILLIAM HOOPER, DARRYL HOOPES, KATHY HOOTEN, GERRI HOOTON, ANN HOOVER, CORBET HOOVER, CYNTHIA HOOVER, FAYE HOPE, WADE HOPE, BARBARA HOPES, DEBORAH HOPKIN, AMANDA HOPKINS, ANDY HOPKINS, DEANNA HOPKINS, JOAN HOPKINS, KELLY HOPKINS, LINDA HOPKINS, OREN HOPKINS, RENE' HOPKINS, CRAIG HOPPER, DAVID HOPPER, SHANA HOPPERSTEAD, JAMES HORAN, JOSEPH HORAN, THOMAS HORGOS, DAWN HORLACHER, RHYS HORMAN, SCOTT HORMAN, GUSTAV HORN, SUMMER HORN, DARIN HORNE, HOLLY HORNE, SUSAN HORNE, HEATHER HORNER, CRAIG HORNING, LAURALEE HORROCKS, SHARILYN HORROCKS, DAVE HORSLEY, DAVID HORSLEY, GREGORY HORSLEY, LINDA HORSLEY, HUGH HORSTMAN, KIMBERLY HORSTMAN, MARK HORSTMEIER, RYAN HORTIN, THOMAS HORTIN, AMANDA HORTON, ELIZABETH HORTON, ELLEN HORTON, JEREMY HORTON, MARGARET HORTON, MILDRED HORTON, NATALIE HORTON, RALPH HORTON, CAROLYN HORTON-CRABTREE, JERRY HORVATH, GREGORY HOSE, CAROLEE HOSFELD, RICHARD HOSIE, JOAN HOSKINS, CHARLES HOSTETLER, ERIC HOTH, GENICE HOTH, MELANIE HOTH, MICHAEL HOTH, QUESTA HOTT, TAMMY HOUCHEN, MARTIN HOUCK, STEVEN HOUD, ERIC HOUGARD, MICHAEL HOUGH, KATHY HOUGHTON, CAROL HOUGNON, KIM HOULE, EVERT HOUSE, LISA HOUSE, ROY HOUSE, VANESSA HOUSE, ANNETTE HOUSTON, CAROL HOUSTON, DOUGLAS HOUSTON, PATRICIA HOUSTON, RONALD HOUSTON, SAMUEL HOUSTON, SHERI HOUSTON, MICHAEL HOUTZ, LISA HOVEY, CHRISTOPHER HOVIK, KJELL HOVIND, CURTIS HOWA, LESLIE HOWA, CAROLINE HOWARD, DAVID HOWARD, GERI HOWARD, JEFFERY HOWARD, JOHN HOWARD, JUDY HOWARD, KIMBERLY HOWARD, LYNETTE HOWARD, MADILYN HOWARD, MARCI HOWARD, MICHAEL HOWARD, MICHAEL HOWARD, NELLENE HOWARD, RAND HOWARD, RICHARD HOWARD, ROBERT HOWARD, SYDNIE HOWARD, HOLLY HOWARTH, CRYSTAL HOWE, DAVID HOWE, JENNIFER HOWE, JULIE HOWE, KRISTIN HOWE, MICHELLE HOWE, PEGGY HOWE, SHELLY HOWE, STEVE HOWE, WILLIAM HOWE, BILL HOWELL, BRYAN HOWELL, EDMUND HOWELL, GINGER HOWELL, JANE HOWELL, JASON HOWELL, JERALD HOWELL, JOHN HOWELL, JON HOWELL, LINDA HOWELL, REGAN HOWELL, ROBERT HOWELL, SANDRA HOWELL, SCOTT HOWELL, SYDNEY HOWELL, THERESA HOWELL, CURT HOWES, RICHARD HOWES, DANE HOWICK, NEAL HOWIE, KRISTEN HOWLETT, DENNIS HOXSIE, SHARON HOY, THOMAS HOY, DEBRA HOYT, HOLLY HOYT, RHEA HRISTOU, DANIELA HRISTOVA, SHIH HSU, WEI-LUN HSU, HEDY HU, TAO HU, MICHAEL HUANG, JOEL HUBBARD, STEVEN HUBBARD, DEAN HUBER, KEVIN HUBER, WILLIAM HUBER, HANS HUBERT, BETTE HUBRICH, DELONNE HUCKS, GINGER HUCKS, JOSEPH HUCKS, DEBRA HUCKSTEP, GREGORY HUDNALL, DAVID HUDSON, HEATHER HUDSON, KYRA HUDSON, GRACIELA HUEFNER, BRUNO HUENERMUND, IAIN HUETON, ANNETTE HUFF, BEN HUFF, JOHN HUFF, BRENT HUFFMAN, CAROL HUFFMAN, JANA HUFFMAN, JOHN HUFFMAN, STEPHEN HUFFMAN, VIRGIE HUFFMAN, DENEECE HUFTALIN, DON HUGGARD, DIANE HUGGENBERGER, DEBORAH HUGGINS, FRANKLIN HUGGINS, COROM HUGHES, ENID HUGHES, GREGORY HUGHES, JILL HUGHES, KATHLEEN HUGHES, LAURA HUGHES, LISA HUGHES, MELISSA HUGHES, NANCY HUGHES, RANDY HUGHES, SHANAUN HUGHES, SIDNEY HUGHES, TERRY HUGHES, THOMAS HUGHES, SHELLY HUGIE, TODD HUGIE, JOHN HUGUS, THOMAS HUIET, JOHANNA HUIJZENDVELD, ADLIN HUISH, CHRIS HUISH, CORINNE HUISH, DEANN HUISH, RENON HULET, DEBRA HULL, JAMES HULL, RANDY HULL, REBECCA HULL, SHARI HULL, SANDRA HULL-TERRY, ROGER HULLINGER, JOHN HULSE, TROY HULSE, WILLIAM HULTERSTROM, FRANCES HUME, GARY HUME, ROBERT HUMITZ, MICHAEL HUMMEL, DIANE HUMPHERYS, LORIE HUMPHERYS, MARY ANN HUMPHERYS, AARON HUMPHREY, BRIAN HUMPHREY, LINDA HUMPHREY, NEAL HUMPHREY, WILLIAM HUMPHREY, WINSTON HUMPHREY, JACOB HUMPHREYS, AUTUMN HUMPHRIES, LISA HUMPHRIES, LUCAS HUMPHRIES, MARK HUMPHRIES, TERRY HUMPHRIES, DONALD HUNSAKER, GARY HUNSAKER, ILONA HUNSAKER, JEFF HUNSAKER, RODNEY HUNSAKER, TERESA HUNSAKER, TIM HUNSAKER, ANDREA HUNT, BEN HUNT, CHARLA HUNT, DAVID HUNT, DAVID HUNT, DAVID HUNT, DEBRA HUNT, DONALD HUNT, HOLLIS HUNT, JASON HUNT, KENNETH HUNT, LANCE HUNT, SANDRA HUNT, SARAH HUNT, STEPHEN HUNT, TERI HUNT, THOMAS HUNT, TONYA HUNT, VERNEITA HUNT, HEATHER HUNT COMPTON, BRUCE HUNTER, CARON HUNTER, CONNIE HUNTER, ERIC HUNTER, GARRY HUNTER, JENNE' HUNTER, JOHN HUNTER, KIMBERLY HUNTER, LONNIE HUNTER, MACKENZIE HUNTER, MARIANNE HUNTER, RENEE HUNTER, ROBERT HUNTER, RONNA HUNTER, ROYLENE HUNTER, SCOTT HUNTER, VADA HUNTER, WESLEY HUNTER, DOROTHY HUNTINGTON, GARN HUNTINGTON, GEOFFREY HUNTSMAN, KIRK HUNTSMAN, LAYNE HUNTSMAN, LESLIE HUNTSMAN, LIZANNE HUNTSMAN, SHEILA HUNTSMAN, ROBERT HURD, DANIEL HURLEY, KAREN HURLEY, SHAYANN HURLEY, TOBY HURLEY, BRYAN HURST, JAYSON HURST, KAREN HURST, RONALD HURST, KENNETH HURT, DAVID HUTCHENS, JUAN HUTCHINGS, PHILLIP HUTCHINGS, JAMI HUTCHINS, RUSSELL HUTCHINS, DAVID HUTCHINSON, DOUGLAS HUTCHINSON, JAMES HUTCHINSON, JOHN HUTCHINSON, JUSTIN HUTCHINSON, KEVIN HUTCHINSON, KENNETH HUTCHISON, TODD HUTCHISON, KENNETH HUTMACHER, TERRY HUTMACHER, JAMES HUTTON, DANIEL HWANG, YEON-JOO HWANG, TEAL HYATT, DUSTIN HYDE, HAZEL HYDE, LORI HYDE, MICHAEL HYDE, MICHELLE HYDE, CAMERON HYER, DARREN HYER, JASON HYER, KENT HYER, LYNETTE HYER, MACKENZIE HYER, NORMA HYER, RICHARD HYER, ROBERT HYJEK JR, GERALDINE HYLAND, VIRGINIA HYLTON, HEIDI HYNES, ANDREW HYPIO, PAT HYTE, ROBERT HYTE • **I** • CHARLES IACONA, KARIN IACONA, LUDMILA IAZYKOVA, PETER ICCABAZZI, JULIE ICKES, FUMIKO IE, KEIKO IENAGA, NIKOLE IHLER, KATHERINE ILARI, DANIEL ILIC, BRIAN ILLARIO, LOUISE ILLES, DAVID ILLSLEY, EVELYN ILLSLEY, CHERI ILLUM, MARK ILLUM, DINA IMAEVA, WAYNE

IMBRESCIA, CAROL ANN IMHOFF, ROBERT IMHOFF, MARK IMLAY, NANCY IMLAY, ROBERT IMMENS, DANIEL IMMERFALL, KENNETH INCE, STEPHANIE INGALLS, HEIDI INGHAM, SCOTT INGHAM, JEANETTE INGLES, JOE INGLES, CAROLE INGLISH, TIMOTHY INGO, MARY INGOLS, CREGG INGRAM, TERESA INGRAM, WILLIAM INGRAM, CHARLES INMAN, KATHLEEN INMAN, SANDY INMAN, BILL INSKEEP, MELANIE INSKEEP, MARCIA INSLEY, TEDDIE IRELAND, TIMOTHY IRISH, JANE IRVINE, MARIE IRVINE, ROBERT IRVINE, VIRGINIA IRWIN, RAY ISAACSON, MICHAEL ISAKSON, HOLLY ISAMAN, VON ISAMAN, SANDRA ISHII, LARRY ISHMAEL, RYAN ISOM, SUSAN ISON, KIMBERLY ISRAELSSON, LINDA ITAMI, SAMPLE ITEMS, JAMES ITO, RICHARD ITOH, CINDY IVERS, TERRY IVERS, SHEILA IVERSEN, ANNE IVERSON, CHAD IVERSON, CHARLES IVERSON, DEWAYNE IVERSON, SHAROLYN IVERSON, HOLLY IVIE, WAINE IVIE, TOMOKO IWANAGA, HILARY IZATT, TONIA IZU • **J** • DEEANN JABBS, STEVEN JABBS, JERRY JACCARD, JILL JACK, STERLING JACK, HAROLD JACKLIN, JENNIFER JACKMAN, ANNA JACKSON, BILLY JACKSON, BRENT JACKSON, CATHARINE JACKSON, CHRISTOPHER JACKSON, CINDI JACKSON, CINDY JACKSON, CLAIR JACKSON, DEBORA JACKSON, ELAINE JACKSON, ELLEN JACKSON, GEORGE JACKSON, GRACE JACKSON, GREGORY JACKSON, HARRY JACKSON, HEATHER JACKSON, MARK JACKSON, MAUREEN JACKSON, PHILLIP JACKSON, ROCHELE JACKSON, RONALD JACKSON, SEAN JACKSON, SUSAN JACKSON, TATYANA JACKSON, WILLIAM JACKSON, MICHAEL JACOBI, BART JACOBS, CARRIE JACOBS, CLARANN JACOBS, DONALD JACOBS, JACQUELINE JACOBS, JENNY JACOBS, JON JACOBS, RIE JACOBS, ANNA JACOBSEN, CAMI JACOBSEN, CAROL JACOBSEN, CHARLOTTE JACOBSEN, DAN JACOBSEN, DAVID JACOBSEN, ELIZABETH JACOBSEN, GAIL JACOBSEN, HEATHER JACOBSEN, JENNIFER JACOBSEN, KARREN JACOBSEN, LARA JACOBSEN, NICHOLAS JACOBSEN, OWEN JACOBSEN, PATRICIA JACOBSEN, THEODORE JACOBSEN, THOMAS JACOBSEN, BRYAN JACOBSON, DIANE JACOBSON, EDWARD JACOBSON, GARY JACOBSON, HOLLY JACOBSON, JENNIFER JACOBSON, JOYCE JACOBSON, PATRICIA JACOBSON, SUSAN JACOBSON, WILLIAM JACOBUS, KEITH JACQUES, RUTH JACQUET, LYNNETTE JACQUEZ, ERIC JAECKEL, CRISTINA JAEGER, LARAINE JAEGER, VAN LARAINE JAEGER, BRENT JAFFA, JOSEPH JAFFIE, MARK JAGIELLO, FLORJAN JAGODIC, BRIAN JAHNE, WALTER JAHRIES, JOHN JAICKS, DALE JAKINS, THUNDER JALILI, CHRISHEL JAMES, DARLENE JAMES, DAVID JAMES, DAVID JAMES, DAVID JAMES, ELLEN JAMES, GREG JAMES, JOLEEN JAMES, KEVIN JAMES, LORI JAMES, LORIANN JAMES, PHOEBE JAMES, JAMILEH JAMESON, ROBERT JAMIESON, PAULA JAMISON, DWIGHT JANERICH, MARY JANERICH, DAVID JANES, SUZAN JANIC, WILLIAM JANIC, ALISSA JANIS, BLAIR JANIS, DARON JANIS, STEVEN JANISCH, LOUISE JANSSEN, PAUL JANTZ, PAIGE JANZEN, JEFF JAQUITH, KENNETH JARDINE, NEVA JARDINE, ROBERT JARDINE, JUNALEE JARQUE, STANLEY JARRELL, HOWARD JARRETT, KELLY JARRETT, MICHAEL JARRETT, SARA JARRETT, JAMIE JARVIS, JOSEPH JARVIS, MARIA JARVIS, RICHARD JARVIS, JILL JASPERSON, MICHAEL JASTER, IRMGARD JAUERNIGG, ERNEST JAUL, HALDON JAUSSI, NELY JAVADOV, CARRIE JAWORSKI, JESSICA JAZEXHIU, MARK JEANBLANC, RUTH ANN JEFFERIES, ALBERT JEFFERY, ALFRED JEFFERY, ALISA JEFFERY, JOHN JEFFERY, KAREN JEFFERY, LINDA JEFFERY, MAVANEE JEFFERY, NANCY JEFFERY, DARLENE JEFFREYS, NONA JEFFRIES-LETHAM, ANNA JEFFS, CAMILLA JEFFS, CLINTON JEFFS, JENNI JELLERSON, ROBERT JELLINGS, AMANDA JENKINS, BARRY JENKINS, BRIAN JENKINS, CAROLYN JENKINS, CRAIG JENKINS, DOUGLAS JENKINS, GEORGANNE JENKINS, JANA JENKINS, JULIE JENKINS, JULIE JENKINS, KATHRYN JENKINS, LON JENKINS, LORNA JENKINS, MARIANNE JENKINS, MARK JENKINS, MARY ANN JENKINS, PAUL JENKINS, SARAH JENKINS, STANLEY JENKINS, WILLIAM JENKINS, DARICE JENKINS-SPACKMAN, CHAD JENKS, PETER JENKS, STEVEN JENN, DOUG JENNINGS, JEREMY JENNINGS, TIFFANI JENNINGS, KAREN JENSE, ALISON JENSEN, ANNA JENSEN, BARBARA JENSEN, BECKY JENSEN, BEN JENSEN, BRANDON JENSEN, BRIAN JENSEN, CHRIS JENSEN, DANIELLE JENSEN, DARWIN JENSEN, DAVID JENSEN, DEANNA JENSEN, DELAN JENSEN, DENISE JENSEN, DENNIS JENSEN, DINNENE JENSEN, DONNA JENSEN, EDWARD JENSEN, ERIC JENSEN, ERIC JENSEN, ERIC JENSEN, FELIECE JENSEN, GRACE JENSEN, JAMES JENSEN, JAMES JENSEN, JAMES JENSEN, JAMIE JENSEN, JASMINE JENSEN, JASON JENSEN, JEAN JENSEN, JENISE JENSEN, JEREMY JENSEN, JERRY JENSEN, JHAN JENSEN, JILL JENSEN, JOANN JENSEN, JOHN JENSEN, JUDY JENSEN, JUDY JENSEN, JULIE JENSEN, KAREN JENSEN, KATHLEEN JENSEN, KAYE JENSEN, KEN JENSEN, KENT JENSEN, KEVIN JENSEN, KRISTINE JENSEN, KURT JENSEN, LEESA JENSEN, LINDA JENSEN, LUANE JENSEN, MARJORIE JENSEN, MARK JENSEN, MARVIN JENSEN, MATTHEW JENSEN, MELISSA JENSEN, MICHAEL JENSEN, MICHAEL JENSEN, NANCY JENSEN, NANCY JENSEN, NITA JENSEN, PATRICIA JENSEN, PENNY JENSEN, RANDON JENSEN, RICHARD JENSEN, RICHELLE JENSEN, RON JENSEN, RONALD E JENSEN, ROXANN JENSEN, SHAWNA JENSEN, SHIRLEY JENSEN, STANLEY JENSEN, SUE JENSEN, SUMMER JENSEN, SUZANNE JENSEN, SUZANNE JENSEN, TED JENSEN, THOMAS JENSEN, TONI JENSEN, TRACI JENSEN, TRACY JENSEN, VALENE JENSEN, VERL JENSEN, ANDREW JENSON, CALEB JENSON, DEBRA JENSON, DOUGLAS JENSON, DUANE JENSON, ELIZABETH JENSON, KEITH JENSON, MERRILL JENSON, RODNEY JENSON, CURTIS JENTZSCH, KARIN JENTZSCH, LARRY JENTZSCH, MATHEW JENTZSCH, RICHARD JEPPERSON, ALAN JEPPESEN, DAVID JEPPESEN, KELLY JEPPESEN, KENT JEPPESEN, MINDY JEPPESEN, SHARON JEPPESEN, MICAH JEPPSEN, BONNIE JEPPSON, BRENDA JEPPSON, JENNIFER JEPPSON, JOHN JEPPSON, LEAH JANE JEPPSON, NEAL JEPPSON, SARA JEPPSON, JAMIE JEPSEN, ROGER JERMAN, STEVE JERMAN, TERI JERMAN, BARBARA JEROME, PETER JEROME, LESLIE JEROMINSKI, JONATHAN JESPERSON, MATTHEW JESPERSON, LAURIE JESS, DEVIN JESSEE, DONALD JESSEE, NORMAN JESSEE, FRANK JESSEN, MELANIE JESSEN, PATRICIA JESSIE, MARK JETTE, DAVID JEVSEVAR, JOHN JEWETT, DAGMAR JEWKES, GREGORY JEWKES, JIM JEWKES, JOSHUA JEWKES, KATHLEEN JEWKES, LISA JEWKES, DON JEX, KYLEY JEX, RODNEY JEX, MOON JI, JANET JIBSON, JEFFERY JILES, CARLOS JIMENEZ, PHILIP JIMENEZ, GLENN JOBE, JOSIANE JOCHMANN, URSULA JOCHMANN, KRISTA JOHANSEN, LESLIE JOHANSEN, MONICA JOHANSEN, PETER JOHANSEN, ERIN JOHANSON, ROWENA JOHANSON, EMILIA JOHANSSON, CAROL JOHN, JEAN JOHN, CATHY JOHNS, FRED JOHNSEN, JARED JOHNSEN, ADAM JOHNSON, ALAN JOHNSON, ALICE JOHNSON, ALISON JOHNSON, ALYSHA JOHNSON, ANDREA JOHNSON, ANGELA JOHNSON, ANN JOHNSON, ANNE MARIE JOHNSON, ANNETTE JOHNSON, ANNETTE JOHNSON, ANNETTE I JOHNSON, ARMINTA JOHNSON, BARRY JOHNSON, BERT JOHNSON, BLAKE JOHNSON, BOBBI JOHNSON, BONNIE JOHNSON, BRAD JOHNSON, BRADLEY JOHNSON, CAROL JOHNSON, CASSIDY JOHNSON, CHARLOTTE JOHNSON, CHRISTENE JOHNSON, CHRISTENE JOHNSON, CHRISTINE JOHNSON, CHRISTOPHER JOHNSON, CHRISTY JOHNSON, CLAYTON JOHNSON, CYNTHIA JOHNSON, DALE JOHNSON, DALE JOHNSON, DANIEL JOHNSON, DARRON JOHNSON, DARWIN JOHNSON, DAVID JOHNSON, DAVID JOHNSON, DAVID JOHNSON, DAVID JOHNSON, DAVID JOHNSON, DAVID JOHNSON, DAVID JOHNSON, DEAN JOHNSON, DEBBIE JOHNSON, DEBRA JOHNSON, DEBRA JOHNSON, DENECE JOHNSON, DENISE JOHNSON, DEREK JOHNSON, DIANE JOHNSON, DJ JOHNSON, DOLORES JOHNSON, EFFIE JOHNSON, ELIZABETH JOHNSON, ELIZABETH JOHNSON, EMILY JOHNSON, EMILY JOHNSON, ERIC JOHNSON, ERIC JOHNSON, FAYE JOHNSON, FRANK JOHNSON, FRIEDA JOHNSON, HANA JOHNSON, JACK JOHNSON, JACK JOHNSON, JAKE JOHNSON, JAMES JOHNSON, JAMES JOHNSON, JAMES JOHNSON, JAMES JOHNSON, JAMES JOHNSON, JAMIE JOHNSON, JANALYN JOHNSON, JANET JOHNSON, JANETTE JOHNSON, JANETTE JOHNSON, JAY JOHNSON, JAY JOHNSON, JEFFERY JOHNSON, JENNI JOHNSON, JERRY JOHNSON, JODY JOHNSON, JOYCE JOHNSON, JOYCE JOHNSON, JUDY JOHNSON, JULIE JOHNSON, JUSTIN JOHNSON, KAREN JOHNSON, KATHRYN JOHNSON, KATHRYN JOHNSON, KATHY JOHNSON, KATHY JOHNSON, KATHY JOHNSON, KAY JOHNSON, KELLY JOHNSON, KENNETH JOHNSON, KENNETH JOHNSON, KENT JOHNSON, KEVIN JOHNSON, KRAIG JOHNSON, LAMAR JOHNSON, LARRY JOHNSON, LAUREL JOHNSON, LAWRENCE JOHNSON, LEEANN JOHNSON, LEONARD JOHNSON, LINDA JOHNSON, LINDA JOHNSON, LISA JOHNSON, LLOYD JOHNSON, MADELYN JOHNSON, MARCIE JOHNSON, MARIA JOHNSON, MARILYN JOHNSON, MARKITA JOHNSON, MATHIUS JOHNSON, MELANIE JOHNSON, MICHAEL JOHNSON, MICHAEL JOHNSON, MICHAEL JOHNSON, MIKE JOHNSON, MONA JOHNSON, NANCY JOHNSON, NATALIE JOHNSON, NORMAN JOHNSON, OLIN JOHNSON, OSCAR JOHNSON, PATRICK JOHNSON, PAUL JOHNSON, PAULINE WEGGELAND- JOHNSON, PIA JOHNSON, POLLY JOHNSON, R CRAIG JOHNSON, RANDY JOHNSON, RAY JOHNSON, RAY JOHNSON, RAY JOHNSON, RAYMOND JOHNSON, REBECCA JOHNSON, REBECCA JOHNSON, RENITA JOHNSON, RHONDA JOHNSON, RICHARD JOHNSON, RICHARD JOHNSON, RICHARD JOHNSON, RICK JOHNSON, ROBERT JOHNSON, RON JOHNSON, RONALD JOHNSON, RONDA JOHNSON, RUSSELL JOHNSON, RUSSELL JOHNSON, RUTHANN JOHNSON, SAMUEL JOHNSON, SAMUEL JOHNSON, SARA JOHNSON, SCOTT JOHNSON, SCOTT JOHNSON, SEAN JOHNSON, SHANDRA JOHNSON, SHARON JOHNSON, SHELDON JOHNSON, SHIRLEY JOHNSON, STEPHANIE JOHNSON, STEPHEN JOHNSON, SUSAN JOHNSON, SUSAN JOHNSON, TERRY JOHNSON, THOMAS JOHNSON, THOMAS JOHNSON, TOD JOHNSON, TODD JOHNSON, TONI JOHNSON, TROY JOHNSON, VAN JOHNSON, WALTER JOHNSON, WHITNEY JOHNSON, WHITNEY JOHNSON, WILLIAM JOHNSON, WILLIAM JOHNSON, WILLIAM JOHNSON, DAVID JOHNSON III, CLYDE JOHNSON JR, ANTHONY JOHNSTON, CHRISTIE JOHNSTON, DANIEL JOHNSTON, GAIL JOHNSTON, GREGORY JOHNSTON, LINDA JOHNSTON, STEPHEN JOHNSTON, SUSAN JOHNSTON, WALTER JOHNSTON, ALAN JOHNSTUN, JANET JOHNSTUN, REGINA JOINER, STEPHEN JOINER, SUE JOINER, ASHLEY JOLLEY, BRIAN JOLLEY, CAMILLE JOLLEY, KRISTIN JOLLEY, LARAIN JOLLEY, MARY JOLLEY, MEGAN JOLLEY, MERLYN JOLLEY, MICHAEL JOLLEY, PAM JOLLEY, SCOTT JOLLEY, ALMA JONES, ALVIN JONES, AMY JONES, ANDREA JONES, ANNE JONES, BETH JONES, BRANDT JONES, BRITTANY JONES, BRYAN JONES, CAROLE JONES, CARRIE JONES, CARTER JONES, CHRIS JONES, CHRISTOPHER JONES, CINDY JONES, CLARK JONES, DARLA JONES, DARON JONES, DARRELL JONES, DARRON JONES, DAVID JONES, DAVID JONES, DAVID JONES, DEBBIE JONES, DEBBIE JONES, GARET JONES, GARY JONES, GARY JONES, GARY JONES, GEORGE JONES, GLENN JONES, GORDON JONES, GREGORY JONES, GUNHILD JONES, HEATHER JONES, JANEEN JONES, JANET JONES, JANINE JONES, JASON JONES, JASON JONES, JEF JONES, JENNIFER JONES, JERILEE JONES, JERRY JONES, JILL JONES, JOSHUA JONES, JOSIE JONES, JOYCE JONES, JUDITH JONES, JULIE JONES, JULIE JONES, KAREN JONES, KAY JONES, KEIKO JONES, KELLY JONES, KENNETH JONES, KENT JONES, KERMA JONES, KEVIN JONES, KEVIN JONES, KIMBERLEE JONES, KIRK JONES, LARRY JONES, LEAH JONES, LEON JONES, LORI JONES, LORRAINE JONES, LYNNE JONES, MARGARET JONES, MARGARET JONES, MARGO JONES, MARY JONES, MARYANN JONES, MATTHEW JONES, MAX JONES, MEGAN JONES, MERRY JONES, MICHAEL JONES, MICHELLE JONES, MIKKEL JONES, NADINE JONES, NANCY JONES, NICOLLE JONES, PATRICIA JONES, PATRICIA JONES, PAUL JONES, PHIL JONES, PHYLLIS JONES, RANDALL JONES, RAY JONES, RHETT JONES, RICHARD JONES, ROBERT JONES, ROBERT JONES, ROBERT JONES, ROBERT C JONES, ROBIN JONES, RODNEY JONES, RONALD D JONES, SANDRA JONES, SARAH JONES, SCOTT JONES, SCOTT JONES, SHALAIR JONES, SHAMRA JONES, SHANNON JONES, SHANNON JONES, SHARRA JONES, SUSAN JONES, SUSAN JONES, SUSAN JONES, THOUIS JONES, TRAVIS JONES, TROY JONES, VENITA JONES, VERNON JONES, WALT JONES, WAYNE JONES, WENDELL JONES, WENDY JONES, WILLIAM E JONES, ARJEN JONKHART, KIMBERLY JONKHART, JOHN JONKMAN, RICHARD JOOS, SHIRLEY JOOS, MARTY JOPLING, HOLLY JORDAN, STEVEN JORDAN, AMANDA JORGENSEN, BRAD JORGENSEN, BRET JORGENSEN, BRETT JORGENSEN, CHRISTIAN JORGENSEN, DEANNE JORGENSEN, ERIC JORGENSEN, JAYME JORGENSEN, KAREN JORGENSEN, KENNA JORGENSEN, KENNETH JORGENSEN, KENNETH JORGENSEN, MICHAEL JORGENSEN, MIKE JORGENSEN, REX JORGENSEN, SANDRA JORGENSEN, SUSAN JORGENSEN, JAMES JORGENSON, DAVID JOSEPH, MEGAN JOSEPHSON, ROZAN JOSEPHSON, RANDALL JOSEY, TROY JOSIE, DENISE JOST, WANPHEN JOTIKABUKKANA, JOSEPH JOYCE, LESLIE JOYCE, ROBERTA JOYCE, STEVEN JOYCE, BRENT JOYNER, BLANKA JUCHELKA, CHRISTENE JUDD, GARR JUDD, KAREN JUDD, NANCY JUDD, NICHOLAS JUDD, SHERRI JUDD, VAL JUDD, JEFFERY JUDKINS, MERLIN JUDKINS, PAULA JUDKINS, JAMES JUDY, JIM JUDY, BRUCE JUHL, CLINTON JUHL, JES JULANDER, DAVID JULIAN, LIZA JULIEN, HOON JIN JUNG, MARILYN JUNK, JENNIFER JURGENS, JOHN JURKOWSKI, BRENT JUSTENSEN, JANE JUSTENSEN • **K** • HANK KAANTA, PANAGIOTA KABOURI, DAVE KADLECK, ANTHONY KADZIUS, BRIDGET KADZIUS, PATRICIA KADZIUS, FLORIAN KAEMPF, DIANNA KAFER, ROBERT KAGGIE, KAREN KAGIE, WAYNE KAHALEKOMO, BARBARA KAHL, RACHEL KAHLER, BRIAN KAHN, CLAUDECORKY KAHN, DAVID KAISER, YUKAKO KAISER, RICHARD KAJMA, CORINE KALAKIS, KRISTI KALASINSKY, LAWRENCE KALKE, FRITZ KALLIN, CHERYL KAMENSKI, JOEY KAMENSKI, KATHY KAMERATH, KEVIN KAMERATH, KENNETH KAMIGAKI, LOU ANN KAMIGAKI, JENNIFER KAMMEYER, MARTIN KAMMEYER, SHARON KAMMEYER, KARUNA KANAGARATNAM, MICHAEL KANE, TIMO KANERVISTO, STANISLAW KANTOWSKI, SUE KAPIS, GRANT KAPP, KRISTIN KAPP, MARK KAPP, WENDI KARBAKHSH, BRUCE KARINEN, SANDRA KARIYA, MARILYN KARJALAINEN, RAULI KARJALAINEN, LAURIE KARLIK, KELEIGH KARLINSEY, LINDA KARLINSEY, NICOLE KARLINSEY, JEANINE KARNS, PETER KARNS, STEVEN KARREN, MARINKA KARTALIJA, KENNETH KARTCHNER, MICHELLE KARTCHNER, ODD KARTOMTEN, ROBERT KARZ, MARK KASCHMITTER, AUDRA KASPARIAN, LAURA KASS, JAMES KASTANIS, LUCILLE KASTANIS, CAMERON KASTELER, LAWRENCE KASTING, MARK KASULEN, SCOTT KATSCHKE, JAMES KATSILAS, MAXINE KATSILAS, JULIE KATYRYNIUK, CONNIE KATZ, GEORGE KATZ, CHRISTINE KATZENBERGER, JONATHAN KAU, CONNIE KAUFMAN, MICHAEL KAURALA, KEVIN KAVANAGH, GERRY KAWAMURA, KATHRYN KAY, MICHAEL KAY, NEWELL KAY, PATRICIA KAY, CRYSTAL KEARL, DEBRA KEARL, JAMES KEARL, RICK KEARL, SYLVIA KEARNEY, MEREDITH KEARSLEY, KATHLEEN KEATE, STEVEN KEATE, SUSAN KEATE, ERIC KECK, DAVID KEDDINGTON, KENRA KEDDINGTON, ROBERT KEDDINGTON, ROGER KEDDINGTON, KRISTEN KEEFE, DAVID KEEFER, ANTHONY KEELE, SAMANTHA KEELE, SHANNA KEELE, CHRISTOPHER KEELER, GAIL KEELER, HYRUM KEELER, JOLENE KEELEY, KAREN KEELEY, MARSHA KEEMER, HOWARD KEEN, JESSE KEENE, WALTER KEESECKER, BRENDA KEESLER, ALFRED KEETCH, ANITA KEETCH, KITSY KEETCH, KRISTA KEETCH, RUSSELL KEETCH, M. JANE KEHL, ANNE KEIL, PAUL KEIL, CARON KEIM, RALPH KEITH, STEPHEN KEITH, THOMAS KEITH, WILLIAM KEITH, NANCY KEITHLEY, CATHERINE KELLEHER, KEELY KELLEHER, MICHAEL KELLEHER, ANN KELLER, BARBARA KELLER, CURTIS KELLER, FLORENCE KELLER, JESSIE KELLER, JONATHAN KELLER, KARREN KELLER, KAY KELLER, LARRY KELLER, LESTER KELLER, MONTIE KELLER, ROGER KELLER, ROGER KELLER, SUSAN KELLER, BOB KELLEY, BURNIS KELLEY, CLINT KELLEY, GLORIA KELLEY, JERI KELLEY, KAREN KELLEY, MELANIE KELLEY, NANCY KELLEY, ROSEMARY KELLEY, WILLIAM KELLEY, ALAN KELLOGG, CHARLES KELLOGG, GILLIAN KELLOGG, SANDE KELLOGG, AILEEN KELLY, BRENDA KELLY, BRIAN KELLY, BURTON KELLY, CAROL KELLY, DAVE KELLY, DEAN KELLY, DENISE KELLY, ELEANOR KELLY, JENNA KELLY, MICHAEL KELLY, PADRAIC KELLY, PHILIP KELLY, SHANE KELLY, VIKKI KELLY, JILL KELSCH, KELLY KELSEY, PHYLLIS KELSEY, SUSAN KELSEY, ANNE KELSTROM, STEPHEN KELTON, CHRISTIAN KEMP, NORBERT KEMP, CHRISTINE KEMPE, SUSAN KEMPFF, DEE ANN KEMPINGER, BONNIE KENDALL, DIANE KENDALL, GARY KENDALL, KIM KENDALL, LARA KENDALL, MARY KENDALL, RICHARD KENDALL, STEPHEN KENDALL, THOMAS KENDALL, CARYN KENDRA, DAVID KENDRICK, ROBERT KENDRICK, COREY KENER, MICHAEL KENISON, MICHIKO KENMOTSU, LON H. KENNARD, BRANDON KENNEDY, DEBRA KENNEDY, KAREN KENNEDY, NANCY KENNEDY, NICOLE KENNEDY, TYLER KENNEDY, VIRGINIA KENNEDY, WILLIAM KENNEDY, CHRISTINE KENNELLY, GEORGE KENNING, KELLY KENNY, MICHAEL KENNY, CAMERON KENT, DEBRA KENT, HENRY KENT, JANALEE KENT, SHOSHANAH KENT, KENT KEOPPEL, PAMELA KEOPPEL, PAUL KEOPPEL, MARILEE KERBY, JOHN KERBY-MILLER, YVONNE KERBY-MILLER, HAROLD KERKMAN, JAMIE KERKMAN, SHARON KERKMAN, JOHN KERN, MATTHEW KERN, WANDA KERN, GRANT KERR, MARY KERR, GARRY KERSHAW, ALLYSON KESLER, RICHARD KESLER, SHIRLYN KESLER, SHERRY KESSEL, MARK KESSLER, ALANE KESTER, BRENDAN KESTER, THOMAS KETTS JR, MATTHEW KEULER, MICHAEL KEULER, ROBERT KEULER, MARY KEY, NANCY KEY, JIM KEYES, FASIHA KHADERI, HASHU KHADERI, ALI KHEFEIFI, TAM KHONG, KEVIN KIDD, RENEE KIDD, VAL ANN KIDD, CLARKE KIDO, KORRY KIEFFER, JIM KIEFHABER, GERD KIESSLING, PATRICIA KIHLSTROM, ELIZABETH KIHM, DARREN KILFOYLE, PATRICK KILGORE, SHARI KILLE, WILLARD KILLE, LARRY KILLIPS, CAROLYN KILLPACK, MINKYOUNG KIM, NAREE KIM, SOHEE KIM, MARIANNE KIMBAL, CAROL KIMBALL, JEANNE KIMBALL, JEFF KIMBALL, JOHN KIMBALL, MATTHEW KIMBALL, PATRICIA KIMBALL, TRACY KIMBALL, PATRICK KIMBER, JOHN KIMBLE, JULIE KIMBLE, DEBRA KIMBROUGH, SIMON KIMCHE, DAVID KIMMEL, MARK KIMMIG, DALE KIMSEY, PATRICIA KIMSEY, MELANIE KIMURA, NADINE KINCAID, PHILIP KINCHINGTON, WINSTON KINDEM, LESLIE KINDRED, CAROLINE KING, DARREN KING, DAVID KING, DENNIS KING, DIANA KING, DWIGHT (SEE COMMENTS) KING, GORDON KING, JAMES KING, JASON KING, JEAN KING, JENNIFER KING, JENNIFER KING, JULIE KING, KENT KING, LANIA KING, LORI KING, MARCIE KING, MARK KING, MICHAEL KING, NOEL KING, NOELLE KING, PAM KING, PATRICK KING, RICHARD KING, RONALD KING, ROYCE KING, SHERRIE KING, STEPHANIE KING, STEVE KING, STEWART KING, TIFFANY KING, TIM KING, TREVOR KING, VERONICA KING, MELANIE KINGDON, JAMES KINGMAN, GEORGE KINGSTON, KATHLEEN KINGSTON, PAUL KINGSTON, JOHN KINNEBERG, BARBARA KINSLEY, LEONA KINZER, JULIE KIPP, RONALD KIPP, BRYAN KIPPEN, HEATHER KIRBY, KRISTIN KIRBY, RICHARD KIRBY, TERRY KIRCH, KATRINA KIRCHER, ANNA KIRCHMEIER, ALAN KIRK, CAROLEE KIRK, CUC KIRK, DAVID KIRK, JOEL KIRK, KARI KIRK, MARK KIRK, MARK KIRK, ESTELLE KIRKHAM, JONATHAN KIRKHAM, MARVIN KIRKHAM, MIRJAM KIRKHAM, TERI KIRKLAND, WILLIAM KIRKLAND, ALICIA KIRKMAN, KELLY KIRKPATRICK, KENT KIRKPATRICK, HEATHER KIRKWOOD, MARY KIRKWOOD, SANDRA KIRSTINE, JOSEPH KIRTON, RICHARD KIRTON JR, SUSAN KIRTS, BROCK KIRWAN, HEATHER KISER, JOHN KISER, RAYMOND KISSEL, WILLIAM KISSELL, ERIKA KITCHEN, TODD KITCHEN, AMANDA KITTELL, EDVARD KJAERAAS, CHAD KJAR, COLLEEN KLAPSTEIN, RICHARD KLATT, JUDITH KLAUTT, WARREN KLAUTT, KAREN KLC, JEFFREY KLECK, JAMES KLECKNER, TROY KLEE, MARTHA KLEFFMAN, RICHARD KLEFFMAN, DEREK KLEIN, DON KLEIN, GRETCHEN KLEIN, KRISTIN KLEIN, NORMAN KLEIN, SUSAN KLEIN, WAYNE KLEIN, WILLIAM KLEIN, ZACHARY KLEINMAN, CHARLENE KLENK, JENNIFER KLETTKE, KURT KLEV, HAROLD KLEVEN, LAURA KLIMOWSKI, PATTIE KLINE, CHADRA KLING, PETER KLINGE JR, LYLE KLIPPEL, JOHN KLISCH, JASON KLOMP, KRISTEN KLOOGH, DIANE KLOS, HANS KLOSSNER, ERIC KLOTZ, KRISTINA KLUETER, JULIE KNAPHUS, ANDREW KNAPP, GAYLE KNAPP, LAURA KNAPP, REINHARD KNAPP, VIRGINIA KNAUB, CHAD KNAVEL, VALERIE KNICKERBOCKER, JANICE KNICKREHM, ANNETTE KNIGHT, BETH KNIGHT, CONNIE KNIGHT, ERIN KNIGHT, JENNIFER KNIGHT, JOHN KNIGHT, JUDITH KNIGHT, KATHRYN KNIGHT, LINDA KNIGHT, NELSON KNIGHT, RANDY KNIGHT, ROSEMAREE KNIGHT, SHELDON KNIGHT, SHERYL KNIGHT, SPENCER KNIGHT, TODD KNIGHT, DEAN KNIGHTON, STEPHANIE KNOPFEL, MARCIA KNORR, BRYAN KNOTTS, CANDICE KNOTTS, RORY KNOTTS, MARJORIE KNOWLDEN, BRIAN KNOWLTON, SHARON KNOWLTON, SUSAN KNOWLTON, TYLER KNOWLTON, ALLISON KNOX, ROGER KNOX, HANS KNUBEL, BRIAN KNUDSEN, CATHY KNUDSEN, CURTIS KNUDSEN, DONNA KNUDSEN, GEORGE KNUDSEN, JONATHAN KNUDSEN, KAREN KNUDSEN, JOHN KNUDSON, LOIS KNUTESON, DEBBIE KNUTSEN, MICHAEL KNUTTI, WILHO KNUUTI, CHU-EN KO, CINDY KOBS, LEROY KOBS, DAVID KOCH, MICHELLE KOCH, ROBERT KOCH, TRAVIS KOCH, LANCE KOCHERHANS, ELIZABETH KOEHLER, SCOTT KOEHLER, SUSAN KOELLIKER, GERD KOERBER, CAROL KOERNER, KARL KOERNER, MARY KOESTER, BRADLEY KOFFORD, JERALD KOFFORD, LAURALYN KOFFORD, CLYDE KOFOED, KRISTOPHER KOFOED, JEFFREY KOFORD, KAREN KOFORD, RODNEY KOFORD, KYUNGRAN KOH, CURTIS KOHLER, DEBBIE KOHLER, JOERG KOHLMANN, FRED KOHOUT, MARY KOHOUT, JERRY KOKESH, KAREN KOKESH, KATY KOLB, KIRK KOLBERG, KARIN KOLBUS, JENNIFER KOLES, GARY KOLMAN, KEN KOMENDARYAN, LEANN KONCAR, DAMIAN KONDAS, BETTY KONG, CANDI KONIECZNY, NOBUE KONNO, SUZANNE KONZ, MARK KOON, SHERRY KOON, JOSEPH KOOS JR, KEVIN KOOYMAN, JULIE KOPLIN, RICHARD KOPLIN, KIMBERLEY KOPLOWITZ, LINDA KOPP, MIKE KOPPY, JOHN KORHONEN, OLGA KORNYUSHYNA, BARBARA KOROUS, JOHN KORPI, HALVARD KORSBERG, BETTY KOSCO, LAWANA KOSEL, JOSEPH KOSIK, APRIL KOSKA, JOHN KOSTER, LORI KOSTER, MEGAN KOURI, DAVID KOVANDA, KAREL KOVAR, CAROLYN KOWALCHIK, PETER KOWALCHIK, LYNN KOWALLIS, KAGEHISA KOYANO, ELAINE KOYLE, JAMIE KOYLE, KENT KOZIMOR, RICHARD KOZLOWSKI, ANNA KOZOLE, KENNETH KOZOLE, BRIAN KRABAK, CONSTANCE HURST KRAFT, EDITH KRAILO, BRANDON KRAINIK, JOANN KRAJESKI, JANET KRAKOW, JEANNE KRAMER, MARK KRANSDORF, ALAN KRAUS, CAROL KRAUS, JENNIFER KRAVITZ, SANDRA KREGER, KAREN KREIFELS, STANLEY KREIFELS, BARB KRELL, ROBYN KREMER, ANARGYROS KREMITSAS, JOHN KREUZER, EVAN KRICHEVSKY, ALIDA KRIEK, MATTHYS KRIEK, AIVAR KRISENKO, BETH KRISTENSON, CAROL KRIZ, JOHN KRIZ, KARL KRIZMANIC, CAROL KROCZKA, NANCY KROGH, ROBERT KROGH, CAROLE KROHN, KADY KRONEBERGER, JIM KROS, CHAD KRUGER, SHELLEY KRUGER, SUSAN KRUGER, DENNIS KRUSE, KRIS KUBICA, JEANETTE KUCHARSKI, KATHY KUDALE, SUSAN KUEHN, MICHAEL KUENNE, JILL KUENZI, KAREN KUGLER, MICHAEL KUHN, NANETTE KUHN, KARL KUHNEN, ANDREA KUHNER, NIEL KUHNER, NADEZHDA KULIKOVA, STEPHEN KULLER, MARY LOUISE KULSICK, CASEY KUNIMURA, KATHRYN KUNKEL, WALTER KUNKLE, GREGORY KUNST, LUKAS KUNZ, MELANIE KUNZ, SARAH KUNZ, DAVID KUNZE, SUZY KUNZE, STEPHEN KUNZLER, TAUNYA KUNZLER, DANIEL KUREK, IRINA KURINSKAJA, BOBBIE KURIVIAL, PATRICK KURIVIAL, MARGARET KURLANDER, ARILYN KUSAKABE, HAJIME KUSAKABE, JENNIFER KUSCH, WILLIAM KUSHNER, DON KUSSEE, KLEIS KUSSEE, KANDI KUTKAS, JEAN KUTNER, DALE KUTTERER, NICHOLAS KUWADA, MARTHA KUZARA, RADOMIR KUZNETSOV, KATHERINE KWIC, JARED KWONG, CHRISTOPHER KYLER • **L** • LINDA L'AI, JAYNE LA FOND, HEATHER LA GIUSA, CAROL LA POINTE, GARRY LA ROSE, KENNETH LABDON, BRIGITTE LABEDAN, HELEN LABELLE, KIMBERLEY LABERTEW, MICHAEL LABERTEW, IVAN LABRUM, JASON LABRUM, JENNETT LABRUM, JO LABRUM, STEPHEN LABRUM, NATALIE LACEY, JANINE LACHANCE, STEVE LACKEY, THOMAS LACY, MARK LADWIG, VERONIQUE LAFLEUR, ERIC LAGE, SALLY LAGOY, NANCY LAGUILLO, GREG LAHR, KEN LAIER, RONDA LAIER, ADAM LAIN, DARLENE LAING, JOSEPH LAIR, ALAN LAKE, LORRAINE LAKEY, ANNE LALONDE, JOHN LALONDE, JACKIE LALOR, DEBORAH LAMARCHE, BRITTEN LAMB, CAROL LAMB, JOHN LAMB, JOSEPH LAMB, KATHRYN LAMB, KEVIN LAMB, MICHAEL LAMB, SCOTT LAMB, SHAWN LAMB, TONDA LAMB, WILLIAM LAMB, WILLIAM LAMB, KEITH LAMBERSON, BRIAN LAMBERT, CHARLES LAMBERT, EUGENE LAMBERT, GARY LAMBERT, JANE LAMBERT, KATHEE LAMBERT, KENNETH LAMBERT, LOREN LAMBERT, NANCY LAMBERT, SCOTT LAMBERT, SEAN LAMBERT, DEBRA LAMBORN, JOHN LAMBORN, TAMARA LAMBORN, KENNETH LAMBRECHT, JEREMY LAMOREAUX, CINDY LAMPH, DEE LAMPH, ELIZABETH LAMPHERE, MONICA LAMPRECHT, JANICE LANCASTER, JASON LANCE, LANA LAND-LAMBERT, JINI LANDER, MARK LANDER, SANDRA LANDIS, BRETT LANDON, CORY LANDON, MICHAEL LANDON, ROSS LANDON, STEVEN LANDON, DENISE LANDVATTER, ERIN LANDVATTER, ALDEN LANEY, BRANDON LANG, CHRISTINA LANG, JOHN LANG, ROBERT LANG, JANICE LANGE, JENNIFER LANGE, MARK LANGE, RHOLAND LANGE, ROBERT LANGE, STACY LANGE, JANINE LANGER, KATHY LANGEVIN, KIRK LANGFORD, LAURA LANGFORD, LEONARD LANGFORD, MIRIAM LANGFORD, REBECCA LANGFORD, ROBERT LANGFORD, TERESA LANGFORD, LAVON LANGLEY, ROBERT LANGSTON, TYLER LANGSTON, KATIE LANGSTRAAT, CATHIE LANHAM, SIDNEY LANHAM, JOYCE LANIEWSKI, RICHARD LANIEWSKI, EMILY LANIN, PATRICK LANIN, AMY LANZEL, TIM LAPAGE, JOHN LAPIC, CRISTEN LAPIERRE, ROBERT LAPINE, ANNIE LAPLANTE, CLAIRE LAPORTE, ROBERT LARABEE, MARCEL LARAMEE, LLOYD LARIMORE, FREDERICK LARKE, BILL LARKIN, JAMES LARKIN, JIM LARKIN, LOUANN LARKIN, PAUL LARKIN, SHARON LARKIN, RICHARD LARKO, LISA LAROCCO, DAIN LAROCHE, TIM LAROS, DAVID LARRABEE, STEPHEN LARRABEE, ALAN LARSEN, ALEHA LARSEN, ALISON LARSEN, BOB LARSEN, BRENDA LARSEN, CAMILLA LARSEN, CATHERINE LARSEN, CATHY LARSEN, DEBORAH LARSEN, DEBRA LARSEN, DEETTE LARSEN, DENNIS LARSEN, DIANE LARSEN, EARL LARSEN, ESTHER LARSEN, FRANCES LARSEN, GORDON LARSEN, GRACE LARSEN, JANNA LARSEN, JORGEN LARSEN, JUDITH LARSEN, KARALEE LARSEN, KAREN LARSEN, KAREN LARSEN, KARI LARSEN, KARIN LARSEN, KATHRYN LARSEN, KENNETH LARSEN, KENT LARSEN, KRISTOFER LARSEN, LEZLE LARSEN, MARJA LARSEN, MARK LARSEN, MARY LARSEN, MARYDA LARSEN, MELISSA LARSEN, MELISSA LARSEN, MELODIE LARSEN, NEIL LARSEN, NOBLE LARSEN, PAUL LARSEN, PAUL LARSEN, RICHARD LARSEN, RICHARD LARSEN, ROBERT LARSEN, ROBERT LARSEN, ROBERT LARSEN, RONALD LARSEN, RUTH LARSEN, SHARON LARSEN, STEPHEN LARSEN, TERESA LARSEN, TRESSA LARSEN, AARON LARSON, ADRIENNE LARSON, ALEXANDER LARSON, ANNETTE LARSON, BYRON LARSON, CAROL LARSON, CHRIS LARSON, CHRISTIAN LARSON, CORINNE LARSON, DEBORAH LARSON, DOUGLAS LARSON, ERIK FINN LARSON, GARY LARSON, JAMES LARSON, JANIFER LARSON, JEANIE LARSON, JEROME LARSON, JODY LARSON, JUSTIN LARSON, KARLA LARSON, KIRSTEN LARSON, KRISTINE LARSON, LAWERENCE LARSON, LEROY LARSON, LEX LARSON, LINDSAY LARSON, LISA LARSON, MARCIA LARSON, MARVIN LARSON, MATTHEW LARSON, PAM LARSON, REBECCA LARSON, ROBIN LARSON, SCOTT LARSON, SHERRIE LARSON, SUSAN LARSON, TANDY LARSON, THAD LARSON, VAUGHN LARSON, WILLIAM LARSON, BERT LARSSON, GERTIE LARSSON, OLAV LARSSON, JAMES LARUE, JOEL LARWAY, EDWARD LASKOWSKI, AMY LASOTA, BJORN LASSERUD, DAVID LASSIG, KARIE LASSON, RAMONA LASSON, CHELSEA LASWELL, KEVIN LATER, MARK LATER, GAYLYN LATIMER, ARTHUR LATOURELLE, MICHAEL LATSHAW, GEORGE LATTA, THOMAS LATTA, MARJORIE LATU, GEORGE LATULIPPE, MARY JO LATULIPPE, MERRILY LAU, EVELYN LAUCK, JOHN LAUCK, CYNTHIA LAUDER, ED LAUDER, DENISE LAUER, TO ' AFA LAUFOU, KATHY LAURENTS, ELIZABETH LAURET, BRAD LAURITZEN, SYLVIE LAUZON, ROBERT LAVERY SR., BONNIE LAW, BRUCE LAW, CARLA LAW, CYNTHIA LAW, FRED LAW, JUDSON LAW, LIN LAW, LINDSEY LAW, SANDRA LAW, SHARON LAW, SHAURI LAW, TIM LAW, VARLIN LAW, DAN LAWLER, GRETCHEN LAWLOR, ANGELA LAWRENCE, ASHLEY LAWRENCE, DANIEL LAWRENCE, DIANA LAWRENCE, DONALD LAWRENCE, ELIZABETH LAWRENCE, ELLIOT LAWRENCE, NICOLE LAWRENCE, ROBERT LAWRENCE, ROBERT LAWRENCE, YVONNE LAWRENCE, CONNIE LAWS, JUDITH LAWS, LLOYD LAWS, BRENDUN LAWSON, JODY LAWSON, JULIE LAWSON, KENNETH LAWSON, KENNETH LAWSON, SHANNON LAWSON, SIDNEY LAWSON, WILLIAM LAWSON, LYLE A. LAWTON, SHERLENE LAWTON, ROBERT LAX, JAMES LAYER, LAUREEN LAYMAN, BRENDA LAYMANCE, CARLA LAYNE, ALLISON LAYPATH, AARON LAYTON, BRYAN LAYTON, CLARK LAYTON, CONNIE LAYTON, MICHAEL LAYTON, MINDY LAYTON, SUSAN LAYTON, TIM LAYTON, WALT LAYTON, DAVID LAZENBY, LO AN LE, PATTI LE CLAIRE, CLAUDETTE LE GENDRE, CYNTHIA LEA, JOYCE LEA, CHELSEA LEADER, LYNN LEADER, RONALD LEADER, KATHLEEN LEAF, REBECCA LEAKE, SHAUNA LEAKE, G. LEAL, LEON LEAL, JOHN LEANING, ROBERT LEAR, GAYLE LEARY, JOHN LEARY, NANCY LEARY, VAL LEARY, SANDRA LEASE, BLAKE LEATHAM, DAVID LEATHAM, JODY LEATHAM, JODY LEATHAM, KRISTINE LEATHAM, MARY LEATHAM, MICHAEL LEATHAM, MYRA LEATHERMAN, ANGELA LEAVENS, LINDA LEAVER, ALISSA LEAVITT, EMILY LEAVITT, JACK LEAVITT, JEFFREY LEAVY, GARN LEBARON, NORMAN LEBARON, CARLISLE LEBARRON, BRECK LEBEGUE, TERRI LEBEGUE, AMY BETH LEBER, LOUIS LEBER II, ELDON LECHTENBERG, LYLE LECHTENBERG, HARRY LECKEMBY, JASON LECKIE, SABRINA LEDDY, BRETT LEE, CAROL LEE, CINDY LEE, DAN LEE, DC LEE, DOROTHY LEE, ERIC LEE, EVETTE LEE, JI YUN LEE, JO LYNN LEE, JOAN LEE, JOEL LEE, JOHN LEE, JON LEE, MARVIN LEE, MATTHEW LEE, MAUGHAN LEE, PAM LEE, RICHARD LEE, RICK LEE, RUTH LEE, SUE LEE, YEONJU LEE, BARRY LEEDER, SHEILA LEEDS, JACQUELINE LEEDY, ALEX LEEMAN, SARAH LEEMASTER, JAMES LEENDERS, LISA LEENDERS, LINDA LEEPER, AMY LEET, JAMES LEFAVOR, GEORGE LEFEUVRE, JENNELYN LEFGREN, AARON LEFOHN, KAREN LEFOHN, VIRGINIA LEFRAK, RENE LEFRANCOIS, JILL LEGAULT, KRISTIN LEGER, MYLINDA LEGRANDE, SHIRLEY LEGUERI, MARY LEHMAN, ROBERT LEHMAN, CINDY LEHMANN, EDWARD LEHNARDT, MARK LEHNARDT, ELIZABETH LEHNER, MICHAEL LEHNER, LANCE LEHNHOF, TAMMY LEHTO, JOSEPH LEIBRAND, FRANK LEICHLITER, SUSAN LEICHLITER, ALBERT LEINWEBER, CARLA LEIS, LORENTZ LEIS, MICHAEL LEISER, CHARLES LEISHMAN, MARGENE LEISHMAN, RICHARD LEISHMAN, TRICIA LEISHMAN, TRAVIS LEITHEAD, CEYLON LEITZEL, SHANNON LEJEUNE, RHEA LEMASTER, MIKE LEMAY, KRISTINE LEMIEUX, PAUL LEMIEUX, GLORIA LEMKE, JOHN LEMKE, LELAND LEMMON, MICHELE LEMMON, PATRICIA LEMMON, ROBERT LEMMON, JUDY LEMMONS, ROBERT LEMON, RYAN LEMONE, BILLIE LEMP, DENNIS LEMP, JOHAN LENIERE, PAUL LENTO, KATHRYN LENTON, ROBERT LENTZ, MARTHA LEO, JEREMY LEONARD, MATHEW LEONARD, MELISSA LEONARD, NICK LEONARD, TAMMY LEONARD, TERRY LEONARD, GEORGIA LEONARDOU, ANNALEE LEONHARDT, KATARZYNA LERCH-BLASZCZAK, THOMAS LERMAN, BLAIR LERNER, JANIE LEROY, WILLIAM LESAR, KATHERINE LESER, DEAN LESHOCK, SUZANNE LESKO, MARINDA LESLIE, LEE LESNESKI, RICK LESSARD, MICHAEL LESTER, ROBERT LESTER, ROSINA LETTRE, JANET LEUNG, CAROLYN LEVALLEY, MARYANNE LEVANDOSKI, JOHN LEVANGER, EDELTRAUD LEVIN, DEAN LEVORSEN, DONALD LEVY, JAMES LEVY, LISA LEVY, SUSAN LEVY, RANDALL LEW, ANDREA LEWIS, ANTHONY LEWIS, ARIAN LEWIS, BENJAMIN LEWIS, BLAIR LEWIS, BRAD LEWIS, COURTNEY LEWIS, DEBBIE LEWIS, DIONA LEWIS, ELIZABETH LEWIS, FRED LEWIS, HOWARD LEWIS, JEANNE LEWIS, JEFFREY LEWIS, JEREMY LEWIS, JODY LEWIS, JOHN LEWIS, JOHN LEWIS, LIZ LEWIS, MARCIA LEWIS, MARIA LEWIS, MATTHEW LEWIS, MELISSA LEWIS, RICHARD LEWIS, RICHARD LEWIS, ROBERT LEWIS, ROBIN LEWIS, SHIRLEY LEWIS, SPENCER LEWIS, STEVEN LEWIS, WESLEY LEWIS, ROBERT LEWSEN, SHENG LI, CHIH-WEI LIAO, GREGORY LIBECCI, GLENN LIBERATORE, JOAN LIBSACK, ANGELA LICAUSI, MARTIN LICCARDO, MELINDA LICHFIELD, STEVEN LICHFIELD, KATIA LICHTVAN, DON LIDDIARD, KATHERINE LIDDLE, STEPHANIE LIDDLE, WILFORD LIEBER, HELENE LIEBMAN, KATHRYN LIECHETY, WENDELL LIECHTY, JOHN LIEGEL, SANDRA LIEPINIS, ANDRIS LIEPNIEKS, ERIKA LIEPNIEKS, GARY LIERD, CHRISTOPHER LIFFERTH, CREG LIFFERTH, KATHY LIFFERTH, MARYJANE LIGAIRI, BILL LIGETY, KENNETH LIGHT, SARA MARIE LIGHT, BRIAN LIGHTHALL, RAINER LILBOK, MARIANNE LILJEBLAD, KYLE LILJENQUIST, YAVONNE LILJENQUIST, ERIC LILLYWHITE, SHAWN LIMA, KARMA LIMB, JEFFREY LIMBACK, JOHANNA LIMBERIS, DANIEL LIN, EVAN LIN, LOURDES LINATO-CRAWFORD, ROBERT LINCOLN, DARREL LIND, JOAN LIND, MARILYN LIND, SUSAN LIND, CHRISTINE LINDE, KATHERINE LINDEMAN, BONNIE LINDER, GARTH LINDER, WAYNE LINDER, BLAINE LINDGREN, MAIVA LINDGREN, KANDA LINDHARDT, WILLIAM LINDHARDT, GARY LINDLEY, GENEVIEVE LINDLEY, KRISTOPHER LINDLEY, DAVID LINDMEIR, GUNNAR LINDNER, CHARLES LINDQUIST, ADAM LINDSAY, ALICE LINDSAY, BETTY LINDSAY, BLYTHE LINDSAY, CHRIS LINDSAY, CHRISTOPHER LINDSAY, DEAN LINDSAY, JAMES LINDSAY, MITCH LINDSAY, PAIVI LINDSAY, ROBERT LINDSAY, STACI LINDSAY, TINAYA LINDSAY, BRYAN LINDSEY, JANICE LINDSEY, LEOMA LINDSEY, RUSSELL LINDSEY, TODD LINDSEY, RICHARD LINDSLEY, JOHN LINDSTROM, LANDON LINDSTROM,

ALLISON LINES, JOY LINES, ADDY LINFORD, AUDREY LINFORD, SHARLENE LINFORD, DORTHY LINGE, SOFIA LINGOS, JON LINGWALL, CAROL LININGTON, RICHARD LININGTON, THOMAS LINK, DONALD LINKE, HAZEL ANN LINKE, TONYA LINKY, GARY LINNELL, KENT LINSLEY, SALLY LINSLEY, JOHN LINTON, JOSHUA LINTON, TRENT LINTON, VICKI LINTON, THEODORE LIOU, DAVID LIPMAN, KAY LIPMAN, ALLAN LIPMAN,JR., RANDALL LIPOSKY, CARL LIPPERT, MELANIE LIPSCOMB, CHRISTINE LIPSCOMBE, CAROL LIPTROT, WILLIAM LISI, LINDA LISTER, MIKE LISTER, CHARLOTTE LISTON, MARK LITCHFIELD, CECIL LITLE, SHARON LITLE, DAVID LITTLE, DON LITTLE, HAROLD LITTLE, JAMES LITTLE, JENNIFER LITTLE, JOLYNN LITTLE, KIMBERLINA LITTLE, MICHAEL LITTLE, PAULA LITTLE, SHARON LITTLE, DAVID LITTLEFIELD, STACEY LITTLEFIELD, BRENT LITTLER, ALLAN LIU, AMY LIU, GUANGYUE LIU, RICK LIU, XUE-DONG LIU, AMY LIVINGSTON, CHARLES LIVINGSTON, DAVID LIVINGSTON, GLENDA LIVINGSTON, JULIA LIVINGSTON, LINDA LIVINGSTON, MARK LIVINGSTON, RICHARD LIVINGSTON, STEPHEN LIVINGSTON, DONALD LIVINGSTONE, HEIDI LIVINGSTONE, NINA LLEWELYN, BRENT LLOYD, GLENNA LLOYD, HELGA LLOYD, HERBERT LLOYD, KATHIE LLOYD, LANGFORD LLOYD, MAX LLOYD, ROBYN LLOYD, SHARON LLOYD, STANFORD LLOYD, WALLY LLOYD, DOROTHY LOADER, JOSEPH LOADER, DOLORES LOBATO-TARR, CATHERINE LOCHER, JAMES LOCK, GARY LOCKE, JOE LOCKE, WESTON LOCKE, BARBARA LOCKHART, BART LOCKHART, JOAN LOCKHART, CADE LOCKWOOD, CHRISTOPHER LOCKWOOD, ROBERT LOCKYER, SHERYL LODDER, WILLIAM LODDER, RICHARD LODMELL, JODI LOECKE, CARLOS LOERA, KAREN LOFGREEN, KIMBERLY LOFGREN, ANGINETTE LOFTIN, CHARLES LOGAN, ISRAEL LOGAN, JENNIFER LOGAN, SIMON LOGAN, GREGORY LOGEAIS, DAVID LOGERSTEDT, RACHEL LOGERSTEDT, ANDREA LOGUE, CLAUDIA LOGUE, FIONA LOHMAN, SYLVIA LOKKEN, WILTON LOLOFIE, LAURIE LOMASNEY, LAILE LOMAX, TAUNIA LOMBARDI, MATT LONDON, SYLVIA LONDON, BOBBY LONG, KENNETH LONG, LOIS LONG, MARY LONG, ROBERT LONG, SHERYL LONG, THEODORE LONG, DANNA LONG-ASAY, ROBERT LONGACRE, JARED LONGHURST, MAX LONGHURST, NYLE LONGHURST, TAMRA LONGHURST, STEVEN LONGNECKER, SUSAN LONGSON, LYNN LONSDALE, BRANDEN LOOCK, JAMES LOOCK, MONICA LOOCK, JOHN LOOMIS, MARGARET LOOMIS, MICHELLE LOOMIS, PAMELA LOOMIS, RICHARD LOOMIS, DAVID LOOS, AARON LOOSLI, BARBARA LOOSLI, JOEL LOOSLI, MARK LOOSLI, RICHARD LOOSLI, BERT LOPANSRI, EDWARD CHARLES LOPEZ, JUSTIN LOPEZ, KARL LOPEZ, VICTOR LOPEZ, WALTER LOPEZ, HARRY LORDS, KEVIN LORDS, MARLOW LORDS, NANCY LORDS, TINA LORDS, JEFFREY LORENZEN, JESSICA LORIMER, MATTHEW LORIMER, JAMES LORIMER IV, GARY LORITZ, SUZANNE LORITZ, KELLY LORSCHEIDER, STEPHEN LORTON, TIMOTHY LOSA, JASON LOSCHER, JAMES LOSEE, MARSHA LOSEE, BENNO LOTZ, KIMBERLY LOTZ, CAROL LOUCKS, JEFFREY LOUDEN, ELLEN LOUDER, JENNIFER LOUDIANA, CAROLYN LOUIE, RAE LOUIE, STEVEN LOUIE, TERESA LOUW, DANA LOVE, OLIVIA LOVE, JARROD LOVELADY, DEREK LOVELAND, JACOB LOVELAND, JIMALEEN LOVELAND, MATTHEW LOVELAND, REBECCA LOVELAND, GLEN LOVELAND JR, DARRELL LOVELL, MAC LOVERIDGE, SHARON LOVERIDGE, JACK LOVETT, MIKE LOVETT, BRIAN LOVING, CHRIS LOW, JAE LOWDER, JANEEA LOWDER, BROOK LOWE, CHRISTIAN LOWE, CINDI LOWE, CRAIG LOWE, KRISTINA LOWE, LORIN LOWE, MATTHEW LOWE, MICHAEL LOWE, RICHARD LOWE, KEVIN LOWELL, JAY LOWER, SHAUNA LOWER, LINDA LOWERY, ARCHIE LOWMAN, DELLENE LOWRY, MARSHALL LOWRY, OLIVER LOWRY, MICHAEL LOWTHER, SAUNDRA LOWTHER, ANGEL LOZANO, KIM LOZIER, REBECCA LUBBERS, THOMAS LUBERSKI, JANET LUCAS, BONNIE LUCERO, ALAN LUCKART, GARY LUCKART, LINDA LUCKART, LORI LUCKART-TOMPKINS, KEVIN LUCUS, JAMES LUDLOW, KELLY LUDLOW, MARK LUDLOW, PAUL LUDLOW, STEVE LUDLOW, CAMERON LUDWIG, KARL LUDWIG, KIRA LUDWIG, DANIEL LUECKLER, FRED LUEDTKE, KATHRYN LUKE, JOYCE LUKER, MARK LUKER, JOYCE LUMBY, CHARLES LUNA, DAVID LUNA, KAREN LUNA, COLLEEN LUNCEFORD, ANNETTE LUND, AUDREY LUND, BART LUND, DELORIS LUND, ISAAC LUND, JAMES LUND, JUDY LUND, KENNETH LUND, LESLIE LUND, MARK LUND, MATTHEW LUND, MATTHEW LUND, MICHAEL LUND, RANDALL LUND, ROBERT LUND, SUSAN LUND, BRENT LUNDBERG, GRANT LUNDBERG, KAREN LUNDBERG, PEGGY LUNDBERG, BONNIE LUNDE, GREGORY LUNDE, KATHLEEN LUNDELL, RYAN LUNDELL, TRAVIS LUNDELL, JEREMY LUNDEVALL, CAROL LUNDGREEN, TOM LUNDGREEN, BONNIE LUNDGREN, STEVE LUNDQUIST, CHERYL LUNDSKOG, KEVIN LUNDY, SUSAN LUNSFORD, DEANNA LUNT, MARIE LUPO, ROSALYN LUPUS, SHANE LUTNER, KENT LUTZ, LAN LUU, MARY LUX, LINDA LUZITANO, CHARLES LYDA, MAUREEN LYDON, LARRY LYM, ERIC LYMAN, GREG LYMAN, K'LYN LYMAN, MARTIN LYMAN, PATRICIA LYMAN, TRINE LYMAN, CHAD LYNCH, DIANNA LYNCH, DORENE LYNCH, JOHN LYNCH, LEIGH LYNCH, LINDA LYNCH, ROBIN LYNCH, TANI LYNCH, JOHN LYNN, KIMBERLY LYNN, BARBARA LYON, BRENDA LYON, CAROLYN LYON, CHRISTINE LYON, JOHN LYON, LEE LYON, ROBERT LYON, PAUL LYON III, LINDSAY LYONS, ROGER LYONS, SUZANNE LYONS, VASYL LYUBARETS • **M** • ANDREW MAAS, BRENT MABEY, CLARK MABEY, DAVID MABEY, MARY MABEY, PAULA MABEY, RALPH MABEY, RICHARD MABEY, RICK MABEY, SYLVIA MABEY, VANYA MABEY, TERRENCE MACARTHUR, CORINNE MACBEAN, THOMAS MACCABE, ANNE MACDONALD, REUEL MACDONALD, TAYLOR MACDONALD, LISA MACE, SANDRA MACE, RODGER MACFARLANE, DEBBI MACFARLANE-CLAYTON, BETTY MACGREGOR, JAMES MACGREGOR, CARLOS MACIAS, EDWARD MACIAS, MICHAEL MACIEJKO, JIM MACINTYRE, DALE MACK, GREG MACK, HALEY MACKAY, SHAWNEEN MACKAY, MARGARET MACKEY, RICHARD MACKEY, TRAVIS MACKEY, DANIEL MACKINTOSH, DEAN MACKINTOSH, NICOLE MACLAREN, GORDON MACLEAN, RICH MACNEILL, ANN MACQUOID, JONATHAN MADDEN, KRISTIN MADDEN, MELISSA MADDEN, MICHELLE MADDEN, DAVID MADDOX, JOHN MADDOX, KATHLEEN MADDOX, SANDRA A. MADDOX, ANNA MADELEINI, J'ANN MADER, DANA MADISON, DOLORES MADRID, LORETTA MADRID, GEORGE MADRON, AARON MADSEN, ALICIA MADSEN, ANGELA MADSEN, ARLIN MADSEN, BENJAMIN MADSEN, BRUCE MADSEN, CORNELIA MADSEN, DAVID MADSEN, GORDON MADSEN, GREGORY MADSEN, JOHN MADSEN, KENDAL MADSEN, MAREN MADSEN, PATRICIA MADSEN, ROBERT MADSEN, RON MADSEN, RONALD MADSEN, RUSSELL MADSEN, SARAH MADSEN, SHARALYNN MADSEN, SYDNEE MADSEN, TODD MADSEN, VALERIE MADSEN, ZIRKA MADSEN, AMANDA MADSON, DAVE MADSON, BENTE MADTSEN, KAMA MAENDL, JENNIFER MAGEE, VICKI MAGER, CURTIS MAGLEBY, DANA MAGLEBY, DAVID MAGLEBY, RICHARD MAGLEBY, SHARON MAGLIETTI, SUSAN MAGNER, KJARTAN MAGNUSSON, CHRISTINE MAGOZSTOVICS, AMY MAH, RICHARD MAH, FRANCINE MAHAK, KURT MAHAN, KEVIN MAHANNAH, CARLENE MAHANY, KATHLEEN MAHAS, GARY MAHER, HEINZ MAHLER, LEE MAHLSTEDE, CLARENCE MAHONEY, KENNETH MAHONEY, LISA MAHONEY, LYNN MAHONEY, RYAN MAHONEY, LELAND MAHOOD, JUDITH MAIER, SAMUEL MAJOR, TERRI MAJOR, COLENE MAKELA, DOUGLAS MAKI, HIROKAZU MAKISHI, HEIDI MAKOWSKI, BOYD MALAN, MARNIE MALAN, SCOTT MALAN, VERNON MALAN, FERNANDO MALDONADO, THOMAS MALEE, GRAZYNA MALEWSKA, KATHY MALINE, MAKALA MALKOVICH, NICHOLAS MALLEK, ROBERT MALLINCKRODT, KATHLEEN MALLIS, KATHERINE MALLORY, LISA MALLORY, DAVID MALMSTROM, MICHAEL MALONEY, COLLEEN MALOUF, CRAIG MALOUF, NIKOLAY MALYAROV, AARON MANCIL, JOEL MANCUSO, RICHARD MANDAHL, MAURICE MANDEL, MELISSA MANDERY, DWAYNE MANFUL, RITA MANFUL, MARTIN MANGAN, JENNIFER MANGELSON, GLORIA MANGIAPANE, ANTHONY MANGUM, JANA MANGUM, SANDRA MANGUM, ANDREW MANN, JOHN MANN, KIM MANN, RAMONA MANN, LUIGI MANNARO, GUENTER MANNEK, KATRI MANNI, ANNA MANNING, DENNIS MANNING, JACQUELINE MANNING, JALYNNE MANNING, JAMES MANNING, REBECCA MANNING, RONALD MANNING, WINDY MANNING, DANIEL MANOOKIN, JANE MANOOKIN, JERRY MANOR, DESSIE MANOUSAKIS, LLOYD MANOWN, MARLENE MANOWN, EMILY MANSEAU, ALYS MANSFIELD, ALYSON MANSFIELD, BONNIE MANSFIELD, DIANE MANSFIELD, FRANCOISE MANUEL, CYNTHIA MANWARING, LAURA MANWARING, MICHELLE MANWARING, PAULA MANWARING, MANETTE MANZ, REBECCA MAQUET, REBECCA MARABLE, LUANN MARCH, SCOTT MARCH, CLARA MARCHANT, MONICA MARCHESCHI, ANNA MARCHI, LAURA MARCHIANDO, MONICA MARCINKO, PATRICK MARCINKO, PATRICK MARCROFT, JANICE MARCUS, LAURA MARCUS, ROBIN MARCUS, SHEREE MARCUS, PETER MARCY, ANTHONY MARES, TYLER MARGETTS, ANDREJ MARICH, ANTHONY MARICONDA, JOAN MARICONDA, DIANE MARIETTI, LINDA MARINCEL, DANIELLE MARINELLI, ANNE MARIE MARINONI, PAUL MARINONI, ALAN MARK, DIANE MARK, LISA MARK, REED MARKHAM, JOHN MARKLE, MARY JANE MARKLE, EMILEE MARKS, FRANCOISE MARKS, KIRSTAN MARKS, JAMES MARLEY, JEANNINE MARLOWE, MICHAEL MARLOWE, GIULIANA MARPLE, DENNIS MARQUARD, KIM MARQUARDT, KIM MARQUARDT, LUCINDA MARQUARDT, MANDI MARQUARDT, SUSAN MARQUARDT, CLAUDIA MARQUES, LINDA MARQUEZ, MARY MARQUEZ, JAY MARQUISS, ANDREW MARRE, DENA MARRIOTT, JILL MARRIOTT, CRAIG MARSDEN, KATHY MARSDEN, LYNN MARSDEN, SARAH MARSE, ALLEN MARSH, BENSON MARSH, CARYL MARSH, CHARLES MARSH, CHRISTOPHER MARSH, FRANKLIN MARSH, JUDY MARSH, LESLIE MARSH, RICHARD MARSH, SANDRA MARSH, STEWART MARSH, TERRY MARSH, WALTER MARSH, DARREN MARSHALL, DEBRA MARSHALL, EILEEN MARSHALL, JASON MARSHALL, JOLENE MARSHALL, KAREN MARSHALL, LARRY MARSHALL, MICHAEL MARSHALL, RICHARD MARSHALL, THOMAS MARSHALL, DEBBIE MARSHALL-PRYDE, SHAUN MARSHALL-PRYDE, ANTHONY MARSING, LESLIE MARSING, TRACI MARSING, MADELINE MARSTON, BRIAN MARTAIN, PHYLLIS MARTELL, CHESLEY MARTIN, DALE MARTIN, DANA MARTIN, DANNY MARTIN, DAWN MARTIN, DIANE MARTIN, DOUGLAS MARTIN, EDWARD MARTIN, FRANZ MARTIN, JAMES MARTIN, JANE MARTIN, JAY MARTIN, JEREMY MARTIN, JESSICA MARTIN, JUDY MARTIN, KATHRYN MARTIN, LAUREL MARTIN, MARK MARTIN, MARY MARTIN, MICHAEL MARTIN, MICHAEL MARTIN, MILDRED MARTIN, PAMELA MARTIN, SHANNON MARTIN, STACY MARTIN, TAMMY MARTIN, WILLIAM MARTIN, YVONNE MARTIN, ANGELA MARTINDALE, EUGENE MARTINDALE, JOHANNA MARTINDALE, MARIANNA MARTINDALE, TRESA MARTINDALE, CHRISTOPHER MARTINEAU, MIKAELA MARTINEAU, SHERRIE MARTINEAU, ALCARIO MARTINEZ, CINDY MARTINEZ, DIANA MARTINEZ, JOE MARTINEZ, JOHN MARTINEZ, JOSEPH MARTINEZ, LARRY MARTINEZ, MANUEL MARTINEZ, MARY MARTINEZ, MONICA MARTINEZ, RICHARD MARTINEZ, RICK MARTINEZ, STEVEN MARTINEZ, TERINA MARTINEZ, RONALD MARTINO, BETTY MARTINSEN, ANDRES MARTINSON, JOSEPH MARTONE, JONATHAN MARUJI, MERRY MARUNO, BONNIE MARURI, LINDA MARVEL, DOROTHY MARYON, LYNETTE MARZ, ROBERT MARZ, SCOTT MARZ, MATT MASARIK, SAL MASCARENAS, SARAH MASINTER, JOSEPH MASON, MARIE MASON, MICHAEL MASON, MONICA MASON, PAUL MASON, ROBERT MASON, WENDY MASON, BRIAN MASSEY, JOSEPH MASSEY, MARILYN MASSEY, EMILY MASSIC, CHARLES MASSON, ROBYNN MASTERS, LAURENCE MASTERSON, REBECCA MASTERSON, MARY MASTIN, REBECCA MATANIC, LIANE MATEAKI, ELLY MATHER, JULIE MATHERLY, KURT MATHERLY, ELISABETH MATHESON, JAMES MATHESON, JENNIFER MATHESON, JENTRIE MATHESON, CAROL MATHEWS, COLETTE MATHEWS, JAMES MATHEWS, KAY JEAN MATHEWS, LISA MATHEWS, LOUISE MATHEWS, MARK MATHEWS, NANCY MATHEWS, NELDON MATHEWS, STEVEN MATHEWS, JESSICA MATHEWSON, PAUL MATHEWSON, GEORGE MATHIS, JENNIFER MATHIS, MARYANN MATHIS, SUSAN MATHIS, AMY MATHRE, ANGELICA MATINKHAH, MELVYN MATIS, MARK MATLEY, CHERYL MATSON, CAROL MATSUKAWA, MILT MATSUSHIMA, SHARON MATT, MARILYN MATTAVICH, GARY MATTESON, JANE MATTESON, INGE MATTEUCCI, LINDA MATTFELDT, CATHERINE MATTHEWS, GAYLENE MATTHEWS, JENNIFER MATTHEWS, MARCIA MATTHEWS, MIKE MATTHEWS, TAMI MATTHEWS, DANIEL MATTOON, BEVERLY MATTSON, CARLY MATTSON, CYNTHIA MATTSON, JOHN MATTSON, JOHN MATTSON, JOHN MATTSON, RAND MATTSON, WENDY MATTSON, MARY MATTURRO, FRAN MATUSZEWSKI, JENNIE MATZEK, CASIE MAUGHAN, DAVID MAUGHAN, FRANK MAUGHAN, GARRETT MAUGHAN, GERALD MAUGHAN, JASON MAUGHAN, KIRSTEN MAUGHAN, MARY MAUGHAN, RICHARD MAUGHAN, SHARALYN MAUGHAN, SHIRLENE MAUGHAN, ZORAN MAUNAGA, JANINE MAURICE, HEATHER MAURO, DAN MAUSS, DIANE MAUSS, MARYANNE MAUSS, ERIC MAUSSER, CHRISOPHER MAUTZ, KENNETH MAWHINNIE, RANDALL MAWHINNIE, SANDRA MAWHINNIE, A SHERLINE MAXFIELD, CATHERINE MAXFIELD, DAVID MAXFIELD, JACKIE MAXFIELD, NEAL MAXFIELD, NORMAN MAXFIELD, RENELLE MAXFIELD, STEVEN MAXFIELD, TIFFANY MAXFIELD, MARYELLEN MAXWELL, MELANIE MAXWELL, SUSAN MAXWELL, DEBRA MAY, MATTHEW MAY, NATALIE MAY, SUSAN MAY, VIRGINIA MAY, SCOTT MAYEDA, DONALD MAYER, KERI MAYER, PATRICIA MAYER, ROBERT MAYER, LESTER MAYERS, NANCY MAYERS, JOHN MAYFIELD, KYLE MAYFIELD, SARAH MAYFIELD, SCOTT MAYFIELD, GUY MAYHEW, JOHN MAYHEW, PHYLLIS MAYHEW, SEAN MAYHEW, THOMAS MAYHEW, TRACY MAYLETT, JAY MAYNARD, SANDRA MAYNARD, EDDIE MAYNE, KAREN MAYNE, WENDY MAYNES, AMANDA MAYO, BRYAN MAYOL, RONDA MAZINGO, MARALYN MAZZA, TONY MAZZELLA, ROBERT MC CARTHY, KRISTINA MCAFEE, LESLIE MCAFFEE, CATHERINE MCALEER, DONNA MCALEER, CHRISTOPHER MCALLISTER, CORTNEY MCALLISTER, LYNN MCALLISTER, TODD MCALLISTER, ALBERTA MCANDREWS, JACKIE MCANINCH, PAULA MCAUGHAN, JOSEPH MCAVOY, JOYCE MCAVOY, CHRISTINE MCBETH, CHRISTOPHER MCBETH, DEE MCBRIDE, NATALIE MCBRIDE, PATRICIA MCBRIDE, RUBY MCBRIDE, WILLIAM MCCAA, MARGIT MCCABE, PATRICIA MCCABE, ROBIN MCCABE, TYLER MCCABE, SHARON MCCAFFREY-BECKERT, SARAH MCCAHILL, ROBERT MCCAIG, SUZANNE MCCALL, JOHN MCCALLISTER, SEAN MCCALLISTER, JULIE MCCANDLESS, PAUL MCCANDLESS, JACK MCCANN, MARIAN MCCANN, LAWRENCE MCCARTER, ERIKA MCCARTHY, GEORGE MCCARTHY, JEREMIAH MCCARTHY, KEVIN MCCARTHY, SHIRLEY MCCARTNEY, BRYAN MCCARTY, BRENDA MCCASLAND, KEITH MCCAULEY, MARIA MCCAULEY, MICHAEL MCCAULEY, WILLIAM MCCAULEY, DANIEL MCCAY, JOCELYN MCCHESNEY, CYNTHIA MCCLATCHY, JACQUELINE MCCLEARY, JOHN MCCLEARY, PATRICIA MCCLEESE, BRUCE MCCLELLAN, JEFFREY MCCLELLAN, MARIE MCCLELLAND, JOHN MCCLENNAN, STEVEN MCCLOSKEY, KOLETTE MCCLURG, TRAVIS MCCLUSKY, DEANNA MCCOARD, HARRY MCCOARD, PAUL MCCOARD, JOHN MCCOLLUM, LYNN MCCOMB, GERALDINE MCCONAUGHY, GLENN MCCONKEY, BRITTANY MCCONKIE, CAROL MCCONKIE, JOANNE MCCONKIE, JULENE MCCONKIE, JULIE MCCONKIE, JAMES MCCONKIE III, KATHLEEN MCCONNEHEY, CLAIRE MCCONNELL, DOLORES MCCONNELL, JAN MCCONNELL, KEN MCCONNELL, BARBARA MCCONVILL, MICHAEL MCCONVILL, JOHN MCCOOMB, KIM MCCOOMB, JACK MCCORD, LAYNE MCCORD, DENNIS MCCORMICK, JANAE MCCORMICK, TORI MCCORMICK, JANIS MCCORQUINDALE, JOHN MCCORQUINDALE, MARY MCCOTTER, TATE MCCOTTER, ANDREW MCCRADY, SUSAN MCCRALEY, JOHN MCCRAY, MICHAEL MCCREA, LAURI MCCREARY, BRIAN MCCULLOUGH, MICHAEL MCCULLOUGH, CINDA MCCULLY, ROBERT MCCULLY, DEANN MCCUNE, RYAN MCCUNE, DANNY MCCURRY, SHARON MCDANIEL, AMBER MCDERMOTT, JENNIFER MCDERMOTT, AMY MCDEVITT, ALLAN MCDONALD, CHARLOTTE MCDONALD, CRAIG MCDONALD, DALLAS MCDONALD, GAIL MCDONALD, GREGORY MCDONALD, KEVIN MCDONALD, LINDA MCDONALD, LINDA Z MCDONALD, NATHAN MCDONALD, SHEILA MCDONALD, SHEILA MCDONALD, SUSAN MCDONALD, JENNA MCDONNEL, PETER MCDONOUGH, MARGARET MCDONOUGH-NAY, SHERRI MCDOUGAL, DAVID MCDOUGAL, JR., SANDRA MCDOUGALL, ANDREW MCDOWELL, CHARLES MCDOWELL, SHEILA MCELVAIN, ERIC MCENTIRE, ERIC MCEVOY, ALAN MCEWAN, PATRICK MCEWEN, JULIE MCFADDEN, MICHAEL MCFADDEN, MICHAEL MCFADDEN, MICHAEL MCFADDEN, RICH MCFADDEN, DON MCFALL, NANCY MCFALL, BARBARA MCFARLAND, DIANA MCFARLAND, ELMER MCFARLAND, JOHN MCFARLAND, KAREN MCFARLAND, MARILYN MCFARLAND, MATTHEW MCFARLAND, PAULA MCFARLAND, SARAH MCFARLAND, TARAN MCFARLAND, ADAM MCFETRIDGE, JULIE MCGARY, MICHAEL MCGARY, AARON MCGAVOCK, LEONARD MCGEE, MARILYNN MCGEEHAN, MATTHEW MCGHIE, BRIAN MCGIBBON, DAWN MCGLADDERY, MADOLYN MCGLINNEN, CECILIA MCGLONE, CHERYL MCGOVERN, KATHERINE MCGOVERN, CHRIS MCGOWN, ERIC MCGRATH, JESSICA MCGRAW, IAN MCGREGOR, MARY JANE MCGREGOR, MORGAN MCGREGOR, SILVIA MCGREW, ALEEN MCGUIRE, DANIEL MCGUIRE, GEOFFREY MCGUIRE, HEATHER MCGUIRE, JOANN MCGUIRE, WILLIAM MCGUIRE, GAYLE MCHENRY, SUSAN MCHENRY, AUDRA MCHOES, CHRIS MCIFF, MATTHEW MCIFF, DUDLEY MCILHENNY, KATHERINE MCILRATH, SARAH MCILROY, JUNE MCINNES, ROBERT MCINNES, SIMONE MCINNIS, LAURIE MCINTOSH, RICHARD MCINTOSH, ANNA MCINTYRE, DONNA MCINTYRE, JAMES MCINTYRE, JAMES MCINTYRE, KATHERINE MCINTYRE, STEVE MCINTYRE, BALALEE MCKAY, CRAIG MCKAY, DAVID MCKAY, KATHY MCKAY, MARJEAN MCKAY, MARK MCKAY, RHONI MCKAY, DANIEL MCKEAN, SALLY MCKEAN, AMANDA MCKEE, SYLVIA MCKEE, BRIDGET MCKEEVER, JAMES MCKENNA, MARLENE MCKENNA, PAULETTE MCKENNA, BRIGHTON MCKENZIE, EMILY MCKENZIE, GARY MCKENZIE, FERGUS MCKIERNAN, CECILIA MCKINLAY, PAULA MCKINLAY, ROBIN MCKINLAY, RUSS MCKINLAY, SHARON MCKINLAY, GILBERT MCKINLEY, BRANDON MCKINNEY, JACKIE MCKINNEY, TIMOTHY MCKINNEY, PAMELA MCKINNON, DENNIS MCKINSTRY, KRISTINE MCKINSTRY, SCOTT MCKINZIE, MARGARET MCKNIGHT, LAURIE MCKRAY, ALLISON MCLACHLAN, BRYAN MCLACHLAN, MARIE MCLACHLAN, ROBERT MCLACHLAN, LAURA MCLAIN, JAMES MCLARTY, CAMILLA MCLAUGHLIN, GAY MCLAUGHLIN, KEVIN MCLAUGHLIN, MICHAEL MCLAUGHLIN, MICHAEL MCLAUGHLIN, TIM MCLAUGHLIN, DEBORAH MCLELLAND, SANDRA MCLELLAND, HELEN MCMAHAN, KATHY MCMAHON, REGINA MCMAHON, ROBERT MCMANN, BETH MCMERRICK, NORMALEE MCMICHAEL, AMY MCMILLAN, ANNETTE MCMILLAN, KATHERINE MCMILLAN, LISA MCMILLAN, KAYDEE MCMILLEN, CHERYL MCMULLIN, DIX MCMULLIN, EMILY MCMULLIN, CATHERINE MCMURRICH, JENNIFER MCNAMARA, PATSY MCNAMARA, DAVID MCNAMEE, MARY JANE MCNAMEE, TAMARA MCNATT, JOAN MCNAUGHTON, KEVIN MCNEELY, KIMBERLEE MCNEELY, COLLEEN MCNEIL, MICHAEL MCNEIL, THOMAS MCNEILIS, KATHRYN MCNEILL, MICHELLE MCNEILL, RICHARD MCNELLIS, GRADY MCNETT, BILL MCNICE, THERESE MCNICHOLAS, DONALD MCOMIE, NETA MCOMIE, RUTH ANN MCOMIE, KENNETH MCPARTLIN, LATEISHA MCPHADEN, CONNIE MCPHEE, DARYLNE MCPHEETERS, JAY MCPHEETERS, DAVID MCPHERSON, LADAWN MCPHERSON, ELDORA 'DOTTIE' MCPHIE, MAXINE MCQUEARY, JENNY MCQUEEN, KEITH MCQUEEN, MATTHEW MCQUEEN, PAULINE MCREAVY, LARRY MCREYNOLDS, PHILIP MCSHINSKY, PAUL MCSWEENEY, STEFAN MCTEE, JUDITH MCVAUGH, ANN MCVEY, JAMES MCVEY, NATHAN MEACHAM, URSULA MEACHAM, CAROL MEAD, GENE MEAD, LINDA MEAD, LUCAS MEAD, AARON MEADOWS, CINDY MEADOWS, JACOB MEADOWS, JIMMIE MEADOWS, THOMAS MEADOWS, CHRISTOPHER MEANS, LAURA MEANS, KAREN MEAR, LINDA MEAUX, ANNA MECHAM, BRADLEY MECHAM, DANNY MECHAM, JANIECE MECHAM, KAREN MECHAM, KERI MECHAM, LEE MECHAM, REBECCA MECHAM, SCOTT MECHAM, ROBERT MEDDAUGH, JOANNE MEDEIROS, PEGGY MEDEIROS, VALERIE MEDEIROS, ROBERT MEDEMA, ALICE MEDINA, MARCO MEDINA, ROBERTO MEDINA, KIMBERLIE MEEHAN, RANDY MEEKS, OHANNES MEGERDICHIAN, WALTER MEHR, MARK MEIDELL, NANCY MEIDELL, AARON MEIER, CHARLES MEIER, DARLEEN MEIER, JANISSE MEIKLE, EARLET MEINERS, PATRICIA MEISMER, TSEGAYE MEKONNEN, PHILIPPE MELBY, ANNETTE MELDRUM, DENISE MELDRUM, ARMANDO MELENDEZ, BONNIE MELENDEZ, CLINT MELENDEZ, DOROTHEA MELENDEZ, ROBERT MELENDEZ, ALEXANDER MELENTIEV, NANCY MELICH, SHARON MELLEN, HOLLY MELLINGER, TRACY MELLISON, BLAKE MELLOR, MARGO MELLOR, SUSAN MELLOR, JOSHUA MELTON, LESLIE MELTON, MARTI MELVILLE, VALERIE MELVILLE, PAULA MEMMOTT, RAMONA MEMMOTT, RICHARD MEMMOTT, OSCAR MENA, RUDOLPH (RUDI) MENA, CODY MENASCO, ALAN MENDEL, CAMILLE MENDEL, JOSEPH MENDENHALL, TIFFANY MENDENHALL, MELISA MENDEZ, NANCI MENDEZ, MARCOS MENENDEZ, MITCHELL MENNING, MARCUS MENTI, ANGELA MERAZ, CHRISTOPHER MERBACK, KADIN MERCER, PATSY MERCER, STACY MERCHANT, REBECCA MEREDITH, STACEY MEREDITH, JOLENE MERICA, VERONICA MERIDITH, BRENDON MERKLEY, BRETT MERKLEY, JANET MERKLEY, KATHLEEN MERKLEY, PATRICIA MERKLEY, MARY MERO, BEVERLY MERRELL, CRAIG MERRELL, MATT MERRELL, MONTY MERRELL, NICHOL MERRELL, RICHARD MERRELL, STEVEN MERRELL, THOMAS MERRELL, TINA MERRETT, CHRISTOPHER MERRILL, DIANA MERRILL, DOUGLAS MERRILL, GAYE MERRILL, GREGORY MERRILL, JANE MERRILL, JUDY MERRILL, KATHY MERRILL, MARDEE MERRILL, ROBERT MERRILL, ROSHEL MERRILL, RYAN MERRILL, SHELA MERRILL, ZANDRIA MERRILL, WESLEY MERRIWETHER, ELVA MERRYWEATHER, SALLY MERRYWEATHER, MONTE MERZ, CYNTHIA MESENBRINK, LINDA KAY MESSENGER, RICHARD MESSENGER, MARK MESSIER, MATT MESSING, MELANIE MESTAS, BEVERLY METCALF, CRAIG METCALF, DONNA METCALF, JOHN METCALF, LINDSAY METCALF, LUND METCALF, VALERIE METCALF, CONSTANCE METHERELL, LINDA METKE, LINDA METOS, CONSTANCE METTLER, JASON METZ, RICKY MEWBORN, JAMES MEYER, JOSEPH MEYER, KANDACE MEYER, KATHERINE MEYER, LISA MEYER, MERILEE MEYER, MICHAEL MEYER, NANNA MEYER, VERNON MEYER, TESSA MEYER SANTIAGO, DAVID MEYERS, DIANA ISTY MEYERS, JUDY MEYERS, LOLA MEYERS, PAUL MEYERS, KARL MEYERSICK, HERBERT MEYRING, MARISA MICHAEL, KEVIN MICHAELIS, TRACY MICHAELIS, PAUL MICHALSKI, IOANNIS-CHRISTOS MICHELIOUDAKIS, KAREN MICHELSON, CARA MICKELSEN, CHARLES MICKELSEN, MIKE MICKELSEN, CALLIE MICKELSON, HEATHER MICKEY, PEGGY MICONI, WILLIAM MIDDLETON, GARY MIDGLEY, LORI MIDGLEY, LISA MIETCHEN, MICHAEL MIETCHEN, PATRICIA MIETCHEN, ROBERT MIETCHEN, JANET MIGLIORE, ANA MIHANOVIC, RENEE MIKKELSEN, PETER MIKKELSON, KATHY MIKLOSSY, JIM MIKOLASH, JOHN MILANO, ROSEANN MILANO, SHEILA MILARDO, BRIANT MILDENHALL, ALMA MILES, KAY MILES, MIKE MILES, RALPH MILES, SUSAN MILES, LAURIE MILEUR, ELLEN MILGROM, SHAUN MILLARD, STEVEN MILLARD, DON MILLBURN, ALAN MILLER, ALISON MILLER, ALLAN MILLER, ALLEN MILLER, ALLISON MILLER, AMY MILLER, ANN MILLER, CAROL MILLER, CAROL MILLER, CATHERINE MILLER, CECILIA MILLER, CINDY MILLER, CLARENCE MILLER, CLIFFORD MILLER, CLYDE MILLER, DARLENE MILLER, DAVID MILLER, DEBORAH MILLER, DIANE MILLER, DOROTHY MILLER, ESTHER MILLER, EVELYN MILLER, FRED MILLER, GAIL MILLER, GARY MILLER, GINGER MILLER, GREG MILLER, GREGORY MILLER, HARRY MILLER, IRAS MILLER, JOAN MILLER, JOHN MILLER, JOSEPH MILLER, KAROL JEAN MILLER, KATHIE MILLER, KENDALL MILLER, KEVIN MILLER, LANCE MILLER, LARRY MILLER, LAWRENCE MILLER, LINDA MILLER, MARILYN MILLER, MARK MILLER, MARK MILLER, MARY MILLER, MICHAEL MILLER, MICHAEL MILLER, MICHAL MILLER, NANCY MILLER, PATRICIA MILLER, PATRICK MILLER, PAULA MILLER, RANDALL MILLER, RANDALL MILLER, RAY MILLER, REX MILLER, RHONDI MILLER, ROBERT MILLER, ROBERT MILLER, ROBERT MILLER, SALLY MILLER, SANDRIA MILLER, SCOTT MILLER, SHIRLEY MILLER, STEVEN MILLER, SUSAN MILLER, SUSANNE MILLER, SUZANNE MILLER, TERRY MILLER, TOBIAS MILLER, TONIE MILLER, TREBY MILLER, WALTER MILLER, WENDY MILLER, WENDY MILLER, BECKY MILLET, CAROLEE MILLET, TERESA MILLET, DENISE MILLIGAN, JEANNE MILLIGAN, DIANN MILLIKAN, CAROL MILLIKEN, LORRAINE MILLIRON, VAUGHN MILLIRON, AARON MILLS, ALAN MILLS, CINDY MILLS, COSETTE MILLS, DEBRA MILLS, GARY MILLS, GRETCHEN MILLS, JUDY MILLS, JULIA MILLS, KAREN MILLS, KATHY MILLS, KIM MILLS, REX MILLS, GORDON MILLS JR, SCOTT MILLSAP, JAMES MILLWARD, RICHARD MILLWARD, ALICIA MILNE, AUD MILNE, BRENDA MILNE, BRENT MILNE, LE ROY MILNE, PATRICK MILNE, RAWLIN MILNE, JOSEPH MILNER, SHIRLEY MILNER, STANLEY MILSTEIN, GAIL MINAGA, RONALD MINARD, CHRISTINE MINCH, THEODORE MINDE, BETSY MINDEN, ANNETTE MINER, GARY MINER, JONATHAN MINER, JUDITH MINER, MARIAN MINER, SUZANNE MINER, TIFFANY MINICHINO, NADIA MINICLIER, MITZI MINJAREZ, HELENE MINOT, MARK MINSON, RICARDO MIRANDA, STEVE MIRISOLA, JOAN MIRKA, HAROLD MISCHLER, TERRENCE MISCHLER, JOYLYNN MISEL, BECKY MITCHELL, DAVID MITCHELL, DEANNE MITCHELL, DEEANN MITCHELL, DICK MITCHELL, GLORIA MITCHELL, JASON MITCHELL, JOANNE MITCHELL, JULIE MITCHELL, LORELEE MITCHELL, MICHAEL MITCHELL, NORMA MITCHELL, REGINA MITCHELL, ROBERT MITCHELL, SCOTT MITCHELL, SUE MITCHELL, TERRIE MITCHELL, WILLIAM MITCHELL, MARSHA MITCHELL-BILLS, KATHRYN MITTELSTADT, INGEBORG MITTENEDER, BRENDA MITTON, BRENT MITTON, LESLIE MIX, TIFFANY MIX, MILES MIYA, RODNEY MIYASAKI, ARTHUR MIYAZAKI, GAYLIN MIYAZAKI, MARIKO MIYAZAKO, PETER MJOS, NORWAN MOALEJI, MARGO MOAREMOFF, MARY MOCK, ROBERT MOCK, RICHARD MOCZYGEMBA, ELTON MODROO, ALBERT MODROVSKY, DEBORAH MODROVSKY, CYNTHIA MOELDER, CHRISTINE MOELLENDORF, JAMES MOELLER, LISA MOELLER, MARCUS MOELLER, MARY MOELLER, GREGORY MOESINGER, AMY MOFFAT, BETSY MOFFAT, BRUCE MOFFAT, RICHARD MOFFAT, DAVID MOFFITT, GERALD MOFFITT, JULIE MOFFITT, SCOTT MOFFITT, SUZANNE MOFFITT, MARK MOGEN, PAUL MOGREN, DAYANG MOHAMMED, JAY MOHLMAN, BOB MOISION, PATRICIA MOJZISIK, BORIS MOKHOV, ANNA MOKHOVA, TERI MOKRANI, SUSAN MOLE, MARILYNN MOLER, WENDY MOLETT, MATTHEW MOLINA, VALERIE MOLLE', KELLY MOLLER, ELISSA MOLLING, GERALD MOLLOY, DENNIS MOLYNEAUX, PAMELA MOLYNEAUX, SUSAN MONGALIER, BROCK MONGER, VERNON MONGER, IRENE MONICAL, JEFF MONROE, JOANN MONROE, JOHN MONROE, ROBERT MONSEY, BRIAN MONSON, DOUGLAS MONSON, ELENA MONSON, FRANCES MONSON, JAMIE MONSON, KELLY MONSON, KENT MONSON, KRISTI MONSON, LARRY MONSON, LORI MONSON, MARILYN MONSON, NANCY MONSON, PAMELA MONSON, PETER MONSON, CLIFF MONTAGNE, JOAN MONTAGNE, ANITA MONTANO, DEIRDRE MONTELLO, JOSE MONTESINOS, CAROL MONTGOMERY, DEBBIE MONTGOMERY, DENNIS MONTGOMERY, JONATHON MONTGOMERY, JOSPEH MONTGOMERY, MARILYN MONTGOMERY, RICHARD MONTGOMERY, SANDRA MONTGOMERY, WENDY MONTGOMERY, KIM MONTI, ROBERTO MONTJOY, DANIEL MONTOYA, ELIZABETH MONTOYA, GILBERT MONTOYA, JUSTIN MONTOYA, KATHLEEN MONTOYA, KATIE MONTOYA, RITCHIE MONUIK, CRESFIELD MOODY, DEBORAH MOODY, ERIC MOODY, JON MOODY, MARGARITA MOODY, PATRICIA MOODY, MARY MOOERS, DEE MOON, MELISSA MOON, VICKI MOON, JULIE MOONEY, BRENDA MOORE, BROOKS MOORE, CAROLYN MOORE, CAROLYN MOORE, DOMINIC MOORE, DONNA MOORE, GALE MOORE, JEAN MOORE, JERRY MOORE, KARI MOORE, KELLY MOORE, KENDALE MOORE, KEVIN MOORE, LANELL MOORE, LARRY MOORE, LAURA MOORE, MARK MOORE, MARYELLEN MOORE, MATTHEW MOORE, ROBERT MOORE, SANDRA MOORE, SHERI MOORE, SULINDA MOORE, TIMOTHY MOORE, TYLER MOORE, JOHN MOORE JR., MICHELLE MOORE-DEWEZ, JACQUELIN MORALES, MARTHA MORAN, MARY MORAN, MELISSA MORAN, JACQUELINE MORASCO-ENGTOW, DENISE MORAVEC, FRANCIS MORAWETZ, GAYLE MORAWETZ, KAREN MORDUE, FAIRY MOREHOUSE, CAROL MORELLI-FARMER, DENNIS MORENO, MICHAEL MORENO, AMBER MORGAN, ANALEE MORGAN, BONNIE MORGAN, BRIAN MORGAN, CANDICE MORGAN, CHERIE MORGAN, CHRISTINE MORGAN, CINDY MORGAN, DALE MORGAN, EMILY MORGAN, ERIC MORGAN, GUY MORGAN, JAMES MORGAN, JENNIFER MORGAN, JUSTIN MORGAN, KAY MORGAN, KEN MORGAN, KRISTY MORGAN, KYLE MORGAN, MEGAN MORGAN, MELINDA MORGAN, MIKE MORGAN, MIKE MORGAN, PAUL MORGAN, PETER MORGAN, RAMON MORGAN, SANDRA MORGAN, SANDRA MORGAN, STEPHEN MORGAN, HOLLY MORHAM, ROBERT MORIARTY, BRIAN MORIN, MARGARET MORIN, GINA MORINAKA, MICKEY MORINAKA, JUANITA MORK, LARRY MORK, DAVID MORLEY, GARY MORLEY, GAIL MORO, LARRY MORO, VANCE MOROSI, STEPHEN MORRELL, YVETTE MORRIBERON, KEELEY MORRICAL, DEAN MORRILL, JENNIFER MORRILL, SCOTT MORRILL, BRENDA MORRIS, BRIAN MORRIS, CAROLYN MORRIS, DEBRA MORRIS, DENNISE MORRIS, HERBERT MORRIS, JUDY MORRIS, KEVIN MORRIS, KIMBERLY MORRIS, LAUREL MORRIS, LEANA MORRIS, LORI MORRIS, MARK MORRIS, MARK MORRIS, MARLAY MORRIS, MICHAEL MORRIS, MICHAEL MORRIS, PETER MORRIS, RAMONA MORRIS, RYAN MORRIS, SUSAN MORRIS, TAYLOR MORRIS, TIMOTHY MORRIS, WENDY MORRIS, ZANE MORRIS, BRETT MORRISON, DEETTE MORRISON, JODY MORRISON, JULIE MORRISON, MICHAEL MORRISON, MIKE MORRISON, NANCY MORRISON, REBECCA MORRISON, STEVE MORRISON, TRACIE MORRISON, DAVID MORROW, MICHAEL MORROW, DENNIS MORSE, DIANA MORSE, HOPE MORSE, JOHN ALLISON MORSE, YVETTE MORSE, KELLY MORSTAD, CAROL MORTENSEN, JEFFREY MORTENSEN, JOLENE MORTENSEN, KAREN MORTENSEN, MARCIA MORTENSEN, MICHAEL MORTENSEN, PAUL MORTENSEN, SUSAN MORTENSEN, TONYA MORTENSEN, BARRY MORTENSON, BRETT MORTENSON, ANITA MORTIMER, WALTER MORTIMER, MARY ELLEN MORTOLA, ELLEN MORTON, JOHN MORTON, KATHERINE MORTON, PAMELA MORTON, ROSEMARY MOSCHEL, ALFRED MOSER, ALYSON MOSER, GENE MOSER, KEN MOSER, LAVERNE MOSER, MILDRED MOSER, PAMELA MOSER, RANDY MOSES, KIM MOSOFF, AARON MOSS, ALAN MOSS, BRANDON MOSS, DAN MOSS, EDWIN MOSS, JANET MOSS, JENNIFER MOSS, JOHN MOSS, KELVIN MOSS, LEE MOSS, LORAINE MOSS, NORVAL MOSS, PAUL MOSS, SCOTT MOSS, STEVEN MOSS, WILLIAM MOSS, BRADFORD MOSTELLER, EILEEN MOTE, TAMARA MOTES, DANIEL MOTT, DIANN MOTT, RANDY MOTT, ALISA MOTZKUS, EDWARD MOULD, CHERYL MOULDING, BRYCE MOULTON, SCOTT MOULTON, KARI MOULTRIE, SANDRA MOULTRIE, JEFF MOUNTEER, LORI MOUNTFORD, LURA MOUNTFORD, GERALD MOUSER, KRISTINA MOUSER, MARIE MOUSER, PATRICIA MOUSER, KRISTIN MOUTY, STEVEN MOUTY, DAVID MOVITZ, TORE MOWATT-LARSSEN, DAVID MOWER, JODIE MOWER, KAYLENE MOWER, LISA MOWER, SCOTT MOWER, TODD MOWER, JOHN MOWRY, JIMMY MOY, JASON MOYER, JANICE MOYES, LAUREL MOYES, RODGER MOYES, JOHN MOYLAN, WAYNE MOYLE, STACEY MOYSH, MADONNA MRZLACK, AL MUDROW, MICHELE MUDROW, JANET MUEHLMANN, ARMIN MUELLER, JILL MUELLER, KIM MUELLER, PAUL MUELLER, ROSS MUELLER, SHELLEY MUELLER, ROBERT MUENCH, BRANDI MUHLESTEIN, DAVID MUIR, GAYLA MUIR, JARIE MUIR, KAARON MUIR, MICHELLE MUIR, RUSS MUIR, DOROTHY MUIRHEAD, PHILLIP MUIRHEAD, CORY MULCOCK, LISA MULCOCK, BRENDA MULDERIG, SHAENA MULDOON, BURDELL MULFORD, TIMOTHY MULHOLLAND, EDWARD MULLANEY, BRADY MULLEN, REBECCA MULLEN, THOMAS MULLEN, VIRGINIA MULLEN, SEILEEN MULLEN MURPHY, IVAN MULLIGAN, MAXENE MULLIGAN, MELVIN MULLIKIN, MAX MULLINER, GAYLA MULLINS, NANCY MULLINS, ROBERT MULLOY, GENEVIEVE MULQUEEN, JODI MULVEY, LINDSAY MUMFORD, REX MUMFORD, CHERILYNN MUNDELL, JEFFREY MUNDEN, DAN MUNGER, JEFF MUNGER, GEORGE MUNK, WILLIAM MUNK, LYNETTE MUNKBERG, GERALD MUNNS, DENNIS MUNOZ, MARY MUNOZ, ALLEN MUNSON, JACE MURAMOTO, AMY MURDOCK, COLLETTE MURDOCK, DOUGLAS MURDOCK, MATHEW MURDOCK, MICHELLE MURDOCK, MICHELLE MURDOCK, MONICA MURDOCK, STEVE MURDOCK, VIVIAN MURDOCK, MARCY MUREN, CAMERON MURIE, DUNCAN MURIE, NATALIE MURILLO, BRIAN MURPHY, BRIAN MURPHY, CINDY MURPHY, COLLEEN MURPHY, DALE MURPHY, DIANA MURPHY, DONNA MURPHY, EMILY MURPHY, JOEL MURPHY, KATHLEEN MURPHY, MARK MURPHY, MARNE MURPHY, SCOTT MURPHY, SHELLEY MURPHY, BEVERLEE MURRAY, CHAD MURRAY, JULIA MURRAY, MALINDA MURRAY, ROBERT MURRAY, SEAN MURRAY, SUSANNA MURRAY, TODD MURRAY, WILLIAM (MARC) MURRI, ROBERT MURRILL, LORINE MURTAGH, NINA MURTAGH, JOSEPH MUSCAT, BRETT MUSE, CHERYL MUSGRAVE, DAN MUSGRAVE, MOHAMMED MUSLEH, MARIANNE MUSTAFA, CAROL MUTERSPAUGH, ELEANOR MUTH, FRED MUTTER, BONNIE MYERS, DEBRA MYERS,

JENNIFER MYERS, JOSEPH MYERS, LAURIE MYERS, ROBERT MYERS, ROBERT MYERS, ROSS MYERS, STEVEN MYERS, SUSAN MYERS, WILLIAM MYERS, HAL MYERS JR, JOHN MYHRA, ALICE MYLI, HOWARD MYLI, DONALD MYRAH SR, ART MYSHRALL • **N** • AMY NACCARATO, DIANNA NACCARATO, ROBERT NACHTWEY, BRANDEE NADAULD, JERALD NADEAU, MICHEAL NADING SR, LAUREN NADLER, IAN NAEF, SANDRA NAEGLE, BONNIE NAETHE, KIMBERLY NAGLE, MASAE NAIDO, SANDRA NAILLON, BRAD NAISBITT, MARGARET NAISBITT, MAYA NAKAIDZE, DONNA NAKASHIMA, JEFFREY NAKASHIMA, MICHIKO NAKASHIMA-LIZARAZO, THIAN NAKASONE, BEVERLEY NALDER, LAREN NALDER, NICOLE NALDER, AMANDA NALL, MELODY NALLEY, TAMMY NALLY, NEEDRA NANAYAKKARA, DOTTI NANCE, PAUL NANCE, ROSALIE NANCE, STANLEY NANCE, VIRGINIA NANCE, BARRY NANGLE, MIRKO NANOT, ANNE NAPER ANDERSEN, DONALD NARDIELLO JR, DANIEL NASCIMENTO, SANDRA NASCIMENTO, CAROLYN NASH, GARETH NASH, STEPHEN NASON, JANICE NATE, MAURA NAUGHTON, MARIO NAUJOKS, JOAN NAUMANN, DANIEL NAVIS, MICHELLE NAY, ALLEN NAYLOR, GERALD NAYLOR, JERRY NAYLOR, KATIE NAYLOR, KERRI NAYLOR, MARCUS NAYLOR, MARISOL NAYLOR, RACHEL NAYLOR, ROXANNA NAYLOR, AMIR NAZARI, LUCY NAZARIAN, DAVID NEBEKER, HEATHER NEBEKER, LANA NEBEKER, LISA NEBEKER, PAT NECHODOM, JEFF NEEDHAM, THOMAS NEEDHAM, SUSAN NEEDLEMAN, DAVID NEELEY, DEBORAH NEELEY, JEFFREY NEELEY, LLOYD NEELEY, TERESA NEELY, LANI NEER, JEANA NEF, JOHN NEFF, KALENE NEFF, MARILYN NEFF, MARJORIE NEFF, MERRIT NEFF, ROBERT NEHREN, MICHAEL NEIBAUR, VALERIE NEIBAUR, BARRY NEIDER, JON NEIDHOLD, DREW NEIL, JOHN NEILL, COURTNEE NEILSEN, MEGAN NEILSEN, ERIC NEILSON, MARLIN NEILSON, REID NEILSON, VINNIE NEILSON, WENDY NEILSON, HAMDO NEIMARLIJA, LINDA NEISWENDER, BONNIE NELL, DAVE NELLIS, ANNE NELSEN, DAVID NELSEN, REBECCA NELSEN, ALYSA NELSON, AMANDA NELSON, ANDREW NELSON, ANITA NELSON, ASHLEE NELSON, BRITT NELSON, CAROL NELSON, CINDY NELSON, DAVID NELSON, DAVID NELSON, DIANA NELSON, DIANNE NELSON, DON NELSON, DOUG NELSON, DOUGLAS NELSON, DOYLE NELSON, ELAINE NELSON, EMILY NELSON, ERIK NELSON, GLEN NELSON, GREGORY NELSON, JAMES NELSON, JAN NELSON, JANET NELSON, JANET NELSON, JARED NELSON, JARED NELSON, JAYNE NELSON, JEAN NELSON, JEFFERY NELSON, JENNIFER NELSON, JEWEL NELSON, JOHN NELSON, KAREL NELSON, KATE NELSON, KATHERINE NELSON, KEVIN NELSON, KIM NELSON, KRISTINE NELSON, LINDA LOU NELSON, LORI NELSON, MARIANNE NELSON, MARIANNE NELSON, MARK NELSON, MAUREEN NELSON, MELINDA NELSON, MITZI NELSON, NANCY NELSON, NATHAN NELSON, NORMAN NELSON, NORMAN NELSON, PAUL NELSON, PAUL NELSON, PEGGY NELSON, PETER NELSON, RANDY NELSON, RICHARD NELSON, ROBERT NELSON, ROBERT NELSON, RON NELSON, RONALD NELSON, RYAN NELSON, SHAREE NELSON, SHAWN NELSON, SHELLY NELSON, SUSAN NELSON, TROY NELSON, TYLER NELSON, TONI NEMANICK, RENATA NEMCOK, MICHAEL NEMELKA, PAIGE NEMROW, ANN NENTWICH, DAVID NERDIN, DENNIS NESBIT, HOLLY NESBIT, CLARENCE NESLEN, ROBERT NESLEN, TODD NESS, TIMOTHY NESTORYAK, NORMA NETTLES, IOANNIS NETTOS, DAVID NEUMAN, DEBBIE Z NEUMANN, JIM NEUMAYER, MARJORIE NEUMAYER, JANE NEUSCHWANDER, KENNETH NEUSCHWANDER, MICHELE NEVARES, TINA NEVERASKI, ARTHUR NEWBERG, MD, CONNIE NEWBOLD, JILLIAN NEWBOLD, KATHLEEN NEWBOLD, MAC NEWBOLD, TAMMY NEWBOLD, ANDREA NEWBOULD, BARBARA NEWBOULD, DAN NEWBOULD, JEFFREY NEWBOULD, JEANINE NEWBY, APRIL NEWELL, CHRIS NEWELL, LARRY NEWELL, DALE NEWEY, LELA NEWEY, MARTY NEWEY, ROBERT NEWEY, DINA NEWHOUSE, BRINTON NEWLAND, JENNIFER NEWLAND, KENNETH NEWLAND, NANCY NEWLIN, JANIE NEWMAN, JEFF NEWMAN, JOHN NEWMAN, LAUREL NEWMAN, LOLA NEWMAN, LOUVONNE NEWMAN, MARSHA NEWMAN, PAT NEWMAN, PAUL NEWMAN, RAY NEWMAN, ROBERT NEWMAN, SARA NEWMAN, WILLARD NEWMAN, JANE NEWSOME, KATHLEEN NEWSOME, MICHAEL NEWSOME, BENJAMIN NEWTON, BRENT NEWTON, DAVE NEWTON, DAVID NEWTON, JANNETTE NEWTON, RICK NEWTON, SANDY NEWTON, SHIRLEY NEWTON, MARK NEY, ALONZO NEZ, JENNIFER NGATUVAI, TRANG NGUYEN, SHERI NIBLEY, LARRY NICCUM, JACQUELYN NICE, BONNIE NICHOL, JACK NICHOL, LINDSIE NICHOL, PAIGE NICHOL, STEVEN NICHOL, CONNIE NICHOLAS, BRYAN NICHOLES, GORDON NICHOLL, JACKIE NICHOLL, AMY NICHOLS, BROOKE NICHOLS, CAROLYN NICHOLS, GARY NICHOLS, GEORGE NICHOLS, JEFF NICHOLS, JOEL NICHOLS, JULIE NICHOLS, KAREN NICHOLS, KAREN NICHOLS, KENT NICHOLS, TIMOTHY NICHOLS, TYLER NICHOLS, DWIGHT NICHOLSON, KARL NICHOLSON, KEITH NICHOLSON, SHARON NICHOLSON, STEPHANIE NICHOLSON, KAREN NICKELL, DENNIS NICKERSON, MATT NICKLAUS, CARL NICKLOS, DONALD NICKMAN, NANCY NICKMAN, SUSAN NICKMAN, DONNA LEE NICKOLAISEN, COURTNEY NICOL, JAY NICOL, KENT NICOL, KEVIN NICOL, MARIE-LOUISE NICOL, PAUL NICOL, TERRY NICOLA, DAVID NICPONSKI, BRYAN NIEBERGALL, JOHN NIEBERGALL, LINDA NIEBERGALL, PAUL NIEBUHR, DIANNE NIEBUHR-JOOS, FRED NIED, BERRIE NIEDERHAUSER, CARSON NIEDERHAUSER, DALE NIEDERHAUSER, PEGGY NIEDERHAUSER, SPENCER NIEDERHAUSER, CINDY NIELD, JUANITA NIELD, LON NIELD, NORMAN NIELD, PAT NIELD, TRICIA NIELD, ANGELA NIELSEN, CAI NIELSEN, CAMILLE NIELSEN, CAROL NIELSEN, CINDY NIELSEN, CRAIG NIELSEN, CURTIS NIELSEN, CYNTHIA NIELSEN, DAVID NIELSEN, DAVID NIELSEN, DAVID NIELSEN, DAVID NIELSEN, DEAN NIELSEN, DENNIS NIELSEN, DOROTHY NIELSEN, FRANKLIN NIELSEN, GRANT NIELSEN, JASON NIELSEN, JAY DEE NIELSEN, JEFF NIELSEN, KATIE NIELSEN, KEN NIELSEN, KENT NIELSEN, KRISTIE NIELSEN, LARRY NIELSEN, LESLIE NIELSEN, LISA ANN NIELSEN, MATTHEW NIELSEN, MICHAEL NIELSEN, MICHAEL NIELSEN, NEPHI NIELSEN, PAULINE NIELSEN, PEGGY NIELSEN, PETER NIELSEN, REBECCA NIELSEN, SUZANNE NIELSEN, TRUDY NIELSEN, VICKI NIELSEN, VICKI NIELSEN, WENDY NIELSEN, ALBERTA NIELSON, ALISON NIELSON, ANTHONY NIELSON, BRENT NIELSON, BRENT NIELSON, BRUCE NIELSON, CHAD NIELSON, CREIG NIELSON, DICK NIELSON, DORIS NIELSON, GORDON NIELSON, J RUSSELL NIELSON, JAMES NIELSON, JANICE NIELSON, JEFFREY NIELSON, KATHY NIELSON, LAWRENCE NIELSON, LYNN NIELSON, MARIANNE NIELSON, MARIE NIELSON, MARILYNN NIELSON, NATALIE NIELSON, REBECCA NIELSON, ROBERT NIELSON, RONALD NIELSON, SAMUEL NIELSON, STEVEN NIELSON, THOMAS NIELSON, LESLIE NIEMANN, RUTH NIEMEYER, PAMELA NIEMI, ROBIN NIEMUTH, MARK NIENSAEDT, STEPHEN NIERNBERGER, DAVE NIGBUR, CONSTANTINOS NIKIFOROS, MARYANN NIKSICH, MICHELLE NILLES, CRYSTALYN NILSON, TARALEE NILSON, JEFF NIMORI, RICHARD NIMORI, SARA NIMORI, LANDY NIPPER, DEBORAH NIVEN, HIROSHI NIWA, BERT NIXON, DANIEL NIXON, JACQUE NIXON, SHIREE NIXON, CINZIA NOBLE, CLARA NOBLE, JIM NOBLE, RANDEL NOBLE, RAJATHI NOEL, RUTHANNE NOEL, WRIGHT NOEL, EMILY NOFFSINGER, ERICA NOFSINGER, GEORGE NOLAN, WILLIAM NOLAND, MARTHA NOLL, LORETTA NOMEIKAITE-WESTON, KENT NOMURA, ARCHIE NOON, IRENE NOORDA, WENDY NORD, LORENE NORDGRAN, SEARI NORDGRAN, RICHARD NORDGREN, ROGER NORDGREN, CINDY NORDLING, DOUG NORDMEYER, DAVID NORDQUIST, DENISE NORDSTROM, LISA NORDSTROM, MARILYN NORDSTROM, ANELA NORIEGA, STEPHANIE NORINE, ANN NORMAN, GARY NORMAN, JOHN NORMAN, MIKI NORMAN, RUSSELL NORMAN, BILL NORR, JOHN NORRIS, KATHERINE NORRIS, MIKE NORSETH, PETER NORSETH, ANGELA NORTH, BRENT NORTH, LUANA NORTH, MICHAEL NORTH, TRENT NORTH, SUSAN NORTHINGTON, DOROTHY NORTON, EDWARD NORTON, GREG NORTON, JACQUELYN NORTON, JAMES NORTON, JORDAN NORTON, LESTER NORTON, LISA NORTON, MELINDA NORTON, RANDY NORTON, RHONDA NORTON, TOSCA NORTON, NANCY NORTZ, CRAIG NORVELL, DEBBIE NOSEWORTHY, LOUIE NOTARIANNI, CINDY NOTTINGHAM, ONDREJ NOVAK, DIANA NOVELLE, LORALEE NOVOSEL, PETER NOWAK, MAURICE NOYES, MICHAEL NOYES, SARAH NOYES, SHELLEY NUDD, MARK NUETZEL, LYNN NUNES, MARIO NUNEZ, JOYCE NUNN, SUSAN NUSINK, JASON NUTTALL, KATHLEEN NUTTALL, MICHAEL NUTTALL, BECKY NYDAM, DAVID NYDAM, ALAN NYE, FREDERICK NYE, KIMBERLY NYE, MANDI NYE, RANDALL NYE, SUSAN NYHUS, ELIZABETH NYMAN • **O** • BONNIE O'BRIEN, JUANITA O'BRIEN, KATHY O'BRIEN, KERRYN O'BRIEN, ROBERT O'BRIEN, ROGER O'BRIEN, VICKI O'BRIEN, JANE O'BRYANT, PATRICK O'CONNELL, PETER O'CONNOR, BRENNAN O'DONNELL, AMANDA O'DRISCOLL, BEVERLY O'FEE, ROSS O'FEE, BRIAN O'HARA, CHARLOTTE O'HARE, GEORGE O'HARE, KATHLEEN O'HARE, STUART O'HARE, ANN O'KEEFE, IVOR O'NEIL, LARRY O'NEIL, DENNIS O'NEILL, JOEL O'NEILL, KYNA O'NEILL, MARY O'NEILL, SHAWN O'NEILL, LAURA O'ROURKE, MARY O'ROURKE, TERESA O'ROURKE, MAUREEN O'ROURKE-ROSS, NATHAN OAK, BRIAN OAKDEN, KELLY OAKDEN, SUSAN OAKDEN, ANGELA OAKES, BARBARA OAKES, KEVIN OAKES, BRIAN OAKESON, LISA OAKESON, KAIRLE OAKS, WAYNE OBERG, JILL OBERNDORFER, DOUGLAS OBLAK, ALISA OBORN, GORDON OBORN, KENT OBORN, DAN OBRADOVICH, GOLDEN OBRAY, JULIE OBRAY, JUN OCHIAI, BARBARA OCHOA, JEFF OCHOA, JOHN OCHOA, SERGIO OCHOA, SUSAN OCHOA, LINDA ODA, SHARON ODELL, GARY ODERDA, NATHALIE ODERNHEIMER, DAVID OEHLER, PAULO OEMIG, TYLER OESTERLE, MARY OFFIELD, DAVID OGDEN, DEBORAH OGDEN, DEBRA OGDEN, DEVON OGDEN, MERYLLEE OGDEN, MICHELLE OGDEN, RANDY OGDEN, TAMRA OGILVIE, WENDY OGILVIE, AMY OGLESBY, WILLIAM OGRAM, JEOUNGHOON OH, DAVID OHLIN, REBECCA OHLRICH, DOUGLAS OHLSON, LINDA OHLSON, RAYMOND OHM, DAWNA OHME, SHANNON OHMERT, JERRY OHRN, ROBYN OHRN, MAURICE OHUMUKINI, MICHELLE OHUMUKINI, RICHELLE OHUMUKINI, TARA OHUMUKINI, THEODORA OIKONOMOU, MICHAEL OJA, CHRES OKI, MARK OKINO, HARALD OLAFSSON, JOSEPH OLAKANGIL, LARS OLAVSON, ALICE OLCH, BARBARA OLCHEK, BRYAN OLCHEK, SCOTT OLCHEK, STEPHEN OLCHEK, SCOTT OLCOTT, CRAIG OLDENBURGER, LINDA OLDENBURGER, HUGH OLDHAM, JAYSEN OLDROYD, KERY OLDROYD, ROSE OLDS, SHAUNA OLDS, WILLIAM OLDS, ANTHONY OLENKIEWICZ, CHARLES OLESEN, KATHY OLESON, KRISTINA OLESON, RONALD OLESON, DEANN OLIEKAN, CHRISTOPHER OLINICK, BRANT OLIPHANT, BRUCE OLIPHANT, MIGNON OLIVE, BEVOLYN OLIVER, DEANNA OLIVER, EDMUND OLIVER, JOE OLIVER, KENT OLIVER, KEVIN OLIVER, MICHAEL OLIVER, PETER OLIVER, REBECCA OLIVER, RICK OLIVER, ROBERT OLIVER, SHELDON OLIVER, STACI OLIVER, TERESA OLIVER, ANDREW OLLERTON, GREGORY OLLIS, TANNIA OLOFSON, NAOMI OLPIN, BYRON OLSCHEWSKI, SHEILA OLSCHEWSKI, AILEEN OLSEN, ALLEN OLSEN, ALONZO OLSEN, BETTY OLSEN, BRENDA OLSEN, BRIAN OLSEN, CARLA OLSEN, CHRIS OLSEN, CRISTINE OLSEN, DAWNA OLSEN, DE ANN OLSEN, DIANA OLSEN, DOROTHY OLSEN, GARY OLSEN, GARY OLSEN, GORDON OLSEN, JANALYN OLSEN, JEFFREY OLSEN, JENNIFER OLSEN, JODIE OLSEN, KAREN OLSEN, KEITH OLSEN, KIM OLSEN, KIRK OLSEN, KRISTEN OLSEN, KRISTEN OLSEN, LINDA OLSEN, LORI OLSEN, MARY OLSEN, MICHAEL OLSEN, MICHAEL OLSEN, MURRAY OLSEN, NOEL OLSEN, PETER OLSEN, RANDY OLSEN, RAYMOND OLSEN, REA OLSEN, RICKIE OLSEN, SCOTT OLSEN, SCOTT OLSEN, SHELLEY OLSEN, SHELLY OLSEN, STACEY OLSEN, STEVE OLSEN, SUSAN OLSEN, TRAVIS OLSEN, BOBETTE OLSON, CANDY OLSON, CINDY OLSON, CRAIGE OLSON, CYNTHIA OLSON, DALANE OLSON, DAVID OLSON, DAVID OLSON, DAVID OLSON, DOUG OLSON, ERIC OLSON, GAYLE OLSON, HEATHER OLSON, ILENE OLSON, JACK OLSON, JARED OLSON, JEFFERY OLSON, JOHN OLSON, KIM OLSON, MELANIE OLSON, MILO OLSON, RAY OLSON, ROXANNE OLSON, RUARK OLSON, SALLY OLSON, SAMUEL OLSON, THOMAS OLSON, TIM OLSON, TYLER OLSON, WENDY OLSON, DANIEL OLYMPIA, RIXA OMAN, KELLY OMANA, ARLENE OMASITS, RACHEL OMENN, DEBRA OMER, ALVARO OMISTE, JENNIFER OMISTE, KATHLEEN ONG, AMY OPENSHAW, JOYCE OPENSHAW, PAMELA OPENSHAW, ANNY OPFAR, JEFFREY OPHEIKENS, KEITH OPP, CHRISTINE ORAM, MARK ORASKOVICH, KAREN ORCHARD, ROBERT (PAUL) ORD, SUSAN ORD, VIRGINIA ORD, DAVID ORDUN, GAIL ORDUN, DRORA OREN, JOE ORGILL, PAUL ORGILL, NATHAN ORIEN, ALISE ORLANDI, RENATO ORLANDIN, BENJAMIN ORME, ERIC ORME, KARIN ORME, NANCY ORME, CHRISTOPHER ORN, ROGER ORN, ELAINE ORR, GORDON ORR, IVA ORR, JANICE ORR, KEVIN ORR, LARRY ORR, MARVIN ORR, SUSAN ORR, TRAVIS ORR, TROY ORR, THOMAS ORROCK, EDWARD ORSCHEL, ROBERT ORTA, EDWARD ORTEGA, JOSIE ORTEGA, STEVE ORTGIESEN, DANNY ORTIZ, ELAINE ORTMAN, BRAD ORTON, ERIC ORTON, HILLARI ORTON, JODIE ORTON, KAY ORTON, RUTH ORTON, STERLING ORTON, STEVEN ORTON, TECIA ORTON, VICKIE ORTON, GAIL OSBORN, JOANN OSBORN, LADAWN OSBORN, RONALD OSBORN, BLAKE OSBORNE, BRENT OSBORNE, CLAY OSBORNE, DARIN OSBORNE, ROBERT OSBORNE, BARBARA OSBOURN, JAMES OSBOURN, GARY OSCARSON, CAROLYN OSENGA, JEREMY OSGOOD, BARBARA OSHUST, ANNETTE OSIEK, ODD OSLAND, MARY OSMOND, MARK OSMUNDSON, BARBARA OSOFSKY, JUDIE OSPITAL, JOSEPH OSTENSON, NANCY OSTERGAR, RYAN OSTERLIND, MELISSA OSTERMILLER, JAMES OSTERUD, ALAN OSTLER, DAVID OSTLER, ELIZABETH OSTLER, KELLI OSTLER, SARAH OSTLER, WENDY OSTLER, DALE OSTLIE, DAVID OSTRANDER, NOEL OSTRANDER, HELEN OTT, JULIE OTT, SUSAN OTTENS, RICHARD OTTESEN, EDWARD OTTO, KATHY OTTO, ROSS OTTO, MARCOS OTTONELLI, JOHN OTTOSEN, PETER OTTOSEN, SHAD OUTSEN, ROBERT OUTWATER, CRAIG OUTZEN, PAUL OUZTS, BRENT OVARD, MAUREEN OVARD, NOELLE OVARD, SUZANNE OVERBY, CHARITY OVERLY, SANDRA OVERMOE, MONA OVERSTEG, HEATHER OVERTON, MICHELLE OVESON, DYLAN OWEN, JULIE OWEN, ROSS OWEN, WAYNE OWEN, WILLIAM OWEN, DIXIE OWENS, JERRY OWENS, JON OWENS, MICHAEL OWENS, NANCY OWENS, PATRICIA OWENS, PHILLIP OWENS, MICHAEL OXBORROW, CHRISTOPHER OXLEY, PHILIP OXLEY, KEVEN OYLER, MELISA OYLER • **P** • VALARIE PABALIS, BEVERLY PACAL, DOUG PACE, JEFFREY PACE, JODY PACE, JOHN PACE, LAURA PACE, NAOMI PACE, STEVEN PACE, WILLIAM PACE, JOHN PACHECANO JR, MARCO PACHECO, KATHLEEN PACHUCKI, CLYDE PACK, JENNIFER PACK, KEVIN PACK, MATTHEW PACK, PRICILLA PACK, ROGER PACK, GLENNA PADFIELD, EMIL PADGETT, REMI PADOIN, ANN PAGE, CATHY PAGE, COLLEEN PAGE, DONALD PAGE, ELEONORE PAGE, ERNEST PAGE, FLOYD PAGE, GAYE LEE PAGE, GEORGE D. PAGE, GWEN PAGE, HOLDEN PAGE, JERAN PAGE, JOAN M. PAGE, LOREN PAGE, LORI PAGE, MARJIE PAGE, MATTHEW PAGE, RONALD PAGE, SHAUNELLE PAGE, MARTHA PAGET, WAH PAI, DANIEL PAIGE, RUSSELL PAIGE, MICHELLE PAINTER, PATRICIA PAKISER, ELSA PALANZA, DAVID PALAZZOLO, SAMUEL PALAZZOLO, MAURICE PALERMO, BARBARA PALMER, BENJAMIN PALMER, BOB PALMER, BRENT PALMER, CHRISTOPHER PALMER, CORRI PALMER, DUSTIN PALMER, ELLIS PALMER, EMILY PALMER, GAYLEN PALMER, JAMES PALMER, JENNIFER PALMER, KAREN PALMER, KATHY PALMER, KELLY PALMER, KORY PALMER, LAUREL PALMER, MICHELLE PALMER, MIKE PALMER, NANCY PALMER, ROSALIE PALMER, RUSSELL PALMER, RYAN PALMER, TRISH PALMER, TUAEFU PALMER, MICHELLE PALOMAKI, TEDDY PALOMAKI, DEMETRIOS PANERAS, JAMES PANGOS, KATHY PANHORST, LIVINGSTON PANHORST, SUI LANG PANOKE, DAVID PANTON, MARK PANTONE, CHARLES PANZA, KITTY PANZA, SHANNON PAOLI, BRUCE PAPE, DARCY PAPENFUSS, DOROTHY PAQUET, GILBERT PAQUET, NICOLE PAQUET, CHRISTOPHER PARADA, DONNA PARADA, MARK PARADISE, KAREN PARARA, KIMBERLEY PARDOE, DAVID PARDUHN, KAYLA PARDUHN, MARIA PAREDES, DIANE PARISI, GERALD PARK, JANNELL PARK, TIMOTHY PARK, JEFFREY PARKE, ARTHUR PARKER, BRAD PARKER, BRIAN PARKER, CAROL PARKER, DAVE PARKER, E. CHARLES PARKER, JEANETTE PARKER, JODI PARKER, JOHN PARKER, LINDA PARKER, LOLA PARKER, LOREN PARKER, NANCY PARKER, NICHOLAS PARKER, NICOLE PARKER, RENEE PARKER, RICHARD PARKER, ROBERT (MICHAEL) PARKER, SUSAN PARKER, RICHARD PARKER DO, ROBERT PARKER JR, SANDI PARKES, STEVEN PARKES, AIMEE PARKIN, BRAD PARKIN, BRENT PARKIN, CRAIG PARKIN, DAN PARKIN, JAKE PARKIN, JAY PARKIN, RICHARD PARKIN, SHARON PARKIN, CAROLYN PARKINS, ADELE PARKINSON, CLARK PARKINSON, GAI PARKINSON, JENNIE PARKINSON, KIRK PARKINSON, PAMELA PARKINSON, SCOTT PARKINSON, BARBARA PARR, KRISTY PARR, SHELDON PARR, VALERIE PARR, MARK PARRA, CHRISTOPHER PARRISH, JEFF PARRISH, LANCE PARRISH, VAL PARRISH, PAMELA PARROT, NANCY PARRY, SHEILA PARRY, ZACHARIAH PARRY, LISA PARSONS, ROYCE PARSONS, JANICE PARTIN, AMY PARTLOW, MARY ANN PASCOE, JAMES PASEK, ALEX PASHLEY, ANDREA PASI, RHONDALEE PASKINS, VICKI PASQUA, MICHAEL PASSARELLA, BRIAN PASSEY, MARK PASSEY, RANDY PASSEY, SHONNIE PASSEY, WENDY PASSEY, GRANT PATCH, MARNA PATCH, MARGARET PATERSON, HAROLD PATRICK, JOEL PATRICK, LYNDA PATRICK, MICHAEL PATRICK, SALLY PATRICK, DAVID PATTEN, JOAN PATTEN, TATIANA PATTEN, DAVID PATTERSON, GERALD PATTERSON, JAMES PATTERSON, JOSEPHINE PATTERSON, MARY PATTERSON, REBEKAH PATTERSON, STUART PATTERSON, SUSAN PATTERSON, SUZANNE PATTERSON, TAYLOR PATTERSON, THOMAS PATTERSON, AARON PATTY, MATTHEW PATZEK, DONALD PAUL, JOHN PAUL, MELODEE PAUL, GREGORY PAUL JR, DIANE PAULL, NANCY PAULL, KATHRYN PAULSEN, VAL PAULSEN, BRAD PAULSON, DONNA PAULSON, HARMONY PAULSON, JUDY PAULSON, JEFF PAVLICK, JULIE PAWLAK, PAUL PAXMAN, DAN PAXTON, KENNETH PAXTON, TAMMIE PAYETTE, DEAN PAYNE, ELEANOR PAYNE, GAVIN PAYNE, JUNE PAYNE, KIM PAYNE, KRISTEN PAYNE, LEEANN PAYNE, PAMELA PAYNE, SUE PAYNE, VALERIE PAYNE, LIRIO PAZ FERNANDEZ, MAGGIE PAZERA, ALYSON PEACOCK, HELEN PEACOCK, KAYE PEACOCK, RYAN PEACOCK, SHERRY PEACOCK, ANN PEARCE, DEXTER PEARCE, LORALIE PEARCE, MARIA PEARCE, VIRGINIA PEARCE, DEBRA PEARL, JAMES PEARL, NORMAN PEARS, DESIREE PEARSON, JODI PEARSON, LUANN PEARSON, MARGARET PEARSON, MARILYN PEARSON, PAMELA PEARSON, RAYMOND PEARSON, REITA PEARSON, RICKY PEARSON, ROGER PEARSON, SHERYL PEARSON, FRANK PEART, MARILYN PEART, VAUGHN PEART, JANICE PEASE, TINA PEASLEE, KEVIN PEAY, DANIEL PECK, DAVID PECK, RANAE PECK, WENDY PECK, KARON PECKHAM, LEENA PECKHAM, GAYE PEDDYCOART, LEE PEDDYCOART, AMBY PEDERSEN, JEREMY PEDERSEN, TORE PEDERSEN, BILL PEDERSON, DAWN PEDERSON, JAMIE PEDERSON, CHRISTIAN PEEL, DENNIS PEERY, SAMUEL PEERY, CHRISTOPHER PEHLER, ERIC PEHRSON, ANDY PEIFFER, GARY PEIRCE, WILLIAM PEIRCE, IAN PEISNER, ELIZABETH PELESS, SCOTT PELLA, MARY PELTO, BRYAN PENDLETON, CYNTHIA PENDLETON, JAYNE PENDLETON, WILLIAM PENDLETON, JESSICA PENG, JUDITH PENHORWOOD, IAN PENICK, RICHARD PENMAN, JOHN PENNEY, DAVID PENNINGTON, DANIEL PENNOCK, GERALD PENNOCK, JOAN PENROD, ROGER PENROSE, GAE PENSABENE, MIKE PENTTILA, TIMOTHY PEPERS, VIVIAN PEPLINSKI, JANEENE PEPPINGER, JAY PEPPINGER, MICHAEL PEPPINGER, LYDIA PERALTA, KATHY JO PERCY, DANA PEREZ, JAVIER PEREZ, MICHAEL PEREZ, QUINN PEREZ, CAMERON PERIGO, KENNETH PERIMAN, ANNETTE PERKINS, CAROLYN PERKINS, CYNTHIA PERKINS, D. KENDALL PERKINS, ERNEST PERKINS, GARY PERKINS, HEATHER PERKINS, SANDRA PERKINS, MARC PERL, DORIS PERLMAN, SVETLANA PERMIAKOVA, DONALD PERO, PATRICK PERRETT, MARY PERRIN, SETH PERRINS, BOB PERRY, BREK PERRY, CHAD PERRY, CHRIS PERRY, DAVID PERRY, DEBORAH PERRY, GARY PERRY, KRISTINE PERRY, LISA PERRY, MARLENE PERRY, MATTHEW PERRY, PATRICK PERRY, ROBERT PERRY, SHARYL PERRY, SUZANNE PERRY, MATTHEW PERSCHON, CYNTHIA PESTOTNIK, LOLA PETERMANN, ALISHA PETERS, ANGELE' PETERS, EUGENE PETERS, NORM PETERS, ROBERT PETERS, DOROTHY PETERS-BRANNON, BARBARA PETERS-GORRY, BOBBIE PETERSEN, CHARLLOT PETERSEN, CHARLOTTE PETERSEN, DARRIN PETERSEN, GAYLE PETERSEN, GLENNA PETERSEN, HEIDI PETERSEN, JAN PETERSEN, JANE PETERSEN, JANET PETERSEN, JANET PETERSEN, JEAN PETERSEN, KAYE LANI PETERSEN, KIMBERLY PETERSEN, LARRY PETERSEN, MARK PETERSEN, MARK PETERSEN, PATRECE PETERSEN, REES PETERSEN, ROGER PETERSEN, RYAN PETERSEN, SHANE PETERSEN, SHELLEY PETERSEN, STEFANIE PETERSEN, WENDY PETERSEN, WILLIAM PETERSEN, ANDREW PETERSON, ANTHONY PETERSON, ANTHONY PETERSON, BECKY PETERSON, BETH PETERSON, BRAD PETERSON, CARL PETERSON, CARRIE PETERSON, CHASE PETERSON, CHUCK PETERSON, COLETTE PETERSON, CONNIE PETERSON, CORY PETERSON, CRISTON PETERSON, DAVID PETERSON, DAVID PETERSON, DEE PETERSON, DEREK PETERSON, ERNEST PETERSON, FREDERICK PETERSON, GREGORY PETERSON, GRETHE PETERSON, HEIDI PETERSON, HOWARD PETERSON, HOWARD PETERSON, JAMES PETERSON, JAMIE PETERSON, JEANNE PETERSON, JEFFREY PETERSON, JESSE PETERSON, JOAN PETERSON, JOAN PETERSON, JODELLE PETERSON, JOHANNA PETERSON, JOHN PETERSON, JOHN PETERSON, JOHN PETERSON, JOY PETERSON, JULIE PETERSON, JUSTIN PETERSON, KENNETH PETERSON, LARRY PETERSON, LISA PETERSON, LISA PETERSON, LISA PETERSON, LORIE PETERSON, LYNN PETERSON, MANDEE PETERSON, MARILYN PETERSON, MARK PETERSON, MARK PETERSON, MARK PETERSON, MARY ELLEN PETERSON, MELINDA PETERSON, MERRILL PETERSON, MICHELLE PETERSON, MONA PETERSON, NANCY PETERSON, NATALIE PETERSON, NEDRA PETERSON, NORALEE PETERSON, OLIVER PETERSON, PATRICIA PETERSON, RANDY PETERSON, REBECCA PETERSON, RICK PETERSON, ROB PETERSON, ROGER PETERSON, RONALD PETERSON, RYAN PETERSON, SCOTT PETERSON, SHIRLEY PETERSON, STEVE PETERSON, SUEANN PETERSON, SUNDEE PETERSON, SUSAN PETERSON, TAMRA PETERSON, TRACY PETERSON, VIRGIL PETERSON, MARY PETIK, OLIVER PETIK, DARRICK PETON, DAVID PETRIE, MELYNDA PETRIE, ROBERT PETRIE, MARK PETRITZ, DAVID PETRON, PAGE PETRUCKA, CAROLE PETRY, GEORGE PETRY, BRIAN PETT, JENNIE PETT, ANNIKEN PETTERSEN, LEE PETTIT, RALPH PETTY, STEVE PETTY, JACOB PETZOLD, KAMBIZ PEZESHKI, ADAM PFAFF, ROXANE PFISTER, ANNE PHELAN, MICHAEL PHELAN, GLADYS PHELPS, JOHN PHELPS, NICHOLAS PHELPS, STEPHANIE PHELPS, BARBARA PHILBRICK, COLLEEN PHILIPP, MARK PHILIPP, PAUL PHILIPS, BELINDA PHILLIPS, CHRISTOPHER PHILLIPS, DAWN PHILLIPS, DEAN PHILLIPS, GREGORY PHILLIPS, JANNA PHILLIPS, JOHN PHILLIPS, KIRK PHILLIPS, KRISTY PHILLIPS, MARCI PHILLIPS, MICHAEL PHILLIPS, MYRNA PHILLIPS, NOLAN PHILLIPS, ROBIN PHILLIPS, SCOTT PHILLIPS, TAMARA PHILLIPS, TAMRA PHILLIPS, TODD PHILLIPS, TRACY PHILLIPS, VALERIE PHILLIPS, JULIA PHILLIPS-HORSLEY, SUSAN PHILLIPS-LEE, JOHN PHIPPEN, PETER PHIPPEN, ALAN PHIPPS, KARLA PHIPPS, RANDY PHIPPS, JANICE PICCOLO, ANDREAS PICHLER, NEIL PICKARD, TERESA PICKERING, GREG PICKETT, REX PICKETT, WILLIAM PIDWELL, MARILYN PIENTKA, JOHN PIEPER, MICHAEL PIEPER, BRADLEY PIERATT, ALLEN PIERCE, BILL PIERCE, CHARLES PIERCE, JAIDI PIERCE, JEFFREY PIERCE, MARK PIERCE, MICHAEL PIERCE, ROBERT PIERCE, SALLY PIERCE, SHARON PIERCE, TRUDY PIERCE, SUZANNE PIERCE-MOORE, LLOYD PIERCY, GENASEE PIERSON, ROSEMARIE PIERSON, MARILYN PIGG, BOB PIHL, KRISTY PIKE, RAY PILAND, JEFFREY PILATO, MELISSA PILATO, MELISSA PILLING, LISA PILLMORE, PEGGY PILLMORE, FRANZ PILZ, JEREMIAH PINEDA, ROBYN PINEGAR, PETER PINETTE, STEVE PINKHAM, KIM PINNEGAR, RANDALL PINSON, KRISTIN PINTER, SANDRA PIPPIN, STUART PIPPIN, TAWNA PIPPIN, SANJIN PIRAGIC, TERESA PIRAMI, PETRA PIRC, AUGUST PIRMANN, RODDY PIROUZNIA, MICHAEL PIRRIE, ROBERT PISCITELLI, JOHN PITCHER, NADINE PITCHER, TAYLOR PITCHER, NANCY PITSTICK, LEAH PITTARD, JUDY PITTMAN, BRIAN PITTS, GREG PITTS, MELINDA PITTS, KATHLEEN PLACE, CRAIG PLANT, DAVID PLANT, BARBARA PLATT, SUSAN PLAUTZ, JUDITH PLAYER, KRISTA PLOTT, SUSAN PLOUZEK, HOWARD PLUIM, STEPHANIE PLUMMER, RAY PLUMMER JR, STEVE POCHE, CLAUS POEHLER, LOREEN POFF, WILLIAM POFF, HEINZ POIKE, YULIYA POKHODNYA, AL POKORNY, MICHAEL POLACEK, JERRY POLASEK, ANTHONY POLETTI, STEVE POLITYKA, SHERRY POLL, LOUISE POLLARD, MELVIN POLLARD, ROBERT POLLARD, WILLIAM POLLEYS, SHAUNA POLLMANN, LINDA POLLOCK-WELLS, SUSAN POLSTER, JESSICA POLYCHRONIS, MARY-ANN POMERLEAU, NANCY POMEROY, GRANT POND, REXANNE POND, KIM PONDER, ALBERT POOL, CATHY POOLE, DOUGLAS POOLE, MARGO POOLE, RONDO POOLE, CAROL POOLEY, JOHN POOLEY, DARWIN POPE, DAVID POPE, GAROLD POPE, GERRI POPE, JILL POPE, KISTI POPE, MARCI POPE, RICK POPIOLEK, PATRICIA POPLAR, JOHN POPPLE, CHRIS POPPLETON, BETSEY PORTER, CAROL PORTER, CHRISTOPHER PORTER, DAVID PORTER, ELAINE PORTER, GARY PORTER, JOHN PORTER, KENYON PORTER, KIMBERLY PORTER, LADAWN PORTER, MELANIE PORTER, MYRON PORTER, NEWELL PORTER, ROBERT PORTER, SANDRA PORTER, SHARON PORTER, SUSAN PORTER, LEONARD PORTOCARRERO, BELVA POST, JACOB POST, JAMIE POST, STANLEY POSTMA, STEVEN POSTMA, CHRIS POTTER, HAROLD POTTER, SARA POTTER, SUMMER POTTER, SUZANNE POTTER, WENDY POTTER, JILL POTTS, MARGARET POTTS, CLAIRE POTVIN, A. LLOYD POULSEN, DENNIS POULSEN, GARY POULSEN, GERALD POULSEN, HEATHER POULSEN, LISA POULSEN, LISA POULSEN, RICHARD POULSEN, YVETTE POULSON, ALLAN KENT POWELL, ALLEN POWELL, BARBARA POWELL, BRENDA POWELL, CINDEE POWELL, ELWOOD POWELL, GARY POWELL, GAYLON POWELL, GENEVA POWELL, GEORGE POWELL, GLEN POWELL, KIM POWELL, KRISTY POWELL, LEE POWELL, LINDSAY POWELL, RICHARD POWELL, SUSAN POWELL, TRENT POWELL, WENDY POWELL, BILL POWERS, CANDACE POWERS, DOLORES POWERS, PATRICIA POWERS, DICK POWNALL, MARY POWNALL, LAWRENCE POZIL, LUCY PRAAST, DIANA PRACHT, DANNY PRAGER, MATTHEW PRALL, CAROL PRATT, CAROLYN PRATT, CHRISTEEN PRATT, DANIEL PRATT, DAVID PRATT, DAVID PRATT, DAVID PRATT, DOUGLAS PRATT, GARY PRATT, STEPHEN PRATT, STEPHEN PRATT, WILLIAM PRATT, GARY PRATT JR, MITCHELL PRATTE, BRANDON PREECE, DAVID PREECE, DEBORAH PREECE, ORAL PREECE, REBECCA PREECE, RUTH PREECE, VICKI PREECE, VICTORIA PREECE, GRETCHEN PREISSER, EDGAR PRESSGROVE, CHRISTOPHER PRESSLER, ANA PRESTON, CHESTER PRESTON, DAVID PRESTON, DENISE PRESTON, LORETTA PRESTON, MACHELLE PRESTON, TERRY PRESTON, KATHARINE PRETTYMAN, AMY PRICE, CAMILLE PRICE, DEBORAH PRICE, DENNIS PRICE, DUSTIN PRICE, GAYLEN PRICE, GORDON PRICE, JENNIFER PRICE, JULIA PRICE, JULIE PRICE, KEN PRICE, LISA PRICE, PAULA PRICE, REGINALD PRICE, RICHARD PRICE, RODNEY PRICE, RONALD PRICE, RONALD PRICE, SARA PRICE, STEPHEN PRICE, STEVEN PRICE, STEVEN PRICE, STEVEN PRICE, TAMARA PRICE, TODD PRICE, TROY PRICE, WALLACE PRICE, CECILEE PRICE-HUISH, BART PRIEST, PAUL PRIETO, SCOTT PRIMAVERA, KAREN PRIMICH, CAROL PRINCE, DAVID PRINCE, JUDY PRINCE, LAURA PRINCE, ROBYN PRINCE, CAMDEN PRINGLE, JAMES PRINGLE, VALERIE PRISBREY, MIKE PRITCHARD, DEBORAH PRITT, LINDA PRIVETT, BARBARA PROBERT, CAROL PROBST, KAY PROBST, KYLE PROBST, ROBYN PROBST, JOHN PROCTER, ADAM PROCTOR, ANITA PROCTOR, LINNITA PROCTOR, PATRICIA PROCTOR, ROBERT PROCTOR, STACEY PROCTOR, STEVE PROCTOR, KRISTY PROESCH, THOMAS PROSCH, ALEX PROTASEVICH, NATALIE PROTASEVICH, FREDERICK PROVONCHA, STERLING PROVOST, RANDY PROVSTGAARD, ROBERT PROVSTGAARD, PAMELA PROWS, ALLAN PRYOR, JAMES PRYOR, JOHN PRYOR, JOHN PRYOR, KRISTINE PRYOR, PATRICIA PRYOR, EVA PRZYBYLA, CARRIE PUCKETT, STEPHANIE PUENTE, LEN PUGH, LISA PUGH, REBECCA PUGH, THOMAS PUGH, MAX PUGMIRE, MARGARET PUGSLEY, PHILIP PUGSLEY, GARY PULHAM, SUZANNE PULHAM, CONNIE PULLEY, LARRY PULLEY, MALENE PULLEY, CHARLES PULLMAN, ANDREA PULLOS, DAVID PULSIPHER, LON PURCELL, LYNN PURCELL, KRISTINA PURVANCE, FRANK PURVIS, GWYNN PURVIS, JAMES PUSATERI, JOHN PUSEY, SHAUNA PUSEY, TERESA PUSKEDRA, DAVID PUTMAN, MARJORIE PUTMAN, BOYD PUTNAM, STEPHEN PUTNAM, ROYCE PYETTE, KENNETH PYFER, DONALD PYKE, JAIMIE PYLE, KIRK PYLE, ELIAS PYLIDIS, MATTHEW PYNE, LEE ANN PYPER, MELISSA PYPER • **Q** • LOUIS QUACKENBUSH, DALTA QUAN, VINCE QUAN, SHARI QUARNBERG, OWEN QUASS, CHRISTOPHER QUATRALE, ROSEMARY QUATRALE, TINA QUAYLE, SUSAN QUENELLE, CARYN QUICK, JOHN QUICK, JOHN QUICK, VIKKI QUICK, COLLEEN QUIGLEY, GARY QUIGLEY, SCOTT QUIGLEY, TYLER QUIGLEY, REX QUILTER, SALLY QUILTER, DAVID QUINN, JENNIFER QUINN, PATRICK QUINN, ALLEN QUINTANA, JACK QUINTANA, RITA QUINTANA, KIMBERLY QUINTERO, ED QUIROGA, CARL QUIST • **R** • CLAUDIA RAAB, JONATHON RAAP, JACQUELINE RABB, DAVID RABIGER, SUSAN RABIGER, HARMONIE RACE, MARY ANN RACINE, LEANNE RACKHAM, ROWENE RADABAUGH, DEBRA RADACK, PAMELA RADANT, ANNE RADCLIFFE, HEATHER RADDATZ, MARK RADDATZ, ALAN RADDON, ALISA RADER, EDWARD RADFORD, GEOFFREY RADFORD, NATHAN RADFORD, RUSSELL RADFORD, WENDY RADKE, KAREN RADLEY, ALAN RADMALL, KRISTIE RADMALL, ANTON RADMAN, IVAN RADMAN, RENEE RADMAN, SHAWN RADMAN, COLLEEN RAFFERTY, RALPH RAFFIN, RISA RAGAN, AUDREY RAICHART, NICHOLAS RAICHART, SALVATORE RAIO, DAVID RAJAMAKI, BRUCE RALEIGH, KATHLEEN RALEIGH, LAURA RALLISON, AMBER RALLS, REBEKA RALPH, ARIA RALSTON, RICHARD RAMAKERS VAN PRAAG, AUDREY RAMBIKUR, JOSEPH RAMETTA, FRANK RAMIREZ, GEORGE RAMJOUE, BRENT RAMMELL, SCOTT RAMMELL, ANTHONY RAMON, BRIAN RAMOS, ROBERT RAMOS, MARCUS RAMPTON, JONATHAN RAMRAS, WILLIAM RAMSAY, NANCY RAMSDELL, DAWN RAMSEY, KELI RAMSEY, RHODA RAMSEY, RON RAMSING, MICHAEL RANAGAN, CLAYTON RAND, ELDON RANDALL, JEFFREY RANDALL, KAREN RANDALL, LORIE RANDALL, NILA RANDALL, TRICIA RANDALL, DAVID RANDLE, JULIE RANDLE, ELAINE RANDOLPH, RICHARD RANDOLPH, LISA RANDS, MARGARET RANGE, JOSEPH RANGEL, MILA RANOVIC, EILEEN RANSON, ISOBEL RAPAICH, ADAM RAPCZYNSKI, LIESE RAPOZO, WALLACE RAPOZO, PATRICIA RAPPLEYE, TROY RAPPLEYE, GARTH RASBAND, JOAN RASBAND, MICK RASBAND, KATHLEEN RASH, CAROLYN RASMUS, ALICIA RASMUSSEN, BOB RASMUSSEN, BRYAN RASMUSSEN, CHRIS RASMUSSEN, DANA RASMUSSEN, JAMES RASMUSSEN, JEANETTE RASMUSSEN, JOHN RASMUSSEN, KERRY RASMUSSEN, LEISHA RASMUSSEN, LONN RASMUSSEN, LONNI RASMUSSEN, LYNETTE RASMUSSEN, LYNN RASMUSSEN, MARK RASMUSSEN, MARY RASMUSSEN, MICHAEL RASMUSSEN, PETER RASMUSSEN, SCOTT RASMUSSEN, SHARON RASMUSSEN, TIMOTHY RASMUSSEN, WADE RASMUSSEN, KISMET RASMUSSON, MICHAEL RATCLIFFE, KIM RATUSHNIAK, BETH RATZLAFF, GRETCHEN RATZLAFF, BRIAN RAU, TIMOTHY RAUENBUSCH, GEORGE RAUSCH, SARI RAUSCHER, JOHNNY RAUZI, LISA RAVELO, EDWARD RAVIZZA, DANIEL T RAVSTEN, RONALD RAWLEY, BRETT RAWLINGS, LARISA RAWLINGS, TREVOR RAWLINGS, CAROL RAWLINS, JEANNE RAWLINS, MARK RAWLINS, RICHARD RAWLINS, ROBERT RAWLINS, RYAN RAWLINS, RICHARD RAWSON, ANNA RAY, BETTY RAY, CHET RAY, DAVID RAY, DAVID RAY, LEOLA RAY, LYNNAE RAY, MICHAEL RAY, TIMOTHY RAY, TOMMY RAY, REBECCA RAYMOND, JIM RAYNOR, ANDREY RAZUVAYEV, JONATHAN REA, TERRI REA, CHERIE READ, CINDY READ, JAMES READ, JILL READ, NANCY READ, SANDY READ, STEPHEN READ, AMY READING, AMY REAM, DAVID REAM, ROBERT REAM, CHRISTEL REAMES, NICOLE REAMES, MARTHA REAVIS, TIMOTHY REAVIS, KAELYN REBER, PAUL REBER, HAROLD REBSCHER, SUSAN REBSCHER, BONNIE RECKSIEK, PAMELA RECKSIEK, LISA RECTOR, DAVID REDD, ELIZABETH REDD, KATHY REDD, PATRICIA REDD, SARAH REDD, KARL REDEKOP, EILEEN REDELL, LOUISE REDFEARN, LISA REDFORD, AMANDA REDINGTON, BOYD REDINGTON II, MELINDA REDMOND, MICHAEL REDMOND, ANGELA REECE, BEVERLY REED, CONNIE REED, DAVID REED, DEBORAH REED, DIANE REED, GARY REED, GEORGEANA REED, GREG REED, HARRY REED, JANET REED, JERRY REED, MARGARET REED, NAYDEAN REED, PAUL REED, RONALD REED, SANDRA REED, STANLEY REED, BENJAMIN REEDER, JOYE REEDER, KAYE REEDER, OWEN REEDER, DAVID REES, DON REES, JASON REES, JERRY REES, ROSE REES, WENDI REES, BRUCE REESE, LUANNE REESE, JONATHAN REESER, KEVIN REEVE, MATTHEW REEVE, RICHARD REEVE, AMY REEVES, BRIAN REEVES, DANIEL REEVES, DEBBIE REEVES, ALISON REGAN, MARY REGAN, LANCE REGIS, MARY JO REHMER, RICHARD REHMER, LEROY REHRER, CATHY REICHMAN, AIMEE REID, ARTHUR REID, CRAIG REID, JEFF REID, KENNETH REID, KIM REID, MARCO REID, ROBERT REID, CHRISTOPHER REIFEL, CONSTANCE REILLY, RENEE REILLY, COLLEEN REIMSCHIISSEL, RICHARD REIMSCHUSSEL, DOUGLAS REINHART, JANET REINHART, BEVERLY REINHOLD, DIANA REISER, FRANCES REISER, REBECCA REISER, MARGARET REMBACZ, TREVOR REMBE, NORMA JEAN REMINGTON, JOEL REMKE, RONALD REMKES, JIMMIE REMLEY, TERESA REMSBERG, MARY REMY, SANDRA REMY, BARBARA RENCHER, ROY RENCHER, DORENE RENDON, JULIE RENEER, NICHOLAS RENFRO, SUZANNE RENFROE, CINDY RENKER, JACK RENNER, ROBERT

RENNER, CARL RENO, DICK RENSCH, MAUREEN RENSHAW, CHERYL RENTERIA, JOSE RENTERIA, JAY RENTMEISTER, ELEANOR REPETTO, TEAM 2002 REPS, DAREN RESCHKE, CLIFFORD REUSCH, PAUL REUTEMAN, FAITH REVELLI, JERRY REVELLI, CHARLENE REVOIR, ANGELA REX, LARISA REX, SAM REX, LARA REYMANN, ASA REYNOLDS, CHARLES REYNOLDS, JAMES REYNOLDS, JOANN REYNOLDS, JOHN REYNOLDS, KIMBERLY REYNOLDS, RYAN REYNOLDS, ELIZABETH RHIEN, AARON RHOADES, BRENDA RHODES, BRITTANY RHODES, CHARLES RHODES, LORETTA RHODES, RYAN RHODES, ERIC RIANDA, JEANETTE RICCI, ALICE RICE, AMY RICE, GREGORY RICE, JAY RICE, JOAN RICE, JOLYNN RICE, JOYCE RICE, KENNETH RICE, LARAINE RICE, LESLI RICE, ROBERT RICE, SALLY RICE, SANDRA RICE, SUSAN RICE, DARLENE RICH, DONALD RICH, DUSTIN RICH, EDWARD RICH, JACOB RICH, KAY RICH, LANCE JR RICH, RAYMOND RICH, SHELLEY RICH, ANN LEE RICHARDS, BRENT RICHARDS, BRENT RICHARDS, CATHY RICHARDS, CHARLES RICHARDS, CINDY RICHARDS, DALE RICHARDS, DAVID RICHARDS, DEBRA RICHARDS, FRANKLIN RICHARDS, GERALD RICHARDS, GERALDINE RICHARDS, JAMIE RICHARDS, JEFFREY RICHARDS, KARRIE RICHARDS, KATHRYN RICHARDS, LESLIE RICHARDS, LINDA RICHARDS, LORI RICHARDS, MARILEE RICHARDS, PHILIP RICHARDS, SAMUEL RICHARDS, SARAH RICHARDS, AARON RICHARDSON, ANDREA RICHARDSON, ANGELA RICHARDSON, ANNA RICHARDSON, BRIAN RICHARDSON, DONNA RICHARDSON, DOROTHY RICHARDSON, ERIC RICHARDSON, JAMES RICHARDSON, JENNIFER RICHARDSON, JERRY RICHARDSON, MELODY RICHARDSON, MIKE RICHARDSON, PEGGY RICHARDSON, RYAN RICHARDSON, SALLIE RICHARDSON, SILVANA RICHARDSON, STUART RICHARDSON, TAMARA RICHARDSON, KEN RICHENS, DEBRA RICHES, DON RICHES, VERNE RICHES, GEORGIA RICHEY, ALISON RICHINS, CHRISTOPHER RICHINS, JOHANNE RICHINS, JUDY RICHINS, KIMBERLEE RICHINS, LINDA RICHINS, MARTIE RICHINS, WALTER RICHMOND, CHRISTINA RICHTER, GLEN RICHTER, PATRICIA RICHTER, KARL RICKER, MARTINA RICKETSON, MICHAEL RICKETTS, VICKI RICKETTS, HOLLY RICKLEFS, ALYSIA RICKS, BENJAMIN RICKS, DENISE RICKS, MARY RICKS, MAUREEN RICKS, PAUL RICKS, TIMOTHY RICO, DEANE RICORD, JAMES RIDD, ETHAN RIDDLE, TARA RIDDLE, JAMES RIDENOUR, SANDRA RIDEOUT, GRETCHEN RIDER, KAREN RIDGE, NATHAN RIDGE, MARY RIDGES, ALLYSON RIDING, BEN RIDING, MICHAEL RIDING, REED RIDING, ROBERT RIDING, WALLACE RIDLEY, CAROLE RIEDEL, ADAM RIEDY, BRIAN RIEKE, YVONNE RIEMERSMA, AMY RIES, DIANNE RIES, VIRGINIA RIES, RUDOLF RIET, SONJA RIFFLE, MAURY RIGANTO, MARZIO RIGAZZI, ALAN RIGBY, BECKY RIGBY, BRADLEY RIGBY, DEBRA RIGBY, KRISTIN RIGBY, ALAN RIGDON, CHRISTINE RIGGLE, SHARON RIGGS, CARL RIGHTER, HELEN RIGHTER, CHRISTOPHER RILEY, DEANNE RILEY, EMILEE RILEY, M BRANDON RILEY, MICHAEL RILEY, PETER RILEY, REBECCA RILEY, TIMOTHY RILEY, RENEE RILEY-CHRISTENSEN, SARIT RIMAL, RITA RIMINGTON, GERALD RINALDI, PEDRO RINCON, JILL RINGEL, BENJAMIN RINGGER, JARED RINGGER, RYAN RINGGER, TODD RINN, NOEL RIOS, RANDALL RIPPLINGER, CRAIG RIRIE, KARI RIRIE, ALBERT RISCH, JOHN RISLEY, SCOTT RISSMANN, STEPHEN RITCHEY, BRENT RITCHIE, BRUCE RITCHIE, DEE RITCHIE, MARGARET RITCHIE, SHERI RITCHIE, WELTON RITCHIE, ELIZABETH RITER, SHANNON RITZMAN, RICHARD RIVARD, JAIR RIVERA, FERNANDO RIVERO, JENNIFER RIVERS, JULIE RIVERS, DEBRA RIX, KARIN RIXON, JONATHAN RIZZO, DENISE ROACH, JAMES ROACH, JANE ROACH, LORI ROACH, ROBERT ROACH, ROBERT ROANE, KAREN ROBARDS, ANN ROBBINS, ARTHUR ROBBINS, JAN ROBBINS, JEAN ROBBINS, KERSTEN ROBBINS, KIRSTIN ROBBINS, LEWIS ROBBINS, MICHELLE ROBBINS, PETER ROBBINS, SUSAN ROBBINS, LIZETTE ROBERSON, SARA ROBERT, CAMI ROBERTS, CLESTA ROBERTS, DENNIS ROBERTS, DIANNE ROBERTS, DONNA ROBERTS, EUGENE ROBERTS, GARY ROBERTS, JAN ROBERTS, JANA ROBERTS, JEFFREY ROBERTS, JERRY ROBERTS, JILL ROBERTS, JIM ROBERTS, JOHN ROBERTS, JUDITH ROBERTS, KARLA ROBERTS, KATIE ROBERTS, KIM ROBERTS, KYLE ROBERTS, MIKE ROBERTS, MIKE ROBERTS, NAVINE ROBERTS, PATRICIA ROBERTS, PATRICIA ROBERTS, RAYMOND ROBERTS, ROBYN ROBERTS, ROSE ROBERTS, STANLEY ROBERTS, THOMAS ROBERTS, TRACI ROBERTS, TRACY ROBERTS, TREVOR ROBERTS, VERONICA ROBERTS, WILLIAM ROBERTS, ALAN ROBERTSON, ANNETTE ROBERTSON, BRIGITA ROBERTSON, CHRISTINE ROBERTSON, COLETTE ROBERTSON, DAVID ROBERTSON, ERIC ROBERTSON, JAMES ROBERTSON, KEVIN ROBERTSON, MATT ROBERTSON, SARA ROBERTSON, TRACIE ROBERTSON, MARK ROBIE, VIRGINIA ROBIE, DEBORA ROBINETTE, HALCYON ROBINS, JENNIFER ROBINS, KENDALL ROBINS, MARC ROBINS, PHYLLIS ROBINS, RACHEL ROBINS, BRENT ROBINSON, BRENT ROBINSON, BROOK ROBINSON, DOUGLAS ROBINSON, ERICA ROBINSON, GARY ROBINSON, GARY ROBINSON, GAYLE ROBINSON, GEORGE ROBINSON, GERALD ROBINSON, GRANT ROBINSON, JAMES ROBINSON, JEANETTE ROBINSON, JILLIAN ROBINSON, JOHN ROBINSON, JOHN W ROBINSON, JOLEEN ROBINSON, JULIANN ROBINSON, KATIE ROBINSON, LAURA ROBINSON, LENNIE ROBINSON, LORRAINE ROBINSON, MICHAEL ROBINSON, PAUL ROBINSON, RANDY ROBINSON, RICHARD ROBINSON, SHAWN ROBINSON, TIMOTHY ROBINSON, WALTER ROBINSON, CONNIE ROBISON, LEE ROBISON, ROSA ROBLES, VINCENT ROCCO, TERRI ROCHE, THOMAS ROCK, TOM ROCK, DONALD ROCKHOLD, CAROL ROCKWELL, GHISLAINE ROCKWOOD, MICHAEL ROCKWOOD, LANITA RODABOUGH, DELYNN RODEBACK, LOUISE RODEBUSH, SHERRI RODERICK, DALE RODGERS, THOMAS RODGERS, MARK RODMAN, AARON RODRIGUEZ, ALEX RODRIGUEZ, ALFREDO RODRIGUEZ, FLORENCIO RODRIGUEZ, JOHN RODRIGUEZ, JONATHAN RODRIGUEZ, LOURDES RODRIGUEZ COOKE, ANDREA ROESBERRY, MARK ROESBERRY, CHRISTINE ROESCH, AARON ROGERS, BRYCE ROGERS, DANIEL ROGERS, DAVID ROGERS, DAWN ROGERS, DON ROGERS, EARL ROGERS, JESSICA ROGERS, JULIA ROGERS, LARRY ROGERS, MARLA ROGERS, MATTHEW ROGERS, ROBERT ROGERS, ROBERT ROGERS, SETH ROGERS, SUSAN ROGERS, TRENT ROGERS, WENDY ROGERS, JAMES ROGERS III, JAMES ROGERSON, RYAN ROGERSON, WILLIAM ROGERSON, PHYLLIS ROGLER, RUSSELL ROGLER, PHILIP ROGOSHESKE, BARON ROHBOCK, MARK ROHDE, WINNIE ROHDE, DARIN ROHEAD, TRELL ROHOVIT, TERESA ROHR, MATT ROHRER, TERRIE ROJAS, JAN ROKICH, JANE ROLEN, BOB ROLLINS, DANIEL ROLLINS, DAVID ROLLINS, JERI ROLLINS, LESLIE ROLLINS, MARCIA ROLLINS, NEWELL ROLLINS, JEANNIE ROLLO, ALEXANDRA ROLSTON, THOMAS ROMAK, ERIC ROMAN, DEBORAH ROMANO, GIORGIA ROMANO, RICHARD ROMANO, AMY ROMANOWSKI, JEREMYAH ROMER, ROBIN ROMER, LOUIS ROMERO, ROBERT ROMERO, VICKIE ROMERO, KENNETH ROMERO JR, TRENT ROMIJN, CLAIRE ROMNEY, KEITH ROMNEY, PAUL ROMNEY, FRANCES ROMNEY-DARR, PAMELA ROMNEY-HELD, BARRY ROMOSER, KATIE ROMRELL, NATALIE ROMRELL, DAVID RONA, MICHAEL RONAN, TRACY RONAN, NANCY ROOK, MARK ROONEY, BRENT ROPELATO, BRENT ROPER, KIM ROPER, SHARILEE ROPER, SHERMAN ROQUIERO, LINDA ROSCOE, CHRISTY ROSE, CONNIE ROSE, CYNTHIA ROSE, IVA ROSE, JAMIE ROSE, JESSIANNA ROSE, JUDITH ROSE, KATHLEEN ROSE, KAY ROSE, ROBERT F. ROSE, THOMAS ROSE, JOHN ROSEN, NANCY ROSEN, KIRSTIE ROSENFIELD, MICAH ROSENFIELD, CRISS ROSENLOF, LEANN ROSENLOF, VERLA ROSEQUIST, CRAIG ROSEVEAR, ELIZABETH ROSEVEAR, KAREN ROSEVEAR, KATHLEEN ROSIER, RYAN ROSIER, DAVID ROSKELLEY, FRANK ROSKELLEY, CHRIS ROSQVIST, VERONICA ROSQVIST, BOB ROSS, CANDICE ROSS, CAROL ROSS, CICI ROSS, DAVID ROSS, DOUGLAS ROSS, JANET ROSS, JOAN ROSS, KAREN ROSS, KATHRYN ROSS, LINDA ROSS, MICHAEL ROSS, PAUL ROSS, STEPHEN ROSS, SYLVIA ROSS, TANYA ROSS, TIM ROSS, TOM ROSS, VICKI ROSS, HAROLD ROSSBERG, ROBERT ROSSBERG, MICHAEL ROSSER, EMANUELE ROSSETTI, KEVAN ROSSETTI, MICHAEL ROSSETTI, GEORGE ROSSI, HUGO ROSSI, LOUIS ROSSI, KIMBERLY ROSSUM, JOHN ROSSWOG, KARL ROSTRON, LYNN ROSVALL, MONICA ROTERMUND, TIMOTHY ROTERT, DANIEL ROTH, DAVE ROTH, GREG ROTH, JIM ROTH, SCOTT ROTH, JEFFREY ROTHCHILD, TISHA ROTHDEUTSCH, EDGAR ROTHE, KATHY ROTHE, TINA ROTHE, GLEN ROTHELL, PATRICIA ROTHHAAR, JANET ROTHMAN, WILLIAM ROTHROCK, WILLIAM ROTTON, JOSEPH ROTUNDO, JEFFREY ROTZ, JULIE ROUGHTON, AMANDA ROUNDS, BRADLEY ROUNDS, PEGGY ROUNDS, ANTONE ROUNDY, BECKY ROUNDY, LAINA ROUNDY, RYAN ROUNDY, THOR ROUNDY, KEITH ROUNKLES, JEFF ROUSE, MATTHEW ROUSH, MARTA ROVIRA, BILLY ROWE, SHON ROWE, MURIEL ROWELL, LINZY ROWETT, KATHY LEE ROWLAND, BRANDON ROWLEY, BRUCE ROWLEY, DAROLD ROWLEY, EVAN ROWLEY, KATHRYN ROWLEY, DAVID ROY, JOHN ROY, KENDALL ROY, CAROL ROYAL, SHERRI ROYAL, ELIZABETH ROYALL, DIANE ROYCE, LESLIE ROYE, CHAD ROYLANCE, KENNETH ROYLANCE, SUSAN ROYLANCE, THOMAS ROYLANCE, REBECCA RUBBELKE, RUSSELL RUBERG, RYAN RUBERG, MARK RUBEY, CORALYN RUBILLOS, MICHAEL RUBIN, IRA RUBINFELD, CARLA RUBINGH, GUILLERMO RUBIO, SERGIO RUBIO, HANS RUBNER, BEVERLY RUDD, ERIC RUDD, JOAN RUDD, MARLON RUDD, STEPHANIE RUDD, LUANN RUDELICH, ADRIENNE RUDERMAN, RAMONA RUDERT, JAMES RUDNICKI, KRISTYNE RUDOLPH, KENNETH RUE, CHARLES RUEBELMANN, REINHOLD RUEGNER, ROMANA RUEMMELE, CECILEE RUESCH, CRYSTAL RUESCH, MARIE RUESCH, MARY RUFF, SHIRLEY RUFFNER, RALPH RUFFOLO, WENDY RUFI, ROBERT RUGG, JOHN RUIZ, KATHRYN RUIZ, KAREN RULE, JOAN RUMP, NATE RUMP, NEDRA RUMSEY, MARY RUNGE, WENDY RUPP, CHRISTY RUSCH, SHANNON RUSCH, SHEILA RUSCH, DIANE RUSCHKE, SHELBY RUSH, ERIN RUSHFORTH, MICHAEL RUSHFORTH, BLAINE RUSHTON, BRUCE RUSHTON, TODD RUSHTON, WENDY RUSIN, RN BSN, JENNIFER RUSK, BONNIE RUSKAUFF, BROOKE RUSSELL, BRUCE RUSSELL, ERIC RUSSELL, GIN RUSSELL, KARI RUSSELL, RONALD RUSSELL, SCOTT RUSSELL, SPENCER RUSSELL, TODD RUSSELL, TODD RUSSELL, VICKI RUSSELL, WAYNE RUSSELL, TAMMI RUSSELL-MORI, ANTHONY RUSSI, JOHN RUSSO, JUSTIN RUSSO, PAMELA RUSSO, CORINNE RUSSON, LAURA RUSSON, JEFFREY RUST, KEITH RUST, JUDY RUSTER, TOM RUSTER, DIANA RUTH, VICKY RUTLEDGE, CAROL RYAN, JAMES RYAN, PATTY RYAN, ROBERT RYAN, WILLIAM RYAN, JACK RYDER, PATRICIA RYLAND, SUSAN RYPIEN, REBECCA RYSER, SUSAN RYSER, IRENA RYSKOVA, MI-KYOUNG RYU, KIYOSHI RYUJIN, KRISTINE RYVER, PIOTR RZEPECKI, PAULA RZOMP • **S** • AL SAAB, SCOTT SABEY, JEREMY SABIN, MICHAEL SABIN, SHARON SABIN, EDWARD SACCO, GRACE SACCO, CHERYL SACHSE, TOM SACHSE, ELIZABETH SACKEWITZ, TAMI SACKS, JEFFERY SADDLER, MARGUERITE SADLER, STEPHEN SADLER, JOSEPH SADOSKI, MARGOT SADOWSKI, JAN SAEED, KAREN SAENGER, MARK SAENGER, ROBIN SAEVA, JOHN SAEZ, SCOT SAFFORD, TERI SAGER, SABINA SAIB, PATRICIA SAINSBURY, FUMIO SAITO, KARL SAKAEDA, MOJDEH SAKAKI, YUKI SAKUMA, JOHNNY SALAS, TERESA SALAS, RICHARD SALAZAR, JOAN SALDIVAR, FRANK SALIMENO, DARLA SALIN, JEANA SALINAS, CLAUDE SALISBURY, PAUL SALISBURY, RICHARD SALLSTROM, CORY SALMELA, JAMES SALMON, JODIE SALMON, KAREN SALMON, MYRA SALMON, RIIKKA SALOKANNEL, MARTHA SAMMOND, ALAXIJANDERA SAMPSON, BONNIE SAMPSON, ERIC SAMPSON, JUDITH SAMPSON, KRISTINE SAMPSON, RALPH SAMPSON, JAMES SAMUELS, KIM SAMUELSON, LAURA SAMUELSON, REGINA SAMUELSON, WAYNE SAMUELSON, DONALD SANBORN, FLORENCE SANBORN, JEFFERY SANBORN, ALICIA SANCHEZ, AMY SANCHEZ, CAROL SANCHEZ, SARAH SANCHEZ, SHANNAN SANCHEZ, STEPHEN SANDALL, ELLEN SANDBERG, HEATHER SANDBERG, HEATHER SANDBERG, KELLY SANDBERG, KIMBERLEY SANDBERG, SARAH SANDBERG, CAROL SANDERS, DARRELL SANDERS, FLOYD SANDERS, PAMELA SANDERS, REV. JOANNE SANDERS, RICHARD SANDERS, SUSAN SANDERS, MICHAEL SANDERSON, PATTIE SANDERSON, TRANNIE SANDERSON, WAYNE SANDERSON, LINDA SANDIFUR, JAMES SANDS, JUDITH SANDSTROM, DALE SANDUSKY, SANDRA SANFACON, DEBBIE SANICH, JOHN SANMIGUEL, BARRY SANNS, DIANNE SANO, SALLY SANSOM, SIU LIN SANTEE, WELSTER SANTOS, ANNA SAPP, ED SAPPINGTON, ANTHONY SARA, RUTH SARANEN, ANDREW SARGENT, HELEN SARGENT, JAN SARGENT, JULIE SARGENT, BOGUSLAW SARNECKI, KEN SARNOWSKI, TRUDY SARTOR, VALERI SASE, JARED SASSER, HEATHER SATHER, LEE SATHER, NELS SATHER, NORMAN SATHER, WENDY SATHER, COURTNEY SATHER-PIROUZNIA, DOUGLAS SATO, KEVIN SATO, NAOMI SATTELBERG, JEAN SAUBERT, DEBRA SAUER, ANTHONY SAUNDERS, KRISTEN SAUNDERS, KYLE SAUNDERS, LYNETTE SAUNDERS, RICK SAUNDERS, TOM SAUNDERS, ROBERT SAURIN, JUDY SAVAGE, LAURETTE SAVAGE-WING, MILOVAN SAVIC, GEORGIA SAVIERS, PHILIP SAVIGNANO, RONALD SAWDEY, ALLISON SAWYER, JULIE SAWYER, RALPH SAWYER, SHELLY SAWYER, CANDICE SAXEY, SCOTT SAXTON, DALE SAYAMA, LINDA SAYRE, WILLIAM SAYRE, GALEN SAYWARD, ROSE MAREE SAZESH, ROSEMARY SCALES, ROEJEAN SCARBROUGH, CRAIG SCHAAF, MANDY SCHAAF, RUBEN SCHAAF, VICKIE SCHAAF, MARK SCHAB, KENNETH SCHADE, KENNETH SCHAECHER, CHESTER SCHAEFER, JAMES SCHAEFER, DAVID SCHAEFERMEYER, LAURA SCHAEFFER, MARK SCHAERRER, STEPHANIE SCHAERRER, TODD SCHAFFLER, LESLIE SCHAG, MELISSA SCHAITBERGER, JAMES SCHALBRACK, CAROLYN SCHARMAN, DANA SCHARMANN, STEVE SCHARMANN, RODNEY SCHEIDECKER, BERTIE SCHEIDELL, MARTIN SCHEIER, CHARLES SCHELL, MARLENA SCHERER, LUCINDA SCHERTING, JAMES SCHERZINGER, MICHAEL SCHEULLER, JANET SCHIAGER, ALPHONSO SCHIAVONE, AIMEE SCHICK, CAROL SCHICK-LYDA, SCOTT SCHIESSWOHL, BARBARA SCHIEVING, ROLAND SCHIFFLER, JESSICA SCHIFFMAN, LYNN SCHIFFMAN, BARBARA SCHILL, MATT SCHILLER, NANCY SCHILLING, SANDRA SCHIRACK-NOSACK, SAM SCHLIEDER, MICHAEL SCHLIER, LISA SCHLOTTMANN, SANDRA SCHLUETER, ROBERT SCHMAD, WAYNE SCHMAD, PATRICIA SCHMAEDEKE, CHARLES SCHMALZ, JOANN SCHMALZ, WILMA SCHMERER, LAWRENCE SCHMIDA, ERWIN SCHMIDT, HERTA SCHMIDT, JEFFREY SCHMIDT, JIM SCHMIDT, KATHLEEN SCHMIDT, LINDA SCHMIDT, SHANNON SCHMIDT, PAUL SCHMIECHEN, CHARLES SCHMITT, CHARLES SCHMITT, KATHY SCHMITZ, JESSICA SCHMUCKER, SIMONE SCHMUDDE, PATRICIA SCHMUHL, DENISE SCHMUTZ, KEN SCHMUTZ, WILLIAM SCHMUTZ, IVY SCHNABEL, LORENA SCHNEBLY, ANN SCHNEIDER, DANIEL SCHNEIDER, EDWIN SCHNEIDER, EVA SCHNEIDER, KATE SCHNEIDER, MARILEE SCHNEIDER, MICHAEL SCHNEIDER, PATRICIA SCHNEIDER, RICHARD SCHNEIDER, RUSSELL SCHNEIDER, WILLIAM SCHNEIDER, SHAWNA SCHNURR, CHRISTINE SCHOCKER, JACK SCHOENFELD, MARY LEE SCHOENFELD, JANICE SCHOFIELD, SHAUN SCHOFIELD, MARY BETH SCHOLAND, EDWIN SCHOLL, JAMES SCHOLL, TODD SCHOLL, TRACY SCHOLL, BROOKE SCHOLZ, DIANE SCHONE, WILLIAM SCHONE, JESICA SCHOOLEY, ASHLIE SCHOONMAKER, TRENT SCHOONMAKER, JOSEPH SCHOONOVER, MICHAEL SCHOUTEN, RYAN SCHOUTEN, ROBERT SCHOVAERS, SCOTT SCHOVAERS, BRETT SCHOW, LAWRENCE SCHOW, CONNIE SCHOWENGERDT, SHERYL SCHOWENGERDT, JAMES SCHRADER, JONI SCHRAGE, CHRISTINE SCHRAMM, KATHRYN SCHRAMM, STEPHEN SCHRANK, ANN SCHRECK, BENJAMIN SCHREITER, JENNIFER SCHREITER, VERONICA SCHRENK, VICKI SCHRODER, BRUCE SCHROEDER, CYNTHIA SCHROEDER, MARY LOU SCHROEDER, ROGER SCHROEDER, STEPHEN SCHROEDER, CRISTIN SCHROEFFEL, JARED SCHRUM, BRIGITA SCHRUMPF, PETER SCHRUMPF, PHILIP SCHRUMPF, JERI SCHRYVER, HEIDI SCHUBERT, ALAN SCHUELER, BRONWYN SCHUETZE, DEAN SCHULMAN, ROBERT SCHULTE, BRIGITTE SCHULTZ, CARL SCHULTZ, CHARLES SCHULTZ, ERIC SCHULTZ, JEANETTE SCHULTZ, JOHN SCHULTZ, SUSAN SCHULTZ, CATHY SCHULZ, LIBBY SCHULZ, THOMAS SCHULZ, MARTY SCHUMACHER, RICK SCHUURMAN, THOMAS D SCHWALL, BRANDY SCHWARTZ, DANIEL SCHWARTZ, KENNETH SCHWARTZ, RUSSELL SCHWARTZ, SANDI SCHWARTZ, RENE SCHWARTZMAN, DEBORAH SCHWARZ, LIS SCHWARZ, WALTER SCHWARZ, CARL SCHWARZER, CLARA SCHWOBE, KRISTEN SCOFIELD, ALICIA SCOLERI, LORI SCOMA, STEPHANIE SCORESBY, AARON SCOTT, ADAM SCOTT, ADENE SCOTT, AUSTIN SCOTT, BRAD SCOTT, BRADLEY SCOTT, BRIANNA SCOTT, BRYAN SCOTT, DANIEL SCOTT, DAVID SCOTT, DIANA SCOTT, DIANE SCOTT, DONALD SCOTT, DOUGLAS SCOTT, JANET SCOTT, JEAN SCOTT, JEFFREY SCOTT, JOHN SCOTT, KENNETH SCOTT, KEVIN SCOTT, LAUREN SCOTT, LONNIE SCOTT, MARTHA SCOTT, MINDY SCOTT, PATRICIA SCOTT, PATRICIA SCOTT, PEGGY SCOTT, RAYNA SCOTT, RICHARD SCOTT, ROBERT SCOTT, RUSSELL SCOTT, SANI SCOTT, SETH SCOTT, SHANDRA SCOTT, SHELLEY SCOTT, STACIA SCOTT, VICTORIA SCOTT, WARREN SCOTT, KIM SCOTT POZIL, AMARIA SCOVIL, MARK SCOVILLE, RYAN SCOVILLE, ANNA SCOW, JANET SCOW, JOE SCRIBNER, KATHRYN SCRIBNER, ROBIN SCRIBNER, TOM SCRIBNER, DERRICK SCRIVEN, JESSE SCROGGINS, LLOYD SCROGGINS, LINDA SCROWTHER, PHILIP SCUTTS, JOSEPH SEAL, EMIL SEAMAN, JOHN SEAMAN, MARY SEAMAN, BRIAN SEAMONS, GAROLD SEAMONS, JOHN SEAMONS, MARGO SEAMONS, MATTHEW SEAMONS, MICHELLE SEAMONS, NANCY SEAMONS, AMY SEARLE, BRENDA SEARLE, GARY SEARLE, GORDON SEARLE, ROBERT SEARLE, CRAIG SEARLS, GALE SEARS, NOLA SEARS, GINA SEASTRAND, DONALD SEATON, RICHELLE SEAWRIGHT, SANDRA SEBBANE, KALYN SECRETAN, LON SECRIST, RAUL SEDAS, JUDY SEDDON, GLEN SEDGWICK, JUDY SEDLACEK, EDWARD SEED, ANTHONY SEEGER, BROCK SEELEY, DOYLE SEELEY, EUGENE SEELEY, RYAN SEELEY, CAROL SEELY, GLEN SEELY, ALBIN SEETHALER, SUSAN SEGATORE, JEANETTE SEGO, PATRICIA SEGUIN, ROBIN SEGUIN, SUSAN SEGUIN, ANNELI SEGURA, JARED SEIBERT, GREG SEIBOLD, TERAP SEID, CYNTHIA SEIDEL, GRACE SEIDLITZ, LEON SEIFERT, RETO SEILER, SPRING SEILER, TAMERA SEILER, HATSUHO SEINO, RUDOLF SEIPEL, SUSAN SEKERET, DRAKE SELF, SHAUNA SELF, LESLIE SELIN, TROY SELK, SCOTT SELLARS, CLAIR SELLEY, VLADIMIR SENIC', TIM SENIOR, MARYANN SENN, PENNY SENRICK, KAREN SEO, LOUIS SEPPI, KATHLEEN SERAFINI, ARA SERJOIE, FRANCO SERRAGLIO, STEPHANIE SERVOSS, RICHARD SESEK, ANNA SESSIONS, DEAN SESSIONS, DEBORA SESSIONS, JANET SESSIONS, LOUISE SESSIONS, MARY LOU SESSIONS, MARY SETTLE, JUDITH SEVCIK, SARAH SEVERINSEN, JAMES SEVERSON, THOMAS SEVY, THOM SEWELL, KELLY SEYMOUR, CAROL SHACKELFORD, JASON SHAFER, JIM SHAFER, LAURA SHAFER, ROBERT SHAFER, ALAN SHAFFER, ALLAN SHAFFER, BRENT SHAFFER, ISABELLA SHAFFER, KARLA SHAFFER, LETA SHAFFER, MARY SHAFFER, SCOTT SHAFFER, SUSIE SHAFT, ROBERT SHAFTER, RETHA SHAIL-SHIRES, MARGE SHAKESPEARE, STEVE SHAKESPEARE, DAVID SHALLENBERGER, IVETA SHALNA, MARYPAT SHANDOR, CRAIG SHANE, ROBERT SHANE, JANET SHANER, JOHN SHANK, LORETTA SHANK, VERLE SHANK, VLADIMIR SHAPOVALOV, ALAN SHARP, CHARLES SHARP, ELIZABETH SHARP, GREG SHARP, LEO SHARP, LISA SHARP, NATHAN SHARP, RACHAEL SHARP, LYNETTE SHARPE, DAVID SHASKEY MD, DOUGLAS SHATTUCK, AMANDA SHAW, CORI SHAW, JOANNE SHAW, JOHNNY SHAW, JUDY SHAW, MICHELLE SHAW, PAUL SHAW, REBECCA SHAW, RONALD SHAW, SANDRA SHAW, SHELLEY SHAW, STANFORD SHAW, TRACY SHAY, VANESSA SHEA, GERALD SHEAR, DAVID SHEARER, CAROL SHEEHAN, FRANK SHEEHAN, INA SHEEHAN, PAMELA SHEELER, JOHN SHEETS, BLAKE SHEFFIELD, RACHAEL SHEFFIELD, SHERRY SHEFFIELD, DAVE SHEFLEY, ROBERT SHEGRUD, ALLYSON SHELBOURNE, HENRY SHELDON, DAVID SHELL, DENNIS SHELL, GINGER SHELL, BRYCE SHELLEY, DAVID SHELLEY, GUY SHELLEY, KRISTEN SHELLEY, MELISSA SHELLEY, RAEANN SHELLEY, ROBERT SHELLEY, DEAN SHELTON, DEBORAH SHELTON, RICHARD SHELTON, TRACI SHEPARD, BRADLEY SHEPHERD, DENISE SHEPHERD, JOHNNY SHEPHERD, KAREN SHEPHERD, LARRY SHEPHERD, MICHAEL SHEPHERD, PAUL SHEPHERD, BRAD SHEPPARD, SALLY SHEPPARD, LARAYE SHERIDAN, YVONNE SHERIDAN, CRAIG SHERMAN, DONALD SHERNER, SCOTT SHERNER, ALICE SHERRY, CLAUDE SHERRY, ELIZABETH SHERRY, JODEE SHERWOOD, JOHN SHERWOOD, STEPHEN SHERWOOD, LESTER SHEWMAKE, WALTER SHEWMAKE, DIANE SHEYA, RICHARD SHEYA, ALMA SHIELDS, JOANN SHIELDS, MARILYN SHIELDS, TERRY SHIELDS, WILLIAM SHIELDS, REBECCA SHIM, JOSEPH SHIMANEK, DAVID SHIMKUS, KATHLEENE SHINAUT, KEN SHINAUT, LINDA SHINGLETON, PAUL SHINGLETON, VLADIMIR SHNAYDERMAN, SUSAN SHOBE, NANCY SHOCKLEY, ALBERTA SHOOK, NANCY SHORE, ALLEN SHORT, KENNETH SHORT, NANCY SHOSTED, GENEVA SHOWALTER, RODNEY SHOWALTER, GLENDA SHRADER, ROBERT SHRADER, CRYSTAL SHUM, LYNNETTE SHUMAN, CLAYTON SHUMWAY, CYNTHIA SHUMWAY, DEBRA SHUMWAY, DIANE SHUMWAY, JEFF SHUMWAY, ROGER SHUMWAY, GORDON SHUPE, JAMES SHUPE, JAYNE SHUPE, JOHN SHUPE, SHERYLL SHUPE, ELAINE SHURTLEFF, CHRISTOPHER SIAVRAKAS, EVELYN SIBBERNSEN, FOREST SICKLES, STEVEN SIEBACH, RUDY SIEBENHAAR, MIKE SIEBER, JEANNE SIEBERT, UWE SIEBKE, ADRIENNE SIEFERT, KELLEY SIEFERT, LYNNE SIEFERT, MARK SIEFERT, SCOTT SIEFERT, PHILLIP SIEVERS, GINNY SIEWERT, SARAH SIFERS, OLGA SIGGINS, TERRY SIGLE, THROSTUR SIGURPSSON, SANDRA SIITER, DAVID SIKICH, ERIN SIKORA, KRISTON SIKORA, KARI SIKORSKI, DAVID SILL, ROSA SILLITO, DEBRA SILLS, ASHLEY SILVA, HEATHER SILVA, JENNIFER SILVA, KARIN SILVA, LARRY SILVER, LYNN SILVER, VIRGINIA SILVER, CAROL SILVERMAN, JOHN SILVERMAN, GIFFORD SILVERSMITH, MIMI SILVERSTEIN, LISA SIM, CREST SIMEON, JOHN SIMKINS, ANN SIMMONS, BRENT SIMMONS, CURT SIMMONS, CURTIS SIMMONS, JENNIFER SIMMONS, JIM SIMMONS, JULIA SIMMONS, LYNETTE SIMMONS, MARIANNE SIMMONS, ROBERT SIMMONS, STEPHEN SIMMONS, ZULENE SIMMONS, MARGARET SIMMONS-CROSS, CHAD SIMON, JULIE SIMONDS, YASMEN SIMONIAN, MARTIN SIMONICH, BRADFORD SIMONS, DANNY SIMONS, ELLA SIMONS, JEROLD SIMONS, JERRY SIMONS, KELSI SIMONS, MARCI SIMONS, SALLY SIMONS, SCOTT SIMONS, STEPHEN SIMONS, TED SIMONS, TYLER SIMONS, ALICE SIMONSEN, DEBRA SIMONSEN, DIXIE SIMONSEN, DON SIMONSEN, HEATHER SIMONSEN, ROBERT SIMONSEN, RON SIMONSEN, SOREN SIMONSEN, INGRID SIMONSON, ANNA SIMPSON, BRETT SIMPSON, DEBBIE SIMPSON, JAMES SIMPSON, JESSICA SIMPSON, MARVEN SIMPSON, MICHAEL SIMPSON, SCOTT SIMPSON, SHELLIE SIMPSON, WILLIAM SIMPSON, ASHLEY SIMS, NOLA SIMS, PAUL SIMS, ANNA SIMS-JONES, IZABELLA SINCA, KIMBERLY SINCAVAGE, ALEXIS SINCLAIR, CHANTE' SINCLAIR, ENOCH SINCLAIR, MARGEAN SINCLAIR, PATRICK SINCLAIR, TONI SINCLAIR, DONNA SINDORF, TEJ SINGH, GRANT SINGLETON, JACQUELINE SINNAEVE, THOMAS SINNAEVE, ARLENE SION, JAMES SIPHERD, CLARENCE SISLER, GLEN SITEMAN, PAMELA SITES, MICHAEL SITKO, KATHLEEN SITTNER, MICHAEL SIZEMORE, JILL SJOBLOM, CHRIS SKAARUP, INGER SKARNAS, JOSTEIN SKATVOLD, LORIE SKEEM, AUDREY SKEEN, DEETT SKEEN, ELIZABETH SKEEN, JENNIFER SKEEN, KAREN SKEEN, RANDALL SKEEN, STEVE SKIDMORE, WILLIAM SKIDMORE, JAMIE SKILLERN, JAMES SKILLINGS, CHARLES SKINNER, COURTNEY SKINNER, WILLIAM SKINNER, MIKHAIL SKLIAR, DAVIN SKOLLINGSBERG, JUNE SKOLLINGSBERG, DANIEL SKOUSEN, PATRICIA SKOUSEN, ROBERT SKOW, SALLY SKROBISZEWSKI, VICTORIA SKURIDINA, EUGENE SKUTACK, RICHARD SLABINSKI, STACY SLACK, CHRIS SLADE, CHRISTOPHER SLADE, JEANNE SLADE, KENT SLADE, LINDA SLADE, JULANNE SLAMA, ALBERT SLANEY, LYNDA SLATER, MICHAEL SLATER, RONDA SLATER, WILLIAM SLAUGHTER, EDWARD SLAWSON, DIXIE SLEEMAN, ARTHUR SLEEPER, SANDRA SLEEPER, MARGARET SLEIGHT, MARK SLETTA, MARK SLETTEN, SHELLY SLEVE, KEVIN SLIDER, GLEN SLIGHT, JENNIFER SLINGERLAND, DOMINIQUE SLOAN, DOUGLAS SLOAN, KEVIN SLOAN, PERRY SLOAN, ROBERT SLOAN, JONATHAN SLOTHOWER, LEO SLOWIKOWSKI, MICHELLE SLUSHER, ROBERT SLY, JEROME SMALL, MARGARET SMALL, MELISSA SMALL, EMILY SMALLEY, MOSIAH SMALLEY, SCOTT SMALLEY, WENDY SMALLEY, CHRIS SMALLWOOD, JIL SMALLWOOD, ALAN SMART, EDIE SMART, ERIC SMART, HEATHER SMART, JAMES SMART, MICHAEL SMART, PAUL SMART, ROSEMARY SMART, SHERYL SMART, KEITH SMEDBERG, ELIZABETH SMEDLEY, GEORGE SMEDLEY, STEVE SMEDLEY, VARCI SMEDLEY, URSULA SMERALDO, DARLA SMETHURST, HELEN SMILEY, ADRIEN SMITH, ALAN SMITH, ALAN SMITH, ALICE SMITH, AMANDA SMITH, AMBER SMITH, AMY SMITH, ANDRE SMITH, ANDREW SMITH, ANNIE SMITH, ARNOLD SMITH, ARTHUR SMITH, BLAINE SMITH, BRADY SMITH, BRANDON SMITH, BRENT SMITH, BRIAN SMITH, BRIAN SMITH, BRIAN SMITH, BRIAN SMITH, BRIAN SMITH, BRUCE SMITH, CATHY SMITH, CHAD SMITH, CHARLENE SMITH, CHARLENE SMITH, CHARLES SMITH, CHERYL SMITH, CHERYL SMITH, CHRISTOPHER SMITH, CINDY SMITH, CONSUELO SMITH, CRAIG SMITH, DAINE SMITH, DALE SMITH, DALLAS SMITH, DAVID SMITH, DAVID SMITH, DAVID SMITH, DAVID SMITH, DAVID SMITH, DEAN SMITH, DEBBIE SMITH, DEBORAH SMITH, DEBORAH SMITH, DEBRA SMITH, DEBY SMITH, DENISE SMITH, DENISE SMITH, DENNIS SMITH, DENNIS SMITH, DENNIS SMITH, DEWITT SMITH, DONALD SMITH, DOUGLAS SMITH, ELAINE SMITH, ELLIOTT SMITH, GALEN SMITH, GARY SMITH, GARY SMITH, GARY SMITH, GEORGE SMITH, GHEETA SMITH, GLENN SMITH, GREGG SMITH, GRETA SMITH, HEATHER SMITH, HEIDI SMITH, HELEN SMITH, IDA SMITH, JACOB SMITH, JAMES SMITH, JAMES SMITH, JAMES SMITH, JANE SMITH, JANET SMITH, JANICE SMITH, JARED SMITH, JASON SMITH, JASON SMITH, JAY SMITH, JC SMITH, JEANELL SMITH, JEFF SMITH, JEFF SMITH, JEREMY SMITH, JOHN SMITH, JONATHAN SMITH, JOSEPH SMITH, JOY SMITH, JOYCE SMITH, JR SMITH, JUDY SMITH, JULIA SMITH, JULIE SMITH, JUNE SMITH, KAREN SMITH, KARIN SMITH, KARYN SMITH, KATHRYN SMITH, KATHRYN SMITH, KAY SMITH, KEITH SMITH, KELLY SMITH, KEN SMITH, KENT SMITH, KERRY SMITH, LEROY SMITH, LESLIE SMITH, LINDA SMITH, LINDA SMITH, LORRAINE SMITH, LYNSIE SMITH, MANDIE SMITH, MARCY SMITH, MARGARET SMITH, MARGO SMITH, MARISA SMITH, MARK SMITH, MARSHA SMITH, MATTHEW SMITH, MICHAEL SMITH, MICHAEL SMITH, MONTE SMITH, MORGAN SMITH, MURRAY SMITH, NATHAN SMITH, NOLA SMITH, NORMAN SMITH, OLIVER SMITH, PAMELA SMITH, PATRICIA SMITH, PEGGY SMITH, PERRY SMITH, RAMONA SMITH, REED SMITH, REX SMITH, RGARY SMITH, RICHARD SMITH, ROBYN SMITH, ROGER SMITH, RUSSELL SMITH, SCOTT SMITH, SCOTT SMITH, SCOTT SMITH, SHARON SMITH, SHAUNA SMITH, SHEILA SMITH, SHELDON SMITH, SHELLEY SMITH, SHERRI SMITH, STACY SMITH, STANTON SMITH, STEPHANIE SMITH, STEPHANIE SMITH, STEPHEN SMITH, TAMARA SMITH, TAMI SMITH, TED SMITH, TERESA SMITH, TERRI SMITH, TERRY SMITH, TERRY SMITH, THOMAS SMITH, TIMOTHY SMITH, TODD SMITH, TONI SMITH, TRACIE SMITH, UDELL SMITH, WALLACE SMITH, WALLACE SMITH, WENDY SMITH, WENDY SMITH, WILFRED SMITH, ZACH SMITH, JAMES SMITH II, MICHAEL SMITH JR, RICHARD SMITH JR., ULRIKA SMITH-SVENSTEDT, OWEN SMOOT, STEPHEN SMOOT, CARRIE SMOTHERMAN, JARRELL SMOTHERMAN, NANCY SMOTHERMAN, STEVE SMOUT, DAVID SMULLIN, FRED SMULLIN, RYAN SNARR, CAROLE SNEDDON, GARY SNEDDON, GEOFFREY SNEED, RYAN SNELSON, CLAY SNITEMAN, HUUB SNOEP, BRADLEY SNOW, BROOKS SNOW, CHRISTOPHER SNOW, DAVID SNOW, GERALDINE SNOW, KATHRYN SNOW, LEE SNOW, LISA SNOW, LOUISE SNOW, MICHAEL SNOW, ROBBIN SNOW, SCOTT SNOW, SYDNEY SNOW, WILLIAM SNOW, JULIE SNOWBALL, KEN SNOY, CHRISTINE SNYDER, DAVID SNYDER, EARL SNYDER, IVETTE SNYDER, JANET SNYDER, KAREN SNYDER, LINDA SNYDER, MATT SNYDER, RENAE SNYDER, SARAH SNYDER, TAMMERA SNYDER, TIMOTHY SNYDER, VALERIE SNYDER, EARL SNYDER SR, JOHN SOBCZAK, DANE SOBEK, BALDUR SOBEL, RICHARD SOBERS, MICHAEL SOBLE, EUGENE SOBOLESKI, DEBBI SOBOTKA, DAVID SOCHA, BECKY SODENKAMP, ELIZABETH SODERQUIST, LESLIE SODERQUIST, CRAIG SOELBERG, STEVEN SOELBERG, NICKI SOFFEL, SARA SOFONIA, DANIEL SOFTLEY, LOUIS SOHAR, PENNY SOHAR, STEIN OLAV SOLHAUG, JOHN SOLIS, MARCIA SOLUM, GJERMUND SOLVANG, STEVEN SOMERS, WILLIAM SOMERS, KENNETH SOMERVILLE, CINDEE SOMMER, HEATHER SOMMER, TIFFANY SOMMER, LISA SOMMERFELDT, KIMBERLY SOMMERS, ZIG SONDELSKI, DOUGLAS SONNENBERG, JANETTE SONNENBERG, ROB SONODA, KATHRYN SONZINI, KIM SOPER, ALLYN SORENSEN, BONNIE SORENSEN, CAMILLE SORENSEN, CAROLYN SORENSEN, CHARLES SORENSEN, CORRIE SORENSEN, GALEN SORENSEN, JILL SORENSEN, JUELLE SORENSEN, KARON SORENSEN, KATHRYN SORENSEN, KENNA SORENSEN, LYNN SORENSEN, LYNN SORENSEN, OLGA SORENSEN, REGEN SORENSEN, ROBERT SORENSEN, RONALD SORENSEN, RONALD SORENSEN, RORY SORENSEN, SHAUN SORENSEN, SHELLEY SORENSEN, SHERI SORENSEN, SOREN SORENSEN, STACEE SORENSEN, STEVEN SORENSEN, SUSAN SORENSEN, TATYANA SORENSEN, THEODORE SORENSEN, VALERIE SORENSEN, ALICIA SORENSON, ANN SORENSON, BERNARD SORENSON, JERI SORENSON, JOAN SORENSON, KARIN SORENSON, LEVI SORENSON, LORI SORENSON, TODD SORENSON, KATHLEEN SORG, BRIAN SORIANO, MICHAEL SOROKINE, STEVEN SORREL, JIM SORY, JOHN SOSMAN, PIERRE SOTTAS, MICHAEL SOUBOTIN, BARBARA SOULIER, SHAUN SOUTH, CAROLYN SOUTHERLIN, ANDREA SOUTHWICK, ANGELA SOUTHWICK, JAMES SOUTHWICK, JANET SOUTHWICK, RODNEY SOUTHWICK, TODD SOUTOR, DAVE SOUTTER, SHARON SOUTTER, MELVIN SOWERBY, SANDRA SOWERBY, WALTER SOWERS, WAYNE SOWERS, JOLENE SPACKMAN, WILLIAM SPACKMAN, DAVID SPALDING, DEREK SPALDING, THOMAS SPANGLER, TOM SPANGLER, TONY SPANOS, CONNIE SPANTON-JEX, PAMELA SPARKMAN, ANNE SPARKS, ERIC SPARKS, KIMBERLY SPARKS, LISA SPARKS, TRUMAN SPARKS, GARY SPARPANA, BRUCE SPARROW, JON SPAUDE, JEFFREY SPAULDING, MONICA SPAULDING, CARL SPEAR, LINDSAY SPEAR, ANGELA SPEASE, JEFFRY SPECKMAN, NANCY SPECTOR, PAUL SPEERS, TIMOTHY SPEICHER, ANDREA SPEIRS, MELANIE SPEIRS, RUSSELL SPEIRS, CHARLES SPENCE, COLIN SPENCE, JACQUELINE SPENCE, JERRY SPENCE, BRENDA SPENCER, CAMILLE SPENCER, CRAIG SPENCER, DARLENE SPENCER, DAVID SPENCER, DAVID SPENCER, DOUGLAS SPENCER, GEORGE SPENCER, GREGORY SPENCER, GUY SPENCER, HEIDI SPENCER, JUDITH SPENCER, KAREN SPENCER, KATHRYN SPENCER, KERRY SPENCER, LORI SPENCER, MARJORIE SPENCER, MICHAEL SPENCER, PAULA SPENCER, RACHEL SPENCER, REED SPENCER, ROBYNN SPENCER, TODD SPENCER, WILLIAM SPENCER, CONNIE SPENCER-ADAMS, BARBARA SPENDLOVE, COLLEEN SPENDLOVE, DIKKI SPENDLOVE, SHAWN SPENDLOVE, MICHELLE SPENS, MIKE SPENS, RON SPERLE, ROBERT SPERLING, ANNA SPERRY, CAROL SPERRY, DIXIE SPERRY, RICHARD SPERRY, DONETTE SPETH, KURT SPIERS, DEBRA SPILMAN, JOANNE SPINA, BRIAN SPITTLER, MARLENE SPITTLER, EDGAR SPIZEL, WALTHER SPJELDVIK, JASON SPJUT, ADRIENNE SPLINTER, CHANA SPOMER, NBC SPORTS, RUBY SPRAGUE, FLOYD SPRAKTES, BRADLEY SPRING, CHARLENE SPRINGER, KIM SPRINGER, GWEN SPRINGMEYER, VENICE SPRINGMEYER, CHARLES SPROUL, LEE SPROUSE, STUART SPROUSE, JOANNE SPRUANCE, SPOTSWOOD SPRUANCE, BRYAN SPUHLER, TANIA SPURKLAND, TOBBEN SPURKLAND, CAROLYN SPURLOCK, HEATHER SPURLOCK, KENNETH SPURLOCK, MARIAN SPURLOCK, WILLIAM SPURZEM, JANIE SQUIRE, KIM SQUIRE, NANCY SQUIRE, SEAN SQUIRE, BARBARA SQUIRES, BRENT SQUIRES, DONNA SQUIRES, GEORGE SQUIRES, JEAN SQUIRES, KAREN SQUIRES, MELANIE SQUIRES, WALTER SROCZYNSKI, MARK ST ANDRE, BONNIE ST JOHN, HENRY ST JOHN, KIRSI ST MARIE, SAMUEL ST PIERRE, JEFFREY ST. CLAIR, MELANIE ST. CLAIR, RUTH ST. GERMAIN, DARRELL STACEY, JULIE STACEY, LESZEK STACHYRA, LEON STACIOKAS, DARLEA STACK, ROBERT STACK, PETER STADLER, KARI STAFFANSON, CYNTHIA STAFFORD, JOHN STAFSHOLT, LINDA STAGE, PATRICIA STAGG, MARCELLA STAHELI, PHIL STAHELI, ANNE STAHMANN, JENNIFER STAIKOS, DUSKO STAJIC, LARRY STAKER, PETER STAKS, EDNA STALEY, MARC STALLINGS, REED STALLINGS, RODNEY STALLINGS, RONNIE STAMM, LEANN STAMOS, LISA STAMPS, LINDA STANDER, STEPHEN STANDIFIRD, JACQUELINE STANDING, JAMES STANDING, JAMES STANFIELD, RONALD STANFIELD, STEPHEN STANFIELD, JOSEPH STANFORD, KENT STANFORD, KERRY STANGER, JOSEPH STANIK, BRUCE STANLEY, JARON STANLEY, JOSEPH STANLEY, DEBRA STANLEY-STEWART, ANGIE STANTON, JODY STANTON, JUDY STANTON, LARRY STANTON, DAVID STAPEL, HEIDI STAPEL, DONA STAPLES, JANNA STAPLES, MARK STAPLES, WENDY STAPLEY, LYNN STARK, LARRY STARKEY, SUSAN STARKWEATHER, BRIAN STARLEY, LYNNE STARLEY, CHRISCHAEL STARR, HEIDE STARR, SANDI STATON, THERESA STAUFFER, BLAINE STAVN, JEFFREY STAY, LAURENCE STAY, LYNNETTE STEAD, MARVIN STEADMAN, PATRICK STEADMAN, JAMIE STECK, KATHLEEN STECK, PEARL STECK, MARTEL STECKLER, RON STECKLER, BARBARA STEED, JOAN STEED, LINA STEED, RODNEY STEED, KENT STEEDMAN, ROCK STEEL, BRYAN STEELE, EMILY STEELE, FRANK STEELE, GERALD STEELE, KANDI STEELE, KEVIN STEELE, MELISA STEELE, PHILLIP STEELE, ROXANNE STEELE, RUSSELL STEELE, WILLIAM STEELE, SPENCER STEENBLIK, ESTHER STEFFEN, HOLLY STEFFEN, JIM STEFFEN, DEE STEFFENSEN, REBECCA STEGGELL, MELVIN STEIGER, GLENN STEIGMEYER, BRYNN STEIMLE, MATTHEW STEIMLE, JOHN STEIN, LYNNE STEINBACH, KAREN

STEINECKERT, BRAD STEINFELDT, TOM STEINHILBER, BRUCE STEINKE, HEINZ STEINMANN, ASHLEIGH STENBERG, KARLA STENHOLM, TIMOTHY STENNER, BILL STENQUIST, CARMA STENQUIST, RUSSELL STENQUIST, BRIAN STENZ, BEVERLEY STEPHAN, TIMOTHY STEPHAN, DEBRA STEPHENS, ERIN STEPHENS, JACOM STEPHENS, JAMES STEPHENS, JAY STEPHENS, LUANN STEPHENS, MARK STEPHENS, ROYCE STEPHENS, TERENCE STEPHENS, TIM STEPHENS, ANTHONY STEPHENSON, NATALIA STEPP, STEPHEN STERRETT, CRAIG STERTZ, THERESA STERTZ, CAROL STERZER, SCOTT STERZER, SUSAN STERZER, MARCO STETICH, DIANE STETTLER, MARCO STEVANONI, ADAM STEVENS, ALLISON STEVENS, BEVERLY STEVENS, CARRINE STEVENS, DAVID STEVENS, DELMAR STEVENS, EVELYN STEVENS, KRISTIN STEVENS, LARRY STEVENS, LOU ANN STEVENS, LYNN STEVENS, MARCI STEVENS, MARGO STEVENS, MARK STEVENS, MARK STEVENS, MICHAEL STEVENS, NICOLE STEVENS, PEGGY STEVENS, PETER STEVENS, RICHARD STEVENS, ROSALEE STEVENS, RUTH STEVENS, SHARON STEVENS, SHAUN STEVENS, SHELLEY STEVENS, WILLIAM STEVENS, YVONNE STEVENS, GREGORY STEVENS, MD, ALLEN STEVENSON, ANDREA STEVENSON, CAROL STEVENSON, CHRISTIAN STEVENSON, CORY STEVENSON, DONALD STEVENSON, FRANKLIN STEVENSON, JO STEVENSON, JUSTIN STEVENSON, KIRK STEVENSON, LYDIA STEVENSON, MARK STEVENSON, MICHAEL STEVENSON, RITA STEVENSON, SCOTT STEVENSON, TAMARA STEVENSON, AMANDA STEWART, ANDREW STEWART, ANNE STEWART, BRIAN STEWART, CAROL STEWART, CHAD STEWART, CHARISSE STEWART, CHRISTINE STEWART, CONNIE STEWART, CONNIE STEWART, DIANN STEWART, JAY STEWART, JEFF STEWART, JULEE STEWART, KATHLEEN STEWART, LAYNE STEWART, LISA STEWART, MAYRENE STEWART, NANCY STEWART, PENEE STEWART, RAYMOND STEWART, STEVEN STEWART, DEBORAH STICINSKI, PATRICIA STICKNEY, DEBBIE STIDHAM, GARY STIDHAM, MARCY STIEGEMEIER, MARK STIEGEMEIER, JENNIFER STIELOW, NANCY STILES, ELIZABETH STILLINGS, ASHLEY STILLMAN, SABRINA STILLWELL, ROBERT STILLWELL JR, DAVID STIMPSON, JO STIMPSON, KIESSA STINGER, JACQUELINE STINNETT, JASON STINNETT, MARILYN STINSON, TYLER STINSON, DANIEL STIREMAN, CHERIE STIRLING, MARGARET STIRLING, FRANCES STITES, CHRISTOPHER STOCK, JASON STOCK, KARI STOCK, KENDALL STOCK, LUZ STOCK, PEGGY STOCK, ROBERT STOCK, THERON STOCK, STEVEN STOCKDALE, DIANA STOCKEBRAND, WAYNE STOCKEBRAND, MARK STOCKER, CHERYL STOCKS, BRENT STODDARD, CHARLES STODDARD, BRETT STODDART, JOAN STODDART, ALICE STOHL, COLLEEN STOHLTON, SVETLANA STOJSIC, DAVID STOKEM, BRENDA STOKER, CANDACE STOKES, JEFF STOKES, KAREN STOKES, KATHALEEN STOKES, KATIE STOKES, KEN STOKES, LINDA STOKES, LUKE STOKES, NATHAN STOKES, SHAELA STOKES, SHELLEICE STOKES, VICKI STOKES, JACOB STOLK, BRUCE STONE, CLEO STONE, DENISE STONE, GORDIE STONE, JUDITH STONE, JULIE STONE, KEN STONE, KENNA STONE, LEE STONE, RICHARD STONE, SHAWNA STONE, TIARERANGI STONE, BRYAN STONE-DALY, ALAN STONELY, TERESA STONELY, JUDITH STONER, SUZANNE STONES, MELINDA STOOR, ROBERT STOOR, ADAM STORHEIM, CAROL STORRS, DEBORAH STOTSENBERG, MAUREEN STOTT, RORIE STOTT, SUZANNE STOTT, KIMBERLY STOUDT, BRENT STOUT, DAWN STOUT, JENNIFER STOUT, KATHY STOUT, KAYNA STOUT, KELLY STOUT, LISA STOUT, LORIN STOUT, MARK STOUT, NATHAN STOUT, AARON STOVER, REBECCA STOVER, CONNIE STOWE, FLORENCE STOWE, GORDON STOWE, THOMAS STOWE, WILLIAM STOWE, JEANNINE STOWELL, KRISTINE STRACHAN, PAUL STRAHL, JONATHAN STRAKER, SANDY STRALEY, RICHARD STRALOW, KATHY STRAND, KIMBERLY STRAND, DAVID STRASDAS, ABE STRATE, BRUCE STRATFORD, CHRISTOPHER STRATFORD, MARK STRATFORD, DANIEL STRATMAN, GLORIA STRATTON, KATHERINE STRATTON, MERI STRATTON, SEAN STRATTON, SUZANNE STRATTON, WENDITH STRATTON, CHRISTOPHER STRAUGHAN, RYAN STRAUSS, SUSAN STRAUSS, AARON STRAW, ANNIE STRAWN, BYRON STRAWN, KELLY STREBEL, CARALYN STREED, GREGORY STREED, AMBER STREET, ANDREA STREET, KAREN STREET, NATALIE STREET, PATRICIA STREET, SHELLEY STREET, GEOFFREY STREETER, TIM STRELICH, WILLIAM STRELOW, KATHY STRETCH, KIMBERLY STRICKLAND, TIFFANY STRICKLAND, DELL STRINGHAM, GINI STRINGHAM, JILL STRINGHAM, MARILYNN STRINGHAM, ROBERT STRINGHAM, ROBYN STRINGHAM, SARA STRINGHAM, SHAWN STRINGHAM, VINCY STRINGHAM, DAVID STROHM, RICHARD STROKES, ED STROMAN, LOUISE STROMBERG, MARC STROMBERG, NORMAN STROMNESS, ANNA STRONG, BECKY STRONG, BRITTNEY STRONG, CHARLENE STRONG, DARYL STRONG, DEBRA STRONG, DONNA STRONG, JAMES STRONG, JAN STRONG, JANET STRONG, JOSHUA STRONG, KELLY STRONG, LAVEE STRONG, LAYNE STRONG, RALPH STRONG, RANDY STRONG, RONALD STRONG, KARLA STRONK, ROBERT STROSHINE, VINCE STROUD, JAMES STROZIER, SHERMAN STRUBLE, MICHELLE STRUEMPH, ELIZABETH STRUTHWOLF, MARK STRUTHWOLF, CHARLES STUART, DAVID STUART, EILEEN STUART, JAMES STUART, LERAE STUART, MELISSA STUART, MICHAEL STUART, PEGGY STUART, SHARON STUART, BERNARD STUDER JR, ALICYN STUDYVIN, PAMELA STUHR, WILLIAM STUMP, BETTY STURDEVANT, ALISON STURGEON, BRIAN STURGIS, STEVEN STURZENEGGER, GEORG STUTZENBERGER, RICHARD STYLES, DANIEL SUAREZ, CAROLYN SUCHALA, AUGUSTIN SUCHAR, JOHN SUCHER, MARIE SUCHYTA, ROBERT SUCHYTA, DAVID SUCKOW, YOSHIKO SUDA, ROCKY SUDLESKY, KATHY SUDWEEKS, BERND SUESS, TAKESHI SUGANUMA, JEANE SUGGS, TRICIA SUGIYAMA, ANNETTE SUITE, CELESTE SUITE, STEVEN SUITE, CASSANDRA SUITE-SMITH, JACQUI SUKER, DANA SULLENS, CARL SULLIVAN, GAYLE SULLIVAN, GEORGIA SULLIVAN, GLENN SULLIVAN, KAORI SULLIVAN, LISA SULLIVAN, MARC SULLIVAN, PATRICIA SULLIVAN, SANDRA SULLIVAN, TIMOTHY SULLIVAN, BENJAMIN SULLY, LARS SUMMERHAYS, MARK SUMMERHAYS, OSA SUMMERHAYS, SPENCER SUMMERHAYS, STEVEN SUMMERILL, TIFFANY SUMMERILL, IOLA SUMMERS, JEREMY SUMMERS, REED SUMMERS, ROBERT SUMMERS, SUELLEN SUMMERS, JANET SUMNER, STEVEN SUMPTER, GRANT SUMSION, JEFF SUMSION, RICHARD SUMSION, EINAR SUNDE, DAVID SUNDERLAND, GEORGE SUNDERLAND, JON SUNDERLAND, MERRILL SUNDERLAND, CHANTELLE SUNDWALL, MUNGHUN SUNG, SERGEY SURENKOV, DEB SUSSMAN, MICHAEL SUSSMAN, JANICE SUSTACHA-KNUTSON, BENJAMIN SUTA, BARBARA SUTHERLAND, DANIEL SUTHERLAND, JOHN SUTHERLAND, JUSTIN SUTHERLAND, KATHLEEN SUTHERLAND, RALINE SUTHERLAND, RANDY SUTHERLAND, STEPHEN SUTHERLAND, TENAY SUTHERLAND, AARON SUTLIFF, LIBBE SUTTER, BONNIE SUTTON, DIANE SUTTON, LISA SUTTON, MICHELLE SUTTON, RICHARD SUTTON, SATOSHI SUZUKI, DAVID SVIR, HELEN SWABY, ALLEN SWAIN, APRIL SWAIN, BOB SWAIN, JUDY SWAIN, KIM SWAIN, PATRICE SWAIN, ADAM SWALBERG, MARY ANN SWALBERG, SINIKA SWALBERG, WILLIAM SWALBERG, JASON SWAN, MARK SWANDBY, CLARENCE SWANER, JOAN SWANER, ELIZABETH SWANK, ROBERT SWANK, MICHAEL SWANN, ANGELA SWANSON, DAVID SWANSON, BEVERLY SWANTY, NORMAN SWANTY, RAELYN SWASEY, FRANK SWAUGER, TYLER SWAVELY, MARGENE SWEAT, JAMES SWEENEY, JOHN SWEENEY, JUNE SWEENEY, MICHAEL SWEENEY, SHARLENE SWEENEY, BRADLEY SWEET, CANDICE SWEET, CHERYL SWEET, DAN SWEET, DEVAN SWEET, KAYLEY SWEET, KRISTEN SWEET, RICHARD SWEET, RODERICK SWEET, RODNEY SWEET, SAMANTHA SWEET, MICHAEL SWEETEN, ALICE SWEETLAND, WILLIAM SWEETLAND III, SANDRA SWEITZER, DAN SWENDSEN, DEBORAH SWENERTON, EMILY SWENSEN, GRETEL SWENSEN, HAROLD SWENSEN, JAMES SWENSEN, LAIRD SWENSEN, LOUISE SWENSEN, NEAL SWENSEN, SWEN SWENSEN, ANCHERIE SWENSON, BRITTANY SWENSON, BURKE SWENSON, CAROL SWENSON, JORDON SWENSON, LEE SWENSON, MARY SWENSON, MICHAEL SWENSON, NANCY SWENSON, PAUL SWENSON, PAUL SWENSON, ROBERT SWENSON, SHELLY SWENSON, VAL SWENSON, STACEY SWETIL-RUST, KAREN SWICORD, NANCY SWIDER-PELTZ, MARJORIE SWIECICKI, LAURALYN SWIM, MARK SWINDEL, IRENE SWINNEA, LAWRENCE SWITAJ, BARBARA SWITZER, EDWIN SWITZER, RUSS SWONSON, JACK SWOPE, CHRISTIAN SYBROWSKY, JACQUELYN SYBROWSKY, CARLA SYDENHAM, BENJAMIN SYKES, DANA SYKORA, DAVID SYKORA, DALE SYLVESTER, MICHAEL SYMALLA, SCOTT SYME, ROCHELLE SYMONS, WENDY SYRETT, WILLIAM SZABO, TERRY SZERSZEN, DAVID SZOKE, HEIDI SZOKE, SIEGFRIED SZOKE, AMBER SZYMANSKI, BECKI SZYMCZAK • **T** • PETER TAAFFE, WILLIAM TABAR, EILEEN TABERT, FEDERICO TABONE, DEBRA TABOR, SHANE TABRIZI, MARK TABRUM, STEVEN TACHIKI, MAKOTO TADACHI, ELLEN TADLOCK, HELEN TAFOYA, COLLEEN TAFT, LINDA TAFT, DIANE TAGGART, LYN TAGGART, RICHARD TAGGART, TIMOTHY TAGGART, LYLE TAGGE, BYRON TAHBO, MARK TAINTER, LOUISE TAINTOR-TEEPLES, BRETT TAIT, JACK TAIT, JON TAIT, KERRY TAIT, KRISTINE TAIT, ALLEN TAKAHASHI, GLADYS TAKASAKI, MAMI TAKEDA, RALYNNE TAKEDA, ARTHUR TALBOT, CLAIR TALBOT, JERRY TALBOT, KATHY TALBOT, KIRK TALBOT, STEVEN TALBOT, VIRGINIA TALBOT, VIVIAN TALBOT, MICHAEL TALL, CHRISTI TALLON, LOK MAN TAM, BRETT TAMAGAWA, JENEILE TAMS, VIRGILINE TANGA, KATHY TANGARO, SONNY TANGARO, TYLER TANGREN, REBECCA TANGUAY, SHERRY TANNAHILL, DAVID TANNEHILL, DANIEL TANNER, HOLLY TANNER, JON TANNER, LYNN TANNER, MICHAEL TANNER, MICHELLE TANNER, NATHAN TANNER, PAMELA TANNER, PEGGY TANNER, ROBERT TANNER, STEPHEN TANNER, TERRY TANSEY, BRIAN TARACENA, CHERYL TARBET, PAUL TARGOSZ, JAMES TARR, JOSE LUIS TARRASO, KENNETH TARZON, NUSRET TASEVAC, GARY TASSAINER, VELYN TASSAINER, BRIAN TASSINARI, LISA TASSINARI, GRACE TASSONE, BENJAMIN TATE, BOB TATE, JOE TATE, MICHAEL TATE, MICHAEL TATE, REBECCA TATE, SETH TATE, VANESSA TATE, IDA TATEOKA, NICOLE TATTERSALL, CANDACE TATTON, JUDITH TATUM, REGINA TAUSINGA, CATHERINE TAUTU, LORELEI TAVEY, STELLA TAVILLA, JONI TAXIN, TERRY TAYE, JARON TAYLER, AMBER TAYLOR, ANDREA TAYLOR, ANGELA TAYLOR, ANNA TAYLOR, BARBARA TAYLOR, BELINDA TAYLOR, BEVERLY TAYLOR, BRENDEN TAYLOR, BRUCE TAYLOR, BRYAN TAYLOR, BYRON TAYLOR, DAVID TAYLOR, DAVID TAYLOR, ELLEN TAYLOR, ERIC TAYLOR, GARY TAYLOR, GARY TAYLOR, GAYLAND TAYLOR, GEORGINA TAYLOR, JAMES TAYLOR, JANET TAYLOR, JANICE TAYLOR, JERALD TAYLOR, JOHN TAYLOR, JOHNNY TAYLOR, JOYCE TAYLOR, JULIE TAYLOR, KAREN TAYLOR, KARINA TAYLOR, KATHERINE TAYLOR, KATHRYN TAYLOR, KATHY TAYLOR, KERRY TAYLOR, KEVIN TAYLOR, KRISTI TAYLOR, LARRY TAYLOR, LINDA TAYLOR, LINDA TAYLOR, LINDA TAYLOR, LINDA TAYLOR, LORI TAYLOR, LYNDA TAYLOR, LYNN TAYLOR, MAE TAYLOR, MARCI TAYLOR, MARK TAYLOR, MARY TAYLOR, MARY TAYLOR, MARY TAYLOR, MERRILYN TAYLOR, MICHAEL TAYLOR, MICKI TAYLOR, MILTON TAYLOR, MILTON TAYLOR, PAMELA TAYLOR, PETER TAYLOR, PRESTON TAYLOR, REBECCA TAYLOR, RENAE TAYLOR, RICHARD TAYLOR, ROBERTA TAYLOR, ROGAN TAYLOR, RONALD TAYLOR, RUSSELL TAYLOR, SHERILYN TAYLOR, SHERMAN TAYLOR, SHIRLEY TAYLOR, SHIRLEY TAYLOR, STACY TAYLOR, STEPHEN TAYLOR, TAMIE TAYLOR, THOMAS TAYLOR, TRAVIS TAYLOR, VAUNA TAYLOR, WARREN TAYLOR, RUSSEL TAYLOR JR, STACI TAYLOR-MEYERS, ALISON TAYSOM, VLADIMIR TCHERNEV, CHARLES TEA, KEVIN TEA, JEAN TEALEY, DOUGLAS TEBBS, KIM TEBBS, COLETTE TECHMEYER, MERINDA TECHMEYER, MICHAEL TECHMEYER, JANICE TEDROW, CRAIG TEEL, KEVIN TEEL, JEFFREY TEEPLES, KAREN TEERLINK, JOSEPH TEFF, KRISTA TEGTMEIER, WILLIAM TEICHERT, SCOTT TEIGEN, LINDA TEKMITCHOV, RUTH TEMPEST, ANDREA TEMPFER, JACQUELINE TENNANT, SAMUEL TENNANT, DIANE TENNEY, KATHRYN TENNEY, MICHAEL TENNEY, JAMES TENSLEY, CHRISTINE TEPLEY-PRATT, BERNADETTE TERCHA, THOMAS TERRELL, CYNTHIA TERRILL, ED TERRIS, KAYELYNNE TERRIS, BYRON TERRY, DAVID TERRY, DAVID TERRY, DONNA TERRY, JANETTE TERRY, JOSEPH TERRY, JOYCE TERRY, KARIN TERRY, KEITH TERRY, LINDA TERRY, MICHAEL TERRY, NATALIE TERRY, STEVEN TERRY, VIRGINIA TERRY, GARY TERUSAKI, BRYAN TESCH, ELAINE TESCH, ANN TESORI, HERMINE TESTARD, PAUL TESTER, RICHARD TETZL, KEVIN TEUSCHER, LESLIE THABES, JAMES THACHER, DEBRA THACKER, ANNE THACKERAY, LAURA THACKERAY, SANDRA THACKERAY, ELAINE THARP, BJOERN THARUN, DANIEL THATCHER, KATHLYN THATCHER, MELINDA THATCHER, PHILLIP THAUT, JOHN THAYER II, DAVID THAYNE, DEONA THAYNE, JEREMY THAYNE, RANDALL THAYNE, ALAN THEIS, LEE THEOBALD, JESSICA THEURER, THOMAS THEYS, JOHN THIBEAULT, MISSY THIEL, JEFF THIELEN, PATTY THIELEN, BRUCE THIELKE, EUGENE THIELMAN, JUDY THIMAKIS, DIANE THINNES, THOMAS S THOLEN JR, HEINZ THOMA, ALLYSON THOMAS, ANGELA THOMAS, BETTY THOMAS, BRUCE THOMAS, CYNTHIA THOMAS, D.SCOTT THOMAS, DEBRA THOMAS, DIANA THOMAS, GOLDEN THOMAS, GUINEVERE THOMAS, JAMES THOMAS, JANET THOMAS, JASON THOMAS, JOANNE THOMAS, JONI THOMAS, JUSTIN THOMAS, KARIDEE THOMAS, KAY THOMAS, KEVIN THOMAS, KRISTEN THOMAS, LARRY THOMAS, LIZ THOMAS, LLOYD THOMAS, MARJORY THOMAS, MICHAEL THOMAS, MYRNA THOMAS, NANCY THOMAS, PERRY THOMAS, RICHARD E THOMAS, ROBIN THOMAS, RUBY THOMAS, SARA THOMAS, SHARLENE THOMAS, SUSAN THOMAS, TARA THOMAS, TOM THOMAS, TRACI THOMAS, RICHARD THOMASON, ALAN THOMPSON, ARTHUR THOMPSON, BRYAN THOMPSON, CAROLYN THOMPSON, CHRISTIAN THOMPSON, CHRISTINE THOMPSON, COLIN THOMPSON, DARRELL THOMPSON, DEBBIE THOMPSON, DIANE THOMPSON, F. MARSHALL THOMPSON, GERALD THOMPSON, IRIS THOMPSON, JANE THOMPSON, JANEEN THOMPSON, JANET THOMPSON, JEFFREY THOMPSON, JEFFREY THOMPSON, JENELLE THOMPSON, JILL THOMPSON, JOAN THOMPSON, KARA THOMPSON, KAREN THOMPSON, KATEY THOMPSON, KATHRYN THOMPSON, KATHRYN THOMPSON, LISA THOMPSON, MARC THOMPSON, MARY ANN THOMPSON, MARY ELLEN THOMPSON, MICHAEL THOMPSON, NOEL THOMPSON, PATRICIA THOMPSON, PHILIP THOMPSON, ROLF THOMPSON, SANDRA THOMPSON, TED THOMPSON, TERESA THOMPSON, TOMMY THOMPSON, TONIA THOMPSON, TRUDY THOMPSON, VIRGIL THOMPSON, WILLIAM THOMPSON, WILLIAM THOMPSON, CAMIE THOMSON, JULIE THOMSON, LORI THOMSON, NEIL THON, EVA THONFELD, SUSAN THORDERSON, SONDRA THORELL, ROD THORESON, SHAWN THORESON, DAVID THORNE, PRESTON THORNE, SCOTT THORNE, SHANNON THORNE, DAVID THORNELL, ELIZABETH THORNELL, LINDA THORNELL, BLAINE THORNOCK, CAROL THORNOCK, HEATHER THORNOCK, ALBERT THORNTON, DIANA THORNTON, EMILY THORNTON, RENEE THORNTON, WILLIAM THORNTON, GREG THORPE, GREG THORPE, JAN THORPE, KARL THORPE, KAYE THORPE, KEVIN THORPE, SYLVIA THORPE, FELISE THORPE MOLL, GIGI THORSEN, ARAINA THORSNESS, RHEA THORSON, PATRICIA THREDGOLD, RAYLENE THUESON, LISA THULIN, KRISTI THUNELL, PATRICIA THUNELL, RANDALL THUNELL, STEVEN THUNELL, RAE THURELL, BEVERLY THURGOOD, CRAIG THURGOOD, DONNA THURGOOD, HOLLY THURGOOD, RICHARD THURGOOD, ROBERT THURGOOD, STEVEN THURGOOD, TIFFANY THURGOOD, GREGORY THURHEIMER, MICHAEL THURMAN, VICKI THURMAN, GARY THURNAU, VALERIE THURNELL, BOB THURSTON, COLLEEN THURSTON, STEPHANIE THYGESEN, LISA TIBBITTS, ROBERT TIBBITTS, TERRY TIBBITTS, ADELA TICHACEK, MICHAEL TICHACEK, KARIN TIDGEWELL, MIKE TIDWELL, THELMA TIDWELL, VERL TIDWELL, JEFF TIEDE, JASON TIEFENBACH, CAROLYN TIERNAN, DRAGOS TIERU-HATU, BECKY TIETZE, CHRISTOPHER TIETZE, CHERYL TILARO, FRANK TILARO, C BRUCE TILLACK, CARROL TILLE, MARY TILLE, JAMES TILLEY, JOSHUA TILLEY, NATASHA REDD TILLEY, LARRY TILLICK, ROBERT TILLMAN, NANCY TILLOTSON, EARL TILLY, DAVID TILTON, REBECCA TILTON, MICHAEL TIMM, STUART TIMM, JAMES TIMMEL, KRISTINE TIMMEL, CASEY TIMMERMAN, ROBERT TIMMERMAN, AMBER TIMMS, CHRISTIE TIMOTHY, LISA TIMOTHY, LORINA TIMOTHY, DAVID TIMPSON, DREW TIMPSON, JILL TIMPSON, MISTI TIMPSON, RICHARD TIMPSON, STEVEN TINGEY, ANN TINKER, MICHELLE TIPPETS, NANCY TIPPETS, RACHEL TIPPETS, BRYAN TIPPETTS, CARRIE TIPPETTS, JASON TIPPETTS, MATTHEW TIPPETTS, JERRY TIREY, WILLIAM TISDALE, GERI TITENSOR, ROBERT TITENSOR, MIKE TITTLE, AARON TITUS, WILLIAM TITUS, KAREN TOBEY, STEPHANIE TOBEY, SHANNON TOBLER, JENA TOCHER, HEATHER TODD, MARK TODD, SHAUNLA TODD, VAL TODD, JEFFREY TOEWE, ARTHUR TOKLE, AL TOKUNAGA, SAMMIE TOLLESTRUP, DONNA LEE TOLLEY, VIOLA TOLLIS, MATTTHEW TOLLISON, ANGIE TOLMAN, BENJAMIN TOLMAN, BRENT TOLMAN, MARK TOLMAN, MICHAEL TOLMAN, SHANNON TOLMAN, TRACEY TOLMAN, KIM TOLSMA, EILEEN TOLSON, DEBBIE TOLTON, ROBERT TOLTON, AIKO TOMA, WINIFRED TOMAN, LAUREL TOMIN, JAMES TOMLINSON, TONI TOMLINSON, RICHARD TOMPSON, DAVID TOMTEN, HEIDI TOMTEN, JESSE TONKS, BILL TOOKE, CAROL TOOKE, ELIZABETH TOOMBS, ANGELA TOONE, CINDY TOONE, JEFFORY TOONE, LYNDA TOONE, LYNN TOONE, TERRY TOONE, CHARLA TOPHAM, CHARLES TOPHAM, CORY TOPHAM, GORDON TOPHAM, JANET TOPHAM, JULIE TOPHAM, MARDELL TOPHAM, JOSEPH TORMAN, CHRISTIAN TORONTO, JAMES TORONTO, JOHN TORONTO, RUSSELL TORONTO, HARUTYUN TOROSYAN, LIDIA TOSCANO, BOB TOTH, ELAINE TOTTEN, JEFFREY TOTTEN, TERRI TOTZKE, CALLI TOULATOS, JANIE TOW, MARK TOWERS, LISA TOWNER, STEVE TOWNER, BRUCE TOWNES, APRIL TOWNSEND, DENNIS TOWNSEND, JAMES TOWNSEND, JOAN TOWNSEND, GARY TOYN, NICHOLAS TOYN, DONALD TRACY, LAURIE TRACY, MICHAEL TRACY, UFFE TRAEDEN, TONHU TRAN, NATHAN TRANCHELL, JILL TRANTER, KENNETH TRASK, DEANNE TRAUBA, STEPHEN TRAUBA, KATHLEEN TRAVERS, BETH TRAVIS, TODD TRAVIS, YVONNE TRAVIS, ROY TRAWICK, ROBERT TREADWAY, JOSEPH TREADWELL, GERALD TREBESCH, TIMOTHY TREBESCH, TERAL TREE, TRUMAN TREGLOWN, PATRICIA TRELA, DANY TREMBLAY, ROGER TREMBLAY, MICHAEL TRESHOW, KYLE TRESNER, VALERIE TREUTING, MICHAEL TRIBBLE, MICHAEL TRIBE, WILLIAM TRIBE, GARY TRICKEY, REBECCA TRIGG, DAVID TRIMBLE, ELDEEN TRIMBLE, JAY TRINNAMAN, TERRI TRINNAMAN, LORI TRIPI, KAY TRIPLETT, KAREN TRIPP, DAVID TROCKMAN, COLLEEN TRONE, DEBBIE TRONIER, DENNIS TROP, DALE TROSTLE, DARCY TROTTER, NANCY TROTTER, BRANT TROWBRIDGE, KURT TROYER, ANN TRUDELL, ALVIN (DICK) TRUE, ALEX TRUESEFF, NATHAN TRUITT, JERRY TRUJILLO, JUDITH TRUJILLO, ALLEN TRUMP, SHARREN TRUMP, KAREN TSUJIMOTO, MALIE TSURUNAGA, CHRISTOPHER TUBBS, AARON TUCK, DARREN TUCKER, DEBORAH TUCKER, HEATHER TUCKER, JANÈT TUCKER, JILL TUCKER, ROD TUCKER, SHEILA TUCKER, VAN TUCKER, NATHAN TUELLER, RENEE TUELLER, KRISTIE TUERO, CARLENE TUFT, STEPHEN TUFT, JOHN TULLIS, KIM TULLIS, SHAUN TULLIS, JOSEPH TULPINSKY, GAIL TUOHIG, DONALD TUOHY, LEIMA MUTI TUPUA, LEO TURCOTTE, STUART TURKANIS, JULIANNE TURKO, ADAM TURLEY, BETH TURLEY, BRENT TURLEY, ELAINE TURLEY, GERALDINE TURLEY, ROBERT TURLEY, TY TURLEY, HAROLD TURLEY JR, RICHARD TURNBOW, ANDREA TURNBULL, LINDSAY TURNBULL, SUSAN TURNBULL, WILLIAM TURNBULL, ALEXANDER TURNER, ANNA TURNER, ANNETTE TURNER, CAMILLE TURNER, CLAUDIA TURNER, DALANE TURNER, DUSTIN TURNER, GARY TURNER, GAYLE TURNER, HEATHER TURNER, JARED TURNER, JEANENE TURNER, JO TURNER, JOANNA TURNER, KATHLEEN TURNER, KATHLEEN TURNER, LANE TURNER, LARRY TURNER, LOLA TURNER, MARTIN TURNER, MEGAN TURNER, NADINE TURNER, RICK TURNER, ROBERT TURNER, SHARON TURNER, TALESE TURNER, TRABERT TURNER, PAUL TURPIN, SUSAN TURPIN, IRA TURUNEN, BEVERLY TURVILLE, TERRY TURVILLE, BILLIE TUTTLE, CAROL TUTTLE, DONALD TUTTLE, RICHARD TUTTLE, STEVEN TUTTLE, TERESA TUTTLE, TERRY TUTTLE, CARLA TWEDT, BRITTNEY TWILLIGEAR, ANGELA TWINING, JEFF TWITCHELL, MARILYN TWITE, RAY TWITE, DEBBIE TYLER, DENEE TYLER, JON TYLER, LARRY TYLER, LOUIS TYLER, MARK TYLER, RICHARD TYLER, TEE TYLER, JAMES TYRRELL, MARK TYSON • **U** • MARC UDA, MARC UDALL, RUTH UDALL, CALVIN UDY, KRISTINE UDY, EPALAHAME UHI, ROBERT ULCH, EVERT ULDRICH, ZARUHI ULIKHANYAN, JENNIFER ULLMAN, CLARK ULRICH, DANIEL ULRICH, KATHY ULRICH, ALEX CHUNG-MIN UM, STEPHEN UNOPULOS, JASON UNRUH, JEFF UNRUH, SHEILA UNSWORTH, WILLIAM UNTHANK, TRACY UPTAIN, MANFRED URBAN, CHARLEE URBANCIC, LAIMIS URBONAS, JUDITH URE, BARRY URRY, SENTI URRY, STEVEN URRY, BRADLEY URSES, EUGENE USHINSKY, ILONA USHINSKY, DRIVERS UTA, JANET UTT, SAMIR UVEJZOVIC, NANCY UYAL, RICHARD UYAL • **V** • RENEE VADEBONCOEUR, SUSAN VAIL, NGATAMAINE VAINERERE, JESSE VALDEZ, TIM VALDEZ, KIM VALEIKA, DAVID VALENTINE, SUSAN VALENTINE, WILLIAM VALENTINE, LUCY VALERIO, VASIL VALKOV, JOHN VALKOVIAK, EUGENE VALLE, GERALD VALLETTE, VALERIE VALLETTE, FRANCINE VALLINE, LYNDA VALLON, JARED VALUM, REBECCA VALVERDE, BARRY VAN, GEORGE VAN, PATRICK VAN AARLE, BARBARA VAN ASDLAN, JOAN VAN ATTA, LAWRENCE VAN ATTA, MARY JUNE VAN BERG, CHRISTIAAN VAN BEUGE, MANJA VAN BIBBER, CHRISTINE VAN BUSKIRK, MICHAEL VAN COUWENBERGHE, DEBORAH VAN DEN BERG, MICHAEL VAN DER BOSCH, LINDLEY VAN DER LINDE, JOHN VAN DINTER, MAUREEN VAN DINTER, TROY VAN DRIMMELEN, MARIANNE VAN DYKE, SUZANNE VAN DYKE, D PETER VAN EENENAAM, NEIL VAN EERDEN, RUTH VAN ERDEN, GRETA VAN ERT, STACY VAN HOOK, NEAL VAN HOUTEN, CURT VAN HOVE, CINDY VAN KLAVEREN, DICK VAN KLAVEREN, JACK VAN KLAVEREN, JUDITH VAN KLAVEREN, DIANE VAN LEEUWEN, RICHARD VAN LEEUWEN, ROSS VAN ORDEN, ELLEN VAN ORMAN, TERRY VAN RAAY, CATHERINE VAN SKYHAWK, TAMMY VAN TASSELL, BARBARA VAN TRUMP, DEAN VAN UITERT, VICTORIA VAN VOORHIS, CHARLOTTE VAN WAGENEN, SHIRLEY VAN WAGENEN, BRYAN VAN WAGONER, STEVEN VAN WAGONER, PETE VAN WYNEN, DARLENE VANAMBURGH, PEGGY VANAMEN, SAM VANAMEN, DAVID VANASSCHE, BRIAN VANBALLEGOOIE, CHRIS VANBROCKLIN, ROBERT VANBROCKLIN, RYAN VANBROCKLIN, ANTHONY VANCE, ARLOU VANCE, BARRY VANCE, DAVID VANCE, DIANNE VANCE, DORAL VANCE, DWAYNE VANCE, JACKIE VANCE, JON VANCE, KOLIN VANCE, MORGAN VANCE, MICHAEL VANCHIERE, LINDA VANCOTT, KARI VANDE MERWE, KIMBERLY VANDE MERWE, DAVID VANDEHEI, NANCY VANDEL, DAVID VANDENBERG, NAOMI VANDENBERG, DIANE VANDENBERGHE, JOHN VANDENBERGHE, JOAN VANDERDOES, CLARK VANDERHOOF, JERRY VANDERPAN, ROXANNE VANDERSLUIS, BRADLEY VANDERSTEK, JAMES VANDERWEST, JOAN VANDERWEST, TRAVIS VANDONGEN, MICHAEL VANDRE, JULIE VANISI, JARED VANLEUVEN, MERJA VANNINEN, OSMO VANNINEN, TIFFANY VANORDEN, LOUWANE VANSOOLEN, TEIA VANSOOLEN, WILLIAM VANT HOF, HERBERT VANVALKENBURGH, PRISCILLA VANVALKENBURGH, JILL VANWAGONER, JASON VANZELLA, BRIAN VARADY, KAREN VARDENY, CHARLENE VARGA, GABRIELA VARGAS, KEVIN VARIAN, DONNA VARNELL, KAREN VARNER, LAWRENCE VASEL, DAN VASQUEZ, DEBBIE VASQUEZ, LUIS VASQUEZ, BONNIE VASSAR, WILLIAM VASSAR, DAN VAUGHAN, ROBYN VAUGHAN, RUTH VAUGHAN, KENT VAUGHN, SUSAN VAUGHN, SUSAN VAUGHN, TRACI VAUGHN, DAVID VAYZER, OLGA VAZQUEZ, PAUL VEASY, STEPHANIE VEASY, JENNIFER VEAZIE, ROBYN VEENEMA, LAMMERT VEENSTRA, VASILIKI VEGIRI, ELENA VEISMAN, GLORIA VELARDE, LILLIAN VELEZ, BRYCE VELLINGA, WILLIAM VELLMURE, REGINA VENABLE, EDWARD VENDELL, BARB VENEMA, SARADHA VENKATRAMAN, MARY VENNETT, RICHARD VENNETT, KENNETH VERDOIA, CATHERINE VERGUET, LAUREL VERHAAREN, MARTIN VERHOEF, MICHAEL VERKLER, ELENI VERNARDAKI, BRYAN VERNETTI, RACHEL VERNON, TRACY VERSLUIS, MICHAEL VERSTEEG, DAVID VESEY, PAUL VESPER, AMBER VEST, JARI VESTERINEN, TROY VETETO, CAROLE VETTER, OTTO VETTER, TEVY VETTER, ANGELA VICCHRILLI, LISA VICCHRILLI ANDERSON, KURT VICKER, KAROLY VICZIAN, JEFF VIELSTICH, LOTHAR VIELSTICH, MICHAEL VIELSTICH, CARLA VIETTI, BIRGIR VIGFZSSON, JUNE VIGIL, MIRIAM VIGIL, MAGNHILD VIK, LISA VILCHEZ, DENISE VILLA, DALBIS VILLALOBOS, KLAUS VILLALOBOS, JAMES VILLALPANDO, STEVE VILLARREAL, BEVERLY VILLATA, VILIAMI VIMAHI, BRIAN VINCENT, DANIEL VINCENT, DARREL VINCENT, DELORES VINCENT, PATRICIA VINCENT, SCOTT VINCENT, SHAWN VINCENT, SUSAN VINCENT, JEFFREY VINLUAN, GERALYN VINSON, KORRIE VINTON, NATHANIEL VINTON, JOSEPH VIRGONA, MICHELLE VIRUS, MICHAEL VISSER, PERRY VLAHOS, VIVIANE VO-DUC, LAWRENCE VOEGELE, JAMES VOGEL, JOAN VOGEL, RICHARD VOGHT, CURTIS VOGT, NORINE VOGT, ROBERT VOGT, STACIE VOGT, ROBERT VOGT, JR., MARY VOIGT, BARBARA VOIGTLAENDER, JACQUELINE VOINOVICH, BRIAN VOLK, GREGORY VOLK, HANK VOLKMAN, LARISA VOLKOVA, TALLEIV VOLLEN, RANDALL VOLLRATH, BARTON VOM DORP, VICTORIA VOMOCIL, BARBARA VON DIETHER, KURT VON PUTTKAMMER, RICHARD VONDRUS, KIM VOORHEES, RODNEY VORIS, ERIC VORLAGE, JANET VORWALLER, SUSAN VOYLES, TYLER VRANES, JAN VREELING, JOAN VRTIS, MICHAEL VUICH, KIRSTI VUOHELAINEN, ELIZABETH VUYK, GERALDINE VYBIRAL, ZDENEK VYMAZAL, ERNEST VYSE, RUTH VYSE • **W** • DAVID WADDELL, JOANN WADDELL, CLEVE WADDOUPS, JANEEN WADDOUPS, KAY WADE, KIP WADE, LYNNE WADE, MICHAEL WADE, MIKEL WADE, OFELIA WADE, PEGGY WADE, STEPHEN WADE, TAMARA WADE, VIVIEN WADE, JAMES WADLEY, LAUREL WADLEY, WAYNE WADMAN, ANN WADSWORTH, DIANE WADSWORTH, JILL WADSWORTH, MARIDAWN WADSWORTH, NICCI WADSWORTH, TAMMY WADSWORTH, JEFFREY WAGER, ROBERT WAGER, MARJORIE WAGGONER, MICHAEL WAGGONER, SANDRA WAGGONER, CORTLAND WAGNER, DAVID WAGNER, JOAN WAGNER, RICHARD WAGNER, SUSAN WAGNER, MARK WAGSTAFF, RUSSELL WAGSTAFF, TERRI WAGSTAFF, DONA WAHL, DOUGLAS WAHL, RAYMOND WAHL, JOY WAHLIN, DOUGLAS WAHLQUIST, DONNA WAHOFF-STICE, JOAN WAIKART, LOUIS WAIKART III, MICHAEL WAINBERG, LANNA WAISATH, EILEEN WAITE, LOREN WAITE, SIDNEY WAITE, BEN WAKE, ANDREW WAKEFIELD, GARY WAKEFIELD, WANDA WAKEFIELD, YING CHIN WAKEFIELD, DARYL WALBECK, DEIDRE WALBECK, LINDA WALBECK, LUCINDA WALD, MARY WALD, AILA WALDOW, EILEEN WALDOW, AMY WALDRON, BARBARA WALDRON, CY WALDRON, KRISTEN WALDRON, LYLE WALDRON, PAUL WALDRON, SCOTT WALDRON, EVERN WALK, ADAM WALKER, BRETT WALKER, BRIAN WALKER, CARLA WALKER, CARLENE WALKER, CAROL WALKER, CECILIA WALKER, CHELSA WALKER, CLAYTON WALKER, CORINNE WALKER, DANNY WALKER, DEAN WALKER, DOUGLAS WALKER, ELIZABETH WALKER, ERIE WALKER, G DAVIES WALKER, GORDON WALKER, GRETCHEN WALKER, JAMES WALKER, JAMES WALKER, JOANNE WALKER, KARL WALKER, KENNETH WALKER, LANA WALKER, LAYNE WALKER, LISA WALKER, LYNN WALKER, MACKENZIE WALKER, MELINDA WALKER, MELISSA WALKER, MICHAEL WALKER, PAUL WALKER, RITA WALKER, RONALD WALKER, RYAN WALKER, SANDY WALKER, STEVE WALKER, STEVE WALKER, SUZANNE WALKER, TROY WALKER, VALERIE WALKER, WHITNEY WALKER, JOSEPH WALKER JR, ALLEN WALL, BARBARA WALL, CORY WALL, DELLAS WALL, GREG WALL, JARED WALL, JON WALL, JUDY WALL, KELLY WALL, MARK WALL, MATTHEW WALL, MERRILL WALL, GARRETT WALL III, ARNIE WALLACE, CATHERINE WALLACE, CHARLENE WALLACE, DAVID WALLACE, DEBORAH WALLACE, GERRIE WALLACE, JANENE WALLACE, JENNIFER WALLACE, JOHN WALLACE, KAREN WALLACE, LYNN WALLACE, MIKE WALLACE, MYRON WALLACE, TRICIA WALLACE, VICKY WALLACE, WAYNE WALLACE, JANICE WALLENTINE, JANICE WALLER, MARLIN WALLER, JOHN WALLERSTEIN, FAITH WALLIN, GARY WALLIN, JOANETTE WALLIN, KATHRYN WALLIN, MELVA WALLIN, ROBERT WALLIN, RUNE WALLIN, CONNIE WALLING, EUGENE WALLING, LIANA WALLMAN, BRETON WALSH, JOSHUA WALSH, MARIE WALSH, CLETHA WALSTRAND, AL WALTER, CLIFTON WALTER, JILL WALTER, MARK WALTER, RAIDA WALTER, APRIL WALTERS, CATHERINE WALTERS, CLARA WALTERS, DARLENE WALTERS, DARREN WALTERS, DEBORAH WALTERS, JOHNNY WALTERS, MELODY WALTERS, RACHAEL WALTERS, SHERIE WALTERS, BRUCE WALTHER, CARA WALTHER, PAT WALTHER, DAVID WALTON, DIANE WALTON, JAMES WALTON, LAVERNE WALTON, LESLIE WALTON, LINDA WALTON, MATTHEW WALTON, MELLISSA WALTON, NATHANIEL WALTON, SANDRA WALTON, GENEVE WANBERG, DAVID WAND, STAN WANEZEK, BJORN WANG, HSIAO-LING WANG, WENSHENG WANG, STEFANI WANICUR, VALERIE WANLASS, LANSIA WANN, JOYCE WANTA, JAMES WARBURTON, JULIE WARBURTON, ROGER WARBURTON, BENJAMIN WARD, BRIAN WARD, BRIAN WARD, CAROL WARD, CHARLES WARD, CHARLES WARD, CLARK WARD, DEBORAH WARD, DENISE WARD, DONALD WARD, DONNA WARD, GLADYS WARD, JEFFREY WARD, JESSE WARD, JILLIAN WARD, JOEL WARD, JONATHAN WARD, LYNN WARD, MARGARET WARD, MARGO WARD, MATTHEW WARD, POLLY WARD, R WARD, SHARON WARD, SHARRON WARD, STANLEY WARD, SUSAN WARD, VALERIE WARD, WILLIAM WARDEN, LARRY WARDLE, DOROTHY WARE, JOAN WARE, JUDY WARE, REUEL WARE, BENJAMIN WARGO, KARI WARING, PAULA WARKENTINE, WENDY WARLAUMONT, DIANNE WARLL, RICHARD WARMBOLD II, HERMAN WARNAS, DANIEL WARNER, DOUGLAS WARNER, HELEN WARNER, MARCIA WARNER, MARILYN WARNER, MARK WARNER, MARK WARNER, MICHAEL WARNER, NEAL WARNER, SHARON WARNER, STACEY WARNER, TAMI WARNER, JULIE WARNICK, KENNETH WARNICK, PAUL WARNICK, EDWARD WARNKE, JANAE WARNOCK, SEAN WARNOCK, MELISSA WARR, CAROLYN WARREN, ROBERT WARREN, DIANE WARSOFF, DOMINIC WARZECHA, SHANE WASDEN, GARALD WASHBURN, POLLY WASHBURN, JOHN WASHINGTON, CYNTHIA WASHIO, RAYMOND WASHIO, PATRICK WASILEWSKI, GRETCHEN WASSER, WILLIAM WASSINK, NORMAN WASSMER, WILLIAM WASSON, MIKA WATABE, MIKI WATANABE, NANCY WATERFALL, GLENN WATERMAN, MIRIAM WATERMAN, ANDREW WATERS, ED WATERS, EVON WATERS, GREG WATERS, JENNIFER WATERS, LESLIE WATERS, ROBERT WATERS, AMBER WATKINS, DAVID WATKINS, DONI WATKINS, GRACE WATKINS, H LEE WATKINS, THOMAS WATKINS, WADE WATKINS, SAMANTHA WATNES, ALENE WATSON, CLAUDIA WATSON, CRAIG WATSON, KARMA WATSON, LINDA WATSON, MARK WATSON, PATRICK WATSON, ROBERT WATSON, ROBIN WATSON, STEPHANIE WATSON, ULYANA WATSON, ADRIAN WATT, KARLIE WATTERSON, BLAINE WATTS, CHRISTI WATTS, JAN WATTS, JANICE WATTS, LELAND WATTS, MICHAEL WATTS, SANDRA WATTS, SCOTT WATTS, WADE WATTS, KATHY WAWRZYNIAK, DANIEL WAYMAN, JOAN WAYMENT, LINDA WAYMENT, MATT WAYMENT, DAN WEATBROOK, MELVIN WEATHERS, DARELL WEAVER, DAVID WEAVER, KAREN WEAVER, LAURIE WEAVER, LYNETTE WEAVER, MICHAEL WEAVER, RAE LYNN WEAVER, REBECCA WEAVER, COLEEN WEBB, DANIEL WEBB, DARRELL WEBB, DAVID WEBB, JACKIE WEBB, JEAN WEBB, LINCOLN WEBB, MARGARET WEBB, RAY WEBB, REBECCA WEBB, RICHARD WEBB, SEAN WEBB, SHANNON WEBB, MARCIA WEBBER, RICHARD WEBBER, MARTI WEBER, NAN WEBER, PAUL WEBER, RICHARD WEBER, STEVEN WEBER, CINDY WEBSTER, DOUGLAS WEBSTER, GARY WEBSTER, JINNI WEBSTER, JULIE WEBSTER, NANCY WEBSTER, TRACY WEBSTER, ERIC WECKENBROCK, CHRISTOPHER WEDDICK, NIKOLAI WEDEKIND, MARK WEDEKING, WILLIAM WEEKES, ALAN WEEKS, ARIANNE WEEKS, CYNTHIA WEEKS, JARROD WEEKS, LOUISE WEEKS, MELANIE WEEKS, JOHN WEGENER, TIM WEIDAUER, TINA WEIDAUER, DREW WEIDMAN, JODI WEIDMAN, JOSEPH WEIDMAN, SHAUNA WEIDMAN, RAY WEIDNER, RYAN WEIERMAN, SUE WEIERMAN, ALEC WEIGHT, CHERYL WEIGHT, ROYLENE WEIGHT, AMY WEILAND, JOHN WEILAND, THADDEUS WEILAND, CHARLES WEILER, JOAN WEILER, MICHAEL WEILER, MICHAEL WEILER, ZABRINA WEILER, ARTHUR WEINFELD, JEFFREY WEINMAN, SALLY WEINRICH, RICHARD WEINSOFT, DANIEL WEIR, DARRIN WEIR, HAROLD WEIR, KAREN WEIR, NANCY WEIR, ROBERT WEIR, ROGER WEIR, HOWARD WEISMAN, JERRY WEISS, JODI WEISS, PAMELA WEISS, PENELOPE WEISS, STACY WEISS, JOAN WEITZEIL, KIRSTIN WEIXLER, TRACI WELBORN, AGNES WELCH, BEVERLY WELCH, CHAD WELCH, DAVID WELCH, JACQUELINE WELCH, JENNIFER WELCH, JILL WELCH, KEITH WELCH, PAMELA WELCH, ROSALEEN ( ROZ ) WELCH, DALE WELCOME, DUARD WELDER, HELENE WELDON, LAUREN WELICZKA, PETER WELKIN, CAROL WELLANDER, BRADFORD WELLER, ROSANNE WELLING, BLAKE WELLING MD, AMBERLIE WELLS, DAVID WELLS, DEBRA WELLS, DIANN WELLS, GLEN WELLS, JOEL WELLS, KIRIN WELLS, ROGER WELLS, SCOTT WELLS, SUSAN WELLS, CHARLES WELSH, JOHN WELSH, MARY WELSH, AMY WELTER, XUEJUN WEN, LYNETTE WENDEL, MERRILEE WENDEL, GLENNISE WENDORF, DARLA WENGER, ANN WENNERLUND, RONALD WENNERLUND, JEAN WENTZEL, MICHELLE WENZBAUER, PAUL WERLEY, JOHN WERNER, SUE WERNER, CLARISSA WERRE, KENNETH

WERTHMANN, BRETT WERTZ, SCOTT WESCHE, TRESA WESCHE, PATTI WESCOTT, CRAIG WEST, DERIK WEST, DONALD WEST, EDITH WEST, FRASER WEST, GEORGIA WEST, JEFF WEST, JENNIFER WEST, JULIE WEST, KRISTOFFER WEST, LAURIE WEST, LINDA WEST, MELISSA WEST, RICHARD WEST, SARA WEST, THELMA WEST, TRENELL WEST, VICKY WEST, WILLIAM WEST, LORI WEST-WEYEN, LINDA WESTBROEK, RUSSEL WESTCOTT, LUCY WESTENBURG, DENISE WESTENSKOW, JAMES WESTENSKOW, RYAN WESTENSKOW, BRENT WESTERGARD, JAY WESTERGARD, SUSAN WESTERGARD, MARYLYN WESTERVELT, MISHA WESTLEY, ROSANN WESTLEY, BRIAN WESTON, HERBERT WESTON, JOANNE WESTON, MARY WESTON, ROBERT WESTON, BENJAMIN WESTOVER, MARY WESTOVER, ROBERT WESTOVER, STEVEN WESTOVER, SUSAN WESTOVER, MATTHEW WESTRICH, LIZ WETMORE, NANCY WETTER, SHON WETTSTEIN, DAVID WETZEL, SANDRA WETZEL, KENNETH WEXLER, JAY WEYLAND, MONICA WHALEN, OLE WHARTON, CAREN WHATCOTT, CRAIG WHATCOTT, MARSHA WHATCOTT, PATRICIA WHEAR, SUSAN WHEATLEY, AMY WHEELER, ANNA WHEELER, CHARLES WHEELER, CLYDE WHEELER, DIANE WHEELER, DUANE WHEELER, JAMES WHEELER, JANALYNNE WHEELER, JUDITH WHEELER, KAREN WHEELER, LINNEA WHEELER, MICHAEL WHEELER, MICHAEL WHEELER, MICHELLE WHEELER, RYAN WHEELER, SCOTT WHEELER, STACIE WHEELER, JASON WHELAN, NANCY WHETMAN, KIRSTEN WHETSTONE, TAMARA WHETTON, BRYAN WHIPPLE, JULIA WHIPPLE, KATHY WHIPPLE, SHELENE WHIPPLE, WALTER WHIPPLE, JO WHIRLEDGE, BETH WHITAKER, LINDA WHITAKER, LINDA WHITAKER, NEIL WHITAKER, SHAWN WHITAKER, TED WHITAKER, THOMAS WHITAKER, WILLIAM WHITAKER, FRANCIS WHITBY, CHARLES WHITCHURCH, MICHAEL WHITCHURCH, THOMAS WHITCHURCH, HILARY WHITCOMB, ALFRED WHITE, ALTAIR WHITE, AMY WHITE, ANNE WHITE, ANTONIA WHITE, BARBARA WHITE, BARNARD WHITE, CAROL WHITE, CAROL WHITE, CATHERINE WHITE, DANIEL WHITE, DENNIS WHITE, DEREK WHITE, DON WHITE, DONALD WHITE, DOUGLAS WHITE, DOUGLAS WHITE, GAY LYN WHITE, GERALD WHITE, GORDON WHITE, HEATHER WHITE, JACQUELINE WHITE, JAMES WHITE, JAMES WHITE, JANAE WHITE, JEFFREY WHITE, JILL WHITE, JOHN WHITE, JOSEPH WHITE, KEITH WHITE, LACHELLE WHITE, LESLIE WHITE, LOWETTA WHITE, MARCIA WHITE, MAUREEN WHITE, PATRICIA WHITE, RICHARD WHITE, ROBIN WHITE, ROCHELLE WHITE, RYAN WHITE, SHANNON WHITE, TRINA WHITE, WILLIAM WHITE, KRISTA WHITE-BLOMSTER, CHERYL WHITEHEAD, GERALD WHITEHEAD, KATHLEEN WHITEHEAD, KATHY WHITEHEAD, PHILLIP WHITEHEAD, WILLIAM WHITEHILL, KARLENE WHITEHOUSE, KATHLEEN WHITEHOUSE, GENETTA WHITEHURST, DANIEL WHITELEATHER, KIMBERLY WHITELEY, STACIE WHITFORD, CLINTON WHITING, DEBBIE WHITING, JAMES WHITING, KRACHEL WHITING, ROSE ANN WHITING, LOYD WHITLOCK, DEBBEE WHITMER, CHRISTA WHITMORE, LORI WHITMORE, WILLIAM WHITMORE, ABBIE WHITNEY, ARVY WHITNEY, BONNIE WHITNEY, BRENDA WHITNEY, BRENT WHITNEY, JANET WHITNEY, JIM WHITNEY, LARRY WHITNEY, PATRICIA WHITNEY, ROBERT WHITNEY, SCOTT WHITNEY, SHONNIE WHITNEY, SPENCER WHITNEY, TIFFANY WHITNEY, VONDA WHITNEY, DARLENE WHITNEY-MORGAN, DIANE WHITTAKER, JED WHITTAKER, LARRY WHITTAKER, LINDA WHITTAKER, RICK WHITTAKER, CARRIE WHITTEN, SHANE WHITTEN, MIKE WHITTENBURG, VILATE WHITTLE, LOUINIA MAE WHITTLESEY, TERESE WHITTY, CONSTANCE WHITWORTH, DOUGLAS WHYTE, DELOS WIBERG, KYLE WIBERG, CATHY WICK, JERRY WICKHAM, LORI WICKHAM, STANLEY WICKS, VIRGINIA WICKS, AMY WIDDISON, FRANCIE WIDDISON, ANDRE WIDMER, MARK WIDMER, SIEGFRIED WIDMER, GAIL WIEBKE, CHARLES WIECZOREK, MARK WIEDEMAN, PETER WIEDEMANN, DON WIEGANDT, FLORENCE WIER, LAWRENCE WIER, KORRYN WIESE, MARK WIESENBERG, SHARON WIEST, EVAN WIGGINS, SHELLY WIGGINS, TED WIGGINS, ANDREW WIGHT, CYNTHEA WIGHT, KRISTEN WIGHT, RICHARD WIGHT, TRACY WIGHT, PAUL WIGHTMAN, ANNIE WIJCKMANS, NEPHI WIJCKMANS, KATHLEEN WIKOFF, PATRICIA WILBURN, CONNIE WILCOX, GARY WILCOX, JOHN WILCOX, LAYNE WILCOX, LESLI WILCOX, LORI WILCOX, ONEAL WILCOX, TORY WILCOX, ROBERT WILD, ANDREA WILDE, BRANDON WILDE, BRITT WILDE, CHRIS WILDE, DAVID WILDE, JACLYN WILDE, JEFFREY WILDE, KRISTINE WILDE, LLOYD WILDE, MARCIE WILDE, MEADOW WILDE, RICH WILDER, MICHELLE WILDING, WENDY WILDING, TERI-LYN WILES, JUSTIN WILEY, LYNNE WILHELM, JAIME WILHELMSEN, SUE WILKERSON, CURTIS WILKEY, JODI WILKEY, JULIE WILKIN, NATALEE WILKINS, PATRICIA WILKINS, SHARON WILKINS, SHERYL WILKINS, ANDREA WILKINSON, BETH WILKINSON, BRADY WILKINSON, BRANDON WILKINSON, CALVIN WILKINSON, CAROL WILKINSON, CHRIS WILKINSON, DAVID WILKINSON, GREGORY WILKINSON, JORIAN WILKINSON, ROBERT WILKINSON, WENDI WILKINSON, BRUCE WILLARD, IAN WILLARD, CURTIS WILLARDSON, LOUISE WILLARDSON, RICHARD WILLARDSON, SUSAN WILLARDSON, ALLEN WILLDEN, GARY WILLDEN, MARY KAYE WILLDEN, LANE WILLE, JEREMY WILLERTON, JOHN WILLERTON, ASHLEE WILLETS, AARON WILLIAMS, ANELISE WILLIAMS, ANGELA WILLIAMS, ANN WILLIAMS, ANN WILLIAMS, APRIL WILLIAMS, ASHLEY WILLIAMS, AVA WILLIAMS, BARBARA WILLIAMS, BRYAN WILLIAMS, CASEY WILLIAMS, CHARLES WILLIAMS, CHARLES WILLIAMS, CHERYL WILLIAMS, CHRIS WILLIAMS, CRAIG WILLIAMS, CYNTHIA WILLIAMS, CYNTHIA WILLIAMS, DALTON WILLIAMS, DAPHNE WILLIAMS, DAVID WILLIAMS, DAYNE WILLIAMS, DELMAR WILLIAMS, DEREK WILLIAMS, DOROTHY WILLIAMS, DOROTHY WILLIAMS, EDWARD WILLIAMS, ELAINE WILLIAMS, ELAINE WILLIAMS, EMILY WILLIAMS, ETHEL WILLIAMS, GLENN WILLIAMS, JAMES WILLIAMS, JANE WILLIAMS, JEFF WILLIAMS, JENNIFER WILLIAMS, JILL WILLIAMS, JOYCE WILLIAMS, JUDI WILLIAMS, KATHLEEN WILLIAMS, KATHRYN WILLIAMS, LAYNE WILLIAMS, LINDA WILLIAMS, LYNN WILLIAMS, MARK WILLIAMS, MATTHEW WILLIAMS, MELISSA WILLIAMS, MICHAEL WILLIAMS, MICHAEL WILLIAMS, NATALIE WILLIAMS, PAMELA WILLIAMS, PAUL WILLIAMS, REGINA WILLIAMS, RHONDA WILLIAMS, ROBERT WILLIAMS, ROBERT WILLIAMS, ROBERT WILLIAMS, ROBYN WILLIAMS, RUTH WILLIAMS, RYAN WILLIAMS, SARAH WILLIAMS, SCOTT WILLIAMS, SHAWN WILLIAMS, STEVE WILLIAMS, SUSAN WILLIAMS, TARA WILLIAMS, TODD WILLIAMS, TYLER WILLIAMS, VANDY WILLIAMS, WAYNE WILLIAMS, WAYNE WILLIAMS, WILLIAM WILLIAMS, HOWELL WILLIAMS III, WILLIAM WILLIAMS III, JOHN WILLIAMSON, KIRT WILLIAMSON, LAWRENCE WILLIAMSON, VICKIE WILLIAMSON, GLEN WILLIE, ROBERT WILLIE, LANCE WILLINGHAM, JOHNNY WILLIS, LINDA WILLIS, MARK WILLIS, MARYLOU WILLIS, SARA WILLIS, DUSTIN WILLMORE, MICHAEL WILLMORE, MELISSA WILLOUGHBY, VANCE WILLSEY, DAVID WILLSON, DIANA WILLSON, CINDY WILMSHURST, AARON WILSON, AMY WILSON, BARBARA WILSON, BARBARA WILSON, CAROLYN WILSON, CHERYL WILSON, DAILE WILSON, DAVID WILSON, DEBORAH WILSON, DIONA WILSON, GAIL WILSON, GARY WILSON, GARY WILSON, GERALD WILSON, GRETCHEN WILSON, J LLOYD WILSON, JAMIE WILSON, JANE WILSON, JASON WILSON, JEFFREY WILSON, JENNIFER WILSON, JENNY WILSON, JONATHAN WILSON, JULIE WILSON, KELLY WILSON, KELLY WILSON, KENT WILSON, KRISSY WILSON, KRISTIE WILSON, LAURA WILSON, LILA WILSON, LYNDA WILSON, MAEGAN WILSON, MARK WILSON, MARY-LOUISE WILSON, MICHAEL WILSON, NATALIE WILSON, PAUL WILSON, RICHARD WILSON, ROBERTA WILSON, ROXANNE WILSON, RYAN WILSON, SANDRA WILSON, SCOTT WILSON, SHANNON WILSON, STEPHEN WILSON, STEVEN WILSON, SUNNY WILSON, SUSAN WILSON, TED WILSON, VICTORIA WILSON, WILLIAM WILSON, WINIFRED WILSON, GEORGE WILSON III, GEORGE WIMER, GERHILD (CONNIE) WIMER, GLENN WIMER, ILENE WIMER, ANDREW WIMMER, CARL WINALSKI, KENT WINDER, MICHAEL WINDER, OWEN WINDER, SHERRI WINDER, ROBERT WINDERS, SHARON WINDERS, ANDREA WINEGAR, ERIKA WINEGAR, NORMA WINEGAR, RICHARD WINEGAR, RONALD WINEGAR, WAYNE WINEGAR, WENDY WINEGAR, JESSICA WING, JOHN WINGELAAR, JOHN WINGER, JUSTIN WINGFIELD, LINDA WINGFIELD, LARRY WININGER, NANCY WININGER, TODD WININGER, ALICIA WINN, CHRISTOPHER WINN, CRISTENE WINN, GARRETT WINN, KAY WINN, MAUREEN WINN, NANCY WINN, ROBERT WINN, MICHAEL WINTER, SHAWNA WINTER, SUNNY WINTER, BRIAN WINTEROWD, CHRISTINE WINTERROTH, CALLIE WINTERS, GARY WINTERS, MARK WINTERS, MEGAN WINTERS, SARA WINTERS, SIDNEY WINTERS, SUSAN WINTERS, GARY WINTERTON, NANCY WINTERTON, VICKI WINTERTON, JOSHUA WINWARD, SIDNEY WINWARD, BRETT WIRICK, JOHN WIRTZ, THOMAS WISCOMB, TARA WISCOTT, SONDRA WISDOM, ANN WISE, WILLIAM WISE, MONICA WISEMAN, SHELLY WISER, JUDITH WISNER, PAUL WISNIEWSKI, THOMAS WITCZAK, SARAH WITHER, DIRK WITKAMP, MARYLYNE WITNEY, KATHLEEN WITRY, CELESTE WITT, LINDSEY WITT, RAYMOND WITZEL, RONALD WITZEL, SHAWN WITZEL, AMY WIXOM, ELLEN WIXOM, MARY WIXOM, ROSEMARY WIXOM, SHANNON WIXOM, GERALD WOHLFORD, PENNY WOHLFORD, KENDRA WOHLGEMUTH, DAVE WOLACH, SARAH WOLACH, MELANIE WOLCOTT KLEIN, DANIEL WOLD, ERIC WOLD, HEATHER WOLD, NANCY WOLD, PEGGY WOLD, BARBARA WOLDBERG, CARRIE WOLF, CHARLES WOLF, CURTIS WOLF, DAVID WOLF, LYNNE WOLF, MILDRED WOLF, BERNADETTE WOLFE, DEANNA WOLFE, MICHAEL WOLFE, PHYLLIS WOLFE, SUSAN WOLFE, WILLIAM WOLFE, RONALD WOLFF, BETH WOLFGRAM, JEANNE WOLFLEY, JONI WOLFLEY, ROSS WOLFLEY, CARL WOLFRAM, HELGARD WOLFRAM, LARA WOLFSON, PAMELA WOLL, GEORGE WOLLASTON, BRIAN WOLSEY, MARY WOLSTENHOLME, PAMELA WOMACK, LARRY WONG, MICHAEL WONG, RINGO WONG, ROY WONG, VAL WONSAVAGE, AMY WOO, ALVIN WOOD, ANDY WOOD, ANGELA WOOD, APRIL WOOD, CAROL WOOD, CHARMION WOOD, CHERYL WOOD, CHRISTINE WOOD, CONNIE WOOD, DANA WOOD, DOUGLAS WOOD, ELLEN WOOD, ELLEN WOOD, FRANK WOOD, JAMES WOOD, JENNETTE WOOD, JOHN WOOD, JONI WOOD, JOY WOOD, JUDY WOOD, KURT WOOD, KURT WOOD, MICHAEL WOOD, MICHAEL WOOD, MONA WOOD, MURRAY WOOD, NITA WOOD, PATRICIA WOOD, ROBERT WOOD, SHELBIE WOOD, STANA WOOD, STEPHANIE WOOD, STEPHEN WOOD, STEVEN WOOD, THOMAS WOOD, WAYNE WOOD, JONNA WOODARD, ROBERT WOODARD, JIM WOODBURNE, CARIE WOODBURY, DAVID WOODBURY, DENISE WOODBURY, JOHN WOODBURY, JONATHAN WOODBURY, KIMBERLY WOODBURY, MICHAEL WOODBURY, NATHAN WOODBURY, SANDRA WOODBURY, WAYNE WOODBURY, ALAN WOODCOX, JANET WOODFIELD, LINDA WOODFIELD, WAYNE WOODFIELD, KATHERINE WOODFORD, JEFFREY WOODHAVE, DAN WOODHEAD, STEPHEN WOODHOUSE, STEVEN WOODHOUSE, LOIS WOODLAND, BRYCEN WOODLEY, LESLIE WOODMANSEE, BRAD WOODRUFF, BRENT WOODRUFF, KATHIE WOODRUFF, KYLE WOODRUFF, LON WOODRUFF, BRENTON WOODS, JIMMY WOODS, KAHILI WOODS, CURTIS WOODWARD, DARRELL WOODWARD, DON WOODWARD, JULIE WOODWARD, KARLA WOODWARD, KATHIE WOODWARD, LUCY WOODWARD, NANCY WOODWARD, ROSEANN WOODWARD, ROSS WOODWARD, SHARON WOODWARD, LISA WOOLEVER, KURTIS WOOLF, MARILYN WOOLF, BRETT WOOLLEY, CHAD WOOLLEY, DWAYNE WOOLLEY, MARGARETTA WOOLLEY, MICHAEL WOOLLEY, TODD WOOLLEY, CAROL WOOLSEY, DENNIS WOOLSTON, DONETTE WOOLSTON, JAMES WOOTEN, LINDY WORDEN, CLAIR WORKMAN, MARC WORKMAN, DENNIS WORKS, HEIDI WORKS, ANNE WORSHAM, MAURINE WORSHAM, SHARON WORSLEY, DAVID WORTHEN, GAIL WORTHEN, JOSEPH WORTHEN, KATHY WORTHEN, KENT WORTHINGTON, PATRICIA WORTHINGTON, JENNIFER WOZAB, DAVID WRAPE, BRIGITTA WRAY, HIDEKO WRAY, JACEN WRAY, KRISTIN WREDEN, COREY WRIDE, JAMIE WRIDE, TIFFANIE WRIDE, WAYNE WRIDE, ADRIENNE WRIGHT, ALLISON WRIGHT, ANDREA WRIGHT, BRENDA WRIGHT, BRUCE WRIGHT, BRYAN WRIGHT, CAROL WRIGHT, CASSITY WRIGHT, DAURI WRIGHT, DAVID WRIGHT, DOUGLAS WRIGHT, EARLENE WRIGHT, GARY WRIGHT, HOLLY WRIGHT, JAMES WRIGHT, JAMIE WRIGHT, JANET WRIGHT, JARED WRIGHT, JENNIFER WRIGHT, JIM WRIGHT, JOHN WRIGHT, JUSTIN WRIGHT, KATHY WRIGHT, KELLY WRIGHT, KENNETH WRIGHT, KIRK WRIGHT, KRISTIE WRIGHT, LANELL WRIGHT, LINDA WRIGHT, MARIA WRIGHT, MARSHALL WRIGHT, MARY WRIGHT, MARY ANN WRIGHT, MATT WRIGHT, PATRICIA WRIGHT, RONNIE WRIGHT, SCOTT WRIGHT, SHERIE WRIGHT, STEPHEN WRIGHT, SUSAN WRIGHT, TAMERA WRIGHT, TAMMY WRIGHT, WILLIAM WRIGHT, JEFFREY WRIGLEY, CORINNE WUNDERLI, EARL WUNDERLI, JOHN WUNDERLI, JENNIFER WUNDERLICH, MINNIE WUNDERLICH, TAMERA WURSTEN, LORENZ WUSTNER, SEAN WYANDT, JAMES WYATT, JANIE WYATT, JASON WYATT, MATTHEW WYBROW, CLAUDIA WYCKOFF, CLINT WYCKOFF, LANCE WYCKOFF, JEFF WYGAL, NANCY WYLIE, ROBERT WYLIE, PERRY WYMORE, G. BRENT WYNN, NOREEN WYNN, DIANNE WYNNE, DANA WYSS, LARENE WYSS, ROBERT WYSS, HENRY WYTHEWINDER, MICHAEL WINDER, OWEN WINDER, SHERRI WINDER, ROBERT WINDERS, SHARON WINDERS, ANDREA WINEGAR, ERIKA WINEGAR, NORMA WINEGAR, RICHARD WINEGAR, RONALD WINEGAR, WAYNE WINEGAR, WENDY WINEGAR, JESSICA WING, JOHN WINGELAAR, JOHN WINGER, JUSTIN WINGFIELD, LINDA WINGFIELD, LARRY WININGER, NANCY WININGER, TODD WININGER, ALICIA WINN, CHRISTOPHER WINN, CRISTENE WINN, GARRETT WINN, KAY WINN, MAUREEN WINN, NANCY WINN, ROBERT WINN, MICHAEL WINTER, SHAWNA WINTER, SUNNY WINTER, BRIAN WINTEROWD, CHRISTINE WINTERROTH, CALLIE WINTERS, GARY WINTERS, MARK WINTERS, MEGAN WINTERS, SARA WINTERS, SIDNEY WINTERS, SUSAN WINTERS, GARY WINTERTON, NANCY WINTERTON, VICKI WINTERTON, JOSHUA WINWARD, SIDNEY WINWARD, BRETT WIRICK, JOHN WIRTZ, THOMAS WISCOMB, TARA WISCOTT, SONDRA WISDOM, ANN WISE, WILLIAM WISE, MONICA WISEMAN, SHELLY WISER, JUDITH WISNER, PAUL WISNIEWSKI, THOMAS WITCZAK, SARAH WITHER, DIRK WITKAMP, MARYLYNE WITNEY, KATHLEEN WITRY, CELESTE WITT, LINDSEY WITT, RAYMOND WITZEL, RONALD WITZEL, SHAWN WITZEL, AMY WIXOM, ELLEN WIXOM, MARY WIXOM, ROSEMARY WIXOM, SHANNON WIXOM, GERALD WOHLFORD, PENNY WOHLFORD, KENDRA WOHLGEMUTH, DAVE WOLACH, SARAH WOLACH, MELANIE WOLCOTT KLEIN, DANIEL WOLD, ERIC WOLD, HEATHER WOLD, NANCY WOLD, PEGGY WOLD, BARBARA WOLDBERG, CARRIE WOLF, CHARLES WOLF, CURTIS WOLF, DAVID WOLF, LYNNE WOLF, MILDRED WOLF, BERNADETTE WOLFE, DEANNA WOLFE, MICHAEL WOLFE, PHYLLIS WOLFE, SUSAN WOLFE, WILLIAM WOLFE, RONALD WOLFF, BETH WOLFGRAM, JEANNE WOLFLEY, JONI WOLFLEY, ROSS WOLFLEY, CARL WOLFRAM, HELGARD WOLFRAM, LARA WOLFSON, PAMELA WOLL, GEORGE WOLLASTON, BRIAN WOLSEY, MARY WOLSTENHOLME, PAMELA WOMACK, LARRY WONG, MICHAEL WONG, RINGO WONG, ROY WONG, VAL WONSAVAGE, AMY WOO, ALVIN WOOD, ANDY WOOD, ANGELA WOOD, APRIL WOOD, CAROL WOOD, CHARMION WOOD, CHERYL WOOD, CHRISTINE WOOD, CONNIE WOOD, DANA WOOD, DOUGLAS WOOD, ELLEN WOOD, ELLEN WOOD, FRANK WOOD, JAMES WOOD, JENNETTE WOOD, JOHN WOOD, JONI WOOD, JOY WOOD, JUDY WOOD, KURT WOOD, KURT WOOD, MICHAEL WOOD, MICHAEL WOOD, MONA WOOD, MURRAY WOOD, NITA WOOD, PATRICIA WOOD, ROBERT WOOD, SHELBIE WOOD, STANA WOOD, STEPHANIE WOOD, STEPHEN WOOD, STEVEN WOOD, THOMAS WOOD, WAYNE WOOD, JONNA WOODARD, ROBERT WOODARD, JIM WOODBURNE, CARIE WOODBURY, DAVID WOODBURY, DENISE WOODBURY, JOHN WOODBURY, JONATHAN WOODBURY, KIMBERLY WOODBURY, MICHAEL WOODBURY, NATHAN WOODBURY, SANDRA WOODBURY, WAYNE WOODBURY, ALAN WOODCOX, JANET WOODFIELD, LINDA WOODFIELD, WAYNE WOODFIELD, KATHERINE WOODFORD, JEFFREY WOODHAVE, DAN WOODHEAD, STEPHEN WOODHOUSE, STEVEN WOODHOUSE, LOIS WOODLAND, BRYCEN WOODLEY, LESLIE WOODMANSEE, BRAD WOODRUFF, BRENT WOODRUFF, KATHIE WOODRUFF, KYLE WOODRUFF, LON WOODRUFF, BRENTON WOODS, JIMMY WOODS, KAHILI WOODS, CURTIS WOODWARD, DARRELL WOODWARD, DON WOODWARD, JULIE WOODWARD, KARLA WOODWARD, KATHIE WOODWARD, LUCY WOODWARD, NANCY WOODWARD, ROSEANN WOODWARD, ROSS WOODWARD, SHARON WOODWARD, LISA WOOLEVER, KURTIS WOOLF, MARILYN WOOLF, BRETT WOOLLEY, CHAD WOOLLEY, DWAYNE WOOLLEY, MARGARETTA WOOLLEY, MICHAEL WOOLLEY, TODD WOOLLEY, CAROL WOOLSEY, DENNIS WOOLSTON, DONETTE WOOLSTON, JAMES WOOTEN, LINDY WORDEN, CLAIR WORKMAN, MARC WORKMAN, DENNIS WORKS, HEIDI WORKS, ANNE WORSHAM, MAURINE WORSHAM, SHARON WORSLEY, DAVID WORTHEN, GAIL WORTHEN, JOSEPH WORTHEN, KATHY WORTHEN, KENT WORTHINGTON, PATRICIA WORTHINGTON, JENNIFER WOZAB, DAVID WRAPE, BRIGITTA WRAY, HIDEKO WRAY, JACEN WRAY, KRISTIN WREDEN, COREY WRIDE, JAMIE WRIDE, TIFFANIE WRIDE, WAYNE WRIDE, ADRIENNE WRIGHT, ALLISON WRIGHT, ANDREA WRIGHT, BRENDA WRIGHT, BRUCE WRIGHT, BRYAN WRIGHT, CAROL WRIGHT, CASSITY WRIGHT, DAURI WRIGHT, DAVID WRIGHT, DOUGLAS WRIGHT, EARLENE WRIGHT, GARY WRIGHT, HOLLY WRIGHT, JAMES WRIGHT, JAMIE WRIGHT, JANET WRIGHT, JARED WRIGHT, JENNIFER WRIGHT, JIM WRIGHT, JOHN WRIGHT, JUSTIN WRIGHT, KATHY WRIGHT, KELLY WRIGHT, KENNETH WRIGHT, KIRK WRIGHT, KRISTIE WRIGHT, LANELL WRIGHT, LINDA WRIGHT, MARIA WRIGHT, MARSHALL WRIGHT, MARY WRIGHT, MARY ANN WRIGHT, MATT WRIGHT, PATRICIA WRIGHT, RONNIE WRIGHT, SCOTT WRIGHT, SHERIE WRIGHT, STEPHEN WRIGHT, SUSAN WRIGHT, TAMERA WRIGHT, TAMMY WRIGHT, WILLIAM WRIGHT, JEFFREY WRIGLEY, CORINNE WUNDERLI, EARL WUNDERLI, JOHN WUNDERLI, JENNIFER WUNDERLICH, MINNIE WUNDERLICH, TAMERA WURSTEN, LORENZ WUSTNER, SEAN WYANDT, JAMES WYATT, JANIE WYATT, JASON WYATT, MATTHEW WYBROW, CLAUDIA WYCKOFF, CLINT WYCKOFF, LANCE WYCKOFF, JEFF WYGAL, NANCY WYLIE, ROBERT WYLIE, PERRY WYMORE, G. BRENT WYNN, NOREEN WYNN, DIANNE WYNNE, DANA WYSS, LARENE WYSS, ROBERT WYSS, HENRY WYTHE, GEORGE XANOS, FAN XIAO, JIA XU, STEVEN YACK, BRETT YADON, ETHAN YAKE, JEANNIE YAMASHITA, YUMI YANAGA, JUSTIN YANCEY, BASIL YANG, BENJAMIN YANG, XUESONG YANG, CHRISTINE YANISIW, CHARLES YANKE, BETH YAPEL, TERRY YARBROUGH, KAYLENE YARDLEY, JOHN YARMAN, CHERIE YATES, KRISTA YATES, SHIRLEY YATES, CAROLYN YAWORSKY, MARK YEARLING, TODD YEATES, TORI YEATES, MARGARET YEE, WING YEE, MARLINA YEE-HALES, KENNETH YEH, KIMBERLY YELDERMAN, MARY YELL, NATALIE YELLIS-KRAUS, SE YEN, LYNNETTE YERBURY, RICHARD YERBURY, AUSTIN YERGENSEN, HELENA YERGENSEN, SEAN YERGENSEN, MYONG YI, BENNY YIH, REBECCA YIH, HALE YILMAZ, JONATHAN YIP, DAVID YNGSDAL, VICKY YOCOM, REGINA YODER, MARC YOE, PETER YOHO, SUYOUNG YOO, CYNTHIA YORGASON, KYLE YORGASON, JOHN YORKEY, WESTON YOUD, AARON YOUNG, ALLEN YOUNG, AMBER YOUNG, ANDREW YOUNG, ANNIE YOUNG, BARBARA YOUNG, BEVEN YOUNG, CHARLOTTE YOUNG, CLAUDE YOUNG, DATHAN YOUNG, DAVID YOUNG, DAVID YOUNG, DIANE YOUNG, DON YOUNG, ELIZABETH YOUNG, GREGORY YOUNG, HEATHER YOUNG, HOLLY YOUNG, HOLLY YOUNG, HOLLY YOUNG, JEFFREY YOUNG, JENNIFER YOUNG, JENNY YOUNG, JERRY YOUNG, JODY YOUNG, JOHN YOUNG, JON YOUNG, JULIE YOUNG, KENNETH YOUNG, KRISTY YOUNG, LEE YOUNG, LEWIS YOUNG, LISA YOUNG, LYNN YOUNG, MARGARET YOUNG, MARGARET YOUNG, MARGARET YOUNG, MICAH YOUNG, MICHAEL YOUNG, MICHEAL YOUNG, NATALIE YOUNG, NED YOUNG, ROBERT YOUNG, ROBERT YOUNG, ROGER YOUNG, SARAH YOUNG, SCOTT YOUNG, STEVE YOUNG, STEVE YOUNG, TERRY YOUNG, THOMAS YOUNG, TROY YOUNG, VALERIE YOUNG, VICKI YOUNG, WILLIAM YOUNG, WILLIAM YOUNG III, VICKI YOUNGBLOOD, GARY YOUNGER, NANCY YOUNT, HONG YU, TIM YUCIS, SUSANA YUEN, ERIC YUHAS, ROBERT YUSCHAK, MELISSA ZABRISKIE, RAMON ZABRISKIE, JOEL ZABRISKIE JR, CARMIE ZACCARDI, VERA ZACCARDI, BREEGE ZACHARY, JODY ZACHMAN, JACQUELINE ZACHRY, BLAIR ZACKON, LINDA ZAFF, PAUL ZAHN, VAJIHE ZAIFNEJAD, FILIPP ZALESSKIY, JONATHAN ZALISK, PAUL ZALUSKY, CHRISTOPHER ZAMBOS, ELAINE ZAMBOS, ARIANA ZAMORA, OSAMA ZANAYED, MACARENA ZANNIER, SCOTT ZAPOTOCKY, JOSEPH ZAPPITELLO, CONSTANCE ZARBOCK, MICHAEL ZARBOCK, RON ZARBOCK, KATHY ZARING, MATTHEW ZARIT, MARK ZAUGG, NATHAN ZAUGG, RONDA ZAUGG, JARMILA ZDANOWICZ, ERIC ZEEMAN, SHIRLEY ZEHNER, LAUREL ZEIBIG, TAWNYA ZEIDLER, ANNE ZEIGLER, WENDY ZEIGLER, DUANE ZELLMER, SUMMER ZEMP, JAMIE ZENGER, JEFF ZENGER, JOHN ZENGER, CYNTHIA ZENT, ADAM ZENTNER, ELIZABETH ZENTNER, BIRGIT ZEPF, MATTHEOS ZERVOS, EMILY ZETTERQUIST, HONGZHI ZHANG, JENNIFER ZHANG, KAI ZHANG, LIANG ZHANG, YUEYING ZHEN, ANTONY ZHONG, BEIBEI ZHU, KIMBERLY ZIEBARTH, PEGGY ZIMMER, VINCE ZIMMER, GINA ZIMMERER, CHERIE ZIMMERMAN, EVELYN ZIMMERMAN, MATHEA ZIMMERMAN, PATTI ZIMMERMAN, RAYMOND ZIMMERMAN, RICHARD ZIMMERMAN, SHAWN ZIMMERMAN, STEVE ZINIK, CHARLES ZINSMASTER, RABBI BENNY ZIPPEL, TRAVIS ZIRKER, ROBERT ZITO, ROBERT ZITO, RUDY ZITZMANN, RAY ZOBRIST, WILLI ZOGG, PACOME ZOKOU, RICHARD ZOLLARS, MARY ZOLLO, JEFF ZORNOW, WEN ZOU, KEITH ZUEHLKE, REED ZUEHLKE, SHIRLEY ZUEHLKE, TRINA ZUEHLSDORFF, CHUCK ZUERCHER, ANGELA ZUFELT, BRIAN ZUFELT, TRUDY ZUFELT, MICHAEL ZUMBRENNEN, PATRICIA ZUMBRENNEN, LORI ZUNDEL, NATHAN ZUNDEL, BETHANY ZURAWICZ, BRITON ZURCHER, CHERYL ZURCHER, DANIEL ZURCHER, MELISSA ZURCHER, WILLARD ZURCHER, CYRIL ZURLINDEN, ANTHONY ZVON, CRISTY ZVONKOVIC, FRED ZWICK, JANET ZWICK, MICHELLE ZWICK • **X** • GEORGE XANOS, FAN XIAO, JIA XU • **Y** • STEVEN YACK, BRETT YADON, ETHAN YAKE, JEANNIE YAMASHITA, YUMI YANAGA, JUSTIN YANCEY, BASIL YANG, BENJAMIN YANG, XUESONG YANG, CHRISTINE YANISIW, CHARLES YANKE, BETH YAPEL, TERRY YARBROUGH, KAYLENE YARDLEY, JOHN YARMAN, CHERIE YATES, KRISTA YATES, SHIRLEY YATES, CAROLYN YAWORSKY, MARK YEARLING, TODD YEATES, TORI YEATES, MARGARET YEE, WING YEE, MARLINA YEE-HALES, KENNETH YEH, KIMBERLY YELDERMAN, MARY YELL, NATALIE YELLIS-KRAUS, SE YEN, LYNNETTE YERBURY, RICHARD YERBURY, AUSTIN YERGENSEN, HELENA YERGENSEN, SEAN YERGENSEN, MYONG YI, BENNY YIH, REBECCA YIH, HALE YILMAZ, JONATHAN YIP, DAVID YNGSDAL, VICKY YOCOM, REGINA YODER, MARC YOE, PETER YOHO, SUYOUNG YOO, CYNTHIA YORGASON, KYLE YORGASON, JOHN YORKEY, WESTON YOUD, AARON YOUNG, ALLEN YOUNG, AMBER YOUNG, ANDREW YOUNG, ANNIE YOUNG, BARBARA YOUNG, BEVEN YOUNG, CHARLOTTE YOUNG, CLAUDE YOUNG, DATHAN YOUNG, DAVID YOUNG, DAVID YOUNG, DIANE YOUNG, DON YOUNG, ELIZABETH YOUNG, GREGORY YOUNG, HEATHER YOUNG, HOLLY YOUNG, HOLLY YOUNG, HOLLY YOUNG, JEFFREY YOUNG, JENNIFER YOUNG, JENNY YOUNG, JERRY YOUNG, JODY YOUNG, JOHN YOUNG, JON YOUNG, JULIE YOUNG, KENNETH YOUNG, KRISTY YOUNG, LEE YOUNG, LEWIS YOUNG, LISA YOUNG, LYNN YOUNG, MARGARET YOUNG, MARGARET YOUNG, MARGARET YOUNG, MICAH YOUNG, MICHAEL YOUNG, MICHEAL YOUNG, NATALIE YOUNG, NED YOUNG, ROBERT YOUNG, ROBERT YOUNG, ROGER YOUNG, SARAH YOUNG, SCOTT YOUNG, STEVE YOUNG, STEVE YOUNG, TERRY YOUNG, THOMAS YOUNG, TROY YOUNG, VALERIE YOUNG, VICKI YOUNG, WILLIAM YOUNG, WILLIAM YOUNG III, VICKI YOUNGBLOOD, GARY YOUNGER, NANCY YOUNT, HONG YU, TIM YUCIS, SUSANA YUEN, ERIC YUHAS, ROBERT YUSCHAK • **Z** • MELISSA ZABRISKIE, RAMON ZABRISKIE, JOEL ZABRISKIE JR, CARMIE ZACCARDI, VERA ZACCARDI, BREEGE ZACHARY, JODY ZACHMAN, JACQUELINE ZACHRY, BLAIR ZACKON, LINDA ZAFF, PAUL ZAHN, VAJIHE ZAIFNEJAD, FILIPP ZALESSKIY, JONATHAN ZALISK, PAUL ZALUSKY, CHRISTOPHER ZAMBOS, ELAINE ZAMBOS, ARIANA ZAMORA, OSAMA ZANAYED, MACARENA ZANNIER, SCOTT ZAPOTOCKY, JOSEPH ZAPPITELLO, CONSTANCE ZARBOCK, MICHAEL ZARBOCK, RON ZARBOCK, KATHY ZARING, MATTHEW ZARIT, MARK ZAUGG, NATHAN ZAUGG, RONDA ZAUGG, JARMILA ZDANOWICZ, ERIC ZEEMAN, SHIRLEY ZEHNER, LAUREL ZEIBIG, TAWNYA ZEIDLER, ANNE ZEIGLER, WENDY ZEIGLER, DUANE ZELLMER, SUMMER ZEMP, JAMIE ZENGER, JEFF ZENGER, JOHN ZENGER, CYNTHIA ZENT, ADAM ZENTNER, ELIZABETH ZENTNER, BIRGIT ZEPF, MATTHEOS ZERVOS, EMILY ZETTERQUIST, HONGZHI ZHANG, JENNIFER ZHANG, KAI ZHANG, LIANG ZHANG, YUEYING ZHEN, ANTONY ZHONG, BEIBEI ZHU, KIMBERLY ZIEBARTH, PEGGY ZIMMER, VINCE ZIMMER, GINA ZIMMERER, CHERIE ZIMMERMAN, EVELYN ZIMMERMAN, MATHEA ZIMMERMAN, PATTI ZIMMERMAN, RAYMOND ZIMMERMAN, RICHARD ZIMMERMAN, SHAWN ZIMMERMAN, STEVE ZINIK, CHARLES ZINSMASTER, RABBI BENNY ZIPPEL, TRAVIS ZIRKER, ROBERT ZITO, ROBERT ZITO, RUDY ZITZMANN, RAY ZOBRIST, WILLI ZOGG, PACOME ZOKOU, RICHARD ZOLLARS, MARY ZOLLO, JEFF ZORNOW, WEN ZOU, KEITH ZUEHLKE, REED ZUEHLKE, SHIRLEY ZUEHLKE, TRINA ZUEHLSDORFF, CHUCK ZUERCHER, ANGELA ZUFELT, BRIAN ZUFELT, TRUDY ZUFELT, MICHAEL ZUMBRENNEN, PATRICIA ZUMBRENNEN, LORI ZUNDEL, NATHAN ZUNDEL, BETHANY ZURAWICZ, BRITON ZURCHER, CHERYL ZURCHER, DANIEL ZURCHER, MELISSA ZURCHER, WILLARD ZURCHER, CYRIL ZURLINDEN, ANTHONY ZVON, CRISTY ZVONKOVIC, FRED ZWICK, JANET ZWICK, MICHELLE ZWICK

**D O N O R S** • **P L A T I N U M** • THE CHURCH OF JESUS CHRIST OF LATTER-DAY SAINTS, GEORGE S. AND DOLORES DORÉ ECCLES FOUNDATION, INTERMOUNTAIN HEALTH CARE • **G O L D** • AUTOLIV, BAIN CAPITAL, KEVIN & GAYLA COMPTON, SPENCER F. ECCLES & CLEONE P. ECCLES, KEM C. AND CAROLYN GARDNER, NANCY ECCLES & HOMER M. HAYWARD FAMILY, RICHARD J. & LISA G. HOWA, JON M. HUNTSMAN, JANET QUINNEY LAWSON, FREDERICK QUINNEY LAWSON, STEVEN AND KALLEEN LUND, BRIAN & JENNIFER MAXWELL, FRED A. MORETON & COMPANY, JERRY & VICKIE MOYES, JOHN & MARCIA PRICE, MITT & ANN ROMNEY, BLAKE & NANCY RONEY, BROOKE & DENICE RONEY, JAMES R. & SUSAN L. SWARTZ, SANDIE N. TILLOTSON • **S I L V E R** • AMERICAN LAFRANCE, DYNATRONICS, GRANITE CONSTRUCTION COMPANY, GREEN, MEREDITH & ROLLINS FAMILIES, HUET FAMILY – JOHN, DONNA & JAMES A., ALAN & LESLIE LAYTON, RICHARD & NANCY MARRIOTT, PIERCE MANUFACTURING, PROMODEL CORPORATION, PUBLICIS DIALOG, REAGAN OUTDOOR ADVERTISING, TATAKA / MOUNTAIN COIN, WORKERS COMPENSATION FUND • **B R O N Z E** • JEFF & DEBI AARTHUN, ATK ALLIANT TECHSYSTEMS, A. SCOTT ANDERSON, JEFF ANDERSON, JOHN & JUDI ANDERSON, AVIS & NICK BADAMI, FORREST S. BAKER, III, SUSAN W. AND JAMES C. BLAIR, TOM & POLLY BREDT, HAL BRIERLY, R. HAROLD BURTON FOUNDATION, CAROL / BRAILEAN FAMILIES, WILLIAM H. & PATRICIA CHILD, CLEAR CHANNEL BROADCASTING OF SALT LAKE CITY, THE COLEMAN COMPANY, CONFERENCE SYSTEMS, INC., SANDRA & STEPHEN R. COVEY & FAMILY, DESERET NEWS, DR. EDWARD & JOANNE DAUER, STEPHEN G. & SUSAN E. DENKERS FAMILY, JIM & GERALYN DREYFOUS, THE THRONTON, RYBERG, DUMKE AND MANSHIP FAMILIES, KATHERINE W. AND EZEKIEL R. DUMKE JR., JACK M. & MARIANNE FERRARO, MICHAEL & PATRICIA FITZPATRICK, MICKEY & SHAREE GALLIVAN, BOB & KATHI GARFF, GMT CORP., MARRITJE & JAMIE GREENE, GROEN BROTHERS, HOFF FAMILY, HORNACEK AND CONDAS FAMILIES, JOEL & SUSAN HYATT, INFORMATION SYSTEMS SUPPORT, JANI-KING INTERNATIONAL, INC., THE WALTER KORTSCHAK FAMILY, KOUREY FAMILY, JOE & LAURIE LACOB, PAUL T. LEONARD JR. FAMILY, LEVINTHAL / MYERS FAMILIES, WORTH & ANDREW LUDWICK & FAMILY, LOUISE & JEFF MANN, EDWARD & GAY MCDONOUGH, BURT & DEEDEE MCMURTRY, RAYMOND AND NANCY MIKULICH, HAL & LOIS MILNER, JOHN AND TASHIA MORGRIDGE, JOE HIDEO MORITA & FAMILY, NORBEST, INC., NEIL PAPIANO, GUS & BARBARA PAULOS, S. DAVID PLUMMER & FAMILY, BILL J. & MARGARET M. POPE, MARK & DIANNE PROTHRO FAMILY, DAVID & SHARI QUINNEY, MEG & ERIC ROACH & FAMILY, HELEN & ROY RYU, THE SALT LAKE TRIBUNE, CARM & NANCY SANTORO, PEGGY & BEN SCHAPIRO, SCOTT MACHINERY COMPANY, STEVE SHERWOOD FAMILY, SHIEBLER FAMILY, DUANE & JODY SHRONTZ, TOM STEMBERG, UNITED SCAFFOLDING, INC., JILL & TOM WERNER, WORLD CUP SUPPLY, YAMAHA

SPECIAL THANKS •

THE INTERNATIONAL OLYMPIC COMMITTEE, THE UNITED STATES OLYMPIC COMMITTEE, THE INTERNATIONAL FEDERATIONS, HALLMARK, BORGE ANDERSON, EASTMAN KODAK, JOHN AALBERG, RESHMA ADVANI, DAVID AMIDON, NATE ANDERSON, HEATHER AUTRY, MARILYN CADENBACH, JULIE CALDWELL, MELINDA CHRISTENSEN, JEFF CHUMAS, TOM CISEWSKI, RICHARD CONNOLLY, CLAIRE DEL NEGRO, HERWIG DEMSCHAR, STEVE DITTMORE, CHRISTOPHE DUBI, KELLY DYER, SPENCER ECCLES, DEBORAH ENGEN, DREW EPSTEIN, ANGIE ERNST, TAUNI EVERETT, ANDY GABEL, SCOTT GIVENS, MATT GOODSON, RAYMOND T. GRANT, FINN GUNDERSEN, GILLIAN HAMBURGER, STINE HELLERUD, JENNY HOLDEN, HEATHER HOLT, ALAN JOHNSON, KAREN KORFANTA, MOLLY LARAMIE, CRAIG LEHTO, HEATHER LINHART ZANG, STEVEN McCARTHY, ANDREA MILLER, PERKINS MILLER, DAN MORO, CONNIE NELSON, LYLE NELSON, JENNIFER NICHOLS, COY NORTH, AIMEE PRESTON, ROBERT RICHARDSON, LIZ RIDLEY, GAIL SEAY, ZIANIBETH SHATTUCK OWEN, MARY KATE SHEA, MARY SHEA TUCKER, LISA SCHOENEBERG, JON STEIN, KELLIE SWIATOCHA, CHRISTA TAYLOR, NICK THOMETZ, SAYRE WISEMAN, MARY YELANJIAN.

*And a very special thanks to* DAVID BRESLAUER, *whose support was instrumental to the success of this book.*

*Dedicated to the memory of* BRUCE DWORSHAK, MATT WALTERS, RANDY MONTGOMERY *and* N. ALAN BARNES.

SPONSORS •

*Worldwide Partners*
THE COCA-COLA COMPANY
EASTMAN KODAK
JOHN HANCOCK FINANCIAL SERVICES
MCDONALD'S
PANASONIC
SAMSUNG
SCHLUMBERGERSEMA
SPORTS ILLUSTRATED
VISA
XEROX

*Salt Lake 2002 Partners*
AT&T
BANK OF AMERICA
BUDWEISER
GENERAL MOTORS
HAVOLINE
QWEST

*Salt Lake 2002 Sponsors*
ALLSTATE
BLUECROSS BLUESHIELD
DELTA AIR LINES
GATEWAY
HALLMARK
JET SET SPORTS
LUCENT TECHNOLOGIES
MARKER
MONSTER.COM
NUSKIN/PHARMANEX
OFFICE DEPOT
SEIKO
SENSORMATIC
THE HOME DEPOT
UTAH POWER
YORK INTERNATIONAL

*Salt Lake 2002 Suppliers*
ACHIEVE GLOBAL
AGGREKO
BOMBARDIER
FETZER/KORBEL
CAMPBELL SOUP COMPANY
CARDINAL HEALTH
CERTIFIED ANGUS BEEF
COMPASS GROUP
DIAMOND OF CALIFORNIA
DRAKE BEAM MORIN
GARRETT METAL DETECTORS
GENERAL MILLS
HARRIS INTERACTIVE
HERMAN MILLER/HENRIKSEN BUTLER
IKANO
KELLOGG COMPANY
KIMBERLY-CLARK
KSL RADIO & TELEVISION
MARRIOTT INTERNATIONAL
MODERN DISPLAY
O.C. TANNER
PFIZER, INC.
POWERBAR
QUESTAR
SCHENKER INTERNATIONAL
SEALY
SEARS, ROEBUCK AND CO.
SMITH'S
SUN MICROSYSTEMS
TICKETS.COM
UNION PACIFIC RAILROAD